The Princeton Review

Cracking the SAT

ADAM ROBINSON AND JOHN KATZMAN

2004 EDITION

RANDOM HOUSE, INC.
NEW YORK

www.PrincetonReview.com

The Independent Education Consultants Association recognizes The Princeton Review as a valuable resource for high school and college students applying to college and graduate school.

Princeton Review Publishing, L.L.C.
2315 Broadway
New York, NY 10024
E-mail: booksupport@review.com

The SAT questions throughout the book were selected from the following publications of the College Entrance Examination Board: *5 SATs, 1981; 6 SATs, 1982; 5 SATs, 1984; 10 SATs, 1983, 5 SATs, 1992*. These questions, as well as test directions throughout the book, are reprinted by permission of Educational Testing Service, the copyright owner of the sample questions. Permission to reprint the material does not constitute review or endorsement by Educational Testing Service or the College Board of this publication as a whole or of any other sample questions or testing information it may contain.

All other questions in the book were created by the authors.

The passage on p. 296 was reprinted from *Memoirs of an Anti-Semite* by Gregor von Rezzori with kind permission of Viking Penguin.

SAT is a registered trademark of the College Entrance Examination Board, which does not endorse this book.

ISBN 0-375-76331-7

Editor: Allegra Burton
Production Editor: Maria Dente
Production Coordinator: Stephen White
Illustrations by: The Production Department of The Princeton Review

Manufactured in the United States of America.

9 8 7 6 5 4 3 2 1

2004 Edition

ACKNOWLEDGMENTS

An SAT course is much more than clever techniques and powerful computer score reports; the reason our results are great is that our teachers care so much about their kids. Many of them have gone out of their way to improve the course, often going so far as to write their own materials, some of which we have incorporated into our course manual as well as into this book. The list of these teachers could fill this page, but special thanks must be given to Lisa Edelstein, Thomas Glass, Len Galla, Rob Cohen, Fred Bernstein, and Jayme Koszyn.

For production and editing help, thanks to Allegra Burton, Morgan Chase, Jeff Rubenstein, Ryan Tozzi, Jennifer Arias, Maria Dente, and Stephen White. Special thanks to Faisel Alam for his expertise.

Thanks go to Alex Freer Balko for sharing her wealth of knowledge on this project. A talented writer with the ability to see the big picture and an amazing eye for detail, Alex always comes through with top-notch work.

The Princeton Review would never have been founded without the advice and support of Bob Scheller. Many of the questions on our practice tests are the result of our joint effort. Bob's program, Pre-test Review, provides the best sort of competition; his fine results make us work all the harder.

Finally, we would like to thank the people who truly have taught us everything we know about the SAT: our students.

Special thanks to Adam Robinson, who conceived of and perfected the Joe Bloggs approach to standardized tests and many of the other successful techniques used by The Princteon Review.

CONTENTS

Foreword

The Princeton Review was formed more than 20 years ago based on a very simple idea: The SAT is not a test of intelligence, aptitude, how good a person you are, or how successful you will be in life. The SAT simply tests how well you take the SAT. And performing well on the SAT takes skill—skill that can be learned, like any other.

When students first take the SAT, many find it hard to believe that a test that claims to cover basic arithmetic, algebra, and geometry could make their lives so difficult. Even students who are very good at math often have difficulty with the SAT. Why? Because while the SAT tests very basic math skills, it tests them in *very* particular ways. Many students find that the particular structure of SAT math problems makes them harder than "ordinary math." In reality, the SAT, far more than measuring your math and English skills, measures your *test-taking skills*. But you've probably never taken a class on test-taking skills in school. This is why a thorough program of test preparation can be so effective.

The SAT was originally designed to be an intelligence test, a test of a student's "scholastic aptitude." (Nobody at the ETS or the College Board has ever been able to explain what that really means.) But this clearly isn't the case. A 1994 Roper Starch study verified that our SAT students increase their scores by an average of 137 points over the course of just a few weeks. This was proof-positive that the SAT did not test "scholastic aptitude" or intelligence—no SAT course can make students significantly smarter. It was also proof-positive that students could learn to take the test well. What The Princeton Review does is teach students how to be better standardized-test takers.

In the past few years, the political landscape surrounding testing has changed. As our society has become more test-savvy, the ETS test writers have responded in more sophisticated ways. They have admitted that the SAT is not an intelligence test, and not really an assessment test, either. This is reflected in the recent name changes of this test. The test writers first changed the name of the test from "Scholastic Aptitude Test" to "Scholastic Assessment Test." Later, they dropped the claim that it was an assessment test, and now it's just called the SAT (which stands for nothing at all). Further, the College Board now not only admits that preparation is advisable, but even recommends it. A College Board official recently remarked, "Just as you wouldn't want to take a driver's test cold, you don't want to go cold into the SAT."

Of course, the test writers still claim that only small improvements can be attributed to test preparation programs, and this may be true of most preparation programs—because most of them only do half the job.

Good test preparation has many elements. First, you need to become familiar with the format of the test and the concepts tested on it, so that you'll know exactly what you're going to see on test day. Second, you should thoroughly review these tested concepts to make sure you understand them fully, and you should review these concepts in the very particular way that they will appear on the test, which may be somewhat different than the way you have seen them in school. Third, you should develop an overall test-taking strategy to help you get the best score you can. Fourth, you should learn some powerful test-taking skills, which will help you think your way through problems *the way they appear on the SAT*. Fifth, you should take several full-length practice tests to put those strategies into practice and to train yourself for the actual test. Sixth, you should try to put yourself into a motivational and supportive environment that will make this learning experience fun. Finally, you should work with people who will help you stay disciplined and focused on your preparation.

The greater the number of these elements found in a preparation program, the more effective that program is likely to be. Our SAT classes are so successful because they combine all of these elements. Read this book very carefully, and learn its strategies. Take the full-length practice tests under actual timed conditions. Log on to our website and take advantage of all the fantastic online tools available to buyers of this book. Study with a friend to stay motivated. The more you take advantage of these resources, the better you'll perform. We're with you all the way.

We wish you the very best of luck in your preparation.

Jeff Rubenstein
Assistant Vice President
Research and Development
The Princeton Review

Introduction

Welcome to the 2004 edition of *Cracking the SAT*. We believe you are holding the most up-to-date book on the new test. If you concentrate on the techniques and strategies in this book, you will perform well on the SAT.

When we first came up with our revolutionary techniques, students would ask us if ETS would change the SAT to counter them. We were a small company back then, so we assured our students that ETS was highly unlikely to change the test just because a few hundred students each year showed impressive score improvements.

By the mid-1980s, however, several hundred students had grown to several thousand. And in 1986, when we revealed our methods to the general public in the first edition of the book you're holding—a book that became a *New York Times* best-seller—our students threw up their hands. "Now you guys have done it," they said. "You've let the secrets out of the bag. ETS is definitely going to change the SAT now to stop your techniques from working."

Well, the test has changed since then, but we've changed with it. Not only do our techniques still work, they're better than ever.

We at The Princeton Review spend almost $10 million every year improving our methods and materials, including our website. We send dozens of teachers into each test administration to make sure nothing slips by us. *Cracking the SAT* incorporates our observations, and gives you the most up-to-date information possible. And we've tied the book into drills and tests on our website—www.PrincetonReview.com—to make the book even more efficient at helping you improve your scores.

Before doing anything else, be sure to go online and follow the log-in instructions on page xiii to get yourself set up. Once you've registered, you'll be able to get detailed score reports for the tests in the back of this book, as well as do drills that will reinforce our techniques. Don't forget that quality practice takes time. You can't learn everything the day before the SAT, so give yourself four or five weeks to practice our techniques. We recommend that you spend six to ten hours per week. Finally, don't forget that *Cracking the SAT* is *not* a textbook; anyone charging you for a course that uses this book is ripping you off. You're better off just buying the book in a bookstore.

This test is important, but you're on the right track. Relax and work hard, and you'll get the SAT scores that the colleges you care about will love. And be sure to log on and take advantage of all the great online tools available to you.

Good luck!

John Katzman
President
The Princeton Review

P.S. If you feel you need more intensive work, you should look into our online and classroom courses. They combine our techniques with small classes run by great teachers. For more information, go online at www.PrincetonReview.com or call us at 1-800-2Review.

GET MORE FROM *CRACKING THE SAT* BY USING OUR FREE ONLINE TOOLS

Buyers of this book receive a free year-long subscription to *Cracking the SAT*'s **online companion course**, which features the latest in interactive tools for test preparation. Go to www.PrincetonReview.com/cracking/sat to register for all the free services we offer to help you improve your test score and find the right college. Once you've logged on, you'll be able to:

- **Take Extra SAT Practice Exams.** Get even more SAT practice by taking full-length SAT practice tests online. After each test, you'll receive a personalized score report that will show you where your strengths and weaknesses are and how well you're pacing yourself. You'll know exactly where you should be concentrating your preparation efforts.

- **Learn Key Test-Taking Skills Through Our Distance Learning Tools.** Some of the key lessons of *Cracking the SAT* will be even clearer after you've spent a few hours seeing and hearing them presented online.

- **Practice New Techniques with Online Drills.** Once you've learned a new technique or concept, you can take online drills to practice and to gauge your mastery.

- **Analyze Your Performance on the Tests in this Book.** By logging on to our website and submitting your answers to the practice tests in this book, you can get personalized score reports that will help you focus your energy on specific areas of weakness.

- **Research and Apply to the Best Colleges for You.** Through PrincetonReview.com, our award-winning college search site, you can access our complete library of information about US colleges, manage your application process, and even apply electronically to more than 800 colleges.

YOU'RE IN COMPLETE CONTROL

Here's what you'll see once you've registered:

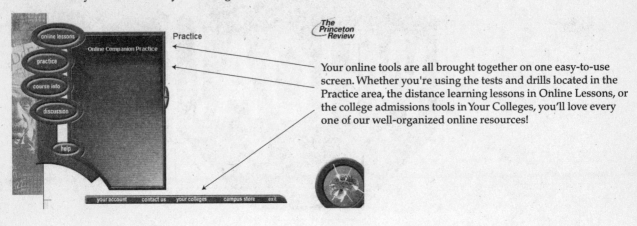

Your online tools are all brought together on one easy-to-use screen. Whether you're using the tests and drills located in the Practice area, the distance learning lessons in Online Lessons, or the college admissions tools in Your Colleges, you'll love every one of our well-organized online resources!

READING YOUR SCORE REPORT

After you take your extra practice exams, here's how to use your score report:

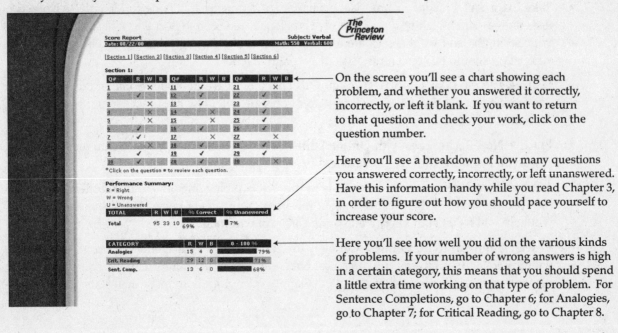

On the screen you'll see a chart showing each problem, and whether you answered it correctly, incorrectly, or left it blank. If you want to return to that question and check your work, click on the question number.

Here you'll see a breakdown of how many questions you answered correctly, incorrectly, or left unanswered. Have this information handy while you read Chapter 3, in order to figure out how you should pace yourself to increase your score.

Here you'll see how well you did on the various kinds of problems. If your number of wrong answers is high in a certain category, this means that you should spend a little extra time working on that type of problem. For Sentence Completions, go to Chapter 6; for Analogies, go to Chapter 7; for Critical Reading, go to Chapter 8.

PART I

Orientation

WHAT IS THE SAT I: REASONING TEST?

The SAT I—from now on, we'll refer to it simply as the SAT—is a three-hour multiple-choice test that is divided into seven sections:

1. Two 30-minute Verbal sections
2. One 15-minute Verbal section
3. Two 30-minute Math sections
4. One 15-minute Math section
5. One 30-minute Experimental section, either Math or Verbal

The 15-minute Verbal section consists of one or two Critical Reading passages followed by thirteen questions. The 15-minute Math section consists of ten multiple-choice math questions.

Only six of the seven sections on the SAT will count toward your scores. The Experimental section on your SAT will look just like a 30-minute Verbal or Math section, but it won't be scored; ETS uses it to try out new SAT questions and to determine whether the test you are taking is harder or easier than ones ETS has given in the past. (Unfortunately, it's *not possible* during the test to figure out which section on your SAT is the Experimental section.)

The Verbal SAT contains three types of questions:

1. Sentence Completions
2. Analogies
3. Critical Reading

The Math SAT also contains three types of questions:

1. Regular multiple-choice math (arithmetic, algebra, and geometry)
2. Quantitative Comparisons
3. Grid-ins

Each of these question types will be dealt with in detail later in the book.

WHERE DOES THE SAT COME FROM?

The SAT is published by the Educational Testing Service (ETS) under the sponsorship of the College Entrance Examination Board (the College Board). ETS and the College Board are both private companies. We'll tell you more about them in Chapter 1.

HOW IS THE SAT SCORED?

Four to five weeks after you take the SAT, you'll receive a report from ETS containing a Verbal score and a Math score. Each score will be reported on a scale that runs from 200 to 800; the best score is 800, and the average student scores around 500. The scores go up or down in increments of ten points.

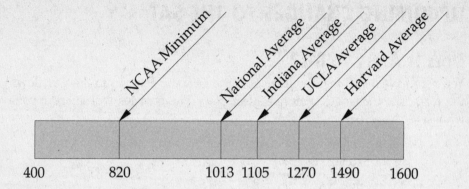

NCAA Minimum · National Average · Indiana Average · UCLA Average · Harvard Average

400   820   1013 1105   1270 1490   1600

RAW SCORES AND PERCENTILES

You may hear about two other kinds of scores in connection with the SAT: raw scores and percentile scores. Your *raw* score is simply the number of questions you answered correctly, minus a fraction of the number of questions you answered incorrectly. It is used to calculate your final *scaled* score. We'll tell you more about raw scores in Chapter 2. A *percentile* score tells you how you did in relation to everyone else who took the test. If your score is in the 60th percentile, it means you did better on the test than 60 percent of the people who took it. People who are disappointed by their SAT scores can sometimes cheer themselves up by looking at their percentile scores.

HOW IMPORTANT ARE SAT SCORES?

The SAT is an important factor when you apply to colleges, but it is not the only one. A rule of thumb: The larger the college, the more important the SAT score. Small liberal arts colleges will give a good deal of weight to your extracurricular activities, your interview, your essays, and your recommendations. Large state universities often admit students based on formulas consisting mostly of just two ingredients: SAT scores and grade point average.

Size Matters

Large schools process more applications, so they rely more heavily on SAT scores. Small schools have the time to read the rest of your application.

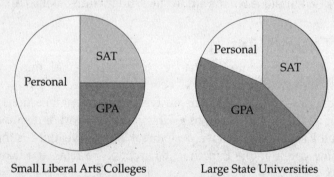

Small Liberal Arts Colleges   Large State Universities

Even at a small liberal arts college, though, SAT scores can be the deciding factor. If your scores fall below a school's usual range, admissions officers will look very critically at the other elements in your application folder. For most college applicants, an SAT score is the equivalent of a first impression. If your scores are good, an admissions officer will be more likely to give you the benefit of the doubt in other areas.

UPCOMING CHANGES TO THE SAT

DOES IT APPLY TO ME?

You may have heard that there are going to be some changes to the SAT down the road. These changes may not affect you. The changes will affect anyone who is:

- Taking the SAT in the spring of 2005 or after (students wishing to start college in 2006)

- Taking the PSAT in the fall of 2004

WHY CHANGE?

The original purpose of the SAT was to measure innate intelligence and not what students were taught in high school. This idea was later reformed and the purpose consequently became to measure a students' ability to reason. "We want people to think out of the box," a College Board vice president argued. It was felt that a student's ability to solve problems quickly could be a good predictor of that student's freshman grades.

So why change?

In February of 2001, the president of the University of California system made a speech asking the University of California to drop the SAT from its admissions requirements because the exam did not fulfill its goals. Understandably, when your biggest client decides to go elsewhere, you change your business philosophy. And this is exactly what the College Board did.

The main complaint against the SAT was that it did not reflect high school curricula and only tested a very narrow type of reasoning skills. To remedy this, the College Board revamped the SAT to reflect the curriculum and instructional practices of high school. Also, they sought to rectify the inability of the SAT to predict freshman grades by adding another dimension to the exam and thereby giving college admissions boards a third measure: writing skills.

AND THE CHANGES ARE...

Before we leap headfirst into the changes, there is one small thing you should be aware of: Students taking the SAT before the 2005 administration may see a few of these "new-look" questions on their Experimental sections (the most noticeable of which are the questions asking you to support or disprove an issue written by an ETS author). No reason to break into a sweat; this simply means that you know you're in the Experimental section. So relax and take a peek at the SAT 2K5.

The first victim of the new look SAT is the Verbal section: it is now named the Critical Reading section, which it essentially becomes. Gone are the frustrating analogies that tortured students about the relationship between two words they'd rarely seen and never used in common conversation. ETS has added more Critical Reading passages to the newly named Critical Reading section. Lucky for you, Sentence Completions have not been touched! Finally, instead of two 30-minute sections and one 15-minute section, there will now be two 25-minute sections and one 20-minute section.

The next change made to the SAT was the elimination of Quantitative Comparisons. This section contained two columns of numerical information and asked students to decide which is larger. Good-bye! If you have older siblings they may remember how much "fun" they had doing this section. Instead of adding a new question format, ETS decided to simply "beef" up the type of math covered by their multiple-choice questions. The new Math section will now include questions pertaining to skills learned in Algebra I, Geometry, and now Algebra II. This, ETS hopes, will align the SAT with standard high school curricula. Finally, just as with the Critical Reading section, there will now be two 25-minute and one 20-minute Math sections instead of the two 30-minute and one 15-minute sections.

Perhaps the most glaring difference is the addition of a Writing Skills section. This will be very similar to (if not exactly like) the SAT II: Writing test. Writing Skills will be made up of two 25-minute sections: one 25-minute essay and one 25-minute multiple-choice Grammar section. If you remember taking the PSAT Writing Skills component, you've already seen the sorts of grammar questions ETS will throw at you. The essay, however, will be based on an idea or maxim that you will have to either agree or disagree with, citing examples to strengthen your position.

The final change to the SAT will be with its scoring. Each section is scored on a 200–800 scale, for a maximum possible score of 2400, instead of 1600. Also, if you were diligent and added up the testing times, you noticed that the total testing time has gone up from 3 hours to a total of 3 hours and 35 minutes.

DON'T WORRY, BE HAPPY

Even though there will be a psychedelic media blitz about the "new" and "improved" SAT, there isn't all that much that is new or improved for you to be worried about. The bottom line is that the test is still coachable and ETS is still only checking a narrow spectrum of knowledge.

And that's why you're holding this book.

WHAT IS THE PRINCETON REVIEW?

The Princeton Review is the nation's fastest-growing test-preparation company. We have conducted courses in roughly 500 locations around the country, and we prepare more students for the SAT than anyone else. We also prepare students for the PSAT/NMSQT, ACT, GRE, GMAT, LSAT, MCAT, and other standardized tests.

The Princeton Review's techniques are unique and powerful. We developed them after spending countless hours scrutinizing real SATs, analyzing them with computers, and proving our theories with real students. Our methods have been widely imitated, but no one else achieves our score improvements.

This book is based on our extensive experience in the classroom. Our techniques for cracking the SAT will help you improve your SAT scores by teaching you to:

1. Think like the test writers at ETS

2. Take full advantage of the limited time allowed

3. Find the answers to questions you don't understand by guessing intelligently

4. Avoid the traps that ETS has laid for you (and use those traps to your advantage)

EVEN ETS KNOWS OUR TECHNIQUES WORK

ETS has spent a great deal of time and money over the years trying to persuade people that the SAT can't be cracked. At the same time, ETS has struggled to find ways of changing the SAT so that The Princeton Review won't be able to crack it—in effect acknowledging what our students have known all along, which is that our techniques really do work. Despite ETS's efforts, the SAT remains highly vulnerable to our techniques. In fact, the current format of the test is more coachable than ever.

A NOTE ABOUT SCORE IMPROVEMENTS

We have found in our courses that students' scores usually don't improve gradually. Instead, they tend to go up in spurts, from one plateau to another. Our students typically achieve score improvements of 100 points or more after mastering the initial concepts of the course. Then, their scores often level off, only to take another jump a few weeks later when they have assimilated more course material.

If you work steadily through this book, you too will find yourself moving from plateau to plateau. But you will have to work. You won't have one of our teachers standing over you, reminding you to review what you have learned.

A WARNING

Many of our techniques for beating the SAT may seem a bit unorthodox. That means using them will sometimes require a leap of faith. In order to get the full benefit from our techniques, you must trust them. The best way to develop this trust is to practice the techniques and convince yourself that they work. But you have to practice them properly. If you try our techniques on the practice questions in most popular SAT coaching books, you will probably decide that they don't work. Why? The practice questions in those books aren't really like the questions on the actual SAT. There may be "analogies" and "quantitative comparisons" in those books, but if you compare them with the questions on real SATs, you will discover that they are different. In contrast, the practice questions on the practice tests in the back of this book and on our website (see Online Tools for information on how to log on) are created using the same writing and testing processes that

Study

If you were getting ready to take a biology test, you'd study biology. If you were preparing for a basketball game, you'd practice basketball. So, if you're preparing for the SAT, study the SAT. ETS can't test everything (in fact, they test very little), so concentrate on learning what they *do* test.

ETS uses. They are then tried out on students to ensure that they are as much like real SAT questions as they can possibly be.

We strongly recommend that you purchase *10 Real SATs,* which is published by the folks who write and administer the SAT (the College Board and ETS). *10 Real SATs* contains ten actual SATs that have been administered over the last few years. This book will give you the opportunity to practice with real SAT questions that were written by the same people at ETS who will write your SAT. By practicing our techniques on real SATs, you will be able to prove to yourself that the techniques really do work. This will increase your confidence when you actually take the test.

If you don't find *10 Real SATs* in your local bookstore, you can order it directly from the College Board (see page 270 for ordering information). You should also ask your guidance counselor for free copies of *Taking the SAT I: Reasoning Test.* This booklet is published by the College Board and contains a full-length practice test.

Are you ready? Let's get cracking!

Shortcuts

The Princeton Review's techniques are the closest thing there is to a shortcut to the SAT. However, there is no shortcut to learning these techniques.

1

How to Think About the SAT

WHAT DOES THE SAT MEASURE?

If you're like most high school students, you think of the SAT as a test of how smart you are. If you score 800 on the Verbal section, you'll probably think of yourself as a "genius"; if you score 200, you may think of yourself as an "idiot." You may even think of an SAT score as a permanent label, like your Social Security number. The Educational Testing Service (ETS), the company that publishes the test, encourages you to think this way by telling you that the test measures your ability to reason and by claiming that you cannot significantly improve your score through special preparation.

Nothing could be farther from the truth.

THE SAT IS NOT A TEST OF REASONING

Closed Loop

The SAT is a test of how well you take the SAT.

The SAT isn't a test of how well you reason, and it isn't a test of how smart you are. More than anything else, it is a test of how good you are at taking the SAT.

Can you learn to be better at taking the SAT? Of course you can. That's what this book is all about. You can improve your SAT score in exactly the same way you would improve your grade in chemistry: by learning the material you are going to be tested on.

LEARN TO THINK LIKE ETS

If you got a D on a chemistry test, what would you do? You'd probably say to yourself, "I should have worked harder" or "I could have done better if I'd studied more." This is exactly the attitude you should have about the SAT. If you were disappointed by your score on the PSAT/NMSQT, you shouldn't say, "I'm stupid." Instead you should say, "I need to get better at taking this test."

You also need to get better at thinking like the people at ETS who write the questions. In your chemistry class, you know how your teacher thinks, and you know that he or she tends to ask certain kinds of questions. You also know what sorts of answers will win you points, and what sorts of answers won't.

You need to learn to think of the SAT in exactly the same terms. The test writers at ETS think in very predictable ways. You can improve your scores by learning to think the way they do and by learning to anticipate the kinds of answers that they think are correct.

WHAT IS ETS?

ETS is a big company. It sells not only the SAT, but also about 500 other tests, including ones for CIA agents, golf pros, travel agents, firefighters, and barbers. ETS is located outside Princeton, New Jersey, on a beautiful 400-acre estate that used to be a hunting club. The buildings where the SAT is written are surrounded by woods and hills. There is a swimming pool, a goose pond, a baseball diamond, lighted tennis courts, jogging trails, an expensive house for the company's president, a chauffeured motor pool, and a private hotel where rooms cost more than $200 a night.

You may have been told that ETS is a government agency or that it's a part of Princeton University. It is neither. ETS is just a private company that makes a lot of money by selling tests. The company that hires ETS to write the SAT is called the College Entrance Examination Board, or the College Board.

THE SAT IS NOT WRITTEN BY GENIUSES

Many people believe that SAT questions are written by famous college professors or experts on secondary education. This is not true. Virtually all questions are written by ordinary company employees or by college students and others who are hired part-time from outside ETS. Sometimes the questions are even written by teenagers. Frances Brodsky, the daughter of an ETS vice president, spent the summer after she graduated from high school writing questions for ETS tests.

Why are we telling you this? Because you should always remember that the test you are going to take was written by real people. The Wizard of Oz turned out not to be a wizard at all; he was just a little man behind a curtain. The same sort of thing is true of the SAT.

HOW TO CRACK THE SYSTEM

In the following chapters we're going to teach you our method for cracking the SAT. Read each chapter carefully. Some of our ideas may seem strange at first. For example, when we tell you that it is sometimes easier to answer hard SAT questions without looking at the questions but only at the answer choices, you may say, "That's not the way I'm taught to think in school."

FORGET ABOUT THE "BEST" ANSWER

The instructions for the SAT tell you to select the "best" answer to every question. What does "best" answer mean? It means the answer that ETS believes to be correct. For that reason, we're not going to talk about "best" answers in this book. Instead, we're going to talk about "ETS's" answers. These are the only answers that will win you points.

THE SAT ISN'T SCHOOL

We're not going to teach you math. We're not going to teach you English. We're going to teach you the SAT.

Why do you need to know the SAT? Because knowledge of the SAT is what the SAT tests.

In the next chapter we're going to lay down a few basic principles. We're going to show you that it is possible to:

- Find a correct answer by eliminating incorrect ones, even if you don't know why your answer is correct

- Take advantage of the SAT's "guessing reward"

- Earn credit for partial information

2

Cracking the SAT: Basic Principles

CRACKING MULTIPLE CHOICE

What's the capital of Malawi? Give up?

Unless you spend your spare time studying an atlas, you may not even know that Malawi is a tiny country in Africa, much less what its capital is. If this question came up on a test, you'd have to skip it, wouldn't you? Well, maybe not. Let's turn this question into a multiple-choice question—the only kind of question you'll find on the SAT Verbal section, and virtually the only kind of question you'll find on the SAT Math section—and see if you can figure out the answer anyway.

1. The capital of Malawi is

   (A) Washington, D.C.
   (B) Paris
   (C) Tokyo
   (D) London
   (E) Lilongwe

The question doesn't seem that hard anymore, does it? Of course, we made our example extremely easy. (By the way, there won't actually be any questions about geography on the SAT.) But you'd be surprised at how many people give up on SAT questions that aren't much more difficult than this one just because they don't know the correct answer right off the top of their heads. "Capital of Malawi? Oh no! I've never heard of Malawi!"

These students don't stop to think that they might be able to find the correct answer simply by eliminating all of the answer choices they know are wrong.

YOU ALREADY KNOW ALMOST ALL OF THE ANSWERS

All but ten of the questions on the SAT are multiple-choice questions, and every multiple-choice question is followed by five (or, in a few cases, four) answer choices. On every single multiple-choice question, one of those choices, and only one, will be the correct answer to the question. You won't have to come up with the answer from scratch. You only have to identify it.

How will you do that?

LOOK FOR THE WRONG ANSWERS INSTEAD OF THE RIGHT ONES

Why? Because wrong answers are usually easier to find. Remember the question about Malawi? Even though you didn't know the answer off the top of your head, you figured it out easily by eliminating the four obviously incorrect choices. You looked for wrong answers first.

In other words, you used the Process of Elimination, which we'll call POE for short. This is an extremely important concept, one we'll come back to again and again. It's one of the keys to improving your SAT score. When you finish reading this book, you will be able to use POE to answer many questions that you don't understand.

A Moral Dilemma

What if someone approached you moments before the SAT began and offered to give you the answers to the test? You'd be shocked. SHOCKED! Right? But what if we told you that the person making the offer was the proctor running the test? The fact is that every student who takes the test gets to see virtually all of the answers ahead of time: They're printed in the test booklet, right underneath each question.

The great artist Michelangelo once said that when he looked at a block of marble, he could see a statue inside it. All he had to do to make a sculpture, he said, was to chip away everything that wasn't part of it. You should approach difficult SAT multiple-choice questions in the same way, by chipping away everything that's not correct. By first eliminating the most obviously incorrect choices on difficult questions, you will be able to focus your attention more effectively on the few choices that remain.

THIS ISN'T THE WAY YOU'RE TAUGHT TO THINK IN SCHOOL

SAT ≠ School

If the SAT is not like the tests you take in high school, then why do colleges want you to take it? Good question.

In school, your teachers expect you to work carefully and thoroughly, spending as long as it takes to understand whatever it is you're working on. They want you to prove not only that you know the answer to a question, but also that you know how to derive it. When your algebra teacher gives you a test in class, he or she wants you to work through every problem, step by logical step. You probably even have to show your work. If you don't know all the steps required to arrive at the solution, you may not receive full credit, even if you somehow manage to come up with the correct answer.

But the SAT is different. It isn't like school. You don't have to prove that you know why your answer is correct. The only thing ETS's scoring machine cares about is the answer you come up with. If you darken the right space on your answer sheet, you'll get credit, even if you didn't quite understand the question.

PROCESS OF ELIMINATION (POE)

There won't be many questions on the SAT in which incorrect choices will be as easy to eliminate as they were on the Malawi question. But if you read this book carefully, you'll learn how to eliminate at least one choice on virtually any SAT multiple-choice question, and two, three, or even four choices on many.

What good is it to eliminate just one or two choices on a four- or five-choice SAT question?

Plenty. In fact, for most students, it's an important key to earning higher scores.

Here's another example:

2. The capital of Qatar is

(A) Paris
(B) Dukhan
(C) Tokyo
(D) Doha
(E) London

On this question you'll almost certainly be able to eliminate three of the five choices by using POE. That means you're still not sure of the answer. You know that the capital of Qatar has to be either Doha or Dukhan, but you don't know which.

Should you skip the question and go on? Or should you guess?

Close Your Eyes and Point

You've probably heard a lot of different advice about guessing on multiple-choice questions on the SAT. Some teachers and guidance counselors tell their students to never guess and to mark an answer only if they're absolutely certain that it's correct. Others tell their students not to guess unless they are able to eliminate two or three of the choices.

Both of these pieces of advice are incorrect.

Even ETS is misleading about guessing. Although it tells you that you *can* guess, it doesn't tell you that you *should*. In fact, if you can eliminate even one incorrect choice on an SAT multiple-choice question, guessing blindly from among the remaining choices will most likely improve your score. And if you can eliminate two or three choices, you'll be even more likely to improve your score by guessing.

Don't Pay Attention to ETS

ETS tries to discourage students from guessing on multiple-choice questions by telling them that there is a "guessing penalty" in the way the test is scored. But this is not true. There is no penalty for guessing on the SAT. Even if you can't eliminate any of the choices, random guessing isn't going to hurt your score in the long run.

There Is No Guessing Penalty on the SAT

Your raw score is the number of questions you got right, minus a fraction of the number you got wrong (except on the ten Grid-Ins, which are scored a little differently). Every time you answer an SAT question correctly, you get one raw point. Every time you leave an SAT question blank, you get zero raw points. Every time you answer an SAT question incorrectly, ETS subtracts one-fourth of a raw point if the question has five answer choices, one-third of a raw point if it has four answer choices, or nothing if it is a Grid-In.

It is the subtracted fraction—one-fourth or one-third, depending on the type of question—that ETS refers to as the "guessing penalty." But it's nothing of the sort. An example should help you understand.

Raw scores are a little confusing, so let's think in terms of money instead. For every question you answer correctly on the SAT, ETS will give you a dollar. For every multiple-choice question you leave blank, ETS will give you nothing. For every multiple-choice question you get wrong, you will have to give twenty-five cents back to ETS. That's exactly the way raw scores work.

What happens to your score if you select the correct answer on one question and incorrect choices on four questions? Remember what we said about money: ETS gives you a dollar for the one answer you guessed correctly; you give ETS a quarter for each of the four questions you missed. Four quarters equal a dollar, so you end up exactly where you started, with nothing—which is the same thing that would have happened if you had left all five questions blank.

In Fact, There's a Guessing Reward

Now, what if you were able to eliminate one incorrect choice on each of four questions? Random odds say you would get one question right—get a dollar—and miss the next three questions—give back 75 cents. You've just gained a quarter! In other words, there would be a guessing reward. All you would have to do to earn this reward is eliminate one choice, close your eyes, and take a shot.

Let's recap: If you eliminate nothing and guess, you break even (earn a dollar, give back four quarters). If you eliminate one or more answer choices, you gain points. So why would anyone hesitate to guess?

One of the most common misconceptions about the SAT is that you're better off leaving a multiple-choice question blank than "taking a chance" on getting it wrong. Some students even believe that they could earn a perfect score on the test by answering just four or five questions correctly and leaving all the others blank. They think they won't lose any points unless they give an answer that is actually wrong.

Nothing could be farther from the truth.

In order to earn the highest scores on the SAT you have to mark an answer for nearly every question, and just about every question you mark has to be correct. If you leave just one question blank in a Math section, for instance, the best Math score you can hope for is 780 or 790; if you leave forty questions blank, then the best score you can get is 400.

Be Test Smart

Many students with good grades get below-average scores because they refuse to guess.

Why This Is True

Let's use money again to illustrate why this is true. When you take the SAT, you start the test with the equivalent of $1,600 ($800 math, $800 verbal) in the bank. If you answer all the questions on each half correctly, you get to keep all $1,600.

For every question you answer incorrectly, though, you lose $10. Now, here's the important part: For every question you leave blank, you still lose $8.

Because of the way ETS calculates raw scores on the SAT, an incorrect answer is only a tiny bit worse than a blank. The one thing you can be certain of is that if you leave a question blank, you are definitely going to lose $8, whereas if you guess, you have the possibility of keeping $10. If you guess incorrectly, you'll lose just $2 more than you would have if you hadn't guessed at all. And if you guess correctly, you'll get to keep your money. That's not much of a gamble, is it?

Credit for Partial Information

We hope we've been able to persuade you that guessing on multiple-choice questions isn't going to hurt you and that, if you learn to do it well, it will help you raise your score. If you're like most people, though, you probably still feel a little funny about it. Earning points for a guess probably seems a little bit like cheating or stealing: You get something you want, but you didn't do anything to earn it.

This is not a useful way to think about the SAT. It's also not true. Look at the following example:

> 3. The sun is a
>
>   (A) main-sequence star
>   (B) meteor
>   (C) asteroid
>   (D) white dwarf star
>   (E) planet

If you've paid any attention at all in school for the past ten years or so, you probably know that the sun is a star. You can easily tell, therefore, that the answer to this question must be either A or D. You can tell this not only because it seems clear from the context that "white dwarf" and "main-sequence" are kinds of stars—as they are—but also because you know for a fact that the sun is not a planet, a meteor, or an asteroid. Still, you aren't sure which of the two possible choices is correct.

HEADS, YOU WIN A DOLLAR; TAILS, YOU LOSE A QUARTER

By using POE you've narrowed your choice down to two possibilities. If you guess randomly you'll have a fifty-fifty chance of being correct—like flipping a coin—heads you win a dollar, tails you lose a quarter. Those are extremely good odds on the SAT. But let's say that, in spite of everything we've told you, you just can't bring yourself to guess. You decide to leave the question blank.

Now, let's say there is a guy sitting next to you who is, to put it politely, no rocket scientist. When it comes to this question, he has no idea what the sun is: planet, asteroid, meteor—he's clueless. So he leaves the question blank, too.

Even though you know more about the sun than this guy, you both earn exactly the same score: zero. According to the SAT, you don't know any more about the sun than he does. (The answer, by the way, is (A). And don't worry, there won't be any questions about astronomy on the SAT.)

If you were in class, this probably wouldn't happen. Your teacher might give you credit for knowing that the sun is some kind of star. In math class, your teacher probably gives you partial credit on a difficult problem if you set it up correctly, even if you make a silly mistake and get the wrong answer.

GUESSING INTELLIGENTLY WILL INCREASE YOUR SCORE

Guessing makes it possible to earn credit for partial information on the SAT. You won't know everything about every question on the test, but there will probably be a lot of questions about which you know something. Doesn't it seem fair that you should be able to earn some sort of credit for what you do know? Shouldn't your score be higher than the score of someone who doesn't know anything?

Of course, there are times you shouldn't guess. We will discuss these in the next chapter. However, if you spend any time working on a problem, you deserve to take a shot at the answer and possibly get credit. Guessing is only unfair if you don't do it—unfair to you, that is. Your SAT score won't be a fair indication of what you know unless you guess and earn some credit for partial information.

TEXTBOOK GRAFITTI

At school you probably aren't allowed to write in your textbooks, unless your school requires you to buy them. You probably even feel a little peculiar about writing in the books you own. Books are supposed to be read, you've been told, and you're not supposed to scrawl all over them.

Because you've been told this so many times, you may be reluctant to write in your test booklet when you take the SAT. Your proctor will tell you that you are supposed to write in it—the booklet is the only scratch paper you'll be allowed to use; it says so right in the instructions from ETS—but you may still feel bad about marking it up.

Don't Be Ridiculous!

Your test booklet is just going to be thrown away when you're finished with it. No one is going to read what you wrote in it and decide that you're stupid because you couldn't remember what 2 + 2 was without writing it down. Your SAT score won't be any higher if you don't make any marks in your booklet. In fact, if you don't take advantage of it, your score will probably be lower than it should be.

Own Your Test Booklet

You paid for your test booklet; act as though you own it. Scratch work is extremely important on the SAT. Don't be embarrassed about it. After all, writing in your test booklet will help you keep your mind on what you're doing.

- When you work on a geometry problem that provides a diagram, don't hesitate to write all over it. What if there's no diagram? Draw one yourself—don't simply try to imagine it. Keep track of your work directly on the diagram to help you avoid making careless mistakes.

- On verbal questions, you will often need to come up with your own word or sentence to help you answer a question. Write it down! Trying to retain information in your head leads to confusion and errors. Your test booklet is your scratch paper—use it.

- When you use POE to eliminate a wrong answer choice, physically cross off the answer choice in your test booklet. Don't leave it there to confuse you. You may often need to carefully consider two remaining answer choices. You want to be clear about which answer choices are left in the running.

- When you answer a question but don't feel entirely certain of your answer, circle the question or put a big question mark in the margin beside it. That way, if you have time later on, you can get back to it without having to search through the entire section.

Write Now

Feel free to write all over this book, too. You need to get in the habit of making the SAT booklet your own. Start now by writing the names of the colleges you really want to attend in the margin below.

You probably think of scratch paper as something that is useful only in arithmetic. But you'll need scratch paper on the SAT Verbal section, too. The Verbal sections of your booklet should be just as marked up as the Math ones.

TRANSFER YOUR ANSWERS AT THE END OF EACH GROUP

Scratch work isn't the only thing we want you to do in your test booklet. We also want you to mark your answers there. In the Verbal sections, you should transfer your answers to the answer sheet when you come to the end of each group of questions. (For example, when you answer a group of Analogies, answer all the questions, then transfer your answers to the answer sheet.) You should transfer your answers a page at a time in the Math sections.

Doing this will save you a great deal of time, because you won't have to look back and forth between your test booklet and your answer sheet every few seconds. You will also be less likely to make mistakes in marking your answers on the answer sheet. However, be sure to give yourself enough time to transfer your answers. Don't wait until the last 5 minutes.

The only exception to this is the Grid-Ins, the ten non–multiple-choice math questions. You will need to grid each answer as you find it. We'll tell you all about Grid-Ins later in the book.

Mark Your Answer

When you take the SAT, you should mark all your answers in your test booklet, with a big letter in the margin beside each problem, and then transfer them later onto your answer sheet.

BASIC PRINCIPLES SUMMARY

1. When you don't know the right answer to a multiple-choice question, look for wrong answers instead. They're usually easier to find.

2. When you find a wrong answer choice, eliminate it. In other words, use POE, the Process of Elimination.

3. ETS doesn't care if you understand the questions on the SAT. All it cares about is whether you darken the correct space on your answer sheet.

4. There is no guessing penalty on the SAT. In fact, there is a guessing reward. If you can eliminate just one incorrect choice on an SAT multiple-choice question, you will most likely improve your score by guessing from among the remaining choices.

5. Leaving a question blank costs you almost as many points as answering it incorrectly.

6. Intelligent guessing on multiple-choice questions enables you to earn credit for partial information.

7. Do not hesitate to use your test booklet for scratch paper.

8. Transfer your answers to your answer sheet all at once when you reach the end of each group of questions in the Verbal sections and a page at a time in the Math sections (except for the Grid-Ins). And remember, give yourself enough time to transfer your answers; don't wait until the last 5 minutes.

3

Cracking the SAT:
Advanced Principles

PUTTING THE BASIC PRINCIPLES TO WORK

In the preceding chapter, we reviewed some basic principles of the SAT. We showed you that it is possible to:

- Find correct answers by using POE, the Process of Elimination, to get rid of incorrect ones

- Take advantage of the SAT's "guessing reward"

- Earn credit for partial information

But how will you know which answers to eliminate? And how will you know when to guess? In this chapter, we'll begin to show you. We will teach you how to:

- Take advantage of the order in which questions are asked

- Make better use of your time by scoring the easy points first

- Use the Joe Bloggs principle to eliminate obviously incorrect choices on difficult questions

- Find the traps that ETS has laid for you

- Turn those traps into points

To show you how this is possible, we first have to tell you something about the way the SAT is arranged.

ORDER OF DIFFICULTY

If you've already taken the SAT once, you probably noticed that the questions got harder as you went along. You probably didn't think much of it at the time, but it's true. Almost every group of questions starts out easy and then gets hard. Critical Reading questions are the exception to this rule.

For example, the 30-minute Verbal sections begin with a group of Sentence Completions. The first of these questions is so easy that you and virtually everyone else will answer it correctly. The second is a bit harder. The eighth is much, much harder, and the last is so hard that most of the people taking the test are unable to answer it correctly.

Is This Always True?

Almost always. Except for the Critical Reading questions, whose difficulty is hard to determine, all SAT questions are arranged in order of difficulty. This makes sense, doesn't it? If your gym teacher wanted to find out how high the people in your gym class could jump, she wouldn't start out by setting the high-jump bar at seven feet. She'd set it at a height that almost everyone could clear, and then she'd gradually raise it from there.

Questions on the SAT work the same way. If they were arranged differently, many students would become discouraged and give up before finding questions they were able to answer.

Easy, Medium, Difficult

Almost every group of questions on the SAT can be divided into three parts according to difficulty:

1. *The easy third*: Questions in the first third of each group are easy. ETS defines an easy question as one that most students answer correctly.

2. *The medium third*: Questions in the middle third are of medium difficulty. ETS defines a medium question as one that about half of all students answer correctly.

3. *The difficult third*: Questions in the last third are difficult. ETS defines a difficult question as one that most students answer incorrectly.

For example, within a group of ten Sentence Completion questions, questions 1 through 3 are easy, questions 4 through 7 are medium, and questions 8 through 10 are difficult. Then, if the next group of questions is a set of thirteen Analogies, questions 11 through 14 are easy, questions 15 through 19 are medium, and questions 20 through 23 are difficult, and so on.

The Princeton Review Difficulty Meter

Before you attack any SAT question, it is important to check out how difficult the question is. To remind you to do this, we will precede each SAT question in this book with The Princeton Review Difficulty Meter.

The Difficulty Meter divides each group of questions into thirds to indicate which question numbers are easy, which are medium, and which are hard. Before you begin working on an example, check the question number against the Difficulty Meter to determine how hard the question is.

Here's how the difficulty meter for a set of ten Sentence Completions would look:

SENTENCE COMPLETIONS		
1 2 3	4 5 6 7	8 9 10
EASY	MEDIUM	HARD

Knowing Question Difficulty Can Raise Your Score

Knowing that SAT questions are presented in order of difficulty can help you in several ways. First, it enables you to make the best use of your limited time. You should never waste time wrestling with the last (and therefore hardest) question in the Sentence Completion group if you still haven't answered the first (and therefore easiest) question in the Analogies group, which follows it. Hard questions aren't worth more than easy ones. Why not do the easiest ones first? Knowing how questions are arranged on the SAT can also help you find ETS's answers to questions you don't understand. To show you why this is true, we need to tell you something about how most people take the SAT and other standardized tests.

Easy to Be Hard

Remember, the SAT isn't a huge intellectual challenge; it's just tricky. When we talk about difficult questions on the SAT, we mean ones that people most often get wrong. Get your hands on an old SAT and look at some of the difficult math questions. Do any of them test anything you didn't learn in high school? Probably not. But do they all resemble the kind of straightforward questions you're used to seeing on a regular test? Probably not. ETS specializes in confusing and misleading test takers.

Rule #1

Answer easy questions first; save hard questions for last.

Choosing Answers That "Seem" Right

When most people take the SAT, they don't have time to do every problem, let alone double-check their work. They tend instead to work a problem as far as they can, then pick the answer that seems right, based on the work they've done. For most people, this method works well at the beginning of a section. They feel confident about the answers they are choosing. However, as they get to the middle of the section, they have more and more trouble solving the problems completely, and feel less and less sure of their guesses. By the time they get to the hard questions, they are often choosing answers not because they know how to solve the questions, but because the answers "seem right."

Should You Choose Answers That "Seem" Right?

That depends on where you are scoring and how hard the questions are.

Rule #2

Easy questions tend to have easy answers; hard questions tend to have hard answers.

- On easy multiple-choice questions, ETS's answers seem right to virtually everyone: high scorers, average scorers, and low scorers.

- On medium questions, ETS's answers seem wrong to low scorers, right to high scorers, and sometimes right and sometimes wrong to average scorers.

- On hard questions, ETS's answers seem right to high scorers and wrong to everyone else.

What we've just said is true by definition. If the correct answer to a difficult question seemed correct to almost everyone, the question wouldn't really be difficult, would it? If the correct answer seemed right to everyone, everyone would pick it. That would make it an easy question. For the average student, an "easy" solution to a hard question will always be wrong.

MEET JOE BLOGGS

We're going to talk a lot about "the average student" from now on. For the sake of convenience, let's give him a name: Joe Bloggs. Joe Bloggs is just the average American high school student. He has average grades and average SAT scores. There's a little bit of him in everyone, and there's a little bit of everyone in him. He isn't brilliant. He isn't dumb. He's exactly average.

How Does Joe Bloggs Approach the SAT?

Joe Bloggs, the average student, approaches the SAT just like everybody else does. Whether the question is hard or easy, he always chooses the answer that seems to be correct.

Here's an example of a very hard question from a real SAT:

PROBLEM SOLVING			
1 2 3 4 5 6 7 8 9 10 11 12 13 14 15 16 17 18 19 20 21 22 23 24 **25**			
EASY	MEDIUM	HARD	

25. A woman drove to work at an average speed of 40 miles per hour and returned along the same route at 30 miles per hour. If her total traveling time was 1 hour, what was the total number of miles in the round trip?

(A) 30

(B) $30\frac{1}{7}$

(C) $34\frac{2}{7}$

(D) 35

(E) 40

This was the last problem in a 25-question Math section. Therefore, according to the order of difficulty, it was the hardest problem in that section. Why was it hard? It was hard because most people answered it incorrectly. In fact, only about one student in ten got it right.

How Did Joe Bloggs Do on This Question?

Joe Bloggs—the average student—got this question wrong. Why? Because if the average student had gotten it right, it wouldn't have been a hard problem, would it?

Which Answer Did Joe Pick?

Joe picked choice D on this question; 35 just seemed like the right answer to him. Joe assumed that the problem required him to calculate the woman's average speed, and 35 is the average of 30 and 40.

But Joe didn't realize that he needed to account for the fact that the woman's trip didn't take the same amount of time in each direction. Her trip to work didn't last as long as her trip home. The answer would be 35 only if the woman had driven for a half-hour at 40 miles an hour and a half-hour at 30 miles an hour, and she did not.

Choice D was a trap: ETS test writers included it among the answer choices because they knew that it would seem right to the average student. They put a trap among the choices because they wanted this problem to be a hard problem, not an easy one. (The answer, by the way, is C. The woman spent more time going 30 mph than she did going 40 mph, so the answer must be a little less than 35.)

Could ETS Have Made This Question Easier?

Yes, by writing different answer choices.

Here's the same question with choices we have substituted to make the correct answer obvious:

1. A woman drove to work at an average speed of 40 miles per hour and returned along the same route at 30 miles per hour. If her total traveling time was 1 hour, what was the total number of miles in the round trip?

   (A) 1 million

   (B) 1 billion

   (C) $34\frac{2}{7}$

   (D) 1 trillion

   (E) 1 zillion

When the problem is written this way, Joe Bloggs can easily see that ETS's answer has to be C. It seems right to Joe, because all the other answers seem obviously wrong.

Remember:

- An SAT question is easy if the correct answer seems correct to the average person—to Joe Bloggs.

- An SAT question is hard if the correct answer seems correct to almost no one.

THE JOE BLOGGS PRINCIPLE

When you take the SAT a few weeks or months from now, you'll have to take it on your own, of course. But suppose for a moment that ETS allowed you to take it with Joe Bloggs as your partner. Would Joe be of any help to you on the SAT?

You Probably Don't Think So

After all, Joe is wrong as often as he is right. He knows the answers to the easy questions, but so do you. You'd like to do better than average on the SAT, and Joe earns only an average score (he's the average person, remember). All things considered, you'd probably prefer to have someone else for your partner.

But Joe might turn out to be a pretty helpful partner, after all. Since his hunches are always wrong on difficult multiple-choice questions, couldn't you improve your chances on those questions simply by finding out what Joe wanted to pick, and then picking something else?

If you could use the Joe Bloggs principle to eliminate one, two, or even three obviously incorrect choices on a hard problem, couldn't you improve your score by guessing among the remaining choices?

ETS's Favorite Wrong Answers

Take another look at question 25. Answer choice D was included to lure Joe Bloggs into a trap. But it isn't the only trap answer choice. Other tempting choices are A and E. Why? Because they are numbers included in the question itself, and Joe Bloggs is most comfortable with familiar numbers. When ETS selects wrong answers to hard questions, it looks for three things:

1. The answer you'd get doing the simplest possible math. In this case, that's D.

2. The answer you'd get after doing some, but not all, of the necessary math.

3. Numbers that are already in the question itself (choices A and E).

ETS doesn't use all of these every time, but there's at least one in every set of difficult answer choices.

How to Navigate with a Broken Compass

If you were lost in the woods, would it do you any good to have a broken compass? It would depend on how the compass was broken. Suppose you had a compass that always pointed south instead of north. Would you throw it away? Of course not. If you wanted to go north, you'd simply see which way the compass was pointing and then walk in the opposite direction.

Joe Bloggs Is Like That Broken Compass

On difficult SAT questions, he always points in the wrong direction. If Joe Bloggs were your partner on the test, you could improve your chances dramatically just by looking to see where he was pointing, and then going a different way.

We're going to teach you how to make Joe Bloggs your partner on the SAT. When you come to difficult questions on the test, you're going to stop and ask yourself, "How would Joe Bloggs answer this question?" And when you see what he would do, you are going to do something else. Why? Because you know that on hard questions, Joe Bloggs is always wrong.

What if Joe Bloggs Is Right?

Remember what we said about Joe Bloggs at the beginning. He is the average person. He thinks the way most people do. If the right answer to a hard question seemed right to most people, the question wouldn't be hard.

Joe Bloggs is right on some questions: the easy ones. But he's always wrong on the hard questions.

Putting Joe Bloggs to Work for You

In the chapters that follow, we're going to teach you many specific problem-solving techniques based on the Joe Bloggs principle. The Joe Bloggs principle will help you:

- Use POE to eliminate incorrect answer choices
- Make up your mind when you have to guess
- Avoid careless mistakes

The more you learn about Joe Bloggs, the more he'll help you on the test. If you make him your partner on the SAT, he'll help you find ETS's answers on problems you never dreamed you'd be able to solve.

Joe's Hunches

Should you always just eliminate any answer that seems to be correct? No! Remember what we said about Joe Bloggs:

1. His hunches are correct on easy questions.
2. His hunches are sometimes correct and sometimes incorrect on medium questions.
3. His hunches are always wrong on difficult questions.

On easy multiple-choice questions, pick the choice that Joe Bloggs would pick. On hard questions, be sure to eliminate the choices that Joe Bloggs would pick.

BECAUSE THIS IS SO IMPORTANT, WE'RE GOING TO SAY IT AGAIN

Here's a summary of how Joe Bloggs thinks:

Question Type	Joe Bloggs Looks For	Joe Bloggs Selects	Time Joe Spends	How Joe Does
Easy	the answer	the one that seems right	very little	mostly right
Medium	the answer	the one that seems right	not much	so-so
Difficult	the answer	the one that seems right	too much	all wrong!

YOU HAVE TO PACE YOURSELF

Rule #3

Any test taker scoring below 700 on either the math section or the verbal section will hurt his or her score by attempting to answer every question.

There are some very difficult questions on the SAT that most test takers shouldn't even bother to read. On the difficult third of every group of questions, there are some questions that almost no one taking the test will understand. Rather than spending time beating your head against these questions, you should enter a guess quickly and focus your attention on questions that you have a chance of figuring out.

Since most test takers try to finish every section ("I had two seconds left over!"), almost every test taker hurts his or her score. The solution, for almost anyone scoring less than 700 on a section, is to slow down.

Most test takers could improve their scores significantly by attempting fewer questions and devoting more time to questions they have a chance of answering correctly. Slow down, score more.

SET THE RIGHT GOAL BEFOREHAND

It's very important to set realistic goals. If you're aiming for a 500 on the Verbal section, your approach to the SAT is going to be different from that of someone who is aiming for an 800. The following charts will give you some idea of what you realistically need to know in order to score at various levels on the SAT. Use the chart to gauge your progress as you work through the practice tests in *10 Real SATs*.

Now before you decide you must get a 700 in Verbal no matter what, do a reality check: To date, what have you scored on the Verbal SAT? The Math? Whatever those numbers are, add 50–90 points to each to determine your goal score. Then get cracking! Work through this book, practice the techniques, and, after a time, take a practice test (timed). If you achieve your goal score on the practice test, great! Could you have worked a little more quickly yet maintained your level of accuracy? If so, increase your goal by another 50 points.

In other words, you must set an attainable goal in order to see any improvement. If you scored a 400 on the last Math SAT you took, and you immediately shoot for a 700, you will be working too quickly to be accurate, and won't see any increase in your score. However, if you instead use the "460–500" pacing guide, you may jump from a 400 to a 480! After that you can work to score over a 500, etc.

Come back to these pages after each practice test you take to reassess your pacing strategy. Remember, accuracy is more important than speed. Finishing is not the goal; getting questions right is! Besides, all the hard problems are at the end. If you are missing easy questions due to your haste to get to the difficult questions, you are throwing points away.

By the way, you may notice that the two charts below present slightly different pacing strategies for the Math and Verbal sections. That's because, on the Math section, it's even more important to take as much time as you need to get each problem right, rather than furiously working through absolutely every problem on the test. The numbers of questions listed in the charts represent how many questions you should do, not how many you need to get right.

Rule #4
Remember, accuracy is more important than speed.

VERBAL PACING CHART

To Get: (scaled score)	You Need: (raw points)	30-question section	35-question section	13-question section	Total Questions
350	11	6	6	2	14
400	18	9	9	4	22
450	27	14	14	6	34
500	35	19	19	7	45
550	44	23	23	9	55
600	54	27	31	10	68
650	62	all	all	all	78
700	68	all	all	all	78
750	72	all	all	all	78
800	76	all	all	all	78

MATH PACING CHART

To Get: (scaled score)	You Need: (raw points)	25-question section	Quant Comp section	Grid-In section	10-question section	Total Questions
350	8	5	4	3	2	14
400	14	7	5	4	4	20
450	21	12	7	4	4	27
500	28	14	9	6	5	34
550	35	16	10	8	7	41
600	42	20	12	8	8	48
650	47	23	12	9	9	53
700	53	All	14	All	All	59
750	57	All	All	All	All	All
800	60	All	All	All	All	All

ADVANCED PRINCIPLES SUMMARY

1. The problems in almost every group of questions on the SAT start out easy and gradually get harder. The first question in a group is often so easy that virtually everyone can find ETS's answer. The last question is so hard that almost no one can.

2. Because number one is true, you should never waste time trying to figure out the answer to a hard question if there are still easy questions that you haven't tried. All questions are worth the same number of points. Why not do the easy ones first?

3. Most every group of questions on the SAT can be divided into thirds by difficulty as follows:

   - On the easy third of each group of questions, the average person gets all the answers right. The answers that seem right to the average person actually are right on these questions.

   - On the medium third of each group, the average person's hunches are right only some of the time. Sometimes the answers that seem right to the average person really are right; sometimes they are wrong.

- On the difficult third, the average person's hunches are usually wrong. The answers that seem right to the average person on these questions invariably turn out to be wrong.

4. Joe Bloggs is the average student. He earns an average score on the SAT. On easy SAT questions, the answers that seem correct to him are always correct. On medium questions, they're sometimes correct and sometimes not. On hard questions, they're always wrong.

5. On hard questions, Joe Bloggs is your partner. Decide what Joe would do, then *do something else*. Cross off Joe Bloggs answers to increase your potential for guessing correctly.

6. Most test takers could improve their scores significantly by attempting fewer questions and devoting more time to questions they have a chance of answering correctly.

7. It's very important to set realistic goals. If you're aiming for a 500 on the Verbal, your approach to the SAT is going to be very different from that of someone who is aiming for an 800.

8. After each practice exam, go back to the pacing chart. You may need to answer more questions on the next exam to earn the score you want.

PART ◆ II

How to Crack the Verbal SAT

A FEW WORDS ABOUT WORDS

The SAT contains seven sections. Three of these will be Verbal, or "English," sections. There may be a fourth Verbal section on your test, but it will be experimental, so it won't count toward your score. Don't worry about trying to identify the Experimental section. Just work at your normal pace.

Each of the three scored Verbal sections on the SAT contains the following three types of questions:

- Sentence Completions
- Analogies
- Critical Reading

WHAT DOES THE VERBAL SAT TEST?

ETS says that the Verbal SAT tests "verbal reasoning abilities" or "higher order reasoning abilities." You may be wondering exactly what these statements mean, but don't sweat it—they're not true anyway. The Verbal SAT is mostly a test of your vocabulary. Even Critical Reading questions often test nothing more than your familiarity with certain words. If you have a big vocabulary, you'll probably do well on the exam. If you have a small vocabulary, you'll have more trouble no matter how many techniques we teach you.

For this reason, it's absolutely essential that you get to work on your vocabulary now! The best way to improve your vocabulary is by reading. Any well-written book is better than television. Even certain periodicals—newspapers and some magazines—can improve your verbal performance if you read them regularly. Keep a notebook and a dictionary by your side as you read. When you encounter words you don't know, write them down, look them up, and try to incorporate them into your life. The dinner table is a good place to throw around new words.

Read What You Like

Some folks think it's necessary to read nothing but books on obscure subjects in order to build a better vocabulary. Not true. Identify something that interests you and find some books on that subject. You'll be spending time on something you enjoy, and hey, you just might learn something.

Building a vocabulary this way can be slow and painful. Most of us have to encounter new words many times before we develop a firm sense of what they mean. You can speed up this process a great deal by taking advantage of the vocabulary section (Part V) in the back of this book. It contains a short list of words that are highly likely to turn up on the SAT, a section on word roots, and some general guidelines about learning new words. If you work through it carefully between now and the time you take the test, you'll have a much easier time on the Verbal SAT. The more SAT words you know, the more our techniques will help you.

Read through the next section and sketch out a vocabulary-building program for yourself. You should follow this program every day, at the same time that you work through the other chapters of this book.

The techniques described in the three Verbal chapters that follow the vocabulary section are intended to help you take full advantage of your growing vocabulary by using partial information to attack hard questions. In a sense, we are going to teach you how to get the maximum possible mileage out of the words you know. Almost all students miss SAT questions that they could have answered correctly if they had used our techniques.

4

Vocabulary

WORDS, WORDS, WORDS

The SAT Verbal section is in large part a vocabulary test. The more words you know on the test, the easier it will be. It's as simple as that. For this reason, it's important that you get to work on your vocabulary *immediately*.

THE HIT PARADE

The Hit Parade list consists of those words that show up most often on the SAT. Each word on the list is accompanied by its definition, a pronunciation guide, and a sentence that uses the word. Your vocabulary-building program should start with these words.

LEARN THE WORDS IN GROUPS

The Hit Parade has been arranged by groups of related words. Learning groups of related words can better help you remember each word's meaning. Even when you don't remember the exact meaning of a word, you may remember what group it is from. This will give you an idea of the word's meaning, which can help you use POE to get to an answer.

Make each group of words a part of your life. Rip out one of the group lists, carry it around with you, and use the words throughout your day. For example, on Monday you may feel like using words of *disdain* (see the "If you can't say anything nice" list), but on Friday you may wish to be more *affable* (see the "Friendly" list).

DON'T MEMORIZE THE DICTIONARY

Only a tiny percentage of all the words in the English language are ever used on the SAT. Generally speaking, the SAT tests the kinds of words that an educated adult—your English teacher, for example—would know without having to look them up. It tests the sort of words that you encounter in your daily reading, from a novel in English class to the newspaper.

HOW TO MEMORIZE NEW WORDS

Here are three effective methods for learning new words.

- **Flash Cards:** You can make your own flash cards out of 3 × 5 index cards. Write a word on one side and the definition on the other. Then quiz yourself on the words, or practice with a friend. You can carry a few cards around with you every day and work on them in spare moments, like when you're riding on the bus.

- **The Image Approach:** The image approach involves letting each new word suggest a wild image to you, then using that image to help you remember the word. For example, the word *enfranchise* means, "to give the right to vote."

Women did not become *enfranchised* in the United States until 1920, when the Nineteenth Amendment to the Constitution guaranteed them the right to vote in state and federal elections.

Franchise might suggest to you a McDonald's franchise: you could remember the new word by imagining people lined up to vote at a McDonald's. The weirder the image, the better you'll remember the word.

- **Mnemonics:** Speaking of "the weirder, the better," another way to learn words is to use mnemonics. A mnemonic is a device or trick, such as a rhyme or a song, that helps you remember something. *In fourteen hundred ninety-two Columbus sailed the ocean blue* is a mnemonic that helps you remember a date in history. The funnier or the stranger you make your mnemonic, the more likely you are to remember it. Write down your mnemonics (your flash cards are a great place for these). Although you may not always be able to think of a mnemonic for *every* Hit Parade word, sometimes you'll end up learning the word just by thinking about the definition long enough.

LOOK IT UP

Well-written general publications—like *The New York Times* and *Sports Illustrated*—are good sources of SAT words. You should read them on a regular basis. When you come across a new word, write it down, look it up, and remember it. You can make flash cards for these words as well.

Before you can memorize the definition of a word you come across in your reading, you have to find out what it means. You'll need a real dictionary for that. ETS uses two dictionaries in writing the SAT: the *American Heritage Dictionary* and the *Webster's New Collegiate Dictionary*. You should own a copy of one or the other. (You'll use it in college, too—it's a good investment.)

Keep in mind that most words have more than one definition. The dictionary will list these in order of frequency, from the most common to the most obscure. ETS will trip you up by testing the second, third, or even the fourth definition of a familiar-sounding word. For example, the word *pedestrian* shows up repeatedly on the SAT. When ETS uses it, though, it never means a person on foot—the definition of *pedestrian* you're probably most familiar with. ETS uses it to mean common, ordinary, banal—a *secondary* definition.

Very often, when you see easy words on hard SAT questions, ETS is testing a second, third, or fourth definition that you may not be familiar with.

ARE YOU TALKIN' TO ME?

assertion   uh SUR shun
> *a declaration or statement*
>> We could not believe John's assertion that he had never seen *Star Wars*.

clarity   KLAR uh tee
> *clearness in thought or expression*
>> Carol spoke with such clarity that her 2-year-old understood exactly what she wanted him to do.

cogent   KO jent
> *convincing; reasonable*
>> Christina's argument was so cogent that even her opponents had to agree with her.

coherent   ko HEER ent
> *logically connected*
>> The old prospector's story was not coherent; he rambled on about different things that had nothing to do with each other.

cohesive   ko HEE siv
> *condition of sticking together*
>> Erik's essay was cohesive because each point flowed nicely into the next point.

didactic   dy DAK tik
> *intended to instruct*
>> The tapes were entertaining and didactic because they amused and instructed children.

discourse   DIS kors
> *verbal expression or exchange; conversation*
>> Their discourse varied widely; they discussed everything from Chaucer to ice fishing.

eloquence   EH lo kwens
> *the ability to speak vividly or persuasively*
>> Cicero's eloquence is legendary; his speeches were well-crafted and convincing.

emphasize   EM fuh size
> *to give special attention to something, to stress*
>> During English class, our instructor emphasized the importance of learning vocabulary.

fluid   FLOO id
> *easily flowing*
>> The two old friends' conversation was fluid; each of them was able to respond quickly and easily to what the other had to say.

implication   im pli KAY shun
>   *the act of suggesting or hinting*
>> When your mother says, "Where were you raised, in a barn?" the implication is that you should close the door.

lucid   LOO sid
>   *easily understood; clear*
>> Our teacher does a good job because he provides lucid explanations of difficult concepts.

pundit   PUN dit
>   *an authority who expresses his/her opinions*
>> The political pundit has made many predictions, but few of them have come true.

rhetoric   RET uh rik
>   *the art of using language effectively and persuasively*
>> Since they are expected to make speeches, most politicians and lawyers are well-versed in the art of rhetoric.

I'LL BE THE JUDGE OF THAT

arbiter   AHR bih ter
>   *a judge who decides a disputed issue*
>> An arbiter was hired to settle the Major League Baseball strike because the owners and players could not come to an agreement.

biased   BYE ist
>   *prejudiced*
>> A judge should not be biased, but should weigh the evidence fairly before making up her mind.

exculpate   EKS kul payt
>   *to free from guilt or blame*
>> When the gold coins discovered in his closet were found to be fake, Dr. Rideau was exculpated and the search for the real thief continued.

impartial   im PAR shul
>   *not in favor of one side or the other, unbiased*
>> The umpire had a hard time remaining impartial; his son was pitching for the home team, and this made it difficult to call the game fairly.

incontrovertible   in kon truh VERT uh bul
>   *indisputable; not open to question*
>> The videotape of the robbery provided incontrovertible evidence against the suspect—he was obviously guilty.

integrity   in TEG rit ee
trustworthiness; completeness
> The integrity of the witness was called into question when her dislike for the defendant was revealed—some jurors suspected that she was not being entirely truthful.

jurisprudence   JER is proo duns
the philosophy or science of law
> Judges and lawyers are longtime students of jurisprudence.

objectivity   ahb jek TIV ih tee
treating facts without influence from personal feelings or prejudices
> It is important that a judge hear all cases with objectivity, so that his personal feelings do not affect his decision.

penitent   PEN ih tunt
expressing remorse for one's misdeeds
> His desire to make amends to the people he had wronged indicated that he was truly penitent, so the parole board let him out of the penitentiary.

plausible   PLAWZ ih bul
seemingly valid or acceptable; credible
> Keith's excuse that he missed school yesterday because he was captured by space aliens was not very plausible.

substantiated   sub STAN shee ay tid
supported with proof or evidence; verified
> The fingerprint evidence substantiated the detective's claim that the suspect had been at the scene of the crime.

vindicated   VIN duh kayt id
freed from blame
> Mrs. Layton was finally vindicated after her husband admitted to the crime.

YOU'RE SO VAIN

condescending   kon de SEND ing
treating people as weak or inferior
> Robert always looked down on his sister and treated her in a condescending manner.

contemptuous   kun TEMP choo us
feeling hatred; scornful
> She was so contemptuous of people who wore fur that she sprayed red paint on them.

despotic   des PAHT ik
exercising absolute power; tyrannical
> He was a despotic ruler whose every law was enforced with threats of violence or death.

dictatorial   dik tuh TOR ee ul

domineering; oppressively overbearing

> The coach had a dictatorial manner and expected people to do whatever he demanded.

disdain   dis DAYN

(n.) contempt, scorn
(v.) to regard or treat with contempt; to look down on

> I felt nothing but disdain for the person who stole my lunch—what a jerk!

haughty   HAW tee

arrogant; vainly proud

> His haughty manner made it clear that he thought he was better than everyone else.

imperious   im PEER ee us

arrogantly domineering or overbearing

> She had a very imperious way about her; she was bossy and treated everyone like they were beneath her.

patronizing   PAY truh ny zing

treating in a condescending manner

> Patrick had such a patronizing attitude that he treated everyone around him like a bunch of little kids.

WHEN THE GOING GETS TOUGH

convoluted   kon vuh LOO tid

intricate; complex

> The directions were so convoluted that we drove all around the city and got lost.

cryptic   KRIP tik

difficult to comprehend

> The writing on the walls of the crypt was cryptic; none of the scientists understood it.

futile   FEW tul

having no useful purpose; pointless

> It is futile to try to explain the difference between right and wrong to your pet.

impede   im PEED

to slow the progress of

> The retreating army constructed barbed-wire fences and destroyed bridges to impede the advance of the enemy.

obscure   ub SKYUR

    (adj.) relatively unknown

    (v.) to conceal or make indistinct

        Scott constantly makes references to obscure cult films, and no one ever gets his jokes.

        The man in front of me was so tall that his head obscured my view of the movie.

quandary   KWAHN dree

    a state of uncertainty or perplexity

        Morgan was in a quandary because he had no soap with which to do his laundry.

I'M A LOSER, BABY

dilatory   DIL uh tor ee

    habitually late

        Always waiting until the last moment to do his work, Stephen was a dilatory student.

indolent   IN duh lunt

    lazy

        Mr. Lan said his students were indolent because none of them had done their homework.

insipid   in SIP id

    uninteresting; unchallenging

        That insipid movie was so boring and predictable that I walked out.

listless   LIST luss

    lacking energy

        Since he is accustomed to an active lifestyle, Mark feels listless when he has nothing to do.

torpor   TOR per

    laziness; inactivity; dullness

        The hot and humid day filled everyone with an activity-halting torpor.

REVOLUTION

alienated   AY lee en ay tid

    removed or disassociated from (friends, family, or homeland)

        Rudolph felt alienated from the other reindeer because they never let him join in their reindeer games.

alliance   uh LY uhns

    a union of two or more groups

        The two countries formed an alliance to stand against their common enemy.

disparity   dis PAR uh tee
  inequality in age, rank or degree; difference
      There is a great disparity between rich and poor in many nations.

servile   SER vul
  submissive; like a servant
      Cameron's servile behavior finally ended when he decided to stand up
      to his older brother.

suppressed   suh PREST
  subdued; kept from being circulated
      The author's book was suppressed because the dictator thought it was
      too critical of his regime.

YOU ARE SO BEAUTIFUL

embellish   em BELL ish
  to make beautiful by ornamenting; to decorate
      We embellished the account of our vacation by including descriptions of
      the many colorful people and places we visited.

florid   FLOR id
  describing flowery or elaborate speech
      The candidate's speech was so florid that although no one could under-
      stand what he was talking about, they all agreed that he sounded good
      saying it.

opulent   AHP yuh lunt
  exhibiting a display of great wealth
      Dances at the king's palace are always very opulent affairs because no
      expense is spared.

ornate   or NAYT
  elaborately decorated
      The carved wood was so ornate that you could examine it several times
      and still notice things you had not seen before.

ostentatious   ah sten TAY shus
  describing a showy or pretentious display
      Whenever the millionaire gave a party, the elaborate decorations and
      enormous amounts of food were always part of his ostentatious display
      of wealth.

poignant   POYN yunt
  profoundly moving; touching
      The most poignant part of the movie was when the father finally made
      peace with his son.

OVERKILL

ebullience   ih BOOL yuns
intense enthusiasm
> A sense of ebullience swept over the crowd when the matador defeated the bull.

effusive   eh FYOO siv
emotionally unrestrained; gushy
> Gwyneth was effusive in her thanks after winning the Oscar; she even burst into tears.

egregious   uh GREE jus
conspicuously bad or offensive
> Forgetting to sterilize surgical tools before an operation would be an egregious error.

flagrant   FLAY grunt
extremely or deliberately shocking or noticeable
> Burning the flag shows flagrant disrespect for the country.

frenetic   freh NEH tik
wildly excited or active
> The pace at the busy office was frenetic; Megan never had a moment to catch her breath.

gratuitous   gruh TOO ih tus
given freely; unearned; unwarranted
> The film was full of gratuitous sex and violence that was not essential to the story.

superfluous   soo PER floo us
extra; unnecessary
> If there is sugar in your tea, adding honey would be superfluous.

IT'S GETTING BETTER

alleviate   uh LEEV ee ayt
to ease a pain or a burden
> John took aspirin to alleviate the pain from the headache he got after taking the SAT.

asylum   uh SY lum
a place of retreat or security
> The soldiers sought asylum from the bombs in the underground shelter.

auspicious   aw SPISH us
favorable; promising
> Our trip to the beach had an auspicious start; the rain stopped just as we started the car.

benevolent   buh NEV uh lunt
  well-meaning; generous
      She was a kind and benevolent queen who was concerned about her
      subjects' well-being.

benign   buh NINE
  kind and gentle
      Uncle Ben is a benign and friendly man who is always willing to help.

emollient   eh MOHL yunt
  (adj.) softening and soothing
  (n.) something that softens or soothes
      His kind words served as an emollient to the pain she had suffered.

mollify   MAHL uh fy
  to calm or soothe
      Anna's apology for scaring her brother did not mollify him; he was mad
      at her all day.

reclamation   rek luh MAY shun
  the act of making something useful again
      Thanks to the reclamation project, the once unusable land became a
      productive farm.

sanction   SANK shun
  to give official authorization or approval
      The students were happy when the principal agreed to sanction the use
      of calculators in math classes.

LIAR, LIAR, PANTS ON FIRE

dubious   DOO bee us
  doubtful; of unlikely authenticity
      Jerry's claim that he could fly like Superman seemed dubious—we didn't
      believe it.

fabricated   FAB ruh kay tid
  made; concocted in order to deceive
      Fabio fabricated the story that he used to play drums for Metallica; he
      had never actually held a drumstick in his life.

hypocrisy   hih POK ruh see
  the practice of pretending to be something one is not; insincerity
      People who claim to be vegetarian but eat chicken and fish are guilty of
      hypocrisy.

slander   SLAN der
  false charges and malicious oral statements about someone
      After the radio host stated that Monica was a space alien, she sued him
      for slander.

spurious   SPUR ee us
  not genuine; false, counterfeit
        The sportscaster made a spurious claim when he said that the San An-
        tonio Spurs were undefeated.

SHE'S CRAFTY

astute   uh STOOT
  shrewd; clever
        Kevin is financially astute; he never falls for the tricks that credit card
        companies play.

camouflage   KAM uh flahzh
  to hide by blending in with surroundings
        The smugglers did not want the trail to their hideout discovered, so they
        camouflaged the entrance with branches and vines.

clandestine   klan DES tin
  secretive
        The spies planned a clandestine maneuver that depended on its secrecy
        to work.

coup   KOO
  a brilliantly executed plan
        It was a coup when I talked the salesperson into selling me this valuable
        cuckoo clock for five dollars.

disingenuous   dis in JEN yoo us
  not straightforward; crafty
        Mr. Gelman was rather disingenuous; although he seemed to be simply
        asking about your health, he was really trying to figure out why you'd
        been absent.

ruse   ROOZ
  a crafty trick
        The offer of a free cruise was merely a ruse to get people to listen to
        their sales pitch.

stratagem   STRAT uh jem
  a clever trick used to deceive or outwit
        Planting microphones in the gangster's home was a clever, but illegal,
        stratagem.

surreptitious   sur ep TISH us
  done by secretive means
        Matt drank the cough syrup surreptitiously because he didn't want
        anyone to know that he was sick.

wary   WAIR ee

on guard; watchful

My father becomes wary whenever a salesman calls him on the phone; he knows that many crooks use the phone so that they can't be charged with mail fraud.

wily   WY lee

cunning

The wily coyote devised all sorts of clever traps to catch the roadrunner.

SITTIN' ON THE FENCE

ambiguous   am BIG yoo us

open to more than one interpretation

His eyes were an ambiguous color: some thought they were brown and some thought they were green.

ambivalent   am BIV uh lunt

simultaneously having opposing feelings; uncertain

She had ambivalent feelings about her dance class: On one hand, she enjoyed the exercise, but on the other hand, she thought the choice of dances could be more interesting.

apathetic   ap uh THET ik

feeling or showing little emotion

When the defendant was found guilty on all charges, her face remained expressionless and she appeared to be entirely apathetic.

arbitrary   AR bih trayr ee

determined by impulse rather than reason

The principal made the arbitrary decision that students could not wear hats in school, without offering any logical reason for the rule.

capricious   kuh PREE shus

impulsive and unpredictable

The referee's capricious behavior angered the players because he was inconsistent in his calls; he would call a foul for minor contact, but ignore elbowing and kicking.

equivocate   eh KWIV uh kayt

to avoid making a definite statement

On critical reading questions, I choose answers that equivocate; they use words such as *could* or *may* that make them hard to disprove.

indifferent   in DIF rent

not caring one way or the other

The old fisherman was completely indifferent to the pain and hunger he felt; his only concern was catching the enormous marlin he had hooked.

spontaneous   spon TAY nee us
  unplanned; naturally occurring
> Dave is such a good musician that he can create a song spontaneously, without having to stop and think about it.

whimsical   WIM zuh kul
  subject to erratic behavior; unpredictable
> Egbert rarely behaved as expected; indeed, he was a whimsical soul whose every decision was anybody's guess.

JUST A LITTLE BIT

inconsequential   in kahn suh KWEN shul
  unimportant
> The cost of the meal was inconsequential to Quentin because he wasn't paying for it.

superficial   soo per FISH ul
  concerned only with what is on the surface or obvious; shallow
> The wound on his leg was only superficial even though it looked like a deep cut.

tenuous   TEN yoo us
  having little substance or strength; shaky; unsure, weak
> Her grasp on reality is tenuous at best; she's not even sure what year it is.

trivial   TRIH vee ul
  of little importance or significance
> Alex says he doesn't like trivia games because the knowledge they test is trivial; he prefers to spend his time learning more important things.

I WILL SURVIVE

assiduous   uh SID yoo us
  hard-working
> Spending hours in the hot sun digging out every tiny weed, Sidney tended her garden with assiduous attention.

compelling   kum PEL ing
  forceful; urgently demanding attention
> By ignoring the problems in the city, the mayor gave people a very compelling reason to vote him out of office.

diligent   DIL uh jent
  marked by painstaking effort; hard-working
> With a lot of diligent effort, they were able to finish the model airplane in record time.

dogged   DOG id
> *stubbornly persevering*
>> Her first few attempts resulted in failure, but her dogged efforts ultimately ended in success.

endure   en DUR
> *to put up with, to survive a hardship*
>> It was difficult to endure the incredibly boring lecture given in class the other day.

intrepid   in TREH pid
> *courageous; fearless*
>> The intrepid young soldier scaled the wall and attacked the enemy forces despite being outnumbered fifty to one.

maverick   MAV uh rik
> *one who is independent and resists adherence to a group*
>> In *Top Gun*, Tom Cruise was a maverick; he often broke the rules and did things his own way.

obdurate   AHB dur ut
> *stubborn; inflexible*
>> Leanna was so obdurate that she was unable to change her way of thinking on even the most minor issues.

obstinate   AHB stin ut
> *stubbornly adhering to an opinion or a course of action*
>> Even though he begged them constantly, Jeremy's parents were obstinate in refusing to buy him a Nintendo.

proliferate   pro LIF er ayt
> *to grow or increase rapidly*
>> Because the number of fax machines, pagers, and cell phones has proliferated in recent years, many new area codes have been created to handle the demand for phone numbers.

tenacity   ten ASS uh tee
> *persistence*
>> With his overwhelming tenacity, Clark was finally able to interview Brad Pitt for the school newspaper.

vitality   vy TA lih tee
> *energy; power to survive*
>> After a few days of rest, the exhausted mountain climber regained his usual vitality.

GO WITH THE FLOW

assimilation   uh sim il AY shun
> *to absorb; to make similar*
>> The unique blend of Mexican culture was formed by the assimilation of the cultures of the Native Americans and the Spanish.

consensus   kun SEN sus
> *general agreement*
>> After much debate, the committee came to a consensus; although they differed on minor points, the members all agreed on the major issue.

context   KAHN tekst
> *circumstances of a situation; environment*
>> The senator complained that his statements had been taken out of context and were therefore misleading; he said that if the newspaper had printed the rest of his speech, it would have explained the statements in question.

derived   de RYVD
> *copied or adapted from a source*
>> Many SAT questions are derived from older questions—the details may have been changed, but the same basic concept is being tested.

incumbent   in KUM bunt
> *imposed as a duty; obligatory*
>> Since you are the host, it is incumbent upon you to see that everyone is having fun.

inevitable   in EV ih tuh bul
> *certain to happen, unavoidable*
>> Gaining a little extra weight during the wintertime is inevitable, especially after the holidays.

malleable   MAL ee uh bul
> *easily shaped or formed; easily influenced*
>> Gold is malleable; it is easy to work with and can be hammered into very thin sheets.

subdue   sub DOO
> *to restrain; to hold back*
>> It took four officers to subdue the fugitive because he fought like a madman.

WAYS OF KNOWING

acquired   uh KWY erd
> *developed or learned; not naturally occurring*
>> A love of opera is an acquired taste; almost nobody likes it the first time
>> he or she hears it.

conception   kun SEP shun
> *the ability to form or understand an idea*
>> Most people have no conception of the enormous amount of genetic
>> information present in a single living cell.

conviction   kun VIK shun
> *a fixed or strong belief*
>> Although he privately held on to his convictions, threats by the church
>> caused Galileo to publicly denounce his theory that the earth orbited
>> the sun.

dogmatic   dog MAT ik
> *stubbornly adhering to insufficiently proved beliefs*
>> Doug was dogmatic in his belief that exercising frequently boosts one's
>> immune system.

enlightening   en LYT uh ning
> *informative; contributing to one's awareness*
>> The Rosetta Stone was enlightening because it allowed linguists to
>> begin to translate Egyptian hieroglyphs, which had previously been a
>> mystery.

impression   im PREH shun
> *a feeling or understanding resulting from an experience*
>> It was my impression that I was supposed to throw a curve ball, but I
>> must have been wrong because the catcher didn't expect it.

intuition   in too ISH un
> *the power of knowing things without thinking; sharp insight*
>> It is said that some people have intuition about future events that allows
>> them to predict disasters.

misconception   mis kun SEP shun
> *an incorrect understanding or interpretation*
>> His belief that storks bring babies was just one of his many misconcep-
>> tions.

perception   per SEP shun
> *awareness; insight*
>> The detective's perception of people's hidden feelings makes it easy for
>> him to catch liars.

perspective per SPEK tiv

point of view

People from the North and South viewed the Civil War from different perspectives—each side's circumstances made it difficult for them to understand the other side.

profound pro FOWND

having great depth or seriousness

There was a profound silence during the ceremony in honor of those who died during World War II.

FEELING AT HOME

inherent in HER ent

inborn; built-in

One of the inherent weaknesses of the SAT is that a multiple-choice test, by definition, cannot allow students to be creative in their answers.

innate in AYT

possessed at birth; inborn

Cats have an innate ability to see well in the dark; they are born with this skill, and do not need to develop it.

inveterate in VET uh rit

long established; deep-rooted; habitual

Stan has always had trouble telling the truth; in fact, he's an inveterate liar.

omnipotent om NIP uh tent

all-powerful

He liked to think that he was an omnipotent manager, but he really had very little control over anything.

proximity prahk SIM ih tee

closeness

I try to sit far away from Roxy—I don't like sitting in proximity to her because she wears too much perfume.

ON THE ROAD AGAIN

elusive il OO siv

difficult to capture, as in something actually fleeting

The girl's expression was elusive; the painter had a hard time recreating it on the canvas.

emigrate EM ih grayt

to leave one country or region and settle in another

Many Jews left Russia and emigrated to Israel after it was founded in 1948.

transient   TRAN zhunt
> *passing away with time; passing from one place to another*
>> Jack Dawson enjoyed his transient lifestyle; with nothing but the clothes on his back and the air in his lungs, he was free to travel wherever he wanted.

transitory   TRAN zih tor ee
> *short-lived or temporary*
>> The sadness she felt was only transitory; the next day her mood improved.

FRIENDLY

affable   AF uh bul
> *easy-going; friendly*
>> We enjoyed spending time with Mr. Lee because he was such a pleasant, affable man.

amenable   uh MEEN uh bul
> *responsive; agreeable*
>> Since we had been working hard all day, the group seemed amenable to my suggestion that we all go home early.

camaraderie   kahm RAH duh ree
> *goodwill between friends*
>> There was great camaraderie among the members of the team; they were friends both on and off the field.

cordial   KOR jul
> *friendly; sincere*
>> Upon my arrival at camp, I received a warm and cordial greeting from the counselors.

facetious   fuh SEE shus
> *playfully humorous*
>> Although the teacher pretended to be insulting his favorite student, he was just being facetious.

UNDER THE WEATHER

impinge   im PINJ
> *hinder; interfere with*
>> By not allowing the students to publish a newspaper, the school was impinging on their right to free speech.

lament   luh MENT
> *express grief for; mourn*
>> After Beowulf had been killed by the dragon, the Geats wept and lamented his fate.

melancholy   MEL un kaw lee
   sadness; depression
         Joy fell into a state of melancholy when her Smashing Pumpkins CD
         got scratched.

sanction   SANK shun
   (n.) an economic or military measure put in place to punish another country
         In 1962, The United States imposed economic sanctions on Cuba to
         protest Castro's dictatorship; travel and trade between the countries are
         severely restricted to this day.

truncated   TRUN kay tid
   shortened; cut off
         The file Chris downloaded from the Internet was truncated; the end of
         it was missing.

I WRITE THE SONGS

aesthetic   es THET ik
   having to do with the appreciation of beauty
         The arrangement of paintings in the museum was due to aesthetic con-
         siderations; as long as paintings looked good together, it didn't matter
         who painted them or when they were painted.

anthology   an THAH luh jee
   a collection of literary pieces
         This anthology contains all of Shakespeare's sonnets, but none of his
         plays.

contemporary   kun TEM po rer ee
   current, modern; from the same time
         Contemporary music is very different from the music of the 1920s.
         Pocahontas and Shakespeare were contemporaries; they lived during the
         same time, though not in the same place.

dilettante   dih luh TAHNT
   one with an amateurish or superficial understanding of a field of knowledge
         You can't trust Betsy's opinion because she's just a dilettante who doesn't
         understand the subtleties of the painting.

eclectic   uh KLEK tik
   made up of a variety of sources or styles
         Lou's taste in music is eclectic because he listens to everything from rap
         to polka.

excerpt   EK serpt
   a selected part of a passage or scene
         We read an excerpt from Romeo and Juliet in which Juliet says, "Romeo,
         Romeo, wherefore art thou Romeo?"

genre   ZHAHN ruh
>*describing a category of artistic endeavor*
>>Gene enjoyed only science fiction movies; in fact, he never went to see anything that was not in that genre.

medley   MED lee
>*an assortment or a mixture, especially of musical pieces*
>>At the concert, the band played a medley of songs from its first album, cutting an hour's worth of music down to five minutes.

mural   MYUR ul
>*a large painting applied directly to a wall or ceiling surface*
>>The mural on the wall of the library showed the signing of the Declaration of Independence.

narrative   NAR uh tiv
>*(adj.) characterized by the telling of a story*
>*(n.) a story*
>>Tony gave us a running narrative of the game, since he was the only one who could see over the fence.

parody   PAR uh dee
>*an artistic work that imitates the style of another work for comic effect*
>>*Mad* magazine is famous for its parodies of popular movies, such as *Star Bores* and *The Umpire Strikes Out*.

realism   REE uh liz um
>*artistic representation that aims for visual accuracy*
>>His photographs have a stark realism that conveys the true horror of the war.

virtuoso   ver choo OH so
>*a tremendously skilled artist*
>>Some people say that Eddie Van Halen is a guitar virtuoso because of his amazing ability—others say that his music is just noise.

COOL IT NOW

decorous   DEK er us
>*proper; marked by good taste*
>>The class was well-behaved and the substitute was grateful for their decorous conduct.

equanimity   ek wuh NIM uh tee
>*the quality of being calm and even-tempered; composure*
>>She showed great equanimity; she did not panic even in the face of catastrophe.

modest   MAH dist
   quiet or humble in manner or appearance
>   Although Mr. Phillips is well-off financially, he lives in a modest, simple home.

propriety   pruh PRY uh tee
   appropriateness of behavior
>   Anyone who blows his nose on the tablecloth has no sense of propriety.

prudent   PROO dunt
   exercising good judgment or common sense
>   It wouldn't be prudent to act until you've considered every possible outcome.

serene   suh REEN
   calm
>   The quiet seaside resort provided a much-needed vacation in a serene locale.

staid   STAYD
   unemotional; serious
>   Mr. Carver had such a staid demeanor that he stayed calm while everyone else celebrated the team's amazing victory.

stoic   STOW ik
   indifferent to pleasure or pain; impassive
>   Not one to complain, Jason was stoic in accepting his punishment.

IF YOU CAN'T SAY ANYTHING NICE

condemn   kun DEM
   to express strong disapproval of; denounce
>   Homer condemned Mayor Quimby for allowing the schoolchildren to drink spoiled milk; he was outraged and let the mayor know it.

discredit   dis CRED it
   to cause to be doubted
>   The claim that π is exactly equal to 3 can be discredited simply by careful measurement.

disparage   dis PAR uj
   to speak of in a slighting way or negatively; to belittle
>   Glen disparaged Wanda by calling her a cheat and a liar.

pejorative   puh JOR uh tiv
   describing words or phrases that belittle or speak negatively of someone
>   Teachers should refrain from using such pejorative terms as "numbskull" when dealing with students who need encouragement.

plagiarism   PLAY juh riz um
> *the act of passing off the ideas or writing of another as one's own*
>> The author was accused of plagiarism when an older manuscript was discovered that contained passages that she had used, word for word, in her own book.

vilify   VIL uh fye
> *to make vicious statements about*
>> Chad issued a series of pamphlets that did nothing but vilify his opponent, but his cruel accusations were not enough to win him the election.

NASTY BOYS

brusque   BRUSK
> *rudely abrupt*
>> Mr. Weir was a brusque teacher who didn't take time to talk to or listen to his students.

caustic   KAW stik
> *bitingly sarcastic or witty*
>> He had a very caustic wit and he seldom told a joke without offending someone.

feral   FEH rul
> *savage; untamed*
>> Although he is usually timid, Murphy becomes feral and attacks the other cats when he is eating fish.

fractious   FRAK shus
> *quarrelsome; unruly*
>> Leonard was a fractious child who disagreed with everything and refused to listen.

incorrigible   in KOR ij uh bul
> *unable to be reformed*
>> She is absolutely incorrigible; no matter how many times you punish her, she goes right ahead and misbehaves.

ingrate   IN grayt
> *an ungrateful person*
>> It is a true ingrate who can accept favor after favor and never offer any thanks.

insolent   IN suh lunt
> *insulting in manner or speech*
>> It was extremely insolent of him to stick his tongue out at the principal.

notorious   no TOR ee us
    known widely and usually unfavorably; infamous
        Al Capone was a notorious gangster in the 1930s; he was feared through-
        out America.

pugnacious   pug NAY shus
    combative; belligerent
        Lorenzo was a pugnacious child who settled his differences by fighting
        with people.

reprehensible   rep ree HEN si bul
    worthy of blame
        It was reprehensible of the girls to spit their gum in their teacher's water
        bottle; they had detention for a week.

PURE EVIL

brittle   BRIT ul
    easily broken when subjected to pressure
        That antique vase is so brittle that it might break at any moment.

deleterious   del uh TEER ee us
    having a harmful effect; injurious
        Although it may seem unlikely, taking too many vitamins can actually
        have a deleterious effect on your health.

enmity   EN muh tee
    mutual hatred or ill-will
        There was great enmity between the opposing generals, and each one
        wanted to destroy the other.

heinous   HAY nus
    hatefully evil; abominable
        To murder someone in cold blood is a heinous crime.

malfeasance   mal FEEZ uns
    misconduct or wrongdoing, especially by a public official
        The mayor was accused of malfeasance because of his questionable use
        of public funds.

malice   MAL is
    extreme ill will or spite
        It was clear that he was acting with malice when he disconnected the
        brakes in his business partner's car.

putrid   PYOO trid
    rotten
        He threw his lunch in the bottom of his locker every day and had a putrid
        mess by the end of the year—rotten bananas, moldy sandwiches, and
        curdled milk were some of the more disgusting ingredients.

rancorous   RANK er us

    hateful; marked by deep seated ill-will

        They had such a rancorous relationship that no one could believe that
        they had ever gotten along.

toxic   TAHK sik

    poisonous

        Since many chemicals are toxic, drinking from random flasks in the
        chemistry lab could be hazardous to your health.

OLD SCHOOL

archaic   ar KAY ik

    characteristic of an earlier period; old-fashioned

        "How dost thou?" is an archaic way of saying "How are you?"

hackneyed   HACK need

    worn-out through overuse; trite

        All my mom could offer in the way of advice were these hackneyed old
        phrases that I'd heard a hundred times before.

medieval   med EE vul

    referring to the Middle Ages, old-fashioned

        His ideas about fashion were positively medieval; he thought that a man
        should always wear a coat and tie, and a woman should always wear a
        dress.

obsolete   ahb suh LEET

    no longer in use; old-fashioned

        Eight-track tape players are obsolete because albums aren't released in
        that format anymore.

BOOORING

austere   aw STEER

    without decoration; strict

        The gray walls and bare floors provided a very austere setting.

mediocrity   mee dee AH krit ee

    the state or quality of being average; of moderate to low quality

        Salieri said that he was the patron saint of mediocrity because his work
        could never measure up to Mozart's.

mundane   mun DAYN

    commonplace; ordinary

        We hated going to class every day because it was so mundane; we never
        did anything interesting.

ponderous   PAHN duh rus
   extremely dull
      That 700-page book on the anatomy of the flea was so ponderous that I
      could not read more than one paragraph.

prosaic   pro ZAY ik
   unimaginative; dull
      Rebecca made a prosaic mosaic—it consisted of only one tile.

sedentary   SEH dun tair ee
   not migratory; settled
      Galatea led a sedentary existence; she never even left her home unless
      she had to.

WHO CAN IT BE NOW?

apprehension   ap reh HEN shun
   anxiety or fear about the future
      My grandmother felt apprehension about nuclear war in the 1960s, so my
      grandfather built a bomb shelter in the backyard to calm her fears.

harbinger   HAR bin jer
   something that indicates what is to come; a forerunner
      When it is going to rain, insects fly lower, so cows lie down to get away
      from the insects; therefore, the sight of cows lying down is a harbinger
      of rain.

ominous   AH min us
   menacing; threatening
      The rattling under the hood sounded ominous, because we were miles
      from the nearest town and would have been stranded if the car had
      broken down.

premonition   prem uh NISH un
   a feeling about the future
      Luckily, my premonition that I would break my neck skiing was un-
      founded; unluckily, I broke my leg instead.

timorous   TIM uh rus
   timid; fearful about the future
      Tiny Tim was timorous; he was afraid that one day he would be crushed
      by a giant.

trepidation   trep uh DAY shun
   uncertainty; apprehension
      We approached Mrs. Fielding with trepidation because we didn't know
      how she would react to our request for a field trip.

NEW SENSATION

innovative   IN no vay tiv
> *introducing something new*
>> The shop on the corner has become known for its innovative use of fruit on its pizzas.

naïve   nah YEEV
> *lacking sophistication*
>> It was naïve of him to think that he could write a novel in one afternoon.

nascent   NAY sunt
> *coming into existence; emerging*
>> If you study Nirvana's first album, you can see their nascent abilities that were brought to maturity on their second recording.

novel   NAH vul
> *strikingly new or unusual*
>> Sharon's novel approach to the problem stunned the scientific community; no one had ever thought to apply game theory to genetics.

novice   NAH vis
> *a beginner*
>> Having only played chess a couple of times, Barry was a novice compared to the contestants who had been playing all their lives.

STRAIGHT UP

candor   KAN der
> *sincerity; openness*
>> It's refreshing to hear Candice's honesty and candor—when asked about her English teacher, she says, "I can't stand her!"

frank   FRANK
> *open and sincere in expression; straightforward*
>> When Frank lost my calculator, he was frank with me; he admitted losing it without trying to make up some excuse.

EARTH, WIND, AND FIRE

arid   AYR id
> *describing a dry, rainless climate*
>> Since they receive little rain, deserts are known for their arid climates.

conflagration   kahn fluh GRAY shun
  a widespread fire
        The protesters burned flags, accidentally starting a fire that developed
        into a conflagration that raged out of control.

nocturnal   nok TER nul
  of or occurring in the night
        Owls are nocturnal animals because they sleep during the day and hunt
        at night.

sonorous   SAH nuh rus
  producing a deep or full sound
        My father's sonorous snoring keeps me up all night unless I close my
        door and wear earplugs.

FULL ON

ample   AM pul
  describing a large amount of something
        Because no one else wanted to try the new soda, Andy was able to have
        an ample sample.

comprehensive   kahm pre HEN siv
  large in scope or content
        The final exam was comprehensive, covering everything that we had
        learned that year.

copious   KO pee us
  plentiful; having a large quantity
        She had taken copious notes during class, using up five large note-
        books.

permeated   PER mee ay tid
  spread or flowing throughout
        After I had my hair professionally curled, the scent of chemicals per-
        meated the air.

pervasive   per VAY siv
  dispersed throughout
        In this part of town, grafitti is pervasive—it's everywhere.

prodigious   pruh DIJ us
  enormous
        The shattered vase required a prodigious amount of glue to repair.

replete   ruh PLEET
  abundantly supplied; filled to capacity
        After a successful night of trick-or-treating, Dee's bag was replete with
        Halloween candy.

R-E-S-P-E-C-T

exemplary   eg ZEM pluh ree
commendable; worthy of imitation
> Jay's behavior was exemplary; his parents wished that his brother Al were more like him.

idealize   eye DEE uh lyze
to consider perfect
> The fans had idealized the new star pitcher; they had such unrealistically high expectations that they were bound to be disappointed.

laudatory   LAW duh tor ee
giving praise
> The principal's speech was laudatory, congratulating the students on their SAT scores.

paramount   PAR uh mount
of chief concern or importance
> The workers had many minor complaints, but the paramount reason for their unhappiness was the low pay.

venerated   VEN er ay tid
highly respected
> Princess Diana was venerated for her dedication to banning land mines around the world; people today still sing her praises.

catalog   KAT uh log
(v.) to make an itemized list of
> He decided to catalog his expenses for the week, hoping that this list would show him where he could cut back his spending.

facile   FAS ul
done or achieved with little effort; easy
> Last night's math homework was such a facile task that I was done in ten minutes.

fastidious   fas TID ee us
possessing careful attention to detail; difficult to please
> Since Kelly was so fastidious, she volunteered to proofread our group's report.

hierarchy   HY er ar kee
a group organized by rank
> With each promotion raising him higher, Archie moved up in his company's hierarchy.

meticulous   muh TIK yuh lus
extremely careful and precise
> The plastic surgeon was meticulous; he didn't want to leave any scars.

pragmatic   prag MAT ik

practical

Never one for wild and unrealistic schemes, Amy took a pragmatic approach to research.

solvent   SAHL vunt

able to pay one's debts

After five years of losing money, the business has finally solved its financial problems and become solvent.

WEIRD SCIENCE

abstract   ab STRAKT

not applied to actual objects

"Justice" is an abstract concept, because it is merely an idea.

apparatus   ap uh RAT us

equipment; a group of machines

The storeroom behind the physics lab was filled with a cumbersome apparatus that has since been replaced by a much smaller and more accurate piece of equipment.

paradigm   PAR a dym

an example or model

The current educational paradigm has students engaged in discovery-based learning, whereas the older theory had teachers lecturing and students merely taking notes.

phenomenon   feh NAH meh nahn

an unusual, observable event

The phenomenon of lightning remained unexplained until scientists discovered electricity.

rational   RASH un ul

logical; motivated by reason rather than feeling

While Joe is more impulsive, Frank is more rational because he thinks things through rather than acting on his feelings.

theoretical   thee oh RET ih kul

lacking application or practical application

Theoretical physics is concerned with ideas, whereas applied physics is concerned with using those ideas.

WORKING FOR THE WEEKEND

cartographer   kar TAH gruh fer
> *one who designs or makes maps*
>> Until the nineteenth century, European cartographers knew very little about the interior of Africa and had to leave it blank on their maps.

vocation   vo KAY shun
> *an occupation or profession*
>> Tristan has always been interested in maps, so he took up a vocation as a cartographer in the army.

OTHER WORDS

As important as Hit Parade words are, they aren't the only words on the SAT. As you go about learning the Hit Parade, you should also try to incorporate other new words into your vocabulary. The Hit Parade will help you determine what kinds of words you should be learning—good solid words that are fairly difficult but not impossible.

One very good source of SAT words is your local paper. Get it, read it, write down the words you don't know, and look them up. (You just may learn something about the world as well.) No one ever got dumber by reading.

ROOTS

Many of the words in the English language were borrowed from other languages at some point in our history. Words that you use every day contain bits and pieces of ancient Greek and Latin words that meant something similar. These bits and pieces are called "roots." The dictionary describes each word's roots by giving its etymology—a "minihistory" of where it came from. For example, the *American Heritage Dictionary* gives the following etymology for *apathy*, a word on the Hit Parade: "Greek *apatheia*, for *apathés*, without feeling: *a-*, without + *pathos*, feeling." Similar-sounding words, like *pathos*, *pathetic*, *sympathy*, and *empathy*, are all related and all have to do with feeling.

Many people say the best way to prepare for the SAT is simply to learn a lot of roots. Students who know a lot of roots, they say, will be able to "translate" any unfamiliar words they encounter on the test. There is some truth in this; the more you know about etymology, the easier it will be to build your vocabulary. But roots can also mislead you. The hardest words on the SAT are often words that seem to contain a familiar root, but actually do not. For example, *audacity*, a hard word sometimes tested on the SAT, means "boldness or daring." It has nothing to do with sound, even though it seems to contain the root *aud-* from a Latin word meaning "to hear"—as in *audio*, *audiovisual*, or *auditorium*. *Audacity* really comes from the Latin word *audax*, courageous.

Still, learning about roots can be helpful—if you do it properly. You should think of roots not as a code that will enable you to decipher unknown words on the SAT, but as a tool for learning new words and making associations between them.

For example, *eloquent, colloquial,* and *circumlocution* all contain the Latin root *loqu/loc,* which means "to speak." Knowing the root and recognizing it in these words will make it easier for you to memorize all of them. You should think of roots as a tool for helping you organize your thoughts as you build your vocabulary.

The worst thing you can do is try to memorize roots all by themselves, apart from words they appear in. In the first place, it can't be done. In the second place, it won't help.

HIT PARADE OF ROOTS

Just as the Hit Parade is a list of the most frequently tested words on the SAT, the Hit Parade of Roots is a list of the roots that show up most often in SAT vocabulary words. You may find it useful in helping you organize your vocabulary study. When approaching the Hit Parade of Roots, focus on the words, using the roots simply as reminders to help you learn or remember the meanings. When you take the SAT, you may be able to prod your memory about the meaning of a particular word by thinking of the related words that you associate with it.

The roots on the Hit Parade of Roots are presented in order of their importance on the SAT. The roots at the top of the list appear more often than the roots at the bottom. Each root is followed by a number of real SAT words that contain it. (What should you do every time you don't know the meaning of a word on the Hit Parade of Roots? Look it up!) Note that roots often have several different forms. Be on the lookout for all of them.

CAP/CIP/CEIPT/CEPT/CEIV/CEIT (take)

capture	exceptionable
intercept	susceptible
receptive	deception
recipient	conception
incipient	receive
perceptive	conceit
percipient	accept
anticipate	emancipate
except	precept
exceptional	

GEN (birth, race, kind)

generous	homogeneous
generate	heterogeneous

degenerate

regenerate

genuine

congenial

ingenious

ingenuous

ingenue

genealogy

indigenous

congenital

gender

engender

genre

progeny

DIC/DICT/DIT (tell, say, word)

predicament

condition

dictate

dictator

abdicate

predict

contradict

addict

malediction

benediction

extradite

verdict

indict

diction

dictum

SPEC/SPIC/SPIT (look, see)

perspective

aspect

spectator

spectacle

suspect

speculation

suspicious

spectrum

specimen

introspection

respite

conspicuous

circumspect

perspicacious

SUPER/SUR/SUM (above)

surpass

superficial

summit

superlative

supernova

supercilious

superstition

superimpose

supersede

superfluous

TENT/TENS/TEND/TENU (stretch, thin)

tension

extend

tendency

tendon

tent

tentative

contend

contention

distend

tenuous

attenuate

portent

tendentious

TRANS (across)

transfer

transaction

transparent

transgress

transport

transform

transition

transitory

transient

transmutation

transcendent

intransigent

traduce

DOC/DUC/DAC (teach, lead)

conduct

reduce

seduce

conducive

inductee

doctrine

document

docile

didactic

indoctrinate

traduce

induce

CO/CON/COM (with, together)

company

collaborate

conjugal

congeal

congenial

convivial

coalesce

contrition

commensurate

conclave

conciliate

comply

congruent

VERS/VERT (turn)

controversy

convert

revert

subvert

inversions

divert

diverse

aversion

extrovert

introvert

inadvertent

versatile

adversity

LOC/LOG/LOQU (word, speech)

eloquent

logic

apology

circumlocution

monologue

neologism

philology

colloquial

eulogy

loquacious

dialogue

prologue

epilogue

SEN (feel, sense)

sensitive

sensation

sentiment

sensory

sensual

resent

consent

dissent

assent

consensus

sentry

sentinel

DE (away, down, off)

denounce

debility

defraud

decry

deplete

defame

delineate

deface

devoid

defile

desecrate

derogatory

NOM/NOUN/NOWN/NAM/NYM (name, order, rule)

name

anonymous

antonym

nominate

economy

renounce

astronomy

ignominy

renown

misnomer

nomenclature

CLA/CLO/CLU (shut, close)

closet

claustrophobia

enclose

disclose

include

conclude

exclusive

preclude

recluse

seclude

cloister

VO/VOC/VOK/VOW (call)

voice

vocal

provocative

advocate

equivocate

vocation

convoke

vociferous

irrevocable

evocative

revoke

avow

MAL (bad)

malicious

malady

dismal

malfunction

malign

malcontent

malodorous

malefactor

malevolent

malediction

maladroit

FRA/FRAC/FRAG (break)

fracture	refraction
fraction	refractory
fragment	infraction
fragmentary	infringe
fragile	fractious
frail	

OB (against)

objective	obstinate
obsolete	obliterate
oblique	oblivious
obscure	obsequious
obstruct	obfuscate

SUB (under)

submissive	subordinate
subsidiary	sublime
subjugation	subtle
subliminal	subversion
subdue	subterfuge

AB (from, away)

abandon	abstain
abhor	absolve
abnormal	abstemious
abstract	abstruse
abdicate	abrogate

GRESS/GRAD (step)

progress	degrade
regress	downgrade
retrogress	aggressor
retrograde	digress
gradual	transgress

SEC/SEQU (follow)

second

sequel

sequence

consequence

inconsequential

execute

subsequent

prosecute

obsequious

PRO (much, for, a lot)

prolific

profuse

propitious

prodigious

profligate

prodigal

protracted

proclivity

propensity

prodigy

QUE/QUIS (ask, seek)

inquire

question

request

quest

query

querulous

acquire

acquisitive

acquisition

exquisite

SACR/SANCT/SECR (sacred)

sacred

sacrifice

sanctuary

sanctify

sanction

sacrosanct

consecrate

desecrate

sacrament

SCRIB/SCRIP (write)

scribble

describe

script

postscript

prescribe

proscribe

ascribe

inscribe

circumscribe

PATHY/PAS/PAT (feeling)

apathy

compassion

sympathy

compatible

empathy

dispassionate

antipathy

impassive

passionate

DIS/DIF (not)

dissonance

dispassionate

discrepancy

disparate

disdain

diffident

dissuade

disparage

dismay

CIRCU (around)

circumference

circuitous

circulation

circumscribe

circumstance

circumvent

circumnavigate

circumlocutory

5

Joe Bloggs and the Verbal SAT

JOE BLOGGS AND THE VERBAL SAT

Joe Bloggs will be a big help to you on the Verbal SAT. By keeping him in mind as you take the test, you will substantially improve your score. Joe will help you identify and eliminate incorrect answer choices before you have a chance to be tempted by them, and he will help you zero in on ETS's answer.

JOE BLOGGS AND THE ORDER OF DIFFICULTY

The Verbal sections of the SAT contain three question types: Sentence Completions, Analogies, and Critical Reading. The analogies and sentence completions are arranged in order of increasing difficulty. That is, in a group of ten sentence completions, the first three or four will be easy, the next three or four will be medium, and the last three or four will be hard. Critical reading questions are not arranged in order of difficulty. They follow the structure of the passage to which they refer. (More on that later.)

How does Joe Bloggs do on verbal questions? As always on the SAT, he gets the easy ones right, does so-so on the medium ones, and crashes and burns on the hard ones. When you take the SAT, you must constantly be aware of where you are in each group of questions. Knowing where a question falls in the order of difficulty will tell you how much faith you can put in your hunches and help you avoid making careless mistakes. In addition, your knowledge of Joe's test-taking habits will enable you to eliminate incorrect choices on the hardest questions, thus greatly improving your odds of guessing ETS's answers.

HOW JOE THINKS

When Joe looks at a Verbal SAT question, he is irresistibly attracted to choices containing easy words that remind him of the question. On easy questions, this tendency serves Joe very well. On hard questions, though, it gets him into trouble every time.

Here's an example. This is a very difficult analogy question. Don't worry if you don't know how to answer a question like this; we'll deal with the SAT Analogies thoroughly in another chapter. For now, all you have to do is look at the words.

ANALOGIES					
10	11	12	13	14	**15**
EASY		MEDIUM		HARD	

15. FLORID : SPEECH ::

    (A) harsh : voice
    (B) fluid : style
    (C) vivid : image
    (D) fertile : soil
    (E) ornate : design

A Reminder

On easy questions, the answers that seem right to Joe really are right; on hard questions, the answers that seem right to Joe are wrong.

Analysis

This is a very hard question from a real SAT. Only about eight percent of test takers answered it correctly. More than twice as many of them would have answered it correctly if they had simply closed their eyes and picked one of the choices at random. Why did the vast majority of test takers—including, of course, Joe Bloggs—do so poorly on this question? Because they all fell into a trap. Like Joe, they didn't know what *florid* means, so they focused their attention on *speech*, an easy word. Then they looked for an answer choice containing something similar. Like Joe, they were immediately drawn to choice A. *Speech* and *voice* seem similar. Joe quickly marked A on his answer sheet.

Was Joe (along with several hundred thousand test takers) correct? No, of course not. Joe never picks the right answer on hard SAT questions.

WHAT DOES THAT MEAN FOR YOU?

It means that on hard questions like this one, you can simply eliminate any answer choice or choices that you know will be attractive to Joe. We'll tell you more about how to do this as we go along. (Incidentally, ETS's answer to this question is E. *Florid* means using flowery or heavily embellished *speech*, and *ornate* means having a fancy or heavily embellished *design*.)

PUTTING JOE TO WORK ON THE VERBAL SAT

Generally speaking, the Joe Bloggs principle teaches you to:

- Trust your hunches on easy questions

- Double-check your hunches on medium questions

- Eliminate Joe Bloggs answers on difficult questions

The next few chapters will teach you how to use your knowledge of Joe Bloggs to add points to your SAT score.

Bloggs Magnets

Joe is irresistibly drawn to easy answer choices containing words that remind him of the question. Therefore, on hard verbal questions, you can eliminate such choices.

6

Sentence Completions

MEMORIZE THE INSTRUCTIONS

Before we begin, take a moment to read the following set of instructions and answer the sample question that comes after it. Both appear here exactly as they do on the real SAT. Be certain that you know and understand these instructions before you take the SAT. If you learn them ahead of time, you won't have to waste valuable seconds reading them on the day you take the test.

Each sentence below has one or two blanks, each blank indicating that something has been omitted. Beneath the sentence are five lettered words or sets of words labeled A through E. Choose the word or set of words that, when inserted in the sentence, best fits the meaning of the sentence as a whole.

Example:

Medieval kingdoms did not become constitutional republics overnight; on the contrary, the change was -------.

(A) unpopular   (B) unexpected   (C) advantageous
        (D) sufficient   (E) gradual

Ⓐ Ⓑ Ⓒ Ⓓ ●

ETS's answer to this sample question is E.

SAT SENTENCE COMPLETIONS: CRACKING THE SYSTEM

It's important to know the instructions printed before each group of sentence completions on the SAT, but it's vastly more important to understand what those instructions mean. ETS's instructions don't tell you everything you need to know about SAT Sentence Completions. The rest of this chapter will teach you what you need to know.

The two 30-minute Verbal sections of your test will contain one group of sentence completions each. One group will have ten sentence completions, the other nine. In each group, the questions will be arranged in order of increasing difficulty. That is, the first question in each group of sentence completions will be the easiest in the group; the last question in each group will be the hardest.

Because our techniques vary depending on the difficulty of the question, we have placed a Difficulty Meter before each example. Look at the meter to determine how hard the example is.

Level of Difficulty

Set of Nine
1–3 Easy
4–6 Medium
7–9 Difficult

Set of Ten
1–3 Easy
4–7 Medium
8–10 Difficult

DETECTIVE WORK: LOOKING FOR CLUES

Sentence completions are sentences from which one or two words have been removed. Your job is to find the missing word or words. How will you do this? By finding the clue ETS has left for you in the sentence. Each sentence completion contains a clue that will tell you the word(s) that goes in the blank(s). All you have to do is find the clue, and you've cracked the question.

Sound too good to be true? Try the following example. The answer choices have been removed so you can concentrate solely on the sentence. Read the sentence, look for the clue, and decide which word goes in the blank.

SENTENCE COMPLETIONS

① 2 3 4 5 6 7 8 9 10

EASY · MEDIUM · HARD

1. Historical buildings in many American cities,
   rather than being destroyed, are now being -------.

Analysis

What word did you come up with? Probably something like *fixed* or *restored*. How did you decide that was the word you needed? Because of the clue. The clue in this sentence is "rather than being destroyed." It tells us that the historical buildings are being *fixed* or *restored* instead of being destroyed.

Now that you have decided on the word that goes in the blank, look at the following answer choices. Cross off the answers that are not close to yours (ones that don't mean *fixed* or *restored*), and pick the best answer.

(A) condemned
(B) constructed
(C) described
(D) renovated
(E) designed

Answer choices A, C, and E are out right away. You may have gotten stuck between B and D, but think about which one is closer to your word. Are the historical buildings being *constructed*? No—they wouldn't be historical if they were only now being constructed. The historical buildings are being *renovated*. ETS's answer is D.

But Why?

You may be wondering why we didn't just plug each answer into the sentence to see which one sounded right. That's because *all* the answers are designed to *sound* right. Look back to the question we just did. The sentence would sound just fine if you plugged in any one of those answer choices. But only one of them is ETS's answer.

More importantly, plugging each word into the sentence is how Joe Bloggs would solve the question. Does Joe get all sentence completion questions correct? No way. Joe doesn't know that ETS has given him a clue in the sentence that tells him exactly what the answer is. He just plugs in choices and takes a guess.

You, on the other hand, know the inside scoop. In each sentence, ETS must include a clue that reveals the answer. If they didn't, no one would agree on the right answer (there wouldn't *be* a right answer) and lots of people would sue.

However, ETS can make the answer choices as attractive as possible, so that the Joe Bloggses of the world get caught by trying to find an answer that sounds right. How can you avoid getting caught in the "sounds right" trap?

COVER UP

**Sentence
Completion
Rule #1**

Cover the answer choices until
you come up with your own
word.

Cover the answer choices before you begin each sentence completion. Place your hand (or your answer sheet) over the five answer choices so that you are not tempted to look at them too soon. Then, read the sentence and find ETS's clue. Decide what you think the word in the blank should be, and then use POE to get to ETS's answer.

Try another example:

4. The onset of the earthquake was gradual, the tremors occurring ------- at first, then with greater frequency.

Here's how to crack it

The clue in any sentence completion is always a short, descriptive phrase that tells you what word goes in the blank. What is the clue in this sentence? Two things give you the full picture: *gradual* and *then with greater frequency.* Since we know the earthquake came on gradually and that the tremors later came with greater frequency, we can assume that the tremors occurred "infrequently" or "gradually" at first.

Now that you have a clue, use POE to get to ETS's answer:

(A) continuously
(B) intensely
(C) sporadically
(D) unexpectedly
(E) chronically

The only word that comes close to meaning "infrequently" or "gradually" is C, *sporadically.* This is ETS's answer.

CLUELESS

The following two examples will further illustrate what we've been talking about. The first is a sentence completion that has no clue. The second is virtually the same sentence, except with ETS's clue added. Which one of the following is easier?

I. The woman told the man, "You're very -------."

(A) rich
(B) correct
(C) preposterous
(D) cloistered
(E) sick

II. The doctor told the man, "You're very -------."

(A) rich
(B) correct
(C) preposterous
(D) cloistered
(E) sick

As you can see, questions I and II are identical, with the exception of a single word. And yet that word makes all the difference in the world. In Question I, several of the choices are possible. In fact, this question cannot be answered (don't worry—you won't have one like this on the SAT). But in Question II, the word *doctor* makes the answer E. The key word *doctor* determines ETS's answer.

ETS will put a clue in every sentence to indicate what goes in the blank. Find it! Once you do, use it to determine the missing word or words.

GET A CLUE

Try the following example. Before you begin, cover up the answer choices. Then read the sentence and underline the clue. Fill in the blank with your own word, then use POE to get to ETS's answer.

4. Some developing nations have become remarkably
-------, using aid from other countries to build
successful industries.

(A) populous
(B) dry
(C) warlike
(D) prosperous
(E) isolated

Here's how to crack it

The clue in this sentence is *build successful industries*. It indicates that some nations "have become remarkably *successful*."

Let's look at each answer choice:

(A) Does *populous* mean *successful*? No. Cross off this answer.
(B) Does *dry* mean *successful*? Not at all. Cross it off.
(C) Does *warlike* mean *successful*? Nope. Ditch it.
(D) Does *prosperous* mean *successful*? Sure does.
(E) Does *isolated* mean *successful*? Nope. Ditch it.

ETS's answer must be D.

SEARCHING FOR CLUES

If you are having trouble finding the clue, ask yourself two simple questions about each sentence:

1. What is the blank talking about?

2. What *else* does the sentence say about this?

For example, look back to the problem we just did. What is the blank talking about? Some nations. What else does the sentence say about the nations? They were able to *build successful industries*. This must be the clue of the sentence, because it refers to the same thing the blank refers to.

Find and underline the clue in the following sentence. Then fill in the blank with your own word. If you have any trouble, ask:

1. What is the blank talking about?

2. What *else* does the sentence say about its subject?

> **1.** Medwick was so outstanding a thinker that her colleagues were often so dazzled by her ------- that they failed to appreciate fully her other virtues.

Analysis

What is the blank talking about? Medwick. What else does the sentence say about Medwick? She was an outstanding thinker. Therefore, her colleagues were dazzled by her *thinking*.

PICK A WORD, ANY WORD

The word you select to fill the blank doesn't have to be an elegant word, or a hard word, or the perfect word. It doesn't even have to be a word; instead, it can be a phrase—even a clunky phrase—as long as it captures the correct meaning.

In an episode of *The Simpsons*, a lawyer couldn't think of the word *mistrial*, so he asked the judge to declare a "bad court thingie." *Bad court thingie* is an accurate enough substitute for *mistrial* on the SAT. With *bad court thingie* as your "word," POE will get you to *mistrial*.

RECYCLE THE CLUE

Instead of coming up with a different word for the blank, you can often just recycle the clue. If you can put the clue itself in the blank, you can be sure that you've put your finger on ETS's answer.

Is the blank always the same as the clue? Sometimes the blank is exactly the same, while other times it is exactly the opposite. You must use the rest of the sentence to determine if the blank and the clue are the same or opposite. In other words, you must be on the lookout for "trigger words."

TRIGGER WORDS

Very often on sentence completions, the most important clue to ETS's answer is a trigger word: a single revealing word or expression that lets you know exactly where ETS is heading. About half of all SAT sentence completions contain trigger words. Combining trigger words with your clue make filling in the blank a breeze.

Some trigger words are change-direction, and some are same-direction. The most important change-direction trigger words are *but, though,* and *although*. These are words that "change the direction" of a sentence. The most important same-direction trigger words are *and* and *because*. These are words that maintain the direction of a sentence.

Change-direction trigger words are more common on the SAT than same-direction trigger words. Both provide terrific clues that you can use to find ETS's answer. To see what we mean, take a look at the following incomplete sentences. For each one, fill in a few words that complete the thought in a plausible way. There's no single correct answer. Just fill in something that makes sense in the context of the entire sentence:

I really like you, *but*_____.

I really like you, *and*_____.

Here's how one of our students filled in the blanks:

I really like you, *but I'm going to leave you.*

I really like you, *and I'm going to hug you.*

Analysis

In the first sentence, the word *but* indicates that the second half of the sentence will contradict the first half. Because the first half of the sentence is positive, the second half must be negative. I like you, *but* I'm going to leave you. The sentence "changes direction" after the trigger word *but*.

In the second sentence, the word *and* indicates that the second half of the sentence will confirm or support the first half. Because the first half of the sentence

If you were directing *Romeo and Juliet,* you'd have to hold auditions in order to find actors. You wouldn't look at all the actors in the world before reading the play, would you? For the role of Juliet, you'd be looking for someone suited to the part. Everybody else would be sent packing.

Sentence completions are the same. You have to read the sentence first and decide what kind of word would fit best *before* you look at the answer choices available. Then, like the director, you would pick the answer choice that is most like what you want and eliminate the ones that are different.

is positive, the second half must be positive as well. I like you, *and* I'm going to hug you. In this case, the sentence continues in the same direction after the trigger word *and*.

OTHER TRIGGERS

Two other same-direction triggers to look for include punctuation triggers, particularly colons and semicolons, and time triggers. Punctuation triggers are important becase they divide the sentence into two pieces: one part with the blank and one without. Ninety-nine percent of the time, the part that does not contain the blank is the clue to what kind of word belongs in the blank. Time triggers denote a change in the sentence with a passage of time and help you fill in the blank with the proper word.

DRILL 1

Circle the trigger word (if there is one) and underline the clue in each of the following sentences. Then, write your own word in the blank. If you have trouble finding the clue, ask yourself, "What is the blank talking about?" and "What else does the sentence say about this?" Don't worry if you can't think of a single, perfect word for the blank; use a phrase that catches ETS's meaning. Once you've finished these questions, go on to Drill 2 and use POE to find ETS's answer. Answers can be found on page 276.

1. Although the critics agreed that the book was brilliant, so few copies were sold that the work brought the author little ------- reward.

6. Sadly, many tropical rain forests are so ------- by agricultural and industrial over-development that they may ------- by the end of the century.

9. My plea is not for drab and ------- technical writing about music but for pertinent information conveyed with as much ------- as possible.

DRILL 2

Here are the same questions, this time with the answer choices. Refer to your notes from Drill 1 and make a choice for each question. Remember to use POE. Answers can be found on page 276.

1. Although the critics agreed that the book was brilliant, so few copies were sold that the work brought the author little ------- reward.

   (A) theoretical (B) thoughtful (C) financial
   (D) abstract (E) informative

6. Sadly, many tropical rain forests are so ------- by agricultural and industrial over-development that they may ------- by the end of the century.

(A) isolated. .separate
(B) threatened. .vanish
(C) consumed. .expand
(D) augmented. .diminish
(E) rejuvenated. .disappear

9. My plea is not for drab and ------- technical writing about music but for pertinent information conveyed with as much ------- as possible.

(A) repetitive. .redundancy
(B) obscure. .felicity
(C) inscrutable. .ambivalence
(D) euphonious. .harmony
(E) provocative. .exhilaration

AND THEN THERE WERE TWO

About half of all sentence completions contain two blanks. Many students fear these questions because they look long and intimidating. But two-blank sentence completions are no more difficult than single-blank sentence completions. The key is to take them one blank at a time.

To crack two-blank sentence completions, read the sentence, circling the trigger word(s) and underlining the clue(s) (there may be a clue for *each* blank). Then fill in whichever blank seems easier to you. Once you have filled in one of the blanks, go to the answer choices and check just the words for that blank, using POE to get rid of answers that are not close to yours. Then go back to the other blank, fill it in, and check the remaining choices. You do not need to check both words at one time. If one of the words doesn't work in a blank, then it doesn't matter what the other word is. One strike and the answer is out.

When eliminating answers, draw a line through the entire answer choice. That way you won't get confused and check it again when you are checking the other blank. Even if you do fill in both blanks the first time you read the sentence, only check one blank at a time. It is much easier to concentrate on one word than on a pair of words. Sometimes you'll be able to get rid of four choices by checking only one blank, and you won't even need to check the other blank.

Here's an example of a two-blank sentence completion:

SENTENCE COMPLETIONS			
1 2 3	4 5 **6** 7	8 9 10	
EASY	MEDIUM	HARD	

6. While the ------- student openly questioned the teacher's explanation, she was not so ------- as to suggest that the teacher was wrong.

(A) complacent . . suspicious
(B) inquisitive . . imprudent
(C) curious . . dispassionate
(D) provocative . . respectful
(E) ineffectual . . brazen

Shoe Store

If you were shopping for shoes and found a pair you liked, you'd ask the clerk to bring you a pair in your size to try on. Say you tried the right shoe first. If it felt horrible, would you even bother to try the left shoe on? No, because even if the left shoe was comfy, you'd have to wear it with the right shoe, which you already know causes you unspeakable pain. You would look for another pair of shoes. Two-blank sentence completions are like shoes. If one doesn't fit, there's no point trying the other one. Half bad is all bad.

Here's how to crack it

Let's start with the first blank. The clue is *openly questioned*, and we can simply recycle the clue and put *questioning* in the blank. Now let's take a look at the first-blank words in the answer choices and eliminate any words that are definitely not a good match for *questioning*. Eliminate choices A and E, because *complacent* and *ineffectual* have nothing to do with *questioning*. All we want to do at this point is eliminate any words that are way off base. Then we can move on to the second blank.

The clue for the second blank is *suggest that the teacher was wrong*. How would you describe a student who accuses the teacher of being wrong? *Bold* or *rude*, maybe? Look at the remaining choices and get rid of any second words that don't mean something like *bold* or *rude*. C is out—*dispassionate* does not mean *bold* or *rude*. Also, D is out since this student is anything but *respectful*. ETS's answer must be B.

Notice that we only had to eliminate one of the words in each answer choice in order to get rid of the entire choice. Attacking this question using POE also made it easier, because we could eliminate four answers without much trouble. If four answers are wrong, the one that's left must be ETS's answer.

THE TRICKY ONES

Every now and then, the clue for one of the blanks in a two-blank sentence completion turns out to be the other blank. What? How can ETS get away with making the clue a *blank*?

Don't worry—if ETS has decided to use one blank as the clue for the other blank, you know they have inserted another way for you to find the answer. Let's look at an example:

7. Most of Rick's friends think his life is unbelievably
------- , but in fact he spends most of his time on
------- activities.

 (A) fruitful . . productive
 (B) wasteful . . useless
 (C) scintillating . . mundane
 (D) varied . . sportive
 (E) callow . . simple

Here's how to crack it

The trigger word in this sentence is *but*. We gather from the sentence that most of Rick's friends think his life is one way, but in fact it is another. We cannot tell if his friends think his life is great and busy while it's really lousy and slow, or vice versa. However, we do know that our blanks are opposites: the first is positive while the second is negative *or* the first is negative while the second is positive.

Knowing this is enough to get us to ETS's answer. Let's look at each answer choice, keeping in mind that we need a pair of words that are opposites:

(A) *Fruitful* is positive, *productive* is positive. Eliminate this choice.

(B) *Wasteful* is negative, *useless* is negative. Cross it off.

(C) *Scintillating* is positive, *mundane* is negative. Keep it.

(D) *Varied* is positive, *sportive* is positive. Cross it off.

(E) *Callow* is negative, *simple* is neutral. A possibility, but not great.

ETS's answer is C: Rick's life may look *scintillating*, but he spends most of his time on *mundane* activities. If the clue of one of the blanks is the other blank in a two-blank sentence completion, look for the trigger and determine the relationship between the blanks. Then use POE to find ETS's answer.

ARE YOU A GOOD WORD OR A BAD WORD?

Notice in the last example that we didn't use *words* to fill in the blanks; instead, we looked for positive and negative. On difficult sentence completions, you may find it hard to determine what the word in the blank is supposed to be. However, you will usually have an idea if that word should be a good word (something positive) or a bad word (something negative). Knowing whether a blank is positive or negative can help you eliminate answer choices. If you are unable to come up with your own word, use + or – to get rid of answers and make smart guesses.

Vocab

Don't eliminate words you've never seen before or cannot readily define. Or, in the words of Bob Dylan, "Don't criticize what you can't understand."

Here's an example:

SENTENCE COMPLETIONS

1	2	3	4	5	6	7	8	9
EASY				MEDIUM			HARD	

8. Ruskin's vitriolic attack was the climax of the ------- heaped on paintings that today seem amazingly -------.

(A) criticism. .unpopular
(B) ridicule. .inoffensive
(C) praise. .amateurish
(D) indifference. .scandalous
(E) acclaim. .creditable

A Gentle Reminder

Your aim is to eliminate wrong answers. Get rid of as many incorrect choices as you can, guess from among the remaining choices, and then move on.

Here's how to crack it

A *vitriolic* attack is something bad (and so is simply an *attack*, if you don't know what *vitriolic* means). The climax of a vitriolic attack must also be bad, and therefore the first blank must be a bad word. Already we can eliminate choices C and E (and possibly choice D). We don't have to worry about the second word in these answer choices, because we already know that the first word is wrong.

Now look at the second blank. The first part of the sentence says that Ruskin thought the paintings were very bad; today, *amazingly*, they seem—what? Bad?

No! The word in the second blank has to be a *good* word. Choices C and E are already crossed out. We can now also eliminate choices A and D (without bothering to look at the first words again) because the second blank words are bad words. The only choice left is B—ETS's answer. You've correctly answered a very hard question simply by figuring out whether the words in ETS's answer were good or bad. Not bad!

The good-word/bad-word method is also helpful when you have anticipated ETS's answer but haven't found a similar word among the choices. Simply decide whether your anticipated answer is positive or negative, then determine whether each of the answer choices is positive or negative. Eliminate the choices that are different, and you'll find ETS's answer.

WHAT ABOUT JOE?

As you know, the last few questions in each group of sentence completions will be quite difficult. On these hard questions, you will find it useful to remember the Joe Bloggs principle and eliminate choices that you know would attract Joe. Here's an example:

9. The phenomenon is called viral ------- because the presence of one kind of virus seems to inhibit infection by any other.

   (A) proliferation
   (B) mutation
   (C) interference
   (D) epidemic
   (E) cooperation

Here's how to crack it

Joe Bloggs is attracted to choices containing words that remind him of the subject matter of the sentence. The words in the sentence that Joe notices are *virus* and *infection*—words related to biology or illness. Which answers attract him? Choices B and D. You can therefore eliminate both.

Where's the clue in this sentence? It's the word *inhibit*. By recycling the clue and putting *inhibit* in the blank, you can anticipate ETS's answer: "The phenomenon is called viral *inhibition* because the presence of one kind of virus seems to inhibit infection by any other." Which answer choice could mean something similar to *inhibition*? *Interference*. ETS's answer is C.

HOW HARD IS IT?

Let's assume you've tried everything: You've looked for the clue and trigger, tried to anticipate ETS's answer, eliminated the Joe Bloggs answers, and used the good-word/bad-word technique. You still can't find ETS's answer. What should you do?

Remember order of difficulty: easy questions have easy answers and hard questions have hard answers. Joe Bloggs tends to avoid choices containing words whose meaning he doesn't understand. As a result, we can be fairly certain that on easy questions (which Joe gets right) ETS's answer will contain easy words. However, on hard questions (which Joe gets wrong) ETS's answer will contain hard words, ones that Joe would never pick.

And an easy word will usually not be the ETS's answer on a hard question.

When you come down to the wire and need to guess on the hardest couple of sentence completions, simply pick the hardest choice—the one with the weirdest, most difficult words. Eliminate any choice whose word or words you can define, and guess from among what's left. No problem!

Important!

Eliminating Joe Bloggs attractors should always be the first thing you do when considering answer choices on a hard sentence completion. If you don't eliminate them immediately, you run the risk of falling for them as you consider the various choices.

DRILL 3

The following two questions contain answer choices from sentence completions. These are both numbers eight out of nine—in other words, tough problems. Eliminate the easy answer choices, then guess the hardest, weirdest answer choices. Answers can be found on page 276.

Answers can be found on page 276.

SENTENCE COMPLETIONS

1 2 3	4 5 6 7 **8** 9
EASY	MEDIUM HARD

8. (A) adjusted
   (B) tainted
   (C) contained
   (D) ignored
   (E) decreased

9. (A) cogent . . perfunctory
   (B) provocative . . poignant
   (C) tactful . . amiable
   (D) predictable . . uninspired
   (E) mundane . . trenchant

SENTENCE COMPLETIONS SUMMARY

1. Cover the answer choices. Learn to anticipate ETS's answer by filling in each blank before you look at the answer choices. If you look at the answer choices first, you will often be misled.

2. Always look for the clue—the key word or words that you need to fill in the blank(s)—and underline it.

3. If you have trouble finding the clue, ask yourself:

   • What is the blank talking about?
   • What else does the sentence say about this subject?

4. Look for trigger words—revealing words or expressions that give you important clues about the meanings of sentences—and circle them. The most important negative trigger words are *but, though,* and *although.* These are words that "change the direction" of a sentence. The most important positive trigger words are *and* and *because.* These are words that maintain the direction of the sentence.

5. Fill in the blank with any word or phrase that will help you get to ETS's answer. Don't worry if you need to use a clunky or awkward phrase. If you can, recycle the clue. If you can't come up with any words for the blank, use + or −. Use POE to get to ETS's answer.

6. Attack two-blank sentence completions by focusing on one blank at a time. Use the same techniques you would use on one-blank questions. If you can eliminate either word in an answer choice, you can cross out the entire choice. If the clue for one of the blanks is the other blank, use the trigger word to determine the relationship between the blanks.

7. Never eliminate a choice unless you are sure of its meaning.

8. Eliminate Joe Bloggs answers. On difficult questions, Joe is attracted to answers containing easy words that remind him of the subject matter of the sentence. Learn to recognize these words and be extremely suspicious of the answer choices in which they appear.

9. Take advantage of the order of difficulty. Easy sentence completions have easy answers, hard ones have hard answers. If you can do nothing else on a hard sentence completion, simply pick the choice with the hardest or weirdest words.

Analogies

MEMORIZE THE INSTRUCTIONS

This chapter is about Analogies, the second of the three types of Verbal SAT questions. There will be at least two groups of analogy questions on the SAT you take, one in each of the two scored 30-minute Verbal sections (of course, if your experimental section is Verbal, you'll have a third set of Analogies).

Before we begin, take a moment to read the instructions and answer the sample question that follows. Both appear here exactly as they do on the real SAT. Be certain that you know and understand these instructions before you take the SAT. If you learn them ahead of time, you won't have to waste valuable seconds reading them on the day you take the test.

Each question below consists of a related pair of words or phrases, followed by five pairs of words or phrases labeled A through E. Select the pair that <u>best</u> expresses a relationship similar to that expressed in the original pair.

Example:

    CRUMB : BREAD ::

    (A) ounce : unit
    (B) splinter : wood
    (C) water : bucket
    (D) twine : rope
    (E) cream : butter   Ⓐ ● Ⓒ Ⓓ Ⓔ

ETS's answer to this sample question is choice B. A CRUMB is a small piece of BREAD just as a *splinter* is a small piece of *wood*.

SAT ANALOGIES: CRACKING THE SYSTEM

Level of Difficulty

Set of 6
10–11 Easy
12–13 Medium
14–15 Difficult
Set of 13
11–14 Easy
15–19 Medium
20–23 Difficult

It's important to know the instructions printed before each Analogy group on the SAT, but it is more important to understand what those instructions mean. ETS's instructions don't tell you everything you need to know about SAT Analogies. The rest of this chapter will teach you what you need to know.

One of your two scored 30-minute Verbal sections will contain a group of six Analogies; the other will contain a group of thirteen. Each group of analogies will be arranged in order of increasing difficulty, from very easy to very hard.

In each group of analogies:

1. The first third will be easy.

2. The middle third will be medium.

3. The final third will be difficult.

Because our techniques vary depending on the difficulty of the question, the examples we use in this chapter will always be preceded by a Difficulty Meter. Always pay attention to where you are on the test when answering SAT questions.

WHAT IS AN ANALOGY?

Every analogy question on the SAT begins with a pair of capitalized words called *stem words*. Your task is to determine how these words are related to each other and then select another pair of words related to each other *in exactly the same way*.

As you can see, determining the relationship between the stem words is pretty important. To get analogy questions right, you need to have more than just a vague idea of how these words are related. How can you determine the relationship between the stem words?

MAKE A SENTENCE

Make a *defining* sentence that connects the stem words. The operative word here is *defining*. You cannot make a sentence about the weather that just happens to include the stem words if you plan to get any of these questions right.

A defining sentence is one that:

- Uses one of the words to define the other

- Is short and simple

- Starts with one word and ends with the other

Write a defining sentence for the following pair of words:

APPLE : FRUIT::

An apple _____ fruit.

The Dictionary, Please

Your sentence should read like a dictionary definition, defining one word in terms of the other. For example, "KENNEL : DOG." If you were to look up *kennel* in the dictionary, you would find something like, "A *kennel* is a place to keep *dogs*."

What did you get?

If you wrote something like, "An apple is a type of fruit," you are on the right track. If you wrote something flowery or descriptive like, "An apple is the most beautiful of all fruits," you are making it too complicated. You want to write a short, simple sentence that clearly indicates the relationship between the two words, as if you were looking them up in the dictionary.

DRILL 1

Practice making good defining sentences for the following pairs of words. Be sure to start each sentence with one of the words and end it with the other. By the way, it doesn't matter which word you place first and which you place second. If you find it easier to make a good sentence by switching the order of the words, go right ahead. Answers can be found on page 277.

Make It Clear

Your sentence should be short, sweet, and to the point. If you are using words like "could," "might," or "sometimes," you are not identifying the defining relationship between the words.

ARCHITECT : BUILDING :: _____

WARDEN : PRISON :: _____

EDUCATION : IGNORANCE :: _____

AQUATIC : WATER :: _____

LETTERS : ALPHABET :: _____

ETS's FAVORITE RELATIONSHIPS

Certain kinds of analogy relationships tend to crop up again and again on the SAT. Here are the four most common types.

Type

These are relationships in which one of the words is a "type of" the other word. For these pairs, your ready-made sentence is, "____ is a type of ____."

Here are some examples:

LOLLIPOP : CANDY

JUICE : BEVERAGE

MAPLE : TREE

Degree

These are relationships in which one of the words is an extreme degree of the other. For each pair, your sentence will be, "____ means extremely ____" or "____ means very little ____."

Here are some examples:

POUR : DRIP

BREEZE : GALE

FAMISHED : HUNGRY

Pour is an extreme form of *drip*. A *gale* is an extremely strong *breeze*. *Famished* means extremely *hungry*.

Means without

In these relationships, one word means "a lack of" the other. Your sentence is, "____ means a lack of ____."

Here are three examples:

SHALLOW : DEPTH

JUVENILE : MATURITY

RANDOM : PATTERN

Shallow means a lack of *depth*. *Juvenile* means a lack of *maturity*. *Random* means a lack of *pattern*.

Use

In these relationships, one word describes the use or the purpose of the other word. "____ is used to____."

Here are three examples:

SCISSORS : CUT

JOKE : AMUSE

BUTTRESS : SUPPORT

Scissors are used to *cut*. The purpose of a *joke* is to *amuse*. A *buttress* is used to *support*.

Characteristic of

In these relationships, one word describes a characteristic of the other word. Your sentence is, "____ is a characteristic of ____."

Here are some examples:

DISHONESTY : LIAR

SPEED : SPRINTER

DOES IT FIT?

Once you've made a sentence, you need to find an answer choice that fits in it. Plug each answer choice into your sentence. Eliminate the answers that don't fit.

Remember that you can flip the order of the stem pair, but if you do, be sure to flip the answer choices as well.

Try the following example:

10. COMPANY : PRESIDENT ::
    (A) team : athlete
    (B) hospital : patient
    (C) airline : passenger
    (D) library : reader
    (E) army : general

Consider the
Possibilities

Read every answer choice
before deciding which is "best."
On question 11, even though
D looked good immediately,
we still tried choice E. If you
answer too quickly, you may
end up with a choice that
sounds all right to you but is
not as good as a choice you
haven't read yet.

Here's how to crack it

First make a defining sentence: "A president is the head of a company." Then plug in the answer choices:

(A) Is an *athlete* the head of a *team*? Well, an athlete is a part of a team, but the head of a team would be a captain. Eliminate.

(B) Is a *patient* the head of a *hospital*? No. Eliminate.

(C) Is a *passenger* the head of an *airline*? No. Eliminate.

(D) Is a *reader* the head of a *library*? No. A reader might use a library, but a librarian is the head of the library. Eliminate.

(E) Is a *general* the head of an *army*? Yes. That's exactly what a general is. This is ETS's answer.

Let's try another one:

11. APPLE : FRUIT ::

    (A) meal : restaurant
    (B) macaroni : cheese
    (C) dessert : vegetable
    (D) beef : meat
    (E) crust : pizza

Here's how to crack it

"An apple is a kind of fruit." Which answer choice fits?

(A) Is a *meal* a kind of *restaurant*? No. A restaurant is a place that serves meals. Eliminate.

(B) Is *macaroni* a kind of *cheese*? No. Eliminate.

(C) Is *dessert* a kind of *vegetable*? No. Eliminate.

(D) Is *beef* a kind of *meat*? Yes. A possibility.

(E) Is *crust* a kind of *pizza*? No. Eliminate.

ETS's answer has to be choice D. It's the only one we weren't able to eliminate.

You can even use this process when you don't know one of the words in an answer choice. Try the example on the following page.

16. DEHYDRATE : WATER ::
    (A) polish : gloss
    (B) soak : liquid
    (C) ???? : steel
    (D) rise : ????
    (E) ???? : color

Here's how to crack it

"Dehydrate means to lose water." Now we will plug in each answer choice. For the choices in which you are missing a word, simply ask if there's a word that *could* mean what the sentence is looking for.

(A) Does *polish* mean to lose *gloss*? No. It might mean to gain it, but this is not our answer. Eliminate.

(B) Does *soak* mean to lose *liquid*? No, it means to place in liquid. Eliminate.

(C) Could *something* mean to lose *steel*? Can you actually lose steel? This sentence doesn't make sense, even though we don't know one of the words. Cross it off.

(D) Could *rise* mean to lose *something*? Rise could probably mean to gain something, but not to lose something. Cross it off.

(E) Could *something* mean to lose *color*? Sure—*fade* means to lose color. Besides, we eliminated everything else. E is ETS's answer.

As you can see, making a good sentence can get you to the answer even when you don't know all the words in the answer choices.

MAKE IT BETTER

Sometimes, after plugging the choices into your sentence, you may find yourself with two or more answers that seem possible. In such cases, you'll have to go back, make your sentence more specific, and try again.

Here's an example:

12. TIGER : ANIMAL ::
    (A) pigeon : hawk
    (B) dinosaur : fossil
    (C) shark : fish
    (D) colt : horse
    (E) tulip : flower

Suppose that your first sentence is "A tiger is a kind of animal." Plug in the choices:

(A) Is a *pigeon* a kind of *hawk*? No. Eliminate.
(B) Is a *dinosaur* a kind of *fossil*? Not really, although some people might think so. We won't eliminate it yet, although it isn't a very good possibility.
(C) Is a *shark* a kind of *fish*? Yes, a possibility.
(D) Is a *colt* a kind of *horse*? Yes, in a way. Another possibility.
(E) Is a *tulip* a kind of *flower*? Yes. Yet another possibility.

As you can see, the initial sentence isn't specific enough.

Good Sentences

The very best sentence is a short and specific one that defines one word in terms of the other. ETS selects one answer for each question. If you come up with more than one, you've done something wrong. And always remember that the Verbal SAT is a *vocabulary* test. Virtually all the relationships tested on SAT Analogies are derived from the definitions of words.

Here's how to crack it
Make your sentence more specific. How do we do that? By keeping in mind *precisely* what the words mean. The important fact about a tiger is not simply that it is a kind of animal, but that it is a ferocious one, or a dangerous one, or a meat-eating one. The only answer choice that fulfills this requirement is C.

THE TOUGHER STUFF
By now you're probably getting pretty good at making defining sentences with the stem words. But what happens when you don't know one of the stem words? You certainly can't make a good sentence with the words if you are not sure what one of them means.

Relax. You can still answer an analogy question correctly, even if you don't know one of the stem words. Sounds impossible? It's not. It's called "Working Backwards."

Working Backwards

If you cannot make a sentence with the stem words, go to the answer choices and try to make defining sentences with each choice. One of two things will happen: either you won't be able to make a good, defining sentence, in which case you can eliminate that answer choice, or you will be able to make a good sentence, which would allow you to plug in the stem word you do know to see if it fits.

Think of it this way:

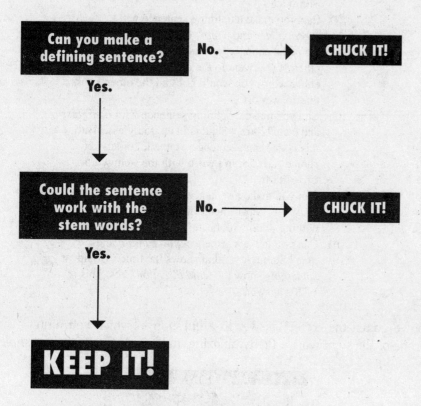

Try the following example:

ANALOGIES

10	**11**	12	13	14	15
EASY		MEDIUM		HARD	

11. ???? : WIND DIRECTION ::

(A) thermometer : mercury
(B) speedometer : pedal
(C) hourglass : sand
(D) barometer : heat
(E) sundial : time

Here's how to crack it

Since you don't know one of the stem words, you can't make a sentence. Instead, you need to work backwards. Let's look at each answer choice:

(A) Can you make a defining sentence with *thermometer* and *mercury*? Sure. "Mercury is in a thermometer." Can this sentence work with the stem word we know? Can *wind direction* be in something? No. This cannot be the answer. Eliminate.

(B) Can you make a defining sentence with *speedometer* and *pedal*? No. The speedometer and the pedal actually have nothing to do with each other. If you went to the dictionary and looked up either word, you would not find the other. Cross this answer off.

(C) Can you make a defining sentence with *hourglass* and *sand*? Sure. "Sand is in an hourglass." But this is the same sentence we made for answer choice A. It doesn't work with the stem words. Cross it off.

(D) Can you make a sentence with *barometer* and *heat*? No. A barometer measures pressure; it has nothing to do with heat. Cross this answer off.

(E) Can you make a sentence with *sundial* and *time*? Sure. "A sundial shows the time." Could *something* show the *wind direction*? Yes. This is ETS's answer.

You've gotten the correct answer to a question in which you didn't even know one of the stem words. Pretty amazing, huh? Let's try another example:

???????? : MOTION ::

(A) numerology : progress
(B) navigation : ocean
(C) astronomy : weather
(D) criminology : perversion
(E) psychology : mind

Here's how to crack it

Since you can't make a sentence of the stem words, go right to the answer choices and work backwards. Let's look at each answer choice:

(A) Can you make a sentence with *numerology* and *progress*? No. Numerology involves numbers, which don't have anything to do with progress (we won't find these words together in the dictionary). Cross this answer off.

(B) Can you make a sentence with *navigation* and *ocean*? Sure. "Navigation is the science used to make one's way across the ocean." Now check the stem words: Is there *something* that means to make one's way across *motion*? No. This cannot be the answer. Eliminate it.

(C) Can you make a sentence with *astronomy* and *weather*? No. Don't confuse *astronomy* with *meteorology*. Cross off this answer.

(D) Can you make a sentence with *criminology* and *perversion*? No. These words don't really have anything to do with each other in a definitional sense (remember to avoid words like "sometimes" and "might"). Cross this off.

(E) Can you make a sentence with *psychology* and *mind*? Sure (not to mention, it's the only answer left). "*Psychology* is the study of the *mind*." Could *something* be the study of *motion*? Sure (it's called dynamics). This is ETS's answer.

DRILL 2

Use the following drill to practice Working Backwards. For each pair of words, decide if there is a definitional relationship. If there is, write a defining sentence in the space provided. If not, write "No relationship" in the blank.

If you aren't absolutely certain of the meaning of a word, look it up, add it to your word list, and make sure you know it before you take the SAT. You can't write a defining sentence if you don't know what the words mean. We've answered the first three questions for you. Be sure to check your answers against the key on page 277.

1. acorn : nut An *acorn* is a type of *nut*.

2. cardiologist : horse No relationship

3. counselor : advice A *counselor's* job is to give *advice*.

4. solar : sun _____

5. sticky : glue _____

6. purr : hunger _____

7. grateful : thanks _____

8. morsel : quantity _____

9. equine : horse _____

10. speculation : profit_____

11. preach : exhortation_____

12. dive : cliff_____

13. alias : identity _____

WHAT IF I DON'T KNOW EITHER WORD?

If you don't know *either* of the words in an *answer choice*, you obviously cannot make a sentence. However, don't simply cross it off! You cannot eliminate
answers simply because you don't know the words. That would be very Joe
Bloggs-like. Instead, leave the choice as a possibility. If you are working on a
very hard question, the hardest answer choice may be your best guess (more on
this later).

If you don't know *either* of the *stem words*, you can still Work Backwards. You
won't be able to check your sentences against the stem words, but you will be able
to eliminate the answer choices for which you could *not* make a good sentence.

Try the following example:

12. ???? : ???? ::

    (A) plentiful : resource
    (B) wealthy : money
    (C) voluntary : result
    (D) neutral : activity
    (E) humorous : movie

Here's how to crack it

Since we have no idea what the given words are, ignore them and go right to the
answer choices. Let's look at the choices one at a time:

    (A) Can we make a defining sentence with *plentiful*
        and *resource*? Not really. Plentiful means "lots
        of something" (not necessarily resources), and
        resources may or may not be plentiful. Cross this
        answer off.
    (B) Can we make a defining sentence with *wealthy*
        and *money*? Yes. "Wealthy means having lots of
        money." This is a possibility.

(C) Can we make a defining sentence with *voluntary* and *result*? Not at all. Eliminate it.

(D) Can we make a sentence with *neutral* and *activity*? No. Cross it off.

(E) Can we make a defining sentence with *humorous* and *movie*? Be careful—some movies are humorous, others are not. And, if you looked up "humorous" in the dictionary, you wouldn't find the word "movie." Eliminate this answer.

ETS's answer has to be B. By Working Backwards, you were able to get this question right without having any idea what the stem words are. (The missing words are MASSIVE : SIZE.)

WILL IT ALWAYS WORK?

You may not always be able to eliminate the four wrong answer choices, but you will always be able to eliminate some answers on analogy questions, even when you don't know either stem word. In addition, Working Backwards can help you stretch your vocabulary. If, for example, you come to a pair of stem words that you *sort of* know (you've seen them before, you kind of know what they mean, but you don't feel entirely comfortable making a sentence), you can Work Backwards instead of trying to make a sentence with the stem words. Eliminate the answers that are not definitionally related. Make sentences with the answers that you can, and then test the stem words. Since you sort of know the meaning of the stem words, testing them in your Working Backwards sentences will be easy.

JOE BLOGGS AND SAT ANALOGIES

As is always true on the SAT, Joe Bloggs finds some answer choices much more appealing than others on analogy questions. Most of all, Joe is attracted to choices containing words that:

- Remind him of one or both of the stem words

- "Just seem to go with" the stem words

- Are easy to understand

ELIMINATING JOE'S ANSWERS ON DIFFICULT QUESTIONS

The Joe Bloggs principle is most useful in helping you eliminate incorrect answer choices on the difficult third of the analogies. To do this, you need to know how to spot choices that seem right to Joe.

Cross It Out

When you eliminate an incorrect answer choice on any SAT question, draw a line through it in your test booklet. On harder questions, you may have to reread the answers several times before you settle on one. If you cross out choices you've eliminated, you won't waste time reconsidering wrong answers over and over again.

Here's an example:

```
                        ANALOGIES
              ⑩   11   12   13   14   15
              EASY      MEDIUM      HARD
```

A Gentle Reminder

Easy questions tend to have easy
answers. Hard questions tend to
have hard answers.

10.   SONG : VERSES ::

(A) moon : phases
(B) tree : roots
(C) battle : soldiers
(D) poem : stanzas
(E) newspaper : reporters

Here's how to crack it

Which choice attracts Joe Bloggs on this question? Choice D. SONGS and VERSES just seem to go with *poems* and *stanzas*. Does that mean choice D is wrong? No! Look at the number of this question. It's a number 10, the easiest in its group. Joe Bloggs gets the easy ones right, and D is ETS's answer.

But Joe's impulse to pick answers that "just seem to go with" the words in capital letters will get him in trouble on hard questions. After all, if Joe knew the answer to a hard analogy, it wouldn't be hard, would it? On the hardest analogy questions, therefore, you can safely eliminate choices that you know would seem attractive to Joe Bloggs. Before you do anything else on a hard question, look for Joe's answers and cross them out.

Try this:

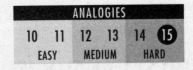

```
                        ANALOGIES
              10   11   12   13   14   ⑮
              EASY      MEDIUM      HARD
```

15.   INFINITESIMAL : SIZE ::

(A) trifling : significance
(B) distant : galaxy
(C) cacophonous : music
(D) lucid : behavior
(E) enormous : mountain

Here's how to crack it

Which choices attract Joe on this question? Choice E definitely does, because *enormous* makes Joe think of SIZE. What does that mean? It means that E cannot possibly be ETS's answer, because this is a hard question and Joe doesn't get the hard questions right.

Joe may also be attracted to choice B: *Galaxies* are large, so in Joe's mind this choice "just seems to go with" the words in capital letters. That means you can also eliminate choice B. Even if you can't eliminate anything else, you've already got a one-in-three chance of guessing ETS's answer.

(ETS's answer is A. INFINITESIMAL means extremely small, or lacking in SIZE, and *trifling* means lacking in *significance*.)

Here's another example:

```
                    ANALOGIES
        10   11   12   13   14   15
          EASY     MEDIUM    HARD
```

14. DESTITUTION : MONEY ::

   (A) budget : options
   (B) sobriety : inebriation
   (C) opulence : wealth
   (D) deficit : finance
   (E) pollution : factory

Here's how to crack it

This is the next-to-last question in its group, which means it's hard. Joe Bloggs will definitely get it wrong.

DESTITUTION is a very hard word. Most people, including Joe Bloggs, don't know what it means. MONEY, however, is an easy word. Joe looks through the choices for a word that seems to go with *money*. He finds three choices that attract him: *budget* in choice A, *wealth* in choice C, and *finance* in choice D. Joe will weigh these three choices and then pick one of them.

With choices A, C, and D out of the way, let's take a look at the remaining choices. Answer choice B has hard words, so it could definitely be the answer. Choice E, on the other hand, has easier words. So you can ask yourself: Can I make a defining sentence with *pollution* and *factory*? Pollution can come from a factory, but does it *have* to come from a factory? If you looked up *pollution* in the dictionary, would the definition be something that comes from a factory? Probably not (look it up and see). Would the definition of *factory* be something that produces pollution? No, that's not what a factory is by definition. If you can't make a defining sentence, it can't be the answer. ETS's answer must be B.

By Working Backwards and using the Joe Bloggs principle, we were once again able to find ETS's answer even without knowing one of the stem words.

HARD QUESTIONS, HARD ANSWERS

Joe Bloggs doesn't like problems that look too hard, and he doesn't like complicated solutions. This means that he has a strong tendency to select choices containing words that he understands and is familiar with. When Joe takes a stab at a question, he picks something easy and familiar.

This can be a big help for you. Because Joe is so irresistibly drawn to easy choices, one of the best places to look for ETS's answer on a hard analogy question is among the hard choices—choices containing words that Joe doesn't understand. When you find yourself stumped on a hard analogy, simply eliminate what you can and then select the remaining choice that contains the hardest and weirdest words.

What's So Hard About That?

If you find that you know most of the words on the SAT, good for you! You've won more than half the battle. You still might get things wrong, though, usually by hastily choosing Joe Bloggs answers. How do you decide which words are hard to Joe, someone with an average vocabulary? Ask yourself, "Did I learn this word in high school or earlier?" Words we learned in high school tend to be harder. The words we've always known tend to be easier.

PICK THE WEIRD ONE

Easy analogies have easy answers; hard analogies have hard answers. If you've eliminated what you can and are guessing on a hard analogy, go with the hardest, *weirdest* answer choice.

DRILL 3

In the following two examples, work backwards to eliminate what you can. Then guess the hardest, weirdest answer for each question. Answers can be found on page 277.

15. ???? : ???? ::
    (A) fabric : weaving
    (B) watercolor : painting
    (C) script : drama
    (D) embellishments : description
    (E) partner : dance

16. ???? : ???? ::
    (A) dither : choice
    (B) dawdle : excuse
    (C) chatter : speech
    (D) mope : laughter
    (E) bustle : arrival

ANALOGIES SUMMARY

We've now given you several effective techniques that you can use to find ETS's answers to analogy questions. To summarize our approach, we're going to show you which techniques to use and when to use them, depending on whether you can make a good sentence with the stem words. If you don't know the meaning of both stem words, then you'll probably have trouble making a sentence. But as you've seen, you can still attack the answer choices.

When you attack any analogy question, you will find yourself in one of the following three situations. Here's the definitive approach for each of them.

When you can make a sentence with the stem words

1. Make a short, specific defining sentence with the stem words. By *defining sentence*, we mean a sentence that:
   - Uses one word to define the other
   - Is short and simple
   - Starts with one word and ends with the other

2. Plug each answer choice into your sentence. Be sure to check *every* answer choice. Cross out any answer choices that don't fit your sentence. ETS's answer will be the answer choice that fits your sentence best.

3. If you find that more than one answer choice works with your sentence, go back and make your sentence more specific. Then try your new sentence with the remaining answer choices.

When you can't make a sentence, but you know at least one of the stem words

1. If you are working on a hard question, eliminate Joe Bloggs answers.

2. Work backwards. Go to each answer choice and try to make a defining sentence. If you can make a sentence, plug in the stem word or words you know to see if they fit. If they do, keep that choice. If not, cross it off.

3. If you cannot make a defining sentence with an answer choice, cross it off.

4. If you are left with more than one possible answer choice after Working Backwards, take a guess (easy questions have easy answers; hard questions have hard answers).

When you can't make a sentence and you don't know either of the stem words

1. Eliminate any Joe Bloggs answers.

2. Work backwards. Try to make a defining sentence with each answer choice. Cross off the answers that do not have a definitional relationship.

3. When all else fails, pick the choice with the hardest, weirdest words that Joe Bloggs would never pick.

8

Critical Reading

MEMORIZE THE INSTRUCTIONS

This chapter is about Critical Reading, the last of the three question types on the verbal SAT. Critical Reading appears in all three verbal sections of the test, and accounts for half of all the points that can be scored on the Verbal SAT, so this chapter is important.

Before we begin, take a moment to read the following set of instructions, which appears exactly as it does on the real SAT.

> Each passage below is followed by questions based on its content. Answer the questions following each passage on the basis of what is stated or implied in that passage and in any introductory material that may be provided.

Be sure that you know and understand these instructions before you take the SAT. If you learn them ahead of time, you won't have to waste valuable seconds reading them on the day you take the test.

SAT CRITICAL READING: CRACKING THE SYSTEM

It's important to know the instructions printed before each group of Critical Reading passages in the SAT, but it's vastly more important to understand what those instructions mean. ETS's instructions don't tell you everything you need to know about critical reading. The rest of this chapter will tell you what you need to know.

Our techniques will enable you to:

1. Read for what you need

2. Eliminate answer choices that could not possibly be correct

3. Take advantage of outside knowledge

4. Take advantage of inside knowledge (about how ETS thinks)

5. Make better use of your limited time by skipping a difficult passage

JUST THE QUESTIONS, PLEASE

The least important part of critical reading is the passage. No, really. The name of the section implies that you will be doing lots of reading, but it doesn't tell you that most of the reading you'll be doing is of the questions. Critical reading is *not* about learning something new and interesting—it's about scoring points by answering questions correctly.

Many students have difficulty with critical reading because they place too much emphasis on the passage and not enough on the questions. In actuality, you could probably answer many questions more effectively if you never read the passage at all.

The Fact Bank

Somebody once asked notorious thief Willie Sutton why he robbed banks. "Because that's where the money is," he replied. While cracking critical reading is safer and slightly more productive than larceny, the same principle applies: Concentrate on the questions and answer choices, because that's where the points are. The passage is just a place for ETS to stash facts and details. You'll find them when you need to. What's the point of memorizing all sixty-seven pesky details about plankton if ETS only asks you about twelve?

Look at the following question. Without so much as a glance at a passage, use your common sense and knowledge of ETS to cross off impossible answers. Then take a guess at ETS's answer.

18. The author believes that federal judges can sometimes be criticized for

    (A) failing to consider the meaning of the law
    (B) ignoring the rights of defendants
    (C) letting their personal opinions influence the outcomes of trials
    (D) slowing the flow of court cases by caring too much about the requirements of justice
    (E) forgetting that the Constitution is the foundation of the American legal system

Here's how to crack it

The question wants to know what an *ETS author* might criticize a federal judge for. The answer, of course, is "not much." ETS is a very pro-American, pro-justice system organization. After all, they as a company are thriving on "the American way." Therefore, ETS is very careful to be respectful of the right people.

Let's look at each answer choice to see if it is possible:

(A) Could ETS criticize federal judges for "failing to consider the meaning of the law"? A federal judge doesn't consider the law? Not likely. This answer is not possible because it would never happen. Even though you have no idea what this passage is about, you can cross off this answer choice.

(B) Could ETS criticize federal judges for "ignoring the rights of defendants"? Another unlikely practice of a federal judge. Even if *you* have a jaded opinion of our federal legal system, *ETS* doesn't. This answer is not possible—cross it off.

(C) Could ETS criticize federal judges for "letting their personal opinions influence the outcomes of trials"? Although this answer seems a little more plausible, it's still pretty unlikely. Federal judges represent the epitome of impartiality, at least according to ETS. Keep it for now, but it is unlikely.

(D) Could ETS criticize federal judges for "slowing the flow of court cases by caring too much about the requirements of justice"? What a laudable error, huh? ETS could criticize them for this honorable mistake. Lookin' good as a choice.

(E) Could ETS criticize federal judges for "forgetting that the Constitution is the foundation of the American legal system"? Would a federal judge simply *forget* about the Constitution? Not likely. Cross this off.

Of the two choices remaining, the most reasonable guess is D. It is also ETS's answer.

GOOD ANSWER

You just answered a critical reading question correctly without ever seeing the passage it was associated with. What does that tell you about critical reading questions? It tells you that there's a lot more to answering a critical reading question than reading the passage. In fact, reading the passage is the least important part of answering critical reading questions.

Will you be answering lots of questions without reading the passage? No, for two reasons: 1) It takes longer to answer a question when you have no knowledge of the passage, and 2) Why should you answer the question this way when all the answers are right there in front of you?

OPEN-BOOK TEST

Critical reading is nothing more than an open-book test. If your history teacher tells you that Friday's exam is going to be an open-book test, what's your reaction? Most people do the "this is gonna be easy" dance when they are told that all the info they need to know will be right in front of them. Okay, you can sit down now.

Well, critical reading is exactly the same as an open-book test. What's more, you only have to scan a few paragraphs to find your answers. For each CR passage, you will do the following:

1. **Read What You Need.** Do a topic search so that you have a clue about the passage's topic and organization.

2. **Translate the Question.** Reword each question so you know exactly what you are being asked.

3. **Put Your Finger on the Answer.** Go back to the passage and find the exact location of the answer you are looking for.

4. **Answer the Question in Your Own Words.** Answer the question in your own words before you read any of the answer choices.

5. **Use POE.** Get rid of answers that are not close to yours.

SAMPLE PASSAGE AND QUESTIONS

Here is an example of what a CR passage and questions look like. We will use this passage to illustrate CR techniques. You may want to stick a paper clip on this page to make it easier to flip back to it.

Questions 16–21 are based on the following passage.

The following passage is a summary of a sociological study concerning groups of Mexican-American women.

The subject of my study is women who are initiating social change in a small region in Texas. The women are Mexican-Americans who are, or
Line were, migrant agricultural workers. There is more
5 than one kind of innovation at work in the region, of course, but I have chosen to focus on three related patterns of family behavior.

The pattern I lifestyle represents how migrant farm workers of all nationalities lived in the past
10 and how many continue to live. I treat this pattern as a baseline with which to compare the changes represented by patterns II and III. Families in pattern I work on farms year-round, migrating for as many as ten months each year. They work and
15 travel in extended kin units, with the eldest male occupying the position of authority. Families are large—eight or nine children are not unusual—and all members are economic contributors in this strategy of family migration. The children receive
20 little formal schooling.

Families in pattern II manifest some differences in behavior while still maintaining aspects of pattern I. They continue to migrate but on a reduced scale, often modifying their schedules of migration to
25 allow children to finish the school year. Parents in this pattern often find temporary local jobs as checkers or clerks to offset lost farming income. Pattern II families usually have fewer children than do pattern I families, and the children make a far
30 smaller contribution to the economic welfare of the family.

The greatest amount of change from pattern I, however, is found in pattern III families, who no longer migrate at all. Both parents work full time in
35 the area, and they have an average of three children. The children attend school for the entire year. In pattern III, the women in particular create new roles for themselves for which no local models exist. They not only work full time but may, in addition,
40 return to school. They also assume a greater responsibility in planning family activities, setting household budgets, and making other domestic decisions than do women in the other patterns.

Although these women are in the minority among
45 residents of the region, they serve as role models for others, causing ripples of change to spread in their communities.

New opportunities have continued to be determined by pre-existing values. When federal
50 jobs became available in the region, most involved working under the direction of female professionals such as teachers or nurses. Such positions were unacceptable to many men in the area because they were not accustomed to being
55 subordinate to women. Women therefore took the jobs, at first, because the income was desperately needed. But some of the women decided to stay at their jobs after their families' distress was over. These women enjoyed their work, its responsibility,
60 and the companionship of fellow women workers. The steady, relatively high income allowed their families to stop migrating. And, as the efficacy of these women became increasingly apparent, they and their families became even more willing to
65 consider changes in their lives that they would not have considered before.

16. Which of the following titles best reflects the main focus of the passage?

   (A) A Study of Three Mexican-American Families at Work in Texas
   (B) Innovative Career Women: Effects on Family Unity
   (C) Changes in the Lifestyles of Migrant Mexican-American Families
   (D) Farming or Family: The Unavoidable Choice for Migrant Farm Workers
   (E) Recent Changes in Methods of Farming in Texas

17. According to the passage, pattern I families are characterized by which of the following?

   (A) Small numbers of children
   (B) Brief periods of migrant labor
   (C) Female figures of family authority
   (D) Commercial as well as agricultural sources of income
   (E) Parents and children working and traveling together

18. All of the following statements about pattern II children express differences between them and pattern I children EXCEPT:

(A) They migrate for part of each year.
(B) They have fewer siblings.
(C) They spend less time contributing to family income.
(D) They spend more months in school.
(E) Their parents sometimes work at jobs other than farming.

19. The word "domestic" in line 43 most nearly means

(A) crucial
(B) native
(C) unspoken
(D) imported
(E) household

20. According to the passage, which of the following is NOT true of women in pattern III families?

(A) They earn a reliable and comparatively high income.
(B) They continue to work solely to meet the urgent needs of their families.
(C) They are more involved in the deciding of family issues than they once were.
(D) They enjoy the fellowship involved in working with other women.
(E) They serve as models of behavior for others in the region.

21. The author's attitude toward the three patterns of behavior mentioned in the passage is best described as one of

(A) great admiration
(B) grudging respect
(C) unbiased objectivity
(D) dissatisfaction
(E) indifference

READ WHAT YOU NEED

What do you need to know about a CR passage before you head to the questions? Three things:

- The author's point
- The author's tone
- The passage layout

Virtually every SAT reading passage has the same basic structure: the author has a point. Her primary purpose is to develop or explain this point. She does this by stating her point and then supporting it with details, facts, examples, metaphors, and secondary ideas. The author also has an attitude toward her subject (she may be *for* something, *against* something, or *neutral*), which she conveys in her tone or style.

You also need to get the gist of how the passage is organized. Remember our open-book test from history class? You may not go home and study for that open-book test, but it would behoove you to organize your notes a bit so you can find answers in a timely fashion. The same holds true for CR passages. You want a sense of where the author put stuff so you can find answers easily.

To access the initial stuff you need from a passage quickly and easily, you're going to do a topic search. To do a topic search, read:

- **The blurb.** Most CR passages are introduced by a brief italicized paragraph that gives you some idea of what the passage is about. Read it carefully.

- **The first few sentences of paragraph one.** Get an idea of what the author is saying. Once you feel you have a clue, jot down a note and move on.

- **The first sentence of the remaining paragraphs.** Jot down a note next to each paragraph so you have a handle on the passage structure.

- **The last sentence.** Read the last sentence so you know how the passage winds up. Jot down a note to yourself about the author's overall point and tone.

Topic Search Test Drive

Flip back to our sample passage on page 117 and try a topic search. Be sure to jot down quick notes to yourself so you know what's going on. Then flip back here to see how you did.

Passage Types

Critical Reading passages come from four broad subject areas:

1. Science: discoveries, controversies, or other topics in physics, chemistry, astronomy, biology, medicine, botany, zoology, and the other sciences.

2. Humanities: excerpts from essays about art, literature, music, philosophy, or folklore; discussions of artists, novelists, or historical figures.

3. Social sciences: topics in politics, economics, sociology, or history.

4. Narrative: usually excerpts from novels, short stories, or humorous essays. (We have yet to see a poem on the SAT.)

ETS usually includes a passage involving a historically overlooked community or social group. This "ethnic" passage, as we call it, is usually either a social science or humanities passage.

Here's how to crack it

First, read the blurb:

The following passage is a summary of a sociological study concerning groups of Mexican-American women.

This sets you on the right track. Now read the first few sentences of the passage:

"The subject of my study is women who are initiating social change in a small region in Texas. The women are Mexican-Americans who are, or were, migrant agricultural workers."

As you read, the following phrases ought to attract your attention: *women who are initiating social change*; *Mexican-American*; *migrant agricultural workers.* The author's point, or most of it, is right here. The main idea might be stated quickly, as "Mexican-American migrant women workers initiating social change," or something similar. Don't sweat the details. Move on.

The structure of this passage is so straightforward that you won't even need so much as the entire first sentence of any succeeding paragraph. By glancing at the first sentence of each paragraph you can figure out that the second paragraph is about *pattern I lifestyle*, the third paragraph is about *pattern II*, and the fourth paragraph is about *pattern III*.

Remember: You aren't looking for details right now. You're looking for the author's point, and you're getting a sense of how the passage is put together. The author is writing about lifestyles, and each of these paragraphs deals with a different one.

The last paragraph is full of details and sociological jargon. Don't get bogged down with big words. Focus on the final sentence. In the future, the women and their families will be "even more willing to consider changes." That's all you need to notice for now.

Jot down a quick note to yourself on the author's point and tone:

- The author's point: Mexican-American women workers are initiating change.

- The author's tone: Neutral-positive.

WHY WRITE IT DOWN?

As you know, when you take a test under pressure, it's easy to forget stuff, lose your focus, and then feel rushed and out of control. The more you write in your test booklet, the less likely you are to do a mental drift, or lose information that "you know you saw *somewhere* in the passage." On critical reading it is imperative that you jot down notes as you go along so you can easily find the info you need when you go back.

HEAD FOR THE QUESTIONS

Your initial search should only take a minute or two. Once you have a clue about the author's point and the layout of the passage, head for the questions.

Unlike the other sections of the SAT, CR questions are *not* arranged in order of difficulty. They are, however, arranged in roughly chronological order. In other words, a question about the first paragraph will come before a question about the second paragraph, and so on. Most of the questions you'll encounter will ask for specific details from the passage. For the most part, you will answer CR questions in the order they are given.

TRANSLATING

The most important reading you will do on the CR section of the test is when you read the questions. ETS has gone out of its way to make CR questions hard to understand. Therefore, before you go searching for answers to any question, put the question in "English" so you know what you are being asked.

Take a look at the following question. What are you being asked?

> 1. According to the passage, the "language of bureaucracy" and the "language of liberation" are alike in that they take into account which one of the following?

Let's simplify this a bit. "According to the passage…" means look at the passage. Cross off this phrase since it is extra and simply adds confusion. "The 'language of bureaucracy' and the 'language of liberation' are alike… ." How are these two languages similar?

The rest of the sentence is fluff ("in that they take into account") followed by a *see the answer choices* phrase ("which one of the following"). Cross off the last part of the sentence. To answer this question, you need to know how the two languages mentioned are similar.

Flip back to our passage on page 117. Read each question and translate it. If there is anything about the question you find confusing, put it into "English." Cross off unnecessary phrases. Make sure you know exactly what you are being asked. When you finish, flip back here to see how you did.

What the questions really ask

16. What's the best title for this passage?

17. What are characteristics of pattern I families?

18. Pattern II children are different from pattern I children in lots of ways. Four of the answer choices are differences. Pick out the answer that is *not* a difference.

19. Clear as written.

20. Four of the answer choices are truths about pattern III women. Which one is *not* true?

21. What's the author's attitude?

Now let's talk about how to answer each of these questions.

In the Form of a Question

One way ETS confuses test takers is by replacing questions with incomplete sentences: "The primary purpose of the passage is…" instead of "What is the primary purpose of the passage?". Many students find it easier to understand what ETS is driving at if they rephrase those incomplete sentences as questions beginning with "What" or "Why." "What" questions ask for things (facts, ideas). "Why" questions ask for reasons.

Once you know what a question is asking, you can head back to the passage to find the answer. For the most part, the only way to answer CR questions correctly is to put your finger on the answer in the passage. Use the notes you jotted down as you searched the passage to help you locate the answers you need. Once you find the part of the passage that contains your answer, translate it into "English." In other words, *answer the question in your own words* before you look at any answer choices.

Translate the following passage excerpt into "English":

> The luminist school of American landscape
> painting drenched the monumental vistas of the
> American West in golden, surreal light, transforming
> already striking scenes into glimpses of Utopia.

In other words, "luminist school painters used lots of light to paint scenes of the West, making the scenes even more beautiful."

ANSWER THE QUESTION

Answering the questions in your own words before looking at any answer choices will keep you from getting trapped by ETS's distractor answers. You can bet that Joe Bloggs isn't answering the questions in his own words. In fact, Joe is reading the passage slowly and carefully, trying to memorize a bunch of facts he hardly understands, and then trying to answer a bunch a questions he hardly understands without going back to the passage. He's sunk from the start.

You, on the other hand, have already searched the passage, translated the question, and are now ready to find your answer. How can you do this?

Questions often contain clues that point to the answer in the passage. In addition to your notes, you can use these clues to zero in on the answers you are looking for.

LINE REFERENCES

The best clue that ETS gives you for finding the answer within a passage is a *line reference*. The majority of the questions in each Critical Reading section will refer to some line or lines in the passage. For example, ETS might ask you to determine what the passage says about "new research in the field of genetics" in lines 21–25.

Line reference questions will be phrased something like this:

> According to paragraph 3 (lines 34–50), scientists
> studied the comet in order to

> In lines 56–75, the narrator is primarily concerned
> with

They Don't Care What You Know

More than one million students take the SAT every year. They can't all have studied the same subjects, so ETS can't expect you to know anything it hasn't told you. This is important to remember on specific questions. All you have to do is find something the passage already states.

The author uses the quote from Johnson's book (line 79) to demonstrate that

According to paragraph 2, the new species of penguins are an "important find" (line 20) because they are

These line references will be a big help when you go back to the passage to look for ETS's answer, because they tell you approximately where to look. We say approximately because, of course, ETS never makes your life that easy. If ETS refers to lines 33–36, the answer will actually be in lines 31–32, or in lines 37–39.

Read at least five lines above and five lines below the lines mentioned in the question in order to be sure that you've found ETS's answer.

VOCABULARY IN CONTEXT

ETS also uses line reference questions to test vocabulary. For example, a question may ask you for the meaning of the word *stupefying* in line 12. Attack these questions aggressively, handling them in exactly the same way we've taught you to handle sentence completions. Even if you don't know the meaning of the word, the context should enable you to eliminate several incorrect choices using POE. Here's our step-by-step strategy:

1. Cover the answer choices so that you won't be influenced by them.

2. Go to the passage and read the sentence that contains the word being tested.

3. Draw a line through the word with your pencil. Read the sentence again and come up with your own word for the blank (just as you would on a sentence completion). If you don't come up with a word on your first try, read one sentence before and one sentence after. Using the context will give you clues.

4. Once you've settled on your own word, uncover the answer choices and use POE to eliminate those choices that are not like your word.

It is very important to use this method in answering these questions. If you simply plug in the choices—Joe Bloggs's favorite technique—you may fall into a trap. ETS's answer will often be a secondary meaning of the word they asked you to define. If you go straight to the choices, you may be irresistibly attracted to one that might be correct in a different context, but is dead wrong in this one. Covering up the answer choices will eliminate temptation. Don't get careless.

Take another look at question 19 from our sample passage.

Heads Up

ETS will try to trip you up by asking questions that seem to have one answer but actually have another. Often the real answer will be hiding behind a trigger word. In writing questions, ETS looks for places in the passage where meanings change. ETS thinks of each of these changes as a trap for a careless reader—for Joe Bloggs. If you pay attention to the trigger words, you will be able to avoid many of ETS's traps. See the Sentence Completions chapter for a review of trigger words.

Vocabulary in Context: The Student's Friend

Since VIC questions are little more than sentence completions, you really don't have to find the main idea of the passage or anything else in order to answer them. Even if you don't plan to answer every critical reading question, you should still try every VIC question. They're short, predictable, and don't require you to read very much. And they earn you the same point you'd earn answering a longer, more complicated question.

19. The word "domestic" in line 43 most nearly means

(A) crucial
(B) native
(C) unspoken
(D) imported
(E) household

Here's how to crack it

Cover up the answer choices. Then find the word in the passage and lightly draw a line through it. Now proceed as though trying to anticipate ETS's answer for a sentence completion problem.

Here's the sentence you are trying to complete:

"They also assume a greater responsibility in planning family activities, setting household budgets, and making other _____ decisions than do women in the other patterns."

The *decisions* in question are *other* decisions, meaning that making them is like *planning family activities* or *setting household budgets*. As a result, the word that belongs in the blank means something like *family* or *household*. Now look at the choices.

(A) Nothing like the word you anticipated. This may be a tempting choice for a test taker who doesn't have any idea what *domestic* means. Joe is drawn to this choice, because he figures that the women's new decisions must be important. Eliminate.

(B) Nothing like the word you anticipated. This is one meaning of *domestic*, but it is not ETS's answer. *Domestic* in the context of the passage does not mean *native* or *from one's own country* (as it might if the paragraph were discussing the difference between domestic and foreign cars).

(C) Nothing like the word you anticipated.

(D) Nothing like the word you anticipated. This is the opposite of a meaning of *domestic* that doesn't apply in this context.

(E) Here's one of the words you anticipated. This is ETS's answer.

Lead words

Some specific questions in the Critical Reading sections will not have line references. For these questions, ETS gives a different clue that tells you where to look for the answer. For example, if a question asked about the author's opinion of the "volcano theory," you would naturally go back to the passage and find the lines that mention the volcano theory. Every specific question that does not have a line reference has a word or phrase that you can use to find ETS's answer in the passage. We call these *lead words*. In our example, *volcano theory* would be the lead words for the question.

Lead word questions are phrased like this:

> The author suggests that science fiction writers
> have a tendency to

> According to the passage, which of the following is
> a feature of architecture in the 1960s?

> The author of the passage suggests that she was
> able to sell her first painting because

> In the passage, the invention of the microchip was
> similar to

In each of the questions above, there is a phrase—*science fiction writers, architecture in the 1960s, sell her first painting, invention of the microchip*—that you could use as lead words to find ETS's answer in the passages. And you won't have to search the whole passage to find where the lead words are mentioned. Since questions about a passage are in chronological order, you can use line reference questions that come before and after a lead word question to help you locate your answer.

As with line references, once you find the lead words in the passage, you must read at least five lines above and five lines below the line that contains the lead words. Keep reading until you can put your finger on ETS's answer. Answer the question in your own words, then eliminate answers that don't match yours.

Take another look at question 17 from our sample passage:

17. According to the passage, pattern I families are
    characterized by which of the following?

    (A) Small numbers of children
    (B) Brief periods of migrant labor
    (C) Female figures of family authority
    (D) Commercial as well as agricultural sources of
        income
    (E) Parents and children working and traveling
        together

Here's how to crack it

Our translated question asks, "What are characteristics of pattern I families?" This question doesn't have a line reference, but it does have some excellent lead words: *pattern I families*. Where did the author discuss pattern I families? Paragraph two. Go back and read what you need. Once you've gotten a handle on the characteristics of pattern I families (a.k.a. answered the question in your own words), go through each answer choice and use POE.

Let's look at each answer choice:

(A) Eliminate. The paragraph says pattern I families *are large—eight or nine children are not unusual.*

(B) Eliminate. Pattern I families migrate *for as many as ten months each year.*

(C) Eliminate. In pattern I families, *the eldest male* is the figure of family authority.

(D) Eliminate. Pattern I families *work on farms year-round.*

(E) This is ETS's answer. The paragraph says that pattern I families *work and travel in extended kin units.* (Besides, we've eliminated everything else.)

THE AUTHOR'S POINT

There are some questions that ask general stuff about the passage. Usually, these questions want to know the author's main idea, tone, etc. Do you need to go back to the passage to answer these questions? No. You already know the author's point from your topic search. Simply use that information plus the information you gather from answering specific questions to answer any general questions you come across.

Let's look at number 16 from our sample passage.

16. Which of the following titles best reflects the main focus of the passage?

   (A) A Study of Three Mexican-American Families at Work in Texas
   (B) Innovative Career Women: Effects on Family Unity
   (C) Changes in the Lifestyles of Migrant Mexican-American Families
   (D) Farming or Family: The Unavoidable Choice for Migrant Farm Workers
   (E) Recent Changes in Methods of Farming in Texas

Here's how to crack it

Our translated question asks, "What the best title for this passage?" Answer the question in your own words before you read ETS's choices. We said the passage was about Mexican-American women workers initiating change, so our title should be something like, "Mexican-American Women Make Changes."

Let's look at each answer choice:

(A) This answer seems close, but it is actually the Joe Bloggs answer. It doesn't mention anything about changes. Be careful of ETS's attractive distractors.

(B) Again, be careful. This answer mentions career women, not *Mexican-American* career women. Also, the passage doesn't focus on family unity. Eliminate this answer choice.

(C) Sounds good.

Cross It Off

On CR questions, it is very likely that you may need to read a few of the answer choices more than once. To avoid confusion, be sure you cross off each answer entirely when you eliminate it. That way, if you have two or three choices you are considering, you can easily tell which choices are left in the running and which you have eliminated.

(D) This passage does not say the women must choose one or the other. Cross this off.

(E) This answer is plain wrong—the passage is not about farming.

ETS's answer is C. Answering the question in your own words before looking at the answer choices saved you from picking the Joe Bloggs answer. Be sure to have a good idea of the answer to a question in your mind before you read any answer choices.

Try number 21 from our sample passage. When you have finished, come back here to check your work.

Here's how to crack it

The question asks for the author's tone, which we said was neutral-positive. You can therefore immediately cross off any extreme or negative choices. This eliminates answers B and D. What about E? Can an author be *indifferent*? If she doesn't care about a subject, she wouldn't write about it. *Indifferent* is never the author's tone. Cross off E.

You are down to A and C. "Great admiration" is very positive—in fact, too positive for our passage. Our author was essentially neutral. ETS's answer is C.

THE TOUGH STUFF

As we mentioned, you will answer most critical reading questions in the order in which they appear. However, there are some CR questions that are harder and more time-consuming to answer than the others. These will be your "later" questions.

Later questions ask you for a lot more than just some basic information from the passage. They may ask you to weaken or strengthen the author's point. They may ask you to identify an underlying assumption the author is making. If you read a question that sounds time-consuming, save it for later. Also, if you read a question and have no clue where to find the answer in the passage, save it for later. The information you learn from answering the other questions about a passage will often make these *later* questions a little easier to do.

There are a few types of *later* questions that come up frequently on a test. Let's take a look at them.

Do It Later

Look at question 18 from our sample passage.

18. All of the following statements about pattern II children express differences between them and pattern I children EXCEPT

(A) They migrate for part of each year.
(B) They have fewer siblings.
(C) They spend less time contributing to family income.
(D) They spend more months in school.
(E) Their parents sometimes work at jobs other than farming.

EXCEPT . . . NOT!
ETS's EXCEPT/LEAST/NOT questions are big time-wasters. Think about it: You're really answering four questions for the price of one. Most of these questions expect you to find four pieces of information in the passage, but only reward you with one measly point. Do them last, if at all.

When we translated our question, we took into account what the word "EXCEPT" means in a question. "EXCEPT" in a question means that *four* of the choices you read will be true, while only *one* of the answer choices will be false. Your job is to identify the false answer choice. This takes a bit more work than a normal question.

To crack an "EXCEPT" question, first go back to the passage. In question 18, we need to know the differences between pattern II children and pattern I children. Go back and read the third paragraph to familiarize yourself with the differences and similarities. Then come back here to answer the question.

Once you have a clue as to what the differences are, read each answer choice and mark it "T" for true if it is a difference between the two groups, or "F" for false if it is not. Don't hesitate to go back to paragraph 3 as often as you need to.

Here's how to crack it

EXCEPT . . . NOT

There's another reason why you should answer EXCEPT/LEAST/NOT questions last. Once you've answered all the other questions, you have a good idea of what facts in the passage are important to ETS and where to find them. By answering other questions, you may also have gathered information that you can use to eliminate wrong answers on EXCEPT/LEAST/NOT questions. You're the one taking the test; make it work for *you*.

Let's look at each answer choice:

(A) False. According to paragraph 3, both groups migrate for part of the year. This is not a difference between the groups.

(B) True. The parents often have fewer children in pattern II than the parents in pattern I.

(C) True. This is stated in paragraph 3.

(D) True. This is also stated in paragraph 3.

(E) True. It says so in the paragraph.

What is the answer to this question? Use the *Sesame Street* method: One of these things is not like the other. ETS's answer is A.

Notice that although getting the answer to this question was not difficult, it was more time-consuming. Leave these questions for later—do them after you have done the shorter, easier questions about a passage.

I, II, III Questions

Occasionally on the SAT, you will find a question like the following:

29. According to the author, which of the following characteristics is (are) common to both literature and biology?

   I. They are concerned with living creatures.
   II. They enrich human experience.
   III. They are guided by scientific principles.

   (A) I only
   (B) II only
   (C) III only
   (D) I and III
   (E) I, II, and III

We call these "I, II, III questions." We could also call them "triple true/false questions," because you are really being asked to determine whether each of three separate statements is true or false. These questions are very time-consuming, and you will receive credit only if you answer all three parts of the question correctly. Therefore, you should save them for last. Still, these questions are excellent for educated guessing, because you can improve your odds dramatically by using POE.

As is usually true on the SAT, the key to success is taking one step at a time. Consider each of the numbered statements individually. If you discover that it's true, you can eliminate any choice that does not contain it. If you discover that it is false, you can eliminate any choice that does contain it.

For example, suppose you know from reading the passage that statement II is false. That means you can eliminate two choices, B and E. Since B and E both contain II, neither can be correct. (Similarly, if you know that one of the statements is correct, you can eliminate any answer choice that does not contain it.) Incidentally, ETS's answer in this case is C.

THE POWER OF COMMON SENSE

Now try question 20 from our sample passage. When you have finished, return here to see how you did.

Here's how to crack it

The fourth paragraph tells you all you need to know about pattern III women. Remember, the question wants to know what is "NOT" true of these women. Use the True/False method to find ETS's answer.

Let's look at each answer choice:

(A) True. This is implied in the passage.

(B) False. They do not work *solely* to meet the needs of the family.

(C) True. See paragraph 4.

(D) ????. You may not be sure about this answer from reading paragraph 4. It sounds possible, but you didn't see it. Leave it as a choice, and deal with it later.

(E) True. It says so in paragraph 4.

You are left with B as false, and D as unknown. Do you need to do more work? No. ETS's answer is B. Since you know that B is false, D doesn't actually matter. If you were to read through the next paragraph, you would find that the women did enjoy the female company (mentioned in lines 59–60). However, you did enough work to make a smart guess without finding out about choice D.

USE THE POWER

What made answer choice B on the last question so obviously false? The word *solely* made the answer choice quite extreme—it said that the *only* thing these women were doing was trying to meet the needs of the family. Even if you weren't 100 percent sure if they were trying to meet the needs of the family, you knew that that wasn't the only thing they were doing. Common sense told you this had to be false.

Don't underestimate the power of common sense. When the ETS team gets together to write up questions and answer choices, it takes them quite a while to come up with the "perfect" ETS answer. If they want to get their work done, they can't spend all day writing tricky wrong answer choices. They just need to make sure the other four choices are clearly wrong. That's where your common sense comes into play.

STUPID ANSWERS

The CR section of the SAT is filled with stupid answers—answers that can't possibly be ETS's answer. Don't assume that you are trying to find the "best" answer from a pool of five good answer choices. Rather, you are trying to find the "least wrong" answer from a pool of pretty bad answer choices. That's why you can sometimes answer a question without even reading the passage to which it refers.

Look at the following example:

16. According to the passage, all of the following are true of living organisms EXCEPT:

(A) They are able to reproduce themselves.
(B) They are past the point of further evolution.
(C) They are capable of growth.
(D) They respond to stimuli.
(E) They are characterized by a capacity for metabolism.

Here's how to crack it

If you know even a little about biology, you will probably be able to answer this question without reading the passage. (Remember that on this question you are asked to look for a statement that is *not* true.) Now let's consider each choice in turn.

(A) The ability to reproduce is one of the obvious differences between living things and nonliving things. Rocks don't reproduce. Eliminate.

(B) Have living organisms stopped evolving? Of course not. This must be ETS's answer.

(C), (D), and (E)

These are all part of the standard biological definition of life. Eliminate.

Without even reading the passage, you could figure out which one of the answer choices had to be ETS's answer.

DON'T GO TO EXTREMES

Likewise, answers that use extreme language or express information that could be argued with are not going to be ETS's answer. If even one percent of the 1.5 million students who take the SAT each year were able to raise a plausible objection to ETS's answer to a question, ETS would have to spend all their time arguing with students. In order to keep this from happening, they try to make the answers impossible to argue with.

How does ETS do that? Let's look at an example:

> Which of the following statements is impossible to argue with?
>
> (A) The population of the world is 4.734 billion people.
> (B) The population of the world is quite large.

Analysis

Statement A sounds precise and scientific; statement B sounds vague and general. Which is impossible to argue with?

Statement B, of course! Does anyone know exactly what the population of the world is? What if some experts say that the population of the world is 4.732 billion people? Doesn't the population of the world change from minute to minute? A number that is correct today will be wrong tomorrow. It's easy to think of dozens of reasons why statement A could be wrong.

Statement B, on the other hand, is so vague and general that no one could argue with it. Anyone can see that it is true. If it were ETS's answer to an SAT critical reading question, no one would be able to quibble with it.

Let's look at an example. Assume that you've already eliminated some of the choices. You can answer this question now without even reading the passage.

> 27. With which of the following statements would the author of the passage probably agree?
>
> (A) No useful purpose is served by examining the achievements of the past.
> (B) A fuller understanding of the present can often be gained from the study of history.
> (C) [eliminated]
> (D) [eliminated]
> (E) Nothing new ever occurs.

Here's how to crack it

Which of these statements is too extreme? Choices A and E. Choice A says that studying the past has *no* useful purpose. This statement is absolute. Once you find just one exception to the statement, you've proven the statement false. Therefore, the author of the passage probably wouldn't be any more likely to agree with it than we would.

Similarly, choice E says that nothing new ever occurs. This, too, is an extreme statement. Therefore, it's easy to raise objections to it. Nothing new ever occurs? Not even once in a while? Surely there must be an exception somewhere. This statement is easy to attack. If we find a single small exception, we have proven the statement wrong.

Choice B, however, is so general and vague that no one could argue with it. A single example would be enough to prove it correct. It must be ETS's answer.

Here's a silly example that makes the point:

20. With which of the following statements would the weather forecaster probably agree?
   (A) It will begin raining tomorrow at 3:36.
   (B) Tuesday's low temperature will be 38 degrees.
   (C) Next year's snowfall will total 45 inches.
   (D) Tomorrow may be cooler than today.
   (E) Next month will be the wettest month of the year.

Here's how to crack it

This question and the answer choices don't refer to an actual reading passage, of course. But even without seeing a passage (or knowing a weather forecaster), you ought to be able to tell that D is the only statement with which our imaginary weather forecaster, or anyone else, would probably agree. *Tomorrow may be cooler than today* is vague enough to be true no matter what. It may be cooler tomorrow, or it may not. All the bases are covered. The other four statements, by contrast, are so specific and absolute that no weather forecaster could make them. If a television weather forecaster said, *It will begin raining tomorrow at 3:36*, your reaction would be, "Oh, yeah? How do you know?"

If a statement says that something is always true, then you need to find only one exception in order to prove it wrong. If a statement says that every child ordered a hot dog, then you need to find only one child with a hamburger to prove it wrong. These words are highly specific, and therefore make the choices that contain them easier for you to attack and, very likely, to eliminate.

WEIRD PASSAGES

NARRATIVES

Some passages you read will be more like stories than like passages. These passages are called Narratives. Why do you care? Because it is tough to do a topic search on a narrative. If you read the blurb of a passage and it sounds like it is going to be an excerpt from a story, use a "Trigger Search" to read what you need. In other words, go through the passage circling trigger words and reading the

---

Choose Vague

The vague choice is usually correct. And the specific choice is usually incorrect. So when you are trying to decide between two choices, both of which seem good, the more specific choice will be much easier to poke holes in. And a choice that is easier to poke holes in will most likely be the wrong choice.

info that comes after each trigger. (See the Sentence Completions chapter for a review of trigger words.) Then attack the questions as usual, looking for answers around the trigger words.

DUAL PASSAGES

Sometimes you will be given two passages for the price of one. You will be asked questions about the first passage, questions about the second passage, and questions about both. Do these passages one at a time. Read the blurb, then read what you need for Passage One. Then, answer the Passage One questions (they will come first).

After you finish the Passage One questions, go back and read what you need for Passage Two. Do the Passage Two questions. Finally, do the questions that involve both passages.

SKIP IT

Finally, critical reading takes longer than any other question type on the SAT. Depending on where you are scoring, it may be to your benefit to skip some or all of a passage. Remember, easy questions are worth just as many points as hard questions. Rushing through analogies to get to critical reading will hurt your accuracy and cost you points.

THE TAIL END

Whether or not you are doing all the critical reading questions, you should definitely do them last of all the question types. In the 30-minute Verbal sections, Critical Reading questions will come after sentence completions and analogies. Be sure to do all the sentence completions and analogies you plan to do before you begin critical reading. If you run out of time on critical reading, no problem—all the easy stuff is already done.

The 15-minute Verbal section consists solely of critical reading. Work this section smartly, not rushing to get through but rather working to answer questions correctly. You can do just as well on critical reading as you can on analogies and sentence completions if you remember to:

- Read what you need
- Translate the questions
- Put your finger on the answers
- Answer the questions in your own words
- Use POE

Do I Offend?

Often ETS will include a passage on the test that talks about a particular ethnic group—normally a group that has been subjugated by our culture. They allegedly put these passages in to make certain groups feel "more comfortable" with the test. Of course, a CR passage doesn't make any student feel more comfortable with an exam that's riddled with biases. However, it does make critical reading a bit easier. If the test writers choose to include an "ethnic" passage, they will most certainly use a positive, inspirational tone. Keep their objective in mind if you see a passage about a traditionally discriminated-against group. Cross off any answers that are offensive or insulting to the group being discussed.

Critical Reading Takes Time

If you were offered a job that paid $10 an hour and another that paid $10 a minute, which one would you choose? Be good to yourself and do critical reading last.

Dual Passage Strategy

1. Read the blurb
2. Passage One
   (A) Read What You Need
   (B) Attack the Passage One questions
3. Passage Two
   (A) Read What You Need
   (B) Attack the Passage Two questions
4. Attack the questions about both passages.

DRILL 1

Use the following dual passage to *put it all together*. Review your strategy for attacking a dual passage before you begin, then crack this passage. Remember, the questions are more important than the passage. Focus on answering questions correctly by putting your finger on each answer in the passage and answering the questions in your own words before looking at any answer choices. Use your common sense and POE to avoid ETS's traps. Answers can be found on page 278.

DUAL PASSAGES—ONE AT A TIME

- Search Passage 1
- Answer only those questions that deal with Passage 1
- Search Passage 2
- Answer only those questions that deal with Passage 2
- Only then should you proceed to questions that deal with both passages.

In 1959, the Hawaiian Islands were admitted into the United States as the fiftieth state. Both of the following passages discuss the United States' annexation of Hawaii.

Passage 1

On January 28, 1893, Americans read in their evening newspapers a bulletin from Honolulu, Hawaii. Two weeks earlier, said the news report, a
Line group of American residents had overthrown a
5 young native queen and formed a provisional government. Marines from the U.S.S. *Boston* had landed at the request of the American minister in order to protect lives and property. Violence had ended quickly. The rebels were in full control and
10 were said to have enthusiastic support from the populace. Most noteworthy of all, they had announced the intention of asking the United States to annex the islands.

The proposal was not as startling as it might
15 have seemed. Most of the large landowners in the islands were Americans or the children of Americans. So too were the men who grew, refined, and shipped the sugar that was Hawaii's principal export. In addition, many of the kingdom's
20 Protestant clergymen, lawyers, bankers, factory owners, and other leading personages were also American citizens. Though numbering only two thousand of the island's total population of around ninety thousand, these Americans had
25 already given Hawaii the appearance of a colony. This influence could be seen as far back as 1854 when they nearly persuaded a native monarch to request annexation by the United States. Subsequently, the American element helped secure
30 tariff reciprocity from the United States while the island ceded a naval station to the United States. Such measures sparked enough concern by the United States to lead presidents from Tyler on down to periodically warn European powers
35 against meddling in Hawaiian affairs. Thus, by

1893, the new proposal might have been characterized as simply a plan to annex a state already Americanized and virtually a protectorate. Nonetheless, the proposition came
40 unexpectedly, and neither politicians nor journalists knew quite what to make of it. Editorials and comments from Capitol Hill were at first noncommittal. The molders of public opinion seemed intent on learning what mold the public
45 wanted.

San Francisco's leading Republican and Democratic dailies, the *Chronicle* and *Examiner*, declared that Hawaii should certainly be accepted as a state. On January 29, the *Chronicle* reported a
50 poll of local businessmen demonstrating overwhelming support for this view. Some businessmen focused on potential profits. Claus Spreckels, for example, who owned Hawaii's largest sugar plantation, hoped to obtain the two-
55 cent-a-pound bounty paid by the United States government to domestic sugar producers. In addition, he anticipated increased freight for his Oceanic Steamship line as well as more plentiful and cheaper raw sugar for his California Sugar
60 Refinery Company.

Businessmen elsewhere on the Pacific coast followed their lead. San Diego, for example, was virtually the property of the Spreckels family. Moreover, in Los Angeles, Fresno, and San Jose,
65 the Spreckelses were allied, to some extent, in the battle against the railroad with merchants, bankers, warehouse owners, real estate dealers, and contractors; and the Chambers of Commerce of Portland and Seattle had long cooperated with that
70 of San Francisco in pressing for national policies advantageous to the West. It was not long before businessmen all along the coast were reported as favoring annexation.

1. In Passage 1, what event occurred "two weeks earlier" (line 3) than January 28, 1893?

   (A) Hawaii became the fiftieth state of the United States.
   (B) The United States annexed the Hawaiian islands.
   (C) American rebels seized governmental control of the Hawaiian islands.
   (D) Marines from the U.S.S. *Boston* arrived to protect the young native queen from rebels.
   (E) Angry Hawaiian natives rebelled against American rule in Honolulu.

2. According to the second paragraph of Passage 1, Americans on the Hawaiian islands

   (A) outnumbered native islanders by about 88,000
   (B) were largely in opposition to the American proposal of an annexation of the islands
   (C) already owned all the land, and thus rightly usurped the power of the monarchy
   (D) had established themselves there in such a way that annexation seemed the next likely step
   (E) were reluctant to establish a tariff reciprocity that would make it difficult to export sugar

3. The word "ceded," as used in line 31, most nearly means

   (A) sowed with new plants
   (B) took as tax
   (C) paid as tax
   (D) donated as charity
   (E) gave over

4. In describing the response of the "molders of public opinion," (line 43) the author of Passage 1 suggests that they

   (A) persuaded the United States government to annex the Hawaiian islands
   (B) really had little to do with the public's opinion on annexation
   (C) were unfamiliar with the politics of the Hawaiian islands
   (D) wanted to learn about the events that took place on the islands
   (E) never spoke out on the possible annexation of Hawaii

5. In Passage 1, the author mentions Claus Spreckels in order to

   (A) present an example of how businessmen would profit from the annexation of Hawaii
   (B) demonstrate that some people in the United States were opposed to annexation
   (C) prove that Hawaiians were predominantly in favor of statehood
   (D) further the argument concerning the ambiguity of public opinion
   (E) show the role that Americans played in Hawaii

6. All of the following served as reasons that Claus Spreckels supported annexation EXCEPT

   (A) the two-cent-a-pound bounty
   (B) more plentiful sugar for his refineries
   (C) support for the railroads
   (D) cheaper sugar for his refineries
   (E) more cargo for his steamship line to carry

Passage 2

President Cleveland was opposed to annexation throughout his term of office. He believed taking the Islands was immoral, and without his support
Line annexationists had no hope. The Provisional
75 Government, however, did not cease to push its cause in Washington—in fact, the vocal commissioner Lorrin Thurston pushed so hard that he was declared *persona non grata*.

When the Cleveland administration rejected
80 annexation, it requested that the Provisional Government restore the monarchy. This request created additional hard feelings in Hawaii, and the new government flatly refused to comply. For a time it appeared that American forces might be
85 called upon to wrest power from the Provisional Government, but the request was not unduly pressed by the United States and tensions soon eased. The Provisional Government now became the Republic of Hawaii. A new constitution was
90 written and the Islands settled down to await more favorable times.

As a consequence of Cleveland's decision, a battle of words raged across the U.S. in the nation's newspapers. Many newspapers
95 supported the royalists while others hailed the Republic. In San Francisco, the *Call* warned that the annexation of Hawaii "will be the open door through which the least desirable elements in Japan will enter upon American citizenship." The
100 *New York Journal and Advertiser* thought Hawaii belonged to the United States: "The acquisition of Hawaii is an imperative patriotic duty."

The most powerful opponent of annexation was the sugar trust, which was comprised of the sugar
105 refiners. The sugar trust was divided into Eastern and Western camps, with Claus Spreckels controlling the West. The refiners subsidized many of the nation's sugar planters. The refiners, therefore, were able not only to name the price
110 mainland farmers received for their crops, but also to control the retail price of sugar as well. The admission of Hawaii created many questions, and the refiners feared a loss of their monopoly control. Perhaps high-grade Hawaiian sugars
115 would not need refining. Certainly all hopes of a tariff barrier would be gone; and it was possible that Hawaiian sugar could be produced at lower costs. All of these things loomed as threats.

The sugar trust lobby in Washington was a
120 powerful one, and its weight was felt in Congress. The lobbyists also conducted a campaign aimed at turning the American public against acquisition of the Islands. One of their favorite suggestions was that a popular vote on
125 annexation be taken in Hawaii. This the Republic of Hawaii wanted to avoid at all costs.

7. According to the first paragraph of Passage 2, in order for Hawaii to be annexed, the annexationists needed

   (A) additional funding
   (B) the support of the president
   (C) to overthrow the Provisional Government
   (D) to eliminate the sugar monopoly
   (E) to gain the backing of major United States newspapers

8. Passage 2 suggests that the Provisional Government of Hawaii

   (A) often caved in to pressure from the mainland
   (B) was merely a puppet of American economic interests
   (C) received a large amount of support from the American government
   (D) persisted despite resistance from the American government
   (E) was completely representative of the people of Hawaii

9. The third paragraph of Passage 2 implies that public opinion as expressed in newspapers on the issue of Hawaii's annexation was

   (A) solidly in favor of annexation
   (B) overwhelmingly opposed to annexation
   (C) unvoiced, and therefore neither favored nor opposed annexation
   (D) split between support for and opposition to annexation
   (E) limited to only a few public elites

10. The discussion of Hawaiian sugars in lines 103–117 suggests that these products were

   (A) clearly superior to domestic sugars
   (B) faced with a high tariff upon entry to the United States
   (C) not controlled by the American sugar trust
   (D) more expensive than domestic products
   (E) not required to undergo a refining process similar to that undergone by domestic sugars

11. The final paragraph of Passage 2 implies that a popular vote on annexation taken in Hawaii would

   (A) have overwhelming success
   (B) most likely fail to gain enough votes for annexation
   (C) have been the political method of choice for the Republic of Hawaii
   (D) not present a true representation of public sentiment
   (E) result in the demise of the Republic of Hawaii

12. Which of the following does the author of Passage 2 cite as possible opposition to annexation that is not mentioned by the author of Passage 1?

   (A) The exiled Hawaiian monarchy
   (B) Marines from the U.S.S. *Boston*
   (C) Politicians and journalists
   (D) The *Chronicle* and *Examiner*
   (E) The president of the United States

13. One major difference between the two passages is that

   (A) while both authors analyze the same events, they appear to reach different conclusions concerning the possibility of Hawaii's annexation
   (B) the author of the first passage fails to provide specific examples of public sentiment similar to those presented in the second passage
   (C) one passage focuses on support for annexation, while the other emphasizes resistance
   (D) the authors disagree over how much Hawaii had already become Americanized
   (E) the authors arrive at different conclusions concerning the importance of sugar as an import

CRITICAL READING SUMMARY

1. Critical reading accounts for half of all the points on the Verbal SAT.

2. The passage is the least important part of every Critical Reading group.

3. Begin by reading what you need. Do a topic search (or a trigger word search on narratives) to determine:
    *   The author's point
    *   The author's tone
    *   The passage layout

4. On critical reading, the questions are *not* presented in order of difficulty.

5. Translate the questions into "English." You can't answer a question if you don't understand what you are being asked.

6. Put your finger on the answer. Go back to the passage and find the answer to each specific question.

7. Use line references and lead words to help you find ETS's answer in the passage. Always read five lines above and five lines below the line reference or the lead words.

8. Answer the questions in your own words before you read ETS's answers. You will avoid Joe Bloggs answer choices by knowing what the answer is before you read any of the choices.

9. Use POE to get rid of choices that don't match yours. Cross out incorrect choices as you go. You should have a definite sense of zeroing in on ETS's answer. If you don't cross out incorrect choices, you'll waste time and energy rereading wrong answer choices.

10. Eliminate answer choices that have extreme wording (*must*, etc.) or violate common sense.

11. Be careful on EXCEPT/LEAST/NOT questions. ETS's answer is the choice that is *not* true. Use the True/False technique. Do these questions last.

12. I, II, III questions are also very time-consuming and should therefore be saved for last. Still, eliminating choices is easy and straightforward.

13. Treat dual passages as two separate passages. The majority of the questions won't require you to think of any connection whatsoever between the two passages.

14. To read what you need for a narrative passage, do a trigger word search. Circle the trigger words and look for important information around the trigger words.

15. Save critical reading for last in each Verbal section of the SAT. These problems take a great deal of time to answer correctly, but they don't earn you any more points than analogies or sentence completions.

16. It's okay to run out of time on critical reading. Most people do. If you are working at the proper pace, the questions you don't have time to tackle are questions you might have missed anyway.

PART III

How to Crack the Math SAT

A FEW WORDS ABOUT NUMBERS

Three of the six scored sections on the SAT are Math sections. Two of the scored Math sections will last 30 minutes each; the third will last 15 minutes. There may be a fourth, 30-minute Math section on your test, but it won't count toward your score. Don't waste time trying to figure out which sections are the scored ones. Just work at your normal pace.

The math questions on your SAT will be drawn from the following three categories:

1. Arithmetic
2. Basic algebra
3. Geometry

The math questions on your SAT will appear in three different formats:

1. Regular multiple-choice questions
2. Quantitative comparisons
3. Grid-ins

Quantitative comparisons are questions in which you are asked to compare two values and determine whether one is greater than the other. Grid-ins are the only non–multiple-choice questions on the SAT; instead of selecting ETS's answer from among several choices, you will have to find ETS's answer independently and mark it in a grid. The quant comps and grid-ins on your test will be drawn from arithmetic, algebra, and geometry, just like regular SAT math questions. But these formats have special characteristics, so we will treat them separately.

WHAT DOES THE MATH SAT MEASURE?

ETS says that the Math SAT measures "mathematical reasoning abilities" or "higher-order reasoning abilities." But this is not true. The Math SAT is merely a brief test of arithmetic, first-year algebra, and a bit of geometry. By a "bit" we mean just that. The principles you'll need to know are few and simple. We'll show you which ones are important. Most of them are listed for you at the beginning of each Math section.

ORDER OF DIFFICULTY

As was true on the Verbal SAT, questions on the Math SAT are arranged in order of difficulty. The first question in each Math section will be the easiest in that section, and the last will be the hardest; in this case, harder doesn't mean tougher—it means trickier. In addition, the questions within the quantitative comparison and grid-in question groups will also be arranged in order of difficulty. The difficulty of a problem will help you determine how to attack it.

You Don't Have to Finish

We've all been taught in school that when you take a test, you have to finish it. If you only answered two-thirds of the questions on a high school math test, you probably wouldn't get a very good grade. But as we've already seen, the SAT is not at all like the tests you take in school. Most students don't know about the difference, so they make the mistake of doing all the problems on each Math section of the SAT.

Since they only have a limited amount of time to answer all the questions, most students are always in a rush to get to the end of the section. At first, this seems reasonable, but think about the order of difficulty for a minute. All the easy questions are at the beginning of a Math section, and the hard questions are at the end. So when students rush through a Math section, they're actually spending less time on the easier questions (which they have a good chance of getting right), just so they can spend more time on the harder questions (which they have very little chance of getting right). Does this make sense? Of course not.

Here's the secret. On the Math SAT, you don't have to answer every question in each section. In fact, unless you're trying to score 600 or more, you shouldn't even look at the difficult last third of the Math questions. The fact is, most students can raise their math scores by concentrating on getting all the easy and medium questions correct. In other words...

Slow Down!

Most students do considerably better on the Math SAT when they slow down and spend less time worrying about the hard questions (and more time working carefully on the easier ones). Haste causes careless errors, and careless errors can ruin your score. In most cases, you can actually *raise* your scores by answering *fewer* questions. That doesn't sound like a bad idea, does it? If you're shooting for an 800, you'll have to answer every question correctly. But if your target is 550, you should ignore the hardest questions in each section and use your limited time wisely.

To make sure you're working at the right pace in each Math section, refer to the Math Pacing Chart on page 30. The chart will tell you how many questions you need to answer in each section in order to achieve your next score goal.

Better Than Average

If you got 70% on a math test in school, you'd feel pretty lousy—that's a C minus, below average. But the SAT is not like school. Getting 42 out of 60 questions correct (70%) would give you a math score of about 600—100 points *above* the national average.

The Princeton Review Approach

We're going to give you the tools you need to handle the easier questions on the Math SAT, along with several great techniques to help you crack some of the more difficult ones. But you must concentrate first on getting the easier questions correct. Don't worry about the difficult third of the Math SAT until you've learned to work carefully and accurately on the easier questions.

When it does come time to look at some of the harder questions, the Joe Bloggs principle will help you once again, this time to zero in on ETS's answer. You'll learn what kinds of answers appeal to Joe in math, and how to avoid those answers. Just as you did in the Verbal section, you'll learn to use POE to find ETS's answer by getting rid of obviously incorrect answers.

Generally speaking, each chapter in the math section of this book begins with the basics and then gradually moves into more advanced principles and techniques. If you find yourself getting lost toward the end of the chapter, don't worry. Concentrate your efforts on principles you can understand but still need to master.

FUNDAMENTALS

Although we'll show you which mathematical concepts are most important to know for the SAT, this book cannot take the place of a basic foundation in math. For example, if you discover as you read this book that you have trouble working with fractions, you'll want to go back and review the fundamentals. Our drills and examples in this book will refresh your memory if you've gotten rusty, but if you have serious difficulty with the following chapters, you should consider getting extra help. For this purpose, we recommend our own *Math Smart*, which is designed to give you a thorough review of all the fundamental math concepts that you'll need to know on the SAT. Always keep in mind that the math tested on the SAT is different from the math taught in school. If you want to raise your score, don't waste time studying math that ETS never tests.

CALCULATORS

Students are permitted (but not required) to use calculators on the SAT. You should definitely bring a calculator to the test. It will be extremely helpful to you, as long as you know how and when to use it and don't get carried away. We'll tell you more about calculators as we go along.

BASIC INFORMATION

Before moving on, you should be certain that you are familiar with some basic terms and concepts that you'll need to know for the Math SAT. This material isn't at all difficult, but you must know it cold. If you don't, you'll waste valuable time on the test and lose points that you easily could have earned.

INTEGERS

Integers are the numbers that most of us are accustomed to thinking of simply as "numbers." They can be either positive or negative. The positive integers are:

1, 2, 3, 4, 5, 6, 7, and so on

The negative integers are:

–1, –2, –3, –4, –5, –6, –7, and so on

Zero (0) is also an integer, but it is neither positive nor negative.

Note that positive integers get bigger as they move away from 0, while negative integers get smaller. In other words, 2 is bigger than 1, but –2 is smaller than –1. This number line should give you a clear idea of how negative numbers work.

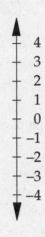

You should also remember the types of numbers that are *not* integers. Here are some examples:

$$-2.7, .625, 15.898, -9.8$$

Basically, integers are numbers that have *no* fractions or decimals. So if you see a number with a fraction or decimal, it's *not* an integer.

DISTINCT NUMBERS

You might see problems on the SAT that mention "distinct numbers." Don't let this throw you. All ETS means by distinct numbers is different numbers. For example, the set of numbers 2, 3, 4, and 5 is a set of distinct numbers, whereas 2, 2, 3, and 4 would not be a set of distinct numbers because 2 appears twice. Easy concept, tricky wording.

DIGITS

There are ten digits:

$$0, 1, 2, 3, 4, 5, 6, 7, 8, 9$$

All integers are made up of digits. In the integer 3,476, the digits are 3, 4, 7, and 6. Digits are to numbers as letters are to words.

The integer 645 is called a "three-digit number" for obvious reasons. Each of its digits has a different name depending on its place in the number:

5 is called the *units* digit

4 is called the *tens* digit

6 is called the *hundreds* digit

Thus the value of any number depends on which digits are in which places. The number 645 could be rewritten as follows:

$$6 \times 100 = 600$$
$$4 \times 10 = 40$$
$$+ 5 \times 1 = + 5$$
$$\overline{ 645}$$

POSITIVE AND NEGATIVE

There are three rules regarding the multiplication of positive and negative numbers:

1. pos × pos = pos
2. neg × neg = pos
3. pos × neg = neg

ODD AND EVEN

Even numbers are integers that can be divided evenly by 2. Here are some examples of even numbers:

−4, −2, 0, 2, 4, 6, 8, 10, and so on

You can always tell at a glance whether a number is even: It is even if its final digit is even. Thus 999,999,999,992 is an even number because 2, the final digit, is an even number.

Odd numbers are integers that cannot be divided evenly by 2. Here are some examples of odd numbers:

−5, −3, −1, 1, 3, 5, 7, 9, and so on

You can always tell at a glance whether a number is odd: It is odd if its final digit is odd. Thus, 222,222,222,229 is an odd number because 9, the final digit, is an odd number.

Several rules always hold true with odd and even numbers:

even + even = even	even × even = even
odd + odd = even	odd × odd = odd
even + odd = odd	even × odd = even

FACTORS

The factors of a number are all of the numbers by which it can be divided evenly. For example, the factors of 30 are 1, 2, 3, 5, 6, 10, 15, and 30.

MULTIPLES

A multiple of a number is any product of an integer and the given number.

REMAINDERS

If a number cannot be divided evenly by another number, the number left over at the end of the division is called the remainder. For example, 25 cannot be divided evenly by 3; 25 divided by 3 is 8 with 1 left over. The 1 is the remainder. Decimals are not remainders.

CONSECUTIVE INTEGERS

Consecutive integers are integers listed in increasing order of size without any integers missing in between. For example, –1, 0, 1, 2, 3, 4, and 5 are consecutive integers; 2, 4, 5, 7, and 8 are not. Nor are –1, –2, –3, and –4 consecutive integers, because they are decreasing in size.

PRIME NUMBERS

A prime number is a positive integer that can be divided evenly only by itself and by 1. For example, the following are all the prime numbers less than 30: 2, 3, 5, 7, 11, 13, 17, 19, 23, 29. (Note: 1 is not prime.)

DIVISIBILITY RULES

You may be called upon to determine whether one number can be divided evenly by another. To do so, use your calculator. If the result is an integer, the number is evenly divisible. Is 4,569 divisible by 3? Simply punch up the numbers on your calculator. The result is 1,523, which is an integer, so you have determined that 4,569 is indeed divisible by 3. Is 1,789 divisible by 3? The result on your calculator is 596.33333, which is not an integer, so 1,789 is not divisible by 3. (Integers don't have decimal points with digits after them.)

STANDARD SYMBOLS

The following standard symbols are used frequently on the SAT:

SYMBOL	MEANING
=	is equal to
≠	is not equal to
<	is less than
>	is greater than
≤	is less than or equal to
≥	is greater than or equal to

Leftovers

Don't try to figure remainders on your calculator. On your calculator, 25 divided by 3 is 8.3333333, but .3333333 is not the remainder. The remainder is 1.

Prime Time

Here are a few important facts about prime numbers:

- 0 and 1 are not prime numbers.
- 2 is the smallest prime number.
- 2 is the only even prime number.
- Not all odd numbers are prime: 1, 9, 15, 21, and many others are *not* prime.

The SAT Formula

Why would ETS give you all those geometric formulas on the test? Because the SAT is not really a geometry test. ETS doesn't care about geometric proofs, because it doesn't want to spend the money grading proofs. So, the test writers dress up arithmetic and algebra with the occasional geometric figure. You need to know some rules of geometry, but not the way you do in a real geometry class.

FINALLY, THE INSTRUCTIONS

Each of the three scored Math sections on your SAT will begin with the same set of instructions. These instructions include a few formulas and other information that you may need to know in order to answer some of the questions. You must learn these instructions ahead of time. You should never have to waste valuable time referring to them during the test.

Still, if you do suddenly blank out on one of the formulas while taking the test, you can always refresh your memory by glancing back at the instructions. Be sure to familiarize yourself with them thoroughly ahead of time, so you'll know which formulas are there.

9

Joe Bloggs and the Math SAT

HEY, JOE!

Joe Bloggs has already been a big help to you on the Verbal SAT questions. By learning to anticipate which answer choices would attract Joe on difficult questions, you now know how to avoid careless mistakes and eliminate obviously incorrect answers.

You can do the same thing on the SAT Math section. In fact, Joe Bloggs answers are even easier to spot on math questions. ETS is quite predictable in the way it writes incorrect answer choices, and this predictability will make it possible for you to zero in on its answers to questions that might have seemed impossible to you before.

HOW JOE THINKS

No Problem

Joe Bloggs is attracted to easy solutions arrived at through methods that he understands.

As was true on the SAT Verbal section, Joe Bloggs gets the easy questions right and the hard questions wrong. In Chapter 3, we introduced Joe by showing you how he approached a particular math problem. That problem, you may remember, involved the calculation of total miles in a trip. Here it is again:

PROBLEM SOLVING
1 2 3 4 5 6 7 8 9 10 11 12 13 14 15 16 17 18 19 20 21 22 23 24 **25**
EASY   MEDIUM   HARD

25. A woman drove to work at an average speed of 40 miles per hour and returned along the same route at 30 miles per hour. If her total traveling time was 1 hour, what was the total number of miles in the round trip?

(A) 30

(B) $30\frac{1}{7}$

(C) $34\frac{2}{7}$

(D) 35

(E) 40

When we showed this problem the first time, you were just learning about Joe Bloggs. Now that you've made him your invisible partner on the SAT, you ought to know a great deal about how he thinks. Your next step is to put Joe to work for you on the Math sections.

Here's how to crack it

This problem was the last in a 25-question Math section. Therefore, it was the hardest problem in that section. Naturally, Joe got it wrong.

The answer choice most attractive to Joe on this problem is D. The question obviously involves an average of some kind, and 35 is the average of 30 and 40, so Joe picked it. Choice D just seemed like the right answer to Joe. (Of course, it wasn't the right answer; Joe gets the hard ones wrong.)

Because this is true, we know which answers we should avoid on hard questions: answers that seem obvious or that can be arrived at simply and quickly. If the answer really were obvious and if finding it really were simple, the question would be easy, not hard.

Joe Bloggs is also attracted to answer choices that simply repeat numbers from the problem. This means, of course, that you should avoid such choices. In the problem about the woman traveling to work, you can also eliminate choices A and E, because 30 and 40 are numbers repeated directly from the problem. Therefore, they are extremely unlikely to be ETS's answer.

We've now eliminated three of the five answer choices. Even if you couldn't figure out anything else about this question, you'd have a fifty-fifty chance of guessing correctly. Those are excellent odds, considering that we really didn't do any math. By eliminating answer choices that we knew were wrong, we were able to beat ETS at its own game. (ETS's answer to this question is C, by the way.)

Avoid Repeats

Joe Bloggs is attracted to answer choices that simply repeat numbers from the problem.

PUTTING JOE TO WORK ON THE MATH SAT

Generally speaking, the Joe Bloggs principle teaches you to:

- Trust your hunches on easy questions

- Double-check your hunches on medium questions

- Eliminate Joe Bloggs answers on difficult questions

The rest of this chapter is devoted to using Joe Bloggs to zero in on ETS's answers to difficult questions. Of course, your main concern is still to answer all easy and medium questions correctly. But if you have some time left at the end of a Math section, the Joe Bloggs principle can help you eliminate answers on a few difficult questions, so that you can venture some good guesses. And as we've already seen, smart guessing means more points. (In Chapter 14, you'll learn how to use Joe Bloggs to answer quantitative comparison questions; in Chapter 15, you'll learn how he can help you with grid-ins.)

BASIC TECHNIQUES

HARD QUESTIONS = HARD ANSWERS

As we've just explained, hard questions on the SAT simply don't have correct answers that are obvious to the average person. Avoiding the "obvious" choices will take some discipline on your part, but you'll lose points if you don't. Even if you're a math whiz, the Joe Bloggs principle will keep you from making careless mistakes.

Here's an example:

Joe Likes to Share

When it comes to the goofy "nonoverlapping region" questions, Joe's own good nature gets the best of him and he assumes that he must divide the figure evenly. That's why he likes to pick C on this problem. But, *nowhere does the question say the regions must be equal in size.* Read carefully.

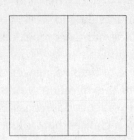

25. The figure above is a square divided into two nonoverlapping regions. What is the greatest number of nonoverlapping regions that can be obtained by drawing any two additional straight lines?

   (A) 4
   (B) 5
   (C) 6
   (D) 7
   (E) 8

Here's how to crack it

This is the last question from a Math section. Therefore, it's extremely difficult. One reason it's so difficult is that it is badly written. (ETS's strengths are mathematical, not verbal.) Here's a clearer way to think of it: The drawing is a pizza cut in half; what's the greatest number of pieces you could end up with if you make just two more cuts with a knife?

The most obvious way to cut the pizza would be to make cuts perpendicular to the center cut, dividing the pizza into six pieces, like this:

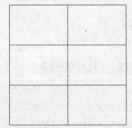

There, that was fast and easy. So that means 6 is ETS's answer, right? Wrong. That was too easy, which means that 6 can't possibly be ETS's answer, and choice C can be eliminated. If finding ETS's answer were that simple, Joe Bloggs would have gotten this question right and it would have been an easy question, not a difficult one.

Will this fact help you eliminate any other choices? Yes. Because you know that if you can divide the pizza into at least six pieces, neither five nor four could be the greatest number of pieces into which it can be divided. Six is a greater number than either 5 or 4; if you can get six pieces you can also get five or four. You can thus eliminate choices A and B as well.

Now you've narrowed it down to two choices. Which will you pick? You shouldn't waste time trying to find the exact answer to a question like this. It isn't testing any mathematical principle, and you won't figure out the trick unless you get lucky. If you can't use another of our techniques to eliminate the remaining wrong answer, you should just guess and go on. Heads you win a dollar, tails you lose a quarter. (ETS's answer is D. Our third technique, incidentally, will enable you to zero in on it exactly. Keep reading.)

In case you're wondering, here's how ETS divides the pizza:

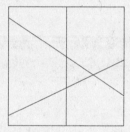

Here's another example:

PROBLEM SOLVING		
1 2 3 4 5 6 7 8	9 10 11 12 13 14 15 16 17	18 19 20 21 22 23 **24** 25
EASY	MEDIUM	HARD

24. A 25-foot ladder is placed against a vertical wall of a building with the bottom of the ladder standing on concrete 7 feet from the base of the building. If the top of the ladder slips down 4 feet, then the bottom of the ladder will slide out how many feet?

(A) 4 ft
(B) 5 ft
(C) 6 ft
(D) 7 ft
(E) 8 ft

Here's how to crack it

Which answer seems simple and obvious? Choice A, of course. If a ladder slips down 4 feet on one end, it seems obvious that it would slide out 4 feet on the other.

What does that mean? It means that we can eliminate choice A. If 4 feet were ETS's answer, Joe Bloggs would get this problem right and it would be an easy question, not one of the hardest in the section.

Choice A also repeats a number from the problem, which means we can be doubly certain that it's wrong. Which other choice repeats a number? Choice D. So we can eliminate that one, too.

If you don't know how to do this problem, working on it further probably won't get you anywhere. You've eliminated two choices; guess and move on. (ETS's answer is E. Use the Pythagorean theorem—see Chapter 13.)

SIMPLE OPERATIONS = WRONG ANSWERS ON HARD QUESTIONS

Since Joe Bloggs doesn't usually think of difficult mathematical operations, he is attracted to solutions that use very simple arithmetic. Therefore, any answer choice that is the result of simple arithmetic should be eliminated on hard SAT math questions.

Here's an example:

PROBLEM SOLVING		
1 2 3 4 5 6 7 8	9 10 11 12 13 14 15 16 17	18 19 **20** 21 22 23 24 25
EASY	MEDIUM	HARD

20. A dress is selling for $100 after a 20 percent discount. What was the original selling price?

   (A) $200
   (B) $125
   (C) $120
   (D) $80
   (E) $75

Here's how to crack it

When Joe Bloggs looks at this problem he sees *20 percent less than $100* and is attracted to choice D. Therefore, you must eliminate it. If finding the answer were that easy, Joe Bloggs would have gotten it right. Joe is also attracted to choice C, which is 20 percent more than $100. Again, eliminate.

With two Joe Bloggs answers out of the way, you ought to be able to solve this problem quickly. The dress is on sale, which means that its original price must have been more than its current price. That means that ETS's answer has to be greater than $100. Two of the remaining choices, A and B, fulfill this requirement. Now you can ask yourself:

   (A) Is $100 20 percent less than $200? No. Eliminate.

   (B) Is $100 20 percent less than $125? Could be. This must be ETS's answer. (It is.)

LEAST/GREATEST

Hard SAT math problems will sometimes ask you to find the least or greatest number that fulfills certain conditions. On such problems, Joe Bloggs is attracted to the answer choice containing the least or greatest number. You can therefore eliminate such choices. (ETS sometimes uses similar words that mean the same thing: *most, maximum, fewest, minimum*, and so on. The same rules apply to problems containing all such terms.)

Look at the square problem on page 152. The question asks you for the greatest number of regions into which the square can be divided. Which choice will therefore attract Joe Bloggs? Choice E. Eight is the greatest number among the choices offered, so it will seem right to Joe. Therefore, you can eliminate it.

Here's another example:

PROBLEM SOLVING																								
1	2	3	4	5	6	7	8	9	10	11	12	13	14	15	16	**17**	18	19	20	21	22	23	24	25
			EASY									MEDIUM										HARD		

17. If 3 parallel lines are cut by 3 nonparallel lines, what is the maximum number of intersections possible?

   (A) 9
   (B) 10
   (C) 11
   (D) 12
   (E) 13

Here's how to crack it

The problem asks you for the *maximum* or greatest number. What is the maximum number among the choices? It is 13; therefore, you can eliminate choice E. By the *simple = wrong* rule that we just discussed, you can also eliminate choice A. Joe's preference for simple arithmetic makes him think that the answer to this problem can be found by multiplying 3 times 3. The simple operation leads quickly to an answer of 9, which must therefore be wrong.

ETS's answer is D. Here's how it's found:

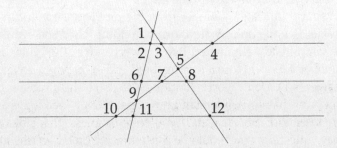

"IT CANNOT BE DETERMINED"

Occasionally on the Math SAT, the fifth answer choice on a problem will be:

(E)   It cannot be determined from the information
       given.

The Joe Bloggs principle makes these questions easy to crack. Why? Joe Bloggs can never determine the correct answer on difficult SAT problems. Therefore, when Joe sees this answer choice on a difficult problem, he is greatly attracted to it.

What does this mean?

It means that if "it cannot be determined" is offered as an answer choice on a difficult problem, it is usually wrong.

Here's an example:

Easy/Medium

Don't automatically eliminate "it cannot be determined" on easy and medium problems. On medium problems, "it cannot be determined" has about one chance in two of being ETS's answer. So, if you are stuck on an easy or medium problem and "it cannot be determined" is one of the choices, pick it and move on. You will have one chance in two of being correct.

When Joe Bloggs picks "It cannot be determined from When Joe Bloggs picks "It cannot be dertermined from the information given" on a hard question, he's thinking, "If I can't get it, no one can."

24. If the average of x, y, and 80 is 6 more than the average of y, z, and 80, what is the value of $x - z$?

(A) 2
(B) 3
(C) 6
(D) 18
(E) It cannot be determined from the information
     given.

Here's how to crack it

This problem is the next-to-last question in a section. It looks absolutely impossible to Joe. Therefore, he assumes that the problem must be impossible to solve. Of course, he's wrong. Eliminate choice E. If E were ETS's answer, Joe would be correct and this would be an easy problem.

Choice C simply repeats a number from the problem, so you can eliminate that choice also. If you couldn't figure out anything else, you would have to guess. Since you already eliminated two answer choices the odds are in your favor. (Remember, tails you lose a quarter, but heads you win a dollar.)

ETS's answer is D. Don't worry about how to solve this problem right now. It's only important that you understand how to eliminate Joe Bloggs answers in order to get closer to ETS's answer. If you have to guess, that's okay. Besides, that was a hard question; you should be concentrating on answering all the easy and medium questions correctly.

JOE BLOGGS AND MATH SUMMARY

1. Joe Bloggs gets the easy math questions right and the hard ones wrong.

2. On difficult problems, Joe Bloggs is attracted to easy solutions arrived at with methods he understands. Therefore, you should eliminate obvious, simple answers on difficult questions.

3. On difficult problems, Joe Bloggs is also attracted to answer choices that simply repeat numbers from the problem. Therefore, you should eliminate any such choices.

4. On difficult problems that ask you to find the least or greatest number that fulfills certain conditions, you can eliminate the answer choice containing the least or greatest number.

5. On difficult problems, you can almost always eliminate any answer choice that says, "It cannot be determined from the information given."

6. The point of Joe Bloggs is not to get to ONE answer choice, it's to improve your odds when you must guess, and eliminate answer choices that could distract you or seem right if you made a careless error.

10

The Calculator

Gee, ETS Must Really
Like Me

Why else would it let you use
a calculator? Well, friend, a
calculator can be a crutch and
an obstacle. ETS hopes that
many test takers will waste
time using their machines to
add 3 + 4. When it comes to
simple calculations, your brain
and pencil are faster than the
fastest calculator.

THE CALCULATOR

You are allowed (but not required) to use a calculator when you take the SAT. You should definitely do so. A calculator can be enormously helpful on certain types of SAT math problems. This chapter will give you general information about how to use your calculator. Other math chapters will give you specific information about using your calculator in particular situations.

You'll need to bring your own calculator when you take the SAT. If you don't own one now, you can buy one for around $15, or you can ask your math teacher about borrowing one. If you do purchase one, buy it far enough ahead of time to practice with it before you take the test. We recommend the Sharp EL-531G Scientific Calculator, which has all the functions you need to answer SAT questions and which meets the guidelines prescribed by ETS for acceptable calculators. Even if you now use a calculator regularly in your math class at school, you should still read this chapter and the other math chapters carefully and practice the techniques we describe.

The only danger in using a calculator on the SAT is that you may be tempted to use it in situations in which it won't help you. Joe Bloggs thinks his calculator will solve all his difficulties with math. It won't. Occasionally, it may even cause him to miss a problem that he might have answered correctly on his own. Your calculator is only as smart as you are. But if you practice and use a little caution, you will find that your calculator will help you a great deal.

What a Calculator Is Good At

Here is a complete list of what a calculator is good at on the SAT:

1. Arithmetic

2. Decimals

3. Fractions

4. Square roots

5. Percentages

6. Nothing else

We'll discuss the calculator's role in most of these areas in the next chapter, which is about SAT arithmetic, and in other chapters.

Calculator Arithmetic

Adding, subtracting, multiplying, and dividing integers and decimals is easy on a calculator. You only need to be careful when you key in the numbers. A calculator will give you an incorrect answer to an arithmetic calculation only if you press the wrong keys. Here are two tips for avoiding mistakes on your calculator:

1. Check every number on the display as you key it in.

2. Press the *on/off* or *clear all* key after you finish each problem or after each separate step.

The main thing to remember about a calculator is that it can't help you find the answer to a question you don't understand. If you wouldn't know how to solve a particular problem using pencil and paper, you won't know how to solve it using a calculator, either. Your calculator will help you, but it won't take the place of a solid understanding of basic SAT mathematics.

Calculators Don't Think

They crunch numbers and often save us a great deal of time and effort, but they are not a substitute for your problem-solving skills.

Use Your Paper First

Before you use your calculator, be sure to set up the problem or equation on paper; this will keep you from getting lost or confused. This is especially important when solving the problem involves a number of separate steps. The basic idea is to use the extra space in your test booklet to make a plan, and then use your calculator to execute it.

Working on scratch paper first will also give you a record of what you have done if you change your mind, run into trouble, or lose your place. If you suddenly find that you need to try a different approach to a problem, you may not have to go all the way back to the beginning. This will also make it easier for you to check your work, if you have time to do so.

Don't use the memory function on your calculator (if it has one). Because you can use your test booklet as scratch paper, you don't need to juggle numbers within the calculator itself. Instead of storing the result of a calculation in the calculator, write it on your scratch paper, clear your calculator, and move to the next step of the problem. A calculator's memory is fleeting; scratch paper is forever.

Order of Operations

In the next chapter, we will discuss the proper order of operations when solving equations in which several operations must be performed. Be sure you understand this information, because it applies to calculators as much as it does to pencil-and-paper computations. (In the next chapter, we will teach you a mnemonic device that will enable you to remember this easily.) You must always perform calculations in the proper order.

Write Things Down

You paid for the test booklet; make the most of it. Keep track of your progress through each problem by writing down each step.

CALCULATOR SUMMARY

1. You should definitely use a calculator on the SAT.

2. Bring your own calculator when you take the test. You don't need a fancy one.

3. Even if you already use a calculator regularly, you should still practice with it before the test.

4. Be careful when you key in numbers on your calculator. Check each number on the display as you key it in. Clear your work after you finish each problem or after each separate step.

5. A calculator can't help you find the answer to a question you don't understand. (It's only as smart as you are!) Be sure to use your calculator as a tool, not a crutch.

6. Set up the problem or equation on paper first. By doing so, you will eliminate the possibility of getting lost or confused.

7. Don't use the memory function on your calculator (if it has one). Scratch paper works better.

8. Whether you are using your calculator or paper and a pencil, you must always perform calculations in the proper order.

9. Make sure your calculator has a fresh battery at test time!

11
Arithmetic

THERE ARE ONLY SIX OPERATIONS

There are only six arithmetic operations that you will ever need to perform on the SAT:

1. Addition (3 + 3)

2. Subtraction (3 – 3)

3. Multiplication (3 × 3 or 3 • 3)

4. Division (3 ÷ 3)

5. Raising to a power (3^3)

6. Finding a square root ($\sqrt{3}$)

If you're like most students, you probably haven't paid much serious attention to these topics since junior high school. You'll need to learn about them again if you want to do well on the SAT. By the time you take the test, using them should be automatic. All the arithmetic concepts are fairly basic, but you'll have to know them cold. You'll also have to know when and how to use your calculator, which will be quite helpful.

In this chapter, we'll deal with each of these six topics.

What Do You Get?

You should know the following arithmetic terms:

1. The result of addition is a *sum* or *total*.

2. The result of subtraction is a *difference*.

3. The result of multiplication is a *product*.

4. The result of division is a *quotient*.

5. In the expression 5^2, the 2 is called an *exponent*.

The Six Operations Must Be Performed in the Proper Order

Do It Yourself

Some calculators automatically take order of operations into account, and some don't. Either way, you can very easily go wrong if you are in the habit of punching in long lines of arithmetic operations. The safe, smart way is to clear the calculator after every individual operation, performing PEMDAS yourself.

Very often, solving an equation on the SAT will require you to perform several different operations, one after another. These operations must be performed in the proper order. In general, the problems are written in such a way that you won't have trouble deciding what comes first. In cases in which you are uncertain, you only need to remember the following sentence:

Please Excuse My Dear Aunt Sally, she limps from *left* to *right*.

That's **PEMDAS**, for short. It stands for Parentheses, Exponents, Multiplication, Division, Addition, Subtraction. First you clear the parentheses; then you take care of the exponents; then you perform all multiplication and division at the same time, from *left* to *right*, followed by addition and subtraction, from *left* to *right*.

The following drill will help you learn the order in which to perform the six operations. First set up the equations on paper. Then use your calculator for the arithmetic. Make sure you perform the operations in the correct order.

DRILL 1

Solve each of the following problems by performing the indicated operations in the proper order. Answers can be found on page 279.

1. $107 + (109 - 107) =$ _____

2. $(7 \times 5) + 3 =$ _____

3. $6 - 3 (6 - 3) =$ _____

4. $2 \times [7 - (6 \div 3)] =$ _____

5. $10 - (9 - 8 - 6) =$ _____

Whichever Comes First

Addition and subtraction are interchangeable in the order of operations. Solve whichever operation comes first, reading left to right. The same is true of multiplication and division. Just remember not to add or subtract before you multiply or divide. Example:
$24 \div 4 \times 6 = 24 \div 24 = 1$
wrong
$24 \div 4 \times 6 = 6 \times 6 = 36$
right

PARENTHESES CAN HELP YOU SOLVE EQUATIONS

Using parentheses to regroup information in SAT arithmetic problems can be very helpful. In order to do this, you need to understand a basic law that you have probably forgotten since the days when you last took arithmetic—*the distributive law*. You don't need to remember the name of the law, but you do need to know how it works.

THE DISTRIBUTIVE LAW

If you're multiplying the sum of two numbers by a third number, you can multiply each number in your sum individually. This comes in handy when you have to multiply the sum of two variables.

If a problem gives you information in "factored form"—$a (b + c)$—then you should distribute the first variable before you do anything else. If you are given information that has already been distributed—$ab + ac$—then you should factor out the common term, putting the information back in factored form. Very often on the SAT, simply doing this will enable you to spot ETS's answer.

For example:

Distributive: $6(53) + 6(47) = 6(53 + 47) = 6(100) = 600$

Multiplication first: $6(53) + 6(47) = 318 + 282 = 600$

You get the same answer each way, so why get involved with ugly arithmetic? If you use the distributive law, you don't even need to use your calculator.

The drill on the following page illustrates the distributive law.

DRILL 2

Rewrite each problem by either distributing or factoring, whichever is called for. Questions 3, 4, and 5 have no numbers in them, therefore, they can't be solved with a calculator. Answers can be found on page 279.

1. $(6 \times 57) + (6 \times 13) =$ _____

2. $51(48) + 51(50) + 51(52) =$ _____

3. $a(b + c - d) =$ _____

4. $xy - xz =$ _____

5. $abc + xyc =$ _____

FRACTIONS

A FRACTION IS JUST ANOTHER WAY OF EXPRESSING DIVISION

Or Use Your Calculator

Another option for solving questions with fractions is to use your calculator.

The expression $\dfrac{x}{y}$ is exactly the same thing as $x \div y$. The expression $\dfrac{1}{2}$ means nothing more than $1 \div 2$. In the fraction $\dfrac{x}{y}$, x is known as the numerator (hereafter referred to as "the top") and y is known as the denominator (hereafter referred to as "the bottom").

ADDING AND SUBTRACTING FRACTIONS WITH THE SAME BOTTOM

To add two or more fractions that all have the same bottom, simply add up the tops and put the sum over the common bottom. For example:

$$\frac{1}{100} + \frac{4}{100} = \frac{1+4}{100} = \frac{5}{100}$$

Subtraction works exactly the same way:

$$\frac{4}{100} - \frac{1}{100} = \frac{4-1}{100} = \frac{3}{100}$$

ADDING AND SUBTRACTING FRACTIONS WITH DIFFERENT BOTTOMS

In school you were taught to add and subtract fractions with different bottoms by finding a common bottom. To do this, you have to multiply each fraction by a number that makes all the bottoms the same. Most students find this process annoying.

Fortunately, we have an approach to adding and subtracting fractions with different bottoms that simplifies the entire process. Use the example below as a model. Just *multiply* in the direction of each arrow, and then either *add* or *subtract* across the top. Lastly, *multiply* across the bottom.

$$\frac{1}{3} + \frac{1}{2} =$$

$$\frac{2+3}{6} = \frac{5}{6}$$

That was easy, wasn't it? We call this procedure the Bowtie because the arrows make it look like a bowtie. Use the Bowtie to add or subtract any pair of fractions without thinking about the common bottom, just by following the steps above.

MULTIPLYING ALL FRACTIONS

Multiplying fractions is easy. Just multiply across the top, then multiply across the bottom.

Here's an example:

$$\frac{4}{5} \times \frac{5}{6} = \frac{20}{30}$$

When you multiply fractions, all you are really doing is performing one multiplication problem on top of another.

You should never multiply two fractions before looking to see if you can reduce either or both. If you reduce first, your final answer will be in the form that ETS is looking for.

$$\frac{63}{6} \times \frac{48}{7} = \frac{\overset{9}{\cancel{63}}}{6} \times \frac{48}{\cancel{7}} = \frac{\overset{9}{\cancel{63}}}{\cancel{6}} \times \frac{\overset{8}{\cancel{48}}}{\cancel{7}} =$$

$$\frac{9}{1} \times \frac{8}{1}$$

$$\frac{72}{1} = 72$$

REDUCING FRACTIONS

When you add or multiply fractions, you will very often end up with a big fraction that is hard to work with. You can almost always reduce such a fraction into one that is easier to handle.

Start Small

It is not easy to see that 26 and 286 have a common factor of 13, but it's pretty clear that they're both divisible by 2.

To reduce a fraction, divide both the top and the bottom by the largest number that is a factor of both. For example, to reduce $\frac{12}{16}$, divide both the top and the bottom by 12, which is the largest number that is a factor of both. Dividing 12 by 12 yields 1; dividing 60 by 12 yields 5. The reduced fraction is $\frac{1}{5}$.

If you can't immediately find the largest number that is a factor of both, find any number that is a factor of both and divide both the top and bottom by that. Your calculations will take a little longer, but you'll end up in the same place. In the previous example, even if you don't see that 12 is a factor of both 12 and 60, you can no doubt see that 6 is a factor of both. Dividing top and bottom by 6 yields $\frac{2}{10}$. Now divide by 2. Doing so yields $\frac{1}{5}$. Once again, you have arrived at ETS's answer.

DIVIDING ALL FRACTIONS

Just Do It

When dividing (don't ask why) just flip the last and multiply.

To divide one fraction by another, invert the second fraction and multiply. To invert a fraction, simply flip it over. Doing this is extremely easy, as long as you remember how it works. Here's an example:

$$\frac{2}{3} \div \frac{4}{3} =$$
$$\frac{2}{3} \times \frac{3}{4} = \frac{6}{12} = \frac{1}{2}$$

Be careful not to cancel or reduce until after you flip the second fraction. You can even do the same thing with fractions whose tops and/or bottoms are fractions. These problems look quite frightening but they're actually easy if you keep your cool.

Here's an example:

$$\frac{\frac{4}{4}}{\frac{3}{3}} =$$
$$\frac{4}{1} \div \frac{4}{3} =$$
$$\frac{4}{1} \times \frac{3}{4} =$$
$$\frac{\cancel{4}}{1} \times \frac{3}{\cancel{4}} =$$
$$\frac{3}{1} = 3$$

CONVERTING MIXED NUMBERS TO FRACTIONS

A mixed number is a number like $2\frac{3}{4}$. It is the sum of an integer and a fraction. When you see mixed numbers on the SAT, you should usually convert them to ordinary fractions. Here's a quick and easy way to convert mixed numbers:

1. Multiply the integer by the bottom of the fraction.
2. Add this product to the top of the fraction.
3. Place this sum over the bottom of the fraction.

For example, let's convert $2\frac{3}{4}$ to a fraction. Multiply 2 (the integer part of the mixed number) times 4 (the bottom of the fraction). That gives us 8. Add that to the 3 (the top of the fraction) to give us 11. Place 11 over 4 to give us $\frac{11}{4}$.

The mixed number $2\frac{3}{4}$ is exactly the same as the fraction $\frac{11}{4}$. We converted the one to the other because fractions are easier to work with than mixed numbers.

Just Don't Mix

For some reason, ETS thinks it's okay to give you mixed numbers as answer choices. On grid-ins, however, if you use a mixed number, ETS won't give you credit.

DRILL 3

Try converting the following mixed numbers. Answers can be found on page 279.

1. $8\frac{1}{3}$

2. $2\frac{3}{7}$

3. $5\frac{4}{9}$

4. $2\frac{1}{2}$

5. $6\frac{2}{3}$

COMPARING FRACTIONS

The SAT sometimes contains problems that require you to compare one fraction with another and determine which is larger. There are two ways to compare fractions: convert them to decimals or use the bowtie.

Using the bowtie to compare fractions is quick and easy. Let's say you are given a problem in which you need to determine which is bigger, $\frac{9}{10}$ or $\frac{10}{11}$. As before, multiply in the direction of the arrows.

$$\frac{9}{10} \underset{}{\overset{99 \qquad 100}{\times}} \frac{10}{11}$$

Notice that you don't need to multiply across the bottom when you are comparing fractions. Since 100 is bigger than 99, $\frac{10}{11}$ is bigger than $\frac{9}{10}$.

If you prefer, you can use your calculator to convert each fraction to a decimal. To do this, perform the division problem the fraction represents. Divide 9 by 10 on your calculator, which gives you 0.9. Then divide 10 by 11, which gives you 0.9090909. Which is bigger?

FRACTIONS BEHAVE IN PECULIAR WAYS

Joe Bloggs has trouble with fractions because they don't always behave the way he thinks they ought to. For example, because 4 is obviously greater than 2, Joe Bloggs sometimes forgets that $\frac{1}{4}$ is less than $\frac{1}{2}$. He becomes especially confused when the top is some number other than 1. For example, $\frac{2}{6}$ is less than $\frac{2}{5}$.

Joe also has a hard time understanding that when you multiply one fraction by another, you will get a fraction that is smaller than either of the first two. For example:

$$\frac{1}{2} \times \frac{1}{4} = \frac{1}{8}$$

$$\frac{1}{8} < \frac{1}{2}$$

$$\frac{1}{8} < \frac{1}{4}$$

A WORD ABOUT FRACTIONS AND CALCULATORS

It's possible to key fractions into many scientific calculators. These calculators allow you to add, subtract, multiply, divide, and reduce fractions, and some also convert mixed numbers to fractions and back again. If you know how to work with fractions on your calculator, go ahead and use it. While you should still understand how to work with fractions the old-fashioned way, your calculator can be a tremendous help if you know how to use it properly. If you plan to use your calculator on fraction problems, make sure you practice with your calculator before the test.

DRILL 4

If you have trouble on any of these problems, go back and review the information just outlined. Answers can be found on page 280.

1. Reduce $\dfrac{18}{6}$ _____

2. Convert $6\dfrac{1}{5}$ to a fraction _____

3. $2\dfrac{1}{3} - 3\dfrac{3}{5} =$ _____

4. $\dfrac{5}{18} \times \dfrac{6}{25} =$ _____

5. $\dfrac{3}{4} \div \dfrac{7}{8} =$ _____

6. $\dfrac{\frac{2}{5}}{5} =$ _____

7. $\dfrac{\frac{1}{3}}{\frac{3}{4}} =$ _____

DECIMALS

A DECIMAL IS JUST ANOTHER WAY OF EXPRESSING A FRACTION

Fractions can be expressed as decimals. To find a fraction's decimal equivalent, simply divide the top by the bottom. (You can do this easily with your calculator.) For example:

$$\frac{3}{5} =$$

$$3 \div 5 = 0.6$$

ADDING, SUBTRACTING, MULTIPLYING, AND DIVIDING DECIMALS

Manipulating decimals is easy with a calculator. Simply punch in the numbers—being especially careful to get the decimal point in the right place every single time—and read the result from the display. A calculator makes these operations easy. In fact, working with decimals is one area on the SAT where your calculator will prevent you from making careless errors. You won't have to line up decimal points or remember what happens when you divide. The calculator will keep track of everything for you, as long as you punch in the correct numbers to begin with. Just be sure to practice carefully before you go to the test center.

DRILL 5

Answers can be found on page 280.

1. $0.43 \times 0.87 =$ _____

2. $\dfrac{43 + 0.731}{0.03} =$ _____

3. $3.72 \div 0.02 =$ _____

4. $0.71 - 3.6 =$ _____

COMPARING DECIMALS

Place Value

Compare decimals place by place, going from left to right.

Some SAT problems will ask you to determine whether one decimal is larger or smaller than another. Many students have trouble doing this. It isn't difficult, though, and you will do fine as long as you remember to line up the decimal points and fill in missing zeros.

Here's an example:

Problem: Which is larger, 0.0099 or 0.01?

Solution: Simply place one decimal over the other with the decimal points lined up, like this:

$$0.0099$$
$$0.01$$

To make the solution seem clearer, you can add two zeros to the right of 0.01. (You can always add zeros to the right of a decimal without changing its value.) Now you have this:

$$0.0099$$
$$0.0100$$

Which decimal is larger? Clearly, 0.0100 is, just as 100 is larger than 99. (Remember that $0.0099 = \dfrac{99}{10,000}$, while $0.0100 = \dfrac{100}{10,000}$. Now the answer seems obvious, doesn't it?)

Analysis

Joe Bloggs has a terrible time on this problem. Because 99 is obviously larger than 1, he tends to think that 0.0099 must be larger than 0.01. But it isn't. Don't get sloppy on problems like this! ETS loves to trip up Joe Bloggs with decimals. In fact, any time you encounter a problem involving the comparison of decimals, you should stop and ask yourself whether you are about to make a Joe Bloggs mistake.

RATIOS AND PROPORTIONS

A Ratio Is a Comparison

Many students get extremely nervous when they are asked to work with ratios. But there's no need to be nervous. A ratio is a comparison between the quantities of ingredients you have in a mixture, be it a class full of people or a bowl of cake batter. Ratios can be written to look like fractions—don't get them confused.

The ratio of x to y can be expressed in the following three ways:

1. $\dfrac{x}{y}$

2. the ratio of x to y

3. $x{:}y$

Part, Part, Whole

Ratios are a lot like fractions. In fact, anything you can do to a fraction (convert it to a decimal or percentage, reduce it, etc.), you can do to a ratio. The difference is that a fraction gives you a part (the top number) over a whole (the bottom number), while a ratio typically gives you two parts (boys to girls, CDs to cassettes, sugar to flour), and it is your job to come up with the whole. For example, if there is one cup of sugar for every two cups of flour in a recipe, that's three cups of stuff. The ratio of sugar to flour is 1:2. Add the parts to get the whole.

Ratios vs. Fractions

Keep in mind that a ratio compares part of something to another part. A fraction compares part of something to the whole thing.

Ratio: $\dfrac{\text{part}}{\text{part}}$

Fraction: $\dfrac{\text{part}}{\text{whole}}$

Ratio to Real

If a class contains 3 students and the ratio of boys to girls in that class is 2:1, how many boys and how many girls are there in the class? Of course: There are 2 boys and 1 girl.

Now, suppose a class contains 24 students and the ratio of boys to girls is still 2:1. How many boys and how many girls are there in the class? This is a little harder, but the answer is easy to find if you think about it. There are 16 boys and 8 girls.

How did we get the answer? We added up the number of "parts" in the ratio (2 parts boys plus 1 part girls, or 3 parts all together) and divided it into the total number of students. In other words, we divided 24 by 3. This told us that the class contained 3 equal parts of 8 students each. From the given ratio (2:1), we knew that two of these parts consisted of boys and one of them consisted of girls.

An easy way to keep track of all this is to use a tool we call the *Ratio Box*. Every time you have a ratio problem, set up a Ratio Box with the information provided in the problem and use it to find ETS's answer.

Here's how it works:

Let's go back to our class containing 24 students, in which the ratio of boys to girls is 2:1. Quickly sketch a table that has columns and rows, like this:

	Boys	Girls	Whole
Ratio (parts)	2	1	3
Multiply By			
Actual Number			24

This is the information you have been given. The ratio is 2:1, so you have 2 parts boys and 1 part girls, for a total of 3 parts. You also know that the actual number of students in the whole class is 24. You start by writing these numbers in proper spaces in your box.

Your goal is to fill in the two empty spaces in the bottom row. To do that, you will multiply each number in the *parts* row by the same number. To find that number, look in the last column. What number would you multiply by 3 to get 24? You should see easily that you would multiply by 8. Therefore, write an 8 in all three blanks in the *multiply by* row. (The spaces in this row will always contain the same number, although of course it won't always be an 8.) Here's what your ratio box should look like now:

	Boys	Girls	Whole
Ratio (parts)	2	1	3
Multiply By	8	8	8
Actual Number			24

The next step is to fill in the empty spaces in the bottom row. You do that the same way you did in the last column, by multiplying. First, multiply the numbers in the boys column ($2 \times 8 = 16$). Then multiply the numbers in the girls column ($1 \times 8 = 8$).

Here's what your box should look like now:

	Boys	Girls	Whole
Ratio (parts)	2	1	3
Multiply By	8	8	8
Actual Number	16	8	24

Now you have enough information to answer any question that ETS might ask you. For example:

- What is the ratio of boys to girls? You can see easily from the ratio (parts) row of the box that the ratio is 2:1.

- What is the ratio of girls to boys? You can see easily from the ratio (parts) row of the box that the ratio is 1:2.

- What is the total number of boys in the class? You can see easily from the bottom row of the box that it is 16.

- What is the total number of girls in the class? You can see easily from the bottom row of the box that it is 8.

- What fractional part of the class is boys? There are 16 boys in a class of 24, so the fraction representing the boys is $\frac{16}{24}$, which can be reduced to $\frac{2}{3}$.

As you can see, the Ratio Box is an easy way to find, organize, and keep track of information on ratio problems. And it works the same no matter what information you are given. Just remember that all the boxes in the *multiply by* row will always contain the same number.

Here's another example:

PROBLEM SOLVING

1	2	3	4	5	6	7	8	9	10	11	12	13	14	15	16	17	**18**	19	20	21	22	23	24	25
		EASY									MEDIUM									HARD				

18. In a jar of red and green jelly beans, the ratio of green jelly beans to red jelly beans is 5:3. If the jar contains a total of 160 jelly beans, how many of them are red?
 (A) 30
 (B) 53
 (C) 60
 (D) 100
 (E) 160

Here's how to crack it

First, sketch out a ratio box:

	Green	Red	Whole
Ratio (parts)	5	3	8
Multiply By			
Actual Number			160

What You Need

Always keep an eye on what you are being asked. You do not want to do more work than necessary. Example 18 never asks about green jelly beans, so leave that box empty.

Now find the multiplier. What do you multiply by 8 to get 160? You multiply 8 by 20. Now write 20 in each box on the *multiply by* row:

	Green	Red	Whole
Ratio (parts)	5	3	8
Multiply By	20	20	20
Actual Number			160

The problem asks you to find how many red jelly beans there are. Go to the red column and multiply 3 by 20. The answer is 60. ETS's answer is C. Notice that you would have set up the box in exactly the same way if the question had asked you to determine how many jelly beans were green. (How many are green? The answer is 5×20, which is 100.)

PROPORTIONS ARE EQUAL RATIOS

Some SAT math problems will contain two proportional, or equal, ratios from which one piece of information is missing.

Here's an example:

PROBLEM SOLVING																								
1	2	3	4	5	6	**7**	8	9	10	11	12	13	14	15	16	17	18	19	20	21	22	23	24	25
			EASY									MEDIUM									HARD			

7. If 2 packages contain a total of 12 doughnuts, how many doughnuts are there in 5 packages?

(A) 12
(B) 24
(C) 30
(D) 36
(E) 60

Here's how to crack it

This problem simply describes two equal ratios, one of which is missing a single piece of information. Here's the given information represented as two equal ratios:

$$\frac{2 \text{ (packages)}}{12 \text{ (doughnuts)}} = \frac{5 \text{ (packages)}}{x \text{ (doughnuts)}}$$

Since ratios are fractions, we can treat them exactly like fractions. To find the answer, all you have to do is figure out what you could plug in for x that would

Careful

You can only cross multiply across an equal sign. You can't reduce across an equal sign.

make $\frac{2}{12} = \frac{5}{x}$. One way to do this is to cross multiply:

$$\frac{2}{12} \diagup\diagdown \frac{5}{x}$$

so, $2x = 60$

$x = 30$

ETS's answer is C.

PERCENTAGES

PERCENTAGES ARE FRACTIONS

There should be nothing frightening about a percentage. It's just a convenient way of expressing a fraction whose bottom is 100.

Percent means "per 100" or "out of 100." If there are 100 questions on your math test and you answer 50 of them, you will have answered 50 out of 100, or

$\frac{50}{100}$, or 50 percent. To think of it another way:

$$\frac{\text{part}}{\text{whole}} = \frac{x}{100} = x \text{ percent}$$

MEMORIZE THESE PERCENTAGE-DECIMAL-FRACTION EQUIVALENTS

$0.01 = \frac{1}{100} = 1$ percent

$0.1 = \frac{1}{10} = 10$ percent

$0.2 = \frac{1}{5} = 20$ percent

$0.25 = \frac{1}{4} = 25$ percent

$0.5 = \frac{1}{2} = 50$ percent

$0.75 = \frac{3}{4} = 75$ percent

CONVERTING PERCENTAGES TO FRACTIONS

To convert a percentage to a fraction, simply put the percentage over 100 and reduce. For example:

$$80 \text{ percent} = \frac{80}{100} = \frac{8}{10} = \frac{4}{5}$$

CONVERTING FRACTIONS TO PERCENTAGES

Since a percentage is just another way to express a fraction, you shouldn't be surprised to see how easy it is to convert a fraction to a percentage. To do so, simply use your calculator to divide the top of the fraction by the bottom of the fraction, and then multiply the result by 100. Here's an example:

> **Problem:** Express $\frac{3}{4}$ as a percentage.

> **Solution:** $\frac{3}{4} = 0.75 \times 100 = 75$ percent.

Converting fractions to percentages is easy with your calculator.

Another Way

You can also convert fractions to percentages by cross multiplying:

$$\frac{3}{4} = \frac{x}{100}$$

$$4x = 3(100)$$

$$x = \frac{3(100)}{4}$$

$$x = 75$$

CONVERTING PERCENTAGES TO DECIMALS

To convert a percentage to a decimal, simply move the decimal point *two places to the left*. For example: 25 percent can be expressed as the decimal 0.25; 50 percent is the same as 0.50 or 0.5; 100 percent is the same as 1.00 or 1.

CONVERTING DECIMALS TO PERCENTAGES

To convert a decimal to a percentage, just do the opposite of what you did in the preceding section. All you have to do is move the decimal point *two places to the right*. Thus, 0.5 = 50 percent; 0.375 = 37.5 percent; 2 = 200 percent.

The following drill will give you practice working with fractions, decimals, and percentages.

DRILL 6

Fill in the missing information in the following table. Answers can be found on page 280.

	Fraction	Decimal	Percent
1.	$\frac{1}{2}$		
2.		3.0	
3.			0.5
4.	$\frac{1}{3}$		

WHAT PERCENT OF WHAT?

Problem: What number is 10 percent greater than 20?

Solution: We know that 10 percent of 20 is 2. So the question really reads: What is 2 greater than 20? The answer is 22.

Analysis

Joe Bloggs gets confused on questions like this. You won't if you take them slowly and solve them one step at a time. The same holds true for problems that ask you what number is a certain percentage less than another number. What number is 10 percent less than 500? Well, 10 percent of 500 is 50. The number that is 10 percent less than 500, therefore, is 500 – 50, or 450. You will see the words *of*, *is*, *product*, *sum*, and *what* pop up a lot in the Math sections of the SAT. Don't let these words fool you, because they all translate into simple math functions. Look at the "Translate" sidebar for The Princeton Review's translation of some terms and get to know them. It will save you time on the test and make your life with the SAT much nicer.

Translate

On a math test like the SAT, we can convert (or translate) words into arithmetic symbols. Here are some of the most common:

Word	Symbol
is	=
of	× (multiply)
percent	/100
what	*n* (variable)

WHAT PERCENT OF WHAT PERCENT OF WHAT?

On harder SAT questions, you may be asked to determine the effect of a series of percentage increases or decreases. The key point to remember on such problems is that each successive increase or decrease is performed on the result of the previous one.

Here's an example:

PROBLEM SOLVING																								
1	2	3	4	5	6	7	8	9	10	11	12	13	14	15	16	17	**18**	19	20	21	22	23	24	25
			EASY								MEDIUM									HARD				

18. A business paid $300 to rent a piece of office equipment for one year. The rent was then increased by 10 percent each year thereafter. How much will the company pay for the first three years it rents the equipment?

(A) $920
(B) $960
(C) $990
(D) $993
(E) $999

> **Bite-Sized Pieces**
> Always handle percentage problems in Bite-Sized Pieces, one piece at a time.

Here's how to crack it

You are being asked to find a business's total rent for a piece of equipment for three years. The easiest way to keep from getting confused on a problem like this is to take it one step at a time. First, make an outline of exactly what you have to find out.

Year 1:

Year 2:

Year 3:

Write this down in the margin of your test booklet. There's one slot for each year's rent; ETS's answer will be the total.

You already know the number that goes in the first slot: 300, because that is what the problem says the business will pay for the first year.

What number goes in the second slot? 330, because 330 equals 300 plus 10 percent of 300.

Now, here's where you have to pay attention. What number goes in the third slot? Not 360! (Cross out choice C!) The rent goes up 10 percent each year. This increase is calculated from the previous year's rent. That means that the rent for the third year is $363, because 363 equals 330 plus 10 percent of 330.

Now you are ready to find ETS's answer:

Year 1:   300

Year 2:   330

Year 3:   <u>363</u>

        993

ETS's answer is thus choice D, $993.

WHAT PERCENT OF WHAT PERCENT OF . . . YIKES!

Sometimes you may find successive percentage problems in which you aren't given actual numbers to work with. In such cases, you need to plug in some numbers.

Here's an example:

PROBLEM SOLVING		
1 2 3 4 5 6 7 8	9 10 11 12 13 14 15 16 17	18 19 20 ㉑ 22 23 24 25
EASY	MEDIUM	HARD

21. A number is increased by 25 percent and then decreased by 20 percent. The result is what percent of the original number?

    (A) 80
    (B) 100
    (C) 105
    (D) 120
    (E) 125

Here's how to crack it

Using the Joe Bloggs principle, you ought to be able to eliminate three choices right off the bat: A, D, and E. Joe loves easy answers. Choices A, D, and E are all equal to 100 plus or minus 20 or 25. All three choices seem right to Joe for different reasons. This is a difficult question, so answers that seem right to Joe must be eliminated. Get rid of them.

A somewhat more subtle Joe Bloggs attractor is choice C. Joe thinks that if you increase a number by 25 percent and then decrease by 20 percent, you end up with a net increase of 5 percent. He has forgotten that in a series of percentage changes (which is what we have here), each successive change is based on the result of the previous one.

We've now eliminated everything but choice B, which is ETS's answer.

Could we have found it without Joe's help? Yes. Here's how:

You aren't given a particular number to work with in this problem—just "a number." Rather than trying to deal with the problem in the abstract, you should immediately plug in a number to work with. What number would be easiest to work with in a percentage problem? Why, 100, of course:

1. 25 percent of 100 is 25, so 100 increased by 25 percent is 125.

2. Now you have to decrease 125 by 20 percent, 20 percent of 125 is 25, so 125 decreased by 20 percent is 100.

3. 100 (our result) is 100 percent of 100 (the number you plugged in), so ETS's answer, once again, is B.

AVERAGES

WHAT IS AN AVERAGE?

On the SAT, the average (also called arithmetic mean) of a set of n numbers is simply the sum of all the numbers divided by n. In other words, if you want to find the average of three numbers, add them up and divide by 3. For example, the average of 3, 7, and 8 is $\frac{(3+7+8)}{3}$, which equals $\frac{18}{3}$, or 6.

That was an easy example, but ETS does not always write average questions with clear solutions. That is, ETS doesn't always give you the information for averages in a way that is easy to work with. For that reason, we have a visual aid, like the Ratio Box for ratios, that helps you organize the information on average questions and find ETS's answer.

We call it the *Average Pie*. Here's what it looks like:

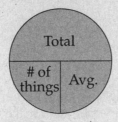

The *total* is the sum of all the numbers you're averaging, and the *number of things* is the number of elements you're averaging. Here's what the Average Pie looks like using the simple average example we just gave you.

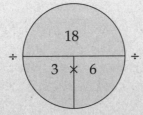

Here's how the Average Pie works mathematically. The line in the middle means *divide*. If you know the total and the number of things, just divide to get the average (18 ÷ 3 = 6). If you know the total and the average, just divide to get the number of things (18 ÷ 6 = 3). If you know the average and the number of things, simply multiply to get the total (6 × 3 = 18). The key to most average questions is finding the total.

Here's another simple example:

Problem: If the average of three test scores is 70, what is the total of all three test scores?

Solution: Just put the number of things (3 tests) and the average (70) in the pie. Then multiply to find the total, which is 210.

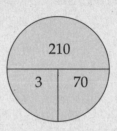

Here's another example:

Problem: What's the average of 10, 10, 10, and 50?

Solution: Simply add up the numbers to find the total, which is 80. The number of things is 4. Then just divide to find the average, which is 20.

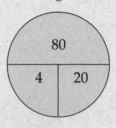

AVERAGES: ADVANCED PRINCIPLES

To solve most difficult average problems, all you have to do is fill out one or more Average Pies. Most of the time you will use them to find the total of the number being averaged. Here's an example:

Problem: Suppose a student has an average of 80 on four tests. If the student scores a 90 on the fifth test, what is her average on all five?

Solution: To find the average of all five tests, you need the total score. You need to start by finding the total of the first *four* tests. Draw an Average Pie and write in the average of the first four tests (80), and the number of things (4):

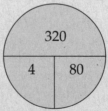

> ## Total
>
> When calculating averages and means, always find the total. It's the one piece of information that ETS loves to withhold.

Then multiply to find the total, which is 320. Now, find the total of all five tests by adding the fifth score to the total of the first four: 320 + 90 = 410. Now draw another Average Pie to find the average of all five tests. Write in the total (410), and the number of things (5). Then divide to find the average: 82.

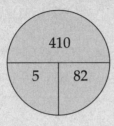

Now let's try a difficult question:

20. If the average (arithmetic mean) of eight numbers
     is 20, and the average of five of these numbers is
     14, what is the average of the other three numbers?

     (A) 14
     (B) 17
     (C) 20
     (D) 30
     (E) 34

Here's how to crack it

Start by drawing an Average Pie for all eight numbers; then multiply to find the total.

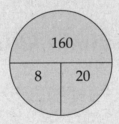

The total of the eight numbers is 160. Now draw another Average Pie for five of the numbers.

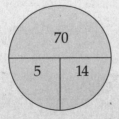

The total of those five numbers is 70. (Remember, those are five out of the original eight numbers.) To find the average of the other three numbers, you need the total of those three numbers. You have the total of all eight numbers, 160, and the total of five of those numbers, 70, so you can find the total of the other three by subtracting 70 from 160. That means the total of the three remaining numbers is 90. It's time to create one more Average Pie to find the average of those three numbers.

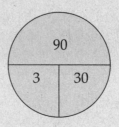

The average is 30, so ETS's answer is D.

On the SAT, you'll also need to know two other topics related to averages: *median* and *mode*.

WHAT IS A *MEDIAN*?

Median Median

To find the median of a set containing an even number of items, take the average of the two middle numbers.

The median of a group of numbers is the number that is exactly in the middle of the group when the group is arranged from smallest to largest, as on a number line. For example, in the group 3, 6, 6, 6, 6, 7, 8, 9, 10, 10, 11, the median is 7. Five numbers come before 7 in the group, and 5 come after. Remember it this way: *median* sounds like *middle*.

WHAT IS A *MODE*?

The mode of a group of numbers is the number in the group that appears most often. In the group 3, 4, 4, 5, 7, 7, 8, 8, 8, 9, 10, the mode is 8, because it appears three times while no other number in the group appears more than twice. Remember it this way: *mode* sounds like *most*.

EXPONENTS AND SQUARE ROOTS

Warning

The rules for multiplying and dividing exponents do not apply to addition or subtraction:
$2^2 + 2^3 = 12$
$(2 \times 2) + (2 \times 2 \times 2) = 12$
It does not equal 2^5 or 32

EXPONENTS ARE A KIND OF SHORTHAND

Many numbers are the product of the same factor multiplied over and over again. For example, $32 = 2 \times 2 \times 2 \times 2 \times 2$. Another way to write this would be $32 = 2^5$, or "thirty-two equals two to the fifth power." The little number, or *exponent*, denotes the number of times that 2 is to be used as a factor. In the same way, $10^3 = 10 \times 10 \times 10$, or 1,000, or "ten to the third power," or "ten cubed." In this example, the 10 is called the *base* and the 3 is called the *exponent*. (You won't need to know these terms on the SAT, but you will need to know them to follow our explanations.)

Multiplying numbers with exponents

When you multiply two numbers with the same base, you simply add the exponents. For example, $2^3 \times 2^5 = 2^{3+5} = 2^8$.

Dividing numbers with exponents

When you divide two numbers with the same base, you simply subtract the exponents. For example, $\frac{2^5}{2^3} = 2^{5-3} = 2^2$.

Raising a power to a power

When you raise a power to a power, you multiply the exponents. For example, $(2^3)^4 = 2^{3 \times 4} = 2^{12}$.

Calculator exponents

You can compute simple exponents on your calculator. Make sure you have a scientific calculator with a y^x key. To find 2^{10}, for example, simply use your y^x key, punching 2 in for the y value and 10 in for the x value. This may be especially useful if you are asked to compare exponents.

The peculiar behavior of exponents

Raising a number to a power can have quite peculiar and unexpected results, depending on what sort of number you start out with. Here are some examples:

1. If you square or cube a number greater than 1, it becomes larger. For example, $2^3 = 8$.

2. If you square or cube a positive fraction smaller than one, it becomes smaller.

   For example, $= \left(\dfrac{1}{2}\right)^3 = \dfrac{1}{8}$

3. A negative number raised to an even power becomes positive. For example, $(-2)^2 = 4$.

4. A negative number raised to an odd power remains negative. For example, $(-2)^3 = -8$.

   You should also have a feel for relative sizes of exponential numbers without calculating them. For example, 2^{10} is much larger than 10^2. ($2^{10} = 1,024$; $10^2 = 100$.) To take another example, 2^5 is twice as large as 2^4, even though 5 seems only a bit larger than 4.

SQUARE ROOTS

The sign indicates the positive square root of a number. For example, $\sqrt{25} = 5$.

The only rules you need to know

Here are the only rules regarding square roots that you need to know for the SAT:

1. $\sqrt{x}\sqrt{y} = \sqrt{xy}$. For example, $\sqrt{3}\sqrt{12} = \sqrt{36} = 6$

2. $\sqrt{\dfrac{x}{y}} = \dfrac{\sqrt{x}}{\sqrt{y}}$. For example, $\sqrt{\dfrac{5}{4}} = \dfrac{\sqrt{5}}{\sqrt{4}} = \dfrac{\sqrt{5}}{2}$

Note that rule 1 works in reverse: $\sqrt{50} = \sqrt{25} \times \sqrt{2} = 5\sqrt{2}$. This is really a kind of factoring. You are using rule 1 to factor a large, clumsy radical into numbers that are easier to work with.

Careless errors

Don't make careless mistakes. Remember that the square root of a number between 0 and 1 is *larger* than the original number. For example, $\sqrt{\dfrac{1}{4}} = \dfrac{1}{2}$, and $\dfrac{1}{2} > \dfrac{1}{4}$.

PROBABILITY

Probability is a mathematical expression of the likelihood of an event. The basis of probability is simple. The likelihood of any event is discussed in terms of all of the possible outcomes. To express the probability of a given event, x, you would count the number of possible outcomes, count the number of outcomes that give you what you want, and arrange them in a fraction, like this:

$$\text{Probability of } x = \frac{\text{number of outcomes that are } x}{\text{total number of possible outcomes}}$$

Every probability is a fraction. The largest a probability can be is 1; a probability of 1 indicates total certainty. The smallest a probability can be is 0, meaning that it's something that cannot happen. Furthermore, you can find the probability that something WILL NOT happen by subtracting the probability that it WILL happen from 1. For example, if the weatherman tells you that there is a 0.3 probability of rain today, then there must be a 0.7 probability that it won't rain, because $1 - 0.3 = 0.7$. Figuring out the probability of any single event is usually simple. When you flip a coin, there are only two possible outcomes, heads and tails; the probability of getting heads is therefore 1 out of 2, or $\dfrac{1}{2}$. When you roll a die, there are six possible outcomes, 1 through 6; the odds of getting a 6 is therefore $\dfrac{1}{6}$. The odds of getting an even result when rolling a die are $\dfrac{1}{2}$ since there are three even results in six possible outcomes.

Here's an example of a probability question:

22. A bag contains 7 blue marbles and 14 marbles that are not blue. If one marble is drawn at random from the bag, what is the probability that the marble is blue?

(A) $\dfrac{1}{7}$

(B) $\dfrac{1}{3}$

(C) $\dfrac{1}{2}$

(D) $\dfrac{2}{3}$

(E) $\dfrac{3}{7}$

Here's how to crack it

Here, there are 21 marbles in the bag, 7 of which are blue. The probability that a marble chosen at random would be blue is therefore $\dfrac{7}{21}$, or $\dfrac{1}{3}$. The correct answer is (B).

PERMUTATIONS

A permutation is an arrangement of objects of a definite order. The simplest sort of permutations question might ask you how many different arrangements are possible for 6 different chairs in a row, or how many different 4-letter arrangements of the letters in the word FUEL are possible. Both of these simple questions can be answered with the same technique.

Just draw a row of boxes corresponding to the positions you have to fill. In the case of the chairs, there are 6 positions, one for each chair. You would make a sketch like this:

Then, in each box, write the number of objects available to be put into that box. Keep in mind that objects put into previous boxes are no longer available. For the chair-arranging example, there would be 6 chairs available for the first box; only 5 left for the second box; 4 for the third, and so on until only one chair remained to be put into the last position. Finally, just multiply the numbers in the boxes together, and the product will be the number of possible arrangements, or permutations:

$$\boxed{6}\ \boxed{5}\ \boxed{4}\ \boxed{3}\ \boxed{2}\ \boxed{1} = 720$$

There are 720 possible permutations of a group of 6 chairs. This number can also be written as 6!. That's not a display of enthusiasm—the exclamation point means factorial. The number is read "six factorial," and it means $6 \cdot 5 \cdot 4 \cdot 3 \cdot 2 \cdot 1$, which equals 720. A factorial is simply the product of a series of integers counting down to 1 from the specified number. For example, the number 70! means $70 \cdot 69 \cdot 68 \ldots 3 \cdot 2 \cdot 1$.

The number of possible arrangements of any group with n members is simply $n!$. In this way, the number of possible arrangements of the letters in FUEL is 4!, because there are 4 letters in the group. That means $4 \cdot 3 \cdot 2 \cdot 1$ arrangements, or 24. If you sketched 4 boxes for the 4 letter positions and filled in the appropriate numbers, that's exactly what you'd get.

ADVANCED PERMUTATIONS

Permutations get a little trickier when you work with smaller arrangements. For example, what if you were asked how many 2-letter arrangements could be made from the letters in FUEL? It's just a modification of the original counting procedure. Sketch 2 boxes for the 2 positions. Then fill in the number of letters available for each position. As before, there are 4 letters available for the first space, and 3 for the second; the only difference is that you're done after two spaces:

$$\boxed{4}\ \boxed{3} = 12$$

As you did before, multiply the numbers in the boxes together to get the total number of arrangements. You should find there are 12 possible 2-letter arrangements from the letters in FUEL.

That's all there is to permutations. The box-counting procedure is the safest way to approach them. Just sketch the number of positions available, and fill in the number of objects available for each position, from first to last—then multiply those numbers together.

COMBINATIONS

Combinations differ from permutations in just one way: In combinations, order doesn't matter. A permutations question might ask you to form different numbers from a set of digits. Order would certainly matter in that case, because 135 is very different from 513. Similarly, a question about seating arrangements would be a permutations question, because the word "arrangements" tells you that order is important. So questions that ask about "schedules" or "orderings" require you to calculate the number of *permutations*.

Combinations questions, on the other hand, deal with groupings in which order *isn't* important. Combinations questions often deal with the selection of committees: Josh–Lisa–Andy isn't any different from Andy–Lisa–Josh, as far as committees go. In the same way, a question about the number of different

3-topping pizzas you could make from a 10-topping list would be a combinations question, because the order in which the toppings are put on is irrelevant. Questions that refer to "teams" or "pairs" are therefore asking about the number of possible *combinations*.

Combination and permutation questions can be very similar in appearance. Always ask yourself carefully whether sequence is important in a certain question before you proceed.

CALCULATING COMBINATIONS

Calculating combinations is surprisingly easy. All you have to do is throw out duplicate answers that count as separate permutations, but not as separate combinations.

Take a look at this example:

pepperoni	sausage
meatballs	anchovies
green peppers	onion
mushrooms	garlic
tomato	broccoli

PROBLEM SOLVING

1 2 3 4 5 6 7 8 9 10 11 12 13 14 15 16 17 18 19 20 21 22 23 24 **25**

EASY   MEDIUM   HARD

25. If a pizza must have 3 toppings chosen from the list above, and no topping may be used more than once on a given pizza, how many different kinds of pizza can be made?

(A) 720
(B) 360
(C) 120
(D) 90
(E) 30

To calculate the number of possible combinations, start by figuring out the number of possible *permutations*:

$$\boxed{10}\ \boxed{9}\ \boxed{8} = 720$$

That tells you that there are 720 possible 3-topping permutations that can be made from a list of 10 toppings. You're not done yet, though. Because this is a list of permutations, it contains many arrangements that duplicate the same group of elements in different orders. For example, those 720 permutations would include these:

pepperoni, mushrooms, onion	mushrooms, onion, pepperoni
pepperoni, onion, mushrooms	onion, pepperoni, mushrooms
mushrooms, pepperoni, onion	onion, mushrooms, pepperoni

All six of these listings are different permutations of the same group. In fact, for every 3-topping combination, there will be 6 different permutations. You've got to divide 720 by 6 to get the true number of combinations, which is 120. The correct answer is (C).

So, how do you know what number to divide permutations by to get combinations? It's simple. For the 3-position question above, we divided by 6, which is 3! That's all there is to it. To calculate a number of possible combinations, calculate the possible permutations first, and divide that number by the number of positions, factorial. Take a look at one more:

PROBLEM SOLVING

1	2	3	4	5	6	7	8	9	10	11	12	13	14	15	16	17	18	19	20	21	22	23	**24**	25
			EASY									MEDIUM										HARD		

24. How many different 4-person teams can be made from a roster of 9 players?

(A) 3,024
(B) 1,512
(C) 378
(D) 254
(E) 126

This is definitely a combination question. Start by sketching 4 boxes for the 4 team positions:

☐☐☐☐

Then fill in the number of possible contestants for each position, and multiply them together. This gives you the number of possible *permutations*:

$$\boxed{9}\ \boxed{8}\ \boxed{7}\ \boxed{6} = 3,024$$

Finally, divide this number by 4!, for the 4 positions you're working with. This gets rid of different permutations of identical groups. You divide 3,024 by 24 and get the number of possible combinations, 126. The correct answer.is (E).

ARITHMETIC SUMMARY

1. There are only six arithmetic operations tested on the SAT: addition, subtraction, multiplication, division, exponents, and square roots.

2. These operations must be performed in the proper order (PEMDAS), beginning with operations inside parentheses.

3. Apply the distributive law whenever possible. Very often, this is enough to find ETS's answer.

4. A fraction is just another way of expressing division.

5. You must know how to add, subtract, multiply, and divide fractions. And don't forget that you can also use your calculator.

6. In any problems involving large or confusing fractions, try to reduce the fractions first. Before you multiply two fractions, for example, see if it's possible to reduce either or both of the fractions.

7. If you know how to work out fractions on your calculator, use it to help you with questions that involve fractions. If you intend to use your calculator for fractions, make sure you practice. You should also know how to work with fractions the old-fashioned way.

8. A decimal is just another way of expressing a fraction.

9. Use a calculator to add, subtract, multiply, and divide decimals.

10. A ratio can be expressed as a fraction, but ratios are not fractions.

11. Use a Ratio Box to solve ratio questions.

12. A percentage is just a convenient way of expressing a fraction whose bottom is 100.

13. To convert a percentage to a fraction, put the percentage over 100 and reduce.

14. To convert a fraction to a percentage, use your calculator to divide the top of the fraction by the bottom of the fraction. Then multiply the result by 100.

15. To convert a percentage to a decimal, move the decimal point two places to the left. To convert a decimal to a percentage, move the decimal point two places to the right.

16. In problems that require you to find a series of percentage increases or decreases, remember that each successive increase or decrease is performed on the result of the previous one.

17. To find the average (or arithmetic mean) of several values, add up the values and divide the total by the number of values.

18. Use the Average Pie to solve problems involving averages. The key to most average problems is finding the total.

19. The median of a group of numbers is the number that is exactly in the middle of the group when the group is arranged from smallest to largest, as on a number line.

20. The mode of a group of numbers is the number in the group that appears most often.

21. Exponents are a kind of shorthand for expressing numbers that are the product of the same factor multiplied over and over again.

22. To multiply two exponential expressions with the same base, add the exponents.

23. To divide two exponential expressions with the same base, subtract the exponents.

24. To raise one exponential expression to another power, multiply the exponents.

25. When you raise a positive number greater than 1 to a power greater than 1, the result is larger. When you raise a positive fraction less than 1 to an exponent greater than 1, the result is smaller. A negative number raised to an even power becomes positive. A negative number raised to an odd power remains negative.

26. When you're asked for the square root of any number $\sqrt{x}$, you're being asked for the positive root only.

27. Here are the only rules regarding square roots that you need to know for the SAT:

   a. $\sqrt{x} \times \sqrt{y} = \sqrt{xy}$

   b. $\sqrt{\dfrac{x}{y}} = \dfrac{\sqrt{x}}{\sqrt{y}}$

12

Algebra:
Cracking the System

PRINCETON REVIEW ALGEBRA

About a third of the math problems on your SAT will involve algebra. Some students are terrified of algebra. Fortunately, we have several techniques that should enable you to solve the most frightening-looking algebra problems—even word problems.

This chapter is divided into three main sections:

1. Plugging In the Answer Choices

2. Plugging In Your Own Numbers

3. Basic Princeton Review Algebra

Princeton Review Algebra is our name for the kind of algebra you need to know to do well on the SAT. It isn't the same as the algebra you were taught in math class. Why did we bother to create our own kind of algebra? Because math-class algebra takes too much time on the SAT. If you want big score improvements, you're going to have to forget about your algebra class and learn the techniques that work on the SAT.

Your biggest scoring gains will come from the sections on Plugging In. These are extremely powerful techniques that work on multiple-choice questions. You won't need to know much algebra in order to use them, but you'll have to stay on your toes.

The third section of this chapter is a summary of basic Princeton Review Algebra. It's dull by comparison with the rest of the chapter, but you should read it carefully, even if you already feel comfortable with algebra. You should think of our summary as a guide to the handful of algebraic concepts you'll need in order to answer problems that can't be solved by Plugging In.

PLUGGING IN THE ANSWER CHOICES

Algebra uses letters to stand for numbers, but no one else does. You don't go to the grocery store to buy x eggs or y gallons of milk. Most people think in terms of numbers, not letters that stand for numbers.

You should think in terms of numbers on the SAT as much as possible. On many SAT algebra problems, even very difficult ones, you will be able to find ETS's answer without using any algebra at all. You will do this by working backward from the answer choices instead of trying to solve the problem using math-class algebra.

Plugging In is a technique for solving word problems whose answer choices are all numbers. Many so-called algebra problems on the SAT can be solved simply and quickly by using this powerful technique.

In algebra class at school, you solve word problems by using equations. Then, if you're careful, you check your solution by Plugging In your answer to see if it works. Why not skip the equations entirely by simply checking the five solutions ETS offers on the multiple-choice questions? One of these has to be correct. You don't have to do *any* algebra, you will seldom have to try more than two choices, and you will never have to try all five. Note that you can only use this technique for questions that ask for a specific amount.

Here's an example:

PROBLEM SOLVING

1	2	3	4	5	6	7	8	9	⑩	11	12	13	14	15	16	17	18	19	20	21	22	23	24	25
			EASY									MEDIUM									HARD			

10. The units digit of a 2-digit number is 3 times the tens digit. If the digits are reversed, the resulting number is 36 more than the original number. What is the original number?

(A) 26
(B) 31
(C) 36
(D) 62
(E) 93

Here's how to crack it

Don't waste time fumbling around all the possible digit combinations. (There are only three, but it can take a while to figure that out.) ETS has limited your decision to five choices—they've already done almost all the work.

What you want to do is look at each answer choice to see if it fulfills the conditions stated in the problem. If it doesn't, you can use POE to get rid of it.

Plugging In on this problem is a piece of cake. You simply take the stated conditions one at a time and try them out against the answer choices.

The first condition stated in the problem is that the units (or ones) digit of the number you are looking for is three times the tens digit. Now you look at the choices:

(A) Is 6 three times 2? Yes. A possibility.

(B) Is 1 three times 3? No. Eliminate.

(C) Is 6 three times 3? No. Eliminate.

(D) Is 2 three times 6? No. Eliminate.

(E) Is 3 three times 9? No. Eliminate.

ETS's answer is A. You found it without even testing the other conditions stated in the problem. Mark your answer and move on.

When you plug in on a question, don't select an answer until you've either tested all the conditions or eliminated all but one of the choices. In this problem, if there had been another choice whose units digit was three times its tens digit, you would have had to move on to the next condition.

Here's another example:

PROBLEM SOLVING

1 2 3 4 5 6 7 8 9 10 **11** 12 13 14 15 16 17 18 19 20 21 22 23 24 25

EASY   MEDIUM   HARD

11. A woman made 5 payments on a loan with each payment being twice the amount of the preceding one. If the total of all 5 payments was $465, how much was the first payment?

   (A) $5
   (B) $15
   (C) $31
   (D) $93
   (E) $155

Here's how to crack it

To solve this problem in math class, you'd have to set up and solve an equation like this:

$$p + 2p + 4p + 8p + 16p = 465$$

Forget it! That's too much work, plus there's a lot of room for error. Why not just try out the answers?

Numeric answer choices on the SAT are always given in order of size. Thus, when you are Plugging In on a problem like this, you should always start out with the number in the middle—choice C. If that number turns out to be too big, you can try a lower number next; if it's too small, you can try a higher one. That way you'll save time.

Let's look at what happens when you try choice C: If the payments double each month, the woman will pay 31 + 62 + 124 + 248 + 496—you can stop right there. You don't have to add up these numbers to see clearly that the total is going to be much more than 465; the fifth number alone is more than that. You need to eliminate this choice, along with choices D and E. Try again with A or B.

Which one should you try? Why not (A), the smaller of the two? It will be easier and faster to work with. If it works, you'll pick it; if it doesn't, you'll eliminate it and pick B.

Here's what you get when you try choice A: 5 + 10 + 20 + 40 + 80. You don't have to add up these numbers to see clearly that they aren't going to come anywhere near 465. ETS's answer must be B. (It is.)

PLUGGING IN: ADVANCED PRINCIPLES

Plugging In is the same on difficult problems as it is on easy and medium ones. You just have to watch your step and make certain you don't make any careless mistakes or fall for Joe Bloggs answers.

Which Way?

Sometimes, it's hard to tell which way to go after eliminating C—higher or lower. Don't fret, just move. Find a choice with an easy-to-manipulate number. It may turn out to be wrong, but it won't take long to find out. It may also tell you whether to go higher or lower.

Here's one of our examples:

PROBLEM SOLVING

1 2 3 4 5 6 7 8 9 10 11 12 13 14 15 16 17 **18** 19 20 21 22 23 24 25

EASY   MEDIUM   HARD

18. Out of a total of 154 games played, a ball team won
     54 more games than it lost. If there were no ties,
     how many games did the team win?

     (A) 94
     (B) 98
     (C) 100
     (D) 102
     (E) 104

Here's how to crack it

What's the Joe Bloggs answer here? It is choice C. Be careful!

To solve the problem all you have to do is plug in. You've eliminated choice
C already, so start with D. If the team won 102 games, how many games did
it lose? It lost 52 ($154 - 102 = 52$). Is 102 (wins) 54 greater than 52 (losses)? No.
$102 - 52 = 50$. You need more wins to make the problem come out right. That
means that ETS's answer must be E. (It is.)

Here's another example we created:

22. Committee A has 18 members and Committee
     B has 3 members. How many members from
     Committee A must switch to Committee B so that
     Committee A will have twice as many members as
     Committee B?

     (A) 4
     (B) 6
     (C) 7
     (D) 9
     (E) 14

Here's how to crack it

This problem represents one of the most difficult principles tested in the SAT
math section. Only a small percentage of students gets it right. But if you plug
in, you won't have any trouble.

This problem is about two committees, so the first thing you should do is quickly draw a picture in your test booklet to keep from getting confused:

Now plug in the answer choices, starting with answer choice C. If you move 7 members out of Committee A, there will be 11 members left in A and 10 members in B. Is 11 twice as many as 10? No, eliminate.

As you work through the choices, keep track of them, like this:

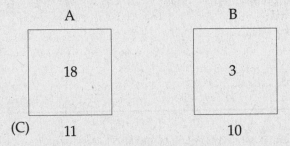

Choice C didn't work. To make the question work out right, you need more members in Committee A and fewer in Committee B. In other words, you need to try a smaller number. Try the smallest one, choice A. Moving 4 members from Committee A will leave 14 in A and 7 in B. Is 14 twice as many as 7? Yes, of course. This is ETS's answer.

PLUGGING IN YOUR OWN NUMBERS

Working Backwards enables you to find ETS's answer on problems whose answer choices are all numbers. What about problems whose answer choices contain letters? On these problems, you will usually be able to find ETS's answer by plugging in your own numbers.

Plugging In is easy. It has three steps:

1. Pick numbers for the letters in the problem.

2. Use *your* numbers to find an answer to the problem.

3. Plug your numbers from step 1 into the answer choices to see which choice equals the answer you found in step 2.

THE BASICS OF PLUGGING IN YOUR OWN NUMBERS

This sort of Plugging In is simple to understand. Here's an example:

PROBLEM SOLVING
1 2 **3** 4 5 6 7 8 9 10 11 12 13 14 15 16 17 18 19 20 21 22 23 24 25
EASY   MEDIUM   HARD

3. Kim was k years of age 2 years ago. In terms of k, how old will Kim be 2 years from now?

(A) $k + 4$

(B) $k + 2$

(C) $2k$

(D) k

(E) $\dfrac{k}{2}$

Here's how to crack it

First, pick a number for k. Pick something easy to work with, like 10. In your test booklet, write 10 directly above the letter k in the problem, so you won't forget.

If $k = 10$, then Kim was 10 years old 2 years ago. That means she's 12 right now. The problem has asked you to find out how old Kim will be in 2 years. She will be 14. Write a nice big 14 in your test booklet and circle it. ETS's answer will be the choice that, when you plug in 10 for k, equals 14.

Now it's time to plug in.

Plugging In 10 for k in answer choice A, you get $10 + 4$, or 14. This is the number you are looking for, so this must be ETS's answer. (It is.) Go ahead and try the other choices just to make sure you're right and to practice Plugging In.

Here's another example:

PROBLEM SOLVING
1 2 3 4 5 6 7 8 9 10 11 12 13 14 15 16 **17** 18 19 20 21 22 23 24 25
EASY   MEDIUM   HARD

17. The sum of two positive consecutive integers is x. In terms of x, what is the value of the smaller of these two integers?

(A) $\dfrac{x}{2} - 1$

(B) $\dfrac{x - 1}{2}$

(C) $\dfrac{x}{2}$

(D) $\dfrac{x + 1}{2}$

(E) $\dfrac{x}{2} + 1$

Get Real

There is nothing abstract about the SAT (except maybe its relevance). So, if the problem says that Tina is x years old, why not plug in your own age? That's real enough. You don't have to change your name to Tina. (Anyway, only ancient Roman children can be x years old.)

When to Plug In

- Phrases like "in terms of k" in the question
- Variable in the answers
- Unspecified values and fractions

Plugging In Works

Don't try to solve problems like this by writing equations and "solving for x" or "solving for y." Plugging In is faster, easier, and less likely to produce errors.

Here's how to crack it

If we pick 2 and 3 for our two positive consecutive integers, then $x = 5$. Write 2, 3, and $x = 5$ in your test booklet.

The smaller of our two integers is 2. Circle it; we are looking for the choice that equals 2 when we plug in 5. Let's try each choice:

(A) Plugging in 5 gives us $\frac{5}{2} - 1$. This won't even be an integer, and 2 is an integer. Eliminate.

(B) Plugging in 5 gives us $\frac{4}{2}$, or 2. This is ETS's answer.

Check all of your choices just to be sure.

WHICH NUMBERS?

Although you can plug in any number, you can make your life much easier by plugging in "good" numbers—numbers that are simple to work with or that make the problem easier to manipulate. Picking a small number, such as 2, will usually make finding the answer easier. If the problem asks for a percentage, plug in 10 or 100. If the problem has to do with minutes, try 60. If you plug in wisely, you can sometimes eliminate computation altogether.

Except in special cases, you should avoid plugging in 0 and 1; these numbers have weird properties. Using them may allow you to eliminate only one or two choices at a time. You should also avoid plugging in any number that appears in the question or in any of the answer choices.

Many times you'll find that there is an advantage to picking a particular number, even a very large one, because it makes solving the problem easier.

Here's an example:

PROBLEM SOLVING																								
1	2	3	4	5	6	7	8	9	10	11	12	13	14	15	16	**17**	18	19	20	21	22	23	24	25
			EASY									MEDIUM									HARD			

17. If 100 equally priced tickets cost a total of d dollars, 5 of these tickets cost how many dollars?

(A) $\dfrac{d}{20}$

(B) $\dfrac{d}{5}$

(C) $5d$

(D) $\dfrac{5}{d}$

(E) $\dfrac{20}{d}$

Be Good

"Good" numbers make a problem less confusing by simplifying the arithmetic. This is your chance to make the SAT easier.

Here's how to crack it

Should you plug in 2 for d? You could, but plugging in 200 would make the problem easier. After all, if 100 tickets cost a total of $200, then each ticket costs $2. Write $d = 200$ in your test booklet.

If each ticket costs $2, then 5 tickets cost $10. Write a 10 in your test booklet and circle it. You are looking for the answer choice that works out to 10 when you plug in 200 for d. Let's try each choice:

$$\text{(A)} \quad \frac{200}{20} = 10$$

That was easy. A quick eyeball of the other choices confirms ETS's answer is A. Here's another example:

PROBLEM SOLVING
1 2 3 4 5 6 7 8 9 10 11 12 13 14 15 16 17 18 19 20 21 22 23 24 **25**
EASY   MEDIUM   HARD

25. A watch loses x minutes every y hours. At this rate, how many hours will the watch lose in one week?

   (A) $7xy$

   (B) $\dfrac{7y}{x}$

   (C) $\dfrac{x}{7y}$

   (D) $\dfrac{14y}{5x}$

   (E) $\dfrac{14x}{5y}$

Here's how to crack it

This is an extremely difficult problem for students who try to solve it the math-class way. You'll be able to find the answer easily, though, if you plug in carefully.

What should you plug in? As always, you can plug in anything, but if you select numbers wisely you'll make things easier on yourself. There are three units of time in this problem: minutes, hours, and weeks. If we plug in 60 for x, we can get it down to two, because 60 minutes equal an hour. Write $x = 60$ in your test booklet.

We can also make things easier for ourselves by plugging in 24 for y. There are 24 hours in a day. What we are saying so far is that the watch loses 60 minutes every 24 hours. In other words, it loses an hour a day. Write $y = 24$ in your test booklet.

At this rate, how many hours will the watch lose in a week? It will lose 7, obviously, because there are 7 days in a week. Write 7 in your test booklet and circle it. We are looking for the answer choice that equals 7 when we plug in 60 for x and 24 for y.

Now let's check each choice:

(A) $7xy = (7)(60)(24)$. Common sense, not computation, tells us that this is way too big. Eliminate.

(B) $7\dfrac{y}{x} = \dfrac{(7)(24)}{(60)} = \dfrac{168}{60} = 2.8$. Eliminate.

(C) $\dfrac{x}{7y} = \dfrac{(60)}{(7)(24)} = \dfrac{60}{168} = 0.35714$. Eliminate.

(D) $\dfrac{14y}{5x} = \dfrac{(14)(24)}{(5)(60)} = \dfrac{336}{300} = 1.12$. Eliminate.

(E) $\dfrac{14x}{5y} = \dfrac{(14)(60)}{(5)(24)} = \dfrac{840}{120} = 7$. This is ETS's answer.

INEQUALITIES

Plugging In works on problems containing inequalities, but you will have to follow some different rules. Plugging In one number is often not enough; to find ETS's answer you may have to plug in several numbers, including weird numbers like: $-1, 0, 1, \dfrac{1}{2}$, and $-\dfrac{1}{2}$.

The five numbers just mentioned all have special properties. Negatives, fractions, 0, and 1 all behave in peculiar ways when, for example, they are squared. Don't forget about them!

Sometimes you can avoid Plugging In altogether by simplifying. Here's an example:

PROBLEM SOLVING																								
1	2	3	4	5	6	7	8	9	**10**	11	12	13	14	15	16	17	18	19	20	21	22	23	24	25
				EASY									MEDIUM								HARD			

10. If $-3x + 6 \geq 18$, which of the following must be true?

(A) $x \leq -4$
(B) $x \leq 6$
(C) $x \geq -4$
(D) $x \geq -6$
(E) $x = 2$

Here's how to crack it

The inequality in the problem can be simplified quite a bit:

$$-3x + 6 \geq 18$$
$$-3x \geq 12$$
$$-x \geq 4$$

We're close to one of the answer choices, but not quite there yet. Multiply both sides by –1 to make x positive. *Remember to change the direction of the inequality sign!* (For more on that, see page 209.)

$$x \leq -4$$

So choice A is ETS's answer.

OTHER SPECIAL CASES

Sometimes SAT algebra problems will require you to determine certain characteristics of a number or numbers. Is x odd or even? Is it small or large? Is it positive or negative?

On questions like this, you will probably have to plug in more than one number and/or plug in weird numbers, just as you do on problems containing inequalities. Sometimes ETS's wording will tip you off. If the problem states only that $x > 0$, you know for certain that x is positive but you don't know that x is an integer. See what happens when you plug in a fraction.

Here are some other tip-offs you should be aware of:

If the problem asked for this	and you plugged in this	also try this, just to be sure
an integer	3	1, 0, or –1
a fraction	$\frac{1}{4}$	$-\frac{1}{4}$
two even numbers	2, 4	2, –2
a number	an integer	a fraction
a number	an even number	an odd number
a number	a small number	a huge number
a multiple of 7	7	7,000 or –7
consecutive numbers	1, 2, 3	–1, 0, 1
$x^2 = 4$	2	–2
$xy > 0$	(2, 4)	(–2, –4)
$x = 2y$	(4, 2)	(–4, –2) or (0, 0)

Gator!

Think of the inequality sign as the mouth of a hungry alligator. The alligator eats the bigger number.

MUST BE TRUE

Try the following problem:

PROBLEM SOLVING

1	2	3	4	5	6	7	8	9	10	11	12	13	14	15	16	17	18	19	20	21	22	23	24	25
		EASY									MEDIUM										HARD			

22. If $x - y$ is a multiple of 3, then which of the following must also be a multiple of 3?

(A) $y - x$

(B) $\dfrac{y - x}{2}$

(C) $\dfrac{x + y}{2}$

(D) $x + y$

(E) xy

Here's how to crack it

Since there are variables in the answer choices, we will plug in. First plug in easy numbers that make the given statement ($x - y$ is a multiple of 3) true. Let's make $x = 6$ and $y = 3$. The question asks which of the following must also be a multiple of 3. Let's plug in our numbers, and cross off any answer choices that are not multiples of 3.

(A) $3 - 6 = -3$ is a multiple of 3, so keep it.

(B) $\dfrac{3 - 6}{2}$ is not a multiple of 3. Cross it off.

(C) $\dfrac{6 + 3}{2}$ is not a multiple of 3. Cross it off.

(D) $6 + 3 = 9$. Keep it.

(E) $(6)(3) = 18$. Keep it.

Since this question asks for something that *must* be true and we are left with three answer choices, we must plug in again. The question asks us for a multiple of 3. The first time we plugged in, we used two other multiples of three ($x = 6$ and $y = 3$) to satisfy the first condition. Let's now use two numbers that make the initial statement true but are *not* multiples of 3. Plug in 5 for x and 2 for y. Now check the answers we didn't eliminate the first time:

(A) $2 - 5 = -3$. It still works, so keep it.

(D) $5 + 2 = 7$. Cross it off.

(E) $(5)(2) = 10$. Cross it off.

ETS's answer is A.

PLUGGING IN: ADVANCED PRINCIPLES

As you have just learned, you should plug in whenever you don't know what a number is. But you can also plug in when you have numbers that are too big, too ugly, or too inconvenient to work with. On such problems you can often find ETS's answer simply by using numbers that aren't as ugly as the ones ETS has given you.

A Little Terminology

Here are some words that you will need to know to follow the rest of this chapter. The words themselves won't show up on the SAT, so after you finish the chapter you can forget about them.

Term: An equation is like a sentence, and a term is the equivalent of a word. For example, 9×2 is a term in the equation $9 \times 2 + 3x = 5y$.

Expression: If an equation is like a sentence, then an expression is like a phrase or a clause. An expression is a combination of terms and mathmatical operations with no equal or inequality sign. For example, $9 \times 2 + 3x$ is an expression.

Polynomial: A polynomial is any expression containing two or more terms. Binomials and trinomials are both known as polynomials.

Here's an example:

20. On the last day of a one-week sale, customers numbered 149 through 201 were waited on. How many customers were waited on that day?

(A) 51
(B) 52
(C) 53
(D) 152
(E) 153

Here's how to crack it

This is a number 20—a difficult question. Finding ETS's answer has to be harder than simply subtracting 149 from 201 to get 52, which means that choice B has to be wrong. Cross it out. (You can also immediately eliminate D and E, which are much, much too big.)

One way to find the answer would be to count this out by hand. But to count from 149 to 201 is an awful lot of counting. You can achieve the same result by using simpler numbers instead.

It doesn't matter which numbers you use. How about 7 and 11? The difference between 7 and 11 is 4. But if you count out the numbers on your hand—7, 8, 9, 10, 11—you see that there are 5 numbers. In other words, if the store had served customers 7 through 11, the number of customers would have been 1 greater than the difference of 7 and 11. ETS's answer, therefore, will be 1 greater than the difference of 149 and 201. ETS's answer, in other words, is C.

Here's another example:

22. $2^{23} - 2^{22} =$

(A) 2^1

(B) $2^{\frac{23}{22}}$

(C) 2^{22}

(D) 2^{23}

(E) 2^{45}

Here's how to crack it

These are big, ugly, inconvenient exponents. No wonder this question is a number 22. But you'll be able to solve it if you plug in easier numbers.

Factoring with Exponents

We can also solve question 22 by factoring 2^{22} out of the parentheses, giving us a new expression: $2^{22}(2^1 - 1) = 2^{22}(2 - 1) = 2^{22}(1) = 2^{22}$

Instead of 2^{23}, let's use 2^4. And instead of 2^{22}, let's use 2^3. Now we can rewrite the problem: $2^4 - 2^3 = 16 - 8 = 8 = 2^3$.

Our answer is the second of the two numbers we started with. ETS's answer, therefore, must be the second number we started with, or 2^{22}, which is choice C. (If you don't believe this always works, try it with 2^3 and 2^2, and with 2^5 and 2^4, or any other similar pair of numbers. By the way, choices A and B are Joe Bloggs answers.)

BASIC PRINCETON REVIEW ALGEBRA

Plugging In will be of enormous help to you on the Math SAT. But it won't be enough to answer every algebra problem. On some problems, you'll have to know the few basic principles of Princeton Review Algebra.

SIMPLIFYING EXPRESSIONS

Something to Hide

Because factoring or unfactoring is usually the key to finding ETS's answer on such problems, learn to recognize expressions that could be either factored or unfactored. This will earn you more points. ETS likes to hide the answers in factors.

If a problem contains an expression that can be factored, you should factor it immediately. For example, if you come upon a problem containing the expression $2x + 2y$, you should factor it immediately to produce the expression $2(x + y)$.

If a problem contains an expression that is already factored, you should multiply it out according to the distributive law to return it to its original unfactored state. For example, if you come upon a problem containing the expression $2(x + y)$, you should unfactor it by multiplying through to produce the expression $2x + 2y$.

Here are five worked examples:

1. $4x + 24 = 4(x) + 4(6) = 4(x + 6)$

2. $\dfrac{10x - 60}{2} = \dfrac{10(x) - 10(6)}{2} = \dfrac{10(x - 6)}{2} = 5(x - 6) = 5x - 30$

3. $\dfrac{x + y}{y} = \dfrac{x}{y} + \dfrac{y}{y} = \dfrac{x}{y} + 1$

4. $2(x + y) + 3(x + y) = (2 + 3)(x + y) = 5(x + y)$

5. $p(r + s) + q(r + s) = (p + q)(r + s)$

MULTIPLYING POLYNOMIALS

Multiplying polynomials is easy. Just be sure to use FOIL (First, Outer, Inner, Last):

$$(x + 2)(x + 4) = (x + 2)(x + 4)$$
$$= (x \times x) + (x \times 4) + (2 \times x) + (2 \times 4)$$
$$\text{FIRST} \quad \text{OUTER} \quad \text{INNER} \quad \text{LAST}$$
$$= x^2 + 4x + 2x + 8$$
$$= x^2 + 6x + 8$$

COMBINE SIMILAR TERMS FIRST

In manipulating long, complicated algebraic expressions, combine all similar terms before doing anything else. In other words, if one of the terms is $5x$ and another is $-3x$, simply combine them into $2x$. Then you won't have as many terms to work with. Here's an example:

$(3x^2 + 3x + 4) + (2 - x) - (6 + 2x) =$

$3x^2 + 3x + 4 + 2 - x - 6 - 2x =$

$3x^2 + (3x - x - 2x) + (4 + 2 - 6) =$

$3x^2$

EVALUATING EXPRESSIONS

Sometimes ETS will give you the value of one of the letters in an algebraic expression and ask you to find the value of the entire expression. All you have to do is plug in the given value and see what you come up with.

Here is an example:

Problem:

If $2x = -1$, then $(2x - 3)^2 = ?$

Solution:

Don't solve for x; simply plug in -1 for $2x$, like this:

$(2x - 3)^2 = (-1 - 3)^2$

$= (-4)^2$

$= 16$

SOLVING EQUATIONS

In algebra class you learned to solve equations by "solving for x" or "solving for y." To do this, you isolate x or y on one side of the equal sign and put everything else on the other side. This is a long, laborious process with many steps and many opportunities for mistakes.

On the SAT, you usually won't need to solve equations this way. You've already learned how to plug in. On the few problems where these techniques don't apply, you should be able to find direct solutions. To demonstrate what we mean, we'll show you the same problem solved two different ways.

Problem:

If $2x = 5$ and $3y = 6$, then $6xy = ?$

> **Learn Them, Love Them**
>
> Don't get bogged down looking for a direct solution. Always ask yourself if there is a simple way to find the answer. If you train yourself to think in terms of shortcuts, you won't waste a lot of time. However, if you don't see a quick solution, get to work. Something may come to you as you labor away.

Math-class solution:

1. Find x

2. Find y

3. Multiply 6 times x times y

Using this procedure, you find that $x = \frac{5}{2}$ and $y = 2$. Therefore, $6xy = (6)\frac{5}{2}(2)$, or 30.

The Princeton Review solution:

You notice that $6xy$ equals $(2x)(3y)$. Therefore, $6xy$ equals $(5)(6)$, or 30.

Analysis

Finding direct solutions will save you time. ETS expects you to perform long, complicated calculations on the SAT. You should always stop and think for a moment before beginning such a process. Look for a trick—a shortcut to the answer.

Here's another example:

> If a, b, c, and d are integers and $ab = 12$,
> $bc = 20$, $cd = 30$, and $ad = 18$, then $abcd = ?$

Here's how to crack it

If you try to solve this the math-class way, you'll end up fiddling forever with the equations, trying to find individual values for a, b, c, and d. Once again, you may get the correct answer, but you'll spend an eternity doing it.

This problem is much simpler if you look for a direct solution. The first thing to notice is that you have been given a lot of information you don't need. For example, the problem would have been much simpler to answer if you had been given only two equations: $ab = 12$ and $cd = 30$. You should know that $(ab)(cd) = abcd$, which means that $abcd = (12)(30)$, which means that the answer is 360.

Solving Inequalities

Warning!

When you multiply or divide an inequality by a negative number, you must reverse the inequality sign.

In an equation, one side equals the other. In an inequality, one side does not equal the other. The following symbols are used in inequalities:

$\neq$ is not equal to

$>$ is greater than

$<$ is less than

$\geq$ is greater than or equal to

$\leq$ is less than or equal to

Solving inequalities is pretty much like solving equations. You can collect similar terms, and you can simplify by doing the same thing to both sides. All you have to remember is that if you multiply or divide both sides of an inequality by a negative number, the direction of the inequality symbol changes. For example, here's a simple inequality:

$$x > y$$

Now, just as you can with an equation, you can multiply both sides of this inequality by the same number. But if the number you multiply by is negative, you have to change the direction of the symbol in the result. For example, if we multiply both sides of the inequality above by –2, we end up with the following:

$$-2x < -2y$$

SOLVING SIMULTANEOUS EQUATIONS

Sometimes on the SAT you will be asked to find the value of an expression based on two given equations. To find ETS's answer on such problems, simply add or subtract the two equations.

Here's an example:

If $4x + y = 14$ and $3x + 2y = 13$, then $x - y = ?$

Here's how to crack it

You've been given two equations here. But instead of being asked to solve for a variable (x or y), you've been asked to solve for an expression ($x - y$). Why? Because there must be a direct solution.

In math class, you're taught to multiply one equation by one number and then subtract equations to find the second variable. Or you're taught to solve one equation for one variable in terms of the other and to substitute that value into the second equation to solve for the other variable, and, having found the other variable, to plug it back into the equation to find the value of the first variable.

Forget it. There's a better way. Just add or subtract the two equations; either addition or subtraction will produce an easy answer. Adding the two equations gives you this:

$$
\begin{array}{r}
4x + \ y = 14 \\
+ \ 3x + 2y = 13 \\
\hline
7x + 3y = 27
\end{array}
$$

This doesn't get us anywhere. So try subtracting:

$$
\begin{array}{r}
4x + \ y = 14 \\
- \ 3x + 2y = 13 \\
\hline
x - \ y = \ 1
\end{array}
$$

The value of ($x - y$) is precisely what you are looking for, so this must be ETS's answer.

Stack 'Em

Don't solve simultaneous equations on the SAT the way you would in school (by multiplying one equation by one number, and then adding or subtracting). We have rarely seen an SAT on which simultaneous equations had to be solved this way. Just stack 'em, and add 'em or subtract 'em.

SOLVING QUADRATIC EQUATIONS

To solve quadratic equations, remember everything you've learned so far: Look for direct solutions and either factor or unfactor when possible.

Here's an example:

$$\text{If } (x+3)2 = (x-2)2, \text{ then } x = ?$$

Here's how to crack it

Since both sides of the equation have been factored, you should unfactor them by multiplying them out:

Left: $(x+3)(x+3) = x^2 + 6x + 9$

Right: $(x-2)(x-2) = x^2 - 4x + 4$

Therefore: $x^2 + 6x + 9 = x^2 - 4x + 4$

Now you can simplify. Eliminate the x^2s since they are on both sides of the equal sign. Move the xs to the left, and the numbers to the right to give you:

$$10x = -5$$

$$x = -\frac{1}{2}$$

Three Common Quadratics

$(x+y)(x-y) = x^2 - y^2$
$(x+y)^2 = x^2 + 2xy + y^2$
$(x-y)^2 = x^2 - 2xy + y^2$

Here's another example:

$$\text{If } x2 - 4 = (18)(14), \text{ then what could x be?}$$

Here's how to crack it

$x^2 - 4$ is actually a common quadratic expression: $x^2 - y^2$. Since $x^2 - y^2 = (x+y)(x-y)$, that means $x^2 - 4$ can be factored in the same way:

$$x^2 - 4 = (x+2)(x-2)$$

Therefore: $(x+2)(x-2) = (18)(14)$

Notice that each side of the equation consists of two terms multiplied by each other. Set the corresponding parts equal to each other and see what you get.

$$(x+2) = 18$$

$$(x-2) = 14$$

Both equations work if x is 16 (–16 also solves the original problem).

Solving Quadratic Equations Set to Zero

If $ab = 0$, what do you know about a and b? You know that at least one of them has to equal 0. You can use this fact in solving some quadratic equations. Here's an example:

> What are all the values of x for which
> $x(x - 3) = 0$?

Here's how to crack it

Because the product of x and $(x - 3)$ is 0, you know that x or $(x - 3)$—or both of them—has to equal 0. To solve the problem, simply ask yourself what x would have to be to make either expression equal 0. The answer is obvious: x could be either 0 or 3.

Functions

When you learned about functions in algebra class, you probably talked about "f of x," or $f(x)$.

The SAT is different. It tests functions, but in a peculiar way. Instead of using $f(x)$, it uses funny symbols to stand for operations. If you understand functions, just remember them when you see the funny symbols. If you don't understand functions, just follow what we tell you.

In a function problem, an arithmetic operation is defined and then you are asked to perform it on a number, a pair of numbers, or an ordered pair of numbers. All you have to do is keep your wits about you, use your booklet as scratch paper, and do as you are told. A function is like a set of instructions: follow it and you'll find ETS's answer.

Here's an example:

Predictable Functions

There are usually two or three function problems on every SAT. The last one will be extremely difficult. If you're not trying to score in the 700s, you should probably skip it. On the others, work very, very carefully.

PROBLEM SOLVING		
1 2 3 4 5 6 7 8	9 10 11 12 13 14 15 16 17 **18** 19 20	21 22 23 24 25
EASY	MEDIUM	HARD

18. If $x \mathbin{\#} y = \dfrac{1}{x - y}$, what is the value of $\dfrac{1}{2} \mathbin{\#} \dfrac{1}{3}$?

(A) 6

(B) $\dfrac{6}{5}$

(C) $\dfrac{1}{6}$

(D) -1

(E) -6

Here's how to crack it

Finding ETS's answers is just a matter of simple substitution. Just substitute $\frac{1}{2}$ and $\frac{1}{3}$ for x and y in the function.

$$\frac{1}{2} \# \frac{1}{3} = \frac{1}{\frac{1}{2} - \frac{1}{3}}$$

$$= \frac{1}{\frac{1}{6}}$$

$$= 6$$

ETS's answer, therefore, is choice A.

Let's try a pair of functions:

Questions 16–17 refer to the following definition:

> For all integers x, let $\odot x = x^2$ if x is negative, and let $\odot x = 2x$ if x is positive.

PROBLEM SOLVING																								
1	2	3	4	5	6	7	8	9	10	11	12	13	14	15	**16**	17	18	19	20	21	22	23	24	25
			EASY									MEDIUM									HARD			

16. $\odot(-5) - \odot 5 =$

 (A) −10
 (B) −5
 (C) 0
 (D) 10
 (E) 15

PROBLEM SOLVING																								
1	2	3	4	5	6	7	8	9	10	11	12	13	14	15	16	**17**	18	19	20	21	22	23	24	25
			EASY									MEDIUM									HARD			

17. What is the value of $\odot(-(\odot x)) - \odot(\odot x)$ when x is equal to −3?

 (A) −18
 (B) −12
 (C) 0
 (D) 18
 (E) 63

Here's how to crack them

If you are given two function problems that refer to the same definition, the second one will be significantly harder than the first. You should feel free to skip the second one if you are having trouble with functions. Let's look at number 16 first.

If x is negative, we are to square it. In this case, our first term is –5. –5 squared equals 25. If x is positive, multiply it by 2. Our second term is 5 so multiply it times 2 to get 10. We now have 25 – 10 or 15. ETS's answer is E.

Number 17 is a bit messier. Just pull it apart one piece at a time. Remember PEMDAS? Do your parentheses first, from the inside out. In this problem we are told that x equals –3. Fill –3 in for x:

$$\odot(-(\odot -3)) - \odot(\odot -3)$$

In the first term, square –3 to get 9. Get rid of the parentheses and you have –9. Square that and you have 81.

In the second term, square –3 to get 9. Multiply 9 times 2 (since 9 is positive) and you have 18. 81 minus 18 equals 63. ETS's answer is E.

Word Problems

Most word problems can be solved quickly by Plugging In. But there will be a few algebra word problems on your SAT that will be more complicated. You'll still be able to answer them, but you should save them for last.

In solving a word problem that can't be done by Plugging In, you should simply translate the problem into an equation. As we said earlier, equations are a kind of shorthand. You will be able to set up equations easily if you train yourself to notice words that are longhand versions of arithmetic symbols. Here are some words and their equivalent symbols:

WORD	SYMBOL
is	=
of, times, product	×
what (or any unknown value)	any letter (x, k, b)
more, sum	+
less, difference	–
ratio, quotient	÷

Here are two examples:

Words: 14 is 5 more than some number

Equation: $14 = 5 + x$

Words: If one-eighth of a number is 3, what is one-half of the same number?

Equation: $\frac{1}{8} n = 3, \ \frac{1}{2} n = ?$

ALGEBRA SUMMARY

1. Ordinary algebra takes too much time on the SAT. Do it our way instead, which is the last thing ETS expects you to do.

2. When Plugging In on an SAT algebra problem, try plugging in each of the numbers in the answer choices into the problem until you find one that works.

3. Plugging in your own numbers is the technique for multiple-choice problems whose answer choices contain variables. It has three steps:

   1. Pick numbers for the variables in the problem.
   2. Use your numbers to find an answer to the problem.
   3. Plug your numbers from step 1 into the answer choices to see which choice equals the answer you found in step 2.

4. When you plug in, use "good" numbers—ones that are simple to work with and that make the problem easier to manipulate.

5. Plugging In works on problems containing inequalities, but you will have to be careful and follow some different rules. Plugging in one number is often not enough; to find ETS's answer you may have to plug in several numbers.

6. You can also plug in when you have numbers that are too big, too ugly, or too inconvenient to work with.

7. If a problem contains an expression that can be factored, factor it. If it contains an expression that already has been factored, unfactor it.

8. Don't "solve for x" or "solve for y" unless you absolutely have to. (Don't worry; your math teacher won't find out.) Instead, look for direct solutions to SAT problems. ETS never uses problems that *necessarily* require time-consuming computations or endless fiddling with big numbers. There's almost always a trick—if you can spot it.

9. To solve simultaneous equations, simply add or subtract the equations.

10. Learn to recognize SAT function problems. They're the ones with the funny symbols. Solve them like playing "Simon Says"—do what you are told.

11. If you come across a word problem you can't beat by Plugging In, simply translate the problem into an equation and solve it.

13

Geometry

SAT GEOMETRY PROBLEMS: CRACKING THE SYSTEM

About a third of the math problems on your SAT will involve geometry. Fortunately, you won't need much specific knowledge of geometry to solve them. You won't have to prove any theorems and you won't need to know many terms. You'll have to use a few formulas, but they will be printed on the first page of each Math section in your test booklet.

In this chapter we will teach you:

- The fundamental facts you must know to solve SAT geometry problems

- How to find ETS's answers and avoid careless mistakes by guesstimating

- How to find ETS's answers by Plugging In

- The advanced principles that will help you on harder problems

BASIC PRINCIPLES: FUNDAMENTALS OF SAT GEOMETRY

The SAT doesn't test any really difficult geometry, but you will need a thorough knowledge of several fundamental rules. You will use these fundamentals in applying the techniques that we will teach you later in the chapter. You don't need to linger over these rules if you have already mastered them. But be sure you understand them completely before you move on. Some of these rules will be provided in the instructions on your SAT, but you should know them before you go to the test center. Consulting the instructions as you work is a waste of time. (On the other hand, if the Pythagorean theorem suddenly vaporizes from your brain while you are taking the test, don't hesitate to peek back at the instructions.)

We divide SAT geometry into four basic topics:

1. Degrees and angles
2. Triangles
3. Circles
4. Rectangles and squares

DEGREES AND ANGLES

1. A circle contains 360 degrees.

Every circle contains 360 degrees. Each degree is $\frac{1}{360}$ of the total distance around the outside of the circle. It doesn't matter whether the circle is large or small; it still has exactly 360 degrees.

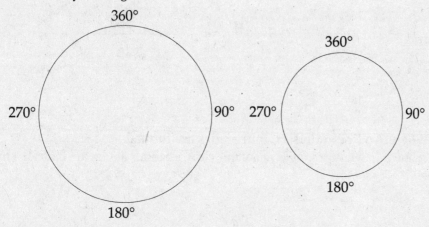

2. When you think about angles, remember circles.

An angle is formed when two line segments extend from a common point. If you think of the point as the center of a circle, the measure of the angle is the number of degrees enclosed by the lines when they pass through the edge of the circle. Once again, the size of the circle doesn't matter; neither does the length of the lines.

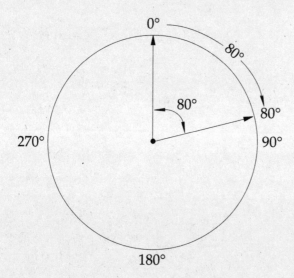

3. A line is a 180-degree angle.

You probably don't think of a line as an angle, but it is one. Think of it as a flat angle. The following drawings should help:

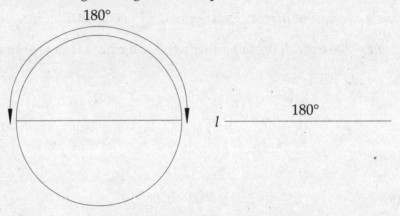

4. When two lines intersect, four angles are formed.

The following diagram should make this clear. The four angles are indicated by letters.

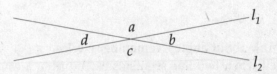

The measures of these four angles add up to 360 degrees. (Remember the circle.)

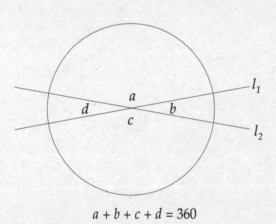

$$a + b + c + d = 360$$

If two lines are perpendicular to each other, each of the four angles formed is 90 degrees. A 90-degree angle is called a right angle.

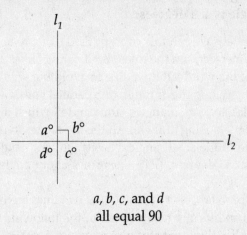

a, b, c, and d
all equal 90

The little box at the intersection of the two lines is the symbol for a right angle. If the lines are not perpendicular to each other, then none of the angles will be right angles.

5. **When two lines intersect, the angles opposite each other will have the same measures.**

Such angles are called vertical angles. In the following diagram, angles a and c are equal; so are angles b and d. The total of all four angles is still 360 degrees.

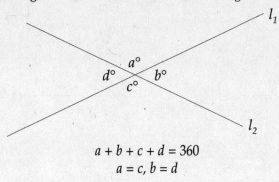

$a + b + c + d = 360$
$a = c, b = d$

It doesn't matter how many lines you intersect through a single point. The total measure of all the angles formed will still be 360 degrees.

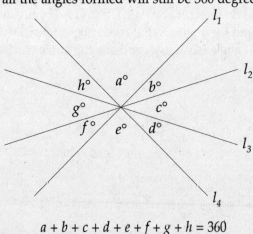

$a + b + c + d + e + f + g + h = 360$
$a = e, b = f, c = g, d = h$

6. **When two parallel lines are cut by a third line, the small angles are equal, the big angles are equal, and the sum of a big angle and a small angle is 180 degrees.**

At The Princeton Review, we call this concept Fred's theorem. Parallel lines are two lines that never intersect, and the rules about parallel lines are usually taught in school with lots of big words. But we like to avoid big words whenever possible. Simply put, when a line cuts through two parallel lines, two kinds of angles are created: big angles and small angles. You can tell which angles are big and which are small just by looking at them. All the big angles look equal, and they are. The same is true of the small angles. Lastly, any big angle plus any small angle always equals 180 degrees. (ETS likes rules about angles that add up to 180 or 360 degrees.)

In any geometry problem, never assume that two lines are parallel unless the question or diagram specifically tells you so. In the following diagram, angle a is a big angle, and it has the same measure as angles c, e, and g, which are also big angles. Angle b is a small angle, and it has the same measure as angles d, f, and h, which are also small angles.

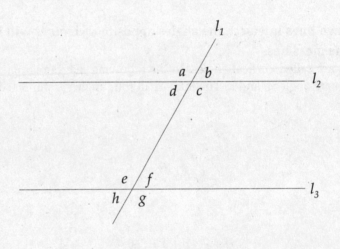

$$a = c = e = g$$
$$b = d = f = h$$

You should be able to see that the degree measures of angles a, b, c, and d add up to 360 degrees. So do those of angles e, f, g, and h. If you have trouble seeing it, draw a circle around the angles. What is the degree measure of a circle? Also, the sum of any small angle (such as d) and any big angle (such as g) is 180°.

TRIANGLES

1. Every triangle contains 180 degrees.

The word *triangle* means "three angles," and every triangle contains three interior angles. The measure of these three angles always adds up to exactly 180 degrees. You don't need to know why this is true or how to prove it. You just need to know it. And we mean *know* it.

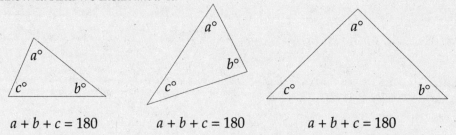

$a + b + c = 180$ $a + b + c = 180$ $a + b + c = 180$

2. An equilateral triangle is one in which all three sides are equal in length.

Because the angles opposite equal sides are also equal, all three angles in an equilateral triangle are equal, too. (Their measures are always 60 degrees each.)

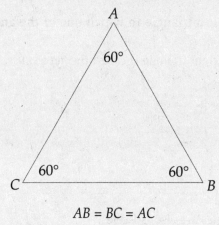

$AB = BC = AC$

Your Friend the Triangle

If ever you are stumped by a geometry problem that deals with a quadrilateral, hexagon, or circle, look for the triangles that you can form by drawing lines through the figure.

3. **An isosceles triangle is one in which two of the sides are equal in length.**

The angles opposite those equal sides are also equal because, as we just mentioned, angles opposite equal sides are also equal.

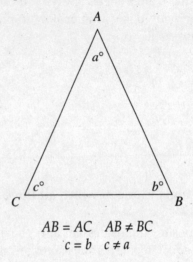

$$AB = AC \quad AB \neq BC$$
$$c = b \quad c \neq a$$

4. **A right triangle is a triangle in which one of the angles is a right angle (90 degrees).**

The longest side of a right triangle is called the *hypotenuse*.

Some right triangles are also isosceles.

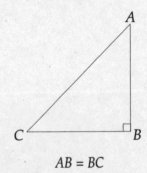

$$AB = BC$$

5. The perimeter of a triangle is the sum of the lengths of its sides.

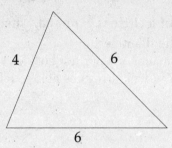

perimeter = 4 + 6 + 6 = 16

6. The area of a triangle is $\frac{1}{2}$ base × height.

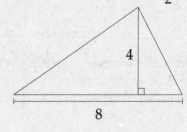

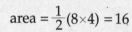

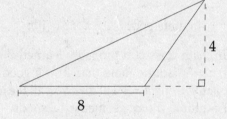

area = $\frac{1}{2}$ (8×4) = 16   area = $\frac{1}{2}$ (8×4) = 16

CIRCLES

Some Formulas

Area = πr^2
Circumfrence = $2\pi r$ or πd
Diameter = $2r$

1. **The circumference of a circle is $2\pi r$ or πd, where r is the radius of the circle and d is the diameter.**

You'll be given this information in your test booklet, so don't stress over memorizing these formulas. You will always be able to refer to your test booklet if you forget them.

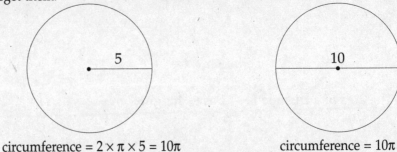

circumference = $2 \times \pi \times 5 = 10\pi$ circumference = 10π

In math class you probably learned that $\pi = 3.14$ (or even 3.14159). On the SAT, $\pi = 3^+$ (a little more than 3) is a good enough approximation. Even with a calculator, using $\pi = 3$ will give you all the information you need to solve difficult SAT multiple-choice geometry questions.

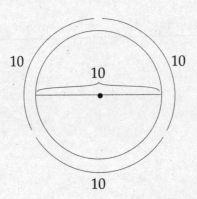

circumference = about 30

2. **The area of a circle is πr^2, where r is the radius of the circle.**

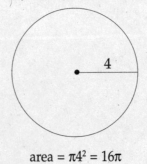

area = $\pi 4^2 = 16\pi$

RECTANGLES AND SQUARES

1. The perimeter of a rectangle is the sum of the lengths of its sides.
Just add them up.

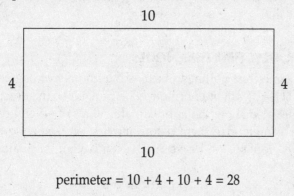

perimeter = 10 + 4 + 10 + 4 = 28

2. The area of a rectangle is length × width.
The area of the preceding rectangle, therefore, is 10 × 4, or 40.

3. A square is a rectangle whose four sides are all equal in length.
The perimeter of a square, therefore, is four times the length of any side. The area is the length of any side squared.

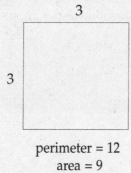

perimeter = 12
area = 9

4. In rectangles and squares all angles are 90° angles.
It can't be a square or a rectangle unless all angles are 90°.

BASIC PRINCIPLES: GUESSTIMATING

On many SAT geometry problems, you will be presented with a drawing in which some information is given and you will be asked to find some of the information that is missing. In most such problems, ETS expects you to apply some formula or perform some calculation, often an algebraic one. But you'll almost always be better off if you look at the drawing and make a rough estimate of ETS's answer (based on the given information) before you try to work it out. We call this *guesstimating*.

Little Boxes

Here's a progression of quadrilaterals from least specific to most specific:

quadrilateral = 4-sided figure
↓
parallelogram = a quadrilateral in which opposite sides are parallel
↓
rectangle = a parallelogram in which all angles = 90°
↓
square = a rectangle in which all sides are equal

Guesstimating is extremely useful on SAT geometry problems. At the very least, it will enable you to avoid careless mistakes by immediately eliminating answers that could not possibly be ETS's answer. In many problems, however, guesstimating will allow you to find ETS's answer without even working out the problem at all.

THE BASIC GUESSTIMATING TOOLS

The basic principles just outlined (such as the number of degrees in a triangle and the fact that $\pi \approx 3$) will be enormously helpful to you in guesstimating on the SAT. You should also know the approximate values of several common square roots. Be sure to memorize them before moving on. Knowing them cold will help you solve problems and save time, even if your calculator has a square root function.

Square Roots

$\sqrt{1} = 1$

$\sqrt{2} \approx 1.4$

$\sqrt{3} \approx 1.7+$

$\sqrt{4} = 2$

You will also find it very helpful if you have a good sense of how large certain common angles are. Study the following examples.

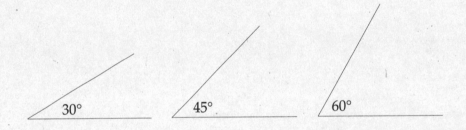

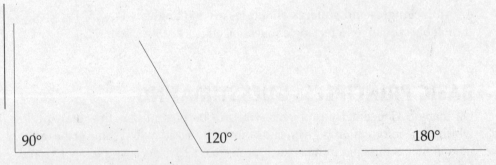

To get a little practice using the material you've memorized to help you guesstimate, do the following drill.

DRILL 1

Guesstimate the following values. Use simple values for $\sqrt{2}$, $\sqrt{3}$, and π (rather than using your calculator) to figure out each value. Answers can be found on page 281.

1. $\sqrt{2} - 1 =$ _____

2. $3\sqrt{\pi} =$ _____

3. $2\sqrt{2} =$ _____

4. $\sqrt{\dfrac{3}{4}} =$ _____

5. $\sqrt{18} =$ _____

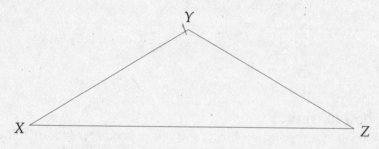

6. In the figure above, given $XY = 16$, estimate all the angles and the lengths of the other sides.

HOW HIGH IS THE CEILING?

If your friend stood next to a wall in your living room and asked you how high the ceiling was, what would you do? Would you get out your trigonometry textbook and try to triangulate using the shadow cast by your pal? Of course not. You'd look at your friend and think something like this: "Dave's about 6 feet tall. The ceiling's a couple of feet higher than he is. It must be about 8 feet high."

Your guesstimation wouldn't be exact, but it would be close. If your mother later claimed that the ceiling in the living room was 15 feet high, you'd be able to tell her with confidence that she was mistaken.

You'll be able to do the same thing on the SAT. Every geometry figure on your test will be drawn exactly to scale unless there is a note in that problem telling you otherwise. That means you can trust the proportions in the drawing. If line segment A has a length of 2 and line segment B is exactly half as long, then the length of line segment B is 1. All such problems are ideal for guesstimating.

The Correct Choice

Remember that the SAT is a multiple-choice test. This means that you don't always have to come up with an answer; you just have to identify the correct one from among the five choices provided.

Look at the following example:

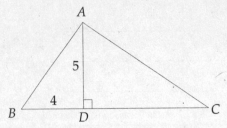

10. If the area of △ABC in the figure above is 30, what is the length of *DC*?

(A) 2
(B) 4
(C) 6
(D) 8
(E) 12

Here's how to crack it

In guesstimation problems like this, it's usually a good idea to start at the edges and work your way in. When an SAT problem has numeric choices, as this one does, they are always given in increasing or decreasing order of size. Choices at either extreme will be the easiest to dispute and hence the easiest to eliminate if they are wrong. Here's what we mean.

Look at the drawing. Line *DC* is obviously a good bit longer than line *BD*. Since *BD* = 4, we know for certain that *DC* has to be greater than 4. That means we can eliminate choices A and B. Just cross them out so you won't waste time thinking about them again. They couldn't possibly be correct.

Now look at *DC* again. Is it 3 times as long as *BD*? No way. That means choice E can be eliminated as well.

We've narrowed it down to choice C or D. Does *DC* look like it's twice as long as *BD*, or like it's one and a half times as long? That's all you have to decide.

(ETS's answer is D. Notice that you found it without having to use the area of the triangle, which was given in the problem.)

Don't Forget to Plug In

You can also plug in the answer choices for this problem using the area formula for a triangle.

Here's another example:

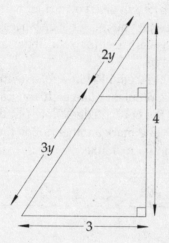

13. In the figure above, what is the value of y?

(A) 1
(B) 2
(C) 3
(D) 4
(E) 5

Here's how to crack it

You can use a number of guesstimating approaches to solve this problem. Here's one of them:

The hypotenuse of the little triangle is $2y$. That means that y equals half the length of the hypotenuse. Is half the length of the small hypotenuse larger or smaller than 3 (the base of the triangle)? Smaller, obviously. Therefore, you can eliminate choices C, D, and E, all of which are too large.

You now know that y has to be either 1 or 2. If y is 2, then the hypotenuse of the small triangle would equal 4, but that's impossible because we just figured out that it must be less than 3. Therefore, ETS's answer must be A.

Another Way

The hypotenuse of this triangle has to be shorter than the sum of the other two sides (this is true of all triangles). So, $5y < 7$. Plug in the answer choices! Only A works.

WHEN YOU CAN'T EYEBALL, MEASURE

Ruler Rule

When making a ruler out of your answer sheet, never mark up the sides. That's where the computer reads your responses, and a stray mark could really foul up your score. Mark the top or bottom, mark lightly, and erase your marks after completing the problem.

Sometimes you won't be able to tell just by looking whether one line is longer than another. In these cases you should actually measure what you need to know. How will you do this? By using the ruler that ETS provides with every answer sheet.

You don't believe that ETS will give you a ruler with your answer sheet? Any piece of paper can be a ruler, if you mark off distances on it. You can use the top or bottom edge of your answer sheet (or your finger or your pencil) to measure distances and solve problems.

Here's how to make a Princeton Review ruler with your answer sheet. Take a look at the first example, problem number 10, on page 228. Take any piece of paper and make a dot on the bottom edge. Now put the dot on point B, lay the edge of the strip along BD, and mark another dot on the edge of the paper beside point D. Here's what it should look like:

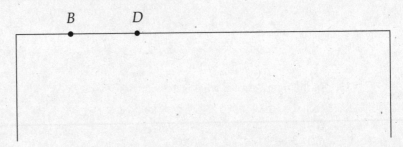

Important Note

You'll have to make a new ruler for each problem on which you need to measure something. ETS figures are drawn to scale (unless they're labeled otherwise), but they aren't all drawn to the *same* scale. A ruler that measures 4 on one diagram won't measure 4 on another.

What's the length of the space between the dots? It's exactly 4, of course—the same as the length of BD in the diagram. You now have a ruler. You can use it to measure the length of DC, which is what the problem asks you for.

You can make your ruler as precise as you need to. By placing the ruler against side AD and noting the difference between its length and the length of BD, you'll be able to mark off your ruler in units of 1.

You can even use your Princeton Review ruler to measure the circumference of a circle or the length of a curved line. Just carefully turn the paper around the curved distance you want to measure, mark off the distance on your ruler with your pencil, and then compare the ruler with some known distance in the problem.

YOU CAN ALSO MEASURE ANGLES

ETS is also kind enough to give you a protractor. Where? On any of the square corners of your answer sheet. The square corner of a sheet of paper is a perfect 90-degree angle, like this:

90°

If you fold the paper on the diagonal, taking care not to leave a crease, you end up with a perfect 45-degree angle, like this:

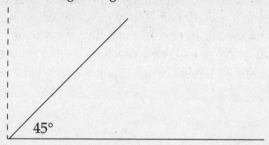

With a tool like this, you'll be able to measure almost any angle with a fair degree of accuracy. Actually, if you practice eyeballing angles, you may never need to consult the corner of your answer sheet. If you spend an hour or so teaching yourself to guesstimate the size of angles just by looking at them, you'll improve your SAT score. In fact, you should be able to answer at least one question on your SAT without doing anything except eyeballing or measuring.

Here's an example:

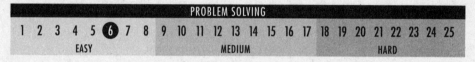

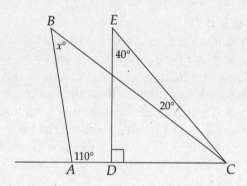

6. In the figure above, what is the value of x?

(A) 15
(B) 20
(C) 30
(D) 40
(E) 50

Here's how to crack it

By using your page-corner protractor you should be able to see that x is a little bit less than 45. (You should also be able to tell this just by eyeballing.) Therefore, you can definitely eliminate answer choices A, B, and E. Your best choice is D. (It is also ETS's answer.)

Take Charge!

Using rulers and protractors will keep you from making careless computational errors on SAT geometry problems. Because measuring the figures enables you to skip the arithmetic, it also enables you to avoid all the traps that ETS has laid for Joe Bloggs.

WHAT IF A DIAGRAM IS NOT DRAWN TO SCALE?

Redraw

Redrawing a figure to exaggerate differences is a great way to crack quant comp problems. See Chapter 14.

Sometimes ETS uses a nonscale drawing because the answer would be obvious even to Joe Bloggs in a scale drawing. In many cases you will simply be able to redraw the diagram in your test booklet and then measure it.

Let's look at an example. Imagine a problem in which you are given a drawing like the one below and asked to determine which is bigger, line segment *AB* or line segment *BC*.

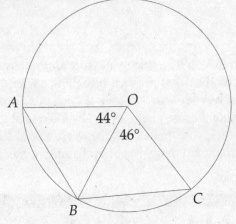

Note: Figure not drawn to scale.

Here's how to crack it

This figure is not drawn to scale, so simply measuring the segments won't help. In addition, ETS has drawn the figure so that the segments seem to be the same length. What should you do? Redraw the figure in your test booklet, exaggerating the difference in the given information. In this case, you are given the measures of two angles. One angle is a little larger than the other, but both seem to be about the same size in the drawing. All you have to do is redraw the figure exaggerating this difference. Since one angle is bigger than the other, you should make it much bigger. Your drawing might look something like this:

Deception

Why would ETS suddenly choose to draw an inaccurate picture? To mislead you, of course! Any figure not drawn to scale is deliberately misleading. Redraw it.

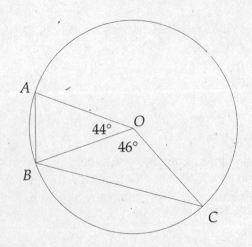

Now you shouldn't have any trouble seeing that line segment *BC* has to be bigger than line segment *AB*. ETS used a nonscale drawing because the answer would have been obvious if the drawing had been to scale.

WHEN YOU CAN'T MEASURE, SKETCH AND GUESSTIMATE

You will sometimes encounter geometry problems that have no diagrams, or that have diagrams containing only partial information. In these cases, you should use the given information to sketch a complete diagram and then use your drawing as a basis for guesstimating. Don't hesitate to fill your test booklet with sketches and scratch work: This is precisely what you are supposed to do. Finding ETS's answer will be much harder, if not impossible, if you don't take full advantage of the information ETS gives you.

Here's an example:

PROBLEM SOLVING

1 2 3 4 5 6 7 8 9 10 11 12 13 14 15 16 17 **18** 19 20 21 22 23 24 25

EASY   MEDIUM   HARD

18. All faces of a cube with a 4-meter edge are covered with striped paper. If the cube is then cut into cubes with 1-meter edges, how many of the 1-meter cubes have striped paper on exactly one face?

   (A) 24
   (B) 36
   (C) 48
   (D) 60
   (E) 72

Here's how to crack it

This problem doesn't have a diagram. It would be much easier to solve if it did. What should you do? Draw a diagram, of course! Just sketch the cube quickly in your test booklet and mark it off into 1-meter cubes as described. Your sketch might look like this:

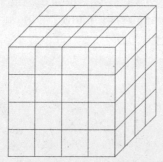

You should be able to see that there are four cubes on each side of the big cube that will have striped paper on only one face (the four center cubes—all the other cubes have at least two exterior sides). Since a cube has six sides, this means that ETS's answer is choice A.

BASIC PRINCIPLES: PLUGGING IN

As you learned in Chapter 11, Plugging In is one of the most powerful techniques for solving SAT algebra problems. It is also very useful on geometry problems. On some problems, you will be able to plug in guesstimated values for missing information and then use the results either to find ETS's answer directly or to eliminate answers that could not possibly be correct.

Here's an example:

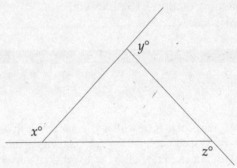

18. In the figure above, what is the value of $x + y + z$?

(A) 90
(B) 180
(C) 270
(D) 360
(E) 450

Here's how to crack it

We don't know the measures of the interior angles of the triangle in the drawing, but we do know that the three interior angles of any triangle add up to 180, and 180 divided by 3 is 60. Now, simply plug in 60 for the value of each interior angle.

This doesn't give you ETS's answer directly; the problem does not ask you for the sum of the interior angles. But Plugging In does enable you to find ETS's answer. Look at the redrawn figure:

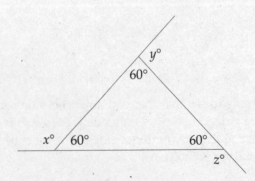

If the marked interior angle is 60, what must x be? Remember that every line is a 180-degree angle. That means that the measure of x must be $180 - 60$, or 120. You can now do the same thing for the other two angles. Using this method you find that x, y, and z each equal 120. That means that $x + y + z = 360$. ETS's answer, therefore, is choice D.

Guesstimating like this won't always give you ETS's answer exactly, but it will usually enable you to eliminate at least three of the four incorrect choices. Other kinds of geometry problems also lend themselves to Plugging In.

Here's another example:

PROBLEM SOLVING

1 2 3 4 5 6 7 8 9 10 11 12 13 14 15 16 17 18 19 20 21 22 23 24 **25**

EASY   MEDIUM   HARD

25. The length of rectangle S is 20 percent longer than the length of square R, and the width of rectangle S is 20 percent shorter than the width of square R. The area of rectangle S is

(A) 20% greater than the area of square R
(B) 4% greater than the area of square R
(C) equal to the area of square R
(D) 4% less than the area of square R
(E) 20% less than the area of square R

Here's how to crack it

This is a hard problem. You should recognize first of all that choices A, C, and E are Joe Bloggs answers and should be eliminated. Even if you don't see this, though, you'll be able to find ETS's answer by sketching and Plugging In.

When Plugging In, always use numbers that are easy to work with. Let's say that the length of square R is 10; that means that the length of rectangle S, which is 20 percent longer, must be 12. You can use 10 again in figuring widths. If the width of square R is 10, then the width of rectangle S, which is 20 percent shorter, must be 8. You should come up with two sketches that look like this:

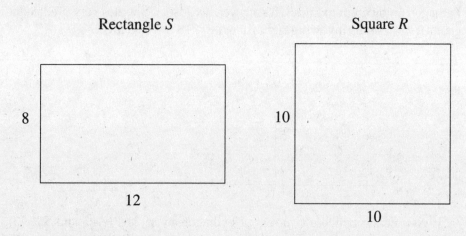

Rectangle S Square R

The area of square R is 100; the area of S is 96. The area of S, which is what the problem asks for, is thus a little bit less than the area of R. In fact, it is 4 percent less. ETS's answer is choice D.

Pythagorean Theorem:

$a^2 + b^2 = c^2$, where c is the hypotenuse of a right triangle. Learn it, love it.

ADVANCED PRINCIPLES: BEYOND THE FUNDAMENTALS

THE PYTHAGOREAN THEOREM

The Pythagorean theorem states that in a right triangle (a triangle with one interior angle that is exactly 90 degrees), the square of the hypotenuse equals the sum of the squares of the other two sides. As we told you earlier, the hypotenuse is the longest side of a right triangle; it's the side opposite the right angle. The square of the hypotenuse is its length squared. Applying the Pythagorean theorem to the following drawing, we find that $c^2 = a^2 + b^2$.

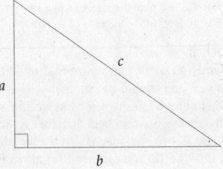

Your Friend the Rectangle

Be on the lookout for problems in which the application of the Pythagorean theorem is not obvious. For example, every rectangle contains two right triangles. That means that if you know the length and width of the rectangle, you also know the length of the diagonal, which is the hypotenuse of both triangles.

If you forget the Pythagorean theorem, you can always look it up in the box at the beginning of the Math section. Very often, however, you won't need to use the Pythagorean theorem to find ETS's answer, because ETS writes very predictable geometry questions involving right triangles. ETS has two favorites:

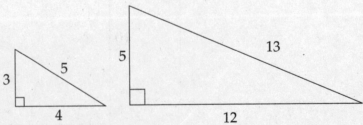

If you memorize these two sets of Pythagorean triplets (3:4:5 and 5:12:13), you'll often be able to find ETS's answer without using the Pythagorean theorem. If ETS gives you a triangle with a side of 3 and a hypotenuse of 5, you know right away that the other side has to be 4. ETS also uses right triangles with sides that are simply multiples of the Pythagorean triplets. For example, ETS likes right triangles with sides of 6, 8, and 10. These sides are simply the sides of a 3:4:5 triangle multiplied by 2.

POLYGONS

Polygons are two-dimensional figures with three or more straight sides. Triangles and rectangles are both polygons. So are figures with five, six, seven, eight, or any greater number of sides. The most important fact to know about polygons is that any one of them can be divided into triangles. This means that you can always determine the sum of the measures of the interior angles of any polygon.

For example, the sum of the interior angles of any four-sided polygon (called a "quadrilateral") is 360 degrees. Why? Because any quadrilateral can be divided into two triangles, and a triangle contains 180 degrees. Look at the following example:

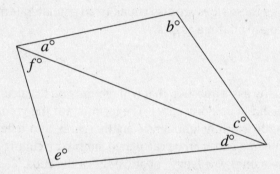

In this polygon, $a + b + c = 180°$; so does $d + e + f$. That means that the sum of the interior angles of the quadrilateral must be 360° $(a + b + c + d + e + f)$.

A *parallelogram* is a quadrilateral whose opposite sides are parallel. In the following parallelogram, side AB is parallel to side DC, and AD is parallel to BC. Because a parallelogram is made of two sets of parallel lines that intersect each other, Fred's theorem applies to it as well: The two big angles are equal, the two small angles are equal, and a big angle plus a small angle equals 180 degrees. In the figure below, big angles A and C are equal, and small angles B and D are equal. Also, since A is a big angle and D is a small angle, $A + D = 180°$.

ANGLE-SIDE RELATIONSHIPS IN TRIANGLES

Another Relationship

It is simply impossible for the third side of a triangle to be longer than the total of the other two sides. Nor can the third side of a triangle be shorter than the difference between the other two sides. Imagine a triangle with sides a, b, and c:

$a - b < c < a + b.$

The longest side of any triangle is opposite the largest interior angle; the shortest side is opposite the smallest angle. In the following triangle, side a is longer than side b, which is longer than side c, because 80 > 60 > 40.

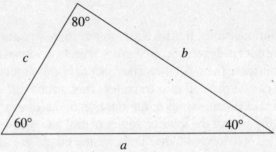

The same rule applies to isosceles and equilateral triangles. An isosceles triangle, remember, is one in which two of the sides are equal in length; therefore, the angles opposite those sides are also equal. In an equilateral triangle, all three sides are equal; so are all three angles.

VOLUME

No Sweat

In the rare case when ETS asks you to find the volume of a figure other than a rectangular solid, the formula will either be provided with the question or will appear in the instructions.

ETS will occasionally ask a question that will require you to calculate the volume of a rectangular solid (a box or a cube). The formula for the volume of a rectangular solid is length width height. Since length, width, and height are equal in a cube, the volume of a cube can be calculated simply by cubing (where do you think they get the name?) the length of any edge of the cube.

Volume = 8 × 4 × 3 = 96

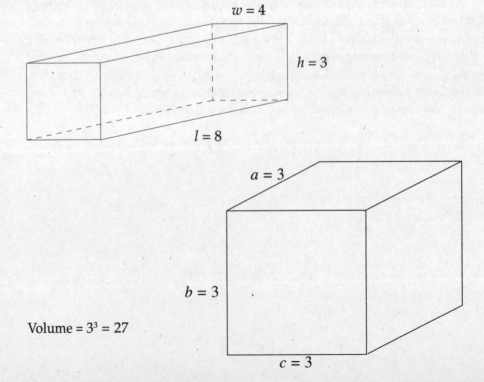

Volume = 3^3 = 27

GRIDS

If you've ever looked for a particular city on a map in an atlas, you're probably familiar with the idea behind grids. You look up Philadelphia in the atlas's index and discover that it is located at D5 on the map of Pennsylvania. On the map itself you find letters of the alphabet running along the top of the page and numbers running down one side. You move your finger straight down from the D at the top of the page until it is at the level of the 5 along the side, and there you are: in Philadelphia.

Grids work the same way. The standard grid is shaped like a cross. The horizontal line is called the *x-axis*; the vertical line is the *y-axis*. The four areas formed by the intersection of the axes are called quadrants. The location of any point can be described with a pair of numbers (*x*, *y*), just the way you would point on a map: (0, 0) are the coordinates of the intersection of the two axes (also called the *origin*); (1, 2) are the coordinates of the point one space to the right and two spaces up; (–1, 5) are the coordinates of the point one space to the left and five spaces up; (–4, –2) are the coordinates of the point four spaces to the left and two spaces down. All these points are located on the following diagram:

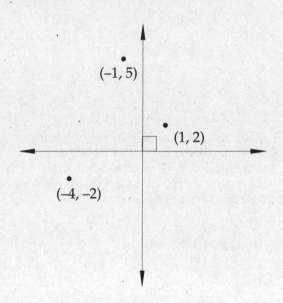

Zones

A grid has four distinct zones, called *quadrants*:

Quadrant I is the upper right-hand corner, where *x* and *y* are both positive.

Quadrant II is the upper left-hand corner, where *x* is negative and *y* is positive.

Quadrant III is the lower left-hand corner, where *x* and *y* are both negative.

Quadrant IV is the lower right-hand corner, where *x* is positive and *y* is negative.

Sometimes, pinning down a coordinate's quadrant is all you need to do to find ETS's answer.

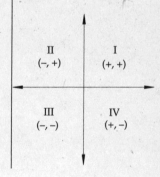

ADVANCED SKETCHING AND GUESSTIMATION

Some extremely difficult SAT geometry problems can be solved quickly and easily through sketching and guesstimation, but you will have to stay on your toes if you want to crack them. The way to do this is always to ask yourself three questions:

1. What information have I been given?

2. What information have I been asked to find?

3. What is the relationship between these two pieces of information?

Here's an example. It was the second-hardest problem on the SAT section in which it appeared:

1 2 3 4 5 6 7 8	9 10 11 12 13 14 15 16 17	18 19 20 21 22 23 24 25
EASY	MEDIUM	HARD

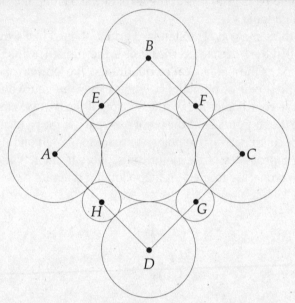

24. Four circles of radius 2 with centers A, B, C, and D are arranged symmetrically around another circle of radius 2, and four smaller equal circles with centers E, F, G, and H each touch three of the larger circles as shown in the figure above. What is the radius of one of the small circles?

(A) $\sqrt{2} - 2$

(B) $\sqrt{2} - 1$

(C) $2\sqrt{2} - 2$

(D) 1

(E) $3\sqrt{2} - 1$

Here's how to crack it

First answer the three questions we mentioned before:

1. I have been given the radius of 5 large identical circles.

2. I have been asked for the radius of a small circle.

3. Both are distances, so both can be measured.

What at first appeared to be an extremely difficult geometry problem turns out to be a simple matter of measurement. Mark off the distance of one large-circle radius along the edge of your answer sheet. This equals 2. Now align your ruler on a small-circle radius. The small-circle radius is smaller, obviously. How much smaller?

You can probably see that it is a little bit less than half as long. That means that the answer to the question is "a little bit less than 1."

Now turn to the answer choices and solve them one at a time:

(A) $\sqrt{2}$, as you know, equals 1.4, so $\sqrt{2} - 2 = -0.6$. A distance cannot be negative. Eliminate.

(B) $\sqrt{2} - 1 = 0.4$ This is less than 1, but a lot less. Not a great possibility.

(C) $2\sqrt{2} - 2 = 0.8$. This is a little bit less than 1. An excellent possibility.

(D) $1 = 1$. One can't be less than 1. Eliminate.

(E) $3\sqrt{2} - 1 = 3.2$. Eliminate.

ETS's answer is C.

GEOMETRY SUMMARY

1. Degrees and angles:

    a. A circle contains 360 degrees.

    b. When you think about angles, remember circles.

    c. A line is a 180-degree angle.

    d. When two lines intersect, four angles are formed; the sum of their measures is 360 degrees.

    e. Fred's theorem: When two parallel lines are cut by a third line, the small angles are equal, the big angles are equal, and the sum of a big angle and a small angle is 180 degrees.

2. Triangles:

    a. Every triangle contains 180 degrees.

    b. An equilateral triangle is one in which all three sides are equal in length, and all three angles are equal in measure (60 degrees).

    c. An isosceles triangle is one in which two of the sides are equal in length, and the two angles opposite the equal sides are equal in measure.

    d. A right triangle is one in which one of the angles is a right angle (90 degrees).

e. The perimeter of a triangle is the sum of the lengths of its sides.

f. The area of a triangle is: $\frac{1}{2}bh$.

3. Circles:

a. The circumference of a circle is $2\pi r$ or d, where r is the radius of the circle and d is the diameter.

b. The area of a circle is πr^2, where r is the radius of the circle.

4. Rectangles and squares:

a. The perimeter of a rectangle is the sum of the lengths of its sides.

b. The area of a rectangle is length × width.

c. A square is a rectangle whose four sides are all equal in length.

5. When you encounter a geometry problem on the SAT, guesstimate the answer before trying to work it out.

6. You must never skip an SAT problem that has a drawing with it.

7. You must know the following values:

$$\pi \approx 3$$
$$\sqrt{2} \approx 1.4$$
$$\sqrt{3} \approx 1.7$$

8. You must also be familiar with the size of certain common angles.

9. Most SAT geometry diagrams are drawn to scale. Use your eyes before you use your pencil. Try to eliminate impossible answers.

10. When your eyes aren't enough, use the edge and corner of your answer sheet as a ruler and a protractor.

11. When a diagram is not drawn to scale, redraw it.

12. When no diagram is provided, make your own; when a provided diagram is incomplete, complete it.

13. When information is missing from a diagram, guesstimate and plug in.

14. The Pythagorean theorem states that in a right triangle, the square of the hypotenuse equals the sum of the squares of the other two sides. Remember ETS's favorite Pythagorean triplets (3:4:5 and 5:12:13).

15. Any polygon can be divided into triangles.

16. The longest side of any triangle is opposite the largest interior angle; the shortest side is opposite the smallest angle.

17. The volume of a rectangular solid is length × width × height. The formulas to compute the volume of other three-dimensional figures are supplied in the instructions at the front of every Math section.

18. You must know how to locate points on a grid.

19. Some extremely difficult SAT geometry problems can be solved quickly and easily through sketching and guesstimation, but you will have to stay on your toes. The way to do this is always to ask yourself three questions:

    a. What information have I been given?

    b. What information have I been asked to find?

    c. What is the relationship between these two pieces of information?

14

Quantitative Comparisons: Cracking the System

WHAT IS A QUANTITATIVE COMPARISON?

One scored Math section on your SAT will contain a group of fifteen quantitative comparison questions (or quant comps, as we call them). These quant comps will be arranged in an order of difficulty, just like in the other Math sections. The first five will be easy, the next five medium, and the last five difficult.

Let's take a look at the instructions for the quant comps as they appear on the SAT.

Directions for Quantitative Comparison Questions

Questions 1–15 each consist of two quantities in boxes, one in Column A and one in Column B. You are to compare the two quantities and on the answer sheet fill in oval

A if the quantity in Column A is greater;
B if the quantity in Column B is greater;
C if the two quantities are equal;
D if the relationship cannot be determined from the information given.

AN E RESPONSE WILL NOT BE SCORED.

Notes:

1. In some questions, information is given about one or both of the quantities to be compared. In such cases, the given information is centered above the two columns and is not boxed.
2. In a given question, a symbol that appears in both columns represents the same thing in Column A as it does in Column B.
3. Letters such as x, n, and k stand for real numbers.

EXAMPLES

	Column A	Column B	Answers
E1.	5^2	20	●ⒷⒸⒹⒺ

150° $x°$

E2.	x	30	ⒶⒷ●ⒹⒺ

r and s are integers.

E3.	$r + 1$	$s - 1$	ⒶⒷⒸ●Ⓔ

Do Not Mark E

There are only four answer choices (A, B, C, and D) on quant comp problems, but your SAT answer sheet has five bubbles (A, B, C, D, and E). If you mark circle E on a quant comp, your answer will be omitted. Check your answer sheet after finishing quant comps. If you marked E, chances are you meant to mark D. Change your answer sheet accordingly.

Make sure that you know these instructions cold before you take the SAT. If you have to consult them each time you answer a question, you'll waste time and rob yourself of points. In every quant comp question, ETS will give you quantities in two columns, A and B. Unlike the regular multiple-choice questions, quant comps have only four answer choices: A, B, C, and D. Here's what each answer choice means:

- Choose A if the quantity in Column A is *always* greater.

- Choose B if the quantity in Column B is *always* greater.

- Choose C if the quantities in Column A and Column B are *always* equal.

- Choose D if you can't figure out the relationship between the two quantities from the information given.

The meaning of each choice is best illustrated with some simple examples.

Let's start with a simple quant comp example:

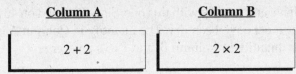

Column A | Column B
2 + 2 | 2 × 2

Your task is to determine the relationship between the quantity in Column A and the quantity in Column B. The quantity in Column A is 4; so is the quantity in Column B. Will this *always* be true? Yes, 2 + 2 will always equal 4, and so will 2 × 2. Therefore, the correct answer is C, "the two quantities are equal."

Suppose we rewrite the problem as follows:

3 + 2 | 2 × 2

The quantity in Column A now equals 5, while the quantity in Column B still equals 4. Because 3 + 2 will always equal 5, and 5 will always be greater than 4, the correct answer now is A, "the quantity in Column A is greater."

Let's rewrite the problem one more time:

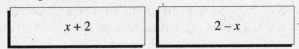

$x + 2$ | $2 - x$

What's the answer now? Suppose that x equals 5. In that case, the quantity in Column A would be greater than the quantity in Column B. But x can be any number; suppose it's 0. In that case, the two quantities would be equal. Now suppose that x equals –2. In that case the quantity in Column B would be greater than the quantity in Column A.

In other words, depending on which numbers we plug in for x, we can make choice A, B, or C seem to be the correct answer. That means that none of these answers is always correct. ETS's answer has to be D, "the relationship cannot be determined from the information given."

THE INFORMATION GIVEN

Many quant comps contain given information that you are supposed to use in solving the problem. This information is placed between the two columns. Here's an example:

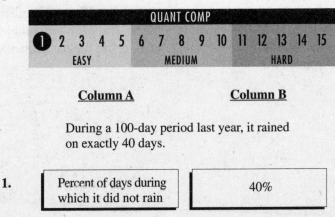

Column A | Column B

During a 100-day period last year, it rained on exactly 40 days.

1. Percent of days during which it did not rain | 40%

Here's how to crack it

You shouldn't have any trouble with this one. Since it rained on 40 percent of the days, 60 percent must have been dry. The quantity in Column A is thus always greater than the quantity in Column B, and ETS's answer is A.

QUANT COMPS ARE QUICK BUT TRICKY

Most students are able to answer quant comps very quickly. Answering quant comps usually takes much less time than answering regular math questions or grid-ins. Because of this, many students breathe a sigh of relief when they come to the quant comp section.

Don't be deceived. Quant comps go quickly because certain answers tend to seem correct immediately. Because of this, Joe Bloggs loves quant comps. When he looks at a question, he doesn't have to think very long before an "obvious" answer choice jumps off the page.

BAD NEWS FOR JOE, GOOD NEWS FOR YOU

Since certain answer choices on quant comps always seem correct to Joe Bloggs, he quickly finds himself in the same predicament as on the rest of the SAT:

1. On easy questions the answers that seem right to him really are right, so he earns points.

2. On medium questions his hunches are sometimes right and sometimes wrong, so he just about breaks even.

3. On difficult questions the answers that seem right to him are always wrong, so he loses points.

This is unlucky for Joe, but very lucky for you. Quant comps are the easiest math questions to crack because the Joe Bloggs answers are easy to spot—if you know what to look for and if you are careful. You can use POE, the Process of Elimination, to eliminate obviously incorrect choices, improve your guessing odds, and zero in on ETS's answer.

MATHEMATICAL CONTENT

In terms of mathematical content, most quant comps will seem familiar to you. You'll find arithmetic problems, algebra problems, and geometry problems. You will be able to solve most of these problems by using the techniques we have already taught you.

SOLVING QUANT COMPS: BASIC PRINCIPLES

Quant comps are a unique problem type, and there are a number of special rules and techniques that apply only to them.

Even on quant comps that can be solved simply by using techniques you already know, there are still some unique features that you need to be familiar with. For instance, some regular techniques must be modified slightly for quant comps. We'll start with some basic principles and then move on to some more advanced ones.

NUMBERS ONLY

If a quant comp problem contains nothing but numbers, choice D cannot be ETS's answer.

In a quant comp that has no variables, it will always be possible to obtain a definite solution. For example, the quantity 2 + 2 can only have one value: 4. The quantity 2 + x, on the other hand, can have an infinite number of values, depending on what you plug in for x.

Here's an example:

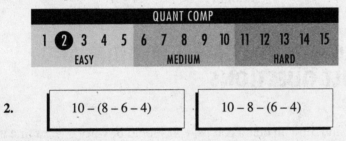

| QUANT COMP |
| 1 **2** 3 4 5 6 7 8 9 10 11 12 13 14 15 |
| EASY MEDIUM HARD |

2. | $10 - (8 - 6 - 4)$ | $10 - 8 - (6 - 4)$ |

Here's how to crack it

This problem contains nothing but numbers. Therefore, it must have a solution, and choice D can be eliminated.

(ETS's answer is A. Because you know you should perform any operations enclosed in parentheses first, you can see that the quantity in Column A equals 12, while the quantity in Column B equals 0.)

EQUATIONS

In the same way that you add or subtract on both sides of an equation, you can add or subtract on both sides of a quant comp. (Just don't multiply or divide on both sides.)

Here's an example:

| QUANT COMP |
| **1** 2 3 4 5 6 7 8 9 10 11 12 13 14 15 |
| EASY MEDIUM HARD |

1. | $\dfrac{1}{4} + \dfrac{1}{2} + \dfrac{1}{13}$ | $\dfrac{1}{13} + \dfrac{1}{2} + \dfrac{1}{3}$ |

Guessing

Even on quant comps, Joe Bloggs gets the hard ones wrong. And because there are only four answer choices, eliminating the Joe Bloggs answer immediately narrows your choices to three. Guess away!

Numbers Only

When you see a quant comp that contains only numbers, eliminate choice D. This tilts the odds in your favor, of course, which means that even if you can't get any further, you should guess from among the remaining choices.

Here's how to crack it

Before doing anything else, you should notice that this quant comp contains nothing but numbers, so choice D cannot possibly be ETS's answer.

Your next impulse may be to find a common denominator for all those fractions. Don't you dare! You can solve this problem in a second by eliminating common terms from both sides.

The quantities in Column A and Column B both include $\frac{1}{2}$ and $\frac{1}{13}$. That means you can subtract both fractions from both sides. Doing so leaves you with the following:

$$\frac{1}{4} \qquad \qquad \frac{1}{3}$$

It should be obvious to you now that ETS's answer has to be B, because $\frac{1}{3}$ is bigger than $\frac{1}{4}$. (Don't make the common careless error of thinking that $\frac{1}{4}$ is bigger than $\frac{1}{3}$ because 4 is bigger than 3!)

SOLVING QUANT COMPS: MEDIUM AND DIFFICULT QUESTIONS

Beware!

On medium and difficult quant comps, you should be wary of your first impulse. Joe Bloggs' first impulse begins to let him down after the easy questions. By the time he reaches the difficult questions, his first impulse is invariably leading him to incorrect choices.

What does this mean for you? It means that on medium and difficult questions, be extremely suspicious of choices that *seem* right. For example, if you're looking at a number 14 quant comp (a hard question) and Column A *looks* bigger than Column B, then A cannot possibly be the answer. Joe Bloggs picks A because it *looks* right to him. But if Joe Bloggs could answer a hard question correctly just by looking at it, it wouldn't be hard, would it? Never choose an answer to a medium or hard quant comp question just because it *looks* right.

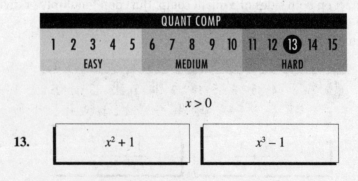

Here's how to crack it

It is easy to think of a value for x that would make the quantity in Column B greater than the quantity in Column A. How about 4? You know that $4^3 - 1$ equals 63, and $4^2 + 1$ equals 17. Because 63 is greater than 17, the correct answer could be B.

But would Column B always have to be greater than Column A? This is what you have to find out. (Before you do, notice that you have already eliminated choices A and C as possibilities: C is out because if one quantity is even sometimes greater than the other, the two quantities cannot always be equal; A is out because if Column B is even sometimes greater than Column A, then Column A cannot always be greater than Column B.)

The easiest number greater than 0 to plug in is 1. Doing so produces a value of 2 for Column A and a value of 0 for Column B. In other words, when you plug in 1, the value in Column A is greater—just the opposite of what happened when you plugged in 4. Since you have now found a case in which Column A could be greater than Column B, you can also eliminate choice B as a possibility. The only choice left is D—ETS's answer.

Maybe Joe Bloggs would pick A because the plus 1 makes Column A look bigger than Column B with its minus 1. On the other hand, maybe Joe would pick B because x^3 looks bigger than x^2. In either case, Joe is wrong. Plugging in two different numbers will help you avoid picking Joe's answers.

PLUGGING IN

When you plug in on quant comps, remember the numbers with special properties: negatives, fractions, 0, and 1.

In ordinary algebra problems on the SAT, you don't have to be very careful about which numbers you plug in. Since you're only looking for numbers that make the equations work, you can just pick numbers that are easy to work with.

Quant comps, though, are a little different. On these questions you are looking for answers that *always* work. A single exception, therefore, is enough to make an answer choice wrong. The key to finding ETS's answer on hard questions is being certain that you've taken into account all possible exceptions. This is why Joe Bloggs has trouble on medium and difficult quant comps.

This is a hard fact for many students to keep in mind. When Plugging In on quant comps, they are attracted naturally to the numbers we use most often: positive whole numbers. But there are many other numbers, and ETS loves to write quant comp problems that depend on the special qualities of these numbers. In fact, many difficult quant comps are difficult only because these numbers must be considered in finding a solution, and Joe Bloggs forgets to consider them.

Because this is true, you should always ask yourself the following question on quant comp plug-ins:

Would my answer be different if I plugged in a negative number, a fraction, 0, or 1?

Always

Before you choose A, B, or C on quant comps, ask yourself: "Is this always the case?" If not, mark D.

Weird Numbers

- negative numbers
- fractions
- 0
- 1

To find out whether you can get more than one result for a quant comp question, try plugging in these special numbers after you've plugged in an easy, positive integer that Joe would think of. In fact, to be sure you've found ETS's answer, you should *always* plug in at least twice.

Here's an example:

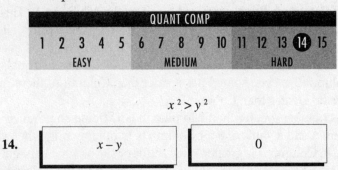

$$x^2 > y^2$$

14.

| $x - y$ | 0 |

Here's how to crack it

When Joe Bloggs solves this problem, he plugs in easy positive integers—say, 3 for x and 2 for y. Because $3 - 2 = 1$, and 1 is greater than 0, he selects A as his answer. What happens? He loses points.

This is a number 14—a very hard question. If finding the answer were as easy as plugging in 3 and 2, Joe Bloggs would get this question right and it would be in the easy third. There must be something Joe has forgotten.

Indeed there is. Joe has forgotten the special cases. If you want to find ETS's answer, you're going to have to remember these special cases.

First, try plugging in negative numbers instead of positive ones: –3 for x and –2 for y. $(-3)^2$ is 9; $(-2)^2$ is 4. Because 9 is greater than 4, you've fulfilled the requirement in the given information. (Important! You *must* plug in numbers that conform to the given information.)

Now look at Column A. What is $x - y$ now? It is –1. Is –1 greater than 0? No, it's less than 0.

Before plugging in negatives, you had already proved that ETS's answer couldn't be B or C. (Do you see why?) Now you've also proved that it can't be A. This means that it must be D.

Drill 1

Do the following quant comp plug-ins. As with most of the examples in this book, the question number indicates the level of difficulty of the problem. Remember, the harder the question, the more work you will need to do. Answers can be found on page 281.

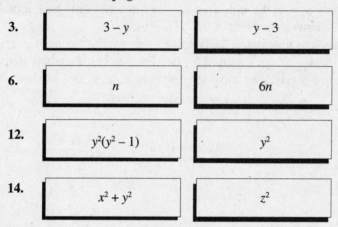

3. $\quad\boxed{3 - y}\qquad\boxed{y - 3}$

6. $\quad\boxed{n}\qquad\boxed{6n}$

12. $\quad\boxed{y^2(y^2 - 1)}\qquad\boxed{y^2}$

14. $\quad\boxed{x^2 + y^2}\qquad\boxed{z^2}$

Sketching and Guesstimating

You must also be very careful about sketching and guesstimating on medium and difficult quant comp geometry problems.

Ordinary guesstimating can occasionally be misleading on these problems for the same reason that ordinary Plugging In can be misleading on quant comp algebra. Because a single exception is enough to disqualify an answer choice, you must be certain that you have considered all the possibilities. Approximate answers are usually good enough on ordinary geometry problems, but they are very often wrong on geometry quant comps.

Here's an example:

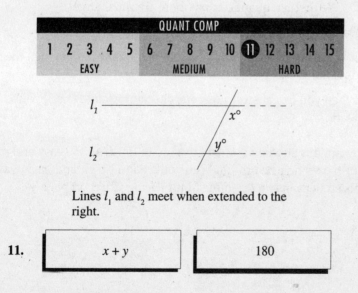

Lines l_1 and l_2 meet when extended to the right.

11. $\quad\boxed{x + y}\qquad\boxed{180}$

Here's how to crack it

By simply eyeballing and guesstimating (or using your Princeton Review protractor) you would decide that $x + y$ equals about 180 degrees. Is ETS's answer therefore C?

No! You know from the information given that the two lines are not parallel, even though they look as though they are. So $x + y$ can only be a little bit less than 180. ETS's answer, therefore, must be B. (It is.)

On problems like this, it will help you to redraw the figure in exaggerated form. The information given says that the two lines meet somewhere to the right. Redraw the figure so that they meet immediately, something like this:

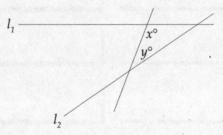

Now you can clearly see why ETS's answer is B. Since x and y are measures of two angles in a triangle, $x + y$ must be less than 180.

PACING AND DIFFICULTY

Quant comps and grid-ins will be in the same section of your SAT. (We'll tell you all you need to know about grid-ins in the next chapter.) Because the hardest quant comps are much harder than the easiest grid-ins, you should not waste time on the hardest quant comps until you have answered the easiest grid-ins. Here's what you should do:

1. Do the first ten quant comps (there are fifteen total).

2. Do the first few grid-ins (there are ten total).

3. If you have time left, do the remaining quant comps, then the remaining grid-ins.

4. When you can answer no more, check or double-check your work.

By following this strategy you will be sure to finish all the easy and medium questions in the section before time runs out. For a quick and easy way to remember this strategy, just refer to the Math Pacing Chart on page 30.

Ugly Pictures

Never trust a picture on medium or difficult quant comps. It may look drawn to scale, but it isn't necessarily perfect. Draw your own version of it to see if you can make it look different.

Order, Order!

Always note the order of difficulty on quant comps. On medium and difficult questions, you should be extremely suspicious of answer choices that seem obvious, or that have misleading diagrams, or that you arrive at quickly without much thought (unless you arrive at them by using our techniques!).

QUANTITATIVE COMPARISONS SUMMARY

1. Quant comps, unlike all other SAT questions, offer only four answer choices: A, B, C, and D. These four choices are always the same. On every quant comp, you will be given two quantities or values and asked to select:

   Choice A if the quantity in Column A is *always* greater.

   Choice B if the quantity in Column B is *always* greater.

   Choice C if the two quantities are *always* equal.

   Choice D if it cannot be determined whether one quantity will always be greater than or equal to the other.

2. Since the answer choices are not given, write out A, B, C, D next to each problem to help you employ POE.

3. Many quant comps provide information that you are supposed to use in solving the problem. This information is placed between the two columns.

4. Quant comps are ideal for POE because the Joe Bloggs attractors are easy to spot—if you know what to look for and if you are careful.

5. Many quant comps can be solved using the techniques that you have already learned.

6. Many quant comps can be solved without any sort of computation. Compare, don't calculate!

7. If a problem contains nothing but numbers, choice D cannot be ETS's answer.

8. You can add and subtract from both Column A and Column B as if they were two sides of an equation.

9. On medium and difficult quant comps, be suspicious of choices that *seem* right.

10. When you plug in on quant comps, remember the numbers with special properties: negatives, fractions, 0, and 1.

11. You must also be very careful about sketching and guesstimating on medium and difficult quant comp geometry problems.

15

Grid-Ins:
Cracking the System

WHAT IS A GRID-IN?

One of the Math sections on your SAT will contain a group of ten problems without multiple-choice answers. ETS calls these problems Student-Produced Responses. We call them *grid-ins*, because you have to mark your answers on a grid printed on your answer sheet. The grid looks like this:

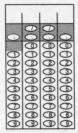

Despite their format, grid-ins are just like other math questions on the SAT, and many of the techniques that you've learned so far still apply. You can still use Plugging In and other great techniques, such as the Ratio Box and the Average Pie. You can still use the order of difficulty and your knowledge of Joe Bloggs to avoid making obvious mistakes on hard questions. Your calculator will still help you out on many problems as well. So grid-ins are nothing to be scared of. In fact, many grid-in questions are simply regular SAT multiple-choice math problems with the answer choices lopped off. The only difference is that you have to arrive at your answer from scratch, rather than choose it from among five possibilities.

You will need to be extra careful when answering grid-in questions, however, because the grid format increases the likelihood of careless errors. It is vitally important that you understand how the grid-in format works before you take the test. In particular, you'll need to memorize ETS's rules about which kinds of answers count, and which don't. The instructions may look complicated, but we've boiled them down to a few rules for you to memorize and practice.

Order of Difficulty: Grid-Ins

16–18 Easy
19–22 Medium
23–25 Difficult

Take a look at the grid again. Because of the way it's arranged, ETS can only use certain types of problems for grid-ins. For example, you'll never see variables (letters) in your answer (although there can be variables in the question), because the grid can only accommodate numbers. This is good for you, because no matter how good you are at algebra, you're better at arithmetic.

Also, this means that your calculator will be useful on several questions. As always, be careful to set up the problem on paper before you carefully punch the numbers into your calculator. Since you have to write in the answer yourself on the grid, you have to be more careful than ever to avoid careless mistakes.

Grid-ins are scored somewhat differently than multiple-choice questions on the SAT. On multiple-choice questions, you lose a fraction of a raw score point for every incorrect answer. This deducted fraction is commonly referred to as a "guessing penalty." We explained earlier in the book why there is really no guessing penalty on SAT multiple-choice questions. For different reasons, there is no guessing penalty for grid-ins, either. Why? Because *nothing* is deducted for an incorrect answer on a grid-in. An incorrect answer on one of these questions is no worse for your score than a question left blank. And, by the same token, a blank is just as costly as an error. Therefore, you *should be very aggressive in answering these questions*. Don't leave a question blank just because you're worried that the answer you've found may not be correct. ETS's scoring computers treat incorrect answers and blanks exactly the same. If you have arrived at an answer, you have a shot at earning points, and if you have a shot at earning points, you should take it.

That doesn't mean that you should guess blindly. Your chance of helping your score with a blind guess on a grid-in is very, very small. You would be better off spending your time either working on problems that you know you can answer or checking your work on problems you have already finished.

THE INSTRUCTIONS

Here are the instructions for grid-in questions as they will appear on your SAT:

Directions for Student-Produced Response Questions

Each of the remaining 10 questions (16–25) requires you to solve the problem and enter your answer by marking the ovals in the special grid, as shown in the examples below.

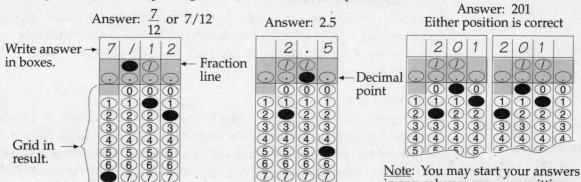

- Mark no more than one oval in any column.

- Because the answer sheet will be machine-scored, **you will receive credit only if the ovals are filled in correctly.**

- Although not required, it is suggested that you write your answer in the boxes at the top of the columns to help you fill in the ovals accurately.

- Some problems may have more than one correct answer. In such cases, grid only one answer.

- No question has a negative answer.

- **Mixed numbers** such as $2\frac{1}{2}$ must be gridded as 2.5 or 5/2. (If ⟨2 1 / 2⟩ is gridded, it will be interpreted as $\frac{21}{2}$, not $2\frac{1}{2}$.)

- **Decimal Accuracy:** If you obtain a decimal answer, **enter the most accurate value the grid will accommodate.** For example, if you obtain an answer such as 0.6666 . . . , you should record the result as .666 or .667. **Less accurate values such as .66 or .67 are not acceptable.**

Acceptable ways to grid $\frac{2}{3}$ = .6666 . . .

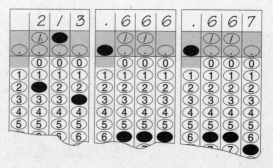

WHAT THE INSTRUCTIONS MEAN

Of all the instructions on the SAT, these are the most important to understand thoroughly before you take the test. Pity the unprepared student who takes the SAT cold and spends ten minutes of potential point-scoring time reading and puzzling over ETS's confusing instructions. We've translated these unnecessarily complicated instructions into a few important rules. Make sure you know them all well.

Fill in the boxes

Watch Out

Negatives, π, and % cannot be gridded in!

Always write your answer in the boxes at the top of the grid before you darken the ovals below. Your written answers won't affect the scoring of your test; if you write the correct answer in the boxes and grid in the wrong ovals, you won't get credit for your answer (and you won't be able to appeal to ETS). However, writing in the answers first makes you less likely to make an error when you grid in, and it also makes it easier to check your work.

Fill in the ovals correctly

As we just pointed out, you receive no credit for writing in the answer at the top of the grid. ETS's computer only cares whether the ovals are filled in correctly. For every number you write into the grid, make sure that you fill in the corresponding oval.

Stay to the left

Keep Left

No matter how many digits in your answer, always start gridding in the left-most column. That way, you'll avoid omitting digits and losing points.

Although you'll receive credit no matter where you put your answer on the grid, you should always begin writing your answer in the far left column of the grid. This ensures that you will have enough space for longer answers when necessary. You'll also cut down on careless errors if you always grid in your answers the same way.

FRACTIONS OR DECIMALS: YOUR CHOICE

You can grid in an answer in either fraction or decimal form. For example, if your answer to a question is $\frac{1}{2}$, you can either grid in $\frac{1}{2}$ or .5. It doesn't matter to ETS, because $\frac{1}{2}$ equals .5; the computer will credit either form of the answer. That means you actually have a choice. If you like fractions, grid in your answers in fraction form. If you like decimals, you can grid in the decimal. If you have a fraction that doesn't fit in the grid, you can simply convert it to a decimal on your calculator and grid in the decimal.

Here's the bottom line: When gridding in fractions or decimals, use whichever form is easier and least likely to cause careless mistakes.

DECIMAL PLACES AND ROUNDING

When you have a decimal answer of a value less than 1, such as .45 or .678, many teachers ask you to write a zero before the decimal point (for example, 0.45 or 0.678).

On grid-in questions, however, ETS doesn't want you to worry about the zero. In fact, there is no 0 in the first column of the grid. If your answer is a decimal less than 1, just write the decimal point in the first column of the grid and then continue from there.

You should also notice that if you put the decimal point in the first column of the grid, you only have three places left to write in numbers. But what if your decimal is longer than three places, such as .87689? In these cases, ETS will give you credit if you round off the decimal so that it fits in the grid. But you'll *also* get credit, however, if you just enter as much of the decimal as will fit.

For example, if you had to grid in .87689, you could just write .876 (which is all that will fit) and then stop. Remember, you only need to grid in whatever is necessary to receive credit for your answer. Don't bother with extra unnecessary steps. You don't have to round off decimals, so don't bother.

If you have a long or repeating decimal, however, be sure to fill up all the spaces in the grid. If your decimal is .666666, you *must* grid in .666. Just gridding in .6 or .66 is not good enough.

REDUCING FRACTIONS

If you decide to grid in a fraction, ETS doesn't care if you reduce the fraction or not. For example, if your answer to a problem is $\frac{4}{6}$, ETS will give you credit if you grid in $\frac{4}{6}$ or reduce it to $\frac{2}{3}$. So if you have to grid in a fraction, and the fraction fits in the grid, don't bother reducing it. Why give yourself more work (and another chance to make a careless error)?

The only time you might have to reduce a fraction is if it doesn't fit in the grid. If your answer to a question is $\frac{15}{25}$, it won't fit in the grid. You have two options: Either reduce the fraction to $\frac{3}{5}$ and grid that in, or use your calculator to convert the fraction to .6. Choose whichever process makes you the most comfortable.

MIXED NUMBERS

ETS's scoring machine does not recognize mixed numbers. If you try to grid in $2\frac{1}{2}$ by writing "2 1/2," the computer will read this number as $\frac{21}{2}$. You have to convert mixed numbers to fractions or decimals before you grid them in. To grid in $2\frac{1}{2}$, either convert it to $\frac{5}{2}$ or its decimal equivalent, which is 2.5. If you have to convert a mixed number in order to grid it in, be very careful not to change its value accidentally.

Lop

Why do extra work for ETS? After all, they won't give you extra points. If your decimal doesn't fit in the grid, lop off the extra digits and grid in what does fit.

Relax

If your answer is a fraction and it fits in the grid (fraction bar included), don't reduce it. Why bother? ETS won't give you an extra point. However, if your fraction doesn't fit, reduce it or turn it into a decimal on your calculator.

Don't Mix

Never grid in a mixed number. Change it into a top-heavy fraction or its decimal equivalent.

DON'T WORRY

The vast majority of grid-in answers will not be difficult to enter in the grid. ETS won't try to trick you by purposely writing questions that are confusing to grid in. Just pay attention to these guidelines and watch out for careless errors.

GRIDDING IN: A TEST DRIVE

To get a feel for this format, let's work through two examples. As you will see, grid-in problems are just regular SAT math problems.

GRID-INS									
16	**17**	18	19	20	21	22	23	24	25
EASY				MEDIUM			HARD		

17. If $a + 2 = 6$ and $b + 3 = 21$, what is the value of $\frac{b}{a}$?

Here's how to crack it

You need to solve the first equation for a and the second equation for b. Start with the first equation, and solve for a. By subtracting 2 from both sides of the equation, you should see that $a = 4$.

Now move to the second equation, and solve for b. By subtracting 3 from both sides of the second equation, you should see that $b = 18$.

The question asked you to find the value of $\frac{b}{a}$. That's easy. The value of b is 18, and the value of a is 4. Therefore, the value of $\frac{b}{a}$ is $\frac{18}{4}$.

That's an ugly-looking fraction. How in the world do you grid it in? Ask yourself: "Does $\frac{18}{4}$ fit?" Yes! Grid in $\frac{18}{4}$. Your math teacher wouldn't like it, but ETS's computer will. You shouldn't waste time reducing $\frac{18}{4}$ to a prettier fraction or converting it to a decimal. Spend that time on another problem instead. The fewer steps you take, the less likely you will be to make a careless mistake.

Here's another example. This one is quite a bit harder.

Take It Your Way

Quant comps and grid-ins appear in the same section of the SAT. Do the first ten quant comps, then the first few grid-ins, then the last five quant comps, then the remaining grid-ins. If you follow that pacing strategy, you won't miss any easy points. If you run out of steam on grid-ins and still have time, go back and work on the hardest quant comps.

Use Joe Bloggs and POE to eliminate incorrect choices and then guess.

GRID-INS

16	17	18	19	20	21	22	**23**	24	25
EASY				MEDIUM			HARD		

23. Forty percent of the members of the sixth-grade class wore white socks. Twenty percent wore black socks. If twenty-five percent of the remaining students wore gray socks, what percent of the sixth-grade class wore socks that were not white, black, or gray? (Disregard the % when gridding your answer.)

Here's how to crack it

The problem doesn't tell you how many students are in the class, so you can plug in any number you like. This is a percentage problem, so the easiest number to plug in is 100. Forty percent of 100 is 40; that means 40 students wore white socks. Twenty percent of 100 is 20. That means that 20 students wore black socks.

Your next piece of information says that 25 percent of the remaining students wore gray socks. How many students remain? Forty, because 60 students wore either white or black socks, and $100 - 60 = 40$. Therefore, 25 percent of these 40—10 students—wore gray socks.

How many students are left? Thirty. Therefore, the percentage of students not wearing white, black, or gray socks is 30 out of 100, or 30 percent. Grid it in, and remember to forget about the percent sign:

ORDER OF DIFFICULTY

Like all other questions on the Math SAT, grid-in problems are arranged in order of increasing difficulty. In each group of ten, the first third is easy, the second third is medium, and the final third is difficult. As always, the order of difficulty will be your guide to how much faith you can place in your hunches.

Guessing is highly unlikely to help you on grid-in questions. For that reason, you must not waste time on questions that are too hard for you to solve. Only students shooting for 700 or above should consider attempting all ten grid-in questions.

Guessing on hard grid-ins is unlikely to get you anywhere, while intelligent guessing on hard quant comps may earn you unexpected points.

Keep in mind, of course, that many of the math techniques that you've learned are still very effective on grid-in questions. Plugging In worked very well on question number 23 on the previous page.

Here's another difficult grid-in question that you can answer effectively by using a technique you've learned before:

GRID-INS		
16 17 18	19 20 21 22 23	24 25
EASY	MEDIUM	HARD

24. Grow-Up potting soil is made from only peat moss and compost in a ratio of 3 pounds of peat moss to 5 pounds of compost. If a bag of Grow-Up potting soil contains 12 pounds of potting soil, how many pounds of peat moss does it contain?

Here's how to crack it

To solve this problem, set up a Ratio Box (the Ratio Box is explained in detail on pages 173–176).

	Peat Moss	Compost	Whole
Ratio (parts)	3	5	8
Multiply By			
Actual Number			12 (lbs)

What do you multiply by 8 to get 12? If you don't know, divide 12 by 8 on your calculator. The answer is 1.5. Write 1.5 in each of the boxes on the Multiply By row of your ratio box, like this:

	Peat Moss	Compost	Whole
Ratio (parts)	3	5	8
Multiply By	1.5	1.5	1.5
Actual Number			12 (lbs)

The problem asks you how many pounds of peat moss are in a bag. To find out, multiply the numbers in the Peat Moss column. That is, multiply 3 × 1.5, and you get 4.5. ETS's answer is 4.5.

	Peat Moss	Compost	Whole
Ratio (parts)	3	5	8
Multiply By	1.5	1.5	1.5
Actual Number	4.5 (lbs)	7.5 (lbs)	12 (lbs)

Grid it in like this:

JOE BLOGGS AND GRID-IN QUESTIONS

On grid-in questions, you obviously can't use the Joe Bloggs principle to eliminate tempting but incorrect answer choices, since there aren't any choices to choose from. But you can—and must—use your knowledge of Joe Bloggs to double-check your work and keep yourself from making careless mistakes or falling into traps.

The basic idea still holds true: Easy questions have easy answers, and hard questions have hard answers. On hard questions, you must be extremely suspicious of answers that come to you easily or through simple calculations.

Unfortunately, your knowledge of Joe Bloggs alone will never lead you all the way to ETS's answers, the way it sometimes does on multiple-choice questions. In order to earn points on grid-in questions, you're going to have to find the real answers, and you're going to have to be extremely careful when you enter your answers on your answer sheet. But Joe Bloggs may help you find the correct path

Say No to Joe

If it takes you four seconds to answer any grid-in question from 23 to 25, you've probably goofed. Check your work. Hard questions have hard answers.

to ETS's answer. On a hard problem, you may be torn between two different approaches, one easy and one hard. Which should you pursue? The harder one. Joe will take the easy path and, as always on hard questions, it will lead him to the wrong answer.

More Than One

Some grid-in questions have several possible correct answers. None is more correct than any other, so grid in the first one you find and move on.

RANGE OF ANSWERS

Some grid-in problems will have many possible correct answers. It won't matter which correct answer you choose, as long as the one you choose really is correct.

Here's an example:

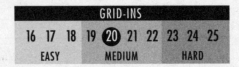

20. What is one possible value of x such that

$$\frac{1}{4} < x < \frac{1}{3}?$$

Here's how to crack it

Joe Bloggs has trouble imagining how anything could squeeze between $\frac{1}{4}$ and $\frac{1}{3}$, but you know there are lots and lots of numbers in there. Any one of them will satisfy ETS.

The numbers in this problem are both fractions, but your answer doesn't have to be. The easiest approach is to forget about math-class solutions and head straight for your calculator (or your mental calculator). Convert $\frac{1}{4}$ to a decimal by dividing 1 by 4, which gives you .25. Now convert $\frac{1}{3}$ to a decimal by dividing 1 by 3, which gives you .333. All you need to answer the question is any number that falls between those two decimals. How about .26? Or .3? Or .331? Your answer merely has to be bigger than .25 and smaller than .333. Pick one, grid it in, and move on.

DRILL 1

Don't lose points to carelessness. Practice by gridding the following numbers in the sample grids below. Answers can be found on page 282.

1. 1.5

2. 5.60

3. 81

4. $\frac{1}{3}$

5. $\frac{8}{11}$

6. 0.33333

7. $4\frac{2}{5}$

8. x, such that $6 < x < 7$

Ungriddable

Some things just won't go in the grid:

- variables
- pi (π)
- negative numbers
- square roots

If they show up in your answer, you've goofed. Redo the problem, or skip it.

GRID-INS SUMMARY

1. One of the Math sections on your SAT will contain a group of ten problems without multiple-choice answers. ETS calls these problems student-produced responses. We call them *grid-ins*, because you have to mark your answers on a grid printed on your answer sheet.

2. Despite their format, grid-ins are really just like other math questions on the SAT, and many of the same techniques that you have learned still apply.

3. The grid format increases the likelihood of careless errors. Know the instructions and check your work carefully.

4. There is no guessing penalty for grid-ins, so you should always grid in your answer, even if you're not sure that it's correct. Blind guessing, however, is very unlikely to improve your score.

5. Always write the numbers in the boxes at the top of grid before you (carefully) fill in the corresponding ovals.

6. Grid in your answer as far to the left as possible.

7. If the answer to a grid-in question contains a fraction or a decimal, you can grid in the answer in either form. When gridding in fractions or decimals, use whichever form is easier and least likely to cause careless mistakes.

8. There's no need to round decimals, even though it is permitted.

9. If you have a long or repeating decimal, be sure to fill up all the spaces in the grid.

10. If a fraction fits in the grid, you don't have to reduce the fraction before gridding it in.

11. ETS's scoring machine does not recognize mixed numbers. Convert mixed numbers to fractions or decimals before gridding them in.

12. The vast majority of grid-in answers will not be difficult to enter in the grid.

13. Some grid-in questions will have more than one correct answer. It doesn't matter which answer you grid in, as long as it's one of the possible answers.

14. Like all other questions on the Math SAT, grid-in problems are arranged in order of increasing difficulty. In each group of ten, the first third is easy, the second third is medium, and the final third is difficult.

15. On grid-ins, as on all other SAT questions, easy questions have easy answers, and hard questions have hard answers. On hard grid-ins, you must be extremely suspicious of answers that come to you easily or through simple calculations.

16. And remember, negatives, π, and % cannot be gridded in.

PART IV

Taking the SAT

THE SAT IS A WEEK AWAY. WHAT SHOULD YOU DO?

First of all, you should practice the techniques we've taught you on real SATs. If you don't own any real SATs, go buy a copy of *10 Real SATs* at your local bookstore. This book is published by the College Board and contains ten actual SATs that have been administered over the last few years. You can also use the full-length practice test in *Taking the SAT I: Reasoning Test*. You can get a free copy of this booklet from either your guidance counselor or ETS.

Get a copy of a full-length SAT from your guidance counselor.

Take and score the three practice tests at the back of this book, as well as the practice tests on our website (see Online Tools at the beginning of the book for information on how to log on). The more full-length SATs you practice, the better.

If you have more than a week, you can order any publications directly from the College Board. Here's the toll-free phone number: (800)-537-3160.

To order *10 Real SATs* by phone, you'll need a credit card. If you prefer, *Taking the SAT I: Reasoning Test* also has a form you can use to order *10 Real SATs* by mail. Here's the address:

College Board SAT Program
Attn: Order Services
Department E59
PO Box 6212
Princeton, NJ 08541-6212

If you want to order by mail, but you don't have a copy of the form, be sure to call the toll-free number to find out how to order.

If you're online, here's how to contact the College Board using the Web: www.collegeboard.com

MORE REAL SATS

If you want to get your hands on more real SATs, in addition to the tests published in *10 Real SATs*, you can obtain copies of the most recent tests that have been released through ETS's Question and Answer Service. You can order copies of these tests directly from the College Board. Here's the address and phone number of the College Board's headquarters:

The College Board
45 Columbus Avenue
New York, NY 10023
(212)-713-8000

Getting Psyched

The SAT is a big deal, but you don't want to let it scare you. Sometimes students get so nervous about doing well that they freeze up on the test and murder their scores. The best thing to do is to think of the SAT as a game. It's a game you can get good at, and beating the test can be fun. When you go into the test center, just think about all those poor slobs who don't know how to eyeball geometry diagrams.

The best way to keep from getting nervous is to build confidence in yourself and in your ability to remember and use our techniques. When you take practice tests, time yourself exactly as you will be timed on the real SAT. Develop a sense of how long 30 minutes is and how much time you can afford to spend on cracking difficult problems. If you know ahead of time what to expect, you won't be as nervous.

Of course, taking a real SAT is much more nerve-racking than taking a practice test. Prepare yourself ahead of time for the fact that 30 minutes will seem to go by a lot faster on a real SAT than it did on your practice tests.

It's all right to be nervous; the point of being prepared is to keep from panicking.

Should You Sleep for 36 Hours?

Some guidance counselors tell their students to get a lot of sleep the night before the SAT. This probably isn't a good idea. If you aren't used to sleeping twelve hours a night, doing so will just make you groggy for the test. The same goes for going out and drinking a lot of beer: People with hangovers are not good test takers.

A much better idea is to get up early each morning for the entire week before the test and do your homework before school. This will get your brain accustomed to functioning at that hour of the morning. You want to be sharp at test time.

Before you go to sleep the night before the test, spend an hour or so reviewing the Hit Parade of vocabulary words listed in the next section. This will make the list fresh in your mind in the morning. You might also practice estimating some angles and looking for direct solutions on a few real SAT math problems. You don't want to exhaust yourself, but it will help to brush up.

FURTHERMORE

Here are a few pointers for test day and beyond:

1. Eat a good breakfast before the test—your brain needs energy.

2. Work out a few SAT problems on the morning of the test to help dust off any cobwebs in your head and get you started thinking analytically.

3. Arrive at the test center early.

#4: Bring ID

A driver's license, a passport, or a school photo ID.

4. You must bring acceptable identification to the test center on the day of the test. According to ETS, acceptable identification must include: "(1) a photograph or a written physical description, (2) your name, and (3) your signature." Acceptable forms of ID include: your driver's license, a school ID with a photo, or a valid passport. If you don't have an official piece of ID with your signature and your photo, you can have your school make an ID for you. Just have your guidance counselor type up a physical description of you on school stationery, which both you and your guidance counselor then have to sign. Complete instructions for making such an ID are contained in ETS's *Registration Bulletin*. According to ETS, the following forms of ID are *unacceptable*: a birth certificate, a credit card, or a Social Security card.

   Make sure you read all of the rules in the *Registration Bulletin*, because conflicts with ETS are just not worth the headache. Your only concern on the day of the test should be beating the SAT. To avoid hassles and unnecessary stress, make *absolutely certain* that you take your admissions ticket and your ID with you on the day of the test.

#5: Bring Equipment

#5 Pencils (at least 12), a watch, a calculator.

5. The only outside materials you are allowed to use on the test are No. 2 pencils (take a dozen, all sharp), a wristwatch (an absolute necessity), and a calculator. Digital watches are best, but if it has a beeper, make sure you turn it off. Proctors will confiscate pocket dictionaries, word lists, portable computers, and the like. Proctors have occasionally also confiscated stopwatches and travel clocks. Technically, you should be permitted to use these, but you can never tell with some proctors. Take a watch and avoid the hassles.

#6: Bring Fruit or Other Energy Food

Grapes or oranges can give you an energy boost if you need it.

6. Some proctors allow students to bring food into the test room; others don't. Take some fruit (especially bananas) with you and see what happens. If you don't flaunt them, they probably won't be confiscated. Save them until your break and eat outside the test room, as discreetly as possible.

7. You are going to be sitting in the same place for more than three hours, so make sure your desk isn't broken or unusually uncomfortable. If you are left-handed, ask for a left-handed desk. (The center may not have one, but it won't hurt to ask.) If the sun is in your eyes, ask to move. If the room is too dark, ask someone to turn on the lights. Don't hesitate to speak up. Some proctors just don't know what they're doing.

#7: Your Desk...

should be comfortable and suited to your needs.

8. Make sure your booklet is complete. Booklets sometimes contain printing errors that make some pages impossible to read. One year more than ten thousand students had to retake the SAT because of a printing error in their booklets. Also, check your answer sheet to make sure it isn't flawed.

#8: Your Test...

should be printed legibly in your booklet.

9. You should get a 5-minute break after the first hour of the test. Ask for it if your proctor doesn't give it to you. You should be allowed to go to the bathroom at this time. You should also be allowed to take a 1-minute break at your desk at the end of the second hour. The breaks are a very good idea. Be sure to get up, move around, and clear your head.

#9: Breaks

You're entitled to two—one after Section 2 and another after Section 4.

10. ETS allows you to cancel your SAT scores. Unfortunately, you can't cancel only your Math or your Verbal score—it's all or nothing. You can cancel scores at the test center by asking your proctor for a "Request to Cancel Test Scores" form. You must complete this form and hand it in before you leave the test center. If you decide to cancel your scores after you leave, you can do so by contacting ETS by cable, overnight delivery, or E-mail (sat@ets.org). The address is in the *Registration Bulletin*, or you can call ETS at (609)-771-7600 to find out where to send your score cancellation request.

#10: Cancel with Care

Don't cancel your scores just because you feel icky. Think it over carefully, and NEVER cancel on the same day as the test. Don't cancel your scores unless you passed out at Section 2 and came to on Section 7!

We recommend that you not cancel your scores unless you know you made so many errors or left out so many questions that your score will be unacceptably low. Don't cancel your scores on test day just because you have a bad feeling—even the best test takers feel a little shaky after the SAT. You've got five days to think it over.

11. Make sure you darken all your responses before the test is over. At the same time, erase any extraneous marks on the answer sheet. **A stray mark in the margin of your answer sheet can result in correct responses being marked as wrong.**

#11: Bubble with Care

A stray mark can hurt your score.

12. Don't assume that your test was scored correctly. Send away for ETS's Question and Answer Service whenever it is offered. It costs money, but it's worth it. You'll get back copies of your answer sheet, a test booklet, and an answer key. Check your answers against the key and complain if you think your test has been scored incorrectly. (Don't throw away the test booklet you

#12: Keep Tabs on ETS

Get a copy of your SAT, your answer sheet, and an answer key. Make sure your score is accurate.

receive from the Question and Answer Service. If you're planning to take the SAT again, save it for practice. If you're not, give it to your guidance counselor or school library.)

#13: We're Here for You

The Princeton Review is proud to advise students who have been mistreated by ETS.

13. You deserve to take your SAT under good conditions. If you feel that your test was not administered properly (the high school band was practicing outside the window, your proctor hovered over your shoulder during the test), call us immediately at (800)-333-0369 and we'll tell you what you can do about it.

PART V

Answer Key to Drills

CHAPTER 6

DRILLS 1 AND 2

1. ETS's answer is C.
   The trigger word *although* indicates a change is coming. "Although . . . the book was brilliant. . . ." The clue in the sentence is *so few copies were sold.* Therefore, the author got little *monetary* reward. The best match for *monetary* is answer choice C, financial.

6. ETS's answer is B.
   Do this question one blank at a time. The trigger word *sadly* tells you that the tone of the sentence is negative. The clue is *over-development.* If there is a lot of over-development, what will happen to the rain forests? They will *disappear.* This word fits perfectly in the second blank. Cross off answers A and C since the second word in each does not mean *disappear.* Answer choice D is weak, but keep it for now.

   In the first blank, we need a word that means something like *hurt.* Look at the remaining answer choices. The first words in both D and E do not mean *hurt,* so cross them off. The answer is B.

9. ETS's answer is B.
   Do this question one blank at a time. In the first blank, the trigger word *and* tells you the blank means the same as *drab.* Go through the answer choices and cross off anything that doesn't mean *drab* or *boring.* If you don't know the meaning of a word, you cannot cross it off. Get rid of E (and C and D if you know what they mean).

   The trigger word *but* tells us the second blank means the opposite of *drab* and *boring.* Look for a second word that means *excitement* or *energy* from among the remaining choices. Redundancy does not mean *excitement,* so get rid of A. Even if you didn't know the first words in C and D, neither of their second words means *excitement.* The answer is B.

DRILL 3

8. B

9. A
   Good second guesses: E, B.

CHAPTER 7

DRILL 1

An ARCHITECT designs a BUILDING.
A WARDEN is in charge of a PRISON.
IGNORANCE means without EDUCATION.
AQUATIC means pertaining to WATER.
LETTERS comprise the ALPHABET.

DRILL 2

4. *Solar* means pertaining to the *sun*.

5. *Glue* is a substance that is *sticky*.

6. No relationship.

7. *Grateful* means giving *thanks*.

8. A *morsel* is a small *quantity*.

9. *Equine* means pertaining to *horses*.

10. No relationship.

11. To *preach* is to engage in *exhortation*.

12. No relationship.

13. An *alias* is a false *identity*.

DRILL 3

15. D

16. A

CHAPTER 8

DRILL 1

1. C
2. D
3. E
4. B
5. A
6. C
7. B
8. D
9. D
10. C
11. B
12. E
13. C

CHAPTER 11

DRILL 1

1. 109
2. 38
3. –3
4. 10
5. 15

DRILL 2

1. $6(57+13) = 6 \times 70 = 420$
2. $51(48 + 50 + 52) = 51(150) = 7{,}650$
3. $ab + ac - ad$
4. $x(y - z)$
5. $c(ab + xy)$

DRILL 3

1. $\dfrac{25}{3}$
2. $\dfrac{17}{7}$
3. $\dfrac{49}{9}$
4. $\dfrac{5}{2}$
5. $\dfrac{20}{3}$

DRILL 4

1. 3

2. $\dfrac{31}{5}$

3. $-1\dfrac{4}{15}$ or $-\dfrac{19}{15}$

4. $\dfrac{1}{15}$

5. $\dfrac{6}{7}$

6. $\dfrac{2}{25}$

7. $\dfrac{4}{9}$

DRILL 5

1. 0.3741

2. 1,457.7

3. 186

4. −2.89

DRILL 6

	Fraction	Decimal	Percent
1.	$\dfrac{1}{2}$	0.5	50
2.	$\dfrac{3}{1}$	3.0	300
3.	$\dfrac{1}{200}$	0.005	0.5
4.	$\dfrac{1}{3}$	$0.333\overline{3}$	$33\dfrac{1}{3}$

CHAPTER 13

Drill 1

1. 0.4
2. a little bit more than 5
3. 2.8
4. a little bit less than 1
5. a little bit more than 4
6. x = about 30°

    y = about 120°

    z = about 30°

    YZ is about 16

    XZ is about 30 (a little less than 32!)

(None of these angle measurements is exact, but remember, you don't have to be exact when you guesstimate. Even a very rough guesstimation will enable you to eliminate one or two answer choices.)

CHAPTER 14

Drill 1

3. D
6. D
12. D
14. D

CHAPTER 15

DRILL 1

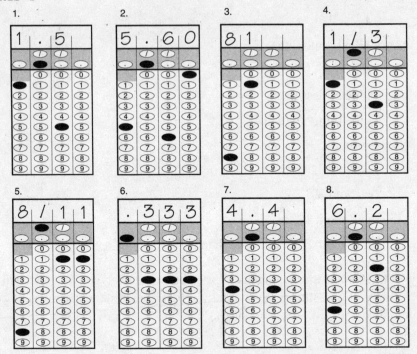

PART **VI**

The Princeton Review
SAT Practice Tests
and Explanations

The best way to learn our techniques for cracking the SAT is to practice them. The following practice tests will give you a chance to do that. The additional practice tests on our website (see Online Tools at the beginning of the book for information on how to log on) will provide even more practice.

These practice tests were designed to be as much like a real SAT as possible. The tests in this book contain three Verbal sections, three Math sections, and an experimental section (two of the sections last for 15 minutes). Our online tests are identical but do not have an experimental section. Our questions test the same concepts that are tested on real SATs.

Since one of the sections on the tests in this book is experimental, none of the questions in it counts toward your final score. The actual SAT will have an experimental section—Verbal or Math—that ETS now euphemistically terms an "equating section."

When you take a practice test, you should try to take it under conditions that are as much like real testing conditions as possible. Take it in a room where you won't be disturbed, and have someone else time you. (It's too easy if you time yourself.) You can give yourself a brief break halfway through, but don't stop for longer than five minutes or so. To put yourself in a proper frame of mind, you might take it on a weekend morning. One more thing: Don't use scrap paper; you will not have any when you take the real SAT.

After taking our test, you'll have a very good idea of what taking the real SAT will be like. In fact, we've found that students' scores on The Princeton Review's practice tests correspond very closely to the scores they earn on real SATs.

The answers to the questions on the tests in this book and a scoring guide can be found beginning on page 331. The answer sheets are in the back of the book.

If you have any questions about the practice test, the SAT, ETS, or The Princeton Review, give us a call, toll-free, at 1-800-2Review.

The following sample tests were written by the authors of this book and are not actual SATs. The directions and format were used by permission of the Educational Testing Service. This permission does not constitute review or endorsement by the Educational Testing Service or the College Board of this publication as a whole or of any sample questions or testing information it may contain.

Keep Working

It is difficult for most people to tell if a section is experimental, so you should treat all of the sections as real sections.

16

Practice Test 1

Time—30 Minutes
25 Questions

In this section, solve each problem using any available space on the page for scratchwork. Then decide which is the best of the choices given and fill in the corresponding oval on the answer sheet.

Notes:

1. The use of a calculator is permitted. All numbers used are real numbers.

2. Figures that accompany problems in this test are intended to provide information useful in solving the problems. They are drawn as accurately as possible EXCEPT when it is stated in a specific problem that the figure is not drawn to scale. All figures lie in a plane unless otherwise indicated.

Reference Information

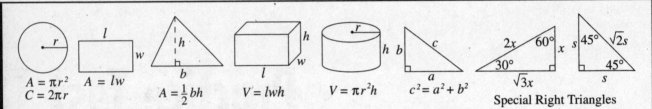

$A = \pi r^2$
$C = 2\pi r$

$A = lw$

$A = \frac{1}{2}bh$

$V = lwh$

$V = \pi r^2 h$

$c^2 = a^2 + b^2$

Special Right Triangles

The number of degrees of arc in a circle is 360.
The measure in degrees of a straight angle is 180.
The sum of the measures in degrees of the angles of a triangle is 180.

1. If $9b = 81$, then $3 \times 3b =$

    (A)   9
    (B)   27
    (C)   81
    (D) 243
    (E) 729

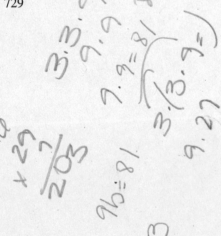

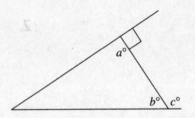

2. In the figure above, what is the sum of $a + b + c$?

    (A) 180
    (B) 240
    (C) 270
    (D) 360
    (E) It cannot be determined from the information given.

GO ON TO THE NEXT PAGE

3. $\dfrac{0.5 + 0.5 + 0.5 + 0.5}{4} =$

(A) 0.05
(B) 0.125
(C) 0.5
(D) 1
(E) 2.0

4. Steve ran a 12-mile race at an average speed of
    8 miles per hour. If Adam ran the same race at
    an average speed of 6 miles per hour, how many
    minutes longer than Steve did Adam take to
    complete the race?

(A) 9
(B) 12
(C) 16
(D) 24
(E) 30

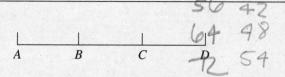

Note: Figure not drawn to scale.

5. If $AB > CD$, which of the following must be true?

   I. $AB > BC$
   II. $AC > BD$
   III. $AC > CD$

(A) I only
(B) II only
(C) III only
(D) II and III only
(E) I, II, and III

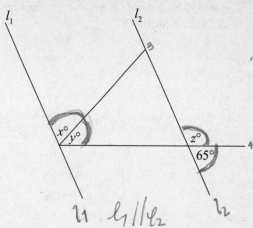

6. In the figure above, $\ell_1 \parallel \ell_2$. What is the value of $x + y$?

(A) 65
(B) 85
(C) 105
(D) 115
(E) It cannot be determined from the information
     given.

7. $\dfrac{4^2}{2^3} + \dfrac{2^3}{4^2} =$

(A) $\dfrac{5}{2}$

(B) 2

(C) 1

(D) $\dfrac{1}{2}$

(E) $\dfrac{1}{4}$

GO ON TO THE NEXT PAGE

8. If 8 and 12 each divide *K* without a remainder, what is the value of *K*?

    (A) 16
    (B) 24
    (C) 48
    (D) 96
    (E) It cannot be determined from the information given.

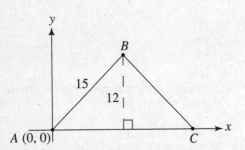

9. In the figure above, side *AB* of triangle *ABC* contains which of the following points?

    (A) (3, 2)
    (B) (3, 5)
    (C) (4, 6)
    (D) (4, 10)
    (E) (6, 8)

10. What is the diameter of a circle with circumference 5?

    (A) $\dfrac{5}{\pi}$

    (B) $\dfrac{10}{\pi}$

    (C) 5

    (D) 5π

    (E) 10π

11. Carol subscribed to four publications that cost $12.90, $16.00, $18.00, and $21.90 per year, respectively. If she made an initial down payment of one-half of the total amount, and paid the rest in 4 equal monthly payments, how much was each of the 4 monthly payments?

    (A) $8.60
    (B) $9.20
    (C) $9.45
    (D) $17.20
    (E) $34.40

GO ON TO THE NEXT PAGE

MERCHANDISE SALES		
Type	Amount of Sales	Percent of Total Sales
Shoes	$12,000	15%
Coats	$20,000	25%
Shirts	$x	40%
Pants	$y	20%

12. According to the table above, what were the sales, in dollars, of shirts and pants combined?

(A) $32,000
(B) $48,000
(C) $60,000
(D) $68,000
(E) $80,000

13. For all integers $n \neq 1$, let $<n> = \dfrac{n+1}{n-1}$. Which of the following has the greatest value?

(A) $<0>$
(B) $<2>$
(C) $<3>$
(D) $<4>$
(E) $<5>$

14. If the product of $(1 + 2)$, $(2 + 3)$, and $(3 + 4)$ is equal to one-half the sum of 20 and x, what is the value of x?

(A) 10
(B) 85
(C) 105
(D) 190
(E) 1,210

15. If $\dfrac{2+x}{5+x} = \dfrac{2}{5} + \dfrac{2}{5}$, what is the value of x?

(A) $\dfrac{2}{5}$

(B) 1

(C) 2

(D) 5

(E) 10

GO ON TO THE NEXT PAGE

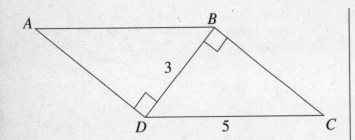

16. In parallelogram *ABCD* above, *BD* = 3 and *CD* = 5. What is the area of *ABCD*?
(A) 12
(B) 15
(C) 18
(D) 20
(E) It cannot be determined from the information given.

17. A survey of Town X found a mean of 3.2 persons per household and a mean of 1.2 televisions per household. If 48,000 people live in Town X, how many televisions are in Town X?

(A) 15,000
(B) 16,000
(C) 18,000
(D) 40,000
(E) 57,600

18. How many numbers from 1 to 200 inclusive are equal to the cube of an integer?

(A) One
(B) Two
(C) Three
(D) Four
(E) Five

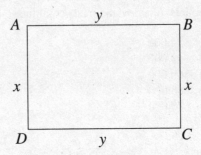

Note: Figure not drawn to scale.

19. If the perimeter of rectangle *ABCD* is equal to *p*, and $x = \dfrac{2}{3}y$, what is the value of *y* in terms of *p*?

(A) $\dfrac{p}{10}$

(B) $\dfrac{3p}{10}$

(C) $\dfrac{p}{3}$

(D) $\dfrac{2p}{5}$

(E) $\dfrac{3p}{5}$

GO ON TO THE NEXT PAGE

20. A basketball team had a ratio of wins to losses of 3:1. After winning six games in a row, the team's ratio of wins to losses was 5:1. How many games had the team won <u>before</u> it won the six games?

(A) 3
(B) 6
(C) 9
(D) 15
(E) 24

21. A college student bought 11 books for fall classes. If the cost of his anatomy textbook was three times the mean cost of the other 10 books, then the cost of the anatomy textbook was what fraction of the total amount he paid for the 11 books?

(A) $\dfrac{2}{13}$

(B) $\dfrac{3}{13}$

(C) $\dfrac{3}{11}$

(D) $\dfrac{3}{10}$

(E) $\dfrac{3}{4}$.

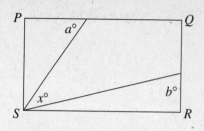

22. In rectangle *PQRS* above, what is the sum of $a + b$ in terms of x?

(A) $90 + x$
(B) $180 - x$
(C) $180 + x$
(D) $270 - x$
(E) $360 - x$

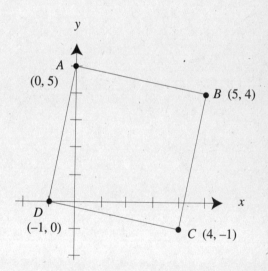

23. What is the area of square *ABCD*?

(A) 25
(B) $18\sqrt{2}$
(C) 26
(D) $25 + \sqrt{2}$
(E) 36

GO ON TO THE NEXT PAGE

24. If 0.1% of m is equal to 10% of n, then m is what percent of $10n$?

(A) $\dfrac{1}{1000}\%$

(B) 10%

(C) 100%

(D) 1,000%

(E) 10,000%

25. If $n \neq 0$, which of the following could be true?

    I. $2n < n^2$
    II. $2n < n$
    III. $n^2 < -n$

(A) None
(B) I only
(C) I and II only
(D) I and III only
(E) I, II, and III

STOP

**If you finish before time is called, you may check your work on this section only.
Do not turn to any other section in the test.**

NO TEST MATERIAL ON THIS PAGE.

Each sentence below has one or two blanks, each blank indicating that something has been omitted. Beneath the sentence are five words or sets of words labeled A through E. Choose the word or set of words that, when inserted in the sentence, best fits the meaning of the sentence as a whole.

Example:

Medieval kingdoms did not become constitutional republics overnight; on the contrary, the change was -------.

(A) unpopular   (B) unexpected   (C) advantageous
(D) sufficient   (E) gradual   Ⓐ Ⓑ Ⓒ Ⓓ ●

1. Since the island soil has been barren for so many years, the natives must now ------- much of their food.

(A) deliver   (B) import   (C) produce
(D) develop   (E) utilize

2. Because Jenkins neither ------- nor defends either management or the striking workers, both sides admire his journalistic ------- .

(A) criticizes. .acumen
(B) attacks. .neutrality
(C) confronts. .aptitude
(D) dismisses. .flair
(E) promotes. .integrity

3. Some anthropologists claim that a few apes have been taught a rudimentary sign language, but skeptics argue that the apes are only ------- their trainers.

(A) imitating   (B) condoning   (C) instructing
(D) acknowledging   (E) belaboring

4. It is ironic that the ------- insights of the great thinkers are voiced so often that they have become mere ------- .

(A) original. .clichés
(B) banal. .beliefs
(C) dubious. .habits
(D) philosophical. .questions
(E) abstract. .ideas

5. The most frustrating periods of any diet are the inevitable -------, when weight loss ------- if not stops.

(A) moods. .accelerates
(B) feasts. .halts
(C) holidays. .contracts
(D) plateaus. .slows
(E) meals. .ceases

6. Since the author's unflattering references to her friends were so -------, she was surprised that her ------- were recognized.

(A) laudatory. .styles
(B) obvious. .anecdotes
(C) oblique. .allusions
(D) critical. .eulogies
(E) apparent. .motives

7. Mark was intent on maintaining his status as first in his class; because even the smallest mistakes infuriated him, he reviewed all his papers ------- before submitting them to his teacher.

(A) explicitly   (B) perfunctorily   (C) honestly
(D) mechanically   (E) assiduously

8. Since many disadvantaged individuals view their situations as ------- as well as intolerable, their attitudes are best described as ------- .

(A) squalid. .obscure
(B) unpleasant. .bellicose
(C) acute. . sanguine
(D) immutable. .resigned
(E) political. .perplexed

9. The subtleties of this novel are evident not so much in the character ------- as they are in its profoundly ------- plot structure.

(A) assessment. .eclectic
(B) development. .trite
(C) portrayal. .aesthetic
(D) delineation. .intricate
(E) illustration. .superficial

GO ON TO THE NEXT PAGE

Each question below consists of a related pair of words or phrases, followed by five pairs of words or phrases labeled A through E. Select the pair that best expresses a relationship similar to that expressed in the original pair.

Example:

CRUMB : BREAD ::

(A) ounce : unit
(B) splinter : wood
(C) water : bucket
(D) twine : rope
(E) cream : butter   Ⓐ ● Ⓒ Ⓓ Ⓔ

10. SHIP : OCEAN ::

(A) fish : gill
(B) plane : air
(C) child : bath
(D) camel : water
(E) car : passengers

11. BOTANY : PLANTS ::

(A) agriculture : herbs
(B) astronomy : stars
(C) philosophy : books
(D) anthropology : religion
(E) forestry : evergreens

12. CENSUS : POPULATION ::

(A) catalog : pictures
(B) inventory : supplies
(C) detonation : explosion
(D) dictionary : words
(E) election : tally

13. CONSTELLATION : STARS ::

(A) earth : moon
(B) center : circle
(C) archipelago : islands
(D) rain : water
(E) maverick : herd

14. REFINE : OIL ::

(A) winnow : wheat
(B) harness : energy
(C) mine : coal
(D) mold : plastic
(E) conserve : resource

15. PERSPICACIOUS : INSIGHT ::

(A) zealous : mobility
(B) audacious : hearing
(C) delicious : taste
(D) avaricious : generosity
(E) amiable : friendliness

GO ON TO THE NEXT PAGE

The passage below is followed by questions based on its content. Answer the questions on the basis of what is <u>stated</u> or <u>implied</u> in the passage and in any introductory material that may be provided.

Questions 16–21 are based on the following passage.

The following passage is an excerpt from a book by novelist Gregor von Rezzori.

Skushno is a Russian word that is difficult to translate. It means more than dreary boredom; a spiritual void that sucks you in like a vague but

Line intensely urgent longing. When I was thirteen, at a
5 phase that educators used to call the awkward age, my parents were at their wits' end. We lived in the Bukovina, today an almost astronomically remote province in southeastern Europe. The story I am telling seems as distant—not only in space but also
10 in time—as if I'd merely dreamed it. Yet it begins as a very ordinary story.

I had been expelled by a *consilium abeundi*—an advisory board with authority to expel unworthy students—from the schools of the then Kingdom
15 of Rumania, whose subjects we had become upon the collapse of the Austro-Hungarian Empire after the first great war. An attempt to harmonize the imbalances in my character by means of strict discipline at a boarding school in Styria (my people
20 still regarded Austria as our cultural homeland) nearly led to the same ignominious end, and only my pseudo-voluntary departure from the institution in the nick of time prevented my final ostracism from the privileged ranks of those for
25 whom the path to higher education was open. Again in the jargon of those assigned the responsible task of raising children to become "useful members of society," I was a "virtually hopeless case." My parents, blind to how the contradictions
30 within me had grown out of the highly charged difference between their own natures, agreed with the schoolmasters; the mix of neurotic sensitivity and a tendency to violence, alert perception and inability to learn, tender need for support and lack
35 of adjustability, would only develop into something criminal.

One of the trivial aphorisms my generation owes to Wilhelm Busch's *Pious Helene* is the homily "Once your reputation's done / You can live a life of fun."
40 But this optimistic notion results more from wishful thinking than from practical experience. In my case, had anyone asked me about my state of mind, I

would have sighed and answered, "*Skushno!*". Even though rebellious thoughts occasionally surged
45 within me, I dragged myself, or rather I let myself be dragged, listlessly through my bleak existence in the snail's pace of days. Nor was I ever free of a sense of guilt, for my feeling guilty was not entirely foisted upon me by others; there were deep reasons
50 I could not explain to myself; had I been able to do so, my life would have been much easier.

16. It can be inferred from the passage that the author's parents were

(A) frustrated by the author's inability to do well in school
(B) oblivious to the author's poor academic performance
(C) wealthy, making them insensitive to the needs of the poor
(D) schoolmasters who believed in the strict disciplining of youth
(E) living in Russia while their son lived in Bukovina

17. Lines 17–25 are used by the author to demonstrate that

(A) the author was an unstable and dangerous person
(B) the schools that the author attended were too difficult
(C) the tactics being used to make the author a more stable person were failing
(D) the author was not accepted well by his classmates
(E) the author's academic career was nearing an end

GO ON TO THE NEXT PAGE

18. The word "ignominious" in line 21 means

    (A) dangerous
    (B) pitiless
    (C) unappreciated
    (D) disgraceful
    (E) honorable

19. In line 24, the word "ostracism" most likely means

    (A) praise
    (B) abuse
    (C) appreciation
    (D) departure
    (E) banishment

20. The passage as a whole suggests that the author felt

    (A) happy because he was separated from his parents
    (B) upset because he was unable to maintain good friends
    (C) melancholy and unsettled in his environment
    (D) suicidal and desperate because of his living in Russia
    (E) hopeful because he'd soon be out of school

21. The passage indicates that the author regarded the aphorism mentioned in the last paragraph with

    (A) relief because it showed him that he would eventually feel better
    (B) disdain because he found it unrealistic
    (C) contempt because he saw it working for others
    (D) bemusement because of his immunity from it
    (E) sorrow because his faith in it nearly killed him

GO ON TO THE NEXT PAGE

The passage below is followed by questions based on its content. Answer the questions on the basis of what is <u>stated</u> or <u>implied</u> in the passage and in any introductory material that may be provided.

Questions 22–30 are based on the following passage.

Fear of communism swept through the United States in the years following the Russian Revolution of 1917. Several states passed espionage acts that restricted political discussion, and radicals of all descriptions were rounded up in so-called Red Raids conducted by the attorney general's office. Some were convicted and imprisoned; others were deported. This was the background of a trial in Chicago involving twenty men charged under Illinois's espionage statute with advocating the violent overthrow of the government. The charge rested on the fact that all the defendants were members of the newly formed Communist Labor party.

The accused in the case were represented by Clarence Darrow, one of the foremost defense attorneys in the country. Throughout his career, Darrow had defended the poor and the despised against exploitation and prejudice. He defended the rights of labor unions, for example, at a time when many sought to outlaw the strike, and he was resolute in defending constitutional freedoms. The following are excerpts from Darrow's summation to the jury.

Members of the Jury . . . If you want to convict these twenty men, then do it. I ask no consideration on behalf of any one of them. They are no better than any other twenty men or women; they are no better
Line
5 than the millions down through the ages who have been prosecuted and convicted in cases like this. And if it is necessary for my clients to show that America is like all the rest, if it is necessary that my clients shall go to prison to show it, then let them go. They
10 can afford it if you members of the jury can; make no mistake about that. . . .
The State says my clients "dare to criticize the Constitution." Yet this police officer (who the State says is a fine, right-living person) twice violated the
15 federal Constitution while a prosecuting attorney was standing by. They entered Mr. Owen's home without a search warrant. They overhauled his papers. They found a flag, a red one, which he had the same right to have in his house that you have
20 to keep a green one, or a yellow one, or any other color, and the officer impudently rolled it up and put another flag on the wall, nailed it there. By what right was that done? What about this kind of

patriotism that violates the Constitution? Has it
25 come to pass in this country that officers of the law can trample on constitutional rights and then excuse it in a court of justice? ...
Most of what has been presented to this jury to stir up feeling in your souls has not the slightest
30 bearing on proving conspiracy in this case. Take Mr. Lloyd's speech in Milwaukee. It had nothing to do with conspiracy.
Whether that speech was a joke or was serious, I will not attempt to discuss. But I will say that if it
35 was serious it was as mild as a summer's shower compared with many of the statements of those who are responsible for working conditions in this country. We have heard from people in high places that those individuals who express sympathy with
40 labor should be stood up against a wall and shot. We have heard people of position declare that individuals who criticize the actions of those who are getting rich should be put in a cement ship with leaden sails and sent out to sea. Every violent
45 appeal that could be conceived by the brain has been used by the powerful and the strong. I repeat, Mr. Lloyd's speech was gentle in comparison ....
My clients are condemned because they say in their platform that, while they vote, they believe the
50 ballot is secondary to education and organization. Counsel suggests that those who get something they did not vote for are sinners, but I suspect you the jury know full well that my clients are right. Most of you have an eight-hour day. Did you get it
55 by any vote you ever cast? No. It came about because workers laid down their tools and said we will no longer work until we get an eight-hour day. That is how they got the twelve-hour day, the ten-hour day, and the eight-hour day—not by voting
60 but by laying down their tools. Then when it was over and the victory won ... then the politicians, in order to get the labor vote, passed legislation creating an eight-hour day. That is how things changed; victory preceded law....
65 You have been told that if you acquit these defendants you will be despised because you will endorse everything they believe. But I am not here to defend my clients' opinions. I am here to defend their right to express their opinions. I ask you, then, to decide this case upon the facts as you have heard

GO ON TO THE NEXT PAGE →

them, in light of the law as you understand it, in light of the history of our country, whose institutions you and I are bound to protect.

22. Clarence Darrow's statement that "They can afford it if you members of the jury can" (lines 9–10) is most probably meant to imply that

(A) the defendants will not be harmed if convicted
(B) if the jurors convict the defendants, they will be harshly criticized
(C) the defendants do not care whether they are convicted
(D) everyone involved in the trial will be affected financially by whatever the jury decides
(E) if the defendants are found guilty, everyone's rights will be threatened

23. Lines 12–27 suggest that the case against Owen would have been dismissed if the judge had interpreted the Constitution in which of the following ways?

(A) Defendants must have their rights read to them when they are arrested.
(B) Giving false testimony in court is a crime.
(C) Evidence gained by illegal means is not admissible in court.
(D) No one can be tried twice for the same crime.
(E) Defendants cannot be forced to give incriminating evidence against themselves.

24. Darrow's defense in lines 28–47 relies mainly on persuading the jury that

(A) the prosecution is using a double standard
(B) the evidence used by the prosecution is unreliable
(C) the defendants' views are similar to those of the jury
(D) labor unions are guaranteed the right to hold a strike
(E) a federal court is a more appropriate place to try the defendants than is a state court

25. Lines 28–47 indicate that the prosecution attempted to characterize Mr. Lloyd's speech as

(A) bitter sarcasm
(B) deceptive propaganda
(C) valid criticism
(D) a frightening threat
(E) a bad joke

26. What does Clarence Darrow accuse "people in high places" (line 38) of doing?

(A) trying to kill Communist Party members
(B) advocating violence against labor sympathizers
(C) lying to the jury
(D) encouraging the use of harsh punishment against criminals
(E) making foolish and insulting suggestions

27. The word "counsel" in line 51 refers to

(A) expert psychologists
(B) the prosecution
(C) an assembly
(D) a recommendation
(E) an expert

GO ON TO THE NEXT PAGE

28. Lines 65–67 imply that the prosecution had told the jury that finding for the innocence of the defendants would be similar to

    (A) denying the validity of the Constitution
    (B) permitting workers to go on strike
    (C) promoting passive resistance
    (D) limiting freedom of expression
    (E) promoting communism

29. In line 73, the word "bound" most nearly means

    (A) intellectually committed
    (B) personally determined
    (C) morally compelled
    (D) violently coerced
    (E) inevitably destined

30. Darrow's defense hinges on the ability of the jurors to

    (A) understand complicated legal terms and procedures
    (B) sympathize with union organizers
    (C) comprehend the beliefs of the Communist Labor party
    (D) separate the defendants' rights from their views
    (E) act in the interest of the national economy

STOP

**If you finish before time is called, you may check your work on this section only.
Do not turn to any other section in the test.**

NO TEST MATERIAL ON THIS PAGE.

Time—30 Minutes 25 Questions	In this section, solve each problem using any available space on the page for scratchwork. Then decide which is the best of the choices given and fill in the corresponding oval on the answer sheet.

Notes:

1.   The use of a calculator is permitted. All numbers used are real numbers.

2.   Figures that accompany problems in this test are intended to provide information useful in solving the problems. They are drawn as accurately as possible EXCEPT when it is stated in a specific problem that the figure is not drawn to scale. All figures lie in a plane unless otherwise indicated.

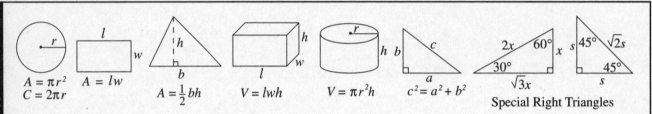

$A = \pi r^2$
$C = 2\pi r$
$A = lw$
$A = \frac{1}{2}bh$
$V = lwh$
$V = \pi r^2 h$
$c^2 = a^2 + b^2$

Special Right Triangles

The number of degrees of arc in a circle is 360.
The measure in degrees of a straight angle is 180.
The sum of the measures in degrees of the angles of a triangle is 180.

Directions for Quantitative Comparison Questions

Questions 1–15 each consist of two quantities in boxes, one in Column A and one in Column B.
You are to compare the two quantities and on the answer sheet fill in oval

A if the quantity in Column A is greater;
B if the quantity in Column B is greater;
C if the two quantities are equal;
D if the relationship cannot be determined from the information given.

AN E RESPONSE WILL NOT BE SCORED.

Notes:

1. In some questions, information is given about one or both of the quantities to be compared. In such cases, the given information is centered above the two columns and is not boxed.
2. In a given question, a symbol that appears in both columns represents the same thing in Column A as it does in Column B.
3. Letters such as x, n, and k stand for real numbers.

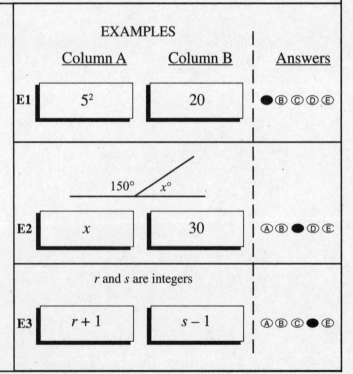

EXAMPLES

	Column A	Column B	Answers
E1	5^2	20	●ⒷⒸⒹⒺ
E2	x	30	ⒶⒷ●ⒹⒺ
E3	$r + 1$	$s - 1$	ⒶⒷⒸ●Ⓔ

150°   x°

r and s are integers

<u>Column A</u>	<u>Column B</u>

1. $\dfrac{3}{7}$ $\dfrac{1}{2}$

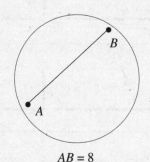

$AB = 8$

2. The radius of the circle   4

$7a > 4b$

3. a b

4. $x + y$ 90

<u>Column A</u>	<u>Column B</u>

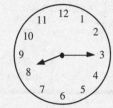

The novelty clock above has hands that move at the correct speed, but counter-clockwise. The clock tells the correct time every 6 hours (at 6:00 and 12:00).

5. 3 hours, 15 minutes   The amount of time that has passed since 12:00

$9^n - 8^n = 1^n$

6.   1 n

A rectangle of area 4 has two sides of lengths r and s, where r and s are integers.

7. $\dfrac{r}{2}$ $2s$

GO ON TO THE NEXT PAGE

SUMMARY DIRECTIONS FOR QUANTITATIVE COMPARISON QUESTIONS

Answer: A if the quantity in Column A is greater;
B if the quantity in Column B is greater;
C if the two quantities are equal;
D if the relationship cannot be determined from the information given.

AN E RESPONSE WILL NOT BE SCORED.

Column A	Column B

In a group of 28 children, there are 6 more girls than boys.

8.

Two times the number of girls	Three times the number of boys

9.

$\dfrac{\frac{3}{2}}{\left(\frac{3}{2}\right)^2}$	$\dfrac{2}{3}$

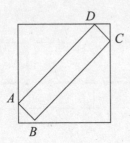

The area of the square is 25. Points *A*, *B*, *C*, and *D* are on the square. *ABCD* is not a square.

10.

The perimeter of rectangle *ABCD*	20

Column A	Column B

x, *y*, and *z* are positive.
$x + y + z = 10$ and $x = y$.

11.

x	5

12.

$\sqrt{3} + \sqrt{4}$	$\sqrt{3} \times \sqrt{4}$

13.

The number of distinct prime factors of 30	The number of distinct prime factors of 60

14.

x^2	$(x + 1)^2$

15.

The percent increase from 99 to 100	The percent decrease from 100 to 99

GO ON TO THE NEXT PAGE

Directions for Student-Produced Response Questions

Each of the remaining 10 questions (16–25) requires you to solve the problem and enter your answer by marking the ovals in the special grid, as shown in the examples below.

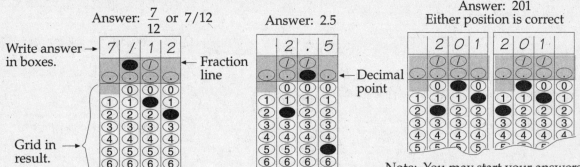

- Mark no more than one oval in any column.
- Because the answer sheet will be machine-scored, **you will receive credit only if the ovals are filled in correctly.**
- Although not required, it is suggested that you write your answer in the boxes at the top of the columns to help you fill in the ovals accurately.
- Some problems may have more than one correct answer. In such cases, grid only one answer.
- No question has a negative answer.
- **Mixed numbers** such as $2\frac{1}{2}$ must be gridded as 2.5 or 5/2. (If is gridded, it will be interpreted as $\frac{21}{2}$, not $2\frac{1}{2}$.)

- **Decimal Accuracy:** If you obtain a decimal answer, **enter the most accurate value the grid will accommodate.** For example, if you obtain an answer such as 0.6666 . . . , you should record the result as .666 or .667. **Less accurate values such as .66 or .67 are not acceptable.**

Acceptable ways to grid $\frac{2}{3}$ = .6666 . . .

16. If $\dfrac{x + 2x + 3x}{2} = 6$, what is the value of x?

17. There are 24 fish in an aquarium. If $\dfrac{1}{8}$ of them are tetras and $\dfrac{2}{3}$ of the remaining fish are guppies, how many guppies are in the aquarium?

GO ON TO THE NEXT PAGE

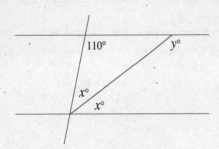

18. If l_1 is parallel to l_2 in the figure above, what is the value of y?

19. The daily newspaper always follows a particular format. Each even-numbered page contains 6 articles and each odd-numbered page contains 7 articles. If today's paper has 36 pages, how many articles does it contain?

20. When n is divided by 5, the remainder is 4. When n is divided by 4, the remainder is 3. If $0 < n < 100$, what is one possible value of n?

21. If $x^2 = 16$ and $y^2 = 4$, what is the greatest possible value of $(x - y)^2$?

22. Segment AB is perpendicular to segment BD. Segment AB and segment CD bisect each other at point X. If $AB = 8$ and $CD = 10$, what is the length of BD?

GO ON TO THE NEXT PAGE

23. At a music store, the price of a CD is three times the price of a cassette tape. If 40 CDs were sold for a total of $480, and the combined sales of CDs and cassette tapes totaled $600, how many cassette tapes were sold?

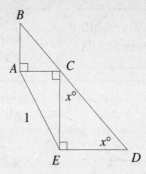

25. In the figure above, if $AE = 1$, what is the sum of the area of $\triangle ABC$ and the area of $\triangle CDE$?

24. At a certain high school, 30 students study French, 40 study Spanish, and 25 study neither. If there are 80 students in the school, how many study both French and Spanish?

STOP

If you finish before time is called, you may check your work on this section only.
Do not turn to any other section in the test.

Time—30 Minutes
35 Questions

For each question in this section, select the best answer from among the choices given and fill in the corresponding oval on the answer sheet.

Each sentence below has one or two blanks, each blank indicating that something has been omitted. Beneath the sentence are five words or sets of words labeled A through E. Choose the word or set of words that, when inserted in the sentence, best fits the meaning of the sentence as a whole.

Example:

Medieval kingdoms did not become constitutional republics overnight; on the contrary, the change was -------.

(A) unpopular
(B) unexpected
(C) advantageous
(D) sufficient
(E) gradual

---

1. If it is true that morality cannot exist without religion, then does not the erosion of religion herald the ------- of morality?

    (A) regulation   (B) basis   (C) belief
     (D) collapse   (E) value

2. Certain animal behaviors, such as mating rituals, seem to be -------, and therefore ------- external factors such as climate changes, food supply, or the presence of other animals of the same species.

    (A) learned. .immune to
    (B) innate. .unaffected by
    (C) intricate. .belong to
    (D) specific. .confused with
    (E) memorized. .controlled by

3. Shaken by two decades of virtual anarchy, the majority of people were ready to buy ------- at any price.

    (A) order   (B) emancipation   (C) hope
     (D) liberty   (E) enfranchisement

4. As a person who combines care with -------, Marisa completed her duties with ------- as well as zeal.

    (A) levity. .resignation
    (B) geniality. .ardor
    (C) vitality. .willingness
    (D) empathy. .rigor
    (E) enthusiasm. .meticulousness

5. Her shrewd campaign managers were responsible for the fact that her political slogans were actually forgotten clichés revived and ------- with new meaning.

    (A) fathomed   (B) instilled   (C) foreclosed
     (D) instigated   (E) foreshadowed

6. The stoic former general led his civilian life as he had his military life, with simplicity and ------- dignity.

    (A) benevolent   (B) informal   (C) austere
     (D) aggressive   (E) succinct

7. Although bound to impose the law, a judge is free to use his discretion to ------- the anachronistic barbarity of some criminal penalties.

    (A) mitigate   (B) understand   (C) condone
     (D) provoke   (E) enforce

8. Henry viewed Melissa as -------; she seemed to be against any position regardless of its merits.

    (A) heretical   (B) disobedient   (C) contrary
     (D) inattentive   (E) harried

GO ON TO THE NEXT PAGE

9. Dr. Schwartz's lecture on art, while detailed and scholarly, focused ------- on the premodern; some students may have appreciated his specialized knowledge, but those with more ------- interests may have been disappointed.

(A) literally. .medieval
(B) completely. .pedantic
(C) expansively. .technical
(D) voluminously. .creative
(E) exclusively. .comprehensive

10. Only when one actually visits the ancient ruins of marvelous bygone civilizations does one truly appreciate the sad ------- of human greatness.

(A) perspicacity   (B) magnitude   (C) artistry
 (D) transience   (E) quiescence

GO ON TO THE NEXT PAGE

4 4 4 4 4 4 4

Each question below consists of a related pair of words or phrases, followed by five pairs of words or phrases labeled A through E. Select the pair that best expresses a relationship similar to that expressed in the original pair.

Example:

CRUMB : BREAD ::

(A) ounce : unit
(B) splinter : wood
(C) water : bucket
(D) twine : rope
(E) cream : butter

Ⓐ ● Ⓒ Ⓓ Ⓔ

11. CAKE : DESSERT ::

(A) coach : football
(B) lawyer : jury
(C) poet : writing
(D) actor : troupe
(E) pediatrician : doctor

12. WEIGHTLIFTER : STRENGTH ::

(A) goalie : skill
(B) dancer : speed
(C) marathoner : endurance
(D) hiker : agility
(E) fisherman : luck

13. BREEZE : HURRICANE ::

(A) water : pebble
(B) gulf : coast
(C) eye : cyclone
(D) sun : cloud
(E) hill : mountain

14. IMMORTAL : DEATH ::

(A) anonymous : fame
(B) hopeless : situation
(C) vital : life
(D) indisputable : agreement
(E) daily : year

15. TAPESTRY : THREAD ::

(A) pizza : pie
(B) mosaic : tiles
(C) ruler : divisions
(D) computer : switch
(E) car : engine

16. LUBRICANT : FRICTION ::

(A) motor : electricity
(B) speed : drag
(C) insulation : heat
(D) adhesive : connection
(E) muffler : noise

17. PARODY : IMITATION ::

(A) stanza : verse
(B) limerick : poem
(C) novel : book
(D) portrait : painting
(E) riddle : puzzle

18. COMET : TAIL ::

(A) traffic : lane
(B) missile : trajectory
(C) vessel : wake
(D) engine : fuel
(E) wave : crest

GO ON TO THE NEXT PAGE

310 ◆ CRACKING THE SAT

19. NEOLOGISM : LANGUAGE ::

   (A) rhetoric : oratory
   (B) syllogism : grammar
   (C) innovation : technology
   (D) iconography : art
   (E) epistemology : philosophy

20. ADDENDUM : BOOK ::

   (A) signature : letter
   (B) vote : constitution
   (C) codicil : will
   (D) heading : folder
   (E) stipulation : contract

21. PENCHANT : INCLINED ::

   (A) loathing : contemptuous
   (B) abhorrence : delighted
   (C) burgeoning : barren
   (D) loss : incessant
   (E) decision : predictable

22. VAGRANT : DOMICILE ::

   (A) pagan : morals
   (B) despot : leadership
   (C) arsonist : fire
   (D) exile : country
   (E) telephone : ear

23. MERITORIOUS : PRAISE ::

   (A) captious : criticism
   (B) kind : admiration
   (C) questionable : response
   (D) reprehensible : censure
   (E) incredible : ecstasy

GO ON TO THE NEXT PAGE

The passage below is followed by questions based on its content. Answer the questions on the basis of what is <u>stated</u> or <u>implied</u> in the passage and in any introductory material that may be provided.

Questions 24–35 are based on the following passage.

The following passage, published in 1986, is from a book written by a zoologist.

The domestic cat is a contradiction. No other animal has developed such an intimate relationship with humanity, while at the same time demanding
Line and getting such independent movement and action.
5 The cat manages to remain a tame animal because of the sequence of its upbringing. By living both with other cats (its mother and littermates) and with humans (the family that has adopted it) during its infancy and kittenhood, it becomes attached to and
10 considers that it belongs to both species. It is like a child that grows up in a foreign country and as a consequence becomes bilingual. The young cat becomes bimental. It may be a cat physically but mentally it is both feline and human. Once it is fully
15 adult, however, most of its responses are feline ones, and it has only one major reaction to its human owners. It treats them as pseudoparents. The reason is that they took over from the real mother at a sensitive stage of the kitten's development and went
20 on giving it milk, solid food, and comfort as it grew up.
    This is rather different from the kind of bond that develops between human and dog. The dog sees its human owners as pseudoparents, as does the cat.
25 On that score the process of attachment is similar. But the dog has an additional link. Canine society is group-organized; feline society is not. Dogs live in packs with tightly controlled status relationships among the individuals. There are top dogs,
30 middle dogs, and bottom dogs, and under natural circumstances they move around together, keeping tabs on one another the whole time. So the adult pet dog sees its human family both as pseudoparents and as the dominant members of the pack, hence its
35 renowned reputation for obedience and its celebrated capacity for loyalty. Cats do have a complex social organization, but they never hunt in packs. In the wild, most of their day is spent in solitary stalking. Going for a walk with a human, therefore, has no
40 appeal for them. And as for "coming to heel" and learning to "sit" and "stay," they are simply not interested. Such maneuvers have no meaning for them.

So the moment a cat manages to persuade a human
45 being to open a door (that most hated of human inventions), it is off and away without a backward glance. As it crosses the threshold, the cat becomes transformed. The kitten-of-human brain is switched off and the wildcat brain is clicked on. The dog, in
50 such a situation, may look back to see if its human packmate is following to join in the fun of exploring, but not the cat. The cat's mind has floated off into another, totally feline world, where strange, bipedal* primates have no place.
55   Because of this difference between domestic cats and domestic dogs, cat-lovers tend to be rather different from dog-lovers. As a rule cat-lovers have a stronger personality bias toward working alone, independent of the larger group. Artists like cats;
60 soldiers like dogs. The much-lauded "group loyalty" phenomenon is alien to both cats and cat-lovers. If you are a company person, a member of the gang, or a person picked for the squad, the chances are that at home there is no cat curled up in front of the fire.
65 The ambitious Yuppie, the aspiring politician, the professional athlete, these are not typical cat-owners. It is hard to picture football players with cats in their laps—much easier to envisage them taking their dogs for walks.
70   Those who have studied cat-owners and dog-owners as two distinct groups report that there is also a gender bias. The majority of cat-lovers are female. This bias is not surprising in view of the division of labor evident in the development
75 of human societies. Prehistoric males became specialized as group-hunters, while the females concentrated on food-gathering and childbearing. This difference contributed to a human male "pack mentality" that is far less marked in females.
80 Wolves, the wild ancestors of domestic dogs, also became pack-hunters, so the modern dog has much more in common with the human male than with the human female.
    The argument will always go on—feline self-
85 sufficiency and individualism versus canine camaraderie and good-fellowship. But it is important to stress that in making a valid point I have caricatured the two positions. In reality there

*bipedal: walking on two feet

GO ON TO THE NEXT PAGE

are many people who enjoy equally the company
90 of both cats and dogs. And all of us, or nearly all
of us, have both feline and canine elements in our
personalities. We have moods when we want to be
alone and thoughtful, and other times when we wish
to be in the center of a crowded, noisy room.

24. The primary purpose of the passage is to

 (A) show the enmity that exists between cats and
     dogs
 (B) advocate dogs as making better pets than cats
 (C) distinguish the different characteristics of
     dogs and cats
 (D) show the inferiority of dogs because of their
     dependent nature
 (E) emphasize the role that human society plays
     in the personalities of domestic pets

25. According to the passage, the domestic cat can be
described as

 (A) a biped because it possesses the characteristics
     of animals with two feet
 (B) a pseudopet because it can't really be tamed
     and will always retain its wild habits
 (C) a contradiction because although it lives
     comfortably with humans, it refuses to be
     dominated by them
 (D) a soldier because it is militant about
     preserving its independence
 (E) a ruler because although it plays the part of a
     pet, it really dominates humans

26. In line 17, the word "pseudoparents" means

 (A) part-time parents that are only partially
     involved with their young
 (B) individuals who act as parents of adults
 (C) parents that neglect their young
 (D) parents that have both the characteristics of
     humans and their pets
 (E) adoptive parents who aren't related to their
     young

27. The author suggests that an important difference
between dogs and cats is that, unlike dogs, cats

 (A) do not regard their owners as the leader of
     their social group
 (B) obey mainly because of their obedient nature
 (C) have a more creative nature
 (D) do not have complex social organizations
 (E) are not skilled hunters

28. It can be inferred from the third paragraph (lines
22–43) that the social structure of dogs is

 (A) flexible
 (B) abstract
 (C) hierarchical
 (D) male-dominated
 (E) somewhat exclusive

29. Lines 39–43 ("Going . . . them.") are used to stress

 (A) the laziness of cats that keeps them from
     being pack animals
 (B) the ignorance of dogs, which makes them
     more obedient pets
 (C) the antipathy that cats feel for humans
 (D) a difference between cats and dogs that
     emphasizes the independent nature of cats
 (E) the stubborn and complacent disposition of
     cats

30. In line 60, "much-lauded" means

 (A) vehemently argued
 (B) overly discussed
 (C) unnecessarily complicated
 (D) typically controversial
 (E) commonly praised

31. The "ambitious Yuppie" mentioned in line 65 is an
example of a person

 (A) who is power-hungry
 (B) who craves virtue
 (C) who is a stereotypical pet-owner
 (D) who has a weak personality
 (E) who seeks group-oriented status

GO ON TO THE NEXT PAGE

32. The sixth paragraph (lines 70–83) indicates that human females

(A) are more like dogs than cats
(B) developed independent roles that didn't require group behavior
(C) had to gather food because they were not strong enough to hunt
(D) are not good owners for the modern dog
(E) were negatively affected by the division of labor of human societies

33. The author uses lines 84–88 ("The argument . . . positions.") to

(A) show that the argument stated in the passage is ultimately futile
(B) disclaim glaring contradictions that are stated in the passage
(C) qualify the generalizations used to make the author's point
(D) ensure that the reader doesn't underestimate the crux of the passage
(E) highlight a difference between individualism and dependency

34. The last four sentences in the passage (lines 86–94) provide

(A) an example of the argument that has been made earlier
(B) a summary of the points made earlier
(C) a reason for the statements made earlier
(D) a modification of the position taken earlier
(E) a rebuttal to opposing views referred to earlier

35. The passage as a whole does all of the following EXCEPT

(A) use a statistic
(B) make parenthetical statements
(C) quote a knowledgeable individual
(D) restate an argument
(E) make a generalization

STOP

**If you finish before time is called, you may check your work on this section only.
Do not turn to any other section in the test.**

NO TEST MATERIAL ON THIS PAGE.

| Time—30 Minutes 25 Questions | In this section, solve each problem using any available space on the page for scratchwork. Then decide which is the best of the choices given and fill in the corresponding oval on the answer sheet. |

Notes:

1. The use of a calculator is permitted. All numbers used are real numbers.

2. Figures that accompany problems in this test are intended to provide information useful in solving the problems. They are drawn as accurately as possible EXCEPT when it is stated in a specific problem that the figure is not drawn to scale. All figures lie in a plane unless otherwise indicated.

Reference Information

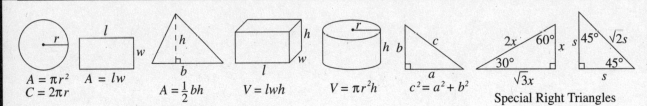

$A = \pi r^2$
$C = 2\pi r$
$A = lw$
$A = \frac{1}{2} bh$
$V = lwh$
$V = \pi r^2 h$
$c^2 = a^2 + b^2$
Special Right Triangles

The number of degrees of arc in a circle is 360.
The measure in degrees of a straight angle is 180.
The sum of the measures in degrees of the angles of a triangle is 180.

1. If $2 + a = 2 - a$, what is the value of a?

    (A) −1
    (B) 0
    (C) 1
    (D) 2
    (E) 4

2. In which of the following patterns is the number of horizontal lines three times the number of vertical lines?

(A)   (B)   (C)

(D)    (E)

GO ON TO THE NEXT PAGE

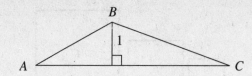

3. If $AC = 4$, what is the area of $\triangle ABC$ above?

(A) $\dfrac{1}{2}$

(B) 2

(C) $\sqrt{7}$

(D) 4

(E) 8

5. If $x + y = z$ and $x = y$, then all of the following are true EXCEPT

(A) $2x + 2y = 2z$

(B) $x - y = 0$

(C) $x - z = y - z$

(D) $x = \dfrac{z}{2}$

(E) $z - y = 2x$

4. If $\dfrac{4}{5}$ of $\dfrac{3}{4}$ is equal to $\dfrac{2}{5}$ of $\dfrac{x}{4}$, what is the value of x?

(A) 12

(B) 6

(C) 3

(D) $\dfrac{3}{2}$

(E) 1

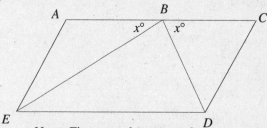

Note: Figure not drawn to scale.

6. In the figure above, $AC \parallel ED$. If the length of BD is 3, what is the length of BE?

(A) 3
(B) 4
(C) 5
(D) $3\sqrt{3}$
(E) It cannot be determined from the information given.

GO ON TO THE NEXT PAGE

7. $\dfrac{900}{10} + \dfrac{90}{100} + \dfrac{9}{1000} =$

(A) 90.09
(B) 90.099
(C) 90.909
(D) 99.09
(E) 999

8. Fifteen percent of the coins in a piggy bank are nickels and five percent are dimes. If there are 220 coins in the bank, how many are <u>not</u> nickels or dimes?

(A) 80
(B) 176
(C) 180
(D) 187
(E) 200

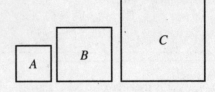

9. In the figure above, the perimeter of square A is $\dfrac{2}{3}$ the perimeter of square B, and the perimeter of square B is $\dfrac{2}{3}$ the perimeter of square C. If the area of square A is 16, what is the area of square C?

(A) 24
(B) 36
(C) 64
(D) 72
(E) 81

10. A bakery uses a special flour mixture that contains corn, wheat, and rye in the ratio of 3:5:2. If a bag of the mixture contains 5 pounds of rye, how many pounds of wheat does it contain?

(A) 2
(B) 5
(C) 7.5
(D) 10
(E) 12.5

GO ON TO THE NEXT PAGE

11. If $a^2b = 12^2$, and b is an odd integer, then a could be divisible by all of the following EXCEPT

(A) 3
(B) 4
(C) 6
(D) 9
(E) 12

12. A coin was flipped 20 times and came up heads 10 times and tails 10 times. If the first and last flips were both heads, what is the greatest number of consecutive heads that could have occurred?

(A) 1
(B) 2
(C) 8
(D) 9
(E) 10

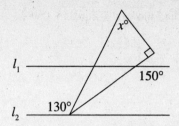

13. If l_1 is parallel to l_2 in the figure above, what is the value of x ?

(A) 20
(B) 50
(C) 70
(D) 80
(E) 90

14. Which of the following must be true?

I. The sum of two consecutive integers is odd.
II. The sum of three consecutive integers is even.
III. The sum of three consecutive integers is a multiple of 3.

(A) I only
(B) II only
(C) I and II only
(D) I and III only
(E) I, II, and III

GO ON TO THE NEXT PAGE

15. Which of the following is equal to .064 ?

(A) $\left(\dfrac{1}{80}\right)^2$

(B) $\left(\dfrac{8}{100}\right)^2$

(C) $\left(\dfrac{1}{8}\right)^2$

(D) $\left(\dfrac{2}{5}\right)^3$

(E) $\left(\dfrac{8}{10}\right)^3$

16. If the average (arithmetic mean) of four distinct positive integers is 11, what is the greatest possible value of any one of the integers?

(A) 35
(B) 38
(C) 40
(D) 41
(E) 44

17. In a list of seven integers, 13 is the lowest member, 37 is the highest member, the mean is 23, the median is 24, and the mode is 18. If the numbers 8 and 43 are then included in the list, which of the following will change?

I.   The mean
II. The median
III. The mode

(A) I only
(B) I and II only
(C) I and III only
(D) II and III only
(E) I, II, and III

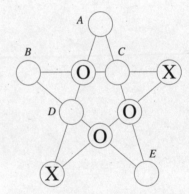

18. If the figure above is filled in so that each row of four circles contains two circles marked with an X and two circles marked with an O, which circle must be marked with an X?

(A) A
(B) B
(C) C
(D) D
(E) E

GO ON TO THE NEXT PAGE

19. If c is positive, what percent of $3c$ is 9?

(A) $\dfrac{c}{100}\%$

(B) $\dfrac{c}{3}\%$

(C) $\dfrac{9}{c}\%$

(D) 3%

(E) $\dfrac{300}{c}\%$

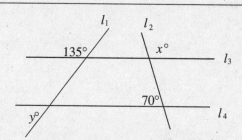

Note: Figure not drawn to scale.

20. If four lines intersect as shown in the figure above, what is the value of $x + y$?

(A)   65
(B)   110
(C)   155
(D)   205
(E)   It cannot be determined from the information given.

21. S is the set of all positive numbers n such that $n < 100$ and $\sqrt{n}$ is an integer. What is the median value of the members of set S ?

(A)   5
(B)   5.5
(C)   25
(D)   50
(E)   99

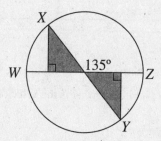

22. If segment WZ and segment XY are diameters with lengths of 12, what is the area of the shaded region?

(A)   36
(B)   30
(C)   18
(D)   12
(E)   9

GO ON TO THE NEXT PAGE

23. At the beginning of 1999, the population of Rockville was 204,000 and the population of Springfield was 216,000. If the population of each city increased by exactly 20% in 1999, how many more people lived in Springfield than in Rockville at the end of 1999?

    (A) 9,600
    (B) 10,000
    (C) 12,000
    (D) 14,400
    (E) 20,000

24. Line a has a slope of $-\dfrac{3}{2}$. If points $(-2, 6)$ and $(m, -9)$ are on line a, what is the value of m?

    (A) 3
    (B) 4
    (C) 6
    (D) 8
    (E) 12

25. A researcher found that a certain student's score on each of a series of tests could be predicted using the formula

    $$P = \frac{310T + (LT)^2}{100}$$

    where P is the number of points scored on the test, T is the number of hours spent studying, L is the number of hours of sleep the night before the test, and where $P \leq 100$. If, before a particular test, this student spent no more than 10 hours studying, what is the least number of hours of sleep she should get if she wants to score at least 80 points?

    (A) 6
    (B) 7
    (C) $\sqrt{56}$
    (D) 8
    (E) $\sqrt{69}$

STOP
**If you finish before time is called, you may check your work on this section only.
Do not turn any other section in the test.**

NO TEST MATERIAL ON THIS PAGE.

Time—15 Minutes
13 Questions

For each question in this section, select the best answer from among the choices given and fill in the corresponding oval on the answer sheet.

The two passages below are followed by questions based on their content and on the relationship between the two passages. Answer the questions on the basis of what is stated or implied in the passages and in any introductory material that may be provided.

Questions 1–13 are based on the following passages.

In Passage 1, the author presents his view of the early years of the silent film industry. In Passage 2, the author draws on her experiences as a mime to generalize about her art. (A mime is a performer who, without speaking, entertains through gesture, facial expression, and movement.)

Passage 1

Talk to those people who first saw films when they were silent, and they will tell you the experience was magic. The silent film had extraordinary powers to
Line draw members of an audience into the story, and an
5 equally potent capacity to make their imaginations work. It required the audience to become engaged— to supply voices and sound effects. The audience was the final, creative contributor to the process of making a film.
10 The finest films of the silent era depended on two elements that we can seldom provide today— a large and receptive audience and a well-orchestrated score. For the audience, the fusion of picture and live music added up to more than the
15 sum of the respective parts.
The one word that sums up the attitude of the silent filmmakers is *enthusiasm*, conveyed most strongly before formulas took shape and when there was more room for experimentation. This
20 enthusiastic uncertainty often resulted in such accidental discoveries as new camera or editing techniques. Some films experimented with players; the 1915 film *Regeneration*, for example, by using real gangsters and streetwalkers, provided startling
25 local color. Other films, particularly those of Thomas Ince, provided tragic endings as often as films by other companies supplied happy ones.
Unfortunately, the vast majority of silent films survive today in inferior prints that no longer reflect
30 the care that the original technicians put into them. The modern versions of silent films may appear jerky and flickery, but the vast picture palaces did not attract four to six thousand people a night by giving

them eyestrain. A silent film depends on its visuals;
35 as soon as you degrade those, you lose elements that go far beyond the image on the surface. The acting in silents was often very subtle and very restrained, despite legends to the contrary.

Passage 2

Mime opens up a new world to the beholder, but
40 it does so insidiously, not by purposely injecting points of interest in the manner of a tour guide. Audiences are not unlike visitors to a foreign land who discover that the modes, manners, and thoughts of its inhabitants are not meaningless oddities, but
45 are sensible in context.
I remember once when an audience seemed perplexed at what I was doing. At first, I tried to gain a more immediate response by using slight exaggerations. I soon realized that these actions had
50 nothing to do with the audience's understanding of the character. What I had believed to be a failure of the audience to respond in the manner I expected was, in fact, only their concentration on what I was doing; they were enjoying a gradual awakening—a
55 slow transference of their understanding from their own time and place to one that appeared so unexpectedly before their eyes. This was evidenced by their growing response to succeeding numbers.
Mime is an elusive art, as its expression is entirely
60 dependent on the ability of the performer to imagine a character and to recreate that character for each performance. As a mime, I am a physical medium, the instrument upon which the figures of my imagination play their dance
65 of life. The individuals in my audience also have responsibilities—they must be alert collaborators. They cannot sit back, mindlessly complacent, and wait to have their emotions titillated by mesmeric musical sounds or visual rhythms or acrobatic feats,
70 or by words that tell them what to think. Mime is

GO ON TO THE NEXT PAGE

an art that, paradoxically, appeals both to those who
respond instinctively to entertainment and to those
whose appreciation is more analytical and complex.
Between these extremes lie those audiences
75 conditioned to resist any collaboration with what is
played before them; and these the mime must seduce
despite themselves. There is only one way to attack
those reluctant minds—take them unaware! They
will be delighted at an unexpected pleasure.

1. Lines 13–15 ("For . . . parts.") indicate that

    (A) music was the most important element of
         silent films
    (B) silent films rely on a combination of music
         and image in affecting an audience
    (C) the importance of music in silent film has
         been overestimated
    (D) live music compensated for the poor quality
         of silent film images
    (E) no film can succeed without a receptive
         audience

2. The "formulas" mentioned in line 18 of the passage
    most probably refer to

    (A) movie theaters
    (B) use of real characters
    (C) standardized film techniques
    (D) the fusion of disparate elements
    (E) contemporary events

3. The author of Passage 1 uses the phrase "enthu-
    siastic uncertainty" in line 20 to suggest that the
    filmmakers were

    (A) excited to be experimenting in an undefined
         area
    (B) delighted at the opportunity to study new
         acting formulas
    (C) optimistic in spite of the obstacles that faced
         them
    (D) eager to challenge existing conventions
    (E) eager to please but unsure of what the public
         wanted

4. The author of Passage 1 uses the phrase "but the
    . . . eyestrain" (lines 32–34) in order to

    (A) indicate his disgust with the incompetence of
         early film technicians
    (B) suggest that audiences today perceive silent
         films incorrectly
    (C) convey his regret about the decline of the old
         picture palaces
    (D) highlight the pitfalls of the silent movie era
    (E) argue for the superiority of modern film
         technology over that of silent movies

5. The word "legends" in line 38 most nearly means

    (A) arguments
    (B) symbolism
    (C) propaganda
    (D) movie stars
    (E) misconceptions

6. The last sentence of Passage 1 implies that

    (A) the stars of silent movies have been criticized
         for overacting
    (B) many silent film actors became legends in
         their own time
    (C) silent film techniques should be studied by
         filmmakers today
    (D) visual effects defined the silent film
    (E) many silent films that exist today are of poor
         quality

7. The word "restrained" (line 37) most nearly means

    (A) sincere
    (B) dramatic
    (C) understated
    (D) inexpressive
    (E) consistent

GO ON TO THE NEXT PAGE

8. The author of Passage 2 mentions the incident in lines 46–58 in order to imply that

   (A) the audience's lack of response was a positive sign and reflected their captivated interest in the performance
   (B) she was forced to resort to stereotypes in order to reach an audience that was otherwise unattainable
   (C) exaggeration is an essential part of mime because it allows the forums used to be fully expressed
   (D) her audience, though not initially appearing knowledgeable, had a good understanding of the subtlety of mime
   (E) although vocalization is not necessary in mime, it is sometimes helpful for slower audiences

9. Lines 46–58 indicate that the author of Passage 2 and the silent filmmakers of Passage 1 were similar because

   (A) neither used many props
   (B) both conveyed universal truths by using sophisticated technology
   (C) for both, trial and error was a part of the learning process
   (D) both used visual effects and dialogue
   (E) both had a loyal following

10. The sentence "As a . . . . life" (lines 62–65) suggests that the author of Passage 2 feels mimes

    (A) cannot control the way audiences interpret their characters
    (B) must suspend their own identities in order to successfully portray their characters
    (C) have to resist outside attempts to define their acting style
    (D) should focus on important events in the lives of specific characters
    (E) know the limitations of performances that do not incorporate either music or speech

11. Which of the following pieces of information makes mime and silent film seem less similar?

    (A) Vaudeville and theatrical presentations were also popular forms of entertainment during the silent film era.
    (B) Silent films presented both fictional drama and factual information.
    (C) Silent film sometimes relied on captions to convey dialogue to the audience.
    (D) Musicians working in movie theaters were usually employed for long periods of time.
    (E) Many of the characters in silent films gained wide popularity among moviegoers.

12. Passages 1 and 2 are similar in that both are mainly concerned with

    (A) the use of special effects
    (B) differences among dramatic styles
    (C) the visual aspects of performance
    (D) the suspension of disbelief in audiences
    (E) nostalgia for a bygone era

13. Which of the following is an element that figures in the success of the dramatic arts described in both passages?

    (A) A successful combination of different dramatic styles
    (B) The exaggeration of certain aspects of a character
    (C) The incorporation of current events in the narrative
    (D) High audience attendance
    (E) The active participation of the audience

STOP

**If you finish before time is called, you may check your work on this section only.
Do not turn to any other section in the test.**

NO TEST MATERIAL ON THIS PAGE.

Time—15 Minutes
10 Questions

In this section, solve each problem using any available space on the page for scratchwork. Then decide which is the best of the choices given and fill in the corresponding oval on the answer sheet.

Notes:

1. The use of a calculator is permitted. All numbers used are real numbers.

2. Figures that accompany problems in this test are intended to provide information useful in solving the problems. They are drawn as accurately as possible EXCEPT when it is stated in a specific problem that the figure is not drawn to scale. All figures lie in a plane unless otherwise indicated.

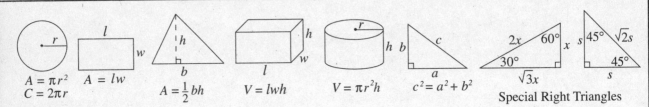
Price of Buttons in Store X	
Color	**Price**
Black	$2 per 5 buttons
Blue	$2 per 6 buttons
Brown	$3 per 8 buttons
Orange	$4 per 12 buttons
Red	$4 per 7 buttons

1. In Store X, which color button costs the most per individual unit?

   (A) Black
   (B) Blue
   (C) Brown
   (D) Orange
   (E) Red

2. Which of the following numbers can be written in the form $6k + 1$, where k is a positive integer?

   (A) 70
   (B) 71
   (C) 72
   (D) 73
   (E) 74

GO ON TO THE NEXT PAGE

3. $\left(\dfrac{4}{5}\times 3\right)\left(\dfrac{3}{4}\times 5\right)\left(\dfrac{5}{3}\times 4\right) =$

(A) 1
(B) 3
(C) 6
(D) 20
(E) 60

4. For which of the following values of x is $\dfrac{x^2}{x^3}$ the LEAST?

(A) 1
(B) −1
(C) −2
(D) −3
(E) −4

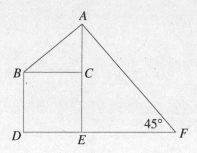

5. If the area of square $BCED = 25$, and the area of $\triangle ABC = 10$, what is the length of EF?

(A) 7
(B) 8
(C) 9
(D) 10
(E) 14

6. The Wilsons drove 450 miles in each direction to Grandmother's house and back again. If their car gets 25 miles per gallon and their cost for gasoline was $1.25 per gallon for the trip to Grandmother's but $1.50 per gallon for the return trip, how much more money did they spend for gasoline returning from Grandmother's than they spent going to Grandmother's?

(A) $2.25
(B) $4.50
(C) $6.25
(D) $9.00
(E) $27.00

7. If the average measure of two angles in a parallelogram is $y°$, what is the average degree measure of the other two angles?

(A) $180 - y$

(B) $180 - \dfrac{y}{2}$

(C) $360 - 2y$

(D) $360 - y$

(E) y

GO ON TO THE NEXT PAGE

8. A swimming pool with a capacity of 36,000 gallons originally contained 9,000 gallons of water. At 10:00 A.M. water begins to flow in at a constant rate. If the pool is exactly three-fourths full at 1:00 P.M. on the same day and the water continues to flow in at the same rate, what is the earliest time the pool will be completely full?

    (A) 1:40 P.M.
    (B) 2:00 P.M.
    (C) 2:30 P.M.
    (D) 3:00 P.M.
    (E) 3:30 P.M.

9. On a map, 1 centimeter represents 6 kilometers. A square on the map with a perimeter of 16 centimeters represents a region with what <u>area</u>?

    (A) 64 square kilometers
    (B) 96 square kilometers
    (C) 256 square kilometers
    (D) 576 square kilometers
    (E) 8,216 square kilometers

10. If $4 < a < 7 < b < 9$, then which of the following best defines $\dfrac{a}{b}$?

    (A) $\dfrac{4}{9} < \dfrac{a}{b} < 1$

    (B) $\dfrac{4}{9} < \dfrac{a}{b} < \dfrac{7}{9}$

    (C) $\dfrac{4}{7} < \dfrac{a}{b} < \dfrac{7}{9}$

    (D) $\dfrac{4}{7} < \dfrac{a}{b} < 1$

    (E) $\dfrac{4}{7} < \dfrac{a}{b} < \dfrac{9}{7}$

STOP

**If you finish before time is called, you may check your work on this section only.
Do not turn to any other section in the test.**

PRACTICE TEST 1 ANSWERS

Section 1	Section 2	Section 3	Section 4	Section 5	Section 6	Section 7
1. C	1. B	1. B	1. D	1. B	1. B	1. E
2. C	2. B	2. A	2. B	2. D	2. C	2. D
3. C	3. A	3. D	3. A	3. B	3. A	3. E
4. E	4. A	4. C	4. E	4. B	4. B	4. B
5. D	5. D	5. B	5. B	5. E	5. E	5. C
6. D	6. C	6. C	6. C	6. A	6. A	6. B
7. A	7. E	7. D	7. A	7. C	7. C	7. A
8. E	8. D	8. A	8. C	8. B	8. A	8. C
9. E	9. D	9. C	9. E	9. E	9. C	9. D
10. A	10. B	10. B	10. D	10. E	10. B	10. A
11. A	11. B	11. B	11. E	11. D	11. C	
12. B	12. B	12. A	12. C	12. D	12. C	
13. B	13. C	13. C	13. E	13. C	13. E	
14. D	14. A	14. D	14. A	14. D		
15. E	15. E	15. A	15. B	15. D		
16. A	16. A	16. 2	16. E	16. B		
17. C	17. C	17. 14	17. B	17. A		
18. E	18. D	18. 145	18. C	18. E		
19. B	19. E	19. 234	19. C	19. E		
20. C	20. C	20. 19, 39,	20. C	20. C		
21. B	21. B	59, 79,	21. A	21. C		
22. A	22. E	or 99	22. D	22. C		
23. C	23. C	21. 36	23. D	23. D		
24. D	24. A	22. 3	24. C	24. D		
25. E	25. D	23. 30	25. C	25. B		
	26. B	24. 15	26. E			
	27. B	25. 1/2	27. A			
	28. E	or .5	28. C			
	29. C		29. D			
	30. D		30. E			
			31. E			
			32. B			
			33. C			
			34. D			
			35. C			

You will find a detailed explanation for each question beginning on page 335.

HOW TO SCORE YOUR PRACTICE TEST

VERBAL

After you have checked your answers to the practice test against the key, you can calculate your score. For the three Verbal sections (Sections 2, 4, and 6), tally up the number of correct answers and the number of incorrect answers. Enter these numbers on the worksheet on the next page. Multiply the number of incorrect answers by $\frac{1}{4}$ and subtract the result from the number of correct answers. Put this number in box A. Then round the number to the nearest whole number and place it in box B.

MATHEMATICS

Figuring your Math score is a little trickier, because some of the questions have five answer choices, some have four, and some have none. In Sections 1 and 7, count the number of correct answers and incorrect answers. Enter these numbers on the worksheet. Multiply the number of incorrect answers by $\frac{1}{4}$ and subtract this from the number of correct answers. Put the result in box C.

Count the number of correct and incorrect answers in Section 3, questions 1–15. (Choice E counts as a blank.) Enter these on the worksheet. Multiply the number of incorrect answers by $\frac{1}{3}$ and subtract this from the number of correct answers in Section 3. Put the result in box D.

Count up the number of correct answers in Section 3, questions 16–25. Put the result in box E. There is no penalty for incorrect grid-in questions.

Note: Section 5 is experimental and should not be scored.

Add up the numbers in boxes C, D, and E, and write the result in box F.

Round F to the nearest whole number, and place the result in box G.

WORKSHEET FOR CALCULATING YOUR SCORE

VERBAL

Correct   Incorrect

A. Sections 2, 4, and 6   _____ – (1/4 × _____) =

| |
| A |

B. Total rounded Verbal raw score

| |
| B |

MATHEMATICS

Correct   Incorrect

C. Sections 1 and 7   _____ – (1/4 × _____) =

| |
| C |

D. Section 3   _____ – (1/3 × _____) =
   (Questions 1–15)

| |
| D |

E. Section 3   _____ =
   (Questions 16–25)

| |
| E |

F. Total unrounded Math raw score (C + D + E)

| |
| F |

G. Total rounded Math raw score

| |
| G |

Use the table on the next page to convert your raw scores to scaled scores. For example, a raw Verbal score of 39 corresponds to Verbal scaled score of 530; a Math raw score of 24 corresponds to a Math scaled score of 470.

Scores on the SAT range from 200 to 800.

Note: Since Section 5 is the experimental section, it does not count toward your score.

SCORE CONVERSION TABLE

Raw Score	Verbal Scaled Score	Math Scaled Score	Raw Score	Verbal Scaled Scored	Math Scaled Score
	800		36	510	560
78	800		35	510	550
77	800		34	500	540
76	800		33	490	530
75	780		32	480	520
74	760		31	480	520
73	750		30	470	510
72	740		29	460	500
71	740		28	460	490
70	730		27	450	480
69	720		26	450	480
68	710		25	440	480
67	700		24	430	470
66	690		23	430	460
65	680		22	420	450
64	670		21	410	440
63	670		20	400	430
62	660		19	390	430
61	660	800	18	380	430
60	650	790	17	380	420
59	640	770	16	370	410
58	640	760	15	360	400
57	630	740	14	350	390
56	620	730	13	350	390
55	620	720	12	340	380
54	610	700	11	330	370
53	600	690	10	310	350
52	600	680	9	300	340
51	600	660	8	290	340
50	590	650	7	270	330
49	590	650	6	270	310
48	580	640	5	230	300
47	570	630	4	230	300
46	570	620	3	230	280
45	560	610	2	230	260
44	560	600	1	230	250
43	550	600	0	230	240
42	550	590	−1	230	220
41	540	580	−2	230	220
40	530	570	−3	230	200
39	530	560	−4	230	200
38	520	560	−5	230	200
37			and below		

17

Answers and Explanations for Practice Test 1

What follows is a detailed explanation for each question in Practice Test 1. Although you will naturally be more curious about the questions you got wrong, don't forget to read the explanations for the questions you left blank. In fact, you should even read the explanations for the questions you got right! Our explanations present the safest, most direct solution to each question. Even though you may have gotten a question right, that does not mean you solved it in the most efficient way.

1. ETS's answer is C.
    This question actually has a one-step solution.
    It isn't necessary to solve for b first, because the
    question is actually asking for the value of $3 \times 3b$,
    which equals $9b$. The question has already told you
    that $9b = 81$.

2. ETS's answer is C.
    The number of degrees in a line is 180. Therefore,
    $b + c = 180$. And since $a + 90 = 180$, $a = 90$. So
    $a + b + c = 270$.

3. ETS's answer is C.

    Here again, as with question 1, the "slow" way to

    solve the question would be to do the arithmetic

    on your calculator. The sum of the numerator is

    2, divided by 4, which equals $\frac{1}{2}$ or 0.5. The point

    of the question was to see if you noticed that four

    equivalent decimals on top divided by 4 equals the

    decimal itself. Therefore, $\frac{4(0.5)}{4} = 0.5$.

4. ETS's answer is E.

    Use the formula for distance:

    $distance = rate \times time$

    Steve runs 12 miles at 8 miles per hour, which

    means that he runs for $1\frac{1}{2}$ hours. (Or 1.5 hours, if

    you're using your calculator.) Adam runs the same

    12 miles at 6 miles per hour, which means that he

    runs for 2 hours. Adam takes half an hour longer to

    complete the race, and half an hour is 30 minutes.

5. ETS's answer is D.
   You should have noticed several things about this question. First, that the figure was not drawn to scale. So a good first step would be to redraw the figure to comply with the condition ($AB >$ CD). Second, the question asks for which of the following *must* be true. *Must* is an important word—which of the following *could* be true would change your analysis completely. So, redrawing the figure, you'd get something like this:

   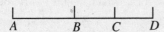

   In this figure, AB is clearly larger than CD. Since Plugging In numbers makes the distance more concrete, you might have made $AB = 3$, for example, and $CD = 2$. Since you don't know the length of BD, however, you'd have to leave it alone. Now, let's check the conditions.
   Option I: Well, this could be true, but it doesn't have to be. So Option I is out. This allows us to eliminate choices A and E.
   Option II: Since we let $AB = 3$ and $CD = 2$, then $AC = 3 + BC$ while $BD = BC + 2$. No matter what BC is, $AC > BD$. Option II is true. This allows us to eliminate choice C, which does not include Option II. We still need to check Option III.
   Option III: Since $AB > CD$, and $AC > AB$, then $AC > CD$. Option III is true; therefore, D is the answer.

6. ETS's answer is D.
   While we can't figure out the values of x or y individually, we can figure out the value of $x +$ y. Since we have two parallel lines and a line that crosses them, we know that $x + y$ is equal to angle z. Since all the angles on a line add up to 180, and since angle z is on a line next to angle of 65 degrees, we know that angle z is equal to 180–65, or 115.

7. ETS's answer is A.
   $$\frac{4^2}{2^3} + \frac{2^3}{4^2} = \frac{16}{8} + \frac{8}{16} = \frac{2}{1} + \frac{1}{2} = 2\frac{1}{2}, \text{ or } \frac{5}{2}$$

   or just use your calculator.

8. ETS's answer is E.
    The best way to solve questions like this is to try choices rather than to reason it out algebraically. Now, trying our choices, B works, but so do C and D. If you chose A, you should review remainders. If you chose B, C, or D, you jumped at an answer too quickly. Remember, this question is already edging into medium territory, so you have to be on your toes.

9. ETS's answer is E.

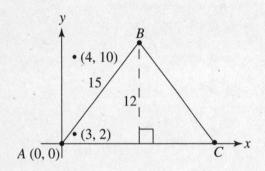

    To solve this problem, you need to figure out the ratio between the x and y values on line segment AB. If you look at the figure, AB is the hypotenuse of a right triangle with a side of 12. Without even using the Pythagorean theorem, you can tell that this triangle is one of ETS's favorite right triangles: a 3:4:5. So this has to be a 9:12:15 triangle, and the coordinates of point B are (9, 12). All the points on line segment AB are in a ratio of 9 to 12 (which is the same as 3 to 4). The only answer with that ratio is E (6, 8).

10. ETS's answer is A.

    The formula for the circumference of a circle is $C = 2\pi r$. (If you forget the formula, you can look it up at the beginning of the section.) The circumference of the circle is 5, so $5 = \pi d$. Now, just solve for d, which equals $\frac{5}{\pi}$. If you picked choice D, you might have thought the question was asking for the circumference instead of the diameter.

11. ETS's answer is A.
    Answer this question in Bite-Sized Pieces. The first step is to use your calculator to compute the sum of the subscriptions: $68.80. The down payment was half that amount, leaving $34.40 to be paid in 4 installments of $8.60 each. If you answered choices D or E, you misread the question.

12. ETS's answer is B.

We're solving for shirts and pants, which constitute 60% of total sales. Since shoes ($12,000) account for 15%, shirts and pants would be four times that amount, or $48,000. The more basic way to solve this is to find out the total value of sales and find 60% of that. If $20,000 represents 25% (or $\frac{1}{4}$) of sales, then the total must be $80,000. Using translation, you'll find that $\frac{60}{100} \times 80,000 = $48,000$.

14. ETS's answer is D.

If you got this question wrong, you either misread it or forgot the correct order of operations. Remember to do parentheses first. Translating the information to an equation, we'd get the following:

$$(1 + 2)(2 + 3)(3 + 4) = \frac{1}{2}(20 + x)$$
$$(3)(5)(7) = \frac{1}{2}(20 + x)$$
$$105 = \frac{1}{2}(20 + x)$$
$$210 = 20 + x$$
$$190 = x$$

13. ETS's answer is B.

You can tell by the question number that you have to be careful on this question. If you selected choice E, you grabbed impulsively at the Joe Bloggs answer. On this question, the safest way—as usual—is to try choices rather than to reason algebraically. Plugging In the choices for n, we get the following results:

(A) $\quad < 0 > \quad = \frac{0+1}{0-1} = \frac{1}{-1} = -1$

(B) $\quad < 2 > \quad = \frac{2+1}{2-1} = \frac{3}{1} = 3$

(C) $\quad < 3 > \quad = \frac{3+1}{3-1} = \frac{4}{2} = 2$

(D) $\quad < 4 > \quad = \frac{4+1}{4-1} = \frac{5}{3} = 1\frac{2}{3}$

(E) $\quad < 5 > \quad = \frac{5+1}{5-1} = \frac{6}{4} = \frac{3}{2} = 1\frac{1}{2}$

B has the greatest value, so that must be the answer.

15. ETS's answer is E.
If you selected choice A, you fell for a Joe Bloggs trap. This question is well into medium territory—check out the difficulty meter. Simplifying the equation, we get the following:

$$\frac{2+x}{5+x} = \frac{2}{5} + \frac{2}{5}$$

$$\frac{2+x}{5+x} = \frac{4}{5}$$

At this point, the fastest solution is to plug in the answer choices until you find the one that works. Using answer choice E:

$$\frac{2+(10)}{5+(10)} = \frac{4}{5}$$

$$\frac{12}{15} = \frac{4}{5}$$

$$\frac{12}{15} = \frac{4}{5}$$

16. ETS's answer is A.
The trick to this question is to notice that this parallelogram is actually made up of two equal triangles. By finding the area of the triangles, you can find the area of the parallelogram. The triangles are both right triangles, and the two sides given to you in the figure follow the 3:4:5 pattern. If you look at triangle DBC from a different angle, the base is 3 and the height is 4. Now you can use the formula for the area of triangle:

$$A = \frac{1}{2}\,bh$$

$$A = \frac{1}{2}\,(3)(4)$$

$$A = 6$$

Since the parallelogram consists of two triangles, its area is 2×6, or 12. (By the way, if you had estimated the area of the parallelogram, the base is 5 and the height is less than 3. The area must be less than 15, and only one answer choice is less than 15: A!)

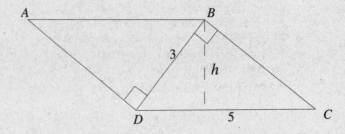

SECTION 1

17. ETS's answer is C.
This is an excellent time to turn on your calculator. Since 48,000 people live in Town X, and each household has 3.2 people, we can determine the number of households:

$$48,000 \div 3.2 = 15,000$$

And since each household has 1.2 televisions, we can now determine the number of televisions:

$$15,000 \times 1.2 = 18,000$$

19. ETS's answer is B.
A Princeton Review student, noticing the algebraic answer choices, would immediately plug in numbers to solve the problem. Since the values we choose for x and y must satisfy the equation, let's let x equal 2 and y equal 3. The perimeter p would then equal $2 + 2 + 3 + 3$, or 10. The target is y, which is equal to 3. Plugging 10 into p in each of the choices, we'd get B as the answer.

Although some of you might have answered this question right by using algebra, doing so might have caused you to make a mistake without realizing it. Trust us. Plugging In is always the safer method for this type of problem. The Joe Bloggs choice, by the way, was C.

18. ETS's answer is E.
Once again, the way *not* to solve an SAT question is to reason algebraically when you can check each of the choices.

Instead, use your calculator to start cubing integers and stop just before you exceed 200.

Integer	Cube	
1	1	
2	8	
3	27	5 integers
4	64	
5	125	
6	216	

20. ETS's answer is C.
And yet again, the slow way to solve a word problem like this is to set up equations. Letting w and l represent the number of wins and losses respectively, the slow method of setting up equations would yield the following:

$$\frac{w}{l} = \frac{3}{1}$$

$$\frac{w+6}{l} = \frac{5}{1}$$

Let's see how Princeton Review students approach this question. Plug in the answer choices, starting in the middle—choice C—and see if it works:

	Before		After	
	Wins	Losses	Wins	Losses
(A)	3			
(B)	6			
(C)	9	3 (3:1)	15	3 (5:1)
(D)	15			
(E)	24			

Bingo! We found the answer on the first try! If C didn't work, we'd move up or down depending on whether the result was too small or too big.

21. ETS's answer is B.
Since we aren't given the cost of any book, we can plug in our own values. Let's say that the average cost of the textbooks, excluding the anatomy textbook, is $10. We can make all the books cost $10 to make the problem easier. The anatomy textbook, then, would cost $30. The total cost of our textbooks would then be $130 (one $30 textbook plus ten $10 textbooks). The anatomy textbook contributes $\frac{\$30}{130}$, or $\frac{3}{13}$ of this amount.

22. ETS's answer is A.

For those students who noticed the variables in the answer choices, this question was easily solved by Plugging In. It was easiest to plug in for a and b first, and then to solve for x. Let $a = 50$ and $b = 70$. Now, the two triangles are right triangles since they are formed from the corners of rectangle $PQRS$, so you can determine the measure of the third angle in each triangle.

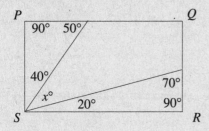

Since $\angle S = 90° = 40° + 20° + x°$
$$x = 30$$

Having computed the value of x, you can now move to the answer choices. $a + b = 50 + 70 = 120$, so you are looking for the answer choice that equals 120. Choice A is $90 + x = 90 + 30 = 120$.

23. ETS's answer is C.

First a little error avoidance: Since 5 is one of the numbers we see, 5^2, or 25 is not going to be the answer. So, eliminate A. Next, let's estimate the area before we try to solve directly. The length of the square's side is a little more than 5, so the area is going to be a little more than 5^2 or 25. Choice E is too large, so before solving the problem, we've eliminated choices A and E. If we couldn't calculate the area exactly, we could guess from among the remaining choices. To determine the area, let's begin by assigning the variable s to indicate the length of the square's side. The area is given by the formula:

$$A = s^2$$

Now, using the Pythagorean theorem, we can determine s^2 directly:

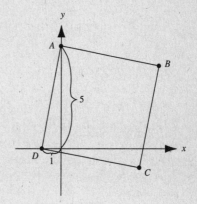

$$s^2 = 5^2 + 1^2$$
$$s^2 = 25 + 1$$
$$s^2 = 26$$

24. ETS's answer is D.

It's time to plug in values for m and n and make use of our translation approach to solving percent problems. We're working with a small percent, so plug in a big number for m. Let's say $m = 2,000$, so 0.1% of 2,000 = $\frac{0.1}{100} \times \frac{2.000}{1} = 2$. Therefore, 10% of n equals 2; rewrite this as $\frac{10}{100} \times n = 2$. Solving for n, you get $n = 20$. Now, translate the rest of the problem: "m is what percent of $10n$" can be written as $2,000 = \frac{x}{100} \times 200$. Now just solve for x, which equals 1,000. The answer is 1,000%.

25. ETS's answer is E.

Plugging In is going to be your best approach. This is a COULD question, so you will want to try several different numbers to attempt to make I, II, and III true. The exponents might have tipped you off that a negative fraction would be a good choice. Plugging In $-\frac{1}{2}$ for n we find:

I. $2n = 2(-\frac{1}{2}) = -1 < n^2 = (-\frac{1}{2})^2 = \frac{1}{4}$. TRUE

II. $2n = 2(-\frac{1}{2}) = -1 < n = -\frac{1}{2}$. TRUE

III. $n^2 = (-\frac{1}{2})^2 = -\frac{1}{2} < -n = -(-\frac{1}{2}) = \frac{1}{2}$. TRUE

Thus, I, II, and III COULD be true, and E is the answer.

1. ETS's answer is B.
   The clue in this sentence is the phrase *barren for so many years*, which provides answer B. If not from the soil, the natives must be getting their food from someplace else.

2. ETS's answer is B.
   The clue for the first blank is *defends* and the trigger word is *nor*, which means that the first blank is the opposite of *defends*. Since you need a negative word for the first blank, you can get rid of choice E. Now look at the second blank. According to the first part of the sentence, Jenkins doesn't do anything positive or negative, which means he must be somewhere in the middle. The word in the answer choices that means *somewhere in the middle* is *neutrality*.

3. ETS's answer is A.
   The clue is *been taught*, which skeptics doubt. So the skeptics must be arguing that the apes have *not* been taught, or are *fooling* their trainers. Choice A works perfectly. If you chose B, *condoning* is too difficult an answer for such an easy question.

4. ETS's answer is A.
   Great thinkers must have *deep* insights; at any rate, the first blank is a positive word. The clue here is *voiced so often*. Things that are voiced often can be called *repetitions*, or some related negative word. The only choice that has a positive word followed by a negative word is A. Once again, choice B would be too difficult in medium territory.

5. ETS's answer is D.
   Let's start with the second blank. The clue is *if not stops*, so the word in the blank must be something just short of stopping, such as *slowing down*. Which word in the second blank means *slowing down*? *Slows*, of course. The first word for D makes sense because a *plateau* is flat, so that means no weight is being gained or lost. Be careful not to choose B or E. The word in the second blank means something just short of stop. It doesn't actually mean *stop*.

6. ETS's answer is C.
   The clues for the sentence are *surprised* and *recognize*. If she's surprised that something was recognized, it must not have been obvious. So you can put *not obvious* in the first blank. That definitely gets rid of B and E. For the second blank, we also need something that means *not obvious*. The best matches for both blanks are in C. Both *oblique* and *allusion* have the sense of *not obvious*.

7. ETS's answer is E.
   The semicolon is a same-direction trigger. Because Mark hates mistakes, he will review his papers *carefully*. We can eliminate choices C and D immediately. If you weren't sure what A, B, or E mean, you had to guess. Give yourself a pat on the back if you guessed A or B rather than leaving the question blank. Even though you got the question wrong, you did the right thing. And in the long run, that's how your score goes up.

8. ETS's answer is D.
The first and second blanks are negative, possibly neutral, words. What's more, you should notice that they are saying similar things. Choice E is the only bad guess; choices A, B, and C are all good guesses. Again, guessing one of these choices would have been better than leaving the question blank.

9. ETS's answer is D.
The clue for this sentence is *subtleties*. You can easily recycle the clue in the second blank and say that the plot structure was profoundly *subtle*. The only word in the second that has a meaning in the same ballpark as *subtle* is *intricate*. Again, at the very least, you would have been better off guessing one of the hard words rather than leaving this question blank. If there were any words that you didn't know in this question, look them up!

10. ETS's answer is B.
A SHIP travels in the OCEAN just as a *plane* travels in the *air*.

11. ETS's answer is B.
BOTANY is the study of PLANTS; *astronomy* is the study of *stars*.

12. ETS's answer is B.
A CENSUS counts the POPULATION; an *inventory* counts the *supplies*. Choice E was close, but it doesn't quite work.

13. ETS's answer is C.
A CONSTELLATION is a group of STARS. You could quickly eliminate A, B, and D. Now, let's say you didn't know what an *archipelago* was. Could it mean a group of islands? Sure, Hawaii is a group of islands; maybe that's what an *archipelago* is. Looking at E, if you weren't sure what a *maverick* was, could it mean a group of herd?
E is a good guess on a hard question like this, so we're proud of you if you guessed it instead of leaving the question blank.

14. ETS's answer is A.
If you weren't sure how to make a sentence with REFINE and OIL we hope you noticed that choices B, C, and E were Joe Bloggs traps, and that D was too easy. To refine oil is to purify it, just as to *winnow* wheat is to *purify* it.

15. ETS's answer is E.
If you had trouble making a sentence, you should have eliminated answer choices with unrelated words and then worked backwards. You can eliminate C right away because the words are much too easy for a hard question. If you know what *zealous* and *audacious* mean, you know that the words in choice A and B are unrelated. If you were able to get rid of even one answer choice, then you should have guessed. (PERSPICACIOUS means having a lot of INSIGHT and *amiable* means having a lot of *friendliness*.)

16. ETS's answer is A.

    The lead words in this question are *the author's parents*. You learn about the author's parents in line 6: *my parents were at their wit's end.* The author mentions his parents again in lines 29–32: *My parents...agreed with the schoolmasters,* who thought the author was a *virtually hopeless case.* Answer choice A paraphrases the answer well (*frustrated*).

    Answer choice B is wrong because the author's parents clearly know that he's got a problem. How could they be oblivious to the fact that he was expelled from several schools?

    Answer choice C has nothing to do with the passage. You might be able to infer that the author's parents were wealthy because they sent him to a boarding school, but their attitude toward the poor has nothing to do with the main idea of the passage.

    Answer choice D confuses several unconnected ideas mentioned in the passage. There is nothing in the passage to suggest that the author's parents were schoolmasters or strict disciplinarians.

    Answer choice E contradicts the passage. The first paragraph states that the author's family lived together in Bukovina.

17. ETS's answer is C.

    According to lines 17–21, *An attempt to harmonize the imbalances in my character by means of strict discipline at a boarding school...nearly led to the same ignominious end.*

    Even if you don't know what *ignominious* means, it should still be clear that the attempt to straighten the author out had the same result as it did the before—it didn't work. This idea is paraphrased in choice C, which says that the *tactics* were *failing.*

    Answer choice A is too extreme. Perhaps the author was a bit *unstable*, but there is nothing in the passage that suggests the author was *dangerous*. And ETS doesn't like dangerous people. Remember, if an answer choice is half bad, it's all bad.

    Answer choice B is one of ETS's traps. Maybe the author did poorly in school partly because the schools were too difficult. Or maybe not. The passage tells us nothing about the difficulty of the schools. All we know is that the author was having a really hard time.

    Answer choice D is another trap. We have no way of knowing from the passage how well the author got along with his peers.

    In answer choice E, ETS is trying to get you to anticipate what will happen to the author in the future. We know that his academic career is in bad shape, but does that mean he'll never finish school?

18. ETS's answer is D.

Go back to the passage, find the word *ignominious*, and cross it out. Then read the sentence and come up with your own word. According to lines 23–24, the author just barely escaped a *final ostracism from the privileged ranks*. If he was about to get thrown out of the privileged ranks, the word that best describes that situation is *disgraceful*.

Answer choice E is wrong, because we definitely need a negative word. The other answer choices are wrong because they don't accurately describe the author's situation as it is described in the passage.

19. ETS's answer is E.

Go back to the passage, find the word *ostracism*, and cross it out. Then read the sentence and come up with your own word. Fortunately, we just worked on this sentence for the previous question. The sentence describes how the author got thrown out of the privileged ranks. The word in the answer choice that best matches *thrown out* is *banishment*.

Choice D is close, but it isn't sufficiently negative. The other answer choices are wrong because they are not negative words.

20. ETS's answer is C.

This is a general question, so you only need to know the main idea of the passage. You know that the author was not happy in the passage, because he says he felt *skushno*, a word that means *more than dreary boredom*.

You can get rid of answer choices A and E because they're positive.

Answer choice D is too extreme. ETS would never suggest that someone was suicidal.

Answer choice B is wrong because the passage never says that the author had trouble with his friends.

21. ETS's answer is B.

Your first clue to the author's attitude toward the aphorism is that he calls it *trivial*. After he quotes the aphorism, the author says, *this optimistic notion results more from wishful thinking than from practical experience*. The author clearly has a very negative opinion of it. Answer choice B gives a perfect paraphrase of *wishful thinking* by saying that the author found the aphorism *unrealistic*.

You can get rid of answer choices A and D because they are positive, and you can eliminate choice E because it refers to his *faith in it*; the author clearly has no faith in the aphorism.

Answer choice C is wrong because the author doesn't say anything about the aphorism working for others.

SECTION 2

22. ETS's answer is E.

After the quoted statement, Darrow goes on to talk about the abuse of constitutional and personal liberty by people in authority. Keeping in mind that ETS loves America, you can see that choice E is the most patriotic answer. If the jury finds the defendants guilty, it will be saying, in effect, that abuses of constitutional rights are okay. This will threaten everybody's freedom. ETS is concerned about constitutional rights in America. Choice E is also most consistent with the main idea of the passage.

Answer choice A is way off base. Whether the defendants will be harmed if convicted is not the issue.

Answer choice B is wrong; there's nothing in the passage to suggest that the jurors would be criticized if they were to convict the defendants. (In fact, the opposite would probably be true.) Remember, the passage is about constitutional rights and abuses of those rights, not the reputation of the jurors.

Answer choice C doesn't make any sense. Of course the defendants care whether they are convicted!

Answer choice D is way off the mark because the passage is not at all about money. Don't forget the main idea.

23. ETS's answer is C.

In lines 12–27, Darrow stresses an inconsistency or contradiction on the part of the prosecution—that it's okay to disregard constitutional rights in order to prosecute someone for violating the Constitution. Answer choice C is ETS's answer because Darrow asserts that the evidence against Owen was obtained by violating his constitutional rights. Therefore, if the judge had interpreted the Constitution as answer choice C suggests, Owen's trial would have been dismissed.

All the other answer choices refer to things that could get a trial dismissed, but none of them is mentioned anywhere in the passage.

24. ETS's answer is A.

You can use the information you gained from answering the previous question to answer this one. Answer choice A is correct here because Darrow believes that the prosecution is using a double standard. Lines 28–47 cite more examples of how Darrow shows that the prosecution is guilty of doing exactly what it has accused the defendants of doing. In this case, the accused are said to have used violent words, and Darrow is giving examples of violent threats that have been aimed at the defendants.

Answer choice B is close, but the evidence is not *unreliable*. Darrow's point is that the evidence was *obtained* by unconstitutional means.

Answer choice C is way off base. There is nothing in the passage to suggest that the jury holds the same view as the defendants. They wouldn't be an impartial jury if they did, would they?

Answer choice D is wrong because the lines cited in the question are about *people in high places*, not about the labor unions. Read the lines again.

Answer choice E comes out of left field. The passage doesn't say anything about state courts versus federal courts.

25. ETS's answer is D.

Line 32 indicates that Lloyd's speech was accused of being a *conspiracy*, and line 47 says that it was *gentle in comparison* to the violent epithets of anti-Communists. But we're not concerned with what Darrow said about the speech. We want to know what the prosecution said about it. Therefore, answer choice D is correct. The violent part of the speech makes it *frightening*, and the conspiratorial nature of the speech makes it a *threat*.

Answer choice C is wrong because the prosecution would never say anything positive about the defendant's speech.

Answer choice E is silly, and answer choice A is not extreme enough.

Answer choice B might be tempting, but the passage never suggests that the speech was in any way *deceptive*.

26. ETS's answer is B.

According to lines 38–40, *We have heard from people in high places that those individuals who express sympathy with labor should be stood up against a wall and shot*. The idea that the people in high places want to shoot people who express sympathy with labor is paraphrased in choice B.

Answer choice A is one of ETS's traps. According to Darrow, people in high places have suggested that labor sympathizers be shot, but that doesn't mean the people in high places have actually killed anyone.

Answer choice C is not mentioned in the passage. The *people in high places* to whom Darrow refers are not testifying in the trial.

Answer choice D is another trap. The people in high places have advocated violence against labor sympathizers, but the labor sympathizers are not necessarily criminals.

Answer choice E doesn't make sense. To suggest that labor sympathizers be stood up against a wall and shot is more than just a *foolish and insulting suggestion*.

27. ETS's answer is B.

Throughout the passage, Darrow has been commenting on the prosecution's double standards, so when he talks about what *counsel suggests*, he is again making a point about what the prosecution has said. So *counsel* refers to *the prosecution*.

Answer choices A and E are wrong because there are no expert psychologists or experts of any other sort mentioned in the passage.

Answer choice C doesn't make sense. There may be an assembly in the court room, but Darrow is not talking about the spectators.

Answer choice D doesn't make sense in context. A recommendation itself doesn't suggest anything; rather, the person making the recommendation does the suggesting.

28. ETS's answer is E.

According to lines 65–67, the jury had been told that if the defendants were to be acquitted, the jury members would be despised for agreeing with the defendants. Since Darrow objects to what the jurors were told, they must have been told this by the prosecution. The idea that people will think that the jury agrees with the defendants' beliefs is paraphrased in choice E as *promoting communism*. Remember, the answer to most specific questions will be an exact *paraphrase* of what the passage says.

The other answer choices are wrong because the question is asking about what the *prosecution* told the jury, and the prosecution is only concerned with one thing—communism.

29. ETS's answer is C.

In line 73, *bound* means *morally compelled*. By reading the last paragraph, you see that Darrow's argument is hinged on the jury's commitment to uphold the law despite how they feel personally about communism. Therefore, *bound* must mean something very compelling, something beyond an intellectual commitment and stopping short of inevitability. *Bound* means tied to something, and in this case Darrow is saying that the jury is tied to upholding the law by a moral obligation.

30.   ETS's answer is D.
      This is the only real general question in the bunch.
      It asks you to determine what Darrow is trying
      to get the jury to do through implication and
      examples. If you're stuck, try looking at a few key
      sentences. The first line of paragraph 2 discusses
      the violation of people's rights by police; the last
      two lines of the whole passage talk again about
      rights. Reading the blurb and a few key sentences
      is all you need to get the idea that Darrow's
      argument relies on the question of civil rights.

1. ETS's answer is B.
   Here's a perfect chance to use the Bowtie:

   $$\frac{3}{7} \diagdown\!\!\!\!\diagup \frac{1}{2}$$

   Since 7 > 6, you know that $\frac{1}{2}$ is greater, so
   Column B is bigger. Another way to answer this
   question is to use your calculator. Divide 3 by 7
   and 1 by 2 and compare.

2. ETS's answer is A.
   Since AB is 8, the diameter of the circle must be
   more than 8. If the diameter is more than 8, the
   radius must be more than 4.

3. ETS's answer is D.
   Try Plugging In numbers for a and b. Since 7(1)
   > 4(1), you can set $a = 1$ and $b = 1$. Therefore,
   the columns could be equal. Eliminate choices A
   and B. You can also say that $a = 2$ and $b = 1$. So
   Column A could be bigger, and you can get more
   than one result.

4. ETS's answer is C.
   Although we don't know what x and y are, we can
   use their vertical angles within the triangle:

   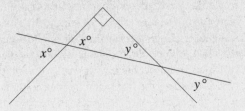

   Since $x + y + 90 = 180$, $x + y = 90$.

5. ETS's answer is B.
   This is a little confusing, but not that difficult if
   we're careful. Moving backward from 12:00, 11:
   00 would be 1 hour, 10:00 would be 2 hours, 9:00
   would be 3 hours, and 8:00 would be 4 hours. 8:15
   is 3 hours and 45 minutes.

6. ETS's answer is C.
Don't be frightened if this looks like some complex equation. The first thing to notice is that the number 1 raised to any power remains 1:
$9^n - 8^n = 1^n$
$9^1 - 8^1 = 1$
The only value of n that satisfies this equation is 1.

7. ETS's answer is D.

The Joe Bloggs response to this question is B, so the answer should be A, C, or D. Joe Bloggs thinks

$2s$ must be greater than $\dfrac{r}{2}$. Now, let's use the

formula for the area of a rectangle:

$A = rs$

$4 = rs$

Let's make $r = 1$ and $s = 4$. Now, compare the

quantities:

$\dfrac{r}{2}$ $2s$

$\dfrac{1}{2}$ $2(4)$

So the answer can't be A or C. If you let $r = 4$ and $s = 1$, the two quantities could be equal. You can get more than one result, so the answer must be D.

8. ETS's answer is A.
If you subtract the 6 girls from the 28 children, there are now 22 children. Half of these kids must be boys, so there must be 11 boys and 11 girls. Now add the 6 girls back, and you have 11 boys and 17 girls. Two times the number of girls (34) is greater than three times the number of boys (33).

9. ETS's answer is C.
First, cross out D because the problem contains only numbers. Then work out Column A:

$$\frac{\dfrac{3}{2}}{\left(\dfrac{3}{2}\right)^2} = \frac{\dfrac{3}{2}}{\dfrac{9}{4}} = \frac{3}{2} \times \frac{4}{9} = \frac{12}{18} = \frac{2}{3}$$

or use your calculator.

The quantities are equal.

10. ETS's answer is B.
If the area of the square is 25, the length of each side is 5. The perimeter of the square, then, is 20. If the perimeter of the square is 20, the perimeter of the inscribed rectangle must be less than 20.

11. ETS's answer is B.
First, plug in some numbers. Let's say $x = 4$. Since $x = y$, that means $y = 4$ also. You know that $x + y + z = 10$, so $z = 2$. That works out, so Column B can be greater. Now, find out if the columns can be equal. If $x = 5$, then $y = 5$ and $z = 0$; that's no good, z has to be positive. Could Column A be greater? If $x = 6$, then $y = 6$ and $z = -2$. That doesn't work either. Column B has to be greater.

12. ETS's answer is A.
The Joe Bloggs response here is B. This problem should give you little trouble on your calculator. Again, D should have been eliminated because there are only numbers.

13. ETS's answer is C.
We can begin by eliminating D. The Joe Bloggs response here, of course, is B. Let's determine the prime factors of 30 and 60:

$$30 = 2 \times 15 \qquad 60 = 2 \times 30$$
$$ = 2 \times 3 \times 5 \qquad = 2 \times 2 \times 15$$
$$ = 2 \times 2 \times 3 \times 5$$

Now, 30 has three distinct prime factors (2, 3, 5) and so does 60. Remember, *distinct* just means *different*.

14. ETS's answer is D.
The classic Joe Bloggs response here, of course, is B. The answer must be A, C, or D. Now, if we let x equal, say, 2, we get the following quantities:

x^2	$(x+1)^2$
2^2	$(2+1)^2$
4	9

Since Column B is greater, the answer cannot be A or C. Only one choice remains: D. (If you had to prove this to yourself, try negative numbers.)

15. ETS's answer is A.
First cross off choice D. The classic Joe Bloggs answer here is C. The increase from 99 to 100 and the decrease from 100 to 99 is 1 in both cases, but the *percent* increase and decrease are different. You're down to A or B. The percent increase from 99 to 100 is:

$$\frac{1}{99} \times 100 = 1.01\%.$$

The percent decrease from 100 to 99 is:

$$\frac{1}{100} \times 100 = 1\%.$$

16. ETS's answer is 2.

$$\frac{x + 2x + 3x}{2} = 6$$
$$\frac{6x}{2} = 6$$
$$6x = 12$$
$$x = 2$$

Grid it like this:

Remember that the first grid-in question returns the difficulty meter to easy.

17. ETS's answer is 14.

Of the 24 fish, 3 are tetras. Of the remaining 21 fish, $\frac{2}{3}$ are guppies.

Two thirds of 21 is 14.

18. ETS's answer is 145.

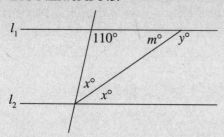

Since the two lines are parallel, $110 + 2x = 180$. Solving this equation for x, we get $x = 35$. Looking at the triangle, the missing angle (m) can be found by solving the equation $110 + x + m = 180$. Since $x = 35$, $m = 35$. Since $m + y = 180$ and $m = 35$, $y = 145$.

19. ETS's answer is 234.
    Since every even-numbered page has 6 articles and every odd-numbered page has 7, there are 13 articles for every two pages. A 36-page paper, then, would contain 18 such paired pages, or $18 \times 13 = 234$ articles.

20. ETS's answer is 19, 39, 59, 79, or 99.
    The simplest way to solve this question would be to find values of n that satisfy the first condition, and then to check which of those also satisfy the second condition. So, let's find some numbers that leave a remainder of 4 when divided by 5:
    9, 14, 19, 24, 29, . . .
    That should be enough. Now, let's check which of these leaves a remainder of 3 when divided by 4.
    $9 \div 4 = 2 \text{ R } 1$
    $14 \div 4 = 3 \text{ R } 2$
    $19 \div 4 = 4 \text{ R } 3$
    Bingo. 19 is one acceptable response.

21. ETS's answer is 36.
   If $x^2 = 16$, then $x = \pm 4$. If $y^2 = 4$, then $y = \pm 2$.
   To maximize $(x - y)^2$, we need to maximize the difference:

   $$(4 - 2)^2 = 2^2 = 4$$
   $$[4 - (-2)]^2 = 6^2 = 36$$
   $$[(-4) - 2]^2 = (-6)^2 = 36$$
   $$[(-4) - (-2)]^2 = (-2)^2 = 4$$

   Thus, the maximum value of the expression is 36.

22. ETS's answer is 3.
   The first step is to draw a diagram, which requires some thought:

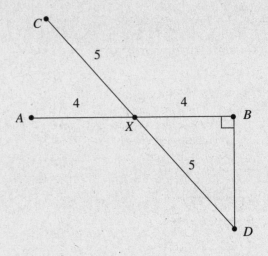

   You should notice that BD is part of one of ETS's favorite right triangles: a 3:4:5 triangle. So $BD = 3$.

SECTION 3

23. ETS's answer is 30.

    Let's proceed step-by-step, starting with the easiest equations to solve. If 40 CDs equal $480, each one equals $12. Since this is three times the cost of a cassette tape, each cassette tape costs $4. Since $600 equals the CDs ($480) and the cassette tapes, the total cassette tape sales were $120. At $4 a cassette tape, 30 cassette tapes were sold.

24. ETS's answer is 15.

    We call these group questions, and we have an easy formula for solving them:

    Total = Group 1 + Group 2 – Both + Neither

    In this question the Total is 80 students, Group 1 is the 30 French students, and Group 2 is the 40 Spanish students. You also know that 25 students study Neither. Now plug those values into the formula:

    $$80 = 30 + 40 - b + 25$$

    Then solve for b, which equals 15.

25. ETS's answer is .5.

First, let's set up equations for the areas of the two triangles:

$$\left(\frac{1}{2}\right)(AC)(AB) + \left(\frac{1}{2}\right)(CE)(ED)$$

Since both triangles are isosceles, $AC = AB$ and $CE = ED$. Thus, the previous equation becomes

$$\left(\frac{1}{2}\right)(AC)^2 + \frac{1}{2}(CE)^2$$

$$\frac{1}{2}[(AC)^2 + (CE)^2]$$

Now, using the Pythagorean theorem, we know that $(AC)^2 + (CE)^2 = 1$

So, the sum of the required areas is $\frac{1}{2}(1)$ or $\frac{1}{2}$.

SECTION 4

1. ETS's answer is D.
   We're looking for a word along the lines of
   erosion; *collapse* is the only choice that fits.

2. ETS's answer is B.
   The clue here is *external factors*. If animal
   behaviors are *innate*, they would be relatively
   unaffected by external factors.

3. ETS's answer is A.
   The clue in this sentence is *anarchy*, which means
   lack of order. If people have been *shaken* by the
   lack of order, they must be ready to buy *order* at
   any price. ETS's answer is, in fact, *order*.

4. ETS's answer is E.
   The clue here is *care* and *zeal*. Even if you don't
   know what *zeal* means, the second blank must
   reflect Marisa's being careful. D and E are the
   only choices that indicate her careful completion
   of duties. *Zeal* means enthusiasm, which locks in
   E as the answer. If you chose A or B, remember
   that this is not yet a difficult question that calls for
   a difficult answer.

5. ETS's answer is B.
   We know that her slogans were *forgotten clichés*.
   Now, even if you aren't sure what a cliché is, you
   know that it has been *revived*. The blank must be
   a positive word and something along the lines of
   given. Choice C is negative; choice E misses the
   clue. Choice D makes absolutely no sense, and for
   a medium question is probably too difficult to be
   the answer anyway. Choice A is way off base.

6. ETS's answer is C.
   We know the general's civilian life is simple,
   dignified, and *stoic*. The only blank that fits is C.
   Choices B and D miss the clue. Choices A and
   E, if you weren't sure what they mean, are good
   guesses, but wrong.

7. ETS's answer is A.
   The clue is *barbarity of some criminal penalties*.
   We're looking for a word that means avoid
   or lessen. Choices B and D miss the point
   completely. If you know what *condone* means, it
   also misses the point; if not, it's not a bad guess.
   Choice E is a Joe Bloggs trap that contradicts the
   clue.

8. ETS's answer is C.
   The clue in this sentence is *against any position*.
   If Melissa is against everything, then she must
   not be very agreeable. The opposite of *agreeable*
   is *contrary*. Choice B may seem close, but the
   sentence says nothing about whether Melissa does
   what she is supposed to do.

9. ETS's answer is E.
The clue for the second blank is *appreciated his specialized knowledge*, and the trigger word is *but*, which tells you that the second part of the sentence must mean the opposite of the clue. If some students didn't appreciate the specialized knowledge, then the *disappointed* students had *non-specialized* interests. The only word in the answer choices that means *non-specialized* is *comprehensive*. The other word in choice E also makes sense, because it fits the clue. We know that the professor has *specialized knowledge*, so if his lecture focused *exclusively* on something, then it was very specialized.

10. ETS's answer is D.
The clues in this sentence are *ancient ruins of marvelous bygone civilizations* and *sad*. What is sad about looking at the ruins of ancient civilizations? Seeing that *human greatness* doesn't last. Therefore, you can put *doesn't last* in the blank, and the best match is *transience*.

11. ETS's answer is E.
A CAKE is a kind of DESSERT just as a *pediatrician* is a kind of *doctor*.

12. ETS's answer is C.
A good WEIGHTLIFTER needs STRENGTH just as a good *marathoner* needs *endurance*. A goalie may need skill, but strength and endurance are more specific.

13. ETS's answer is E.
A HURRICANE is a larger version of a BREEZE just as a *mountain* is a larger version of a *hill*.

14. ETS's answer is A.
IMMORTAL means without DEATH, just as *anonymous* means without *fame*.

15. ETS's answer is B.
A TAPESTRY is made of THREAD. A *mosaic* is made of *tiles*. If you had trouble making a sentence, you should have eliminated answer choices with unrelated words and then Worked Backward. The words in choice D do not have a clear relationship. *Pizza* comes in the shape of a *pie*. Does a TAPESTRY come in the shape of a THREAD? That doesn't make any sense. A *ruler* is separated into *divisions*. Is a TAPESTRY separated into THREADs? That doesn't make sense either. A *car* is powered by an *engine*. Is a TAPESTRY powered by a THREAD? That's ridiculous. Choices A, C, and E can each be eliminated by working backward, leaving choice B, which is the answer.

16. ETS's answer is E.
A LUBRICANT reduces FRICTION, and a *muffler* reduces *noise*. If you had trouble making a sentence, try using POE. A *motor* can be powered by *electricity*, but nothing can be powered by FRICTION. Eliminate A. *Speed* and *drag* have no relationship. Eliminate B. *Insulation* keeps in *heat*. Could something keep in FRICTION? Not likely. Eliminate C. You could say that an *adhesive* makes a *connection*, but that's a weak relationship, which means E is a better choice.

17. ETS's answer is B.
A PARODY is a humorous IMITATION just as a *limerick* is a humorous *poem*. If you chose C, D, or E, your sentence may not have been specific enough.

18. ETS's answer is C.
A COMET is followed by a TAIL, and a *vessel* is followed by a *wake*. Did you use POE? A *lane* is for a single line of *traffic*. A TAIL is not for a single line of COMET. Eliminate A. A *trajectory* is the path that a *missile* travels along. A TAIL is not the path a COMET travels along. Eliminate B. An *engine* runs on *fuel*. A COMET doesn't run on TAIL. The *crest* is the top of a *wave*. The TAIL is not the top of a COMET.

19. ETS's answer is C.
First of all, choice B is a Joe Bloggs trap because *grammar* makes Joe think of LANGUAGE. Unless you know what a NEOLOGISM is, you're better off Working Backward to answer this question. You can come up with a sentence for choice C: An *innovation* is a new development in *technology*. Could a NEOLOGISM be a new development in LANGUAGE? Sure. Choice C is your best guess, even if you didn't know some of the words in the other answer choices.

20. ETS's answer is C.
This is a hard question, so you can eliminate choices A and D because *letter* and *folder* make Joe think of BOOK. You can eliminate choice B because *vote* and *constitution* do not have a clear relationship. If you simply guessed the hardest word, *codicil*, you would have found the answer, although E would not have been a bad guess. (An ADDENDUM is an addition to a BOOK and *codicil* is an addition to a *will*.)

21. ETS's answer is A.
The words in choices D and E have no relationship, so those choices can be eliminated. Here's a way to decide among the remaining choices: The words in choices B and C have opposite meanings (one word is positive and the other word is negative), while the words in choice A have similar meanings (both words are negative). Choice A is the odd one out, which would make it the best guess. (Having a PENCHANT means being very INCLINED. *Loathing* means being very *contemptuous*.)

22. ETS's answer is D.
The words in E are too easy for a hard question, so you can eliminate them. If you know what a *pagan* is, you know it has no relationship with *morals*, so you can eliminate A. An *arsonist* starts a *fire*. Does a VAGRANT start a DOMICILE? No. Eliminate C. An *exile* is a person without a *country*. Is a VAGRANT a person without a DOMICILE? Yup.

23. ETS's answer is D.
Joe Bloggs picks B, so eliminate that right away. The words in choices C and E have no relationship, so eliminate them. Now you're down to a fifty-fifty guess. Not bad. *Reprehensible* means deserving *censure* and MERITORIOUS means deserving PRAISE.

24. ETS's answer is C.

This is a general question, so you only need to know the main idea of the passage. In simple terms, the passage talks about the difference between cats and dogs. This is exactly what choice C says.

Notice that the author presents both sides of the issue and doesn't advocate one animal over the other. That's why answer choices B and D are wrong.

Answer choice A is way too extreme. If you don't know what *enmity* means, look it up and you'll see.

Answer choice E is too specific and only covers one section of the passage, not the primary purpose of the passage as a whole.

25. ETS's answer is C.

The lead words in this question are *the domestic cat*, which should lead you to the second paragraph. According to lines 12–14, *The young cat becomes bimental. It may be a cat physically, but mentally it is both feline and human.* To be both feline and human is definitely a *contradiction.*

Common sense kills answer choice A, because cats don't have two feet.

Answer choice B is wrong because domestic cats are tame by definition. Otherwise, they would be wild.

Answer choice D is wrong because cats aren't soldiers.

Answer choice E doesn't make any sense. Do cats dominate humans? No way!

26. ETS's answer is E.

According to the passage, the cat treats its human owners as *pseudoparents* because *they took over from the real mother at a sensitive stage of the kitten's development.* That means the human owners are obviously not the kitten's real parents, but rather like adoptive parents that took over from the kitten's real mother. Choice E says exactly that.

Answer choice A is wrong because *pseudo-* doesn't mean *part-time*. Human owners can be full-time parents to a cat, but that doesn't make them the cat's *real* parents.

Answer choice B misses the mark because the passage is talking about the parents of cats, not the parents of adults.

Answer choice C is wrong because the passage doesn't say anything about *neglect.*

Answer choice D makes no sense. How can someone have the characteristics of both humans and cats?

27. ETS's answer is A.

The lead words in this question are *difference between dogs and cats*, which should lead you right to the beginning of the third paragraph. According to lines 32–38, *the adult pet dog sees its human family as both pseudoparents and dominant members of the pack.*

On the other hand, cats *never hunt in packs*, and *most of their day is spend in solitary stalking.* So while dogs see their owners as leaders of the pack, cats do not because they're solitary. This is paraphrased in choice A.

Answer choice B has it backward. Dogs are obedient, not cats.

Answer choice C comes out of nowhere. Where does it say that cats are creative?

Answer choice D directly contradicts the passage. According to lines 36–38, *Cats do have a complex social organization.* Read carefully.

Answer choice E also contradicts the passage. According to line 38, cats spend most of their time *in solitary stalking*, which means they must be good hunters.

28. ETS's answer is C.

According to the lines 27–30, *Dogs live in packs with tightly controlled status relationships among the individuals. There are top dogs, middle dogs, and bottom dogs...* This describes a social structure that is *hierarchical*. (If you don't know what *hierarchical* means, look it up!)

The other answer choices are wrong because none of them accurately describes the social structure in the lines quoted above. There is nothing *abstract* or *flexible* about *tightly controlled status relationships*, nor is there any mention of male domination in the passage. And *exclusivity* is certainly not the issue.

29. ETS's answer is D.

The third paragraph is all about the difference between cats and dogs. Lines 39–43 emphasize the solitary nature of cats, which differs from the group-oriented nature of dogs. This is exactly what choice D says.

Answer choice A comes out of left field. Where does it say that cats are lazy? According to the passage, cats don't hunt in packs because they are *solitary* creatures, not because they are lazy.

Answer choice B is rude. To say that dogs are ignorant is insulting to dog owners, and ETS never insults anybody. Can you imagine all the angry phone calls they would get if this choice were the answer?

Answer choice C is way too extreme. *Antipathy* is a very strong word. (If you don't know what it means, look it up and you'll see.) Cat owners would certainly be angry if this choice were the answer.

Answer choice E is also rude to cat owners. Remember, ETS doesn't like to upset people.

30. ETS's answer is E.

Go back to the passage, find *much-lauded*, and cross it out. Then read the sentence and come up with your own word. *Much-lauded* is describing the "group loyalty" phenomenon. From the context, there is no reason to believe that the "group loyalty" phenomenon is *overly discussed*, *complicated*, or *controversial*, so you can get rid of B, C, and D. Choice A is too extreme, which only leaves E.

31. ETS's answer is E.

According to the passage, an *ambitious Yuppie* is an example of someone who is not a typical cat owner. Since cat-owners are solitary people, that means the *ambitious Yuppie* must be a group-oriented person. Accordingly, choice E is the answer.

Answer choices A and D are insulting to Yuppies, and ETS wants to avoid controversy.

Answer choice B doesn't make any sense, and there is no mention of virtue anywhere in the passage.

Answer choice C might be tempting, but ETS likes to avoid *stereotypes* because they can get it in trouble.

32. ETS's answer is B.

You can immediately eliminate choices A, C, D, and E because ETS would never say anything negative about women. According to the sixth paragraph, the differences between the roles of prehistoric men and women *contributed to a human male "pack mentality" that is far less marked in females*. This idea is paraphrased in choice B.

33. ETS's answer is C.

To answer this question, you have to know what *caricatured* means. A caricature is an exaggerated drawing, so the author is saying that he exaggerated in the passage. He is thus qualifying some of the generalizations he has made in the passage.

   Answer choice A is too extreme. ETS would never suggest that the author of one of her passages made a *futile* argument.

   Answer choice B is also too extreme. ETS doesn't deal with *glaring contradictions*.

   Answer choice D goes in the wrong direction. In the lines cited in the question, the author admits that he exaggerated in order to make his point, so he's trying to ensure that readers don't overestimate what he said in the passage.

   Answer choice E sounds like psychobabble, and it also has nothing to do with what the author is saying at the end of the passage.

34. ETS's answer is D.

You can use the answer to question 33 to help you answer this question. Since the author is qualifying some of the generalizations he made, he's modifying the position he took earlier.

   There are no *examples* or *summaries* in the last four sentences of the passage, so kill answer choices A and B.

   Answer choice C is wrong because there are no *reasons* in lines 86–94, and answer choice E is wrong because there are no *rebuttals* or *opposing views* anywhere in the passage.

35. ETS's answer is C.

This is a general question, but it is also an EXCEPT question, so do it last. The only way to answer this question is to search through the passage for each of the answer choices. Remember, you're looking for the answer choice that is *not* there. The passage uses a *statistic* in line 70–73, makes a *parenthetical statement* in lines 45–46, restates an *argument* in lines 84–86, and makes *generalizations* throughout the passage. Answer C is the only one left.

SECTION 5

1. ETS's answer is B.

   This simple equation should present us with little difficulty, although beware: It is on precisely such questions that our guard comes down and we become careless! Plugging In the answer choices is safest.

   Only B works:

   $$2 + (0) = 2 - (0)$$
   $$2 = 2$$

2. ETS's answer is D.

   If you missed this question, you either misread the question or miscounted the lines. Choice D has 6 horizontal lines and 2 vertical ones. Remember, horizontal means side to side, and vertical means up and down.

3. ETS's answer is B.

   As the instructions to every Math section remind us, the area of a triangle is given by the formula:

   $$A = \frac{1}{2}bh$$

   Since the base is 4 and the height is 1, the area is 2.

   $$A = \frac{1}{2}(4)(1)$$

4. ETS's answer is B.

   Translating the word *of* as *times*, we get the following equation:

   $$\left(\frac{3}{5}\right) = \left(\frac{x}{10}\right)$$

   $$\left(\frac{3}{5}\right) = \left(\frac{x}{10}\right)$$

   $$5x = 30$$
   $$x = 6$$

5. ETS's answer is E.
   With algebraic answer choices, we should plug in numbers. Let's let $x = y = 2$, which makes $z = 4$. Plugging these values into the choices, we'd get the following:

   [Yes]   (A) $2(2) + 2(2) = 2(4)$

   [Yes]   (B) $2 - 2 = 0$

   [Yes]   (C) $2 - 4 = 2 - 4$

   [Yes]   (D) $2 = \dfrac{4}{2}$

   [No]   (E) $4 - 2 = 2(2)$

6. ETS's answer is A.
   Keep in mind that this figure is not drawn to scale. Since $AC \parallel ED$, we know that the following angles are equal:

   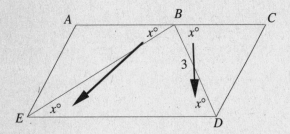

   Since $\triangle EBD$ has two equal angles, the opposing sides are also equal. Therefore, $BE = BD = 3$.

7. ETS's answer is C.
   If you missed this question, you should review decimal place values:

   $$\frac{900}{10} = 90$$

   $$\frac{90}{100} = 0.9$$

   $$\frac{9}{1000} = 0.009$$

   $$\begin{array}{r} 90 \\ 0.9 \\ +\ 0.009 \\ \hline 90.909 \end{array}$$

   Remember, you can use your calculator to help you solve this problem.

8. ETS's answer is B.
   Twenty percent of the coins are either nickels or dimes, so 80% are neither. Eighty percent of 220 equals 176. Use your calculator!

9. ETS's answer is E.
    If the area of square *A* is 16, the length of each side is 4 and the perimeter is 16. We are told that this is two-thirds of *B*'s perimeter, which we can calculate:

    $$16 = \frac{2}{3}B$$

    $$\left(\frac{3}{2}\right)16 = B$$

    $$24 = B$$

    Now that we know the perimeter of *B*, we can calculate the perimeter of *C*:

    $$24 = \frac{2}{3}C$$

    $$\left(\frac{3}{2}\right)(24) = C$$

    $$36 = C$$

    If the perimeter of *C* is 36, each side is 9 and the area of *C* is 9^2, or 81. If you chose B, you need to read the question more carefully.

10. ETS's answer is E.
    First, by estimation, we know that the mixture contains more wheat than rye; so wheat must be more than 5. So let's eliminate choices A and B. Use the Ratio Box.

Corn	Wheat	Rye	Total
3	5	2	10
	2.5	2.5	
	12.5	5	

11. ETS's answer is D.
    Note first that this is an EXCEPT question. Now, since $a^2b = 12^2$, and *b* is an odd integer, let's see what we can come up with. The first value for *b* that occurs to us is 1, so we get the following:
    $a^2b = 12^2$
    $(a^2)(1) = 12^2$
    $a^2 = 12^2$
    $a = 12$
    If *a* equals 12, it is divisible by 1, 2, 3, 4, 6, and 12. So the only choice that remains is D.

12. ETS's answer is D.
    If the first and last flips were heads, we could have 9 consecutive heads, followed by 10 consecutive tails and the final head.

13. ETS's answer is C.

Estimating first, x is less than 90 and more than 20. So we can eliminate choices A and E. Now let's examine the figure:

Since $l_1 \parallel l_2$, 130 plus the other angle in the triangle is 150. So the other angle in the triangle must be 20, which means that x is 70.

15. ETS's answer is D.

If you use your calculator, this problem should not give you any trouble. You can convert each of the fractions to decimals with your calculator and then apply the exponent. In choice D:

$$\left(\frac{2}{5}\right)^3 = (.4)^3 = .064.$$

14. ETS's answer is D.

Note before we begin that the question asks for what *must* be true. Let's start with the first option:

I. $2 + 3 = 5$
    $3 + 4 = 7$

Option I must be true. Eliminate choice B.
Let's check the second option:

II. $2 + 3 + 4 = 9$

Option II is false. Eliminate choices C and E.
We still need to check the third option:

III. $2 + 3 + 4 = 9$
      $3 + 4 + 5 = 12$
      $4 + 5 + 6 = 15$

Option III must be true. Eliminate choice A.

16. ETS's answer is B.
Use an Average Pie to solve this one. Write in the number of things, which is 4, and the average, which is 11.

Multiply to find the total, which is 44. Now you have to be careful with the vocabulary in the question. We know that the four *distinct positive integers* add up to 44. To find the greatest possible value of one of them, you need to figure out the smallest possible value of the other three. Since distinct means different, the other three numbers have to be the smallest positive integers: 1, 2, and 3. Those add up to 6, so the fourth number must be 44 – 6, or 38.

17. ETS's answer is A.
Do NOT try to figure out the seven numbers in the original list! The median is the middle number in a list of numbers. Since 8 is lower than every other number, and 43 is higher, they won't change the value of the median. This means that option II is wrong, so we can eliminate choices B, D, and E. Since choices A and C both include I, we know it must be true without even checking it. Let's focus on option III. The mode is the number repeated most often. Well, since 8 and 43 weren't in the original list, they can't change the mode. Eliminate choice C and pick choice A.

18. ETS's answer is E.
This problem is probably best approached by the brute force method of trial and error. (On the SAT, with the clock ticking away, you'll often find that you don't have the time to be logical.) Eventually, you'd discover that circle E is the answer. If you were logical, you'd notice that rows BE and AE are identical. That being the case, circle A equals circle B, and circle D equals circle C. The odd man out is circle E.

19. ETS's answer is E.
Plug in 3 for c. The question is now asking what percent of 9 is 9. The answer would be 100. Whichever choice gives you 100 when 3 is plugged in for c is the answer. Therefore E is the answer. Remember, Plugging In good numbers will make your life much easier!

20. ETS's answer is C.
We trust you noticed that choice D is too simple an answer for this question since it can be arrived at by adding the only two numbers we are given. Likewise, choice E is another Joe Bloggs choice. Looking at the figure, we should not assume that the lines are parallel. (Did you?) Instead, we must use vertical angles to compute the following values:

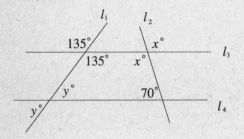

Since the sum of a quadrilateral's interior angles is 360°, we get the following equation:
$135 + x + 70 + y = 360$
$205 + x + y = 360$
$x + y = 155$

21. ETS's answer is C.
First, we need to compute all possible values of n:

$\sqrt{n}$	n
1	1
2	4
3	9
4	16
5	25
6	36
7	49
8	64
9	81

Now, careful! The median value for $\sqrt{n}$ is 5, but the median value for n is 25.

22. ETS's answer is C.

You can find the answer to this question by using the side of your answer sheet as a ruler and guesstimating. Since $XY = 12$, the hypotenuse of each triangle is 6. Now mark off the length of 6 with your homemade ruler and compare that to a side of one of the triangles. You can guesstimate that the side is about 4. Using that approximation, calculate that since the base and height of both triangles is 4, the area of each triangle is $\frac{1}{2}(4)(4)$, or 8. The area of both triangles together is 16, which is closest to 18, in choice C. Remember, ETS wants you to do complicated geometry, but all you care about is finding the answer.

23. ETS's answer is D.
Take out your calculator:
216,000 + 20% of 216,000 = 259,200
204,000 + 20% of 204,000 = 244,800
                                14,400
Another route to the answer is to take the difference immediately (216,000 − 204,000 = 12,000) and then to increase that by 20%. On a calculator, either solution is equally effective.

24. ETS's answer is D.

The formula for slope is $\frac{y_2 - y_1}{x_2 - x_1}$. Plugging In our given points, we can solve for m.

$$\frac{6 - (9)}{-2 - m} = \frac{-3}{2}$$

$$\frac{15}{-2 - m} = \frac{-3}{2}$$

$$30 = (-3)(-2 - m)$$
$$-10 = -2 - m$$
$$-8 = -m$$
$$8 = m$$

25. ETS's answer is B.

Substituting 10 for T and 80 for P, we get the following equation to solve:

$$80 = \frac{(3100) + (10L)^2}{100}$$
$$8000 = 3100 + (10L)^2$$
$$4900 = 100L^2$$
$$49 = L^2$$

1. ETS's answer is B.

   According to lines 13–15, the combination of live music and pictures adds up to something truly spectacular and affecting. The phrase in the passage, *the fusion of picture and live music* is paraphrased in choice B as *a combination of music and image.*

   Answer choice A is wrong because there's nothing in the passage to indicate that the author believes music is the most important element in silent films. In fact, this answer choice directly contradicts the lines cited in the questions, which tell us that there was a *fusion* of picture and music.

   Answer choices C and D are wrong for the same reason. According to the passage, music and pictures in silent film are of equal importance, and one is not better or worse than the other.

   Answer choice E is way off. The lines cited in the question are about *music* and *pictures*.

2. ETS's answer is C.

   According to lines 16–19, the enthusiasm of the filmmakers was more evident *before formulas took shape and when there was more room for experimentation.* So *formulas* must have been followed after the period of experimentation, which means that *formulas* are the opposite of *experimentation.* In choice C, *standardized film techniques* are the opposite of experimentation.

   Answer choices A and E don't make any sense. How can *events* or *theaters* be *formulas*? Use common sense.

   Answer choice B is an example of *experimentation,* not a *formula.*

   Answer choice D is not mentioned anywhere in the third paragraph.

3. ETS's answer is A.

   According to lines 20–22, the *enthusiastic uncertainty* led to *such accidental discoveries as new camera or editing techniques.* Thus, the filmmakers were excited to be trying new things.

   Answer choice B confuses several ideas. The *enthusiastic uncertainty* existed *before* formulas took shape.

   Answer choice C is wrong because there are no *obstacles* mentioned in the third paragraph.

   Answer choice D is wrong for the same reason that choice B is wrong. The passage is talking about the time *before* formulas and conventions, back when filmmakers still experimented.

   Answer choice E is way off base. The passage says nothing about filmmakers being *eager to please* or *unsure what the public wanted.* Go back to the passage and read more carefully.

4. ETS's answer is B.

   According to lines 28–34, the prints of silent films that exist today are of poor quality, but the prints they used in the movie houses originally must have been of high quality in order to attract so many people. So the poor prints we have today don't show us what the films really looked like back them. This idea is best paraphrased in answer choice B.

   Answer choice A is much too extreme. ETS's authors are never *disgusted.*

   Answer choice C also expresses an emotion that ETS doesn't like. *Regret* is too negative.

   Answer choice D is wrong because the passage never mentions any *pitfalls.*

   Answer choice E completely contradicts the main idea of the passage. The author is clearly a big fan of silent films.

5. ETS's answer is E.
Go back to the passage, find *legends*, and cross it out. Then read the sentence and come up with your own word. The clue, in effect, is *to the contrary*, so you can put *contradiction* in the blank. The best match in the answer choices is *misconceptions*.

    Answer choices B, C, D make no sense whatsoever in context. Would you say *despite movie stars to the contrary*? Of course not.

    Answer choice A might be tempting, but it doesn't match the clue in the passage.

6. ETS's answer is A.
You can use the last question to help you answer this question. The last sentence says that the acting in silent movies was very subtle and restrained, although people now have precisely the opposite view of it. The opposite of subtle and restrained acting is *overacting*, which is exactly what choice A is about.

    Answer choice B mixes up the ideas in the last sentence. The *legends* were about the acting of silent film actors, not about the actors themselves.

    Answer choice C is very wrong. The last sentence says nothing about what today's filmmakers should do.

    Answer choice D is wrong because the last sentence says nothing about *visual effects*.

    Answer choice E is mentioned earlier in the paragraph, but this is not what the last sentence says.

7. ETS's answer is C.
Again, you can use the previous question to answer this question. The last sentence says that the acting in silent movies was actually very *subtle* and *restrained*, and in the last question we said that this was the opposite of *overacting*. So *restrained* acting must be, in some sense, *underacting*. Therefore, the best match is *understated*.

    Answer choices A and B miss by a long shot because *restrained* doesn't mean *sincere* or *dramatic* in any context.

    Answer choice D is close, but something can be *expressive* even if it's *subtle* and *restrained*.

    Answer choice E doesn't fit in the context of the passage at all.

8. ETS's answer is A.
In lines 51–54, the author says, *What I believed to be a failure of the audience to respond in the manner I expected was, in fact, only their concentration on what I was doing.* So, although the author originally thought that she wasn't getting through to the audience, it turned out that they were actually paying very close attention to what she was doing. The best paraphrase for this idea is in choice A.

    Answer choice B is wrong because ETS's authors never *resort to stereotypes*.

    The author never says that exaggeration is an *essential* part of mime, so you can cross off C.

    Answer choice D is close, but the author is talking about the how well the audience responded to mime, not how much they knew about it.

    Answer choice E is ridiculous. The whole point of mime is that the actor remains completely silent!

9. ETS's answer is C.
You can use what you learned from the last question to help you answer this question. The author of the second passage originally thought she was failing with her audience, but it turned out she had actually succeeded. The previous passage mentions experimentation and accidental discovery (look back at question 3). So the filmmakers in Passage 1 and the author of Passage 2 both used trial and error to make new discoveries. If you look at the other answer choices, they all apply to only one of the two passages.

Answer choice is A is wrong because props are not mentioned in either passage. If it's not mentioned in the passage, it's not ETS's answer.

Answer choice B makes no sense. Does a mime use sophisticated technology? Certainly not. Don't forget to use common sense.

Answer choice D completely contradicts the main idea of both passages. Both silent film and mime are *silent*. That means there's no *dialogue*!

Answer choice E is wrong because the lines cited in the question make no mention of *loyal followings*.

10. ETS's answer is B.
The sentence in question refers to mime as a *physical medium*. In this case, a medium is the material that an artist uses to create art. For example, a painter uses paint and a canvas as a medium. But for a mime, her own body is the physical medium through which *the figures of my imagination play their dance of life*. So she allows her characters (figuratively) to take over her body. The best paraphrase of this idea is in choice B.

Answer choice A is wrong because ETS would never suggest that artists have no control.

Answer choices C and D are not mentioned anywhere in the passage.

Answer choice E contradicts the main idea of the passage. The author is a mime, which means she doesn't use speech or music. So why would she suggest that such performances have limitations?

11. ETS's answer is C.
The connection between the topics of the two passages is that both mimes and silent films communicate without words. But if it were true that silent films actually used words, then the two arts would not be as similar as they seem. Choice C introduces this fact and, therefore, makes mime and silent film seem less similar.

Answer choice A gets completely off the topic. What do vaudeville and theater have to do with the similarity between mime and silent film?

Answer choice B doesn't lessen the similarity. Can't mime also present fictional drama and factual information?

Answer choice D is ridiculous. What could this possibly have to do the comparison between silent film and mime? Just because ETS wrote the answer choice doesn't mean you have to take it seriously.

Answer choice E also misses the mark. What does popularity of silent film have to do with its relationship to mime? Not much.

12. ETS's answer is C.
As you know from the previous question, the similarity between silent film and mime is that they are both *silent*. If you're not using your ears to enjoy silent film and mime, then you must be using your *eyes*. So the similarity lies in the *visual* aspect, which leads you to answer choice C.

Answer choice A is silly. Do mimes use special effects? Of course not.

Answer choice B might be tempting, but the passages are not about *differences* in dramatic styles.

Answer choice D is not mentioned anywhere in either passage. Remember, this is a main idea question. How can something that is never mentioned be the main idea?

Answer choice E is wrong because there is no *nostalgia* in Passage 2.

SECTION 6

13. ETS's answer is E.

     According to line 12 in Passage 1, silent films depended on a *large and receptive audience*. The author of Passage 2 says, *The individuals in my audience also have responsibilities—they must be collaborators* (lines 65–66). So the common element is audience participation.

     Answer choice A is wrong because there is no mention of *different dramatic styles* in either passage. If it's not in the passage, then it's not ETS's answer.

     Passage 1 never mentions any *exaggeration*, so cross off answer choice B.

     Answer choices C and D are wrong because Passage 2 never mentions *current events* or *high audience attendance*.

1. ETS's answer is E.
    This is an excellent calculator question.

    Here are the costs per unit for each color:

    Black = $\dfrac{2}{5}$ = .40 per button

    Blue = $\dfrac{2}{6}$ = .33 per button

    Brown = $\dfrac{3}{8}$ = .375 per button

    Orange = $\dfrac{4}{12}$ = .33 per button

    Red = $\dfrac{4}{7}$ = .57 per button

2. ETS's answer is D.
    To answer this just start Plugging In values of k
    until you get into the 70–74 range:
    $6(12) + 1 = 73$

3. ETS's answer is E.
    A calculator might actually slow you down on this
    question. Instead, simply reduce the expression
    before calculation:

    $$= \left(\dfrac{4}{5} \times 3\right)\left(\dfrac{3}{4} \times 5\right)\left(\dfrac{5}{3} \times 4\right) =$$
    $$= \dfrac{4 \cdot 3 \cdot \cancel{3} \cdot \cancel{5} \cdot 5 \cdot \cancel{4}}{\cancel{3} \cdot \cancel{5} \cdot \cancel{4}}$$
    $$= 60$$

4. ETS's answer is B.
    Again, before you reach for your calculator, reduce
    the expression:

    $$\dfrac{x^2}{x^3} = \dfrac{\cancel{x} \cdot \cancel{x}}{\cancel{x} \cdot \cancel{x} \cdot x} = \dfrac{1}{x}$$

    then simply try each choice; $\dfrac{1}{-1}$ is the least value.

    If you selected E, you didn't work out each choice.

SECTION 7

5. ETS's answer is C.
    First, we can estimate. Since square *BCED* has an area of 25, *DE* equals 5 and *EF* looks to be less than twice *DE*, or in the 7–9 range. Thus, we can eliminate D and E.

    Now, we're looking for the length of *EF*. Since angle *AEF* is a right angle, angle *EAF* must be 45°. So we know that *AE* = *EF*.

    We know that the area of triangle *ABC* is 10, and that its base (*BC*) is 5. Using the formula for area, we can calculate *AC*:

    $$A = \frac{1}{2}bh$$
    $$10 = (\frac{1}{2})(5)(h)$$
    $$4 = h$$

    So, *AE* = *EF* = (5 + 4) = 9.

6. ETS's answer is B.
    First, let's calculate how many gallons are consumed in each direction: $\frac{450}{25} = 18$
    Now each of the 18 gallons cost us $0.25 more returning than going.
    (18)(0.25) = $4.50

7. ETS's answer is A.
    Let's begin by drawing a parallelogram and Plugging In a number for *y*, say 50:

    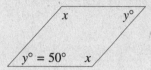

    Since there are 360° in a quadrilateral, we know that $2x + 100° = 360°$, which means $x = 130°$. So, we're looking for the choice that gives us 130 when *y* = 50°. We simply plug 50 into the answer choices until we find our answer.

8. ETS's answer is C.
    Let's start by drawing a picture of the situation.

    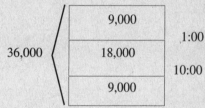

    We know that by 1:00 the pool is three-fourths full. Three-fourths of 36,000 is 27,000. Since we started with 9,000 gallons, we added 18,000 gallons in 3 hours, or 6,000 gallons per hour. To fill the remaining 9,000 gallons at this rate will take 1.5 hours (9,000 ÷ 6,000). One and a half hours later would be 2:30.

9. ETS's answer is D.
    This is a tricky question.
    Let's draw a picture:

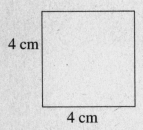

4 cm

4 cm

Since 1 centimeter equals 6 kilometers, 4 centimeters equals 24 kilometers:

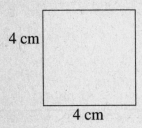

4 cm

4 cm

The area of this region is 24^2 or 576.

10. ETS's answer is A.

    We're looking for the range of the fraction $\frac{a}{b}$, from its minimum to its maximum value. The maximum value $\frac{a}{b}$ would be when a is as large as possible and b is as small as possible. Thus, $\frac{a}{b}$ must be less than $\frac{7}{7}$. Eliminate choices B, C, and E. At the other extreme, $\frac{a}{b}$ achieves its minimum value when a is as small as possible and b is as large as possible. Thus, $\frac{a}{b}$ must be greater than $\frac{4}{9}$.

18

Practice Test 2

Time—30 Minutes
25 Questions

In this section, solve each problem using any available space on the page for scratchwork. Then decide which is the best of the choices given and fill in the corresponding oval on the answer sheet.

Notes:

1. The use of a calculator is permitted. All numbers used are real numbers.

2. Figures that accompany problems in this test are intended to provide information useful in solving the problems. They are drawn as accurately as possible EXCEPT when it is stated in a specific problem that the figure is not drawn to scale. All figures lie in a plane unless otherwise indicated.

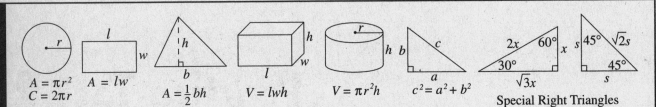

Reference Information

$A = \pi r^2$
$C = 2\pi r$

$A = lw$

$A = \frac{1}{2} bh$

$V = lwh$

$V = \pi r^2 h$

$c^2 = a^2 + b^2$

Special Right Triangles

The number of degrees of arc in a circle is 360.
The measure in degrees of a straight angle is 180.
The sum of the measures in degrees of the angles of a triangle is 180.

1. If $\dfrac{12}{4} = x$, what is the value of $4x + 2$?

    (A) 2
    (B) 3
    (C) 4
    (D) 12
    (E) 14

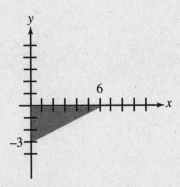

2. In the figure above, which of the following points lies within the shaded region?

    (A) $(-1, 1)$
    (B) $(1, -2)$
    (C) $(4, 3)$
    (D) $(5, -4)$
    (E) $(7, 0)$

GO ON TO THE NEXT PAGE

3. If n is an even integer, which of the following must be an odd integer?

(A) $3n - 2$

(B) $3(n + 1)$

(C) $n - 2$

(D) $\dfrac{n}{3}$

(E) n^2

4. $x\sqrt{4} - x\sqrt{9} =$

(A) $-5x$
(B) $-x\sqrt{5}$
(C) $-x$
(D) x
(E) $3x$

5. Six cups of flour are required to make a batch of cookies. How many cups of flour are needed to make enough cookies to fill 12 cookie jars, if each cookie jar holds 1.5 batches?

(A) 108
(B) 90
(C) 81
(D) 78
(E) 72

6. If Circle O has a diameter of 9, then what is the area of Circle O ?

(A) 81π

(B) $\dfrac{9}{2}\pi$

(C) $\dfrac{81}{4}\pi$

(D) 18π

(E) 9π

7. Cindy has a collection of 80 records. If 40 percent of her records are jazz records, and the rest are blues records, how many blues records does she have?

(A) 32
(B) 40
(C) 42
(D) 48
(E) 50

8. How many even integers are there between 2 and 100, not including 2 and 100?

(A) 98
(B) 97
(C) 50
(D) 49
(E) 48

GO ON TO THE NEXT PAGE

9. If *b* equals 40 percent of *a*, then, in terms of *b*, 40 percent of 4*a* is equal to which of the following?

(A) $\dfrac{b}{40}$

(B) $\dfrac{b}{4}$

(C) *b*

(D) 4*b*

(E) 16*b*

11. In triangle *ABC* above, if *AC* is equal to 8, what is the length of *BC*?

(A) $8\sqrt{2}$
(B) 8
(C) 6
(D) $4\sqrt{2}$
(E) $3\sqrt{2}$

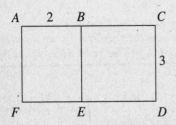

10. In the figure above, the perimeter of square *BCDE* is how much smaller than the perimeter of rectangle *ACDF*?

(A) 2
(B) 3
(C) 4
(D) 7
(E) 16

	Number Sold	Average Weight per Parrot (in pounds)
Red Parrots	5	2
Blue Parrots	4	3

12. The chart above shows the number of red and blue parrots Toby sold in May and the average weight of each type of bird sold. If Toby sold no other parrots, what was the average (arithmetic mean) weight of a parrot in pounds that Toby sold in May?

(A) 2

(B) $2\dfrac{4}{9}$

(C) $2\dfrac{1}{2}$

(D) 5

(E) 9

GO ON TO THE NEXT PAGE

13. If $999 \times 111 = 3 \times 3 \times n^2$, then which of the following could be the value of n?

(A)   9
(B)   37
(C) 111
(D) 222
(E) 333

14. If $x + 6 > 0$ and $1 - 2x > -1$, then x could equal each of the following EXCEPT

(A) –6

(B) –4

(C) –2

(D) 0

(E) $\dfrac{1}{2}$

15. In 1998, Andrei had a collection of 48 baseball caps. Since then he has given away 13 caps, purchased 17 new caps, and traded 6 of his caps to Pierre for 8 of Pierre's caps. Since 1998, what has been the net percent increase in Andrei's collection?

(A) 6%

(B) $12\dfrac{1}{2}\%$

(C) $16\dfrac{2}{3}\%$

(D) 25%

(E) $28\dfrac{1}{2}\%$

Questions 16–17 refer to the following definition: For all real numbers x, let $\otimes x$ be defined as $2x^2 + 4$.

16. What is the value of $\otimes 4$?

(A) 16
(B) 18
(C) 20
(D) 36
(E) 72

17. Which of the following is equal to $\otimes 3 + \otimes 5$?

(A) $\otimes 4$
(B) $\otimes 6$
(C) $\otimes 8$
(D) $\otimes 10$
(E) $\otimes 15$

18. What is the greatest number of regions into which an equilateral triangle can be divided using exactly three straight lines?

(A) 4
(B) 6
(C) 7
(D) 8
(E) 9

GO ON TO THE NEXT PAGE

19. Elsa has a pitcher containing x ounces of root beer. If she pours y ounces of root beer into each of z glasses, how much root beer will remain in the pitcher?

(A) $\dfrac{x}{y} + z$

(B) $xy - z$

(C) $\dfrac{x}{yz}$

(D) $x - yz$

(E) $\dfrac{x}{y} - z$

20. A bag contains 4 red hammers, 10 blue hammers, and 6 yellow hammers. If three hammers are removed at random and no hammer is returned to the bag after removal, what is the probability that all three hammers will be blue?

(A) $\dfrac{1}{2}$

(B) $\dfrac{1}{8}$

(C) $\dfrac{3}{20}$

(D) $\dfrac{2}{19}$

(E) $\dfrac{3}{8}$

21. There are k gallons of gasoline available to fill a tank. After d gallons have been pumped, then in terms of k and d, what percent of the gasoline has been pumped?

(A) $\dfrac{100d}{k}\%$

(B) $\dfrac{k}{100d}\%$

(C) $\dfrac{100k}{d}\%$

(D) $\dfrac{k}{100(k-d)}\%$

(E) $\dfrac{100(k-d)}{k}\%$

22. If $a = 4b + 26$, and b is a positive integer, then a could be divisible by all of the following EXCEPT

(A) 2
(B) 4
(C) 5
(D) 6
(E) 7

GO ON TO THE NEXT PAGE

23. Ray and Jane live 150 miles apart. They each drive toward the other's house along a straight road connecting the two, Ray at a constant rate of 30 miles per hour and Jane at a constant rate of 50 miles per hour. If Ray and Jane leave their houses at the same time, how many miles are they from Ray's house when they meet?

(A) 40

(B) $51\frac{1}{2}$

(C) $56\frac{1}{4}$

(D) 75

(E) $93\frac{1}{4}$

24. If $x = y + 1$ and $y \geq 1$, then which of the following must be equal to $x^2 - y^2$?

(A) $(x - y)^2$
(B) $x^2 - y - 1$
(C) $x + y$
(D) $x^2 - 1$
(E) $y^2 + 1$

25. If x is an integer, which of the following could be x^3 ?

(A) 2.7×10^{11}
(B) 2.7×10^{12}
(C) 2.7×10^{13}
(D) 2.7×10^{14}
(E) 2.7×10^{15}

STOP
**If you finish before time is called, you may check your work on this section only.
Do not turn to any other section in the test.**

Time—30 Minutes
30 Questions

For each question in this section, select the best answer from among the choices given and fill in the corresponding oval on the answer sheet.

Each sentence below has one or two blanks, each blank indicating that something has been omitted. Beneath the sentence are five words or sets of words labeled A through E. Choose the word or set of words that, when inserted in the sentence, best fits the meaning of the sentence as a whole.

Example:

Medieval kingdoms did not become constitutional republics overnight; on the contrary, the change was -------.

(A) unpopular (B) unexpected (C) advantageous
 (D) sufficient (E) gradual   Ⓐ Ⓑ Ⓒ Ⓓ ●

---

1. Nuclear power plants are some of the largest producers of ------- wastes, with each plant producing barrels of radioactive material that must be stored in special protective containers.

   (A) biodegradable (B) artificial
    (C) reasonable (D) durable (E) hazardous

2. The scientific community was ------- when a living specimen of the coelacanth, long thought to be ----- , was discovered by deep-sea fishermen.

   (A) perplexed. .common
   (B) overjoyed. .dangerous
   (C) unconcerned. .local
   (D) astounded. .extinct
   (E) dismayed. .alive

3. After the governor's third trip overseas, voters complained that he was paying too little attention to ------- affairs.

   (A) intellectual (B) foreign (C) professional
         (D) aesthetic (E) domestic

4. The Roman Emperor Claudius was viewed with ------ by generations of historians until newly discovered evidence showed him to be ------- administrator.

   (A) suspicion. .a clever
   (B) reluctance. .an inept
   (C) antagonism. .an eager
   (D) indignation. .an incompetent
   (E) disdain. .a capable

5. Communities in primitive areas where natural ------ is scarce must be resourceful in order to secure adequate nutrition.

   (A) education (B) competition (C) sustenance
      (D) agriculture (E) assistance

6. Anthony's ------- expression masked an essentially cheerful nature.

   (A) jubilant (B) inevitable (C) dour
      (D) pert (E) serene

7. Morgan's interest was focused on ------- the division between theory and empiricism; she was convinced that a ------- of philosophy and applied science was possible and necessary.

   (A) eliminating. .synthesis
   (B) maintaining. .restoration
   (C) crossing. .stabilization
   (D) ignoring. .duplicity
   (E) denying. .delineation

8. The professor highlighted the importance of ------- the experiences of many different ethnic groups when he warned against ------- policies that fail to consider the wide variety of cultural standards.

   (A) portraying. .discriminatory
   (B) considering. .myopic
   (C) remembering. .alluring
   (D) delineating. .captivating
   (E) disparaging. .pedantic

9. Although at times Nikolai could be disagreeable and even -------, more often than not he was the most ------- person you could hope to meet.

   (A) contentious. .complaisant
   (B) disgruntled. .befuddled
   (C) contradictory. .disconcerted
   (D) misguided. .solicitous
   (E) curmudgeonly. .didactic

GO ON TO THE NEXT PAGE →

Each question below consists of a related pair of words or phrases, followed by five pairs of words or phrases labeled A through E. Select the pair that best expresses a relationship similar to that expressed in the original pair.

Example:

CRUMB : BREAD ::

(A) ounce : unit
(B) splinter : wood
(C) water : bucket
(D) twine : rope
(E) cream : butter

10. SHEPHERD : SHEEP ::

(A) sociologist : statistics
(B) driver : conveyances
(C) gardener : plants
(D) critic : reviews
(E) artist : murals

11. VANDAL : DAMAGE ::

(A) victim : crime
(B) pest : annoyance
(C) temper : shouting
(D) addiction : weakness
(E) arbitrator : dispute

12. SNARE : ANIMAL ::

(A) nest : bird
(B) pouch : kangaroo
(C) net : fish
(D) kennel : dog
(E) forest : raccoon

13. CACOPHONOUS : EAR ::

(A) outrageous : order
(B) objectionable : commotion
(C) erroneous : mind
(D) noisome : mouth
(E) rank : nose

14. BELLIGERENCE : AGGRESSOR ::

(A) insensitivity : boor
(B) confidence : prelate
(C) irascibility : pacifist
(D) truculence : ingrate
(E) affectation : shrew

15. INCORRIGIBLE : REFORM ::

(A) immutable : speak
(B) intractable : manage
(C) impartial : decide
(D) intolerable : criticize
(E) intangible : understand

GO ON TO THE NEXT PAGE

Each passage below is followed by questions based on its content. Answer the questions following each passage on the basis of what is <u>stated</u> or <u>implied</u> in that passage and in any introductory material that may be provided.

Questions 16–22 are based on the following passage.

A parable is a symbolic story that, like a fable, teaches a moral lesson. The parable below was written by the Czech author Franz Kafka and was published in 1935.

Poseidon sat at his desk, doing figures. The administration of all the waters gave him endless work. He could have had assistants, as many as he
Line wanted—and he did have very many—but since he
5 took his job very seriously, he would in the end go over all the figures and calculations himself, and thus his assistants were of little help to him. It cannot be said that he enjoyed his work; he did it only because it had been assigned to him; in fact, he had already
10 filed petitions for—as he put it—more cheerful work, but every time the offer of something different was made to him it would turn out that nothing suited him quite as well as his present position. And anyhow, it was quite difficult to find something
15 different for him. After all, it was impossible to assign him to a particular sea; aside from the fact that even then the work with figures would not become less but only pettier, the great Poseidon could in any case only occupy an executive position.
20 And when a job away from the water was offered to him he would get sick at the very prospect, his divine breathing would become troubled and his brazen chest would begin to tremble. Besides, his complaints were not really taken seriously; when
25 one of the mighty is vexatious the appearance of an effort must be made to placate him, even when the case is most hopeless. In actuality, a shift of posts was unthinkable for Poseidon—he had been appointed God of the Sea in the beginning, and that
30 he had to remain.
What irritated him most—and it was this that was chiefly responsible for his dissatisfaction with his job—was to hear of the conceptions formed about him: how he was always riding about through the
35 tides with his trident. When all the while he sat here in the depths of the world-ocean, doing figures uninterruptedly, with now and then a trip to Jupiter as the only break in the monotony—a trip, moreover, from which he usually returned in a
40 rage. Thus he had hardly seen the sea—had seen it fleetingly in the course of hurried ascents to Olympus, and he had never actually traveled around it. He was in the habit of saying that what he was waiting for was the fall of the world; then,
45 probably, a quiet moment would yet be granted in which, just before the end and after having checked the last row of figures, he would be able to make a quick little tour.
Poseidon became bored with the sea. He let fall
50 his trident. Silently he sat on the rocky coast and a gull, dazed by his presence, described wavering circles around his head.

16. Lines 7–9 ("It . . . him") suggest that Poseidon regarded his work with

(A) resignation
(B) enthusiasm
(C) indifference
(D) intimidation
(E) destructiveness

17. In line 25, the word "vexatious" most nearly means

(A) pleased
(B) cursed
(C) doomed
(D) troubled
(E) indisposed

18. The word "conceptions" as used in line 33 most nearly means

(A) origins
(B) opinions
(C) discussions
(D) plans
(E) explanations

GO ON TO THE NEXT PAGE

19. It can be inferred from the author's description of Poseidon's routine (lines 40–43) that

    (A) Poseidon prefers performing his duties to visiting Jupiter
    (B) Poseidon is too busy to familiarize himself with his kingdom
    (C) Poseidon requires silence for the performance of his duties
    (D) if the world falls, Poseidon will no longer be able to travel
    (E) Poseidon's dissatisfaction with his job detracts from his efficiency

20. According to the passage, Poseidon's dissatisfaction with his job primarily stems from

    (A) the constant travel that is required of him
    (B) the lack of seriousness with which his complaints are received
    (C) the constantly changing nature of his duties
    (D) others' mistaken notions of his routine
    (E) his assistants' inability to perform simple bookkeeping tasks

21. The author of the passage portrays the god Poseidon as

    (A) a dissatisfied bureaucrat
    (B) a powerful deity
    (C) a disgruntled vagabond
    (D) a capable accountant
    (E) a ruthless tyrant

22. Poseidon is unable to change occupations for all of the following reasons EXCEPT

    (A) his appointment as God of the Sea is inherently unchangeable
    (B) he has fallen into disfavor with the gods on Mount Olympus
    (C) he cannot imagine a life away from the water
    (D) nothing else suits him as well as his present position
    (E) his job must be appropriate to his elevated status

GO ON TO THE NEXT PAGE

Each passage below is followed by questions based on its content. Answer the questions following each passage on the basis of what is <u>stated</u> or <u>implied</u> in that passage and in any introductory material that may be provided.

Questions 23–30 are based on the following passage.

The following passage was excerpted from a book called The Extraordinary Origins of Everyday Things, *which was published in 1987.*

Because early man viewed illness as divine punishment and healing as purification, medicine and religion were inextricably linked for centuries.
Line This notion is apparent in the origin of our word
5 "pharmacy," which comes from the Greek *pharmakon*, meaning "purification through purging."
By 3500 B.C., the Sumerians in the Tigris-Euphrates Valley had developed virtually all of our modern methods of administering drugs. They used gargles,
10 inhalations, pills, lotions, ointments, and plasters. The first drug catalog, or pharmacopoeia, was written at that time by an unknown Sumerian physician. Preserved in cuneiform script on a single clay tablet are the names of dozens of drugs to treat ailments
15 that still afflict us today.
The Egyptians added to the ancient medicine chest. The Ebers Papyrus, a scroll dating from 1900 B.C. and named after the German Egyptologist George Ebers, reveals the trial-and-error know-how acquired
20 by early Egyptian physicians. To relieve indigestion, a chew of peppermint leaves and carbonates (known today as antacids) was prescribed, and to numb the pain of tooth extraction, Egyptian doctors temporarily stupefied a patient with ethyl alcohol.
25 The scroll also provides a rare glimpse into the hierarchy of ancient drug preparation. The "chief of the preparers of drugs" was the equivalent of a head pharmacist, who supervised the "collectors of drugs," field workers who gathered essential minerals and
30 herbs. The "preparers' aides" (technicians) dried and pulverized ingredients, which were blended according to certain formulas by the "preparers." And the "conservator of drugs" oversaw the storehouse where local and imported mineral, herb,
35 and animal-organ ingredients were kept.
By the seventh century B.C., the Greeks had adopted a sophisticated mind-body view of medicine. They believed that a physician must pursue the diagnosis and treatment of the physical (body) causes
40 of disease within a scientific framework, as well as cure the supernatural (mind) components involved. Thus, the early Greek physician emphasized something of a holistic approach to health, even if the suspected "mental" causes of disease were not
45 recognized as stress and depression but interpreted as curses from displeased deities.

The modern era of pharmacology began in the sixteenth century, ushered in by the first major discoveries in chemistry. The understanding of how
50 chemicals interact to produce certain effects within the body would eventually remove much of the guesswork and magic from medicine.
Drugs had been launched on a scientific course, but centuries would pass before superstition was
55 displaced by scientific fact. One major reason was that physicians, unaware of the existence of disease-causing pathogens such as bacteria and viruses, continued to dream up imaginary causative evils. And though new chemical compounds emerged,
60 their effectiveness in treating disease was still based largely on trial and error.
Many standard, common drugs in the medicine chest developed in this trial-and-error environment. Such is the complexity of disease and human
65 biochemistry that even today, despite enormous strides in medical science, many of the latest sophisticated additions to our medicine chest shelves were accidental finds.

23. The author cites the literal definition of the Greek word pharmakon in line 6 in order to

(A) show that ancient civilizations had an advanced form of medical science
(B) point out that many of the beliefs of ancient civilizations are still held today
(C) illustrate that early man thought recovery from illness was linked to internal cleansing
(D) stress the mental and physical causes of disease
(E) emphasize the primitive nature of Greek medical science

24. It was possible to identify a number of early Sumerian drugs because

(A) traces of these drugs were discovered during archaeological excavations
(B) the ancient Egyptians later adopted the same medications
(C) Sumerian religious texts explained many drug-making techniques
(D) a pharmacopoeia in Europe contained detailed recipes for ancient drugs
(E) a list of drugs and preparations was compiled by an ancient Sumerian

GO ON TO THE NEXT PAGE

25. The passage suggests that which of the following is a similarity between ancient Sumerian drugs and modern drugs?

    (A) Ancient Sumerian drugs were made of the same chemicals as modern drugs.
    (B) Like modern drugs, ancient Sumerian drugs were used for both mental and physical disorders.
    (C) The delivery of ancient Sumerian drugs is similar to that of modern drugs.
    (D) Both ancient Sumerian drugs and modern drugs are products of sophisticated laboratory research.
    (E) Hierarchically organized groups of laborers are responsible for the preparation of both ancient Sumerian and modern drugs.

26. The "hierarchy" referred to in line 26 is an example of

    (A) a superstitious practice
    (B) the relative severity of ancient diseases
    (C) the role of physicians in Egyptian society
    (D) a complex division of labor
    (E) a recipe for ancient drugs

27. According to the passage, the seventh-century Greeks' view of medicine differed from that of the Sumerians in that the Greeks

    (A) discovered more advanced chemical applications of drugs
    (B) acknowledged both the mental and physical roots of illness
    (C) attributed disease to psychological, rather than physical, causes
    (D) established a rigid hierarchy for the preparation of drugs
    (E) developed most of the precursors of modern drugs

28. In line 43, the word "holistic" most nearly means

    (A) psychological
    (B) modern
    (C) physiological
    (D) integrated
    (E) religious

29. The passage indicates that advances in medical science during the modern era of pharmacology may have been delayed by

    (A) a lack of understanding of the origins of disease
    (B) primitive surgical methods
    (C) a shortage of chemical treatments for disease
    (D) an inaccuracy in pharmaceutical preparation
    (E) an over-emphasis on the psychological causes of disease

30. In the final paragraph, the author makes which of the following observations about scientific discovery?

    (A) Human biochemistry is such a complex science that important discoveries are uncommon.
    (B) Chance events have led to the discovery of many modern drugs.
    (C) Many cures for common diseases have yet to be discovered.
    (D) Trial and error is the best avenue to scientific discovery.
    (E) Most of the important discoveries made in the scientific community have been inadvertent.

STOP
**If you finish before time is called, you may check your work on this section only.
Do not turn to any other section in the test.**

Time—30 Minutes 25 Questions	In this section, solve each problem using any available space on the page for scratchwork. Then decide which is the best of the choices given and fill in the corresponding oval on the answer sheet.

Notes:

1.   The use of a calculator is permitted. All numbers used are real numbers.

2.   Figures that accompany problems in this test are intended to provide information useful in solving the problems. They are drawn as accurately as possible EXCEPT when it is stated in a specific problem that the figure is not drawn to scale. All figures lie in a plane unless otherwise indicated.

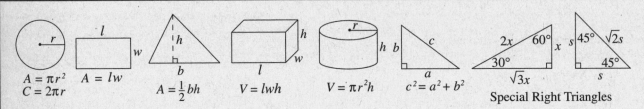

$A = \pi r^2$ $A = lw$
$C = 2\pi r$
                              $A = \frac{1}{2}bh$ $V = lwh$ $V = \pi r^2 h$ $c^2 = a^2 + b^2$
Special Right Triangles

The number of degrees of arc in a circle is 360.
The measure in degrees of a straight angle is 180.
The sum of the measures in degrees of the angles of a triangle is 180.

Directions for Quantitative Comparison Questions

Questions 1–15 each consist of two quantities in boxes, one in Column A and one in Column B.
You are to compare the two quantities and on the answer sheet fill in oval

A   if the quantity in Column A is greater;
B   if the quantity in Column B is greater;
C   if the two quantities are equal;
D   if the relationship cannot be determined from the information given.

AN E RESPONSE WILL NOT BE SCORED.

Notes:

1.   In some questions, information is given about one or both of the quantities to be compared. In such cases, the given information is centered above the two columns and is not boxed.
2.   In a given question, a symbol that appears in both columns represents the same thing in Column A as it does in Column B.
3.   Letters such as x, n, and k stand for real numbers.

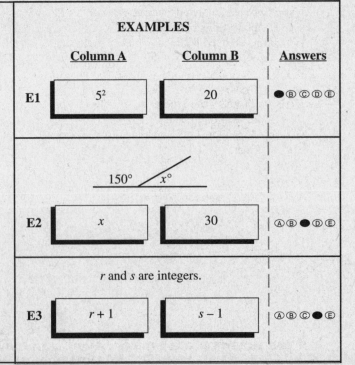

EXAMPLES

	Column A	Column B	Answers
E1	5^2	20	●ⒷⒸⒹⒺ
E2	x	30	ⒶⒷ●ⒹⒺ
E3	$r + 1$	$s - 1$	ⒶⒷⒸ●Ⓔ

E2: $150°$ $x°$

E3: r and s are integers.

SUMMARY DIRECTIONS FOR QUANTITATIVE COMPARISON QUESTIONS

Answer: A if the quantity in Column A is greater;
          B if the quantity in Column B is greater;
          C if the two quantities are equal;
          D if the relationship cannot be determined from the information given.

AN E RESPONSE WILL NOT BE SCORED.

Column A	Column B

$x = 3$

1.
$$\frac{x}{10}$$
$$\frac{x}{100}$$

2.
The average (arithmetic mean) of 1, 199, and 700

The average (arithmetic mean) of 10, 90, and 800

$-3 < z < 0$

3.
$3 - z$
$z - 3$

4.

$110°$ $a°$

$111°$
$b°$

a
b

Column A	Column B

$3 > p > 1$

5.
$$\frac{p}{2}$$
$$\frac{p+2}{4}$$

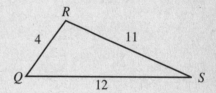

6.
The area of triangle QRS

The perimeter of triangle QRS

$ABCD$ is a square.

7.
the length of AC
the length of AD

2

GO ON TO THE NEXT PAGE

Column A   **Column B**

Line segments FG and JK intersect at point X such that $FX = \frac{1}{2}GX$.

8. | JX | $\frac{1}{2}KX$ |

1,000 milliliters = 1 liter

9. | The number of 1.9 milliliter portions that can be poured from a bottle containing 0.8 liters of fluid | 400 |

a is the average (arithmetic mean) of two consecutive positive even integers.

10. | The remainder when a is divided by 2 | 1 |

Column A   **Column B**

Questions 11–12 refer to the following definition:

For all numbers n, let $\{n\}$ be defined as $n^3 + 2n^2 - n$.

11. | $\{-2\}$ | $\{-1\}$ |

12. | $\{x\}$ | $\{x+1\}$ |

13. | The ratio of nickels to dimes in Jar A, where there are 4 more nickels than dimes | The ratio of nickels to dimes in Jar B, where there are 4 more dimes than nickels |

14. | The area of a parallelogram with base 8 and perimeter 36 | The area of a parallelogram with base 16 and perimeter 36 |

$$a + b = c$$
$$a - c = 5$$
$$b - c = 3$$

15. | c | 0 |

3 3 3 3 3 3 3 3 3

Directions for Student-Produced Response Questions

Each of the remaining 10 questions (16–25) requires you to solve the problem and enter your answer by marking the ovals in the special grid, as shown in the examples below.

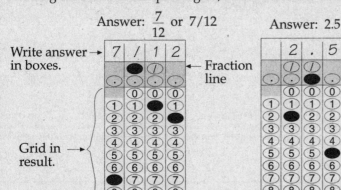

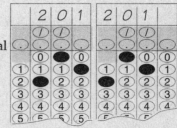

Answer: 201
Either position is correct

Note: You may start your answers in any column, space permitting. Columns not needed should be left blank.

- Mark no more than one oval in any column.
- Because the answer sheet will be machine-scored, **you will receive credit only if the ovals are filled in correctly.**
- Although not required, it is suggested that you write your answer in the boxes at the top of the columns to help you fill in the ovals accurately.
- Some problems may have more than one correct answer. In such cases, grid only one answer.
- No question has a negative answer.
- **Mixed numbers** such as $2\frac{1}{2}$ must be gridded as 2.5 or 5/2. (If [2 1 / 2] is gridded, it will be interpreted as $\frac{21}{2}$, not $2\frac{1}{2}$.)

- **Decimal Accuracy:** If you obtain a decimal answer, **enter the most accurate value the grid will accommodate.** For example, if you obtain an answer such as 0.6666 . . . , you should record the result as .666 or .667. **Less accurate values such as .66 or .67 are not acceptable.**

Acceptable ways to grid $\frac{2}{3}$ = .6666 . . .

16. If $3x = 12$, what is the value of $8 \div x$?

17. In the figure above, what is the value of $a + b + c$?

GO ON TO THE NEXT PAGE

PRACTICE TEST 2 ◆ 397

18. Twenty bottles contain a total of 8 liters of apple juice. If each bottle contains the same amount of apple juice, how much juice (in liters) is in each bottle?

19. If $4x + 2y = 24$ and $\dfrac{7y}{2x} = 7$, what is the value of x?

20. What is the sum of the positive even factors of 12?

21. Y is a point on segment XZ such that $XY = \dfrac{1}{2}XZ$. If the length of YZ is $4a + 6$, and the length of XZ is 68, what is the value of a?

22. One-fifth of the cars in a parking lot are blue and $\dfrac{1}{2}$ of the blue cars are convertibles. If $\dfrac{1}{4}$ of the convertibles in the parking lot are blue, then what percent of the cars in the lot are neither blue nor convertibles? (Disregard the percent sign when gridding your answer.)

GO ON TO THE NEXT PAGE

23. Three numbers are considered a "prime set" if their sum is a prime number. If 31, –8, and n are a prime set, what is the least possible positive value for n?

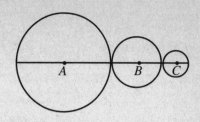

25. In the figure above, the radius of the circle with center A is twice the radius of the circle with center B and four times the radius of the circle with center C. If the sum of the areas of the three circles is 84π, what is the length of AC?

24. A ball bounces up $\dfrac{3}{4}$ of the distance it falls when dropped, and on each bounce thereafter, it bounces $\dfrac{3}{4}$ of the previous height. If it is dropped from a height of 64 feet, how many feet will it have traveled when it hits the ground the fourth time?

STOP
If you finish before time is called, you may check your work on this section only.
Do not turn to any other section in the test.

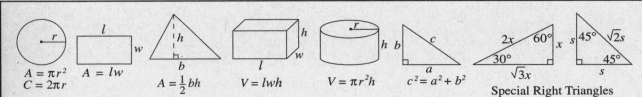

4 4 4 4 4 4 4

Time—30 Minutes
25 Questions

This section contains two types of questions. You have 30 minutes to complete both types. You may use any available space for scratchwork.

Notes:

1. The use of a calculator is permitted. All numbers used are real numbers.

2. Figures that accompany problems in this test are intended to provide information useful in solving the problems. They are drawn as accurately as possible EXCEPT when it is stated in a specific problem that the figure is not drawn to scale. All figures lie in a plane unless otherwise indicated.

Reference Information

$A = \pi r^2$
$C = 2\pi r$
$A = lw$
$A = \frac{1}{2}bh$
$V = lwh$
$V = \pi r^2 h$
$c^2 = a^2 + b^2$

Special Right Triangles

The number of degrees of arc in a circle is 360.
The measure in degrees of a straight angle is 180.
The sum of the measures in degrees of the angles of a triangle is 180.

Directions for Quantitative Comparison Questions

Questions 1–15 each consist of two quantities in boxes, one in Column A and one in Column B.
You are to compare the two quantities and on the answer sheet fill in oval

A if the quantity in Column A is greater;
B if the quantity in Column B is greater;
C if the two quantities are equal;
D if the relationship cannot be determined from the information given.

AN E RESPONSE WILL NOT BE SCORED.

Notes:

1. In some questions, information is given about one or both of the quantities to be compared. In such cases, the given information is centered above the two columns and is not boxed.
2. In a given question, a symbol that appears in both columns represents the same thing in Column A as it does in Column B.
3. Letters such as x, n, and k stand for real numbers.

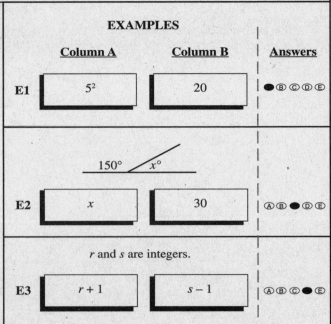

EXAMPLES

	Column A	Column B	Answers
E1	5^2	20	●ⒷⒸⒹⒺ
E2	x	30	ⒶⒷ●ⒹⒺ
E3	$r + 1$	$s - 1$	ⒶⒷⒸ●Ⓔ

(E2: $150°$ $x°$)
(E3: r and s are integers.)

SUMMARY DIRECTIONS FOR COMPARISON QUESTIONS

Answer: A if the quantity in Column A is greater;
         B if the quantity in Column B is greater;
         C if the two quantities are equal;
         D if the relationship cannot be determined from the information given.

Column A	Column B

$3x + 5 = 20$

1.
$6x$	40

The average of positive integers p and q is 3.

2.
p	q

10% of x is 20% of 100.

3.
x	50

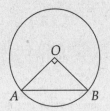

O is the center of the circle.

4.
The measure of $\angle OAB$	The measure of $\angle OBA$

Column A	Column B

On Sunday, 200 customers visited a gas station. Every 20th customer received a free fill-up. Every 30th customer received a discount tune-up.

5.
The number of customers who received both a free fill-up and a discount tune-up	4

$x^2 > 17$

6.
$x + 4$	8

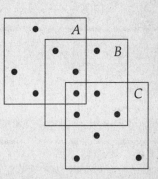

7.
In squares A, B, and C above, the number of points that lie in exactly two squares	6

GO ON TO THE NEXT PAGE

SUMMARY DIRECTIONS FOR COMPARISON QUESTIONS

Answer: A if the quantity in Column A is greater;
         B if the quantity in Column B is greater;
         C if the two quantities are equal;
         D if the relationship cannot be determined from the information given.

Column A	Column B

$x \geq 1$

8. $x^{(x+2)}$ | $(x+2)^x$

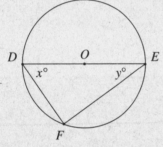

Note: Figure not drawn to scale.

O is the center of the circle with $DF = EF$.
Segment DE passes through point O.

9. x | 60

10. The area of a triangle with base $3x$ and height $2x$ | The area of a circle with radius x

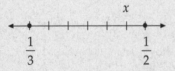

On the number line above, the marks are equally spaced.

11. x | $\dfrac{17}{37}$

Column A	Column B

12. The number of distinct 3-player teams that can be drawn from a pool of 5 players | 12

PN and *OM* are line segments.

13. $g + h$ | $i + j$

Set A: $\{2, -1, 7, -4, 11, 3\}$
Set B: $\{10, 5, -3, 4, 7, -8\}$

14. The median of Set A | The average (arithmetic mean) of Set B

$ax \neq 0$

15. $(x - a)^2$ | $-2ax$

GO ON TO THE NEXT PAGE →

Directions for Student-Produced Response Questions

Each of the remaining 10 questions (16–25) requires you to solve the problem and enter your answer by marking the ovals in the special grid, as shown in the examples below.

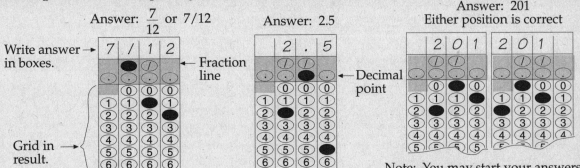

Answer: $\frac{7}{12}$ or 7/12

Write answer in boxes.

Fraction line

Grid in result.

Answer: 2.5

Decimal point

Answer: 201
Either position is correct

<u>Note</u>: You may start your answers in any column, space permitting. Columns not needed should be left blank.

- Mark no more than one oval in any column.

- Because the answer sheet will be machine-scored, **you will receive credit only if the ovals are filled in correctly.**

- Although not required, it is suggested that you write your answer in the boxes at the top of the columns to help you fill in the ovals accurately.

- Some problems may have more than one correct answer. In such cases, grid only one answer.

- No question has a negative answer.

- **Mixed numbers** such as $2\frac{1}{2}$ must be gridded as 2.5 or 5/2. (If $\boxed{2\ 1\ /\ 2}$ is gridded, it will be interpreted as $\frac{21}{2}$, not $2\frac{1}{2}$.)

- <u>**Decimal Accuracy:**</u> If you obtain a decimal answer, **enter the most accurate value the grid will accommodate.** For example, if you obtain an answer such as 0.6666 . . . , you should record the result as .666 or .667. **Less accurate values such as .66 or .67 are not acceptable.**

Acceptable ways to grid $\frac{2}{3}$ = .6666 . . .

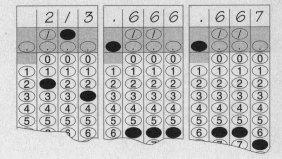

---

16. A certain clothing store sells only T-shirts, sweatshirts, and turtlenecks. On Wednesday, the store sells T-shirts, sweatshirts, and turtlenecks in a ratio of 2 to 3 to 5. If the store sells 30 sweatshirts on that day, what is the total number of garments that the store sells on Wednesday?

17. A rectangular packing crate has a height of 4.5 inches and a base with an area of 18 square inches. What is the volume of the crate in cubic inches?

GO ON TO THE NEXT PAGE →

18. If $5x - 4 = x - 1$, what is the value of x?

19. A box of donuts contains 3 plain, 5 cream-filled, and 4 chocolate donuts. If one of the donuts is chosen at random from the box, what is the probability that it will NOT be cream-filled?

20. If b is a prime integer such that $3b > 10 > \dfrac{5}{6}b$, what is one possible value of b?

21. The Tyler Jackson Dance Company plans to perform a piece that requires two dancers. If there are 7 dancers in the company, how many possible pairs of dancers could perform the piece?

GO ON TO THE NEXT PAGE

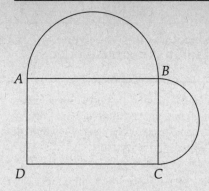

22. In the figure above, if semicircular arc AB has length 6π and semicircular arc BC has length 4π, what is the area of rectangle $ABCD$?

23. Let $\overset{\heartsuit}{x}$ be defined for all positive integers x as

the product of the distinct prime factors of x. What

is the value of $\dfrac{\overset{\heartsuit}{6}}{\overset{\heartsuit}{81}}$?

SPICE PRICES OF DISTRIBUTOR D

Spice	Price per pound
cinnamon	$8.00
nutmeg	$9.00
ginger	$7.00
cloves	$10.00

24. The owner of a spice store buys 3 pounds each of cinnamon, nutmeg, ginger, and cloves from Distributor D. She then sells all of the spices at $2.00 per ounce. What, in dollars, is her total profit (1 pound = 16 ounces)?

25. Points E, F, G, and H lie on a line in that order. If $EG = \dfrac{5}{3}EF$ and $HF = 5FG$, then what is $\dfrac{EF}{HG}$?

STOP
**If you finish before time is called, you may check your work on this section only.
Do not turn to any other section in the test.**

Time—30 Minutes	For each question in this section, select the best answer
35 Questions	from among the choices given and fill in the corresponding oval on the answer sheet.

Each sentence below has one or two blanks, each blank indicating that something has been omitted. Beneath the sentence are five words or sets of words labeled A through E. Choose the word or set of words that, when inserted in the sentence, best fits the meaning of the sentence as a whole.

Example:

Medieval kingdoms did not become constitutional republics overnight; on the contrary, the change was -------.

(A) unpopular (B) unexpected (C) advantageous
(D) sufficient (E) gradual

1. Plants that grow in the desert or on high rocky ledges can survive long periods of ------- because they hoard water in their leaves, stems, and root systems.

    (A) darkness (B) inactivity (C) dormancy
    (D) warmth (E) drought

2. Thanks to his eloquence and logic, Liam spoke ------- and made it difficult for even his bitterest opponents to ------- his opinions.

    (A) monotonously. .clash with
    (B) charmingly. .yield to
    (C) tediously. .contend with
    (D) abhorrently. .concede to
    (E) persuasively. .disagree with

3. Many myths and legends, however -------, often possess a grain of truth.

    (A) delightful (B) accurate (C) eternal
    (D) unbelievable (E) important

4. Ancient Greek playwrights often included the device of divine intervention in their work; just as circumstances became dire, a ------- would descend from Olympus and rescue the hero from almost certain death.

    (A) hero (B) warrior (C) luminary
    (D) deity (E) liberator

5. The apparent ------- with which professional skiers descend the slopes is deceptive; this activity requires ------- effort and intense concentration.

    (A) trepidation. .conscious
    (B) focus. .resolute
    (C) nonchalance. .strenuous
    (D) consideration. .unpredictable
    (E) insouciance. .minimal

6. Miranda, in her desire to foster -------, often felt compelled to ------- readily to others in tense situations.

    (A) cooperation. .object
    (B) consistency. .defer
    (C) dissension. .surrender
    (D) discourse. .appeal
    (E) harmony. .acquiesce

7. Early psychoanalysts challenged many of the most ------- notions of human behavior and compelled many to alter their dearly held assumptions about human nature.

    (A) elusive (B) derided (C) volatile
    (D) cherished (E) contemplative

8. Although detractors labeled Margaret Thatcher's policies -------, she asserted that her ideas moved the United Kingdom forward.

    (A) premature (B) autocratic (C) regressive
    (D) democratic (E) radical

GO ON TO THE NEXT PAGE

9. Some subatomic particles, ------- only through their effects on other bodies, have been compared to outer planets whose ------- was first deduced from eccentricities in other planets' orbits.

    (A) feasible. .irregularity
    (B) palpable. .creation
    (C) imaginable. .falsity
    (D) perceptible. .existence
    (E) verifiable. .proximity

10. Wary of unorthodox treatments, many doctors are reluctant to concede that nutritionists have a ------- argument for the use of dietary regulation as preventive medicine.

    (A) cogent (B) cursory (C) vacillating
       (D) feckless (E) vehement

GO ON TO THE NEXT PAGE

Each question below consists of a related pair of words or phrases, followed by five pairs of words or phrases labeled A through E. Select the pair that <u>best</u> expresses a relationship similar to that expressed in the original pair.

Example:

CRUMB : BREAD ::

(A) ounce : unit
(B) splinter : wood
(C) water : bucket
(D) twine : rope

11. STOCKING : LEG ::

(A) waistband : skirt
(B) ankle : foot
(C) button : lapel
(D) cast : body
(E) glove : hand

12. PARK : RECREATION ::

(A) kitchen : cooking
(B) fence : sitting
(C) tree : climbing
(D) yard : playing
(E) bus : driving

13. OUNCE : WEIGHT ::

(A) acre : area
(B) scale : mass
(C) inch : yard
(D) menu : portion
(E) variety : difference

14. CREST : WAVE ::

(A) climax : action
(B) elegy : memory
(C) example : paradigm
(D) milestone : distance
(E) landmark : territory

15. LOW : COW ::

(A) gosling : goose
(B) swarm : bee
(C) hutch : rabbit
(D) chirp : bird
(E) bed : oyster

16. HAMLET : VILLAGE ::

(A) street : sidewalk
(B) convertible : car
(C) building : skyscraper
(D) photograph : portrait
(E) cottage : house

17. MALLEABLE : SHAPED ::

(A) flexible : bullied
(B) amenable : persuaded
(C) tolerable : handled
(D) pliable : hardened
(E) negotiable : sold

18. ANALGESIC : PAIN ::

(A) anesthetic : surgery
(B) palliative : violence
(C) operation : health
(D) enthusiasm : anger
(E) prosthesis : limb

19. NOVICE : EXPERIENCE ::

(A) questioner : knowledge
(B) invader : bravery
(C) narrator : objectivity
(D) ingenue : talent
(E) rube : sophistication

GO ON TO THE NEXT PAGE ⟹

20. GRISLY : DISGUST ::
    (A) happy : grief
    (B) endearing : affection
    (C) redolent : joy
    (D) boring : interest
    (E) bitter : repulsion

21. DIATRIBE : ABUSIVE ::
    (A) rant : condemnatory
    (B) doctrine : orthodox
    (C) eulogy : laudatory
    (D) refrain : musical
    (E) judgment : fearful

22. SECRETE : FIND ::
    (A) muffle : hear
    (B) cover : open
    (C) exude : ignore
    (D) smile : sadden
    (E) explain : comprehend

23. INDELIBLE : PERMANENCE ::
    (A) united : individuality
    (B) qualified : employment
    (C) unavoidable : toleration
    (D) inconsistent : compatibility
    (E) flimsy : tenuousness

GO ON TO THE NEXT PAGE

The passage below is followed by questions based on its content. Answer the questions following the passage on the basis of what is <u>stated</u> or <u>implied</u> in the passage and in any introductory material that may be provided.

Questions 24–35 are based on the following passage.

The role of women has historically been different in different cultures. The following passage presents an analysis of women in Frankish society by Suzanne Fonay Wemple.

Although the laws and customs in lands under Frankish domination emphasized the biological function and sexual nature of women, they did not
Line deprive women of opportunities to find personal
5 fulfillment in a variety of roles. Frankish women could sublimate their sexual drives and motherly instincts in ways not available to women in ancient societies. Their labor, moreover, was not as exploited as it had been in primitive tribal societies. Queens
10 had access to power not only through their husbands but also through churchmen and secular officials whom they patronized. As widows, acting as regents for their sons, they could exercise political power directly. The wives of magnates issued donations
15 jointly with their husbands, founded monasteries, endowed churches, cultivated interfamilial ties, transmitted clan ideology to their children, supervised the household, and administered the family's estates when their husbands were away.
20 Whether they contracted a formal union or entered into a quasi-marriage, their children could inherit. As widows, they acted as guardians of their minor children, arranged their marriages, and in the absence of sons, wielded economic power as well. In the
25 dependent classes, women shared their husbands' work, produced textiles and articles of clothing both for their family's and the lords' use, and were instrumental in bringing about the merger of the free and slave elements in society.
30 For those who wished to free their bodies, souls, and brains from male domination and devote their lives to the service of God, Christianity provided an alternative way of life. Although, in relation to the total population, women in religious life remained
35 a small minority even in the seventh and eighth centuries, when many female communities were founded, their roles, social functions, and cultural contributions have an importance for the history of women that outweighs their numbers. This
40 alternative way of life was available not only to the unmarried but also to widows. Monasteries served as places of refuge for married women as well. The rich and the poor, at least until the late eighth century, were accepted as members. Women from
45 all walks of life, as well as relatives, friends, and dependents of the foundresses and abbesses, were invited to join the new congregations. Freed from the need to compete for the attention of men, women in these communities sustained each other in spiritual,
50 intellectual, scholarly, artistic, and charitable pursuits. Writings by early medieval nuns reveal that female ideals and modes of conduct were upheld as the way to salvation and as models of sanctity in the monasteries led by women. By facilitating the
55 escape of women from the male-dominated society to congregations where they could give expression to their own emotions, ascetic ideals, and spiritual strivings, Christianity became a liberating force in the lives of women. Historians have often overlooked
60 these positive effects and concentrated instead on the misogynistic sentiments perpetuated by the male hierarchy.

24. The passage suggests that women under Frankish law were

    (A) confined to narrow social roles
    (B) cut off from religious communities
    (C) exploited as slaves and servants
    (D) defined in physical or biological terms
    (E) valued but essentially powerless

25. According to the passage, which of the following describes a difference between Frankish society and more primitive cultures?

    (A) Frankish society did not encourage childbearing.
    (B) Women in Frankish society were not taken advantage of for their labor.
    (C) Women in Frankish society had more social and political power over their husbands.
    (D) Women in Frankish society were less likely to work within their homes.
    (E) Frankish society defined gender differences in biological terms.

GO ON TO THE NEXT PAGE

26. The passage suggests that the "access to power" (line 10) enjoyed by Frankish queens

    (A) surpassed the influence wielded by their sons and husbands
    (B) was greatly increased by their relationship to the church
    (C) did not extend beyond the boundaries of their households
    (D) permitted them to exercise power, but only indirectly
    (E) was based on their relationships to male figures of power

27. The word "transmitted" as used in line 17 most nearly means

    (A) announced
    (B) taught
    (C) enforced
    (D) distributed
    (E) broadcast

28. It can be inferred from the passage that marriage in Frankish society

    (A) was the only means of exchanging wealth
    (B) could be entered formally or informally
    (C) raised women to positions of influence
    (D) held greater importance than in primitive societies
    (E) was generally arranged by the bride's mother

29. The word "instrumental" as used in line 28 most nearly means

    (A) helpful
    (B) skilled
    (C) harmonious
    (D) resistant
    (E) vital

30. Which of the following best describes the difference between "wives of magnates" (line 14) and wives in the "dependent classes" (line 25)?

    (A) Wives in the dependent classes cooperated with their husbands, while the wives of magnates did not.
    (B) Wives in the dependent classes were powerless in their own households, while the wives of magnates wielded considerable power in theirs.
    (C) Wives in the dependent classes were forced by their husbands to perform strenuous tasks, while wives of magnates were not.
    (D) Wives of magnates were less likely than wives in the dependent classes to turn to religious communities for refuge and liberation.
    (E) Wives of magnates had greater power to administrate their own households than did wives in the dependent classes.

31. According to the author, female religious communities in Frankish society had "importance for the history of women" (lines 38–39) because

    (A) Frankish women entered these religious groups in great numbers
    (B) they increased the political influence of all Frankish women
    (C) women in these communities received superior education
    (D) they introduced women to diverse cultural and social activities
    (E) they eliminated the rift between married and unmarried women

GO ON TO THE NEXT PAGE

32. The passage implies that Frankish women outside religious communities

(A) felt obliged to compete for male attention
(B) were not inclined to religious feeling
(C) had greatly diminished economic power
(D) did not contribute to Frankish culture
(E) relied on males for emotional support

33. In line 52, "upheld" most nearly means

(A) delayed
(B) endorsed
(C) suspended
(D) enforced
(E) announced

34. According to the passage, Christianity facilitated the "escape of women from the male-dominated society" (lines 54–55) by doing all of the following EXCEPT

(A) permitting women self-expression
(B) insulating women from physical hardship
(C) diversifying women's social roles
(D) removing male social pressures
(E) putting pressure on women to study

35. The passage is best described as

(A) a study of class conflict in a medieval society
(B) an example of religion's influence on secular life
(C) a discussion of the roles of a social group
(D) a demonstration of the need for religious communities
(E) a refutation of a popular misconception

STOP

**If you finish before time is called, you may check your work on this section only.
Do not turn to any other section in the test.**

NO TEST MATERIAL ON THIS PAGE.

Time—15 Minutes 10 Questions	In this section, solve each problem using any available space on the page for scratchwork. Then decide which is the best of the choices given and fill in the corresponding oval on the answer sheet.

Notes:

1. The use of a calculator is permitted. All numbers used are real numbers.

2. Figures that accompany problems in this test are intended to provide information useful in solving the problems. They are drawn as accurately as possible EXCEPT when it is stated in a specific problem that the figure is not drawn to scale. All figures lie in a plane unless otherwise indicated.

Reference Information

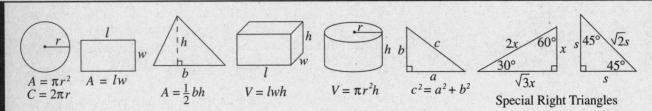

$A = \pi r^2$
$C = 2\pi r$ $A = lw$ $A = \frac{1}{2}bh$ $V = lwh$ $V = \pi r^2 h$ $c^2 = a^2 + b^2$ Special Right Triangles

The number of degrees of arc in a circle is 360.
The measure in degrees of a straight angle is 180.
The sum of the measures in degrees of the angles of a triangle is 180.

1. If $6 - y = 2y - 6$, what is the value of y ?

 (A) 0
 (B   2
 (C) 4
 (D) 6
 (E) 12

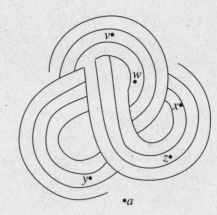

2. Which of the following points can be connected to point a by a continuous path without crossing any line or curve of the figure above?

 (A) v
 (B) w
 (C) x
 (D) y
 (E) z

GO ON TO THE NEXT PAGE

Computer Production		
	Morning Shift	**Afternoon Shift**
Monday	200	375
Tuesday	245	330
Wednesday	255	340
Thursday	250	315
Friday	225	360

3. If the above chart shows the number of computers produced at a factory during each shift, on which day is the total number of computers produced greatest?

(A) Monday
(B) Tuesday
(C) Wednesday
(D) Thursday
(E) Friday

4. If a rectangular swimming pool has a volume of 16,500 cubic feet, a depth of 10 feet, and a length of 75 feet, what is the width of the pool, in feet?

(A) 22
(B) 26
(C) 32
(D) 110
(E) 1,650

5. A science class has a ratio of girls to boys of 4 to 3. If the class has a total of 35 students, how many more girls are there than boys?

(A) 20
(B) 15
(C) 7
(D) 5
(E) 1

6. If $\frac{n}{8}$ has a remainder of 5, then which of the following has a remainder of 7 ?

(A) $\frac{n+1}{8}$

(B) $\frac{n+2}{8}$

(C) $\frac{n+3}{8}$

(D) $\frac{n+5}{8}$

(E) $\frac{n+7}{8}$

7. For positive integer x, 10 percent of x percent of 1,000 is equal to which of the following?

(A) x
(B) $10x$
(C) $100x$
(D) $1,000x$
(E) $10,000x$

GO ON TO THE NEXT PAGE

8. Nails are sold in 8-ounce and 20-ounce boxes. If 50 boxes of nails were sold and the total weight of the nails sold was less than 600 ounces, what is the greatest possible number of 20-ounce boxes that could have been sold?

(A) 34
(B) 33
(C) 25
(D) 17
(E) 16

9. If $c = \dfrac{1}{x} + \dfrac{1}{y}$ and $x > y > 0$, then which of the following is equal to $\dfrac{1}{c}$?

(A) $x + y$

(B) $x - y$

(C) $\dfrac{xy}{x + y}$

(D) $\dfrac{xy}{x + y}$

(E) $\dfrac{1}{x} - \dfrac{1}{y}$

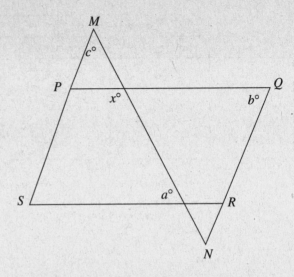

10. If $PQRS$ is a parallelogram and MN is a line segment, then which of the following must be equal to x?

(A) $180 - b$
(B) $180 - c$
(C) $a + b$
(D) $a + c$
(E) $b + c$

STOP

**If you finish before time is called, you may check your work on this section only.
Do not turn to any other section in the test.**

NO TEST MATERIAL ON THIS PAGE.

The two passages below are followed by questions based on their content and on the relationship between the two passages. Answer the questions on the basis of what is <u>stated</u> or <u>implied</u> in the passages and in any introductory material that may be provided.

Questions 1–13 are based on the following passages.

The discipline of physics has seen a number of changes in the last 100 years. The following passages discuss two of those changes.

Passage 1

It is mandatory to preface any discussion of atoms by paying homage to Democritus, an Ionian philosopher of the fifth century B.C., the earliest
Line known proponent of an atomic theory. Though
5 Democritus' ideas were in many ways strikingly modern and were promulgated by his more celebrated successor Epicurus, his theory never gained wide acceptance in Greek thought. It had largely been forgotten by the time of the late
10 Renaissance rebirth of science. While the dramatic rise of the atomic theory over the last century and a half seems to have vindicated Democritus, only the Greek name atom ("indivisible") remains to establish his claim as the father of the theory.
15 Nonetheless, Democritus' thinking contained the seed of the idea that has dominated twentieth-century physical thought. He was one of the first to perceive that nature on a sufficiently small scale might be qualitatively different in a striking way
20 from the world of our ordinary experience. And he was the first to voice the hope, today almost an obsession, that underlying all the complex richness, texture, and variety of our everyday life might be a level of reality of stark simplicity, with the turmoil
25 we perceive representing only the nearly infinite arrangements of a smaller number of constituents.
Today, the notion that simplicity is to be found by searching nature on a smaller level is embedded in physical thought to the point where few physicists
30 can imagine any other approach.
Democritus' ideas were popular among the philosophically sophisticated founders of modern physics. Galileo, Newton, and most of their contemporaries were atomists, but their beliefs were
35 based more on intuition than on concrete evidence. Moreover, the invention of calculus had eliminated

the difficulties with continuity that had in part motivated the Greek atomists, so the theory received little attention in the century following
40 Newton's work. Still, the atomic theory remained a popular speculation among physicists, because it offered the hope that all the properties of matter might ultimately be explained in terms of the motion of the atoms themselves.
45 It remained for the chemists of the early nineteenth century to find the first solid empirical support for atomism. Without stretching the point too far, it is fair to say that in 1800 the atomic theory was something physicists believed but couldn't prove,
50 while the chemists were proving it but didn't believe it.

Passage 2

The discovery that the universe is expanding was one of the great intellectual revelations of the twentieth century. With hindsight, it is easy
55 to wonder why no one had thought of it before. Newton, and others, should have realized that a static universe would soon start to contract under the influence of gravity. But suppose instead the universe is expanding. If it was expanding fairly
60 slowly, the force of gravity would cause it eventually to stop expanding and then to start contracting. However, if it was expanding at more than a certain critical rate, gravity would never be strong enough to stop it, and the universe would continue
65 to expand forever. This is a bit like what happens when one fires a rocket upward from the surface of the earth. If it has a fairly low speed, gravity will eventually stop the rocket and it will start falling back. On the other hand, if the rocket has more
70 than a certain critical speed (about seven miles per second), gravity will not be strong enough to pull

GO ON TO THE NEXT PAGE →

it back, so it will keep going away from the earth forever. This behavior of the universe could have been predicted from Newton's theory of gravity at
75 any time in the nineteenth, the eighteenth, or even the late seventeenth centuries. Yet so strong was the belief in a static universe that it persisted into the early twentieth century. Even Einstein, when he formulated the general theory of relativity in
80 1915, was so sure that the universe had to be static that he modified his theory to make this possible, introducing a so-called cosmological constant into his equations. Einstein introduced a new "antigravity" force, which, unlike other forces, did
85 not come from any particular source, but was built into the very fabric of space-time. He claimed that space-time had an inbuilt tendency to expand, and this could be made to balance exactly the attraction of all the matter in the universe, so that a static
90 universe would result.

1. In line 6, the word "promulgated" most nearly means

   (A) plagiarized
   (B) dismissed
   (C) protected
   (D) obscured
   (E) promoted

2. From the information presented in Passage 1, which of the following can be properly inferred about Democritus?

   (A) Although his view was initially met with skepticism, Democritus was among the first to advocate an atomic theory.
   (B) Although he was more known for his work in politics, Democritus also made important scientific discoveries.
   (C) His ideas were incompatible with those of Galileo and Newton.
   (D) Democritus was unduly credited with being the father of Greek atomism.
   (E) Democritus was more known for his discovery of calculus than for his theory of atomism.

3. Which of the following does the author of Passage 1 suggest about the physical world?

   (A) The composition of everyday things will remain a mystery forever.
   (B) Understanding matter is much simpler than scientists once believed.
   (C) Despite the diversity of the physical world, all matter may have a single underlying component.
   (D) Although physicists use simple models to describe matter, the principles underlying the models point to a more complex reality.
   (E) The theories developed by Democritus accurately explain all aspects of everyday matter.

4. The "obsession" that the author describes in line 22 can best be described as

   (A) Democritus' desire to see his ideas accepted by the scientific community
   (B) physicists' search for Democritus' original writings on atoms
   (C) the author's own search for the principles underlying matter
   (D) early-nineteenth-century chemists' search for the first solid evidence of atomism
   (E) modern scientists' quest for a simple unifying property of everyday matter

5. Which of the following can be inferred from Passage 2 about the expanding universe?

   (A) It was incompatible with a theory widely accepted in the nineteenth century.
   (B) Newton discovered it during his work with gravity.
   (C) Most scientists believe that the idea is no longer tenable.
   (D) The existence of gravity makes it impossible for the universe to expand.
   (E) The expanding universe theory cannot be proven.

GO ON TO THE NEXT PAGE

6. In lines 62–63, the term "certain critical rate" refers to

   (A) the rate at which scientific knowledge is growing
   (B) an urgent problem which needs solving
   (C) the speed at which a rocket must travel in order to move away from the earth
   (D) the speed necessary to equal the force of gravity's pull
   (E) the meeting point of gravity and the universe

7. The author of Passage 2 mentions Newton in order to

   (A) point out the ignorance of many physicists
   (B) give one example of a proponent of the expanding universe theory
   (C) illustrate the point that the expanding universe theory might have been discovered earlier
   (D) provide evidence that the universe is not expanding
   (E) show the consequences of a scientist's disregard for a new theory

8. The author's reference to a rocket (lines 66–72) serves to illustrate

   (A) the implications of an expanding universe
   (B) the forces governing the universe's gradual expansion
   (C) the similarity of the energy released by the universe and that released by rockets
   (D) the way in which gravity prevents the universe from expanding
   (E) the theory of a static universe

9. In Passage 2, the author's description of Einstein's general theory of relativity serves to

   (A) bolster the author's theory that the universe is expanding
   (B) show that modern scientists were reluctant to abandon the theory of a static universe
   (C) indicate the creativity that Einstein brought to his work
   (D) question the validity of the theory of the expanding universe
   (E) underscore Einstein's reliance on Newtonian physics

10. The term "cosmological constant" (lines 82–83) refers to

    (A) a mathematical constant employed by Einstein to bring his theories in line with the idea of a static universe
    (B) an equation used by Einstein to debunk Newton's ideas about universal expansion
    (C) a theory developed by opponents of Einstein's general theory of relativity
    (D) the mathematical model that was used to disprove Newtonian physics
    (E) the theory that the mass of all matter in the universe must remain the same

11. In the last line of Passage 2, the word "static" most nearly means

    (A) charged
    (B) conflicting
    (C) particulate
    (D) unchanging
    (E) dynamic

GO ON TO THE NEXT PAGE ⟶

12. The authors of both passages would most probably agree with which of the following statements?

(A) Democritus and Newton both struggled to see their theories accepted by others.

(B) Neither Democritus nor Newton received credit for his theories.

(C) Newton, Einstein, and Democritus are all responsible in part for setting back modern physics.

(D) The atomic model of matter and the theory of the expanding universe are mutually exclusive.

(E) Scientists may adopt particular theories in spite of weak or contradictory evidence.

13. Based on the information in both passages, a difference between atomism and the expanding universe theory is

(A) the idea of atomism can be traced to the ancient Greeks, while the model of the expanding universe is a relatively recent theory

(B) atomism is easier to understand and explore than the static universe theory

(C) atomism was developed for political reasons, while the static universe theory is purely scientific

(D) the theory of atomism has been proven, while the static universe theory is now thought to be incorrect

(E) the static universe theory is more adaptable to modern science than is the atomistic theory

STOP
**If you finish before time is called, you may check your work on this section only.
Do not turn to any other section in the test.**

PRACTICE TEST 2 ANSWERS

Section 1	Section 2	Section 3	Section 4	Section 5	Section 6	Section 7
1. E	1. E	1. A	1. B	1. E	1. C	1. E
2. B	2. D	2. C	2. D	2. E	2. B	2. A
3. B	3. E	3. A	3. A	3. D	3. C	3. C
4. C	4. E	4. A	4. C	4. D	4. A	4. E
5. A	5. C	5. D	5. B	5. C	5. D	5. A
6. C	6. C	6. B	6. D	6. E	6. B	6. D
7. D	7. A	7. B	7. B	7. D	7. A	7. C
8. E	8. B	8. D	8. D	8. C	8. E	8. B
9. D	9. A	9. A	9. B	9. D	9. C	9. B
10. C	10. C	10. C	10. B	10. A	10. E	10. A
11. D	11. B	11. C	11. A	11. E		11. D
12. B	12. C	12. D	12. B	12. A		12. E
13. C	13. E	13. A	13. D	13. A		13. A
14. A	14. A	14. D	14. C	14. A		
15. B	15. B	15. B	15. A	15. D		
16. D	16. A	16. 2	16. 100	16. E		
17. B	17. D	17. 270	17. 81	17. B		
18. C	18. B	18. .4	18. .75	18. B		
19. D	19. B	or 2/5	or 3/4	19. E		
20. D	20. D	19. 3	19. .583	20. B		
21. A	21. A	20. 24	or	21. C		
22. B	22. B	21. 7	7/12	22. A		
23. C	23. C	22. 50	20. 5, 7,	23. E		
24. C	24. E	23. 6	or 11	24. D		
25. C	25. C	24. 286	21. 21	25. B		
	26. D	25. 18	22. 96	26. E		
	27. B		23. 2	27. B		
	28. D		24. 282	28. B		
	29. A		25. .375 or	29. E		
	30. B		3/8	30. E		
				31. D		
				32. A		
				33. B		
				34. E		
				35. C		

You will find a detailed explanation for each question beginning on page 427.

HOW TO SCORE YOUR PRACTICE TEST

VERBAL

After you have checked your answers to the practice test against the key, you can calculate your score. For the three Verbal sections (Sections 2, 5, and 7), tally up the number of correct answers and the number of incorrect answers. Enter these numbers on the worksheet on the next page. Multiply the number of incorrect answers by $\frac{1}{4}$ and subtract the result from the number of correct answers. Put this number in box A. Then round the numbers to the nearest whole number and place it in box B.

MATHEMATICS

Figuring your Math score is a little trickier, because some of the questions have five answer choices, some have four, and some have none. In Sections 1 and 6, count the number of correct answers and incorrect answers. Enter these numbers on the worksheet. Multiply the number of incorrect answers by $\frac{1}{4}$ and subtract this from the number of correct answers. Put the result in box C.

Count the number of correct and incorrect answers in Section 3, questions 1–15. (Choice E counts as a blank.) Enter these on the worksheet. Multiply the number of incorrect answers by $\frac{1}{3}$ and subtract this from the number of correct answers. Put the result in box D.

Count up the number of correct answers in Section 3, questions 16–25. Put the result in box E. There is no penalty for incorrect grid-in questions.

Note: Section 4 is experimental and should not be scored.

Add up the numbers in boxes C, D, and E, and write the result in box F.

Round F to the nearest whole number, and place the result in box G.

WORKSHEET FOR CALCULATING YOUR SCORE

VERBAL

	Correct	Incorrect	
A. Sections 2, 5, and 7	_____	– (1/4 × _____) =	A
B. Total rounded Verbal raw score			B

MATHEMATICS

	Correct	Incorrect	
C. Sections 1 and 6	_____	– (1/4 × _____) =	C
D. Section 3 (Questions 1–15)	_____	– (1/3 × _____) =	D
E. Section 3 (Questions 16–25)	_____	=	E
F. Total unrounded Math raw score (C + D + E)			F
G. Total rounded Math raw score			G

Use the table on the next page to convert your raw score to scaled scores. For example, a raw Verbal score of 39 corresponds to a Verbal scaled score of 530; a Math raw score of 24 corresponds to a Math scaled score of 470.

Scores on the SAT range from 200 to 800.

Note: Since Section 4 is the experimental section, it does not count toward your score.

SCORE CONVERSION TABLE

Raw Score	Verbal Scaled Score	Math Scaled Score	Raw Score	Verbal Scaled Score	Math Scaled Score
78	800		36	510	560
77	800		35	510	550
76	800		34	500	540
75	800		33	490	530
74	780		32	480	520
73	760		31	480	520
72	750		30	470	510
71	740		29	460	500
70	740		28	460	490
69	730		27	450	480
68	720		26	450	480
67	710		25	440	480
66	700		24	430	470
65	690		23	430	460
64	680		22	420	450
63	670		21	410	440
62	670		20	400	430
61	660		19	390	430
60	660	800	18	380	430
59	650	790	17	380	420
58	640	770	16	370	410
57	640	760	15	360	400
56	630	740	14	350	390
55	620	730	13	350	390
54	620	720	12	340	380
53	610	700	11	330	370
52	600	690	10	310	350
51	600	680	9	300	340
50	600	660	8	290	340
49	590	650	7	270	330
48	590	650	6	270	310
47	580	640	5	230	300
46	570	630	4	230	300
45	570	620	3	230	280
44	560	610	2	230	260
43	560	600	1	230	250
42	550	600	0	230	240
41	550	590	−1	230	220
40	540	580	−2	230	220
39	530	570	−3	230	200
38	530	560	−4	230	200
37	520	560	−5 and below	230	200

19

Answers and Explanations for Practice Test 2

What follows is a detailed explanation for each question on Practice Test 2. Although you will naturally be more curious about the questions you got wrong, don't forget to read the explanations for the questions you left blank. In fact, you should even read the explanations for the questions you got right! Our explanations present the safest, most direct solution to each question. Even though you may have gotten a question right, that does not mean you solved it in the most efficient way.

1. ETS's answer is E.

   If you divide 12 by 4, you'll see that $x = 3$. When you plug $x = 3$ into the term, you'll see that $4(3) + 2 = 12 + 2 = 14$.

2. ETS's answer is B.

   The shaded region lies in the quadrant where x is positive and y is negative. Given this, you can get rid of answer choices A, C, and E. If you plot answer choices B and D, you'll find that $(1, -2)$ is inside the shaded region, while $(5, -4)$ is not.

3. ETS's answer is B.

   There are variables in the answer choices, so this is a plug-in question. If $n = 2$, then answer choice B is the only answer choice that gives you an odd integer:
   $$3(n + 1) = 3(2 + 1) = 3(3) = 9.$$

4. ETS's answer is C.

   This question is much easier if you work out the square roots first. We know that $\sqrt{4} = 2$ and $\sqrt{9} = 3$, so we can rewrite the question like this: $2x - 3x = -x$.

5. ETS's answer is A.

   You need to take this question one step at a time. First, figure out how many batches there are in 12 jars of cookies. If one jar holds 1.5 batches, then twelve jars will hold 12×1.5, or 18 batches. Now you need to figure out how much flour is needed for 18 batches. If you need six cups of flour for one batch, then for 18 batches you will need 18×6, or 108 cups.

6. ETS's answer is C.

   The formula for the area of a circle is πr^2, so we need to find the radius of the circle. We know that the diameter is 9, and the radius is half of the diameter, so the radius is $\dfrac{9}{2}$. Since there are fractions in the answer choices, you might as well keep the radius as a fraction. The area of the circle is $\left(\dfrac{9}{2}\right)^2 \pi$, which equals $\dfrac{81}{4}\pi$.

7. ETS's answer is D.

   The idea of "the rest" in this question can save you from doing unnecessary arithmetic. If 40 percent of the records are jazz, then the rest, or 60 percent, are blues. Since there are 80 records, just use your calculator to find 60 percent of 80, which is 48.

8. ETS's answer is E.

   From 1 to 100, there are 50 even integers. If we don't include 2 and 100, then there are only 48.

9. ETS's answer is D.

   If there are variables in the answer choices you should…plug in! First, cross out that phrase "in terms of b," because we don't need it. Next, let's plug in a number for a. This is a percent question, so let $a = 100$. Since b is 40 percent of a, that means $b = 40$. If $a = 100$, then $4a = 400$. Use your calculator to find 40 percent of 400, which is 160. That's your target answer. Since $b = 40$, answer choice D gives you 160.

10. ETS's answer is C.

    Remember that the perimeter is the sum of all the sides. $BCDE$ is a square, so all the sides are equal. Since $CD = 3$, each side of the square is 3. Add up all four sides to find the perimeter, which is 12. $ACDF$ is a rectangle, which means that the opposite sides are equal. $AB = 2$, so $FE = 2$ also. BE is a side of square $BCDE$, so BE equals 3, but it's also the side of the rectangle, and that means the opposite side, AF, also equals 3. Add up all the sides of $ACDF$ to find the perimeter: $2 + 2 + 3 + 3 = 16$. To find out how much smaller the perimeter of $BCDE$ is, just subtract: $16 - 12 = 4$.

11. ETS's answer is D.

    The sides of a 45:45:90 triangle have a special pattern, which you can find in the gray box at the beginning of every Math section. Each leg of a 45:45:90 triangle is equal to the hypotenuse divided by $\sqrt{2}$. Since the hypotenuse in triangle ABC is 8, BC must be equal to $\frac{8}{\sqrt{2}}$. You can't have a square root on the bottom of a fraction; multiply the top and the bottom by $\sqrt{2}$. That gives you $\frac{8\sqrt{2}}{2}$, which equals $4\sqrt{2}$. Also, you could have used Ballparking to eliminate A and B. Since the hypotenuse of a right triangle is always the longest of the three sides, BC must be less than 8.

12. ETS's answer is B.
Use Average Pies:
In the first pie you have the number of red parrots sold, which is 5, and the average weight, which is 2. That gives you a total weight of 10 pounds. In the second pie you have the number of blue parrots, which is 4, and the average weight, which is 3. That gives you a total weight of 12. To find the average weight of all the parrots, you need to find the total weight of all the parrots. This is simply the total of the red plus the total of the blue. In the last pie you have the total number of parrots, which is 9, and the total weight of all the parrots, which is 22. This gives you an average weight of $\frac{22}{9}$, or $2\frac{4}{9}$.

13. ETS's answer is C.
This question can be solved easily, using your calculator. Just punch in 111×999 and you get 110,889. Then plug in the answer choices, starting with C. If $n = 111$, then $3 \times 3 \times (111)^2 = 110,889$.

14. ETS's answer is A.
The question is essentially asking which of the answer choices cannot be a value of x. So just try each answer choice one at a time by plugging the number into each of the two inequalities in the question, and see which one doesn't fit. If $x = -6$, is $-6 + 6 > 0$? No, because zero is not greater than zero. So -6 is the exception.

15. ETS's answer is B.
This question has several steps, so don't try to do it all at once. Take it one step at a time. Andrei starts out with 48 baseball caps. In the first step, Andrei gives away 13 caps, so he has 35 left. In the next step, he buys 17 new caps, so now he has 52. Then Andrei gives Pierre 6 caps (46 left) and gets 8 caps in return. In the end, Andrei has 54 baseball caps, which is 6 more caps than he had originally. The percent increase is $\frac{6}{48}$. You can change this to a percent by converting the fraction to a decimal and then multiplying by 100 on your calculator:
$\frac{6}{48} \times 100 = 0.125 \times 100 = 12.5\%$.

16. ETS's answer is D.
According to the function, $\otimes\, x = 2x^2 + 4$. To find the value of $\otimes\, 4$, just substitute 4 for x:

$$2(4)^2 + 4 = 2(16) + 4 = 32 + 4 = 36$$

17. ETS's answer is B.
To find the value of $\otimes\, 3 + \otimes\, 5$, find the values of 3 and 5 separately: $\otimes\, 3 = 2(3)^2 + 4 = 22$; and $\otimes\, 5 = 2(5)^2 + 4 = 54$. So $\otimes\, 3 + \otimes\, 5 = 76$. You already know that $\otimes\, 4 = 36$ from question 16, so you can cross out A. Answer choice C is the Joe Bloggs answer, because Joe simply adds 3 and 5, and it can't be that easy. If you Ballpark answer choices D and E, putting 10 or 15 in the function will give you a number bigger than 100, and you're looking for 76, so D and E are too big. That means the answer is B by POE.

18. ETS's answer is C.
The Joe Bloggs answer is E, because Joe simply chooses the greatest number. If you draw three straight lines through the center of the triangle, you get six regions, so you know that you can have at least six. Therefore, you can eliminate A. But that was too easy. That means the answer must be 7 or 8. If you don't have time, you can guess between C and D. Here's how you can actually get seven regions:

19. ETS's answer is D.
Whenever there are variables in the answer choices, you should always plug in. Let's say $x = 20$, which means there are 20 ounces of root beer in the pitcher. Next, let's make $y = 3$ and $z = 4$. That means Elsa pours 3 ounces into each of 4 glasses, so she pours a total of 12 ounces. The question asks how much root beer remains in the pitcher, so your target answer is $20 - 12$, or 8. Go to the answer choices and plug in $x = 20$, $y = 3$, and $z = 4$. In answer choice D, $x - yz = 20 - (3)(4) = 20 - 12 = 8$.

20. ETS's answer is D.

To figure out probability, you need to work with fractions; the total number of possible outcomes goes on the bottom, and the number of desired outcomes goes on the top. To figure out the probability of selecting three blue hammers, you need to figure out the probability of getting a blue hammer each time a hammer is selected. The first time, there are total of 20 hammers and 10 of them are blue, so the probability of getting a blue hammer is $\frac{10}{20}$, or $\frac{1}{2}$. When the second hammer is selected, there are only 19 hammers left, and only 9 of them are blue. So the probability of getting a blue hammer the second time is $\frac{9}{19}$. When the third hammer is selected, there are a total of 18 hammers left and 8 are blue, so the probability of getting a blue hammer on the third try is $\frac{8}{18}$, or $\frac{4}{9}$. To find the probability of selecting three blue hammers, you need to multiply the three separate probabilities: $\frac{1}{2} \times \frac{9}{19} \times \frac{4}{9} = \frac{2}{19}$. By the way, A and B are Joe Bloggs answers.

21. ETS's answer is A.

    Variables in the answer choices? Plug in! This is a percent question, so make $k = 100$ and $d = 40$. If 40 out of the 100 gallons have been pumped, that equals 40%. So 40% is your target answer. When you plug $k = 100$ and $d = 40$ into the answer choices, A gives you 40. Plugging In turns a hard question into a much easier question.

22. ETS's answer is B.

    To find out what numbers a could be divisible by, you need to try different values of b. If $b = 1$, then $a = 4(1) + 26 = 30$. In this case, a is divisible by 2, 5, and 6, so you can cross out A, C, and D. If $b = 4$, then $a = 42$, which is divisible by 7, so cross out choice E. That only leaves choice B, which must be the answer.

23. ETS's answer is C.

    For this question you need to know the distance formula: distance = rate × time. This is also a perfect question for which to plug in the answer choices. The question asks how far Ray and Jane will be from Ray's house when they meet. Start with C: if they are $56\frac{1}{4}$ miles away from Ray's house, and Ray traveled from home at 30 miles per hour, then you can figure out the time he traveled using the "rate × time = distance" formula (and your calculator): $56\frac{1}{4} = 30 \times$ time. In this case Ray has traveled for $1\frac{7}{8}$ hours. Jane has been traveling for the same amount of time at a rate of 50 miles an hour, so you can figure out how far Jane has traveled: distance $= 50 \times 1\frac{7}{8}$. If Jane has traveled $93\frac{3}{4}$ and Ray has traveled $56\frac{1}{4}$, then they have traveled a total of 150 miles when they meet.

    Bingo! You're done.

24. ETS's answer is C.

    Whenever there are variables in the answer choices, you must plug in. Since $x = y + 1$ and $y \geq 1$, we can make $x = 5$ and $y = 4$. In that case $x^2 - y^2 = 25 - 16 = 9$, so 9 is your target answer. When you plug $x = 5$ and $y = 4$ into the answer choices, C gives you 9. Plugging In turns a hard question into a much easier question.

25. ETS's answer is C.

    The question asks which of the answer choices could be x^3. If x is an integer, then the cube root of one of the answer choices should be an integer. You should be able to find the cube root on most scientific calculators. Here, the answer is C: $2.7 \times 10^{13} = 27 \times 10^{12}$ and $3\sqrt{27 \times 12^{12}} = 3 \times 10^4$, which equals 30,000 (an integer).

SECTION 2

1. ETS's answer is E.
   The blank in this sentence is a word that describes the wastes produced by nuclear power plants. What do we know about the wastes? The wastes are *radioactive materials* that have to be stored in *protective containers*, which means they must be dangerous, so *dangerous* would be a good word for the blank. Answer choice E, *hazardous*, is the best match for *dangerous*.

2. ETS's answer is D.
   Let's start with the second blank. The clues for this blank are *living specimen* and *long thought*. If they found a *living* specimen, and the whole scientific community is talking about it, then the creature must have been long thought *dead*. So we can put *dead* in the second blank, and the only second blank word that matches *dead* is *extinct*, in answer choice D. The first blank word, *astounded*, makes sense because you would certainly be surprised if something you thought was dead turned out to be alive.

3. ETS's answer is E.
   The clues here are *third trip overseas* and *voters complained*. Why would the voters complain about the governor taking a lot of trips abroad? If he's always away in a foreign country, then he probably isn't paying a lot of attention to the affairs of his own country. So we can put *his own country* in the blank. Looking to the answer choices, *domestic* is the best match; it means the opposite of *foreign*.

4. ETS's answer is E.
   For this question we need to figure out the relationship between the blanks. Claudius was viewed one way by generations of historians, *until newly discovered evidence* changed everyone's mind. So the words in the blanks must be opposites. We can get rid of answer choices B and D, because the words aren't opposites. In choices A, C, and E, the first word is negative and the second is positive, so they are all possibilities. To narrow it down, let's look at the second blank, which describes Claudius' ability as an administrator. Would it make sense to call him *an eager* administrator? Not really, so get rid of C. Between A and E, the best answer is E because it makes more sense to say that they used to think of Claudius with *disdain*, and now they think of him as *capable*. In answer choice A, *suspicion* and *clever* aren't really opposites.

5. ETS's answer is C.
The clues in this sentence are *scarce* and *nutrition*. In these primitive areas, something is scarce, so they have to be resourceful in order to find nutrition. What is scarce? It must be nutrition, that's why they have to be resourceful in order to find it. So we can recycle the clue and put *nutrition* in the blank. Looking at the answer choices, *sustenance* is the best match for *nutrition*. Answer choice D, *agriculture*, is close, but *agriculture* doesn't mean *nutrition*.

6. ETS's answer is C.
The clues in this sentence are *masked* and *cheerful nature*. If Anthony's cheerful nature is masked, then he must not be very cheerful at the moment. We can recycle the clue and put *not cheerful* in the blank. The best match for *not cheerful* in the answer choices is *dour*. If you didn't know what all the words meant, you should at least have been able to eliminate any words you did know that didn't match our word for the blank.

7. ETS's answer is A.
Let's start with the first blank. The first clue in the sentence is *division between*. Morgan wants to do something with the division between *theory* and *empiricism*. In the second part of the sentence we learn that she thinks doing something with philosophy and applied science is *possible and necessary*. If doing something with both things together is possible and necessary, then she must be *against* the division, so the word in the first blank is negative. That means we can get rid of answer choice B. Since Morgan is against the *division*, she must be convinced that a *combination* is possible and necessary, so we can put *combination* in the second blank. Looking at the answer choices, the best match for *combination* in the second blank is *synthesis* in answer choice A.

8. ETS's answer is B.
Let's start with the second blank. The professor is warning against policies that fail to consider the *wide variety* of cultural standpoints, so the policies must be *narrow*. That means we can put *narrow* in our second blank. We can cross out answer choices C, D, and E, because none of the second words in those blanks means *narrow*. *Discriminatory* in choice A fits the topic of the sentence, but *discriminatory* doesn't mean *narrow*. Also, this is a difficult question; *myopic*, in B, is definitely a difficult word. In the first blank, it makes sense to say that the professor wants to *consider* the experiences of different groups, because he's against policies that *fail to consider* them. So B is the best answer.

9. ETS's answer is A.
Let's start with the second blank. The clue in this sentence is *disagreeable*, and the trigger word for the second blank is *although*, which means that the word in the second blank is the opposite of *disagreeable*. Therefore we can put *agreeable* in the second blank. Looking at the answer choices, the only word that matches *agreeable* is *complaisant*.

SECTION 2

10. ETS's answer is C.
A SHEPHERD tends SHEEP, and a *gardener* tends *plants*.

11. ETS's answer is B.
A VANDAL causes DAMAGE, and a *pest* causes *annoyance*.

12. ETS's answer is C.
A SNARE is used to trap an ANIMAL, and a *net* is used to trap a *fish*.

13. ETS's answer is E.
CACOPHONOUS means unpleasant to the EAR. *Rank* means unpleasant to the *nose*. If you weren't able to make a sentence, you should have eliminated any unrelated answer choices. For example, *erroneous* means mistaken, and that has nothing to do with *mind*. As it turns out, the only answer choice that has a clear relationship is E.

14. ETS's answer is A.
We can make a better sentence if we reverse the order of the words. An AGGRESSOR shows BELLIGERENCE. A *boor* shows *insensitivity*. If you weren't able to make a sentence, you should have eliminated any unrelated answer choices. As it turns out, the only answer choice that has a clear relationship is A.

15. ETS's answer is B.
INCORRIGIBLE means difficult to REFORM and *intractable* means difficult to *manage*. If you weren't able to make a sentence, you should have eliminated any unrelated answer choices. For example, *impartial* means not taking sides, and that has nothing to do with *decide*. As it turns out, the only answer choice that has a clear relationship is B.

16. ETS's answer is A.

In lines 7–9, the passage says, *It cannot be said that he enjoyed his work; he did it only because it had been assigned to him.* Poseidon is clearly not very happy with his job, but he does it anyway. The word that best describes this attitude is *resignation.*

Answer choice B is wrong because the passage says the Poseidon *filed petitions for … more cheerful work,* so he definitely wasn't enthusiastic about his job.

Answer choice C is wrong because Poseidon certainly had an opinion about his job. He didn't like it.

Answer choice D is way off. Poseidon wasn't happy, but there's nothing in the passage to indicate that he was intimidated by his work. After all, he's a god.

Answer choice E can't be right, because the passage never says that Poseidon was destructive.

17. ETS's answer is D.

Vocabulary-in-context questions should be answered like sentence completions. Go back to the passage, find the word *vexatious,* and cross it out. Then read the sentence and come up with your own word. The sentence says that *his complaints were not really taken seriously.* We're talking about Poseidon's *complaints,* so ETS's word must have a similar meaning. The best match for *complaints* is *troubled.*

Answer choice A is wrong, because *pleased* is a positive word and you can figure out from the context that *vexatious* is negative.

Answer choices B and C are wrong because they're *too* negative. Poseidon complained and he was unhappy, but things weren't *that* bad.

Answer choice E has nothing to do with the meaning of *vexatious.* If you don't know what *indisposed* means, look it up.

18. ETS's answer is B.

Here's another vocabulary-in-context question. Go back to the passage, find the word *conceptions,* and cross it out. Then read the sentence and come up with your own word. The sentence in the passage tells us that Poseidon was *irritated* when he found out that people thought he *was always riding about through the tides with his trident.* If he's upset about what people think about him, that means he's upset about their *opinions* of him.

Answer choice A is a Joe Bloggs answer. Joe doesn't look at the word in context. He just chooses an answer that reminds him of the word. In this case, *conceptions* makes Joe think of conceiving an idea (or, perhaps, a child). That makes him think of *origins.*

Answer choices C, D, and E don't make sense in context. It wouldn't make sense to say that Poseidon didn't like to hear about the *discussions* formed about him, or the *plans* formed about him, or the *explanations* formed about him.

19. ETS's answer is B.

In lines 40–43, the passage says, *Thus he had hardly seen the sea—had seen it only fleetingly . . . and he had never actually traveled around it.* If you read further, you also learn that Poseidon was waiting for the fall of the world so he would have a *quiet moment* to *make a quick little tour* of the sea. From that we can infer that Poseidon is too busy to see his own kingdom, so ETS's answer must be B.

Answer choice A gets it backward. The passage says that Poseidon's trips to visit Jupiter are the *only break in the monotony* of his jobs, so if anything, he *prefers* the trips to his duties, not the other way around.

Answer choice C is wrong because the passage doesn't say anything about Poseidon needing silence.

Answer choice D contradicts the passage. Poseidon is waiting for the fall of the world so that he can finally get out and *make a quick little tour* of his domain, which he has never had a chance to see.

Answer choice E is wrong because the passage doesn't say anything to suggest that Poseidon is inefficient.

20. ETS's answer is D.
The lead word for this question is *dissatisfaction*, so you should go back to the passage and find where it mentions Poseidon's dissatisfaction. Lines 31–35 describe what is *chiefly responsible for his dissatisfaction*. He does not like *to hear of the conceptions formed about him: how he was always riding about through the tides with his trident.* According to the passage, Poseidon doesn't actually get out much at all, so people have the wrong idea about what he actually does. This is exactly what answer choice D says.

Answer choice A contradicts the passage. Poseidon was so irritated by the false idea people had that he was always riding around with his trident.

Answer choice B is a trap. The question asks what is *primarily* responsible for Poseidon's dissatisfaction. Although something similar to choice B is mentioned earlier in the passage, it's not *chiefly responsible for his dissatisfaction* (line 32). Use the lead words to make sure you are reading in the right place.

Answer choice C contradicts the passage. Poseidon does the exact same thing every day. That's why he's so bored and unhappy.

Answer choice E is incorrect because the passage says that Poseidon actually did most of the bookkeeping tasks himself, leaving little for his assistants to do (lines 5–7).

21. ETS's answer is A.
This is a general question, so you only need to know the main idea of the passage. The passage portrays Poseidon as someone who sits around working out *figures* all day and doesn't go out much. Poseidon is also clearly unhappy (as we learned in questions 19 and 20), so he is best described as a *dissatisfied bureaucrat*.

The other answer choices are wrong because they don't fit the main idea of the passage. Poseidon may be a *deity*, but the passage doesn't characterize him as being *powerful*. Poseidon is definitely not a *vagabond*, and he's definitely not a *tyrant*. Answer choice D is half-wrong, which means that it's all wrong. Although the description of Poseidon's duties make him sound like an *accountant*, the passage focuses on his unhappiness, not his *capabilities* as an accountant.

22. ETS's answer is B.
This is an EXCEPT question, so you should definitely save it for last. We need to know why Poseidon is unable to change his job, so we need to go back to the passage and find where that is discussed. Remember, we're looking for the reason that is *not* mentioned, so we can eliminate answer choices that are mentioned.

The passage mentions answer choice A in lines 29–30: *he had been appointed God of the Sea in the beginning, and that he had to remain.* Answer choice C is in lines 20–21: *when a job away from the water was offered to him he would get sick at the very prospect.* Answer choice D is in lines 12–13 (*nothing suited him quite as well as his present position*), and answer choice E is in lines 18–19 (*Poseidon could in any case only occupy an executive position*). Therefore B must be the answer.

23. ETS's answer is C.

According to the first paragraph, *early man viewed ... healing as purification,* and this *notion is apparent in the origin of our word for "pharmacy."* The passage then gives the meaning of the Greek word *pharmakon*, which is *purification through purging*. Therefore, the literal definition is cited in order to give an example of how early man thought of healing as *purging*, or *internal cleansing*, as it is paraphrased in answer choice C. Remember, the answer to most specific questions will be an exact *paraphrase* of what the passage says.

Answer choice A doesn't make any sense. Did *ancient* civilization have an *advanced* form of medical science? No way. Don't forget to use your common sense.

Answer choice B doesn't answer the question, and it is irrelevant. We're talking about ancient medicine, not ancient beliefs in general.

Answer choice D is wrong because the passage doesn't say anything in the first paragraph about the mental and physical causes of diseases. This is mentioned much later in the passage. Make sure you're reading in the right place.

Answer choice E is too extreme, and it actually contradicts the passage. In lines 36–37, the passage says that *the Greeks had adopted a sophisticated mind-body view of medicine*, so they were certainly not *primitive*.

24. ETS's answer is E.

The lead words in this question are *early Sumerian drugs*, which should lead you back to the second paragraph. According to lines 11–15, the *first drug catalog, or pharmacopoeia, was written... by an unknown Sumerian physician. Preserved in cuneiform script on a single clay tablet are the names of dozens of drugs to treat ailments that still afflict us today.* So it was possible to identify a number of early Sumerian drugs because somebody back then wrote them all down, which is exactly what answer choice E says.

Answer choice A is wrong because the passage doesn't say anything at all about traces of the drugs being found in archeological excavations. If it's not in the passage, then it's not ETS's answer.

Answer choice B is wrong because the passage says in line 16 that the Egyptians *added* to the ancient knowledge of medicine. The passage doesn't say that they used the *same* medications as the Sumerians.

Answer choice C is wrong because the passage doesn't say anything at all about *Sumerian religious texts*.

Answer choice D is way off the topic. The passage is about ancient civilizations, *not* about Europe. Modern Europe didn't even exist back then. Read the answer choices carefully.

25. ETS's answer is C.

This question asks about Sumerian drugs again, so you need to go back to the second paragraph. This time the question is looking for a similarity between Sumerian drugs and modern drugs. According to lines 7–9, *the Sumerians in the Tigris-Euphrates Valley had developed virtually all of our modern methods of administering drugs.* So the similarity between Sumerian and modern drugs is in the *methods of administering drugs*, which is paraphrased in answer choice C as the *delivery* of drugs. Remember, the answer to most specific questions will be an exact *paraphrase* of what the passage says.

Answer choice A is wrong because the passage says that the Sumerians had the same methods of *administering* drugs, not that they used the same chemicals. Besides, it doesn't make any sense to say that an ancient civilization had the same chemicals that we do now. They didn't have penicillin, or anything like that, did they? Don't forget about common sense.

Answer choice B is wrong because the passage doesn't talk about mental and physical disorders until much later in the passage. Use the lead words to make sure you are reading in the right place.

Answer choice D doesn't make any sense at all. Were ancient Sumerian drugs the products of *sophisticated laboratory research*? No way! Use common sense.

Answer choice E is wrong because a hierarchy of drug producers was part of *Egyptian* society, not *Sumerian* society.

26. ETS's answer is D.

For this question, you should read before and after the word *hierarchy* to give yourself some context. In the fourth paragraph, the passage talks about the *hierarchy of ancient drug preparation.* In lines 26–35, the passage describes the different people involved in the process of making drugs, including the *chief of the preparers of drugs*, the *collectors of drugs*, the *preparers*, the *preparers' aides*, and the *conservator of drugs.* With all these different jobs, the *hierarchy* must be an example of a *division of labor.*

Answer choice A is wrong because the fourth paragraph doesn't say anything about superstitious practices.

Answer choice B is wrong because the passage doesn't say anything about the severity of ancient diseases.

Answer choice C is close, but the fourth paragraph is about the people who *made drugs* in ancient Egypt, not the doctors who administered the drugs.

Answer choice E is also wrong because the fourth paragraph is about the people who made the drugs, not the recipes for the drugs themselves. Read carefully.

27. ETS's answer is B.

The lead words in this question are *the seventh-century Greeks*, which should lead you to the fifth paragraph. The question asks how the view of medicine *differed* between the Greeks and the Sumerians. According to lines 36–37, *By the seventh century B.C., the Greeks had adopted a sophisticated mind-body view of medicine.* If this view was newly adopted by the Greeks, it must have been different from what the Sumerians thought. So the difference is that the Greeks had a *mind-body* view. *Mind-body* is paraphrased in answer choice B as *the mental and physical roots of illness*.

Answer choice A is wrong because the passage doesn't say anything about *advanced chemical applications*. Read carefully.

Answer choice C contradicts the passage. The Greeks believed that it was necessary to treat the mind *and* the body. That is the point of the fifth paragraph. Go back and read it again.

Answer choice E is wrong because the word *most* makes it a *must* answer. The Greeks didn't develop *most* of the precursors of modern drugs. What about the Egyptians and the Sumerians?

28. ETS's answer is D.

Go back to the passage, find the word *holistic*, and cross it out. Then read the sentence and come up with your own word. The paragraph is talking about how the Greeks had a *mind-body* view of medicine, meaning they believed it was important to treat the mind as well as the body. Since they believed in treating the whole person, that means they *emphasized* an *approach to health* that included everything. So we use *included everything* in place of the *holistic*. The best match in the answer choices is *integrated*.

Answer choices A and C are wrong because *holistic* doesn't just describe the psychological perspective or just the physiological perspective, but both together.

Answer choice B gets the time frame wrong. The Greeks were *ancient*, not *modern*.

Answer choice E misinterprets the passage. The Greeks had a holistic perspective *despite* their belief in deities.

29. ETS's answer is A.

The lead words in this sentence are *modern era of pharmacology*, which should lead you to the sixth paragraph. This paragraph talks about how the modern era of pharmacology began, but the question asks what delayed *advances in medical science* during the modern era.

So you need to keep reading into the next paragraph to find the answer: *physicians, unaware of the existence of disease-causing pathogens such as bacteria and viruses, continued to dream up imaginary causative evils*. So the problem was that doctors didn't really know what caused diseases, and that is exactly what answer choice A says.

The other answer choices are wrong because none of them is mentioned anywhere in the passage. Go back and read the second to last paragraph carefully.

30. ETS's answer is B.

To answer this question, you just need to read the final paragraph and find out what the passage says about *scientific discovery*. According to the last paragraph, *many of the latest sophisticated additions to our medicine chest shelves were accidental finds*. In other words, many modern drugs were discovered by accident. Answer choice B paraphrases the idea of *accidental finds* as *chance events*.

Answer choice A doesn't make any sense. Are discoveries in biochemistry *uncommon*? Most biochemists would probably disagree. Don't forget to use common sense.

Answer choice C may actually be true, but the passage doesn't mention it, so it can't be ETS's answer. Remember, ETS's answers come right out of the passage. You don't need any outside knowledge.

Answer choice D is wrong because the word *best* makes this a *must* answer. How do we know that trial and error is the *best* way to make scientific discoveries? The passage never says that it's the best way.

Answer choice E is wrong because it is also a *must* answer. Is it really true that *most* of the important scientific discoveries have been accidents? Besides, we're only talking about *drugs* here!

SECTION 3

1. ETS's answer is A.

   Begin by eliminating D. You can solve this

   question easily on your calculator. Just convert both

   of the fractions to decimals by dividing the top of

   the fraction by the bottom: $\frac{3}{10} = .3$ and $\frac{3}{100} = .03$.

   Since .3 is greater than .03, Column A is greater.

2. ETS's answer is C.
   In Column A, the sum of the numbers is 900. There
   are three numbers, so you need to divide 900 by 3,
   which gives you an average of 300. For Column
   B, the sum of the numbers is also 900, and there
   are also three numbers, so the average must be the
   same.

3. ETS's answer is A.
   Always be sure to plug in twice for quant comp
   questions. You need to plug in numbers for z that
   are between −3 and 0. If $z = −2$, then Column A is
   5 and Column B is −5. Since Column A is bigger,
   you can cross out choices B and C. Now plug in
   a weird number. If $z = −1.5$, then Column A is 4.5
   and Column B is negative −4.5. Since Column A
   is still greater and this is an easy question, you can
   be sure that A is the answer.

4. ETS's answer is A.
   Cross off D right off the bat. This question tests the
   Rule of 180 (not Fred's theorem). There are 180
   degrees in a straight line. So $a + 110 = 180$, which
   means $a = 70$, and $b + 111 = 180$, so $b = 69$. Since
   70 is greater than 69, Column A is greater than
   Column B.

5. ETS's answer is D.
   Always be sure to plug in twice for quant comp
   questions. You need to plug in numbers for p that
   are between 3 and 1. If $p = 2$, then Column A is
   1 and Column B is 1. Since the columns can be
   equal, you can cross out choice A and B. Now plug
   in a weird number. If $p = 1.5$ (use your calculator),
   then Column A is .75 and Column B is .875. The
   columns are no longer equal, so you can get more
   than one result. That means the answer must be D.

6. ETS's answer is B.
   First, draw a line segment from point R

   perpendicular to QS. This is the altitude of triangle

   QRS, and it must be less than 4. The formula for

   the area of a triangle is $\frac{1}{2} \times$ base $\times$ height. The

   base is 12, and if the height were 4, the area would

   be 24. Since the height is actually less than 4, the

   area must be less than 24. You don't have to find

   the actual value of area, though. Whatever the

   area is, the perimeter (the sum of all the sides) is

   27. Compare, don't calculate! Column B is bigger

   regardless of the exact value of Column A.

7. ETS's answer is B.
   Since we don't know what the side of the square
   is, we can plug in a value. Let's say the side is 3.
   The diagonal of the square divides it into two 45:
   45:90 triangles. If you look in the gray box at the
   beginning of the section, it tells you that the sides
   of a 45:45:90 triangle are in a ratio of $1:1:\sqrt{2}$. If
   the side of the square is 3, the diagonal must be
   $3\sqrt{2}$. Therefore $\frac{AC}{AD} = \frac{3\sqrt{2}}{3}$, or $\sqrt{2}$. Since $\sqrt{2}$
   is less than 2, Column B is bigger.

SECTION 3

8. ETS's answer is D.

The question tells you how *JK* divides up *FG*, since it says $FX = \frac{1}{2}GX$. But you have no idea how *JK* itself gets divided up when the two lines cross. *JX* might equal $\frac{1}{2}KX$, or maybe not. So the answer must be D. Since question 8 is pretty close to the difficult third of quant comp, C would be the Joe Bloggs answer.

9. ETS's answer is A.
You need to attack this question one step at a time, with the help of your calculator. First you need to figure out how many milliliters are in .8 liters. To do this, you can set up a proportion:

$$\frac{1}{1,000} = \frac{.8}{x}$$

Solve for *x*, and you get 800. If there are 800 milliliters of fluid, and you want to divide it into 1.9 milliliter portions, you simply divide 800 by 1.9, which gives you 421.05. So Column A is greater than Column B.

10. ETS's answer is C.
Since you don't know what the two consecutive positive even integers are, you can plug in values for them. Let's use 2 and 4. *a* is the average of 2 and 4, so *a* = 3. In Column A, when 3 is divided by 2 the remainder is 1, so the columns are equal. If you plug in different numbers, the results are the same.

11. ETS's answer is C.
Make sure you start by crossing out B, which is the Joe Bloggs answer because –1 is greater than –2. This function question is just a substitution exercise. We know that $\{n\} = n^3 + 2n^2 - n$, so $\{-2\} = 2$ and $\{-1\} = 2$. Since $\{-2\} = 2$ and $\{-1\} = 2$, the answer must be C.

12. ETS's answer is D.
Joe Bloggs picks B, because $\{x + 1\}$ looks bigger, so you should cross out B immediately. Since this question has variables, you can plug in, but you must be sure to plug in at least twice. Start with an easy number. If *x* = 2, then $\{2\} = 14$ and $\{3\} = 42$. Since Column B is bigger, you can cross out choices A and C. Since you already crossed out B, the answer must be D. But you can prove it by Plugging In a weird number (like the number in question 11). If *x* = –2, then $\{-2\} = 2$ and $\{-1\} = 2$. Now the columns are equal.

13. ETS's answer is A.

You don't know how many dimes or nickels there are, so you can plug in some numbers. In Jar A, there are 4 more nickels than dimes, so we can say there are 7 nickels and 3 dimes. In that case, the ratio of nickels to dimes in A would be 7 to 3, or $\frac{7}{3}$. In Jar B, there are 4 more dimes than nickels, so we can say that there are 3 nickels and 7 dimes, so the ratio of nickels to dimes would be 3 to 7. Column A is bigger because $\frac{7}{3}$ is bigger than $\frac{3}{7}$. You can't plug in negative numbers, fractions, or zero, because you're talking about quantities of nickels and dimes, and you can't have half a nickel. If you plug in again, you will get the same result.

SECTION 3

14. ETS's answer is D.

The formula for the area of a parallelogram is base × height. Even though the parallelogram in Column B has a bigger base, you have no idea what the height of either parallelogram is, so you can't say for sure what the area of either one is. Of course, the parallelogram in B could be bigger. But if the parallelogram in Column A had a height of 6, and the parallelogram in B had a tiny height, such as 1, then the one in B would be smaller than the one in A. Since either parallelogram can be bigger, depending on what you make the height, the answer must be D. Joe Bloggs thinks B is bigger because it has a bigger base. But this is a hard question. Just Say No to Joe.

15. ETS's answer is B.

Joe Bloggs thinks this question is impossible. He picks D because he thinks D means "I don't know." But you know better than Joe. You can use the first two equations as simultaneous equations. In the second equation, add c to both sides so the c's are in the same place. Then line up the equations like this:

$a + b = c$
$a = c + 5$

When you subtract the equations, you end up with $b = -5$. You need to know the value of c for Column A. Since you know the value of b, just pop it into the third equation: $-5 - c = 3$. So $c = -8$.
Column B is greater.

16. ETS's answer is 2.

First, solve for x. Divide both sides of the equation by 3, and you get $x = 4$. Then divide 8 by 4, which gives you 2.

17. ETS's answer is 270.

The trick here is that ETS is not asking for the value of a, b, or c. It just wants to know what they add up to. ETS is only testing the Rule of 360. All the angles in the figure make up a circle, so they all add up to 360. The right angle is 90 degrees, so $90 + a + b + c = 360$. Therefore $a + b + c = 270$.

18. ETS's answer is .4 or $\frac{2}{5}$.

You can solve this question by setting up a proportion. There are 8 liters in 20 bottles of juice and you need to find out how many liters are in one bottle. Here's what the proportion looks like:

$$\frac{8}{20} = \frac{x}{1}$$

Solve for x, and your answer is $\frac{2}{5}$ or .4.

19. ETS's answer is 3.

You can solve this question using simultaneous equations, because you have two equations with two variables. First, you need to rearrange the equations a bit:

$4x + 2y = 24$ divided by 2 on both sides becomes $2x + y = 12$. $\frac{7y}{2x} = 7$, multiplied by $2x$ on both sides, becomes $7y = 14x$. This, divided by 7 on both sides, becomes $y = 2x$, which can be manipulated into $2x - y = 0$.

Now you can add the equations:

$$2x + y = 12$$
$$+\ 2x - y = 0$$
$$\overline{4x\ = 12}$$
$$x\ =\ 3$$

21. ETS's answer is 7.

It would definitely help to draw out this question:

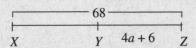

If $XY = \frac{1}{2}XZ$, that means Y is the midpoint of XZ. So $XY = YZ$, and therefore $YZ = \frac{1}{2}XZ$. If $YZ = 4a + 6$ and $XZ = 68$, then $4a + 6 = \frac{1}{2}(68)$. Now just solve for a:

$$4a + 6 = \frac{1}{2}(68)$$
$$4a + 6 = 34$$
$$4a = 28$$
$$a = 7$$

20. ETS's answer is 24.

For this question you need your math vocabulary. First, list all the factors of 12: 1, 2, 3, 4, 6, 12. Make sure that you don't miss any factors. Now add up the even factors: $2 + 4 + 6 + 12 = 24$.

22. ETS's answer is 50.

You don't know how many cars are in the parking lot, so you can plug in a number. Let's say there are 40 cars in the parking lot. Now read through the question; if $\frac{1}{5}$ of the cars are blue, there are 8 blue cars. If $\frac{1}{2}$ of the blue cars are convertibles, there are 4 blue convertibles. If $\frac{1}{4}$ of all the convertibles are blue, and there are 4 blue convertibles, that means there are 16 convertibles all together. The question asks what percent of the cars are neither blue nor convertibles. At this point, the question becomes a group question, and we have a formula for solving such questions:

total = group 1 + group 2 − both + neither

In this question, the total is 40 cars, group 1 is the 8 blue cars, and group 2 is the 16 convertibles. You also know that 4 cars are both blue and convertibles. Now just plug those values into the formula: $40 = 16 + 8 - 4 + n$. Then solve for n, which equals 20. So 20 out of the total 40 cars are neither blue nor convertibles: $\frac{20}{40} = \frac{1}{2} = 50\%$.

23. ETS's answer is 6.

Since 31 and −8 add up to 23, that means $23 + n$ has to be a prime number in order for 31, −8, and n to be a prime set. You're looking for the smallest positive value of n, so start with $n = 1$ and keep trying numbers until you get a prime number as a result:

$n = 1$	$23 + 1 = 24$ (not prime)
$n = 2$	$23 + 2 = 25$ (not prime)
$n = 3$	$23 + 3 = 26$ (not prime)
$n = 4$	$23 + 4 = 27$ (not prime)
$n = 5$	$23 + 5 = 28$ (not prime)
$n = 6$	$23 + 6 = 29$

Since 29 is the first prime number we got as a result, that means 6 is the least possible positive value of n.

24. ETS's answer is 286.

It would definitely be helpful to draw out this question. If the ball is dropped from a height of 64 feet, it will travel 64 feet before it hits the ground the first time. Then it will bounce up $\frac{3}{4}$ of 64, or 48 feet. It will then travel down 48 feet, hit the ground a second time, and bounce back up $\frac{3}{4}$ of 48, or 36 feet. The ball travels back down 36 feet, hits the ground a third time, and then bounces up $\frac{3}{4}$ of 36, or 27 feet. Finally, the ball travels 27 feet to hit the ground a fourth time. All together, the ball has gone down 64, up 48, down 48, up 36, down 36, up 27, and down 27. So $64 + 48 + 48 + 36 + 36 + 27 + 27 = 286$.

25. ETS's answer is 18.

To answer this question you have to set up an equation. If the radius of C is r, then the radius of B is $2r$ and the radius of A is $4r$. The formula for the area of a circle is πr^2. Since 84π is the sum of the areas of the circles, this is your equation:

$$\pi r^2 + \pi(2r)^2 + \pi(4r)^2 = 84\pi$$
$$r^2 + 4r^2 + 16r^2 = 84$$
$$21r^2 = 84$$
$$r^2 = 4$$
$$r = 2$$

If $r = 2$, then the radius of C is 2, the radius of B is 4, and the radius of A is 8. Line segment AC is made up of the radius of A, the diameter of B, and the radius of C, so the $AC = 8 + 4 + 4 + 2 = 18$.

SECTION 4

1. ETS's answer is B.

   Eliminate D. It is not necessary to solve for x to answer this question. If you subtract 5 from both sides of the question, you get $3x = 15$. Then just multiply both sides by 2, and you get $6x = 30$. So Column A is 30. Therefore, Column B is greater.

2. ETS's answer is D.

   Use an Average Pie. If the average of two numbers, p and q, is 3, then the sum of those numbers is 6. Therefore, $p + q = 6$. But that's all you know. It's possible that $p = 3$ and $q = 3$, in which case the columns are equal. But it's also possible that $p = 4$ and $q = 2$, in which case Column A is greater. Since you can get more than one result, the answer must be D.

3. ETS's answer is A.

   Just translate the expression:

   $\left(\dfrac{10}{100}\right)x = \left(\dfrac{20}{100}\right)100$. Then use your calculator

   to solve for x, which equals 200. So Column A is

   greater.

4. ETS's answer is C.

   The trick to this question is making a connection between the circle and the triangle. OA and OB are the sides of the triangle, but they are *also* radii of the circle, which means they must be equal. If two sides of the triangle are equal, then you have an isosceles triangle. Since angle OAB and angle OBA are opposite the equal sides of the triangle, they must be equal angles.

5. ETS's answer is B.

   Column A asks for the number of customers who received *both* a free fill-up and a discount tune-up. If every 20th customer got the fill-up and every 30th customer got the tune-up, then the first customer to get both was the 60th customer. The next customer to get both was the 120th customer, and the last customer to get both was the 180th customer. Essentially, you are just looking for numbers that are multiples of both 20 and 30. So only three customers got both a tune-up and a fill-up, which means that Column B is greater.

SECTION 4

6. ETS's answer is D.
You must always plug in *at least twice* for quant comp questions. Since x^2 has to be greater than 17, you can make $x = 5$. In that case, Column A is 9, which is greater than Column B. But is there any way that Column B can be greater? To find out, you need to try one of the special numbers. Can x be negative? Sure. If $x = -5$, then x^2 is still greater than 17. In that case, Column A is -1, which means that Column B is greater. Since you got more than one result, the answer must be D.

7. ETS's answer is B.
This is not really a math question. We call these visual perception problems. You just need to look at the figure very carefully. There are two points in the area where squares A and B overlap. There are also three points in the area where squares B and C overlap. Now, be careful. Squares A and C actually overlap inside of square B, which means that there are three squares overlapping in that area, so that point doesn't count. There are only five points all together, which means that Column B is greater.

8. ETS's answer is D.
You must always plug in *at least twice* for quant comp questions. Since x can be 1, you should start by trying $x = 1$. In that case, Column A equals $1^{(1+2)}$, or 1^3, which is 1. Column B equals $(1 + 2)^1$, or 3^1, which is 3. So Column B can be greater. What if $x = 2$? In that case, Column A equals $2^{(2+2)}$, or 2^4, which is 16. Column B equals $(2 + 2)^2$, or 4^2, which is 16. So the columns can be equal. You can get more than one result, so the answer is D.

9. ETS's answer is B.
The most important thing to notice in this question is that the figure is not drawn to scale. That means you can't trust it. You can only trust what the question says. According to the question, $DF = EF$, which means that you have an isosceles triangle, even though it doesn't look that way. Therefore, x and y are equal, because they are opposite the equal sides. DE is the diameter of the circle, so angle DFE must be a right angle. We also know that angle DFE is a right angle because any angle inscribed within a semicircle is 90 degrees. Therefore, x and y both equal 45, which means that Column B is greater.

450 ◆ CRACKING THE SAT

10. ETS's answer is B.

Start by Plugging In a number for x. Let's say $x = 4$. In that case, the base of the triangle is 3×4, or 12, and the height is 2×4, or 8. Now use the formula for the area of a triangle: $\frac{1}{2} \times \text{base} \times \text{height} = \frac{1}{2}(12)(8) = 48$. So Column A is 48. If $x = 4$, the area of circle with a radius of 4 is 16π. Now, since this is a quant comp question, you need to be careful with approximating the value of π. We need to be a little more precise and say that π is about 3.14. In that case, the area of the circle is 16×3.14, which is 50.24. So Column B is greater.

11. ETS's answer is A.

First, find the distance between $\frac{1}{3}$ and $\frac{1}{2}$, which is $\frac{1}{3} - \frac{1}{2}$, or $\frac{1}{6}$. If you count the intervals on the number line between $\frac{1}{3}$ and $\frac{1}{2}$, you'll find that there are six. So you need to divide $\frac{1}{6}$ by 6, which gives you $\frac{1}{36}$. That means each interval is $\frac{1}{36}$. Since x is one interval less than $\frac{1}{2}$, that means $x = \frac{1}{2} - \frac{1}{36} = \frac{17}{36}$. Now, be careful. The best thing to do is convert both fractions to decimals on your calculator: $\frac{17}{36} = .472$ and $\frac{17}{37} = .459$. Since .472 is greater than .459, Column A is greater.

12. ETS's answer is B.
Imagine you have five players: A, B, C, D, and E. How many different ways can you combine them in groups of three?

This is a combination question. The number of *permutations* of 5 players in 3 spaces is $\boxed{5}\,\boxed{4}\,\boxed{3} = 60$. To find the number of combinations, divide 60 by $3 \cdot 2 \cdot 1$, or 6. You get 10, so there are ten different ways to make 3-player teams out of the five players. So Column B is greater.

13. ETS's answer is D.
Remember, the figures in difficult quant comp questions are designed to trick you. You know that $g = j$ because they are vertical angles. But does $h = i$? You have no idea! Joe Bloggs thinks that they are equal because they *look* that way. But this is a hard question, and Joe is always wrong. You can't answer a hard quant comp question by saying, "It looks that way." That's why the answer is D, not C.

14. ETS's answer is C.
Remember, the median of a group of numbers is the number that is exactly in the middle of the group when the group is arranged from smallest to largest. To find the median of set A, you have to put the numbers in order: $-4, -1, 2, 3, 7, 11$. Since there are only six numbers, you have to take the average of the two middle numbers, 2 and 3. The average of 2 and 3 is 2.5. To find the average of set B, add up all the numbers and divide by six, because there are six numbers. The sum of the numbers in set B is 15, and 15 divided by 6 is 2.5. So the columns are equal.

SECTION 4

15. ETS's answer is A.
Plug in some numbers! If $ax \neq 0$, that means a and x cannot be 0. If $x = 3$ and $a = 2$, then Column A is 1 and Column B is –12. So Column A can be greater. What if $x = -3$ and $a = -2$? In that case, Column A is still 1 and Column B is still –12. How about if $x = 1$ and $a = 1$? In that case, Column A is 0 and Column B is –2. Column A is still greater. As it turns out, no matter what numbers you plug in for a and x, Column A is always greater.

16. ETS's answer is 100.
Use a Ratio Box:

T-shirts	Sweatshirts	Turtlenecks	Total
2	3	5	10
10	10	10	10
	30		100

You only need to work out the *total* column to figure out the total number of garments that the store sold, which is 100.

17. ETS's answer is 81.
The formula for the volume of a box is length × width × height. But the question gives you the area of the base of the crate, so you already know that length × width = 18. The volume of the crate, then, is simply the area of the base times the height: $18 \times 4.5 = 81$

18. ETS's answer is .75 or $\frac{3}{4}$.

All you have to do is simply solve for x:
$$5x - 4 = x - 1$$
$$5x = x + 3$$
$$4x = 3$$

$$x = \frac{3}{4} \text{ (or .75)}$$

19. ETS's answer is .583 or $\frac{7}{12}$.

There are 3 plain, 5 cream-filled, and 4 chocolate donuts, which means there are 12 donuts all together. Of those 12 donuts, 7 of them are NOT cream-filled (3 plain + 4 chocolate = 7). So the probability of randomly selecting a donut that is not cream-filled is simply 7 out of 12, or $\frac{7}{12}$.

20. ETS's answer is 5, 7, or 11.

First, think of a prime number that will make $3b$ greater than 10. How about 5? To see if that fits the other side of the inequality, you need to find the value of $\frac{5}{6}b$. If $b = 5$, then $\frac{5}{6}(5) = \frac{25}{6}$, or 4.166, which is definitely less than 10. Since 5 fits both sides of the inequality, it must be one of ETS's answers. Remember, you only need to find *one* possible value of b.

21. ETS's answer is 21.

Let's say you have seven dancers: A, B, C, D, E, F, and G. How many different ways can you pair them up? This is a combination question. Start by sketching two boxes for the pair: ☐☐ Then fill in the number of possible dancers for each position, and multiply them together. This gives you the number of possible *permutations*: $\boxed{7}\,\boxed{6} = 42$. Finally, divide this number by 2 for the 2 positions we're looking for.

There are 21 possible combinations.

22. ETS's answer is 96.

You know that AB is a semicircle, which means it's half a circle. So the circumference of the entire circle would be $6\pi \times 2$, or 12π. Therefore, the diameter of that circle is 12. Since AB is the diameter, you know that the length of rectangle ABCD is 12. You can also use the same trick to find the width. If the length of semicircle BC is 4π, then the circumference of the entire circle would be 8π. That means the diameter is 8, and since BC is the diameter, the width of the rectangle is 8. Now you can find the area of the rectangle: length × width = 12 × 8 = 96.

23. ETS's answer is 2.

This is a function question, and the definition of the function is given to you. Whenever you see $\boxed{x}$, it means you have to find the product all the distinct prime factors of x. To find the value of $\heartsuit 6$, you need to find all the distinct prime factors of 6 and then multiply them. First, list the factors of 6: 1, 6, 2, 3. Of those numbers, only 2 and 3 are prime. So $\heartsuit 6 = 2 \times 3 = 6$. To find the value of $\heartsuit 81$, list the factors of 81: 1, 81, 9, 3, 27. Of those numbers, only 3 is prime, so the value of $\heartsuit 81$ is just 3. So value of $\dfrac{\heartsuit 6}{\heartsuit 81}$ is $\dfrac{6}{3}$, or 2.

24. ETS's answer is 282.

This is a hard question, so you have stay on your toes. If the owner buys 3 pounds of each spice, that means she pays the following amounts for each spice:

cinnamon: $8 \times 3 = \$24$
nutmeg: $9 \times 3 = \$27$
ginger: $7 \times 3 = \$21$
cloves: $10 \times 3 = \$30$

So she pays a total of 24 + 27 + 21 + 30, or 102 dollars for 12 pounds of spices. She then sells the spices per *ounce*, so you have to figure out first how many ounces of spices she has. If 1 pound is 16 ounces, then 12 pounds is 12×16, or 192 ounces. She sells all the spices at 2 dollars per ounce, so she makes $192 \times \$2$, or \$384. To figure out her profit, subtract the amount she paid for the spices from the amount she made selling them: $384 - 102 = 282$.

25. ETS's answer is .375 or $\frac{3}{8}$.

   Since the question doesn't give you a figure, you should draw one. Then plug in some values.

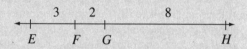

   If $EG = \frac{5}{3}EF$, then you can make $EF = 3$ and

   $EG = 5$. That means FG must be 2. If $HF = 5FG$,

   then $HF = 5(2) = 10$. If $HF = 10$ and $FG = 2$, then

   $HG = 8$. So $\frac{EF}{HG} = \frac{3}{8}$.

1. ETS's answer is E.
   The clue in this sentence is *they hoard water in their leaves*. If the plants are hoarding water, they must be doing it to survive long periods without water. So you can put *without water* in the blank, in which case the best match is *drought*.

2. ETS's answer is E.
   The clue for this sentence is *eloquence and logic*. If Liam is eloquent and logical, he must speak very well; therefore, you can eliminate choices A, C, and D because they're negative. Liam's eloquence and logic probably made it difficult for his bitterest opponents to *contradict* his opinions. The best match for *contradict* is *disagree with*, in answer choice E. It also makes sense that Liam's eloquence and logic made him speak *persuasively*.

3. ETS's answer is D.
   The clue is for this sentence is *possess a grain of truth*, and the trigger word is *however*, which means the word that fills the blank will have the opposite meaning of the clue. The opposite of *possess a grain of truth* is *unbelievable*.

4. ETS's answer is D.
   The clue in this sentence is *the device of divine intervention*. *Divine* means having to do with a god, so it must be a god that intervened at the last moment in Greek dramas. That means you can put *god* in the blank. Looking at answer choices, *deity* means *god*.

5. ETS's answer is C.
   The clues in this sentence are *apparent* and *deceptive*. Professional skiers descend the slopes with apparent *ease*, but this *apparent* ease is *deceptive*. Therefore, it must actually be difficult to ski well. The best way to complete the second part of the sentence is to say that skiing "requires *great* effort and intense concentration." So we can put *great* in the second blank. That gets rid of answer choice E. Then we have *ease* in the first blank, and the best match among the remaining answers is *nonchalance*.

6. ETS's answer is E.
   The clues in this sentence are *foster* and *in tense situations*. Since *foster* is a positive word, the word in the first blank must be positive; you can get rid of C and D because they have negative words. If Miranda wants to foster something good, then in tense situations she is probably compelled to give in to others. You can use *give in* for the second blank, which means you can eliminate A. Between B and E, you can eliminate B because *consistency* doesn't make any sense in the first blank. Remember, it's often easier to figure out which answer is wrong than to figure out which one is right.

7. ETS's answer is D.
   The clue in this sentence is *compelled many to alter their dearly held assumptions about human nature*, and the trigger word is *and*, which tells you that the blank will agree with the clue. Here you can simply recycle the clue: The *notions of human behavior* that psychoanalysis compelled people to change must have been *dearly held* notions. If you put *dearly held* in the blank, the best match is *cherished*.

8. ETS's answer is C.

The clue in this sentence is *moved the United Kingdom forward*, and the trigger word is *although*, which means the blank must be the opposite of *moved forward*. If you put *moved backwards* in the blank, the best match is *regressive*.

9. ETS's answer is D.

The clue in this sentence is *first deduced from eccentricities in other planets' orbits*. If subatomic particles are being compared to the outer planets, then these particles must have been *deduced* through their effects on other particles. If you put *deducible* in the first blank, you can get rid of choices A and C. What was deduced about the outer planets and subatomic particles? That they *existed*. So you can put *existence* in the second blank, which means choice D must be the answer. Notice that it would not make sense to talk about the outer planets' *proximity*, or their *creation*, since they are neither close by nor recently created.

10. ETS's answer is A.

The clue in this sentence is *many doctors are reluctant to concede*. If the doctors are reluctant to concede something about the nutritionists' argument, then the nutritionists must have a good argument. So the doctors don't want to concede that the nutritionists' argument is *good*, which means a positive word goes in the blank. If you cross out all the negative words in the answer choices, you're left with A.

11. ETS's answer is E.

A STOCKING covers your LEG. If you had trouble choosing between D and E, you should have made a more specific sentence. A STOCKING is a *piece of clothing* that covers your LEG. A *glove* is a piece of clothing that *covers* your hand.

12. ETS's answer is A.

A PARK is a place for RECREATION. A *kitchen* is a place for *cooking*. If you had trouble narrowing down the choices, then you were probably missing the idea of *place* in your sentence. Whenever more than one answer fits your sentence, make a more specific sentence.

13. ETS's answer is A.

An OUNCE is a unit of WEIGHT. An *acre* is a unit of *area*. Remember, an ounce doesn't measure weight. A scale measures weight.

14. ETS's answer is A.

The CREST is the peak of the WAVE. The *climax* is the peak in the *action*.

SECTION 5

15. **ETS's answer is D.**
LOW is the sound of a COW. *Chirp* is the sound of a *bird*. If you had trouble making a sentence, you should have eliminated answer choices with unrelated words and then worked backwards. A *gosling* is a baby *goose*. Is a LOW a baby COW? No, eliminate A. A *swarm* is a group of *bees*. Is a LOW a group of COWs? No, eliminate B. A *hutch* is a home for a *rabbit*. Is a LOW a home for a COW? No, Eliminate C. A *chirp* is the sound of a *bird*. Is a LOW the sound of a COW? If you don't know the word for the sound a cow makes, then this is a possibility. A *bed* is a place where *oysters* live. Is a LOW a place where COWs live? No, eliminate E.

16. **ETS's answer is E.**
A HAMLET is a small VILLAGE. A *cottage* is a small *house*. If you had trouble making a sentence, you should have eliminated answer choices with unrelated words and then worked backwards. *Street* and *sidewalk* are unrelated, because not all streets have sidewalks next to them; eliminate A. A *convertible* is a *car* with a removable top. Is a HAMLET a VILLAGE with a removable top? Certainly not. Eliminate B. A *skyscraper* is a very tall *building*. Is a VILLAGE a very tall HAMLET? No, eliminate C. You could say that a *photograph* is a type of *portrait*, but VILLAGE and HAMLET have a more specific relationship.

17. **ETS's answer is B.**
MALLEABLE means easily SHAPED. *Amenable* means easily *persuaded*. If you had trouble making a sentence, you should have eliminated answer choices with unrelated words and then worked backward. As it turns out, the only answer choice with a pair of words that have a clear relationship is B.

18. **ETS's answer is B.**
An ANALGESIC eases PAIN. A *palliative* eases *violence*. If you had trouble making a sentence, you should have eliminated any unrelated answer choices and then worked backward. An *anesthetic* can be used to prevent pain during *surgery*, but does it make sense to say that an ANALGESIC prevents pain during PAIN? No. Eliminate A. An *operation* is not necessarily related to *health*, so you can eliminate C, and *enthusiasm* and *anger* have no relationship, so you can eliminate D. A *prosthesis* is an artificial *limb*. Is an ANALGESIC an artificial PAIN? No, so you can eliminate E.

19. **ETS's answer is E.**
A NOVICE lacks EXPERIENCE. A *rube* lacks *sophistication*. If you eliminate all the answer choices that contain unrelated words, E is the only answer choice left.

20. **ETS's answer is B.**
GRISLY means inspiring DISGUST. *Endearing* means inspiring *affection*. If you had trouble making a sentence, you could have used the fact that GRISLY and DISGUST have similar meanings. In other words, they are both negative. *Happy* and *grief* have different meanings (one is positive and one is negative), and so do *boring* and *interest*, so you can eliminate A and D. *Redolent* and *joy* have no relationship, and neither do *bitter* and *repulsion*, which gets rid of C and E. Since this is a difficult question, you could have eliminated E, which is a Joe Bloggs answer, because *repulsion* reminds Joe Bloggs of DISGUST.

SECTION 5

21. ETS's answer is C.
A DIATRIBE is an ABUSIVE speech. A *eulogy* is a laudatory *speech*. If you had trouble making a sentence, you should have eliminated answer choices with unrelated words and then worked backward. The words in answer choice A and E have no relationship, so you can eliminate them.

22. ETS's answer is A.
SECRETE means to make difficult to FIND. *Muffle* means to make difficult to *hear*. If you had trouble making a sentence, you should have eliminated answer choices with unrelated words and then worked backward. Answer choices B, C, and D all contain unrelated pairs. *Explain* means to make easier to *comprehend*, but SECRETE does not mean make easier to FIND, so you can eliminate E.

23. ETS's answer is E.
INDELIBLE means having PERMANENCE. *Flimsy* means having *tenuousness*. If you eliminate all the answer choices that contain unrelated words, only E is left.

24. ETS's answer is D.
The lead words in this question are *Frankish law*, which should lead you to the beginning of the passage. According to lines 1–3, *the laws and customs in lands under Frankish domination emphasized the biological function and sexual nature of women*. These lines are perfectly paraphrased in answer choice D, which says that women were *defined in physical or biological terms*.
   Answer choice A contradicts the passage. Frankish society *did not deprive women of opportunities to find personal fulfillment in a variety of roles* (lines 3–5).
   Answer choice B completely contradicts the second half of the passage, which is all about women in religious communities. Always keep in mind the main idea of the passage.
   Answer choice C contradicts lines 8–9, which tell us that Frankish society did not exploit women.
   Answer choice E is wrong because lines 9–30 say that women had access to power in several different ways.

25. ETS's answer is B.
The lead words in this question are *ancient societies*, which should lead you back to line 9, where *primitive tribal societies* are mentioned. According to lines 8–9, women's *labor... was not as exploited as it had been in primitive tribal societies*. So the difference between Frankish society and more ancient societies is that women's labor was not exploited. This idea is paraphrased in answer choice B, which says that women were *not taken advantage of for their labor*.
   Answer choice A doesn't make any sense. How can it be true that Frankish society did not encourage childbearing? How would they have children? Don't forget to use your common sense.
   Answer choice C doesn't make any sense either. Although Frankish women had access to power through their husbands, the passage doesn't say that they had *more* power.
   Answer choice D is wrong because the passage never suggests that Frankish women did not work in their homes.
   Answer choice E contradicts itself. Gender differences are, by definition, biological differences.

26. ETS's answer is E.
According to lines 9–12, *Queens had access to power not only through their husbands but also through churchmen and secular officials whom they patronized.* Since Frankish queens had *access to power* through their husbands, churchmen, and secular officials, their access to power was *based on their relationships to male figures of power.*

Answer choice A is wrong for the same reason that choice C was wrong in the previous question. Although Frankish women had influence through their sons and husbands, they did not have *more* influence. Also, the word *surpassed* makes this a *must* answer.

Answer choice B is wrong because the phrase *greatly increased* is too extreme, and therefore this is not the kind of answer that ETS would choose.

Answer choice C contradicts the passage. The power of Frankish women *did* extend beyond their households. According to the passage, they had access to power through *churchmen and secular officials whom they patronized,* and this definitely represents power outside the home.

Answer choice D also contradicts the passages. According to lines 12–14, *As widows, acting for their sons, they could exercise political power directly.*

27. ETS's answer is B.
Go back to the passage, find the word *transmitted,* and cross it out. Then read the sentence and come up with your own word. Since the word in context has something to do with *clan ideology* and *children,* a good substitute for the word might be *taught,* since it would make sense that the *wives of magnates* taught clan ideology to their children. If you look in the answers, *taught* is actually a choice.

The other answer choices are wrong because they don't make any sense in context. Choice E is a Joe Bloggs answer, because *transmitted* makes Joe think of *broadcast.*

28. ETS's answer is B.
The lead word in this question is *marriage,* which should lead to lines 20–21. According to these lines, in Frankish society people either *contracted a formal union or entered into a quasi-marriage.* Answer choice B paraphrases this sentence by saying that marriage *could be entered formally or informally.*

Answer choice A is wrong because the word *only* makes this a *must* answer, so it can't be ETS's answer. Besides, does it make sense to say that marriage was the *only* means of exchanging wealth?

Answer choice C implies that marriage always raised women to positions of power, which is definitely not the case.

Answer choice D is wrong because there is no comparison made in the passage between marriage in primitive society and marriage within Frankish society. Read carefully.

Answer choice E is wrong because the passage doesn't say anything about arranged marriages.

29. ETS's answer is E.
Go back to the passage, find the word *instrumental,* and cross it out. Then read the sentence and come up with your own word. According to the passage, women played a role *in bringing about the merger of free and slave elements in society.* ETS would be much more likely to say that women played a *vital* role than she would to say that they were merely *helpful.*

Joe likes answer choice C because *instruments* make Joe think of *harmony.* The other choices are wrong because they don't make any sense in context.

30. ETS's answer is E.

According to lines 14–19, the *wives of magnates ... administered the family's estates when their husbands were away.* If you read farther down you'll find that wives in *dependent classes* did not have this power. That is the difference described in answer choice E. Another way to answer this question is to eliminate wrong answers.

Answer choice A is a very extreme statement. How can it be true that wives of magnates did not cooperate with their husbands? Not even one wife cooperated with her husband? Not ever?

Answer choice B is also a very extreme statement. Were the wives in the dependent classes completely *powerless* in their own homes? That doesn't seem very likely.

Answer choice C is too extreme, and the passage doesn't say anything of the sort.

Answer choice D contradicts what the passage says in lines 44–47.

31. ETS's answer is D.

The answer to this question does not come until lines 48–50, so if you stopped reading, you wouldn't have found the answer. According to the passage, *women in these communities sustained each other in spiritual, intellectual, scholarly, artistic, and charitable pursuits.* This is paraphrased in answer choice D.

Answer choice A contradicts line 35, which says that women in religious life were still a *small minority.*

Answer choice B is wrong because the passage doesn't say anything about *political influence* in connection with female religious communities.

Answer choice C is too extreme because of the word *superior.*

Answer choice E is wrong because the passage doesn't say anything about a rift between married and unmarried women, and even so, it would be much too extreme to say that this rift was *eliminated.*

32. ETS's answer is A.

The only answer choice that comes from something stated in the passage is A. According to lines 47–49, *Freed from the need to compete for the attention of men, women in these communities....* If women in the Frankish religious communities were freed from the need to compete for male attention, that means women outside the communities must have had to compete for the attention of men.

Answer choice B doesn't make any sense. How can it be true that women outside the religious community were not inclined to any religious feeling at all? Just because they weren't nuns doesn't mean they weren't religious.

Answer choice C is wrong because it makes no sense to say that women outside the religious community had *less* economic power. If anything, the opposite would be true.

Answer choice D is too extreme and too offensive. ETS would never say that women outside religious communities did not contribute to Frankish culture at all.

Answer choice E is wrong because ETS would never suggest that women had to rely on men for emotional support. Besides, the passage never says that. Read carefully.

33. ETS's answer is B.

Go back to the passage, find the word *upheld*, and cross it out. Then read the sentence and come up with your own word. According to the passage, *female ideals and modes of conduct* had some direct connection with *the way to salvation* and *models of sanctity in the monasteries led by women.* So we could put *were given* or *were taught* in the blank. The best match is *endorsed.*

Answer choice C is a Joe Bloggs answer because *upheld* makes Joe think of *suspended.* The other choices are wrong because they don't make sense in context.

34. ETS's answer is E.

   This is an EXCEPT question, so you should definitely save it for last. ETS is asking how Christianity allowed women to escape from male-dominated society, so you have to go back to the passage and find where that is discussed. Remember, you are looking for the answer choice that is *not* mentioned.

   Answer choice A is mentioned in line 57; answer choice B is mentioned in lines 41–42; answer choice C is mentioned in line 37; answer choice D is mentioned in lines 47–48. That leaves choice E.

35. ETS's answer is C.

   This is a general question, so you only need to know the main idea of the passage. The best way to attack this question is to get rid of wrong answers using POE. The passage is not about *class conflict*, so you can get rid of A. It's not about the influence of religion on secular life, so you can get rid of B. It's not strictly about the *need for religious communities*, so you can toss D out. Finally, the passage does not discuss any *misconceptions*, so E is out. The passage is about the roles of women in Frankish society or, in other words, *the roles of a social group*.

SECTION 6

1. ETS's answer is C.
   To solve for y, begin by adding y to both sides of the equation, which gives you $6 = 3y - 6$. Then add 6 to both sides, which gives you $12 = 3y$. Now divide both sides by 3, and you find that $y = 4$. You can also plug in the answer choices for any question that asks you to solve for a variable: $6 - 4 = 2(4) - 6$.

2. ETS's answer is B.
   This is what we call a visual perception problem. It's like a maze. Just put your pencil on a and see which other letter you can connect to a without crossing any lines. The only letter you can reach directly is w, all the way in the middle.

3. ETS's answer is C.
   This is a perfect calculator question. Just add up the morning shift and the afternoon shift for each day and see which total is the greatest. The total for Wednesday (the greatest) is 595.

4. ETS's answer is A.
   For this question, you need to know that volume equals length × width × height. You know that the volume is 16,500, the depth, or the height, is 10, and the length is 75. Just put those numbers in the formula: $16,500 = 75 \times w \times 10$.
   Use your calculator to solve for w, which equals 22.

5. ETS's answer is D.
   Use a Ratio Box:

Girls	Boys	Total
4	3	7
5	5	5
20	15	35

There are 20 girls and 15 boys, so there are 5 more girls than boys.

6. ETS's answer is B.

Get ready to plug in: You need a number for n that gives you a remainder of 5 when you divide it by 8. Let's say $n = 21$. The question asks you which of the answer choices has a remainder of 7. Since $n = 21$, answer choice B equals $\frac{23}{8}$, which gives you a remainder of 7 when you divide.

7. ETS's answer is A.
Once again, plug in: Let's say $x = 50$. Now we can translate the question:

$$\frac{10}{100} \times \frac{50}{100} \times 1000 =$$

If you work this out on your calculator, you should get 50 as your target answer. Since we said $x = 50$, the answer is A.

8. ETS's answer is E.
This is a perfect question for Plugging In the answer choices. The question asks for the greatest possible number of 20-ounce boxes. Start with answer choice C. If there are twenty-five 20-ounce boxes, then there are twenty-five 8-ounce boxes, because a total of 50 boxes was purchased. In this case, the twenty-five 20-ounce boxes weigh 500 ounces, and the twenty-five 8-ounce boxes weigh 200 ounces; the total is 700 ounces. This is too big, because the question says the total weight was less than 600. If C is too big, A and B must also be too big; eliminate all three choices. If you try answer choice D, the total weight is 604 ounces, which is still too big. So the answer must be E.

9. ETS's answer is C.

Here's yet another chance to plug in because of the variables in the answer choices. In this case, you have several variables. You should start by Plugging In values for x and y, and then work out c. Since $x > y > 0$, let's say $x = 6$ and $y = 3$. Therefore, $c = \frac{1}{6} + \frac{1}{3}$, which equals $\frac{1}{2}$. The question asks for the value of $\frac{1}{c}$, which is the reciprocal of $\frac{1}{2}$, which is 2. This is your target answer. If you plug $x = 6$ and $y = 3$ into all of the answer choices, you'll find that answer choice C equals 2.

10. ETS's answer is E.
There are variables in the answer choices again, so plug in. However, you can't plug in a value for all the variables at once, because you must follow the rules of geometry. (Makes sense, right? It's the last question in the section.) Let's start by saying $a = 70$ and $b = 60$. Since $PQRS$ is a parallelogram, angle Q must equal angle S, so angle S also equals 60. If you look at the big triangle that contains a and c, you already know that two of the angles are 60 and 70, so the third angle, c, must be 50. We know that PQ and SR are parallel and, using Fred's theorem, we can see that x is a big angle and a is a small angle. So $a + x = 180$. Since $a = 70$, that means $x = 110$. Therefore, your target answer is 110. Plug your values for a, b, and c into the answer choices and you'll find that answer choice E equals 110.

SECTION 7

1. ETS's answer is E.
   Go back to the passage, find the word *promulgated*, and cross it out. Then read the sentence and come up with your own word. The first part of the sentence is saying something very positive about Democritus's ideas, so we need a positive word. That means you can eliminate A, B, and D. It doesn't make sense to say that Democritus's ideas were *protected*, so you can cross out C. E is the only choice left.

2. ETS's answer is A.
   The best way to find the answer to this question is to use POE.
   Answer choice B says that Democritus was known for his work in politics, but this is not mentioned anywhere in the passage.
   Answer choice C says that his ideas were incompatible with those of Galileo and Newton, which contradicts lines 33–35.
   Answer choice D says that Democritus was unduly credited, but the passage is all about giving him proper credit.
   Answer choice E says that Democritus was known for his discovery of calculus, which is not said anywhere in the passage, and it also happens to be completely false.
   That only leaves A.

3. ETS's answer is C.
   According to lines 22–26, *underlying all the complex richness, texture, and variety of our everyday life might be a level of reality of stark simplicity, with the turmoil we perceive representing only the nearly infinite arrangements of a smaller number of constituents.* This sentence is paraphrased perfectly in answer choice C.
   Another way to answer this question is to use POE.
   Answer choice A is much too extreme. Will the composition of everyday things remain a mystery *forever*? Forever is a very long time.
   Answer choice B confuses the idea of simplicity in the passage. Even if all matter does have a single underlying component, that doesn't mean that *understanding* it is simple.
   Answer choice D contradicts the lines from the passage we quoted above. Scientists hope their models point to an underlying *simplicity*, not an underlying *complexity*.
   Answer choice E is also too extreme. Did Democritus's theories explain everything about matter? Not likely.

4. ETS's answer is E.
   The same lines that we just used for question 3 contain the answer to this question as well. The *obsession* referred to in the passage is the search for *a level of stark simplicity* underlying all *the complex richness* of our everyday life. This idea is paraphrased perfectly in answer choice E, which says that scientists are on a quest for *a simple unifying property of everyday matter*.
   The passage is talking about something that is *today almost an obsession*, so choices A and D are wrong because they are not about modern science.
   Choices C and D are wrong because they aren't mentioned anywhere in the passage. If it's not in the passage, then it's not ETS's answer.

SECTION 7

5. **ETS's answer is A.**

According to the first sentence of the passage, *the discovery that the universe is expanding was one of the great intellectual revelations of the twentieth century*.

Answer choice B is wrong because Newton wasn't alive in the twentieth century.

Answer choice C isn't right because the idea was discovered, and is still accepted, by modern physicists.

You can eliminate answer choice D because it's too extreme and contradicts the passage.

Lastly, answer choice E is also too extreme. That only leaves choice A.

6. **ETS's answer is D.**

According to lines 59–64, if the universe *was expanding fairy slowly, the force of gravity would cause it eventually to stop expanding …. However, if it was expanding at more than a certain critical rate, gravity would never be strong enough to stop it*.

So the *critical rate* is the rate at which the universe would need to be expanding in order to overcome the force of gravity. This idea is perfectly paraphrased in answer choice D.

Answer choices A and B are wrong because neither is mentioned in the passage.

The passage mentions a critical speed necessary for a rocket to escape earth's gravity, but that's in line 70, not line 63; therefore, choice C doesn't answer the question.

Answer choice E doesn't make sense because it confuses several of the concepts discussed in the passage. Go back and read carefully.

7. **ETS's answer is C.**

Go back to the passage and find where Newton is mentioned. According to lines 54–58, *With hindsight, it is easy to wonder why no one thought of it before. Newton, and others, should have realized that a static universe would soon start to contract under the influence of gravity*.

So the passage uses Newton as an example of a scientist who might have come up with the idea of an expanding universe before it was actually discovered in the twentieth century. This idea is paraphrased in answer choice C.

Answer choice A is wrong because ETS would never suggest that many physicists are *ignorant*. Remember, ETS has great respect for scientists.

Newton wasn't a proponent of the expanding-universe theory, so you can discount answer choice B.

Answer choice D contradicts the main idea of the passage. According to the author, the universe *is* expanding. Go back and read the first sentence of the passage.

Answer choice E is wrong because Newton didn't *disregard* the expanding-universe theory. There was no such theory back then!

8. **ETS's answer is B.**

According to lines 62–66, if the universe *was expanding at more than a certain critical rate, gravity would never be strong enough to stop it…This is a bit like what happens when one fires a rocket upward from the surface of the earth*. So the rocket is being used as an example of how the force of gravity applies to the idea of an expanding universe. Choice B paraphrases this nicely.

Answer choice A is wrong because the rocket example is not an *implication* of the expanding universe. The rocket is simply an example used to illustrate the implications of *gravity* on the expanding-universe theory.

Answer choice C makes no sense. Is the energy released by a rocket similar to the energy released by an entire universe? No way!

Answer choices D and E contradict the main idea of Passage 2. According to the author, the universe *is* expanding.

9. ETS's answer is B.

The lead words for this question are *Einstein's general theory of relativity*, which should lead you back to lines 78–82. According to these lines, *Even Einstein, when he formulated the general theory of relativity in 1915, was so sure that the universe had to be static that he modified his theory to make this possible.*

So the passage is showing us that, among modern scientists, even Einstein wanted to maintain the idea that the universe is static. He even changed his famous theory of relativity to make this possible. This idea is perfectly paraphrased in answer choice B.

Answer choice A is wrong because the expanding-universe theory is not the *author's* theory.

Answer choice C is incorrect because the passage says nothing about Einstein's creativity. The point is that Einstein disagreed with the expanding-universe theory.

Answer choice D is wrong because the passage never suggests that the expanding-universe theory may not be valid. Just because Einstein didn't agree with the theory doesn't mean it's wrong.

Answer choice E strays too far from the main idea. Remember, the passage is about the expanding-universe theory, not about Einstein's relation to Newton.

10. ETS's answer is A.

According to lines 78–82, Einstein wanted so much to maintain the idea of the static universe that he changed his theory of relativity to make this possible. The change he made was to introduce the *so-called cosmological constant*. That is exactly what answer choice A says.

Answer choice B is wrong because Newton didn't have any ideas about the expanding-universe theory. The theory didn't exist back in Newton's time!

Answer choice C is off the mark because the *cosmological constant* is *part* of Einstein's theory of relativity, not an idea developed by his opponents. Read more carefully.

You can't pick answer choice D either, because Newtonian physics has never been disproved, and this is not suggested anywhere in the passage. Remember, the passage is about the expanding-universe theory. Don't forget the main idea.

Answer choice E is incorrect because the passage is not about the *mass* of all matter. Again, everything in the passage relates to the expanding-universe theory.

11. ETS's answer is D.

Go back to the passage, find the word *static*, and cross it out. Then read the sentence and come up with your own word. According to the passage, Einstein and many other modern scientists were against the idea of an expanding universe. That means they must have believed in a universe that wasn't expanding. So we can put *not expanding* in place of *static*. The best match for *not expanding* in the answer choices is *unchanging*.

The other answer choices are wrong because they don't make any sense in context.

12. ETS's answer is E.
Since this question involves both passages, you should definitely do it last. The easiest way to answer this question is to use POE.

Answer choice A is only about Passage 1, so you can eliminate it. Newton certainly received credit for his theories, so you can eliminate choice B. Answer choice C is rather insulting to all three scientists mentioned (and ETS never insults scientists), so you can eliminate it. Between choices D and E, choice E is better because it's a *may* answer, and ETS likes wishy-washy answers.

13. ETS's answer is A.
According to the passages, Democritus, an ancient Greek scientist, first came up with the theory of atomism, while the expanding-universe theory was first put forth in the twentieth century. That is one clear difference between the two theories, and it also happens to be exactly what answer choice A says.

Choice B is wrong because the passages never suggest that atomism is *easier* to understand than the expanding-universe theory. The comparison is never made. Choice C is way off base. There is no mention of *politics* anywhere in either passage.

Choice D is too extreme. The passage never says that the theory of atomism had been *proven*. Remember, it's just a theory.

Choice E contradicts the main idea of the passage. Modern science has rejected the static-universe theory in favor of the expanding-universe theory.

20

Practice Test 3

**Time—30 Minutes
25 Questions**

In this section, solve each problem using any available space on the page for scratchwork. Then decide which is the best of the choices given and fill in the corresponding oval on the answer sheet.

Notes:

1. The use of a calculator is permitted. All numbers used are real numbers.

2. Figures that accompany problems in this test are intended to provide information useful in solving the problems. They are drawn as accurately as possible EXCEPT when it is stated in a specific problem that the figure is not drawn to scale. All figures lie in a plane unless otherwise indicated.

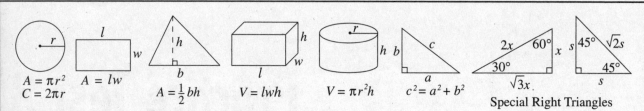

$A = \pi r^2$
$C = 2\pi r$

$A = lw$

$A = \frac{1}{2}bh$

$V = lwh$

$V = \pi r^2 h$

$c^2 = a^2 + b^2$

Special Right Triangles

The number of degrees of arc in a circle is 360.
The measure in degrees of a straight angle is 180.
The sum of the measures in degrees of the angles of a triangle is 180.

1. If $4y + 8 = 12y + 24$, then $y =$

(A) −2
(B) −1
(C) 1
(D) 2
(E) 4

2. If a, b, c and d are consecutive multiples of 5, where $a < b < c < d$, what is the value of $(a - c)(d - b)$?

(A) −100
(B) −25
(C) 0
(D) 50
(E) 100

3. A store sells a box of 6 light bulbs for $30, or a box of 12 light bulbs for $48. The price per bulb is what percent less when purchased in a box of 12 than in a box of 6?

(A) 80%
(B) 75%
(C) 50%
(D) 25%
(E) 20%

GO ON TO THE NEXT PAGE

4. If the remainder when x is divided by 5 equals the remainder when x is divided by 4, the x could be any of the following EXCEPT

(A) 20
(B) 21
(C) 22
(D) 23
(E) 24

5. What is the least integer n such that $n^4 < 605$?

(A) −5
(B) −4
(C) −3
(D) 1
(E) 5

6. If 3 more than x is 2 more than y, what is x in terms of y?

(A) $y - 5$
(B) $y - 1$
(C) $y + 1$
(D) $y + 5$
(E) $y + 6$

7. If x and y are integers such that $4x - 8 > 0$ and $4y + 8 < 0$, then which of the following must be true?

(A) xy is even
(B) xy is odd
(C) $xy < 0$
(D) $xy > 0$
(E) $xy = 0$

8. A rectangle with length 16 and width 6 has an area that is 3 times the area of a triangle with height 8. What is the length of the base of the triangle?

(A) 4
(B) 8
(C) 12
(D) 16
(E) 22

9. If the average (arithmetic mean) of a, b, 6, a, and b is 14, what is the value of $a + b$?

(A) 20
(B) 28
(C) 32
(D) 36
(E) 40

GO ON TO THE NEXT PAGE

10. If $x > 0$ and $(3 - \sqrt{x})(3 + \sqrt{x}) = 7$, what is the value of x?

(A) 4
(B) 3
(C) 2
(D) 1
(E) 0

11. $ABCD$ is a quadrilateral such that $AB = BC$, $AD = \frac{1}{2}CD$, and $AD = \frac{1}{4}AB$. If $BC = 12$, what is the perimeter of $ABCD$?

(A) 44
(B) 42
(C) 40
(D) 36
(E) 33

$$A8$$
$$\times A3$$
$$\overline{8B}$$
$$\underline{5C0}$$
$$CBB$$

12. In the correctly solved multiplication problem above, where A, B, and C are distinct digits, what digit does A represent?

(A) 1
(B) 2
(C) 4
(D) 6
(E) 7

13. Which of the following is equivalent to $-9 \le 3b + 3 \le 18$?

(A) $-4 \le b \le 5$
(B) $-4 \le b \le 6$
(C) $-3 \le b \le 5$
(D) $3 \le b \le 5$
(E) $4 \le b \le 6$

14. The lengths of two sides of a triangle are 5 and 7. If the length of the third side is an integer, what is the least possible perimeter of the triangle?

(A) 12
(B) 13
(C) 14
(D) 15
(E) 17

GO ON TO THE NEXT PAGE

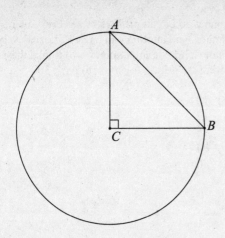

15. In the figure above, *AC* and *BC* are radii of the circle with center *C*. If triangle *ABC* has area 18, what is the circumference of the circle?

(A) 6π
(B) 9π
(C) 12π
(D) 18π
(E) 36π

Questions 16–17 refer to the following table, which shows the amount of rain that fell during a 30-day period in 1998.

Rainfall	
Rainfall (in inches)	**Number of Days**
0	17
1	5
2	3
3	3
4	2

16. What is the mode of the amount of rainfall, in inches, over these 30 days?

(A) 0
(B) 1
(C) 2
(D) 3
(E) 4

17. If 200 inches of rainfall were expected to fall during all of 1998, what percent of the expected yearly rainfall was reached during this 30-day period?

(A) 56%
(B) 42%
(C) 28%
(D) 14%
(E)   7%

18. If the ratio of *r* to *s* is 5 to 6, which of the following could be true?

(A) $r = 0, s = \dfrac{5}{6}$

(B) $r = \dfrac{5}{2}, s = 3$

(C) $r = 6, s = 7$

(D) $r = 12, s = 10$

(E) $r = 25, s = 36$

GO ON TO THE NEXT PAGE

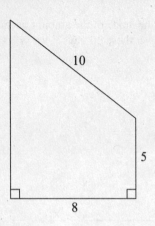

19. What is the area of the figure above?

(A) 60
(B) 64
(C) 70
(D) 80
(E) 88

20. If $x^2 - x = 12$ and $y^2 - y = 12$, what is the greatest possible value of $x - y$?

(A) 0
(B) 4
(C) 7
(D) 12
(E) 24

21. If one worker can pack 15 boxes every two minutes, and another can pack 15 boxes every three minutes, how many minutes will it take these two workers, working together, to pack 300 boxes?

(A) 10
(B) 12
(C) 15
(D) 24
(E) 30

22. A jar contains a number of jellybeans of which 58 are red, 78 are green, and the rest are blue. If the probability of choosing a blue jellybean from this jar at random is $\frac{1}{5}$, how many blue jellybeans are in the jar?

(A) 34
(B) 56
(C) 78
(D) 102
(E) 152

GO ON TO THE NEXT PAGE

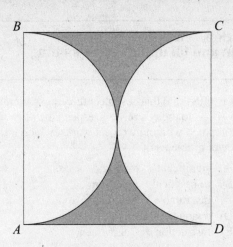

23. In the figure above, *ABCD* is a square with side of length 2. The square contains two semicircles with diameters *AB* and *CD*. What is the sum of the areas of the two shaded regions?

(A) $2 - \dfrac{\pi}{2}$

(B) $2 - \pi$

(C) $4 - \pi$

(D) $4 - 2\pi$

(E) $4 - \dfrac{\pi}{4}$

24. The product of integers *x* and *y* is divisible by 36. If *x* is divisible by 6, which of the following must be true?

    I. *y* is divisible by *x*

    II. *y* is divisible by 6

    III. $\dfrac{y}{6}$ is divisible by 6

(A) None
(B) I only
(C) II only
(D) I and III only
(E) II and III only

25. Jennifer ran from her house to school at an average speed of 6 miles per hour and returned along the same route at an average speed of 4 miles per hour. If the total time it took her to run to the school and back was one hour, how many minutes did it take her to run from her house to school?

(A) 16
(B) 18
(C) 20
(D) 22
(E) 24

STOP

**If you finish before time is called, you may check your work on this section only.
Do not turn to any other section in the test.**

Time—30 Minutes
30 Questions

**Time—30 Minutes
30 Questions**

For each question in this section, select the best answer from among the choices given and fill in the corresponding oval on the answer sheet.

Each sentence below has one or two blanks, each blank indicating that something has been omitted. Beneath the sentence are five words or sets of words labeled A through E. Choose the word or set of words that, when inserted in the sentence, <u>best</u> fits the meaning of the sentence as a whole.

Example:

Medieval kingdoms did not become constitutional republics overnight; on the contrary, the change was -------.

(A) unpopular (B) unexpected (C) advantageous
(D) sufficient (E) gradual   Ⓐ Ⓑ Ⓒ Ⓓ ●

---

1. While Sarah may have been rather quiet, she was by no means a -------, for she often spent evenings with other people and considered that time to be quite -------.

   (A) recluse . . enjoyable
   (B) conservative . . diplomatic
   (C) reformer . . irritating
   (D) barbarian . . confusing
   (E) critic . . demanding

2. The improvements made on the new automobile are largely -------; although the exterior has been changed, the engine has remained unchanged.

   (A) mechanical (B) ornamental (C) economical
   (D) environmental (E) expensive

3. One of the serious ------- of meteorology is that natural weather patterns cannot be ------- in the laboratory for investigation.

   (A) successes . . achieved
   (B) complexities . . broadened
   (C) premises . . acknowledged
   (D) weaknesses . . recreated
   (E) advantages . . analyzed

4. It is often said that seventeenth-century literature is ------- to today's readers, especially when compared with more recent works, which introduce fewer problems of -------.

   (A) significant . . writing
   (B) impractical . . tradition
   (C) inscrutable . . comprehension
   (D) opaque . . thought
   (E) instructional . . agreement

5. The playwright ------- realism and fantasy in her work so well that the audience is never sure whether the characters' experiences are ------- or imaginary.

   (A) intermingles . . actual
   (B) explains . . enjoyable
   (C) combines . . obvious
   (D) delineates . . questionable
   (E) exposes . . correct

6. While his writing demonstrated the difficulties of living a ------- life within the confines of a corrupt society, Darius Holmes never despaired, and he continued to ------- his ideal of virtue.

   (A) complete . . attack
   (B) neutral . . allude to
   (C) sanguine . . consider
   (D) moral . . pursue
   (E) grandiose . . struggle with

7. Zora Neale Hurston's talent at convincing her readers to believe in the world as she describes it in her novels is due to her ability to create extremely ------- characters.

   (A) unsavory
   (B) restrained
   (C) ambiguous
   (D) unilateral
   (E) credible

GO ON TO THE NEXT PAGE

8. Jacobs was much more than a ------- member of the group; he was chosen in light of his extraordinary analytical skills and strong staff management skills.

    (A) token
    (B) perceptive
    (C) feasible
    (D) paradoxical
    (E) vitriolic

9. Some educators view television as an entirely ------- presence in society, virtually disregarding the idea that television has the potential to be -------.

    (A) pernicious . . understood
    (B) auxiliary . . discontinued
    (C) deleterious . . beneficial
    (D) cohesive . . informative
    (E) stabilizing . . hidden

GO ON TO THE NEXT PAGE

Each question below consists of a related pair of words or phrases, followed by five pairs of words or phrases labeled A through E. Select the pair that <u>best</u> expresses a relationship similar to that expressed in the original pair.

Example:

CRUMB : BREAD ::

(A) ounce : unit
(B) splinter : wood
(C) water : bucket
(D) twine : rope
(E) cream : butter

10. CUT : KNIFE ::

(A) dig : shovel
(B) fill : lock
(C) twist : screw
(D) open : door
(E) buy : store

11. CHOREOGRAPHER : DANCER ::

(A) athlete : coach
(B) playwright : line
(C) mathematician : genius
(D) conductor : musician
(E) sculptor : artist

12. TUNDRA : FROZEN ::

(A) ocean : deep
(B) metropolis : smoggy
(C) desert : arid
(D) mountain : towering
(E) moon : nocturnal

13. MUSEUM : ARTIFACTS ::

(A) train : passengers
(B) gallery : portraits
(C) circus : clowns
(D) infirmary : patients
(E) building : architects

14. IMPOSTER : IDENTITY ::

(A) policeman : law
(B) spy : border
(C) lawyer : client
(D) singer : performance
(E) plagiarist : idea

15. UNFETTERED : RESTRAINT ::

(A) intimidated : fear
(B) expunged : clarity
(C) embittered : rage
(D) inclined : behavior
(E) exonerated : blame

GO ON TO THE NEXT PAGE

The passage below is followed by questions based on its content. Answer the questions following each passage on the basis of what is <u>stated</u> or <u>implied</u> in that passage and in any introductory material that may be provided.

Questions 16–21 are based on the following passage.

The following passage is about the art and recreation of Southeastern Indians.

The ceremonies and rituals of the Southeastern Indians seem bizarre, outlandish, even irrational, until viewed against the background of their belief
Line system. When seen in their original context, the
5 ceremonies and rituals of the Southeastern Indians are no more irrational than our own. We encounter the same sort of problem in understanding the art forms and games of the Southeastern Indians, and likewise we find the solution to be similar. Our best
10 road to understanding their artistic and recreational forms is to view them as the outward expressions of their belief system.

In some ways the task of understanding the artistic and recreational forms of the Southeastern Indians
15 is more difficult than understanding their ceremonial life. One problem is that they reached their highest artistic development in the late prehistoric and early historic period. De Soto saw architectural forms and artistic creations that surpassed anything witnessed
20 by the Europeans who came after him, and because many of these creations were made of perishable materials, they did not survive. Hence perhaps the best Southeastern Indian art is irretrievably gone.

A further difficulty in dealing with the artistic and
25 recreational forms of the Southeastern Indians is that all of these are intimately imbedded in other social and cultural institutions. They are neither as self-contained nor as separable from other institutions as are the art forms and games in our own culture.
30 For instance, the Southeastern Indians placed a high value on men who could use words skillfully. Jack and Anna Kilpatrick have discussed the condensed poetry in some of the Cherokee magical formulas, some of them containing a single word, compound
35 in form, which might be likened to tiny imagist poems. Another form of verbal artistry was oratory, the words of a gifted speaker that could move contentious men to reach consensus or the timid and hesitant to go against the enemy. And yet oratory can
40 hardly be separated from the political institutions of the Southeastern Indians.

In looking at the art and recreation of the Southeastern Indians, we will often wish that we knew more about underlying social factors. For
45 example, even though we know much about the Southeastern Indian ball game, we do no know the precise nature of the social and political forces which led them to play it with such ferocity. To a lesser extent we know the basic rules of chunkey
50 but what we do not understand is why the Indians would sometimes bet the last thing they owned on the outcome of a game. In general, we sense that the players of these games were motivated by social factors which lay outside the playing field, but we
55 cannot often be specific about what they were.

16. According to the author, the Southeastern Indians were

(A) ferocious and cruel
(B) intelligent but unmotivated
(C) creative and competitive
(D) mysterious and threatening
(E) timid and hesitant

17. The main purpose of the passage is to

(A) show how bizarre certain Southeastern Indian ceremonies and rituals are
(B) explain the rules of several games played by the Southeastern Indians
(C) describe the difficulties inherent in appreciating the Southeastern Indians' artistic and recreational forms
(D) explore the mysticism of the ceremonies and rituals in the Southeastern Indian belief system
(E) delineate the difference between the artistic forms of the Southeastern Indians and the Cherokee Indians

GO ON TO THE NEXT PAGE

18. Which of the following best describes the "problem" mentioned in line 7?

   (A) The belief system of the Southeastern Indians was irrational and therefore impossible to understand.
   (B) It is difficult to comprehend the artistic and recreational expression of the Southeastern Indians without understanding their belief system.
   (C) A superficial examination of the ceremonies and rituals of the Southeastern Indians make them appear similar to our own.
   (D) Since we have virtually no understanding of the beliefs of the Southeastern Indians, it is unlikely we will ever understand the significance of their art.
   (E) Scholars are unwilling to acquaint themselves sufficiently with the artistic and recreational forms of the Southeastern Indians.

19. According to the passage, the Southeastern Indians viewed oratorical abilities with

   (A) suspicion
   (B) admiration
   (C) curiosity
   (D) thankfulness
   (E) belligerence

20. According to the passage, which of the following was an advantage of skilled oratory?

   (A) It was effective in enhancing one's athletic ability.
   (B) An orator was responsible for composing the magical formulas used in spiritual rituals.
   (C) Orators were usually the most powerful warriors among the Southeastern Indians.
   (D) Timid and hesitant speakers could soothe anxious tempers.
   (E) A skilled speaker could mend differences between opposing parties.

21. The author mentions the game "chunkey" in line 49 primarily in order to

   (A) prove that the Southeastern Indians were more concerned with politics than with organized competition
   (B) show how social politics and ferocious violence were interconnected in the lives of the Southeastern Indians
   (C) explain how the Southeastern Indians' interest in competition and artistic endeavors were dictated by separate social factors
   (D) provide an example of how the Southeastern Indians' competitive nature was motivated by social influences
   (E) describe the unusual and ambiguous rules of a little-known competition

GO ON TO THE NEXT PAGE

The passage below is followed by questions based on its content. Answer the questions following each passage on the basis of what is <u>stated</u> or <u>implied</u> in that passage and in any introductory material that may be provided.

Questions 22–30 are based on the following passage.

The following passage discusses the history and some of the characteristics of jazz.

Like the blues, jazz emphasizes individualism. The performer is at the same time the composer, shaping the music into style and form. A traditional melody
Line or harmonic framework may serve as the takeoff
5 point for improvisation, but it is the personality of the player and the way he or she improvises that produces the music. Performances of the same work differ from player to player, for each recreates the music in his or her own individual way. Jazz is
10 learned through oral tradition, as is folk song, and those who would learn to play it do so primarily by listening to others playing jazz.

Although improvisational in nature, jazz nonetheless contains recognizable elements that
15 derive from older musical traditions. The influence of ragtime is represented in jazz by the emphasis on syncopation and the presence of the piano in the ensemble. The influence of the brass band reveals itself in the jazz instrumentation*, in the roles
20 assigned to each instrument, and in the resulting musical texture. In the classic New Orleans band, for example, three instruments are given melodic roles; the cornet typically plays the lead, the clarinet plays a counter melody, and the trombone plays the
25 lower voice of the trio. The other instruments—the drums, banjos, guitars, and basses—function as the rhythm section. Although pianos were added to jazz bands from the beginning, and often a second cornet as well, the instruments remained basically the same
30 as in brass bands. Later, trumpets took the place of cornets and saxophones were added or used in place of clarinets. The addition of saxophones suggests the influence of the syncopated dance orchestra which used saxophones early in its development.
35 The brass band emphasized the ensemble sound, as distinguished from solo music, and this tradition, too, passed over into the performances of early jazz bands. In many jazz performances of the early 1920s, for example, all of the instruments play
40 throughout the piece, the cornet always retaining the lead melody. In performances that include solo passages, the other instruments typically give firm support, particularly the rhythm section. The ensemble sound of the brass band was basically
45 polyphonic in nature, not chordal. As many as two

or three clearly defined melodic lines dominated the texture, and frequently the rhythm instruments furnished little counter melodies.
The polyphonic texture of the music was a result
50 of "collective improvisation" with each melody player improvising his or her part in such a way that the parts combined into a balanced, integrated whole. The concept of jazz improvisation changed its implications over the years. In this early period,
55 the performer embellished the melody, adding extra tones and altering note values, but in such a manner as to retain the essential shape of the original melody.
The most salient features of jazz derive directly
60 from the blues; its soloists approximate the voice with their instruments, but try to recreate its singing style and blue notes by using scooping, sliding, whining, growling, and falsetto effects. Finally, jazz uses the call-and-response style of the blues, by
65 employing an antiphonal relationship between two solo instruments or between solo and ensemble.
Jazz is created from the synthesis of certain elements in the style of its precursors. Its most striking feature is its exotic sound, which is
70 produced not only by the kinds of instruments used in the orchestra, but also from the manner in which intonation is used. Instead of obtaining exact pitches, the players glide freely from one note to another (or through long series of notes in glissandos) and
75 frequently fluctuate the pitches (i.e., use a wide vibrato).

*Instrumentation refers to the choice of instruments within a musical group.

22. The main purpose of the passage is to show that

(A) three instrument melodies were not the dominant style of jazz
(B) the call-and-response style of the blues was highly successful
(C) blues was a uniquely American form of music with a completely original style
(D) the New Orleans band was the single greatest influence on the evolution of jazz
(E) jazz is a complex musical form with a complicated history

GO ON TO THE NEXT PAGE

23. The author uses the examples of ragtime and brass bands to illustrate

   (A) that jazz is not entirely an original creation
   (B) the diversity of elements from which jazz was created
   (C) the origins of certain jazz compositions
   (D) the relative growth in popularity of modern jazz
   (E) the long, illustrious history that led to the creation of jazz

24. The influence of the brass band on jazz performance includes all of the following EXCEPT

   (A) the playing of the lead melody by the cornet
   (B) emphasis on the ensemble sound
   (C) polyphonic music rather than chordal music
   (D) the playing of all the instruments throughout the song
   (E) the exotic sound of improvisational jazz

25. One of the "salient features" of jazz (line 59) would be that

   (A) the instruments mimic human voices
   (B) jazz is dominated by singers
   (C) music lovers prefer the blues to jazz
   (D) the music is composed with singers in mind
   (E) every jazz musician is also a jazz singer

26. Which is most similar to the "call-and-response style of the blues" mentioned in line 64?

   (A) The replacement of the cornet by the trumpet
   (B) Two people having a dialogue
   (C) The echo of a ringing bell
   (D) A crowd of people chanting
   (E) The contrast between a growl and a falsetto

27. The word "striking" in line 69 most nearly means

   (A) removing
   (B) pounding
   (C) thoughtful
   (D) remarkable
   (E) believable

28. The exotic sound of jazz is primarily a result of

   (A) the selection of instruments and the ways in which sounds are manipulated
   (B) the influences of ragtime and brass bands
   (C) the use of syncopated rhythms
   (D) the addition of extra tones and the replacement of one note with another
   (E) the first and third beat percussion work

29. In line 75, the word "pitches" most nearly means

   (A) tosses
   (B) tones
   (C) volume
   (D) proposals
   (E) styles

30. According to the passage, the development of jazz was influenced by all of the following EXCEPT

   (A) ragtime bands
   (B) dance orchestras
   (C) brass bands
   (D) folk music
   (E) blues singing

STOP

**If you finish before time is called, you may check your work on this section only.
Do not turn to any other section in the test.**

NO TEST MATERIAL ON THIS PAGE.

<table>
<tr><td>

Time—30 Minutes
25 Questions
</td><td>

In this section, solve each problem, using any available space on the page for scratchwork. Then decide which is the best of the choices given and fill in the corresponding oval on the answer sheet.
</td></tr>
</table>

<u>Notes:</u>

1.   The use of a calculator is permitted. All numbers used are real numbers.

2.   Figures that accompany problems in this test are intended to provide information useful in solving the problems. They are drawn as accurately as possible EXCEPT when it is stated in a specific problem that the figure is not drawn to scale. All figures lie in a plane unless otherwise indicated.

Reference Information

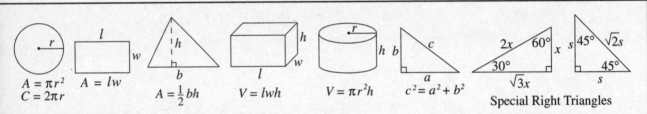

$A = \pi r^2$
$C = 2\pi r$

$A = lw$

$A = \frac{1}{2}bh$

$V = lwh$

$V = \pi r^2 h$

$c^2 = a^2 + b^2$

Special Right Triangles

The number of degrees of arc in a circle is 360.
The measure in degrees of a straight angle is 180.
The sum of the measures in degrees of the angles of a triangle is 180.

Directions for Quantitative Comparison Questions

<u>Questions 1–15</u> each consist of two quantities in boxes, one in Column A and one in Column B.
You are to compare the two quantities and on the answer sheet fill in oval

A   if the quantity in Column A is greater;
B   if the quantity in Column B is greater;
C   if the two quantities are equal;
D   if the relationship cannot be determined from the information given.

AN E RESPONSE WILL NOT BE SCORED.

<u>Notes:</u>

1.   In some questions, information is given about one or both of the quantities to be compared. In such cases, the given information is centered above the two columns and is not boxed.
2.   In a given question, a symbol that appears in both columns represents the same thing in Column A as it does in Column B.
3.   Letters such as x, n, and k stand for real numbers.

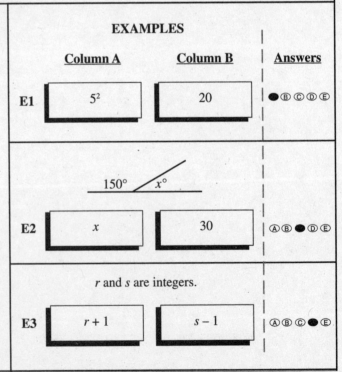

EXAMPLES

SUMMARY DIRECTIONS FOR QUANTITATIVE COMPARISON QUESTIONS

Answer: A if the quantity in Column A is greater;
B if the quantity in Column B is greater;
C if the two quantities are equal;
D if the relationship cannot be determined from the information given.

AN E RESPONSE WILL NOT BE SCORED.

Column A	Column B

1. $5\frac{3}{5}+9\frac{1}{6}$ $5\frac{1}{6}+9\frac{3}{5}$

2. 2% of 200   1% of 800

a and *b* are positive

3. a^2 b^3

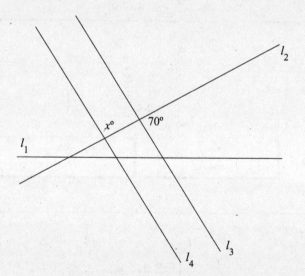

Note: Figure not drawn to scale. $\ell_3 \parallel \ell_4$

4. 70 x

Column A	Column B

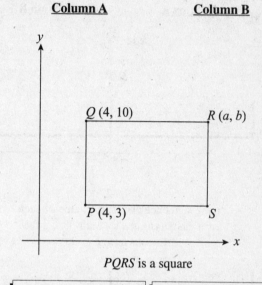

$PQRS$ is a square

5. a 10

The area of circle J is 9π
The area of circle L is 36π

6. $\dfrac{\text{radius of circle } J}{\text{radius of circle } L}$ $\dfrac{1}{4}$

7. $2x(y-2y^2)$ $2y(x-2xy)$

GO ON TO THE NEXT PAGE

GO ON TO THE NEXT PAGE

SUMMARY DIRECTIONS FOR QUANTITATIVE COMPARISON QUESTIONS

Answer: A if the quantity in Column A is greater;
B if the quantity in Column B is greater;
C if the two quantities are equal;
D if the relationship cannot be determined from the information given.

AN E RESPONSE WILL NOT BE SCORED.

Column A	Column B

8.
$12a = 2b$
$15c = 5b$
$a > 0$

Column A: a Column B: c

9.
$1, -3, 9, -27, \ldots$
In the sequence above, the value of each term is determined by multiplying the previous term by -3.

Column A: The 27th term of the sequence Column B: The 28th term of the sequence

10.
$x + 4 > 2y$
$z - y < 2y$

Column A: $x + z$ Column B: y

11.
$3(-2n + 4) - 3 = 9 - 6n$

Column A: 1 Column B: n

12.
A is the set of integers between 0 and 100 that are squares of an odd integer

Column A: The number of integers in set A that have a remainder of 1 when divided by 4 Column B: The number of integers in set A

13.
$x, y,$ and z are integers.
$x < y < z < 3x$

Column A: x Column B: 1

14.
$\dfrac{m}{n} = \dfrac{2}{3}$
$n \neq 3$

Column A: $\dfrac{m+3}{n+3}$ Column B: $\dfrac{5}{6}$

15.
$\dfrac{q}{2} + 1 = m$

Column A: $3q$ Column B: $6m - 6$

Directions for Student-Produced Response Questions

Each of the remaining 10 questions (16–25) requires you to solve the problem and enter your answer by marking the ovals in the special grid, as shown in the examples below.

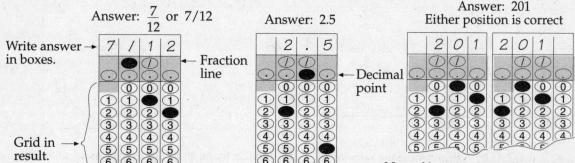

- Mark no more than one oval in any column.
- Because the answer sheet will be machine-scored, **you will receive credit only if the ovals are filled in correctly.**
- Although not required, it is suggested that you write your answer in the boxes at the top of the columns to help you fill in the ovals accurately.
- Some problems may have more than one correct answer. In such cases, grid only one answer.
- No question has a negative answer.
- **Mixed numbers** such as $2\frac{1}{2}$ must be gridded as 2.5 or 5/2. (If [2 1 / 2] is gridded, it will be interpreted as $\frac{21}{2}$, not $2\frac{1}{2}$.)

- **Decimal Accuracy:** If you obtain a decimal answer, **enter the most accurate value the grid will accommodate.** For example, if you obtain an answer such as 0.6666 . . . , you should record the result as .666 or .667. **Less accurate values such as .66 or .67 are not acceptable.**

Acceptable ways to grid $\frac{2}{3}$ = .6666 . . .

Note: You may start your answers in any column, space permitting. Columns not needed should be left blank.

---

16. If $x - 8 = 5y$ and $x = 23$, then $x - y =$

17. During her summer vacation, Vanessa got a job for which she earned $100 per week. If she worked for six weeks, and then did not work for two weeks, what was the average (arithmetic mean) number of dollars she earned per week over the entire eight-week period? (Ignore the dollar sign when gridding your answer.)

GO ON TO THE NEXT PAGE

18. If a rectangle has a length of 5 and a diagonal of 13, what is its perimeter?

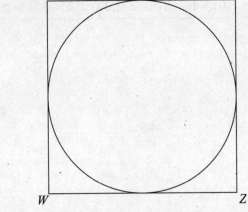

19. If 14,7*B*2 is divisible by 7, then what is the value of the digit *B*?

20. In the figure above, a circle is inscribed in square *WXYZ*. If the area of the circle is 400π, what is the area of *WXYZ*?

21. If Alexandra pays $56.65 for a table, and this amount includes a tax of 3% on the price of the table, how much money, in dollars, does she pay in tax? (Ignore the dollar sign when gridding your answer.)

GO ON TO THE NEXT PAGE

22. Jeannette's average (arithmetic mean) score for six tests was 92. If the sum of the scores of two of her tests was 188, then what was her average score for the other four tests?

23. There were 320 students at a school assembly attended only by juniors and seniors. If there were 60 more juniors than seniors and if there were 30 more female juniors than male juniors, how many male juniors were at the assembly?

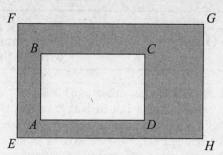

Note: Figure not drawn to scale.

24. In the figure above, the area of the shaded region is $\frac{1}{4}$ the area of rectangle *ABCD*. What is the value of

$$\frac{\text{area of } EFGH}{\text{area of } ABCD}?$$

25. If $-1 \le a \le 2$ and $-3 \le b \le 2$, what is the greatest possible value of $(a + b)(b - a)$?

STOP
**If you finish before time is called, you may check your work on this section only.
Do not turn to any other section in the test.**

Time—30 Minutes
35 Questions

For each question in this section, select the best answer from among the choices given and fill in the corresponding oval on the answer sheet.

Each sentence below has one or two blanks, each blank indicating that something has been omitted. Beneath the sentence are five words or sets of words labeled A through E. Choose the word or set of words that, when inserted in the sentence, best fits the meaning of the sentence as a whole.

Example:

Medieval kingdoms did not become constitutional republics overnight; on the contrary, the change was -------.

(A) unpopular (B) unexpected (C) advantageous
(D) sufficient (E) gradual

Ⓐ Ⓑ Ⓒ Ⓓ ●

1. The two teams reached an agreement that was -------: they promised to exchange players of comparable talent.

    (A) equitable (B) variable (C) hypocritical
    (D) inopportune (E) extended

2. Their daughter's story was so entirely implausible that the parents believe it to be -------.

    (A) an explanation (B) an intimidation
    (C) a fabrication (D) a rationalization
    (E) a confirmation

3. Professor Yang's article was unusually -------, but its brevity did not conceal the importance of her discovery.

    (A) complex (B) cerebral (C) irrelevant
    (D) terse (E) ambitious

4. While industry in the late twentieth century believed itself ------- in its treatment of laborers, Cesar Chavez made a career of revealing the ------- experienced by farm workers.

    (A) generous . . injustices
    (B) just . . satisfaction
    (C) vindictive . . challenges
    (D) superior . . relationships
    (E) immutable . . consistency

5. The judge proposed several ------- means of settling the case, but the defendant resolved to ------- the government's authority and refused to acknowledge the legitimacy of the court.

    (A) unorthodox . . eliminate
    (B) comprehensive . . assuage
    (C) impartial . . demonstrate
    (D) political . . temper
    (E) amicable . . subvert

6. Isabella's ------- style is best seen in her architecture, which combines elements of Byzantine, Greek, Roman, and Gothic periods.

    (A) reticent (B) eclectic (C) mystical
    (D) formulaic (E) eminent

7. Though his earlier books contained relatively subtle criticisms of the inequalities in his country, Wynn's later novels were much more ------- in their approach.

    (A) jubilant (B) veiled (C) trenchant
    (D) indirect (E) mundane

8. The Black Plague was so ------- that in a few short years it had reduced the population of medieval Europe substantially.

    (A) lenient (B) susceptible (C) suppressed
    (D) maudlin (E) virulent

GO ON TO THE NEXT PAGE ➡

9. Her promotional tour was ------- by missteps, but the increasing appreciation for her works suggests that the effects of these blunders were -------.

   (A) strengthened . . destructive
   (B) avoided . . ancillary
   (C) surrounded . . perceptive
   (D) beleaguered . . negligible
   (E) besmirched . . unquestionable

10. While the ambassador was not ------- about the path that his country was taking, he did not believe that its economic politics would cause a significant amount of -------.

    (A) excited . . bliss
    (B) sanguine . . distress
    (C) impartial . . neutrality
    (D) despondent . . despair
    (E) agitated . . upheaval

GO ON TO THE NEXT PAGE

Each question below consists of a related pair of words or phrases, followed by five pairs of words or phrases labeled A through E. Select the pair that best expresses a relationship similar to that expressed in the original pair.

Example:

CRUMB : BREAD ::

(A) ounce : unit
(B) splinter : wood
(C) water : bucket
(D) twine : rope
(E) cream : butter   Ⓐ ● Ⓒ Ⓓ Ⓔ

11. MARBLE : SCULPTOR ::

(A) clay : potter
(B) typewriter : poet
(C) blueprint : technician
(D) wrench : plumber
(E) ocean : sailor

12. SILO : GRAIN ::

(A) chorus : soprano
(B) loft : barn
(C) saddle : horse
(D) armory : weapon
(E) doctor : hospital

13. CARICATURE : PORTRAIT ::

(A) satire : writing
(B) misfortune : comedy
(C) attack : enemy
(D) comedian : joke
(E) deception : hoax

14. VULNERABLE : DEFEATED ::

(A) oblivious : educated
(B) impulsive : detached
(C) audible : heard
(D) accessible : delayed
(E) irrational : believed

15. LAX : FIRMNESS ::

(A) frugal : money
(B) pretentious : modesty
(C) disgruntled : resentment
(D) pivotal : essence
(E) detrimental : harm

16. SECTOR : CIRCLE ::

(A) dormitory : student
(B) calculation : computer
(C) construction : builder
(D) sphere : influence
(E) province : country

17. ITINERARY : JOURNEY ::

(A) figure : accounting
(B) schematic : blueprint
(C) employment : career
(D) agenda : meeting
(E) application : business

18. ANTHOLOGY : WORKS ::

(A) program : editions
(B) qualification : abilities
(C) director : films
(D) lexicon : words
(E) orchestra : symphonies

19. FLOW : DELUGE ::

(A) evaporate : water
(B) revolve : orbit
(C) disarm : defense
(D) reflect : beam
(E) burn : conflagration

20. REFUTE : THEORY ::

(A) verify : idea
(B) approve : plan
(C) substitute : corollary
(D) integrate : resource
(E) debunk : myth

21. IOTA : AMOUNT ::

(A) aroma : smell
(B) sliver : portion
(C) blade : grass
(D) shoe : pair
(E) notch : belt

GO ON TO THE NEXT PAGE →

22. DEBASE : DEGRADATION ::

 (A) engender : destruction
 (B) abash : embarrassment
 (C) converse : isolation
 (D) inculpate : liberation
 (E) collude : protection

23. VAIN : FLATTERY ::

 (A) ingenuous : competition
 (B) zealous : investigation
 (C) gregarious : company
 (D) bulbous : security
 (E) logical : entertainment

GO ON TO THE NEXT PAGE

The passage below is followed by questions based on its content. Answer the questions following the passage on the basis of what is <u>stated</u> or <u>implied</u> in the passage and in any introductory material that may be provided.

Questions 24–35 are based on the following passage.

The following passage written in 1989 is taken from A Year in Provence *by Peter Mayle. In this excerpt, we follow a family's first exposure to the French district.*

The proprietor of Le Simiane wished us a happy new year and hovered in the doorway as we stood in the narrow street, blinking into the sun.

Line
5 "Not bad, eh?" he said, with a flourish of one velvet-clad arm which took in the village. "One is fortunate to be in Provence."

Yes indeed, we thought, one certainly was. If this was winter, we wouldn't be needing all the foul-weather paraphernalia—boots and coats and
10 inch-thick sweaters—that we had brought over from England. We drove home, warm and well fed, making bets on how soon we could take the first swim of the year, and feeling a smug sympathy for those poor souls in harsher climates who had to
15 suffer real winters.

Meanwhile, a thousand miles to the north, the wind that had started in Siberia was picking up speed for the final part of its journey. We had heard stories about the Mistral. It drove people, and animals,
20 mad; it was an extenuating circumstance in crimes of violence. It blew for fifteen days on end, uprooting trees, overturning cars, smashing windows, tossing old ladies into the gutter, splintering telegraph poles, moaning through houses like a cold and baleful
25 ghost—every problem in Provence that couldn't be blamed on the politicians was the fault of the *sacre vent* which the Provençeaux spoke about with a kind of masochistic pride.

Typical Gallic exaggeration, we thought. If
30 they had to put up with the gales that come off the English Channel and bend the rain so that it hits you in the face almost horizontally, then they might know what a real wind was like. We listened to their stories and, to humor the tellers, pretended to be
35 impressed.

And so we were poorly prepared when the first Mistral of the year came howling down the Rhône valley, turned left, and smacked into the west side of the house with enough force to skim roof tiles
40 into the swimming pool and rip a window that

had carelessly been left open off its hinges. The temperature dropped twenty degrees in twenty-four hours. It went to zero, then six below. Readings taken in Marseilles showed a wind speed of 180
45 kilometers an hour. And then one morning, with the sound of branches snapping, the pipes burst one after the other under the pressure of water that had frozen in them overnight.

They hung off the wall, swollen and stopped up
50 with ice, and Monsieur Menicucci studied them with his professional plumber's eye.

"*Oh là là,*" he said. "*Oh là là.*" He turned to his young apprentice, whom he invariably addressed as *jeune homme* or *jeune*. "You see what we have here,
55 *jeune*. Naked pipes. No insulation. Côte d'Azur plumbing. In Cannes, in Nice, it would do, but here ..."

He made a clucking sound of disapproval and wagged his finger under *jeune's* nose to underline the
60 difference between the soft winters of the coast and the biting cold in which we were now standing, and pulled his woolen bonnet firmly down over his ears. He was short and compact, built for plumbing, as he would say, because he could squeeze himself into
65 constricted spaces that more ungainly men would find inaccessible. While we waited for *jeune* to set up the blowtorch, Monsieur Menicucci delivered the first of a series of lectures and collected *pensées* which I would listen to with increasing enjoyment
70 throughout the coming year. Today, we had a geophysical dissertation on the increasing severity of Provençal winters.

For three years in a row, winters had been noticeably harder than anyone could remember—
75 cold enough, in fact, to kill ancient olive trees. But why? Monsieur Menicucci gave me a token two seconds to ponder this phenomenon before warming to his thesis, tapping me with a finger from time to time to make sure I was paying attention.

80 It was clear, he said, that the winds which brought the cold down from Russia were arriving in Provence with greater velocity than before, taking less time to reach their destination and therefore having less time to warm up en route. And the
85 reason for this—Monsieur Menicucci allowed

GO ON TO THE NEXT PAGE

himself a brief but dramatic pause—was a change
in the configuration of the Earth's crust. *Mais
oui.* Somewhere between Siberia and Ménerbes
the curvature of the Earth had flattened, enabling
90 the wind to take a more direct route south. It was
entirely logical. Unfortunately, part two of the
lecture (Why the Earth Is Becoming Flatter) was
interrupted by a crack of another burst pipe, and my
education was put aside for some virtuoso work with
95 the blowtorch.

The effect of the weather on the inhabitants of
Provence is immediate and obvious. They expect
every day to be sunny, and their disposition suffers
when it isn't. Rain they take as a personal affront,
shaking their heads and commiserating with each
other in the cafés, looking with profound suspicion
at the sky as though a plague of locusts is about to
descend, and picking their way with distaste through
the puddles on the pavement.

24. The author's comment about the family "making
bets on how soon we could take the first swim of
the year" (lines 12–13) refers to

(A) the vain desire to partake of the French waters
(B) the longing for real pleasure on an otherwise
dull French vacation
(C) the hope that a return to the British shore
would cure their homesickness
(D) the faith that the powerful Mistral would soon
vanish and allow them to swim happily once
again
(E) the anticipation of warm weather that would
make it conceivable to swim, despite the
season

25. The word "poor" in line 14 most nearly means

(A) humble
(B) underprivileged
(C) inferior
(D) destitute
(E) unfortunate

26. The author describes the Mistral as "an extenuating
circumstance in crimes of violence" in lines 20–21
in order to

(A) explain the problems attributed to their
politicians
(B) illustrate that the sole cause of problems in
Provence is natural disasters beyond human
control
(C) explain how the Mistral strangely caused
damage at the same moment that politicians
caused harm
(D) emphasize that damage caused by any natural
disaster is negligible compared to that caused
by juvenile delinquents
(E) illustrate the severity of the effects of the
Mistral on people

27. The word "baleful" in line 24 most nearly means

(A) lonely
(B) ambitious
(C) sprightly
(D) deadly
(E) rambunctious

28. In lines 30–33 the author implies that "the gales
that come off the English Channel"

(A) prevent most nautical vessels from reaching
their destination
(B) can combine with a Mistral and cause
unimaginable havoc across the European
countryside
(C) have greater force than their French
counterparts
(D) bend the rain into horizontal streams only
under certain storm conditions
(E) cause damage only around the English
Channel

29. The "clucking sound of disapproval" (line 58)
made by Monsieur Menicucci signifies

(A) his belief that the plumbing installation was
inappropriate for the climate conditions
(B) his disdain for the English visitors
(C) his opinion of his assistant's work ethic
(D) his preference for the warmer winters of the
coast
(E) his sense that the plumbing in Cannes and
Nice is superior to that in Provence

GO ON TO THE NEXT PAGE

30. Judging from the author's description in lines 58–70, Monsieur Menicucci can best be characterized as

(A) a diligent and somber figure who has a passing interest in plumbing
(B) an enthusiastic workman who yearns for the more temperate climates of Nice and Cannes
(C) an eccentric and entertaining personality whose physique seems to suit his profession
(D) a comic worker who depends on his younger co-worker for guidance
(E) a solemn figure whose tedious work has turned him into a hardened man

31. The author implies that Monsieur Menicucci offers the "token two seconds" (lines 76–77)

(A) as an effrontery to the author whose opinion was not regarded with sufficient consideration
(B) in sincere hope that the author might be able to shed some light on the mystery
(C) simply as a courtesy, since Menicucci believes he can provide the definitive theory on the phenomenon's cause
(D) in confusion, momentarily forgetting what he had been discussing
(E) to reveal his own ignorance to such matters as the Mistral's capacity for destruction

32. Which of the following best describes Menicucci's theory about the Earth's crust?

(A) The burst pipes were the result of the increased velocity of the Mistral.
(B) Siberia is gradually moving closer to Provence.
(C) The presence of wind in most regions is completely determined by the curvature of the Earth.
(D) Wind slows down across a flat plain since it wants to change directions.
(E) A deviation in the Earth's shape results in shorter distances for the cold Siberian wind to travel.

33. The author's comment *"Mais oui,"* translated to mean "But, of course," suggests the author regards Menicucci as a

(A) highly educated thinker whose theory is provocative
(B) confused character who cannot adequately articulate his ideas
(C) slightly pompous comic figure who perceives himself to be overly knowledgeable
(D) plumber whose grasp of the English language is impressive
(E) deceitful man interested in misleading the author into believing fanciful tales

34. The author most likely thinks of Monsieur Menicucci with feelings of

(A) disgust
(B) pity
(C) sorrow
(D) indifference
(E) amusement

35. Which of the following best expresses how the Provençeaux population regards rain?

(A) It is a personal insult which they tend to avoid by hiding away in cafes.
(B) It represents a refreshing change from the common weather patterns.
(C) It affects the citizens by damaging the land which is vulnerable to excessive moisture.
(D) It is an unwelcome guest to a region which depends on it.
(E) It is an inconvenience, introducing an unwelcome variety to a static community.

STOP
**If you finish before time is called, you may check your work on this section only.
Do not turn to any other section in the test.**

NO TEST MATERIAL ON THIS PAGE.

Time—30 Minutes
35 Questions

For each question in this section, select the best answer from among the choices given and fill in the corresponding oval on the answer sheet.

Each sentence below has one or two blanks, each blank indicating that something has been omitted. Beneath the sentence are five words or sets of words labeled A through E. Choose the word or set of words that, when inserted in the sentence, best fits the meaning of the sentence as a whole.

Example:

Medieval kingdoms did not become constitutional republics overnight; on the contrary, the change was -------.

(A) unpopular (B) unexpected (C) advantageous
(D) sufficient (E) gradual   Ⓐ Ⓑ Ⓒ Ⓓ ●

1. The fireworks display created so much ------- that the night sky was completely -------, almost as if it were the middle of the day.

    (A) heat . . exploded
    (B) gunpowder . . polluted
    (C) color . . decorated
    (D) refuse . . detonated
    (E) light . . illuminated

2. In speech and in action she was never haughty or -------; she was always willing to ------- any recommendations, even if she did not agree with them at first.

    (A) persistent . . deny
    (B) conceited . . consider
    (C) ornery . . oppose
    (D) openminded . . embrace
    (E) accommodating . . ignore

3. Believing that a writer has ------- responsibilities, Simon Le Boq hopes that his work ------- the differences between right and wrong.

    (A) contradictory . . explains
    (B) textual . . blames
    (C) principal . . indicates
    (D) required . . contains
    (E) ethical . . demonstrates

4. Most animals respond with excessive violence to insignificant threats; in contrast, some remain ------- when facing serious physical danger.

    (A) menacing (B) hostile (C) inane
    (D) placid (E) jubilant

5. Anthropologists had long assumed that hunter-gatherers moved continually in their search for food; however, recent findings indicate that during the Mesolithic period such groups were often quite -------.

    (A) prudent (B) sedentary (C) industrious
    (D) indigent (E) superstitious

6. Although it has begun to garner -------, until recently, African drum music was virtually ------- by all but those with the most esoteric tastes.

    (A) acclaim . . overlooked
    (B) respect . . praised
    (C) criticism . . ignored
    (D) recognition . . played
    (E) censure . . disregarded

7. Presidents of large companies have traditionally been very -------; they rarely suggest radical new ideas unless all other options have been investigated and found to be impossible.

    (A) inventive (B) conservative (C) gentrified
    (D) ingenuous (E) gratuitous

8. While writing her latest novel, Samantha experienced periods where she was quite -------, but these were interrupted by dry spells during which she found she could write nothing.

    (A) stagnant (B) abstruse (C) prolific
    (D) flamboyant (E) urbane

9. Since none of the original doors or windows of the Mayan Indian homes have survived, restoration work on these portions of these buildings has been largely -------.

    (A) exquisite (B) impertinent (C) speculative
    (D) appeased (E) abstract

10. While many health-conscious individuals have stopped eating eggs, dietitians say that in appropriate quantities eggs can be quite -------.

    (A) injurious (B) erudite (C) convenient
    (D) perfunctory (E) salubrious

GO ON TO THE NEXT PAGE ▷

Each question below consists of a related pair of words or phrases, followed by five pairs of words or phrases labeled A through E. Select the pair that best expresses a relationship similar to that expressed in the original pair.

Example:

CRUMB : BREAD ::

(A) ounce : unit
(B) splinter : wood
(C) water : bucket
(D) twine : rope
(E) cream : butter

 Ⓐ ● Ⓒ Ⓓ Ⓔ

11. AIRPORT : PLANES ::

(A) pedal : bicycles
(B) tunnel : headlights
(C) store : groceries
(D) harbor : boats
(E) mechanic : cars

12. MEASURE : MUSIC ::

(A) oven : food
(B) sentence : writing
(C) bow : violin
(D) sprinkle : salt
(E) puddle : pond

13. RENEGE : PROMISE ::

(A) betray : confidence
(B) disobey : punishment
(C) understand : instruction
(D) evaluate : position
(E) condemn : viewpoint

14. COWARD : INTIMIDATED ::

(A) egotist : humbled
(B) dupe : deceived
(C) politician : opinionated
(D) child : punished
(E) celebrity : appreciated

15. SANCTUARY : WORSHIP ::

(A) gymnasium : exercise
(B) office : meeting
(C) lectern : debate
(D) platform : politician
(E) television : performer

16. INTRACTABLE : GOVERN ::

(A) unfaithful : promise
(B) hopeful : anticipate
(C) immobile : motivate
(D) obstinate : persuade
(E) minimal : achieve

17. MAVERICK : INDIVIDUALISM ::

(A) litigant : persecution
(B) winner : competition
(C) criminal : innocence
(D) prevaricator : dishonesty
(E) dullard : levity

18. ILLUSORY : DECEPTION ::

(A) realistic : disbelief
(B) didactic : confusion
(C) soporific : sleep
(D) intrinsic : value
(E) majestic : view

GO ON TO THE NEXT PAGE →

19. ENIGMA : UNDERSTAND ::

    (A) alternative : choose
    (B) ideology : believe
    (C) physician : diagnose
    (D) colleague : distrust
    (E) recidivist : reform

20. RAVENOUS : HUNGRY ::

    (A) vehement : insistent
    (B) dubious : preposterous
    (C) insipid : vapid
    (D) foreign : alien
    (E) delinquent : obedient

21. PUERILE : INFANT ::

    (A) melancholy : artist
    (B) venerable : novice
    (C) punctilious : perfectionist
    (D) laudatory : orator
    (E) chastened : ambassador

22. MELLIFLUOUS : EUPHONY ::

    (A) monotonous : lecture
    (B) belligerent : hostility
    (C) offensive : language
    (D) agile : weakness
    (E) turbulent : calm

23. FRIVOLITY : SERIOUSNESS ::

    (A) reticence : verbosity
    (B) maturity : extravagance
    (C) lassitude : apathy
    (D) agreement : coercion
    (E) dissention : eagerness

GO ON TO THE NEXT PAGE →

The passage below is followed by questions based on its content. Answer the questions following the passage on the basis of what is stated or implied in the passage and in any introductory material that may be provided.

Questions 24–35 are based on the following passage.

In this excerpt from the book The Brain *written in 1984, Dr. Richard M. Restak discusses two different schools of thought in brain research: those who believe there is a strong relationship between the brain and the mind, and those who do not. By citing various neuroscientists, Restak conveys the struggle many scientists have with the issue.*

Two years before his death at age eighty-four, neurosurgeon Wilder Penfield was writing his final book, *The Mystery of the Mind.* During moments
Line away from his desk, Penfield continued to ponder
5 the theme of his book: the relationship of mind, brain, and science.
One weekend while at his farm outside of Montreal, Penfield began painting on a huge rock. On one side, he painted a Greek word for
10 "spirit" along with a solid line connecting it to an Aesculapian torch, which represented science. The line continued around the rock to the other side, where he drew an outline of a human head with a brain drawn inside, which contained, at its center, a
15 question mark. At this point, Penfield was satisfied: brain studies, if properly conducted, would lead inevitably to an understanding of the mind.
But as Penfield progressed with his book, he became less certain that the study of the brain, a field
20 in which he had done pioneering work earlier in his career, would ever lead to an understanding of the mind. Finally, six months before he died, he reached a conclusion.
Donning six sweaters to protect himself from the
25 harsh Canadian wind, Penfield returned to the rock and, with shaking hands, converted the solid line connecting the spirit and brain into an interrupted one. This alteration expressed, in a form for all to see, Penfield's doubts that an understanding of the
30 brain would ever lead to an explanation of the mind.
Among neuroscientists, Penfield is not alone in undergoing, later in life, a change in belief about the relationship of the mind to the brain. Sir John Eccles, a Nobel Prize winner has teamed up in
35 recent years with Karl Popper. Together they have written *The Self and Its Brain*, an updated plea for dualism: the belief that the mind and the brain are

distinct entities. Brain researcher Karl Pribram is currently collaborating with physicist David Bohm
40 in an attempt to integrate mind and consciousness with ideas drawn from quantum physics. Together they are searching for a model capable of integrating matter and consciousness into a holistic worldview.
Why should these brain researchers have a change
45 of heart late in their careers about the adequacy of our present knowledge of the brain to provide an "explanation" for mind and consciousness? What compels them toward a mystical bent?
Interest and enthusiasm regarding the brain can't
50 be the only explanations why neuroscientists are susceptible to a mystical bent, since only a small number of them end up waxing philosophical. But the nature of their research and the kinds of questions asked undoubtedly contribute to
55 later "conversions." Penfield's work involved neurosurgical explorations into the temporal lobes. In response to Penfield's electrical probe, his patients reported familiar feelings and vivid memories. In essence, these patients reported experiences
60 that did not correspond to actual events in the operating theater, but rather were the result of direct stimulation of neural tissues. Does this mean that our conscious experience can be understood solely in terms of electrical impulses?
65 Researchers like Wilder Penfield and Roger Sperry are examples of brain researchers who have become disillusioned with claims that the mind can "be explained" in terms of brain functioning. They have revolted against what another neuroscientist
70 calls the "Peter Pan School of Neuroscience" with its "bloodless dance of action potentials" and its "hurrying to and fro of molecules."
Common to all these brain scientists is a willingness to adapt innovative attitudes as well as
75 pursue unorthodox lines of inquiry. They have also been open to transcendental influences. Eccles, for instance, had a "sudden overwhelming experience" at age eighteen that aroused an intense interest in the mind-brain problem. He attributes his choice of
80 career in the neurosciences to this experience.
Brain researchers with a "mystical bent" have also been comfortable sharing their findings and

GO ON TO THE NEXT PAGE

ideas with specialists in other fields. Penfield's
book, *The Mystery of the Mind*, was encouraged by
85 Charles Hendle, professor of philosophy at Yale.
It was a much-needed encouragement, since the
other neuroscientists to whom Penfield had shown
his early draft discouraged him from proceeding
with the project. To them, Penfield's speculative
90 leap from neurophysiologist to philosopher was
"unscientific." At Hendle's urging, Penfield
proceeded to detail "how I came to take seriously,
even to believe, that the consciousness of man,
the mind, is something not to be reduced to brain
95 mechanisms."

24. In line 10, Penfield uses the Greek word for "spirit" to represent

(A) alcohol
(B) mood
(C) ghost
(D) consciousness
(E) animation

25. The "solid line" painted by Penfield (line 10) represents

(A) Penfield's desire to link art and science within one discipline
(B) his reluctance to make any connections between the mind and the brain
(C) his conclusion that experiments had proven the link between the brain and the mind
(D) an example of Penfield's mental confusion
(E) Penfield's confidence that the mind would eventually be understood through study of the brain

26. The author mentions that Penfield is not alone in his change of belief (lines 31–32) in order to show that

(A) several neuroscientists believe that the mind cannot be reduced to facts about the brain
(B) most scientists believe that the brain and the mind are strongly linked
(C) new scientific evidence proves that the brain and the mind are distinct entities
(D) a number of scientists believe that neuroscience alone cannot explain the mind
(E) scientists must work together in order to understand dualism

27. It can be inferred from the passage that Pribram and Bohm decided to collaborate because

(A) they felt that a holistic world view could explain quantum physics
(B) they felt that consciousness might better be understood by unorthodox avenues of inquiry
(C) they wanted to expand on the findings of Eccles and Popper
(D) new findings in the field of quantum physics had convinced them that matter and consciousness could serve as a model for the brain's mechanisms
(E) Penfield's book contained factual errors that they felt they must correct

28. The collaborative work of Pribram and Bohm would most likely indicate that

(A) the separation of mind and brain is unmistakable yet impossible to prove
(B) investigations of human consciousness are the primary way to gain information on the brain
(C) a combination of the abstract and the concrete is vital in order to create a complete and universal theory
(D) Eccles' work could have no effect on their own investigations
(E) Popper and Eccles' belief in the separateness of the brain and the mind is still unfounded

29. Which of the following most clearly defines the meaning of the word "bent" in line 51?

(A) tendency
(B) distortion
(C) determination
(D) talent
(E) explanation

GO ON TO THE NEXT PAGE

30. The phrase "experiences that did not correspond to actual events" in line 60 refers to

    (A) sensations and memories unrelated to what was really happening
    (B) inexplicable patient perceptions that were not caused by Penfield's electrical probe
    (C) the patients' confusion about the point of Penfield's research
    (D) the discrepancies between different patients' memories of the experimental procedure
    (E) a transfer of feelings and memories from one area of the temporal lobes to another

31. It can be inferred that skeptics believe that advocates of the "Peter Pan School of Neuroscience"

    (A) succeed in creating a definitive technique for neurosurgeons to follow
    (B) fail to take brain study seriously as a field of endeavor
    (C) misunderstand the importance of brain waves in the study of the mind
    (D) rely too much on the physiological to explain the workings of the mind
    (E) believe that abstract aspects of the mind cannot be explained scientifically

32. The main distinction between orthodox and unorthodox neuroscientists is that

    (A) the former believe in enlarging the pool of research topics, while the latter tend to stay within their own field
    (B) the latter seek out alternative sources for research, while the former only regard those with a mystical bent as worthy
    (C) the former encourage "unscientific" research, while the latter concern themselves primarily with mystical phenomena
    (D) the latter regard the former with contempt, while the former consider the latter to be colleagues
    (E) the former tend to ignore research that is not based in science, while the latter support exploration that calls on various sources

33. The author mentions Eccles' "sudden overwhelming experience" (line 77) in order to

    (A) demonstrate that Eccles' own brain problems led him to the field of neuroscience
    (B) provide an example of the pressure and stress associated with the study of the mind-brain problem
    (C) show that Eccles' unusual experience may have left him more open to nonscientific discussions of the mind
    (D) show how experience is closely linked to brain mechanisms
    (E) strengthen his contention that all great brain researchers have had unusual experiences

GO ON TO THE NEXT PAGE

34. Which of the following is the closest parallel to the transformation that Penfield went through in his scientific career?

   (A) A professor prepares a lecture on the Reformation, recalls a collection of slides in the library that is helpful, and decides to incorporate them into his lecture.

   (B) An officer is given the opportunity to lead his troops into the heat of battle, but refrains because of a mystical dream that predicts a devastating loss.

   (C) A teacher punishes a disruptive student, meets with his angry parents, and ultimately decides that her actions were appropriate, despite the criticism of her colleagues.

   (D) An artist who believes that realism is the only legitimate style, but later understands that there are other ways to understand art.

   (E) A religious leader who cites mainly from the book of Numbers for his sermons decides to use references from Genesis as well, and incorporates them successfully.

35. Wilder Penfield would most likely consider which of the following investigations of the mind and brain insufficient?

   (A) An article written in a science journal that pleads for the inclusion of a philosopher's input into future research

   (B) A seminar in which an expert on mysticism speaks to students of neuroscience

   (C) An experiment that deals solely with the concrete and tangible data available to researchers

   (D) A book that includes both "scientific" data and philosophy

   (E) A researcher who is willing to use ideas based upon non-scientific sources

STOP

If you finish before time is called, you may check your work on this section only. Do not turn to any other section in the test.

NO TEST MATERIAL ON THIS PAGE.

<table>
<tr><td>Time—15 Minutes
10 Questions</td><td>In this section, solve each problem using any available space on the page for scratchwork. Then decide which is the best of the choices given and fill in the corresponding oval on the answer sheet.</td></tr>
</table>

Notes:

1. The use of a calculator is permitted. All numbers used are real numbers.

2. Figures that accompany problems in this test are intended to provide information useful in solving the problems. They are drawn as accurately as possible EXCEPT when it is stated in a specific problem that the figure is not drawn to scale. All figures lie in a plane unless otherwise indicated.

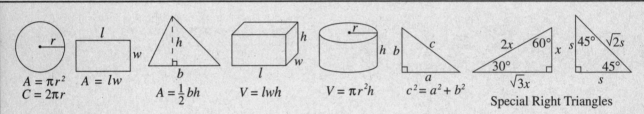

$A = \pi r^2$
$C = 2\pi r$ $A = lw$ $A = \frac{1}{2}bh$ $V = lwh$ $V = \pi r^2 h$ $c^2 = a^2 + b^2$

Special Right Triangles

The number of degrees of arc in a circle is 360.
The measure in degrees of a straight angle is 180.
The sum of the measures in degrees of the angles of a triangle is 180.

1. During the past week, a factory produced 10,000 computer disks, of which 30 were found to be defective. At this rate, if the factory produced 1,000,000 computer disks, approximately how many would be defective?

    (A) 3
    (B) 30
    (C) 300
    (D) 3,000
    (E) 30,000

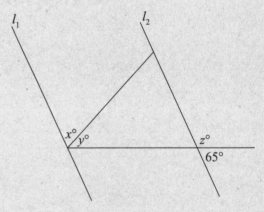

3. In the figure above, if ℓ_1 is parallel to ℓ_2, and $x = 55$, then $y + z =$

    (A) 120
    (B) 145
    (C) 175
    (D) 180
    (E) 195

2. If $3a + 2b + c = 22$, $b + c = 8$, and $c = 6$, what is the value of $a + b + c$?

    (A) 4
    (B) 8
    (C) 12
    (D) 18
    (E) 36

GO ON TO THE NEXT PAGE ➔

4. If b is a positive number not equal to 1, which of the following must also be positive?

(A) $\dfrac{b}{b+1}$

(B) $\dfrac{b+6}{b-3}$

(C) $\dfrac{1}{2b-2}$

(D) $2-b$

(E) $2b-1$

5. Eighty students went on a class trip. If there were fourteen more boys than girls on the trip, how many girls were on the trip?

(A) 26
(B) 33
(C) 40
(D) 47
(E) 66

6. Which of the following is equal to the sum of two consecutive even integers?

(A) 224
(B) 226
(C) 227
(D) 228
(E) 229

7. If it costs z dollars to buy n pizzas, how much will it cost, in dollars, to buy b pizzas at the same rate?

(A) $\dfrac{zb}{n}$

(B) $\dfrac{b}{zn}$

(C) $\dfrac{nb}{z}$

(D) $\dfrac{zn}{b}$

(E) znb

GO ON TO THE NEXT PAGE

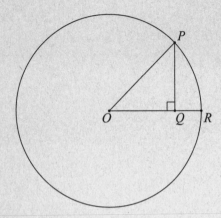

8. In the circle above with center O, $OQ = QR$. If the radius of the circle is 8, what is the area of triangle OPQ?

(A) 4
(B) $4\sqrt{3}$
(C) 8
(D) $8\sqrt{3}$
(E) 16

9. For all x, $\lozenge x = (10 - x)^2$. If $p = \lozenge 6$, which of the following is equal to $4p$?

(A) $\lozenge 24$
(B) $\lozenge 18$
(C) $\lozenge 12$
(D) $\lozenge 8$
(E) $\lozenge 4$

$n,$ _____ $, 2n,$ _____

10. The first number in the sequence above is n, and each number after the first is p units greater than the previous number. In terms of p, what is the sixth number in the sequence?

(A) $3p$
(B) $4p$
(C) $5p$
(D) $6p$
(E) $7p$

STOP

If you finish before time is called, you may check your work on this section only. Do not turn to any other section in the test.

NO TEST MATERIAL ON THIS PAGE.

Time—15 Minutes
13 Questions

For each question in this section, select the best answer from among the choices given and fill in the corresponding oval on the answer sheet.

The two passages below are followed by questions based on their content and on the relationship between the two passages. Answer the questions on the basis of what is <u>stated</u> or <u>implied</u> in the passages and in any introductory material that may be provided.

Questions 1–13 are based on the following passages.

The following passages deal with the question of air pollution. Passage 1 gives a broad historical overview, and passage 2 discusses one type of pollutant.

Passage 1

Even before there were people, there were cases of air pollution. Volcanoes erupted, spewing ash and poisonous gases into the atmosphere. There
Line were dust storms. Gases collected over marshes.
5 When people appeared on the scene and began their conquest of nature, they also began to pollute the air. They cleared land, which made possible even larger dust storms. They built cities, and the soot from their hearths and the stench from their waste filled the
10 air. The Roman author Seneca wrote in A.D. 61 of the "stink, soot and heavy air" of the imperial city. In 1257, the Queen of England was forced to move away from the city of Nottingham because the heavy smoke was unendurable.
15   The industrial revolution brought even worse air pollution. Coal was burned to power factories and to heat homes. Soot, smoke, and sulfur dioxide filled the air. The good old days? Not in the factory towns. But there were large rural areas unaffected by air
20 pollution.
  With increasing population, the entire world is becoming more urban. It is the huge megalopolises that are most affected by air pollution. But rural areas are not unaffected. In the neighborhoods
25 around smoky factories, there is evidence of increased rates of spontaneous abortion and of poor wool quality in sheep, decreased egg production and high mortality in chickens, and increased food and care required for cattle. The giant Ponderosa pines
30 are dying over a hundred miles from the smog-plagued Los Angeles basin. Orbiting astronauts visually traced drifting blobs of Los Angeles smog as far east as western Colorado. Other astronauts, over 100 kilometers up, were able to see the plume
35 of smoke from the Four Corners power plant near

Farmington, New Mexico. This was the only evidence from that distance that Earth is inhabited.
  Traffic police in Tokyo have to wear gas masks and take "oxygen breaks"—breathing occasionally
40 from tanks of oxygen. Smog in Athens at times has forced factory closings and traffic restrictions. Acid rain in Canada is spawned by air pollution in the United States, contributing to strained relationships between the two countries. Sydney, Rome, Tehran,
45 Ankara, Mexico City, and most other major cities in the world have had frightening episodes of air pollution.

Passage 2

One of the two major types of smog—consisting of smoke, fog, sulfur dioxide, sulfuric acid (H_2SO_4),
50 ash, and soot—is called London smog. Indeed, the word smog is thought to have originated in England in 1905 as a contraction of the words "smoke" and "fog."
  Probably the most notorious case of smog in
55 history started in London on Thursday, 4 December, 1952. A large cold air mass moved into the valley of the Thames River. A temperature inversion placed a blanket of warm air over the cold air. With nightfall, a dense fog and below-freezing temperatures caused
60 the people of London to heap coal into their small stoves. Millions of these fires burned throughout the night, pouring sulfur dioxide and smoke into the air. The next day, Friday, the people continued to burn coal when the temperature remained below freezing.
65 The factories added their smoke and chemical fumes to the atmosphere.
  Saturday was a day of darkness. For twenty miles around London, no light came through the smog. The air was cold and still. And the coal fires
70 continued to burn throughout the weekend. On Monday, 8 December, more than one hundred people died of heart attacks while trying desperately to breathe. The city's hospitals were overflowing with patients with respiratory diseases.

GO ON TO THE NEXT PAGE

75 By the time a breeze cleared the air on Tuesday,
9 December, more than 4,000 deaths had been
attributed to the smog. This is more people than
were ever killed in any single tornado, mine disaster,
shipwreck, or airplane crash. This is more people
80 than were killed in the attack on Pearl Harbor in
1941. Air pollution episodes may not be as dramatic
as other disasters, but they can be just as deadly.
   Soot and ash can be removed by electrostatic
precipitators. These devices induce an electric
85 charge on the particles, which then are attracted
to oppositely charged plates and deposited.
Unfortunately, electrostatic precipitators use large
amounts of electricity, and the electrical energy has
to come from somewhere. Fly ash removed from
90 the air has to be put on the land or water, although
it could be used in some way. Increasingly, fly ash
is being used to replace part of the clay in making
cement.
   The elimination of sulfur dioxide is more difficult.
95 Low-sulfur coal is scarce and expensive. The most
plentiful fuel that exists is low-grade, high-sulfur
coal. Pilot runs have shown that sulfur can be
washed from finely pulverized coal, but the process
is expensive. There are also processes for converting
100 dirty coal to clean liquid and gaseous fuels. These
processes may hold promise for the future, but they
are too expensive to compete economically with
other fuels at present. They also waste a part of the
coal's energy.

1. Passage 1 implies that air pollution
   (A) was originally caused by the industrial
       revolution
   (B) affects only urban areas
   (C) has natural as well as manmade causes
   (D) can be eliminated through the use of better
       fuels
   (E) seriously affects the nervous systems of both
       people and animals

2. The author of Passage 1 uses both the Roman
   author Seneca and the Queen of England (lines
   10–14) as evidence that
   (A) civilization has necessarily caused air
       pollution
   (B) air pollution was troublesome in early cities
   (C) urban air pollution is not just a modern
       problem
   (D) humanity disregards its environment
   (E) recently, the level of air pollution has risen
       dramatically

3. The orbiting astronauts are discussed by the author
   (lines 31–36) in order to
   (A) demonstrate the increased urbanization of
       modern civilization
   (B) prove that air pollution is an inevitable
       consequence of human progress
   (C) support the claim that pollution has become
       the defining characteristic of modern
       society
   (D) provide evidence that pollution is no longer
       restricted to urban areas
   (E) further the argument that large urban areas are
       most affected by air pollution

4. The last paragraph of Passage 1 suggests that air
   pollution causes all of the following EXCEPT
   (A) difficulties in international relations
   (B) otherwise unnecessary closings of businesses
   (C) changes in the quality of some water
   (D) changes in work habits
   (E) high levels of lung disease

5. The evidence of pollution offered in Passage 1
   provides support for which one of the following
   claims?
   (A) If society continues along the same path of
       development, air pollution will most likely
       continue to increase.
   (B) If nothing is done to control air pollution,
       civilization will eventually destroy both
       itself and its environment.
   (C) Unless society decentralizes its major
       urban regions, these areas will become
       uninhabitable.
   (D) If all the major industrialized nations cannot
       agree to control pollution, none will be able
       to succeed.
   (E) Only if society can learn how to control
       pollution will society be able to continue to
       grow.

GO ON TO THE NEXT PAGE

6. The author of Passage 2 discusses the 1952 out-
    break of London smog in order to

    (A) demonstrate that smog has serious effects that
        are not controllable by human action
    (B) point out that air pollution is a major threat to
        human health in the long run
    (C) describe an example of the lethal potential of
        air pollution
    (D) support the claim that air pollution must be
        controlled
    (E) prove that the toxic effects of air pollution
        are far worse in Europe than in the United
        States

7. According to Passage 2, London smog can best be
    described as

    (A) a deadly type of air pollution that cannot be
        completely eliminated
    (B) a phenomenon responsible for more deaths
        than from any other natural cause
    (C) a combination of fog conditions and heavy
        accumulations of smoke from fossil fuel
        fires
    (D) a threat to human health that we are often
        unaware of
    (E) a new, mostly uninvestigated, type of air
        pollution

8. The statistics cited in lines 75–82 imply that

    (A) any effects of a serious air pollution episode
        cannot be seen until some time after the
        episode
    (B) in the short run, air pollution can only produce
        non-traumatic health problems
    (C) approximately half the fatalities from air
        pollution may not occur during an air
        pollution episode
    (D) air pollution episodes can be among the most
        devastating types of disasters
    (E) it is impossible to know the total death rate
        from a given episode of air pollution

9. Passage 2 suggests that electrostatic precipitators
    work by a process in which

    (A) electricity is attracted to particles
    (B) charged particles are attracted to plates with
        the opposite charge
    (C) a large amount of electricity ionizes the air
    (D) induction acts on charged particles
    (E) ash and soot are naturally charged particles

10. The author of Passage 2 believes that the removal
    of sulfur dioxide from air pollution is difficult
    because

    (A) the technology to remove sulfur dioxide is
        only currently in development
    (B) any successful process utilizes more natural
        resources than it produces
    (C) sulfur is made up of very resilient molecules
        that cannot be broken down easily
    (D) the available methods are costly and involve
        some waste
    (E) sulfur is a basic compound in all fuels that are
        currently used

11. It can be inferred that the author of Passage 1
    would agree with which statement about the cost of
    pollution control discussed in Passage 2?

    (A) Society must be prepared to spend whatever it
        takes to eliminate all forms of air pollution.
    (B) The cost of pollution control is too high to
        make it economically efficient with current
        technology.
    (C) We should not be concerned with limiting the
        effects of pollution but rather we should try
        to eliminate the sources of pollution.
    (D) Dealing with pollution can be a significant
        challenge for urban populations.
    (E) The cost of pollution control is much higher
        than the cost of changing to better energy
        sources.

GO ON TO THE NEXT PAGE

12. Which factor mentioned in Passage 1 contributed to the environmental disaster described in Passage 2?

(A) The industrial revolution
(B) Natural sources of air pollution
(C) Land clearing
(D) Heavy smoke from Nottingham
(E) Improper disposal of solid waste

13. The author of Passage 1 and the author of Passage 2 would most likely agree that

(A) air pollution is the foremost problem facing modern civilization
(B) pollution can be controlled using manmade scientific techniques
(C) air pollution represents a serious threat to human life
(D) air pollution is no longer solely a problem of urban areas
(E) air pollution control is too costly to implement at the current time

STOP
**If you finish before time is called, you may check your work on this section only.
Do not turn to any other section in the test.**

PRACTICE TEST 3 ANSWERS

Section 1	Section 2	Section 3	Section 4	Section 5	Section 6	Section 7
1. A	1. A	1. C	1. A	1. E	1. D	1. C
2. A	2. B	2. B	2. C	2. B	2. C	2. C
3. E	3. D	3. D	3. D	3. E	3. C	3. D
4. E	4. C	4. B	4. A	4. D	4. A	4. E
5. B	5. A	5. A	5. E	5. B	5. B	5. A
6. B	6. D	6. A	6. B	6. A	6. B	6. C
7. C	7. E	7. C	7. C	7. B	7. A	7. C
8. B	8. A	8. B	8. E	8. C	8. D	8. D
9. C	9. C	9. A	9. D	9. C	9. B	9. B
10. C	10. A	10. D	10. B	10. E	10. E	10. D
11. E	11. D	11. D	11. A	11. D		11. D
12. B	12. C	12. C	12. D	12. B		12. A
13. A	13. B	13. A	13. A	13. A		13. C
14. D	14. E	14. D	14. C	14. B		
15. C	15. E	15. C	15. B	15. A		
16. A	16. C	16. 20	16. E	16. D		
17. D	17. C	17. 75	17. D	17. D		
18. B	18. B	18. 34	18. D	18. C		
19. B	19. B	19. 4	19. E	19. E		
20. C	20. E	20. 1600	20. E	20. A		
21. D	21. D	21. 1.65	21. B	21. C		
22. A	22. E	22. 91	22. B	22. B		
23. C	23. A	23. 80	23. C	23. A		
24. A	24. E	24. 1.25	24. E	24. D		
25. E	25. A	25. 9	25. E	25. E		
	26. B		26. E	26. A		
	27. D		27. D	27. B		
	28. A		28. C	28. C		
	29. B		29. A	29. A		
	30. D		30. C	30. A		
			31. C	31. D		
			32. E	32. E		
			33. C	33. C		
			34. E	34. D		
			35. A	35. C		

You will find a detailed explanation for each question beginning on page 519.

HOW TO SCORE YOUR PRACTICE TEST

VERBAL

After you have checked your answers to the practice test against the key, you can calculate your score. For the three Verbal sections (sections 2, 5, and 7), tally up the number of correct answers and the number of incorrect answers. Enter these numbers on the worksheet on the next page. Multiply the number of incorrect answers by $\frac{1}{4}$ and subtract the result from the number of correct answers. Put this number in box A. Then round the numbers to the nearest whole number and place it in box B.

MATHEMATICS

Figuring your Math score is a little trickier, because some of the questions have five answer choices, some have four, and some have none. In Sections 1 and 6, count the number of correct answers and incorrect answers. Enter these numbers on the worksheet. Multiply the number of incorrect answers by $\frac{1}{4}$ and subtract this from the number of correct answers. Put the result in box C.

Count the number of correct and incorrect answers in Section 3, questions 1–15. (Choice E counts as a blank.) Enter these on the worksheet. Multiply the number of incorrect answers by $\frac{1}{3}$ and subtract this from the number of correct answers. Put the result in box D.

Count up the number of correct answers in Section 3, questions 16–25. Put the result in box E. There is no penalty for incorrect grid-in questions.

Note: Section 4 is experimental and should not be scored.

Add up the numbers in boxes C, D, and E, and write the result in box F.

Round F to the nearest whole number, and place the result in box G.

WORKSHEET FOR CALCULATING YOUR SCORE

VERBAL

	Correct	Incorrect	
A. Sections 2, 5, and 7	_____ – (1/4 × _____) =		A
B. Total rounded Verbal raw score			B

MATHEMATICS

	Correct	Incorrect	
C. Sections 1 and 6	_____ – (1/4 × _____) =		C
D. Section 3 (Questions 1–15)	_____ – (1/3 × _____) =		D
E. Section 3 (Questions 16–25)	_____ =		E
F. Total unrounded Math raw score (C + D + E)			F
G. Total rounded Math raw score			G

Use the table on the next page to convert your raw score to scaled scores. For example, a raw Verbal score of 39 corresponds to a Verbal scaled score of 530; a Math raw score of 24 corresponds to a Math scaled score of 470.

Scores on the SAT range from 200 to 800.

Note: Since Section 4 is the experimental section, it does not count toward your score.

SCORE CONVERSION TABLE

Raw Score	Verbal Scaled Score	Math Scaled Score	Raw Score	Verbal Scaled Score	Math Scaled Score
78	800		36	510	560
77	800		35	510	550
76	800		34	500	540
75	800		33	490	530
74	780		32	480	520
73	760		31	480	520
72	750		30	470	510
71	740		29	460	500
70	740		28	460	490
69	730		27	450	480
68	720		26	450	480
67	710		25	440	480
66	700		24	430	470
65	690		23	430	460
64	680		22	420	450
63	670		21	410	440
62	670		20	400	430
61	660		19	390	430
60	660	800	18	380	430
59	650	790	17	380	420
58	640	770	16	370	410
57	640	760	15	360	400
56	630	740	14	350	390
55	620	730	13	350	390
54	620	720	12	340	380
53	610	700	11	330	370
52	600	690	10	310	350
51	600	680	9	300	340
50	600	660	8	290	340
49	590	650	7	270	330
48	590	650	6	270	310
47	580	640	5	230	300
46	570	630	4	230	300
45	570	620	3	230	280
44	560	610	2	230	260
43	560	600	1	230	250
42	550	600	0	230	240
41	550	590	−1	230	220
40	540	580	−2	230	220
39	530	570	−3	230	200
38	530	560	−4	230	200
37	520	560	−5 and below	230	200

21

Answers and Explanations for Practice Test 3

What follows is a detailed explanation for each question on Practice Test 3. Although you will naturally be more curious about the questions you got wrong, don't forget to read the explanations for the questions you left blank. In fact, you should even read the explanations for the questions you got right! Our explanations present the safest, most direct solution to each question. Even though you may have gotten a question right, that does not mean you solved it in the most efficient way.

1. ETS's answer is A.

   To solve for y, we should start by moving all the ys to one side of the equation. If we subtract $4y$ from each side, we get

   $$8 = 8y + 24$$

   Now let's subtract 24 from each side of the equation, to give us

   $$-16 = 8y$$

   Finally we should divide each side by 8, which gives us

   $$-2 = y$$

2. ETS's answer is A.

   Since it's much easier working with numbers than with variables, let's plug in some consecutive multiples of 5. Let's say that $a = 5$, $b = 10$, $c = 15$, and $d = 20$. The question then asks for the value of $(a - c)(d - b)$. Using the numbers we just plugged in, this becomes $(5 - 15)(20 - 10)$, or $(-10)(10)$, which equals -100.

3. ETS's answer is E.

   Let's start by finding the amount per bulb when bought in a pack of 6: If you can buy 6 bulbs for $30, then each bulb will cost $30 ÷ 6, or $5. In a box of 12, each bulb will cost $48 ÷ 12, or $4.

   Now we need to figure out the percentage difference between $5 and $4. The formula for percentage difference is $\dfrac{difference}{original}$. In this case, a reduction from $5 to $4 is a difference of $1 over an original price of $5. So the percentage difference is $\dfrac{1}{5}$, or 20 percent.

4. ETS's answer is E.

   One of the safest ways to solve this problem is by Plugging In the answer choices. While we normally start with choice C, we don't want to forget that this is an EXCEPT question, so let's just start with choice A and go straight through to choice E. Assume $x = 20$. Is the remainder when 20 is divided by 5 the same as the remainder when 20 is divided by 4? Sure, the remainder is 0 in each case. So we can cross off choice A. (This is an EXCEPT question, don't forget!). How about choice B? If $x = 21$, is the remainder the same? Yes, the remainder is 1 when 21 is divided by 4 and when it is divided by 5. How about choice C? If $x = 22$, the remainder is 2 when divided by 4 and when divided by 5. How about choice D? If $x = 23$, then the remainder is 3 when divided by 4 and when divided by 5. If $x = 24$, however, the remainder when 24 is divided by 4 is 0, while the remainder when 24 is divided by 5 is 4. So E is our answer.

5. ETS's answer is B.

   This is another good problem for Plugging In the answer choices. Again, we'd normally start with choice C, but in this case we're looking for the smallest integer possible, so we'd be better off starting on the low end with choice A. If $n = -5$, then $n^4 = 625$. This is not less than 605, so we can eliminate choice A. How about choice B? If $n = -4$, then $n^4 = 256$. Therefore B is our answer.

6. ETS's answer is B.

   Whenever you see variables in the answer choices, you must plug in. Let's start by Plugging In a number for x. If $x = 10$, then 3 more than 10 is 13. Now you know that 13 is 2 more than y, so $y = 11$. This is your target answer. When you plug in 11 for y in all the answer choices, choice B is the only one that works.

7. ETS's answer is C.

Let's start by figuring out what the vales of x and y could be. We know that $4x - 8 > 0$. If we add 8 to each side of the equation, we get

$$4x > 8$$

which means that $x > 2$. So x could be 3, 3.5, 4, or any value larger than 2. Likewise, we know that $4y + 8 < 0$. If we subtract 8 from each side of this equation, we get

$$4y < -8$$

which means that $y < -2$. So y could be -3, -3.5, -4, or any value less than -2. Neither x nor y can be zero, so the product xy cannot be zero. This means we can eliminate choice E. And since we don't know whether x and y are odd or even (or even that they are integers) we can also eliminate choices A and B. We do know, though, that x will always be positive and y will always be negative, so whatever numbers x and y are, we know their product will always be negative.

8. ETS's answer is B.

If a rectangle has length 16 and width 6, then its area will be the length times the width, or 16×6, which equals 96. If this is 3 times the area of a triangle, then the triangle will have an area of 32.

If a triangle with area 32 has height of 8, we can use the triangle formula: $\frac{1}{2} \times base \times height = area$, so $base \times 4 = 32$. This means that the base is equal to 8.

9. ETS's answer is C.

Remember to use the Average Pie: We know that the average is 14, and that the number of elements we have is 5. The Average Pie shows us that the total of these items must be equal to 70. So $70 = a + b + 6 + a + b$. If we subtract 6 from each side of the equation, we get $a + b + a + b = 64$. This means that $2a + 2b = 64$. Now we can just divide the whole thing by 2 to get $a + b = 32$.

10. ETS's answer is C.

Let's multiply out what we have in parentheses using FOIL. This gives us $9 + 3\sqrt{x} - 3\sqrt{x} + x$, or $9 + x$. So our equation now reads $9 + x = 7$. This makes $x = 2$.

11. ETS's answer is E.

Don't assume that the figure $ABCD$ must be a rectangle; it doesn't have to be. All we need to do here is follow the rules: We know that $AB = BC$ and that $BC = 12$, so we now know two of the four sides (sides AB and BC) are equal to 12. We know that AD is going to be one-quarter of AB, so AD must be equal to 3. Finally, we know that AD is one-half of CD, so CD must be equal to 6. This makes the total perimeter $12 + 12 + 3 + 6$, or 33.

12. ETS's answer is B.

The best way to solve digit problems is by Plugging In the answer choices. Let's start with choice C. If $A = 4$, then we get $48 \times 43 = 2,064$. Since we need a three-digit result, this is too big; eliminate choices C, D and E. Let's try choice B; if $A = 2$, then we get $28 \times 23 = 84 + 560 = 644$. All of the digits make sense ($A = 2$, $B = 4$, $C = 6$), so B is the answer.

13. ETS's answer is A.

Let's take this one step at a time. First, just concentrate on the right side: $3b + 3 \leq 18$. We can simply treat this just like an equation: if we subtract 3 from each side, we get $3b \leq 15$. Now we can divide 3 from each side to get $b \leq 5$. This will allow us to eliminate choices B and E. Now let's focus on the left side: $-9 \leq 3b + 3$. Again, let's subtract 3 from each side, which gives us $-12 \leq 3b$. By dividing 3 from each side, we get $-4 \leq b$. This will eliminate choices C and D, so our answer must be A.

14. ETS's answer is D.

    We know that any two sides of a triangle must have a sum which is larger than the third side. This means that whatever the third side of the triangle is, its value + 5 must be larger than 7. This means that the third side must be larger than 2. Since the question specifies that the third side has an integer value, the smallest integer larger than 2 is 3. So the third side will measure 3, and the perimeter will be $3 + 5 + 7 = 15$.

15. ETS's answer is C.

    Since AC and BC are each radii of the circle, we know they are equal. This means that the triangle ABC must be isosceles, and the base and the height are equal. What base and height would give the triangle an area of 18? The base and height would each have to be equal to 6. Since the circumference of the circle is equal to $2\pi r$, the circumference will be equal to $12\pi r$.

16. ETS's answer is A.

    Remember that the mode is the number that appears most often in a list. The number that appears most often (17 times) in the rainfall chart is 0.

17. ETS's answer is D.

    If we add up the amount of rainfall accounted for in the chart, this makes:

    5 days of 1 inch = 5 total inches of rain
    3 days of 2 inches = 6 total inches of rain
    3 days of 3 inches = 9 total inches of rain
    2 days of 4 inches = 8 total inches of rain

    for a grand total of 28 inches. If we expect 200 inches in a year, what percent of 200 is 28 inches?

    Translate this into algebra as $\frac{x}{100} \times 200 = 28$, and

    we get $x = 14\%$.

18. ETS's answer is B.

    One good way to approach this question is to place each choice into a ratio of r to s and see which gives us $\frac{5}{6}$. For choice A, is zero over $\frac{5}{6}$ equal to $\frac{5}{6}$? Nope. How about choice B? Is $\frac{\frac{5}{2}}{3}$ equal to $\frac{5}{6}$? Yes, it is, so B is our answer.

19. ETS's answer is B.

    To work with a strange figure, try to break it up into figures you know. If we draw a line across the middle of this figure, we can break it into a rectangle and a triangle. The rectangle will be 8 by 5, and the triangle will have a base of 8 and a hypotenuse of 10. The area of the rectangle is 8 times 5, or 40. We can figure out the area of the triangle by finding its height. If you recognize a 6:8:10 triangle as one of the Pythagorean triples, you'll know that the height of the triangle must be 6. So the area of the triangle is $\frac{1}{2} \times 6 \times 8$, or 24. Therefore the area of the whole figure is 40 + 24, or 64.

20. ETS's answer is C.

    A good rule of thumb on the SAT is: if it looks like a quadratic equation, try to make it into a quadratic equation. If we try to solve for x, the best way is to move 12 to the same side of the equation, and then factor. $x^2 - x - 12 = 0$ will factor as $(x - 4)(x + 3)$. This means that x could be 4 or −3. We can factor for y in the same way, so y could also be 4 or −3. The greatest value for $x - y$ will be if $x = 4$ and $y = -3$, which is a difference of 7.

21. ETS's answer is D.

The easiest way to solve this problem is to get to a common rate. We know that one packer packs 15 boxes every 2 minutes, and the other packs 15 boxes every 3 minutes. If we put these in terms of 6-minute intervals, the first packer will pack 45 boxes in 6 minutes, while the other packs 30 every 6 minutes. This means that together they will pack 75 boxes in 6 minutes and 150 boxes in 12 minutes, and thus 300 boxes in 24 minutes.

22. ETS's answer is A.

If the probability of picking a blue jellybean is $\frac{1}{5}$ then we know that $\frac{1}{5}$ of the beans in the jar are blue. Let's try Plugging In the answer choices. If there are 78 blue jellybeans, then we would have a total of $58 + 78 + 78 = 214$ beans in the jar. Is 78 equal to $\frac{1}{5}$ of 214? Nope, so choice C cannot be right. Let's try choice B. If there are 56 blue jellybeans, then we would have a total of $58 + 78 + 56 = 192$ beans in the jar. Is 56 equal to $\frac{1}{5}$ of 192? Nope. So let's try choice A. If there are 34 blue jellybeans, then there will be a total of $58 + 78 + 34 = 170$ jellybeans. Is 34 equal to $\frac{1}{5}$ of 170? Yes, so A is our answer.

23. ETS's answer is C.

Choices B and D have negative values, so we can eliminate them right away. Let's start with the area of the whole figure. The square has a side of 2, so its area is 4. Now let's remove the area of the two semi-circles (which is the same as the area of one whole circle). These semi-circles have a radius of 1, so the area of one whole circle will be π. So the area of the shaded region will be $4 - \pi$.

24. ETS's answer is A.

Let's try Plugging In some numbers for this problem. Let's start by choosing 18 for x and 2 for y. This makes their product equal to 36, which is divisible by 36. We also made sure to pick a value for x which is divisible by 6. Using these numbers, let's look at Statements I, II, and III. Are they true? Statement I is not true, since 2 cannot be evenly divided by 18; since Statement I is not true, we can eliminate choices B and D. Now what about Statement II? It's also false, so we can cross off choices C and E. This means our answer must be A.

25. ETS's answer is E.

Let's plug in the answer choices, starting with C. 20 minutes is $\frac{1}{3}$ of an hour, so (using rate × time = distance) Jennifer ran $6 \times \frac{1}{3} = 2$ miles to school. If she returned at 4 miles per hour, we can find the time for her return trip from $4 \times t = 2$. Her return time is $\frac{1}{2}$ hour, or 30 minutes. Her total time is supposed to be one hour, but here it's only 50 minutes. Let's eliminate choices A, B, and C because they're too small. Let's skip to choice E; that multiple of 6 looks like it will work better with clock numbers than will 22. 24 minutes is $\frac{2}{5}$ of an hour, so Jennifer ran $6 \times \frac{2}{5} = 2.4$ miles to school. If she returned at 4 miles per hour, we can find the time for her return trip from $4 \times t = 2.4$. Her return time is $\frac{3}{5}$ hour, or 36 minutes. Her total time is indeed one hour, so E is the answer.

1. ETS's answer is A.

   For the second blank, a good clue is *rather quiet* combined with the trigger *while*. This tells us that whatever comes in the second blank must mean that she was the opposite of rather quiet; in fact, she must have liked being around people. This will allow us to eliminate choices C, D, and E. For the first blank, we need a word that goes along with the idea of being quiet. That makes B impossible, so our best answer is A.

2. ETS's answer is B.

   The key to this question is the semicolon; this trigger tells us that whatever follows the semicolon describes the word in the blank. What follows says that the exterior is different but the interior is the same. This would mean that a word like *superficial* or *decorative* should go in the blank. The closest choice is B.

3. ETS's answer is D.

   Even if you can't find an exact word for the first blank, you can probably tell that it's going to be a negative word because of the clue *natural weather patterns cannot be —— in the laboratory*. So the first blank is probably discussing a *problem* with meteorology. This will allow us to eliminate choices A, C, and E. What might be a problem with meteorology? Probably if natural weather patterns cannot be *studied* or *created* in a lab. This will eliminate choice B, and makes D our best answer.

4. ETS's answer is C.

   From the clue that today's works introduce fewer problems for readers, we know that the first blank should describe a problem of seventeenth-century literature—a word like *difficult for readers*. This will eliminate A and E. For the second blank, we will need to say that it is *not difficult for readers*. Choices B and D don't really have anything to do with *reading,* so our best answer is C.

5. ETS's answer is A.

   In this sentence we have the contrasting ideas of *realism* and *fantasy* so the second blank should be a word like *real* that contrasts with the word *imaginary*. This eliminates choices B, C, and D. For the first blank, what kind of word would describe what a playwright could do in order to make the audience uncertain? That playwright might *combine* realism and fantasy. Therefore A is our best answer.

6. ETS's answer is D.

   For the first blank, we know that the word in the blank describes something it is *difficult* to do *within the confines of a corrupt society*, so the word in the first blank must be something like *just* or *upstanding*. Choice D works very well, but let's say you don't know the word *sanguine*. For the second blank, even though the task was *difficult*, Holmes continued to do it, so the word in the blank must be a word like *strive for*. This makes D our best choice.

7. ETS's answer is E.

   In this sentence the clue is *convincing her readers to believe*. This means that she must be able to create extremely *believable* characters. What word comes closest to this idea? E does.

8. ETS's answer is A.

   The clue in this sentence is *chosen in light of his extraordinary analytical skills*. This means that Jacobs was chosen for his intelligence, and not for some other reason. So the word we're looking for is a word that makes the opening part of the sentence say that Jacobs was *not* chosen for a silly reason, something like *meaningless*. This makes A our best answer.

9. ETS's answer is C.
This is a toughie. In this case, pay attention to the values of the words in the blanks. They need to be opposites; either educators view it as bad while it actually has the power to be good, or educators view it as good while ignoring the fact that it can be bad. Knowing this, we can eliminate any answer pairs whose words are not strongly opposed—choices such as A, B, D, and E. The only answer choice which contains two strongly opposed words is C.

10. ETS's answer is A.
It's probably easier to make a sentence with these words in reverse. A KNIFE is used to CUT. Is a *shovel* used to *dig*? Yes. Is a *lock* used to *fill*? No. Is a *screw* used to *twist*? Not quite—a screw is usually something that is twisted by a screwdriver. Is a *door* used to *open*? No. Is a *store* used to *buy*? While you might buy something at a store, you don't use a store to buy something. We've eliminated choices B, C, D, and E, so ETS's answer must be A.

11. ETS's answer is D.
A CHOREOGRAPHER is someone who directs a DANCER. Does an *athlete* direct a *coach*? Probably not—it's usually the other way around. Does a *playwright* direct a *line*? If not, we can eliminate choice B as well. Does a *mathematician* direct a *genius*? Nope, we can cross off choice C. Does a *conductor* direct a *musician*? Sure. Does a *sculptor* direct an *artist*? A sculptor is a kind of artist, so we can cross off choice E. This leaves us with D as our answer.

12. ETS's answer is C.
FROZEN is a characteristic of a TUNDRA. Is *deep* a characteristic of an *ocean*? Yeah, usually. Is *smoggy* a characteristic of a *metropolis*? Not necessarily. Is *arid* a characteristic of a *desert*? Yes. Is *towering* a characteristic of a *mountain*? Not always. Is *nocturnal* a characteristic of a *moon*? No, the moon can appear during the daytime. So we've eliminated choices B, D, and E. Let's make a more specific sentence: A *tundra* is a *frozen* environment. For A, deep doesn't really describe an ocean in the same way; acquatic would make more sense. C fits best.

13. ETS's answer is B.
Let's reverse the words: ARTIFACTS are displayed in a MUSEUM. Are *passengers* displayed in a *train*? No. Are *portraits* displayed in a *gallery*? Yes. Are *clowns* displayed in a *circus*? Sort of, but choice B is better. Are *patients* displayed in an *infirmary*? No. Are *architects* displayed in a *building*? No.

14. ETS's answer is E.
An IMPOSTER steals an IDENTITY. Does a *policeman* steal a *law*? Hopefully not. Does a *spy* steal a *border*? No. Does a *lawyer* steal a *client*? Not usually. Does a *singer* steal a *performance*? On exceptional nights you can say that someone "stole the show," but that's not part of the meaning of the word. Does a *plagiarist* steal an *idea*? Yes, that's exactly what a plagiarist does.

15. ETS's answer is E.
This is a hard analogy, so we may need to Work Backwards or resort to using Side of the Fence. If you know these words, you can make a sentence: UNFETTERED means to be freed from RESTRAINT. Likewise, in choice E, *exonerated* means to be freed from *blame*. However, even if you weren't sure of the words, you could have crossed out B and D, since these pairs have no good relationship.

16. ETS's answer is C.
Let's use POE to answer this question. Choices A and E are too extreme; eliminate these. Nowhere in the passage are Southeastern Indians described as either *threatening* or *unmotivated*, so eliminate choices B and D. Our best answer is C.

17. ETS's answer is C.
From the introductory blurb, we know that the passage is about the art and recreation of the Southeastern Indians. Choice A is too extreme. Choice B isn't the main purpose of the passage; in fact, no rules were explained. Choice D doesn't mention art and recreation; eliminate it. For choice E, the Cherokee Indians were mentioned only as a detail. This makes our best answer C.

SECTION 2

18. **ETS's answer is B.**
If we read about the *problem* in context, the passage says that we need to view the art and games *as the outward expressions of their belief system.* That is, we need to understand their beliefs to understand their art and recreation. Choice A is close to this, but it's too extreme, whereas B says precisely this.

19. **ETS's answer is B.**
In lines 30–31 the passage says that *the Southeastern Indians placed a high value on men who could use words skillfully.* This best supports choice B.

20. **ETS's answer is E.**
We know that the answer to this question will follow shortly after the answer to the previous question in the passage, so we know approximately where in the passage to look. In lines 37–38 the passage says that *the words of a gifted speaker... could move contentious men to reach consensus.* Choice E is a paraphrase of these lines.

21. **ETS's answer is D.**
In lines 45–48 the author says *even though we know much about the Southeastern Indian ball games, we do not know the precise nature of the social and political forces which led them to play it with such ferocity.* This best supports choice D.

22. **ETS's answer is E.**
From the introductory blurb we know that this passage is primarily about jazz. This means that B and C can't be the answer, so eliminate them. Choice A is just too narrow to be right; the passage is not primarily about three instrument melodies. Likewise, the New Orleans band is a detail of the passage, but not the main idea. After crossing off A and D, we are left with E.

23. **ETS's answer is A.**
The lead words here are *ragtime* and *brass bands*. We can find these mentioned on the first lines of the second paragraph. There it says that jazz *contains . . . elements that derive from older musical traditions.* A is a paraphrase of this idea.

24. **ETS's answer is E.**
This could be a time-consuming question, so save it for last. From answering the previous question, we know that the answers should be found in the second paragraph. There we can find A, B, C, and D mentioned. This means our answer must be E.

25. **ETS's answer is A.**
Since this question has a line reference, let's go to that line and read it in context. There the passage says that jazz tries to imitate blues by *recreating its singing style.* This best supports choice A.

26. **ETS's answer is B.**
In the previous question, we saw that the passage says that jazz tries to recreate the voices of people with their instruments. Lines 63–64 then say that *jazz uses the call-and-response style* with two solo instruments or a solo instrument and the ensemble. This means that the individual instruments are used like human voices, as though two of them were having a discussion. This makes B the best choice.

27. **ETS's answer is D.**
For a vocab-in-context question, cover the word you're being asked about, reread the sentence, and pick the word you think fits the blank. You'll probably pick a word like *interesting* or *distinctive.* Which choice comes closest to this idea? D does.

28. **ETS's answer is A.**
The lead words here are *exotic sound.* We can find these in the beginning of the final paragraph of the passage, which says that *the kinds of instruments used* and *the manner in which intonation is used* are characteristic of jazz. The best paraphrase of this idea is A.

29. ETS's answer is B.
   This is another vocab-in-context question. If we reread the passage at that point, we would probably put in a word like *notes*. Choice B comes closest to this idea.

30. ETS's answer is D.
   Since this question will take a lot of time, we should save it for last. We can find evidence that jazz was heavily influenced by ragtime, brass bands, and dance orchestras in the second paragraph. In the next-to-last paragraph we see evidence that it was heavily influenced by blues. This allows us to eliminate choices A, B, C, and E, which leaves D as our best answer.

1. ETS's answer is C.
   Start by crossing off D. You can certainly do the addition here and you'll find that the two columns are equal, but you don't actually have to add up these numbers. Remember that comparing the two sides is all you really need to do; each column has the same values in it, so the two sides must be equal.

2. ETS's answer is B.
   Cross off D. Probably the easiest way to do this is with your calculator: key in .02 × 200 and .01 × 800 and you'll get 4 on the left and 8 on the right.

3. ETS's answer is D.
   Since there are variables in this problem, let's plug in. To start, let's try some easy numbers. Let's plug in $a = 2$ and $b = 3$. In this case, column A is equal to 4 and column B is equal to 27. Since column B is larger than column A, we can cross off choices A and C. Now let's try some weird numbers. We know that a and b are both positive, so we can't use zero, but what if a and b are each equal to 1? In this case, column A is equal to 1 and column B is equal to 1. This means that we can cross off choice B, and the answer must be D.

4. ETS's answer is B.
   The figure is misleading because it isn't drawn to scale. Since lines 3 and 4 are parallel, and line 2 crosses them, we know that all of the large angles have the same measure and all of the small angles have the same measure. The angles adjacent to the angle of 70 degrees will measure 110 degrees. Angle x is one of the large angles, so it must measure 110. Therefore column B is larger.

5. ETS's answer is A.
   Since $PQRS$ is a square, we know that all the sides have the same measure. Since side QP goes from point $(4, 3)$ to $(4, 10)$, we know that QP measures 7. This means that all sides must measure 7. We can use this to figure out point R, since it must be 7 units from point Q. Point Q is at $(4, 10)$ and point R is 7 points further along the x-axis, so point R must be at $(11, 10)$. Therefore a is equal to 11.

6. ETS's answer is A.

   To figure out what column A equals, we'll need to use the formula $area = \pi r^2$. Since the area of circle J is 9π, we know that its radius must be 3. Since the area of circle L is 36π, we know that its radius must be 6. This makes column A equal to $\frac{3}{6}$, which is larger than column B.

7. ETS's answer is C.
   To see this, we'll need to multiply out the expressions in columns A and B. When we multiply out column A, we get $2xy - 4xy^2$. When we multiply out column B, we get $2xy - 4xy^2$. ETS often likes to hide similar expressions in complicated algebra, so be on the lookout for problems that look like they require a lot of work.

8. ETS's answer is B.
   Since we have variables in this problem, we should plug in. If we plug in $a = 2$, we'll be able to solve for b. Since $12a = 2b$, once we plug in $a = 2$, we know that b must be equal to 12. Now we can figure out c, since $15c = 5b$. This means that c will be equal to 4. Since c is larger, we can eliminate choices A and C. We can try Plugging In weird numbers, but since we can't use negatives or zero, the answer will always be B.

9. ETS's answer is A.
   Of course, ETS can't be looking for you to multiply by −3 all the way through to the 28th term in the sequence. Whenever you get a question that seems to require a lot of work, there must be a pattern. If you want to write out a few more numbers in the sequence to make sure that you understand the pattern, you can; you'll quickly see that every odd-numbered term is positive, and every even-numbered term is negative. This means that the 27th term will be positive, and the 28th term will be negative. This means that column A will be bigger than column B.

10. ETS's answer is D.

    Since we have variables in this question, we should plug in. We just have to make sure that we pick numbers that follow the rules in the problem: namely that $x + 4 > 2y$ and $z - y < 2y$. Let's start by Plugging In 6 for x, 3 for y, and 2 for z. These follow all the rules in the problem; in this case, column A is 8 and column B is 3. In this case, column A is larger so we can eliminate choices B and C. Can we pick different numbers and get a different answer? We can plug in 6 for x, 3 for y, and –6 for z. These numbers also follow the rules in the problem. In this case, column A is 0 and column B is 3. This makes D our answer.

11. ETS's answer is D.

    If we multiply out both sides of the equation, we get $9 - 6n = 9 - 6n$, which is true for any value of n. That is, n could be 1, but it could also be 0 or 2. We could also try Plugging In any number for n, and we find that the equation is always true. So n could be any number.

12. ETS's answer is C.

    First cross off D. The number of integers between 0 and 100 that are squares of an odd integer are very few: only 1^2, 3^2, 5^2, 7^2, 9^2, or 1, 9, 25, 49, and 81. So column B is 5. How many of these have a remainder of 1 when divided by 4? All of them do, so column A is also 5.

13. ETS's answer is A.

    What kind of integers could we plug in for x, y, and z that satisfy the statement $x < y < z < 3x$? We can't plug in a negative number or zero for x, because then we'd violate the condition that $x < 3x$. We can't plug in 1 for x, because then we'd have no way to pick integers y and z that were between 1 and 3. Therefore x must be larger than 1.

14. ETS's answer is D.

    This question has variables in it, so we should plug in. We simply have to obey the rules that $\dfrac{m}{n} = \dfrac{2}{3}$ and $n \neq 3$. Let's start with $m = 4$ and $n = 6$. In this case, column A becomes $\dfrac{7}{9}$, which is less than $\dfrac{5}{6}$, so we can eliminate A and C. Now let's try some weird numbers. How about $m = -6$ and $n = -9$? These satisfy the condition that $\dfrac{m}{n} = \dfrac{2}{3}$. In this case, column A becomes $\dfrac{-3}{-6}$, which is equal to $\dfrac{1}{2}$. This is larger than column B, so we can eliminate B, and our answer must be D.

15. ETS's answer is C.

    Whenever we have variables in a problem, we should plug in, so let's try that now. What if we make $q = 4$? According to the equation $\dfrac{q}{2} + 1 = m$, we know that m must be equal to 3. This makes column A and column B both equal to 12. So we can eliminate A and B. Now can we find a different number to plug in for q that gives us a different answer? How about zero? If $q = 0$, then $m = 1$. This makes column A and column B both equal to zero. Once again they're equal. Try a fraction, too; if we keep finding that the columns are equal, then we pick C.

16. ETS's answer is 20.

If we plug in 23 for x, then the equation becomes $23 - 8 = 5y$, or $15 = 5y$. This makes $y = 3$, so $x - y = 23 - 3$, or 20.

17. ETS's answer is 75.

Vanessa earned a total of $600 during these 8 weeks, since she made $100 per week for each of the six weeks she worked, and she made nothing the other two weeks. The question asks for the average for the whole 8 weeks. To find the average, we take the total she made over the 8 weeks, and divide by the number of weeks, which gives us

$\frac{600}{8}$, or 75.

18. ETS's answer is 34.

If a rectangle has a length of 5 and a diagonal of 13, this means that its other side must be 12, since 5:12:13 is a Pythagorean triple. Therefore the perimeter of the rectangle will be $5 + 12 + 5 + 12 = 34$.

19. ETS's answer is 4.

There are only 10 digits that B could be; the trick here is to make an educated guess rather than trying all ten possibilities. Since we know that 14,000 can be divided by 7, and we know that 700 can be divided by 7, the first three digits of the number 14,7B2 are actually irrelevant. We can just look at the last 2 digits alone. What digit would probably work for B? We know that 42 can be divided by 7, so it's a good bet that B is the digit 4. Try it in your calculator to verify.

20. ETS's answer is 1600.

If the area of the circle is 400π, then we can figure out its radius, which must be 20. The diameter of the circle is twice the radius, or 40. Since this circle is inscribed in the square, we know that the diameter of the circle is equal to one side of the square, so we know that each side is equal to 40. The area of the square is $40 \times 40 = 1600$.

21. ETS's answer is 1.65.

The best way to approach this problem is to set up an equation. There is some price such that if we add 3% of it, we get $56.65. This means that we can set up an equation: $x + 3\%$ of $x = 56.65$. Now we can just solve for x, and we get that the original price was $55 and the tax $1.65.

22. ETS's answer is 91.

Let's begin by using our Average Pie. If her average on 6 tests was 92, then we know that her total score on all six tests must be $92 \times 6 = 552$. Two of those tests have scores that add up to 188; if we remove those two tests, the other four tests must have a sum which adds up to $552 - 188$, or 364. So the average of these four tests will be $364 \div 4$, or 91.

23. ETS's answer is 80.

We know that the total number of students is 320. Since we know that there are 60 more juniors than seniors, the easy way to find out how many of each there is is to take half of 320 (which is 160) and then add half of 60 to get the number of juniors, and subtract half of 60 to get the number of seniors. This means that the number of juniors is 190 and the number of seniors is 130. (Their difference is 60 and their sum is 320.) So there are 190 juniors. Knowing that there are 30 more female juniors than male juniors, we can find out the number of male juniors the same way—take half of 190 (which is 95) and subtract half of 30. $95 - 15 = 80$.

24. ETS's answer is 1.25.

Let's say the area of *ABCD* = 4. Since the area of the shaded region is one-quarter of this, it will have area 1. Then the rectangle *EFGH* will have a total area of 5. So the $\dfrac{\text{area of } EFGH}{\text{area of } ABCD}$ will be equal to $\dfrac{5}{4}$ or 1.25.

25. ETS's answer is 9.

This looks suspiciously like a quadratic equation, and if we multiply it out it's equivalent to $b^2 - a^2$. We want to make this as large as possible, so we want b^2 to be large and a^2 to be small. If $b = -3$, $b^2 = 9$; if $a = 0$, $a^2 = 0$. So $b^2 - a^2$ can be as large as 9.

SECTION 4

1. ETS's answer is A.
   The clue is *comparable*; the trade was fair or equitable.

2. ETS's answer is C.
   The clue is *entirely implausible*. A good word for the blank might be falsehood.

3. ETS's answer is D.
   A good clue for this blank is *brevity*—the sentence says that the article's brevity didn't detract from its importance, so we know that the article was brief. What is another word for brief? D is.

4. ETS's answer is A.
   This sentence starts with the trigger *while*. So we know that the two blanks need to be contrasting ideas. The only pair that has a strong opposite relationship is choice A.

5. ETS's answer is E.
   For the second blank, we know that the defendant *refused to acknowledge* so the word in the blank must be something like *resist*. This eliminates B, C, and D. Now for the first blank. We have the trigger word *but* in the middle of the sentence, so the first blank must mean the opposite of *resist*. This makes E the best choice.

6. ETS's answer is B.
   The clue here is *combines elements of Byzantine, Greek, Roman, and Gothic*. We need a word that means *combines different elements*. The word which best matches this is B.

7. ETS's answer is C.
   The clue here is *relatively subtle*. This combined with the trigger word *though* means that the second blank should be the opposite of subtle. The opposite of subtle would be *blunt* or *obvious*. Which word best matches this idea? Choice C does.

8. ETS's answer is E.
   Here we have a great clue: *reduced the population substantially*. So we need a word that means *very deadly*. The choice that most nearly means this is E.

9. ETS's answer is D.
   For the second blank we know that there was an *increasing appreciation* for her work, so the blunders must have been *unimportant* or *insignificant*. This will allow us to eliminate choices A, C, and E. The trigger word *but* tells us that the first blank should be opposed to this idea, so the first blank should say that she was hurt by the missteps. This makes D the best choice.

10. ETS's answer is B.
    Let's look at the relationship between the blanks. We could be looking for a pair of words like *happy* and *harm*, or we could be looking for a pair like *sad* and *good*. So we're looking for opposites. Eliminate A, C, D, and E.

11. ETS's answer is A.
    MARBLE is shaped by a SCULPTOR. Is *clay* shaped by a *potter*? Yes. Is a *typewriter* shaped by a *poet*? No. Is a *blueprint* shaped by *technician*? No. Is a *wrench* shaped by a *plumber*? No. Is an *ocean* shaped by a *sailor*? No. So A is the answer.

12. ETS's answer is D.
    A SILO is something that stores GRAIN. Does a *chorus* store a *soprano*? A soprano might be one of its members, but we can't really say that a chorus stores a soprano. Does a *loft* store a *barn*? Does a *saddle* store a *horse*? Does an *armory* store a *weapon*? Yes. Does a *doctor* store a *hospital*? No. So D is the answer.

13. ETS's answer is A.
    A CARICATURE is a humorous PORTRAIT. Is *satire* humorous *writing*? Absolutely. Is a *misfortune* a humorous *comedy*? Nope. Is an *attack* a humorous *enemy*? No. Is a *comedian* a humorous *joke*? That doesn't make any sense. Is a *deception* a humorous *hoax*? Nope. So A is our answer.

14. ETS's answer is C.
Someone VULNERABLE is easily DEFEATED. Is someone *oblivious* easily *educated*? Not especially. Is someone *impulsive* easily *detached*? No. Is someone *audible* easily *heard*? Yes. Is someone *accessible* easily *delayed*? Not really. Is someone *irrational* easily *believed*? Definitely not. So C is our best answer.

15. ETS's answer is B.
LAX means lacking FIRMNESS. Does *frugal* mean lacking *money*? Not quite—it means unwilling to spend money. Does *pretentious* mean lacking *modesty*? Yes. Does *disgruntled* mean lacking *resentment*? Exactly the opposite—it means having a lot of resentment. Does *pivotal* mean lacking *essence*? Nope. Does *detrimental* mean lacking *harm*? Exactly the opposite—it means causing harm. So B is our answer.

16. ETS's answer is E.
A SECTOR is a part of a CIRCLE. Is a *dormitory* a part of a *student*? Nope. Is a *calculation* part of a *computer*? A computer might make a calculation, but a calculation isn't a piece of a computer. Is a *construction* part of a *builder*? No. Is a *sphere* part of an *influence*? You might know the phrase "sphere of influence" but this isn't a defining sentence. Don't be tempted by math vocab. Is a *province* part of a *country*? Yes, so E is our answer.

17. ETS's answer is D.
An ITINERARY is a plan for a JOURNEY. Is a *figure* a plan for *accounting*? No, they are used in accounting but they aren't a plan. Is a *schematic* a plan for a *blueprint*? Nope, though a blueprint is a plan for something else. Is *employment* a plan for a *career*? You might plan to be employed, but an employment isn't itself a plan for anything. Is an *agenda* a plan for a *meeting*? Yes. Is an *application* a plan for a *business*? No, so D is ETS's answer.

18. ETS's answer is D.
An ANTHOLOGY is a collection of WORKS. Is a *program* a collection of *editions*? Nope. Is a *qualification* a collection of *abilities*? A qualification might be an ability, but it's not a collection of abilities. Is a *director* a collection of *films*? Definitely not. Is a *lexicon* a collection of *words*? Absolutely. Is an *orchestra* a collection of *symphonies*? No. An orchestra plays symphonies. Pick D.

19. ETS's answer is E.
A DELUGE FLOWS strongly. Does *water evaporate* strongly? No. Does an *orbit revolve* strongly? No. Does a *defense disarm* strongly? No. Does a *beam reflect* strongly? No. Does a *conflagration burn* strongly? Yes. Finally!

20. ETS's answer is E.
To REFUTE is to disprove a THEORY. Does to *verify* mean to disprove an *idea*? No, exactly the opposite. Does to *approve* mean to disprove a *plan*? No, also the opposite. Does to *substitute* mean to disprove a *corollary*? Nope. Does to *integrate* mean to disprove a *resource*? That doesn't sound right. Does to *debunk* mean to disprove a *myth*? Exactly.

21. ETS's answer is B.
An IOTA is a very small AMOUNT. Is an *aroma* a very small *smell*? Nope. Is a *sliver* a very small *portion*? Yes. Is a *blade* a very small *grass*? Nope. Is a *shoe* a very small *pair*? Nope. Is a *notch* a very small *belt*? Nope.

22. ETS's answer is B.
These are difficult words, so if you're not sure of them, you can Work Backwards or skip this question. If you know the words in A and C, you can eliminate these choices, since they really don't have defining sentences. To DEBASE means to cause DEGRADATION. Likewise, to *abash* means to cause *embarrassment*.

23. ETS's answer is C.
Even if you're not sure of the words here, if you try Working Backwards, you can probably eliminate B, D, and E since these words have no defining relationships. Then you can guess from among the remaining choices. Someone VAIN likes FLATTERY. Similarly, someone *gregarious* likes *company*.

24. ETS's answer is E.
Just following these lines the author says that his family felt *a smug sympathy for those poor souls in harsher climates who had to suffer real winters.* This means that he was discussing the warmth of the weather he was used to. Choice E is the best paraphrase of this idea.

25. ETS's answer is E.
For a vocab-in-context question, we should cover the word in question, reread the line, and put our own word into the blank. In this case, we'd probably use a word like *unhappy*. The closest choice is E.

26. ETS's answer is E.
If we read these lines in context, we see that they are followed by a list of problems that the wind causes: uprooted trees, overturned cars, and the like. These all illustrate how powerful and destructive the wind is, which best supports E.

27. ETS's answer is D.
Here we have another vocab-in-context question. If we cover up the word *baleful* and try to use our own word in its place, we'd probably choose a word like *destructive*. Which choice comes closest to this idea? D does.

28. ETS's answer is C.
In the previous lines, the author discusses how certain people complained about the wind in Provence, and that they would think differently *if they had to put up with the gales that come off the English Channel.* The author is thereby saying that the gales off the English Channel are worse than anything in Provence. This best supports C.

29. ETS's answer is A.
For this question we know from lines 46–48 that Menicucci was concerned that *the pipes burst... under the pressure of the water that had frozen in them overnight*, we also know that Menicucci was a plumber (so he would naturally be working on the pipes). These best support A.

30. ETS's answer is C.
If we reread the description of Menicucci carefully, we see in line 63 that *He was short and compact, built for plumbing....* This supports choice C. While choices A and E have some support (he does seem solemn) there is no evidence that he has only a passing interest in plumbing, or that he was a hardened man, so we can eliminate these two choices. There is also no reason to believe that he is incompetent, so choice D can be crossed off. Therefore C is our best choice.

31. ETS's answer is C.
In the first lines of the next-to-last paragraph, we find Menicucci clearly expounding on his theory of why the winds were so bitterly cold. He therefore thinks he knows the answer, which allows us to eliminate choices B, D, and E. Choice A is extreme, so we should avoid it as well. This leaves us with C as our best choice.

32. ETS's answer is E.
This is a tough question, so we should expect to solve it by POE. From the next-to-last paragraph we know that Menicucci thinks that the harsher wind was due to a flattening of the curvature of the earth, which enabled *the wind to take a more direct route south* from Siberia to Provence. Since the pipes have nothing to do with this question, choice A should be crossed off. B, C, and D look tempting but if you reread the paragraph you'll see that Menicucci never said any of these things. Choice E sounds just like his theory and is the best answer.

33. ETS's answer is C.
Remember that every question will have some support in the passage. Immediately prior to saying *Mais oui* the passage says that Menicucci *allowed himself a brief but dramatic pause.* This indicates that he was being somewhat theatrical and pompous. This best supports C.

34. ETS's answer is E.
The author clearly finds Menicucci entertaining and the author's tone with respect to this character is upbeat so we can eliminate choices A, B, and C. As for choice D, if the author felt indifferent about Menicucci, why would he have chosen to write about him? E is the best answer.

35. ETS's answer is A.
In the final paragraph, the passage says that people in Provence take rain *as a personal affront, shaking their heads and commiserating with each other in the cafes.* This is paraphrased by A.

SECTION 5

1. ETS's answer is E.
   The clue here is *almost as if it were the middle of the day*. This tells us that the second blank must be a word like *lit up*. This makes E our best choice.

2. ETS's answer is B.
   A good clue for the first blank is *haughty*. We know that the first blank has to be a negative word that goes along with *haughty*—a word like *stubborn* or *arrogant*. This will eliminate D and E. The second blank needs to be an opposing idea, something like *willing to listen*. This will eliminate A and C, which leaves us with B.

3. ETS's answer is E.
   A good clue here is *the differences between right and wrong*. What kind of book would this describe? Perhaps a *moral* book. This will allow us to eliminate every choice except E.

4. ETS's answer is D.
   The clue is *excessive violence* and our trigger is *in contrast to*. So we need a word which is the opposite of violent. This will eliminate A, B, and C. Since we're contrasting an idea with *excess*, we need a word that means *restraint* or *being relaxed*. This makes D the closest choice.

5. ETS's answer is B.
   Our clue here is *had assumed that the hunter-gatherers moved* combined with the trigger *however*. So we need a word in the blank that means the opposite of *moving*—a word that means *staying in one place*. The word that best fits this idea is B.

6. ETS's answer is A.
   The trigger word *although* tells us that the words in the blanks should have opposite meanings. Choices B, C, D, and E are all pairs which have similar meanings, so they can be eliminated. This leaves us with A.

7. ETS's answer is B.
   In this sentence we have trigger punctuation (the semicolon) that tells us that the word in the blank will mean *rarely suggest radical new ideas*. Choice B, *conservative*, fits the bill.

8. ETS's answer is C.
   The trigger word *but* combined with the clue *dry spells during which she found she could write nothing* tells us that the word in the blank should mean *writes a lot*. Choice C comes closest in meaning to this idea.

9. ETS's answer is C.
   The clue here is *none of the original doors or windows…survived*. In that case, the restoration is largely guesswork. C is the best choice.

10. ETS's answer is E.
    The trigger word *while* combined with *health-conscious individuals have stopped eating eggs* means that the word in the blank must be a word that means *healthy* (or at least not unhealthy.) Choice E means exactly this.

11. ETS's answer is D.
    An AIRPORT is a place where PLANES are kept. Is a *pedal* a place where *bicycles* are kept? No. Is a *tunnel* a place where *headlights* are kept? Definitely not. Is a *store* a place where *groceries* are kept? Yes, so let's leave it in. Is a *harbor* a place where *boats* are kept? Yes, so let's leave this one in too. Is a *mechanic* a place where *cars* are kept? Nope. So we're down to C and D. This means that we need to make a more specific sentence. An AIRPORT is a place where you also go to board a PLANE. Likewise, a *harbor* is a place where you go to board a *boat*. This makes D the best choice.

SECTION 5

12. **ETS's answer is B.**
Let's make the sentence in reverse: MUSIC is divided into MEASURES. Is *food* divided into *ovens*? Nope. Is *writing* divided into *sentences*? Yes. Is a *violin* divided into *bows*? Definitely not. Is *salt* divided into *sprinkles*? Maybe, so let's leave it in. Is a *pond* divided into *puddles*? No, unless you jump in it. So now let's make a more specific sentence: MUSIC is divided into MEASURES when it is written. Likewise, *writing* is divided into *sentences* when it is written. This makes B our best choice.

13. **ETS's answer is A.**
To RENEGE is to betray a PROMISE. Does to *betray* mean to betray a *confidence*? Yes, if you know the secondary definition of confidence. Does to *disobey* mean to betray a *punishment*? No. Does to *understand* mean to betray an *instruction*? Nope. Does to *evaluate* mean to betray a *position*? No. No relationship there. Does to *condemn* mean to betray a *viewpoint*? No.

14. **ETS's answer is B.**
A COWARD is easily INTIMIDATED. Is an *egoist* easily *humbled*? No, exactly the opposite. Is a *dupe* easily *deceived*? Yes. Is a *politician* easily *opinionated*? Maybe, but that's not really a definition of the word politician. Is a *child* easily *punished*? Perhaps, but again, that's not part of the meaning of the word child. Is a *celebrity* easily *appreciated*? Once more, that's not really part of the meaning of the word celebrity. This makes B our best choice.

15. **ETS's answer is A.**
A SANCTUARY is a place for WORSHIP. Likewise, a *gymnasium* is a place for *exercise*. Choice B is tempting, but offices are places for all kinds of work (not merely for meetings).

16. **ETS's answer is D.**
INTRACTABLE means difficult to GOVERN. Does *unfaithful* mean difficult to *promise*? Nope. Does *hopeful* mean difficult to *anticipate*? Definitely not. Does *immobile* mean difficult to *motivate*? Not great. Does *obstinate* mean difficult to *persuade*? Absolutely. Does *minimal* mean difficult to *achieve*? No. So D is our answer.

17. **ETS's answer is D.**
A MAVERICK has the characteristic of INDIVIDUALISM. Likewise, a *prevaricator* has the characteristic of *dishonesty*.

18. **ETS's answer is C.**
Something ILLUSORY is intended to cause DECEPTION. Likewise, something *soporific* is intended to cause *sleep*.

19. **ETS's answer is E.**
An ENIGMA is hard to UNDERSTAND. Is an *alternative* hard to *choose*? No. Is an *ideology* hard to *believe*? Nope. Is a *physician* hard to *diagnose*? Definitely not. Is a *colleague* hard to *distrust*? That's certainly not part of the meaning of the word colleague. Is a *recidivist* hard to *reform*? That's exactly what a recidivist is. So E is our answer.

20. **ETS's answer is A.**
RAVENOUS means to be extremely HUNGRY. Choice B is tempting, and Joe Bloggs may have chosen it, but it is backwards: *preposterous* means extremely *dubious*. However, *vehement* means very *insistent*, so A is ETS's answer.

21. **ETS's answer is C.**
If you Work Backwards, you can probably use POE to eliminate A and E since these have no relationship. PUERILE means like an INFANT. Likewise, *punctilious* means like a *perfectionist*. Therefore C is ETS's answer.

22. ETS's answer is B.
These words are difficult. If you know the words in the answer choices you can use POE to eliminate A and C, since these words have no defining relationships. You can also use side of the fence; if you know that MELLIFLUOUS and EUPHONY are on the same side of the fence, you can eliminate D and E, which are on opposite sides. This leaves B as our answer. MELLIFLUOUS means having the property of EUPHONY. Likewise, *belligerent* means having the property of *hostility*.

23. ETS's answer is A.
If you have some sense of these words, you may know that they are roughly opposite: FRIVOLITY means lacking SERIOUSNESS. Choices B and E have no defining relationship, and C is a pair of words with similar meanings, so these can be eliminated. *Reticence* means lacking *verbosity*, which is why A is ETS's answer.

24. ETS's answer is D.
From the last line of the second paragraph we know that Penfield believed that *brain studies, if properly conducted, would lead inevitably to an understanding of the mind.* Since one side of Penfield's drawing was a picture of the human brain and the other was the Greek symbol for "spirit," we know that the Greek symbol for spirit was standing in for the idea of the mind. This makes D our best choice.

25. ETS's answer is E.
This is a line reference question, so we should read these lines in context to find the answer. We know from answering question 24 that Penfield believed *brain studies...would lead inevitably to an understanding of the mind.* The correct answer will be a paraphrase of this idea. Choice E says exactly this.

26. ETS's answer is A.
This is a great time to use POE. Even if you're not sure about A, if we know that the other choices can't be right, we can pick A with confidence. B is the opposite of what the paragraph tries to show—namely that many scientists believe that *the mind and the brain are distinct.* Choices C, D and E aren't stated in the fifth paragraph, so we can eliminate them as well. This leaves us with A.

27. ETS's answer is B.
Pribram's and Bohm's collaboration is discussed in paragraph 5. Reread the paragraph and then use POE. Choices A, C, D, and E may sound tempting but none of them are actually stated. Choice B is a nice, general choice, which sums up the scientists' intentions.

28. ETS's answer is C.
In this question the lead words are *Pribram* and *Bohm*. We can find them discussed in paragraph 5. There we find that they are making an attempt *to integrate mind and consciousness with ideas drawn from quantum physics...searching for a model capable of integrating matter and consciousness into a holistic worldview.* That is, they are combining two different areas of study to try to find a single explanation. C is a paraphrase of this idea.

29. ETS's answer is A.
For a vocab-in-context question like this one, we should cover the word *bent*, reread the sentence, and put our own word in the blank. In this sentence we would probably insert a word like *belief* or *inclination*. The word that best fits this idea is A.

30. ETS's answer is A.
Let's read these lines in context to get our answer. In paragraph 7 we see *patients reported familiar feelings and vivid memories* even though their brains were simply being activated by electrical impulses. That is, they were having feelings for things that were simply generated artificially and which were not actually happening in the room. A is our answer.

31. ETS's answer is D.
"Peter Pan School of Neuroscience" is mentioned in paragraph 8. If we read the rest of the paragraph for context, we see that the point of the paragraph is that researchers *become disillusioned with claims that the mind can "be explained" in terms of brain functioning.* Which choice best paraphrases this idea? D does.

32. ETS's answer is E.
Unorthodox research is mentioned at the beginning of paragraph 9. There it states that unorthodox researchers were open to *innovative attitudes* and *transcendental influences.* E paraphrases this idea.

33. ETS's answer is C.
If we reread paragraph 9 we see that nowhere is there mention made of Eccles' brain problems (choice A), pressure and stress (choice B), or the idea that *all great brain researchers have had unusual experiences* (choice E). Eliminate these and we are left with C and D. Reading back around the line where Eccles is mentioned, we see that Eccles is described as a scientist who was *open to transcendental influences.* C best expresses this idea.

34. ETS's answer is D.
According to the passage, at the beginning of his career, Penfield believed that science and only science could explain the nature of the mind. Later he gave up this idea and came to believe that science may not be the best way to understand the mind. Choice D best paraphrases this, where a similar change in belief takes place.

35. ETS's answer is C.
In the paragraph that discusses Penfield and Sperry (paragraph 8) the author says that they have *become disillusioned with claims that the mind can "be explained" in terms of brain functioning.* So an explanation that would be insufficient would be one that tried to explain the mind exclusively in terms of scientific brain evidence. The choice that paraphrases this idea is C.

1. ETS's answer is D.
   We can set up a proportion, or simply notice that 1,000,000 is 10,000 × 100. So if we multiply 30 by 100 we get 3,000.

2. ETS's answer is C.
   If $c = 6$ and $b + c = 8$, then we know that $b = 2$. Since we know that $c = 6$ and $b = 2$, we can solve for a: If $3a + 2b + c = 22$, then $3a + 4 + 6 = 22$, so $3a = 12$, and $a = 4$. Therefore $a + b + c = 4 + 2 + 6$, or 12.

3. ETS's answer is C.
   Since we have parallel lines, let's identify the big and small angles. The small angles measure 65°, so the big angles measure 115°. So $x + y = z = 115$. If we add everything together and substitute $x = 55$, we get $55 + y + z = 230$, so $y + z = 175$.

4. ETS's answer is A.
   Be sure to read the question carefully; the key here is *must be positive*. Let's try Plugging In an easy number for b. If we make $b = 2$, then let's see which of the choices is positive. Choice A becomes $\frac{2}{3}$, choice B becomes $\frac{8}{-1}$, choice C becomes $\frac{1}{2}$, choice D becomes 0, and choice E becomes 3. We can cross off B and D, since they aren't positive. Now let's try making $b = \frac{1}{2}$. In this case, A becomes $\frac{1}{3}$, C becomes -1, and E becomes 0. We can now cross off C and E, which leaves us with A.

5. ETS's answer is B.
   This is a great problem to solve by Plugging In the answer choices. Let's start with choice C. Could the number of girls on the trip be 40? If there are 14 more boys than girls, then there must be $40 + 14 = 54$ boys. But that makes a total of 94 students, which is more than the 80 the problem says we should have. So we can cross off C, D, and E. Let's try choice B. Could there be 33 girls? In this case there will be $33 + 14 = 47$ boys, and $33 + 47$ equals 80. So B is the answer.

6. ETS's answer is B.
   We can estimate what the numbers should be by going for two consecutive even numbers which are about half of 225, which means we want to try numbers around 112. Let's try these: $110 + 112 = 222$, which isn't on our list. $112 + 114 = 226$, which is choice B.

7. ETS's answer is A.
   This is a great problem for Plugging In. Let's try using $z = 2$, $n = 5$, and $b = 15$. If $2 will buy 5 pizzas, then how much will 15 pizzas cost? $6. Now we just need to figure out which choice says $6. Try calculating each of the answer choices, and you'll find that A makes $6.

8. ETS's answer is D.
   Since OP is a radius of the circle, $OP = 8$. Since OR is a radius of the circle, $OQ = QR = 4$. Using the Pythagorean theorem—or recognizing the ratio of sides in a 30:60:90 triangle—will give us the value of PQ: $4\sqrt{3}$. Since area $= \frac{1}{2} \times$ base $\times$ height, the area is $\frac{1}{2} \times 4 \times 4\sqrt{3} = 8\sqrt{3}$.

9. ETS's answer is B.

Let's start by solving for p. We know that $p = \lozenge 6$, which means that it will be equal to $(10 - 6)^2$, or 16. So $4p$ will be equal to $4(16)$, or 64. Now we simply have to figure out which choice says 64. $\lozenge 18$ will equal $(10 - 18)^2$, which is 64. So B is the answer.

10. ETS's answer is E.

We know that the first number in the sequence is n, and the next number will be p more than it, so the second number will be $n + p$. Likewise, the third number will be p more than the second number, so the third number will be $n + p + p$. But we also know that the third number is equal to $2n$, so we know that $n + p + p = 2n$. By solving for n, we get $n = 2p$. Therefore the first number in the sequence is $2p$, and each following number is p more than it. So the second number is $3p$, the third number is $4p$, the fourth number is $5p$, the fifth number is $6p$, and the sixth number will be $7p$. You might be able to plug in on this question, but you'd have to do a bit of work before you knew which numbers you could use.

SECTION 7

1. **ETS's answer is C.**
According to the first paragraph, some of the causes of pollution included the eruption of volcanoes, dust storms, and marsh gases. In the lines just following, the passage states that humans were also responsible for pollution. C restates these ideas.

2. **ETS's answer is C.**
Let's go back to the passage and read the lines in question. They mention ancient cities that had pollution problems. This sounds a lot like either B or C. Both of these are plausible, so we should pick the one that is more general and defensible based on what the passage says. Earlier in the passage the author tells us that people early on *began to pollute the air*. The passage doesn't say that the air pollution was troublesome, just that it existed even in ancient times. This makes C a better choice than B.

3. **ETS's answer is D.**
If we read these lines in context, we find in lines 32–33 that the astronauts *traced drifting blobs of Los Angeles smog as far east as western Colorado*. This means that the smog has spread from a big city to the countryside. This is paraphrased by choice D. Choices B and C, while tempting, are much too extreme to be correct.

4. **ETS's answer is E.**
This is an EXCEPT question, so it's best left for last. The final paragraph of Passage 1 mentions strained relationships between the US and Canada, factory closings, and acid rain. This means we can eliminate A, B, and C. The passage also mentions a change in the work habits of traffic police, so choice D can also be eliminated. This leaves E as our best answer.

5. **ETS's answer is A.**
B, C, and D are all quite extreme, so we should avoid these. Since the author doesn't really say that pollution will limit growth, choice E can also be eliminated. The passage does say that air pollution has been increasing over the years, which is basically what A says.

6. **ETS's answer is C.**
Remember to look back to the passage for evidence to support your answer. Choice A is quite extreme, so we should avoid it. Choice B is tempting, but the passage never really talks about the *long run*. Instead, it only mentions a particular historical event. Lines 76–77 say that *more than 4,000 deaths had been attributed to the smog*, which makes C our best answer.

7. **ETS's answer is C.**
The lead words here are *London smog*. We can find London smog described in the first paragraph of Passage 2, where we are told it was a combination of *smoke, fog, sulfur dioxide, sulfuric acid (H_2SO_4), ash, and soot*. This is best paraphrased by C.

8. **ETS's answer is D.**
The opening lines of this paragraph say that air pollution has killed *more people than were ever killed in any single tornado*. In other words, air pollution is extremely dangerous and deadly. Choice D is a paraphrase of this idea.

9. **ETS's answer is B.**
For a detail question like this one, be sure to look back to find the answer in the passage. Lines 84–86 say that electrostatic precipitators *induce an electric charge on the particles, which are then attracted to oppositely charged plates and deposited*. This makes B the best choice.

10. **ETS's answer is D.**
Again, let's look back to the passage. In lines 98–105 we find that the processes to remove sulfur dioxide from air pollution are *expensive* and *waste a part of the coal's energy*. Choice D says exactly this.

11. **ETS's answer is D.**
     This is a difficult problem, so save it for last and plan to use POE. Choices A and B are extreme, so we should avoid them. Neither author discusses *eliminating* the sources of pollution, so we can also cross off choice C. Finally, neither author says that *the cost of pollution control is much higher than the cost of changing to better energy sources*, so we can eliminate E as well. Choice D is a nice SAT-type answer, since it's fairly general and hard to argue with.

12. **ETS's answer is A.**
     In lines 15–18, the first passage says *The industrial revolution brought even worse air pollution ... Soot, smoke and sulfur dioxide filled the air.* This explains why sulfur dioxide and soot created London smog. This makes A our answer.

13. **ETS's answer is C.**
     If the two passages are to agree on something, we need to find something that each passage talks about. Only the second passage discusses scientific techniques for controlling pollution, so B can be eliminated. Only the first passage discusses the spread of pollution to rural areas, so D can also be eliminated. Neither author says *air pollution control is too costly to implement at the current time*, so we can cross off choice E. A is really extreme, which makes it implausible that either author really says something like that. What's left? Choice C.

Afterword

ABOUT THE PRINCETON REVIEW COURSE

The Princeton Review course is a six-week course that prepares students for the SAT. Students are assigned to small classes (eight to twelve students) grouped by ability. Everyone in your Math class is scoring at your Math level; everyone in your Verbal class is scoring at your Verbal level. This enables the teacher to focus each lesson on your problems, because everybody is in the same boat.

Each week you cover one Math area and one Verbal area. If you don't understand a particular topic, some other courses expect you to listen to audiocassettes. Not so with The Princeton Review. If you want more work on a topic, you can request free private tutoring with your instructor.

Four times during the course you will take a practice test that is computer-evaluated. Each practice test is constructed according to the statistical design of actual SATs. Indeed, some of our questions are actual questions licensed directly from ETS.

The computer evaluation of your practice tests is used to assign you to your class, as well as to measure your progress. The computer evaluation tells you what specific areas you need to concentrate on. We don't ask you to spend time on topics you already know well.

Princeton Review instructors undergo a strict selection process and a rigorous training period. All of them have done exceedingly well on the SAT, and most of them have gone to highly competitive colleges. All Princeton Review instructors are chosen because we believe they can make the course an enjoyable learning experience.

Finally, Princeton Review materials are updated every year. Each student is given a manual and workbook. Each person receives materials that are challenging but not overwhelming.

Is This Book Just Like Your Course?

Since the book came out, many students and teachers have asked us, "Is this book just like your course?" The answer is no.

We like to think that this book is fun, informative, and well written, but no book can capture the magic of our instructors and course structure. Each Princeton Review instructor has attended a top college and has excelled on the SAT. Moreover, each of our instructors undergoes several weeks of rigorous training.

It isn't easy to raise SAT scores. Our course is more than fifty hours long and requires class participation, quizzes, homework, four practice examinations, and possibly additional tutoring.

Also, for a number of reasons, this book cannot contain all of the techniques we teach in our course. Some of our techniques are too difficult to include in a book, without a trained and experienced Princeton Review teacher to explain and demonstrate them. Moreover, this book is written for the average student. Classes in our course are grouped by ability so that we can gear our techniques to each student's level. What a 900-level Princeton Review student learns is different from what a 1400- or 1600-level student learns.

We're Flattered, But...

Some tutors and schools use this book to run their own "Princeton Review course." While we are flattered, we are also concerned.

It has taken us many years of teaching tens of thousands of students across the country to develop our SAT program, and we're still learning. Many teachers think that our course is simply a collection of techniques that can be taught by anyone. It isn't that easy.

We train each Princeton Review instructor for many hours for every hour he or she will teach class. Each of the instructors is monitored, evaluated, and supervised throughout the course.

Another concern is that many of our techniques conflict with traditional math and English techniques as taught in high school. For example, in the Math section, we tell our students to avoid setting up algebraic equations. Can you imagine your math teacher telling you that? And in the Verbal section, we tell our students not to read the passage too carefully. Can you imagine your English teacher telling you that?

While we also teach traditional math and English in our course, some teachers may not completely agree with some of our approaches.

BEWARE OF PRINCETON REVIEW CLONES

We have nothing against people who use our techniques, but we do object to tutors or high schools who claim to "teach The Princeton Review method." If you want to find out whether your teacher has been trained by The Princeton Review or whether you're taking an official Princeton Review course, call us toll-free at 1-800-2Review.

IF YOU'D LIKE MORE INFORMATION

Princeton Review sites are in dozens of cities around the country. For the office nearest you, call 1-800-2Review.

A Parting Shot from FairTest

Now that you are well-prepped for the SAT, there are a few things you should know to help keep the test in perspective. First, your score on the SAT is not a measure of your intelligence; it is a measure of how well you take these kinds of fill-in-the-bubble exams.

Fortunately, in the real world very few people care a fig about whether you know how "mendicant" relates to "beggar." So even if you aren't great at taking multiple-choice tests, you, too, could still become a corporate CEO, a rock 'n' roll star, or president of the United States.

Second, if you choose to apply to colleges that use SAT scores to make admissions decisions, you don't need scores that are astronomical, just within the requisite range. This book will help you reach that goal.

If you've worked hard but your test scores still don't meet your expectations, do not despair: many good schools still want you. Today, more than 200 enlightened colleges and universities have adopted a test score–optional policy for some or all of their applicants. These schools will consider your scores if you submit them, but they won't hold it against you if you don't. They include some of the nation's best schools, ranging from small private liberal arts colleges to large public systems in Oregon and California. They judge students based on years of high school coursework, not on a three-and-a-half-hour standardized test.

Colleges have made the tests optional to attract students who perform well in other areas, but not on standardized tests. By all reports, they are pleased with the results. For example, both Bowdoin and Bates, two small liberal arts colleges, experienced strong growth in the number of minority applicants. At both colleges, applicants who did not submit test scores were accepted at about the same rate as those who did. Students from both groups had very similar grade point averages in college and graduated at about the same rate.

These results may surprise some who think the SAT is an important predictor of performance. Think again. Despite the hype surrounding the SAT, the test adds very little to the ability of college admissions officers to forecast student success. The sole stated purpose of the SAT is to predict first-year college grades. It doesn't do a great job of meeting even that modest objective. Despite the enormous range of grading practices, high school records still provide a more accurate picture of how well students will fare in their first year of college. The SAT is even less reliable as a predictor of grades in the second and third years of college and beyond.

So why do so many colleges still rely on the test? Many do so in order to maintain an aura of selectivity—to achieve that coveted spot on the college rankings charts. Another reason is convenience. Some highly selective schools attract such well-qualified pools of applicants that a large percentage of those denied entrance could perform well academically. Rejecting students who have modest test scores gives them a relatively cheap and easy way to thin the ranks of applicants. Of course, that practice also harms otherwise qualified students who don't happen to do well on tests, but that's why you bought this book, isn't it?

At FairTest, the National Center for Fair & Open Testing, we are committed to fighting the abuses and misuses of standardized tests. Princeton Review staff have been helpful allies in this fight. They live and breathe the SAT, so they know just how flawed and limited it really is. And they don't mind saying so publicly. So prepare well and "crack" the SAT, but understand that there are good colleges and universities that want you whether you ace the test or not.

For more information about FairTest, or to obtain a list of the test score–optional four-year colleges and universities, send an SASE to 342 Broadway, Cambridge, MA, 02139.

ABOUT THE AUTHORS

Adam Robinson was born in 1955, and lives in New York City.

John Katzman was born in 1959. He graduated from Princeton University in 1980. After working briefly on Wall Street, he founded The Princeton Review in 1981. Having begun with nineteen high school students in his parents' apartment, Katzman now oversees courses that prepare tens of thousands of high school and college students annually for tests, including the SAT, GRE, GMAT, and LSAT. He lives in New York City.

Completely darken bubbles with a No. 2 pencil. If you make a mistake, be sure to erase mark completely. Erase all stray marks.

1

YOUR NAME: _____
(Print)
Last   First   M.I.

SIGNATURE: _____   **DATE:** ___ / ___ / ___

HOME ADDRESS: _____
(Print)
Number and Street

_____
City   State   Zip Code

PHONE NO.: _____
(Print)

IMPORTANT: Please fill in these boxes exactly as shown on the back cover of your test book.

2. TEST FORM
_____

6. DATE OF BIRTH

Month		Day		Year		
☐ JAN						
☐ FEB						
☐ MAR	⊂0⊃	⊂0⊃	⊂0⊃	⊂0⊃		
☐ APR	⊂1⊃	⊂1⊃	⊂1⊃	⊂1⊃		
☐ MAY	⊂2⊃	⊂2⊃	⊂2⊃	⊂2⊃		
☐ JUN	⊂3⊃	⊂3⊃	⊂3⊃	⊂3⊃		
☐ JUL		⊂4⊃	⊂4⊃	⊂4⊃		
☐ AUG		⊂5⊃	⊂5⊃	⊂5⊃		
☐ SEP		⊂6⊃	⊂6⊃	⊂6⊃		
☐ OCT		⊂7⊃	⊂7⊃	⊂7⊃		
☐ NOV		⊂8⊃	⊂8⊃	⊂8⊃		
☐ DEC		⊂9⊃	⊂9⊃	⊂9⊃		

3. TEST CODE   4. REGISTRATION NUMBER

⊂0⊃	⊂A⊃	⊂0⊃	⊂0⊃	⊂0⊃	⊂0⊃	⊂0⊃	⊂0⊃	⊂0⊃	⊂0⊃	⊂0⊃
⊂1⊃	⊂B⊃	⊂1⊃	⊂1⊃	⊂1⊃	⊂1⊃	⊂1⊃	⊂1⊃	⊂1⊃	⊂1⊃	⊂1⊃
⊂2⊃	⊂C⊃	⊂2⊃	⊂2⊃	⊂2⊃	⊂2⊃	⊂2⊃	⊂2⊃	⊂2⊃	⊂2⊃	⊂2⊃
⊂3⊃	⊂D⊃	⊂3⊃	⊂3⊃	⊂3⊃	⊂3⊃	⊂3⊃	⊂3⊃	⊂3⊃	⊂3⊃	⊂3⊃
⊂4⊃	⊂E⊃	⊂4⊃	⊂4⊃	⊂4⊃	⊂4⊃	⊂4⊃	⊂4⊃	⊂4⊃	⊂4⊃	⊂4⊃
⊂5⊃	⊂F⊃	⊂5⊃	⊂5⊃	⊂5⊃	⊂5⊃	⊂5⊃	⊂5⊃	⊂5⊃	⊂5⊃	⊂5⊃
⊂6⊃	⊂G⊃	⊂6⊃	⊂6⊃	⊂6⊃	⊂6⊃	⊂6⊃	⊂6⊃	⊂6⊃	⊂6⊃	⊂6⊃
⊂7⊃		⊂7⊃	⊂7⊃	⊂7⊃	⊂7⊃	⊂7⊃	⊂7⊃	⊂7⊃	⊂7⊃	⊂7⊃
⊂8⊃		⊂8⊃	⊂8⊃	⊂8⊃	⊂8⊃	⊂8⊃	⊂8⊃	⊂8⊃	⊂8⊃	⊂8⊃
⊂9⊃		⊂9⊃	⊂9⊃	⊂9⊃	⊂9⊃	⊂9⊃	⊂9⊃	⊂9⊃	⊂9⊃	⊂9⊃

7. SEX
☐ MALE
☐ FEMALE

The Princeton Review

5. YOUR NAME

First 4 letters of last name				FIRST INIT	MID INIT
⊂A⊃	⊂A⊃	⊂A⊃	⊂A⊃	⊂A⊃	⊂A⊃
⊂B⊃	⊂B⊃	⊂B⊃	⊂B⊃	⊂B⊃	⊂B⊃
⊂C⊃	⊂C⊃	⊂C⊃	⊂C⊃	⊂C⊃	⊂C⊃
⊂D⊃	⊂D⊃	⊂D⊃	⊂D⊃	⊂D⊃	⊂D⊃
⊂E⊃	⊂E⊃	⊂E⊃	⊂E⊃	⊂E⊃	⊂E⊃
⊂F⊃	⊂F⊃	⊂F⊃	⊂F⊃	⊂F⊃	⊂F⊃
⊂G⊃	⊂G⊃	⊂G⊃	⊂G⊃	⊂G⊃	⊂G⊃
⊂H⊃	⊂H⊃	⊂H⊃	⊂H⊃	⊂H⊃	⊂H⊃
⊂I⊃	⊂I⊃	⊂I⊃	⊂I⊃	⊂I⊃	⊂I⊃
⊂J⊃	⊂J⊃	⊂J⊃	⊂J⊃	⊂J⊃	⊂J⊃
⊂K⊃	⊂K⊃	⊂K⊃	⊂K⊃	⊂K⊃	⊂K⊃
⊂L⊃	⊂L⊃	⊂L⊃	⊂L⊃	⊂L⊃	⊂L⊃
⊂M⊃	⊂M⊃	⊂M⊃	⊂M⊃	⊂M⊃	⊂M⊃
⊂N⊃	⊂N⊃	⊂N⊃	⊂N⊃	⊂N⊃	⊂N⊃
⊂O⊃	⊂O⊃	⊂O⊃	⊂O⊃	⊂O⊃	⊂O⊃
⊂P⊃	⊂P⊃	⊂P⊃	⊂P⊃	⊂P⊃	⊂P⊃
⊂Q⊃	⊂Q⊃	⊂Q⊃	⊂Q⊃	⊂Q⊃	⊂Q⊃
⊂R⊃	⊂R⊃	⊂R⊃	⊂R⊃	⊂R⊃	⊂R⊃
⊂S⊃	⊂S⊃	⊂S⊃	⊂S⊃	⊂S⊃	⊂S⊃
⊂T⊃	⊂T⊃	⊂T⊃	⊂T⊃	⊂T⊃	⊂T⊃
⊂U⊃	⊂U⊃	⊂U⊃	⊂U⊃	⊂U⊃	⊂U⊃
⊂V⊃	⊂V⊃	⊂V⊃	⊂V⊃	⊂V⊃	⊂V⊃
⊂W⊃	⊂W⊃	⊂W⊃	⊂W⊃	⊂W⊃	⊂W⊃
⊂X⊃	⊂X⊃	⊂X⊃	⊂X⊃	⊂X⊃	⊂X⊃
⊂Y⊃	⊂Y⊃	⊂Y⊃	⊂Y⊃	⊂Y⊃	⊂Y⊃
⊂Z⊃	⊂Z⊃	⊂Z⊃	⊂Z⊃	⊂Z⊃	⊂Z⊃

Start with number 1 for each new section. If a section has fewer questions than answer spaces, leave the extra answer spaces blank.

SECTION 1

1 ⊂A⊃ ⊂B⊃ ⊂C⊃ ⊂D⊃ ⊂E⊃   11 ⊂A⊃ ⊂B⊃ ⊂C⊃ ⊂D⊃ ⊂E⊃   21 ⊂A⊃ ⊂B⊃ ⊂C⊃ ⊂D⊃ ⊂E⊃   31 ⊂A⊃ ⊂B⊃ ⊂C⊃ ⊂D⊃ ⊂E⊃
2 ⊂A⊃ ⊂B⊃ ⊂C⊃ ⊂D⊃ ⊂E⊃   12 ⊂A⊃ ⊂B⊃ ⊂C⊃ ⊂D⊃ ⊂E⊃   22 ⊂A⊃ ⊂B⊃ ⊂C⊃ ⊂D⊃ ⊂E⊃   32 ⊂A⊃ ⊂B⊃ ⊂C⊃ ⊂D⊃ ⊂E⊃
3 ⊂A⊃ ⊂B⊃ ⊂C⊃ ⊂D⊃ ⊂E⊃   13 ⊂A⊃ ⊂B⊃ ⊂C⊃ ⊂D⊃ ⊂E⊃   23 ⊂A⊃ ⊂B⊃ ⊂C⊃ ⊂D⊃ ⊂E⊃   33 ⊂A⊃ ⊂B⊃ ⊂C⊃ ⊂D⊃ ⊂E⊃
4 ⊂A⊃ ⊂B⊃ ⊂C⊃ ⊂D⊃ ⊂E⊃   14 ⊂A⊃ ⊂B⊃ ⊂C⊃ ⊂D⊃ ⊂E⊃   24 ⊂A⊃ ⊂B⊃ ⊂C⊃ ⊂D⊃ ⊂E⊃   34 ⊂A⊃ ⊂B⊃ ⊂C⊃ ⊂D⊃ ⊂E⊃
5 ⊂A⊃ ⊂B⊃ ⊂C⊃ ⊂D⊃ ⊂E⊃   15 ⊂A⊃ ⊂B⊃ ⊂C⊃ ⊂D⊃ ⊂E⊃   25 ⊂A⊃ ⊂B⊃ ⊂C⊃ ⊂D⊃ ⊂E⊃   35 ⊂A⊃ ⊂B⊃ ⊂C⊃ ⊂D⊃ ⊂E⊃
6 ⊂A⊃ ⊂B⊃ ⊂C⊃ ⊂D⊃ ⊂E⊃   16 ⊂A⊃ ⊂B⊃ ⊂C⊃ ⊂D⊃ ⊂E⊃   26 ⊂A⊃ ⊂B⊃ ⊂C⊃ ⊂D⊃ ⊂E⊃   36 ⊂A⊃ ⊂B⊃ ⊂C⊃ ⊂D⊃ ⊂E⊃
7 ⊂A⊃ ⊂B⊃ ⊂C⊃ ⊂D⊃ ⊂E⊃   17 ⊂A⊃ ⊂B⊃ ⊂C⊃ ⊂D⊃ ⊂E⊃   27 ⊂A⊃ ⊂B⊃ ⊂C⊃ ⊂D⊃ ⊂E⊃   37 ⊂A⊃ ⊂B⊃ ⊂C⊃ ⊂D⊃ ⊂E⊃
8 ⊂A⊃ ⊂B⊃ ⊂C⊃ ⊂D⊃ ⊂E⊃   18 ⊂A⊃ ⊂B⊃ ⊂C⊃ ⊂D⊃ ⊂E⊃   28 ⊂A⊃ ⊂B⊃ ⊂C⊃ ⊂D⊃ ⊂E⊃   38 ⊂A⊃ ⊂B⊃ ⊂C⊃ ⊂D⊃ ⊂E⊃
9 ⊂A⊃ ⊂B⊃ ⊂C⊃ ⊂D⊃ ⊂E⊃   19 ⊂A⊃ ⊂B⊃ ⊂C⊃ ⊂D⊃ ⊂E⊃   29 ⊂A⊃ ⊂B⊃ ⊂C⊃ ⊂D⊃ ⊂E⊃   39 ⊂A⊃ ⊂B⊃ ⊂C⊃ ⊂D⊃ ⊂E⊃
10 ⊂A⊃ ⊂B⊃ ⊂C⊃ ⊂D⊃ ⊂E⊃   20 ⊂A⊃ ⊂B⊃ ⊂C⊃ ⊂D⊃ ⊂E⊃   30 ⊂A⊃ ⊂B⊃ ⊂C⊃ ⊂D⊃ ⊂E⊃   40 ⊂A⊃ ⊂B⊃ ⊂C⊃ ⊂D⊃ ⊂E⊃

SECTION 2

1 ⊂A⊃ ⊂B⊃ ⊂C⊃ ⊂D⊃ ⊂E⊃   11 ⊂A⊃ ⊂B⊃ ⊂C⊃ ⊂D⊃ ⊂E⊃   21 ⊂A⊃ ⊂B⊃ ⊂C⊃ ⊂D⊃ ⊂E⊃   31 ⊂A⊃ ⊂B⊃ ⊂C⊃ ⊂D⊃ ⊂E⊃
2 ⊂A⊃ ⊂B⊃ ⊂C⊃ ⊂D⊃ ⊂E⊃   12 ⊂A⊃ ⊂B⊃ ⊂C⊃ ⊂D⊃ ⊂E⊃   22 ⊂A⊃ ⊂B⊃ ⊂C⊃ ⊂D⊃ ⊂E⊃   32 ⊂A⊃ ⊂B⊃ ⊂C⊃ ⊂D⊃ ⊂E⊃
3 ⊂A⊃ ⊂B⊃ ⊂C⊃ ⊂D⊃ ⊂E⊃   13 ⊂A⊃ ⊂B⊃ ⊂C⊃ ⊂D⊃ ⊂E⊃   23 ⊂A⊃ ⊂B⊃ ⊂C⊃ ⊂D⊃ ⊂E⊃   33 ⊂A⊃ ⊂B⊃ ⊂C⊃ ⊂D⊃ ⊂E⊃
4 ⊂A⊃ ⊂B⊃ ⊂C⊃ ⊂D⊃ ⊂E⊃   14 ⊂A⊃ ⊂B⊃ ⊂C⊃ ⊂D⊃ ⊂E⊃   24 ⊂A⊃ ⊂B⊃ ⊂C⊃ ⊂D⊃ ⊂E⊃   34 ⊂A⊃ ⊂B⊃ ⊂C⊃ ⊂D⊃ ⊂E⊃
5 ⊂A⊃ ⊂B⊃ ⊂C⊃ ⊂D⊃ ⊂E⊃   15 ⊂A⊃ ⊂B⊃ ⊂C⊃ ⊂D⊃ ⊂E⊃   25 ⊂A⊃ ⊂B⊃ ⊂C⊃ ⊂D⊃ ⊂E⊃   35 ⊂A⊃ ⊂B⊃ ⊂C⊃ ⊂D⊃ ⊂E⊃
6 ⊂A⊃ ⊂B⊃ ⊂C⊃ ⊂D⊃ ⊂E⊃   16 ⊂A⊃ ⊂B⊃ ⊂C⊃ ⊂D⊃ ⊂E⊃   26 ⊂A⊃ ⊂B⊃ ⊂C⊃ ⊂D⊃ ⊂E⊃   36 ⊂A⊃ ⊂B⊃ ⊂C⊃ ⊂D⊃ ⊂E⊃
7 ⊂A⊃ ⊂B⊃ ⊂C⊃ ⊂D⊃ ⊂E⊃   17 ⊂A⊃ ⊂B⊃ ⊂C⊃ ⊂D⊃ ⊂E⊃   27 ⊂A⊃ ⊂B⊃ ⊂C⊃ ⊂D⊃ ⊂E⊃   37 ⊂A⊃ ⊂B⊃ ⊂C⊃ ⊂D⊃ ⊂E⊃
8 ⊂A⊃ ⊂B⊃ ⊂C⊃ ⊂D⊃ ⊂E⊃   18 ⊂A⊃ ⊂B⊃ ⊂C⊃ ⊂D⊃ ⊂E⊃   28 ⊂A⊃ ⊂B⊃ ⊂C⊃ ⊂D⊃ ⊂E⊃   38 ⊂A⊃ ⊂B⊃ ⊂C⊃ ⊂D⊃ ⊂E⊃
9 ⊂A⊃ ⊂B⊃ ⊂C⊃ ⊂D⊃ ⊂E⊃   19 ⊂A⊃ ⊂B⊃ ⊂C⊃ ⊂D⊃ ⊂E⊃   29 ⊂A⊃ ⊂B⊃ ⊂C⊃ ⊂D⊃ ⊂E⊃   39 ⊂A⊃ ⊂B⊃ ⊂C⊃ ⊂D⊃ ⊂E⊃
10 ⊂A⊃ ⊂B⊃ ⊂C⊃ ⊂D⊃ ⊂E⊃   20 ⊂A⊃ ⊂B⊃ ⊂C⊃ ⊂D⊃ ⊂E⊃   30 ⊂A⊃ ⊂B⊃ ⊂C⊃ ⊂D⊃ ⊂E⊃   40 ⊂A⊃ ⊂B⊃ ⊂C⊃ ⊂D⊃ ⊂E⊃

DO NOT MARK IN THIS AREA
⊂ ⊃ ⊂ ⊃ ⊂ ⊃ ⊂ ⊃ ⊂ ⊃ ⊂ ⊃ ⊂ ⊃ ⊂ ⊃ ⊂ ⊃ ⊂ ⊃ ⊂ ⊃ ⊂ ⊃ ⊂ ⊃ ⊂ ⊃ ⊂ ⊃ ⊂ ⊃ ⊂ ⊃

Start with number 1 for each new section. If a section has fewer questions than answer spaces, leave the extra answer spaces blank.

SECTION 3

1 (A) (B) (C) (D) (E)	16 (A) (B) (C) (D) (E)	31 (A) (B) (C) (D) (E)
2 (A) (B) (C) (D) (E)	17 (A) (B) (C) (D) (E)	32 (A) (B) (C) (D) (E)
3 (A) (B) (C) (D) (E)	18 (A) (B) (C) (D) (E)	33 (A) (B) (C) (D) (E)
4 (A) (B) (C) (D) (E)	19 (A) (B) (C) (D) (E)	34 (A) (B) (C) (D) (E)
5 (A) (B) (C) (D) (E)	20 (A) (B) (C) (D) (E)	35 (A) (B) (C) (D) (E)
6 (A) (B) (C) (D) (E)	21 (A) (B) (C) (D) (E)	36 (A) (B) (C) (D) (E)
7 (A) (B) (C) (D) (E)	22 (A) (B) (C) (D) (E)	37 (A) (B) (C) (D) (E)
8 (A) (B) (C) (D) (E)	23 (A) (B) (C) (D) (E)	38 (A) (B) (C) (D) (E)
9 (A) (B) (C) (D) (E)	24 (A) (B) (C) (D) (E)	39 (A) (B) (C) (D) (E)
10 (A) (B) (C) (D) (E)	25 (A) (B) (C) (D) (E)	40 (A) (B) (C) (D) (E)
11 (A) (B) (C) (D) (E)	26 (A) (B) (C) (D) (E)	
12 (A) (B) (C) (D) (E)	27 (A) (B) (C) (D) (E)	
13 (A) (B) (C) (D) (E)	28 (A) (B) (C) (D) (E)	
14 (A) (B) (C) (D) (E)	29 (A) (B) (C) (D) (E)	
15 (A) (B) (C) (D) (E)	30 (A) (B) (C) (D) (E)	

If section 3 of your test booklet has math questions that are not multiple-choice, continue to item 16 below. Otherwise, continue to item 16 above.

ONLY ANSWERS ENTERED IN THE OVALS IN EACH GRID AREA WILL BE SCORED.
YOU WILL NOT RECEIVE CREDIT FOR ANYTHING WRITTEN IN THE BOXES ABOVE THE OVALS.

16   17   18   19   20

[Grid-in answer fields with fractions (/), decimal (.), and digits 0–9]

21   22   23   24   25

[Grid-in answer fields with fractions (/), decimal (.), and digits 0–9]

BE SURE TO ERASE ANY ERRORS OR STRAY MARKS COMPLETELY.

PLEASE PRINT YOUR INITIALS

First   Middle   Last

Use a No. 2 pencil only. Be sure each mark is dark and completely fills the intended oval. Completely erase any errors or stray marks.

Start with number 1 for each new section. If a section has fewer questions than answer spaces, leave the extra answer spaces blank.

SECTION 4

	A	B	C	D	E		A	B	C	D	E		A	B	C	D	E		A	B	C	D	E
1	⊂A⊃	⊂B⊃	⊂C⊃	⊂D⊃	⊂E⊃	11	⊂A⊃	⊂B⊃	⊂C⊃	⊂D⊃	⊂E⊃	21	⊂A⊃	⊂B⊃	⊂C⊃	⊂D⊃	⊂E⊃	31	⊂A⊃	⊂B⊃	⊂C⊃	⊂D⊃	⊂E⊃
2	⊂A⊃	⊂B⊃	⊂C⊃	⊂D⊃	⊂E⊃	12	⊂A⊃	⊂B⊃	⊂C⊃	⊂D⊃	⊂E⊃	22	⊂A⊃	⊂B⊃	⊂C⊃	⊂D⊃	⊂E⊃	32	⊂A⊃	⊂B⊃	⊂C⊃	⊂D⊃	⊂E⊃
3	⊂A⊃	⊂B⊃	⊂C⊃	⊂D⊃	⊂E⊃	13	⊂A⊃	⊂B⊃	⊂C⊃	⊂D⊃	⊂E⊃	23	⊂A⊃	⊂B⊃	⊂C⊃	⊂D⊃	⊂E⊃	33	⊂A⊃	⊂B⊃	⊂C⊃	⊂D⊃	⊂E⊃
4	⊂A⊃	⊂B⊃	⊂C⊃	⊂D⊃	⊂E⊃	14	⊂A⊃	⊂B⊃	⊂C⊃	⊂D⊃	⊂E⊃	24	⊂A⊃	⊂B⊃	⊂C⊃	⊂D⊃	⊂E⊃	34	⊂A⊃	⊂B⊃	⊂C⊃	⊂D⊃	⊂E⊃
5	⊂A⊃	⊂B⊃	⊂C⊃	⊂D⊃	⊂E⊃	15	⊂A⊃	⊂B⊃	⊂C⊃	⊂D⊃	⊂E⊃	25	⊂A⊃	⊂B⊃	⊂C⊃	⊂D⊃	⊂E⊃	35	⊂A⊃	⊂B⊃	⊂C⊃	⊂D⊃	⊂E⊃
6	⊂A⊃	⊂B⊃	⊂C⊃	⊂D⊃	⊂E⊃	16	⊂A⊃	⊂B⊃	⊂C⊃	⊂D⊃	⊂E⊃	26	⊂A⊃	⊂B⊃	⊂C⊃	⊂D⊃	⊂E⊃	36	⊂A⊃	⊂B⊃	⊂C⊃	⊂D⊃	⊂E⊃
7	⊂A⊃	⊂B⊃	⊂C⊃	⊂D⊃	⊂E⊃	17	⊂A⊃	⊂B⊃	⊂C⊃	⊂D⊃	⊂E⊃	27	⊂A⊃	⊂B⊃	⊂C⊃	⊂D⊃	⊂E⊃	37	⊂A⊃	⊂B⊃	⊂C⊃	⊂D⊃	⊂E⊃
8	⊂A⊃	⊂B⊃	⊂C⊃	⊂D⊃	⊂E⊃	18	⊂A⊃	⊂B⊃	⊂C⊃	⊂D⊃	⊂E⊃	28	⊂A⊃	⊂B⊃	⊂C⊃	⊂D⊃	⊂E⊃	38	⊂A⊃	⊂B⊃	⊂C⊃	⊂D⊃	⊂E⊃
9	⊂A⊃	⊂B⊃	⊂C⊃	⊂D⊃	⊂E⊃	19	⊂A⊃	⊂B⊃	⊂C⊃	⊂D⊃	⊂E⊃	29	⊂A⊃	⊂B⊃	⊂C⊃	⊂D⊃	⊂E⊃	39	⊂A⊃	⊂B⊃	⊂C⊃	⊂D⊃	⊂E⊃
10	⊂A⊃	⊂B⊃	⊂C⊃	⊂D⊃	⊂E⊃	20	⊂A⊃	⊂B⊃	⊂C⊃	⊂D⊃	⊂E⊃	30	⊂A⊃	⊂B⊃	⊂C⊃	⊂D⊃	⊂E⊃	40	⊂A⊃	⊂B⊃	⊂C⊃	⊂D⊃	⊂E⊃

SECTION 5

(Questions 1–40, answer ovals A B C D E for each, identical layout to Section 4.)

SECTION 6

(Questions 1–40, answer ovals A B C D E for each, identical layout to Section 4.)

SECTION 7

(Questions 1–40, answer ovals A B C D E for each, identical layout to Section 4.)

The Princeton Review

1

YOUR NAME: _____
(Print)   Last   First   M.I.

SIGNATURE: _____ DATE: __ / __ / __

HOME ADDRESS: _____
(Print)   Number and Street

_____
          City   State   Zip Code

PHONE NO.: _____
(Print)

IMPORTANT: Please fill in these boxes exactly as shown on the back cover of your test book.

2. TEST FORM
_____

6. DATE OF BIRTH

Month		Day		Year	
◯ JAN					
◯ FEB					
◯ MAR	⊂0⊃	⊂0⊃	⊂0⊃	⊂0⊃
◯ APR	⊂1⊃	⊂1⊃	⊂1⊃	⊂1⊃
◯ MAY	⊂2⊃	⊂2⊃	⊂2⊃	⊂2⊃
◯ JUN	⊂3⊃	⊂3⊃	⊂3⊃	⊂3⊃
◯ JUL		⊂4⊃	⊂4⊃	⊂4⊃
◯ AUG		⊂5⊃	⊂5⊃	⊂5⊃
◯ SEP		⊂6⊃	⊂6⊃	⊂6⊃
◯ OCT		⊂7⊃	⊂7⊃	⊂7⊃
◯ NOV		⊂8⊃	⊂8⊃	⊂8⊃
◯ DEC		⊂9⊃	⊂9⊃	⊂9⊃

3. TEST CODE

⊂0⊃ ⊂A⊃ ⊂0⊃ ⊂0⊃ ⊂0⊃
⊂1⊃ ⊂B⊃ ⊂1⊃ ⊂1⊃ ⊂1⊃
⊂2⊃ ⊂C⊃ ⊂2⊃ ⊂2⊃ ⊂2⊃
⊂3⊃ ⊂D⊃ ⊂3⊃ ⊂3⊃ ⊂3⊃
⊂4⊃ ⊂E⊃ ⊂4⊃ ⊂4⊃ ⊂4⊃
⊂5⊃ ⊂F⊃ ⊂5⊃ ⊂5⊃ ⊂5⊃
⊂6⊃ ⊂G⊃ ⊂6⊃ ⊂6⊃ ⊂6⊃
      ⊂7⊃ ⊂7⊃ ⊂7⊃
      ⊂8⊃ ⊂8⊃ ⊂8⊃
      ⊂9⊃ ⊂9⊃ ⊂9⊃

4. REGISTRATION NUMBER

⊂0⊃ ⊂0⊃ ⊂0⊃ ⊂0⊃ ⊂0⊃ ⊂0⊃ ⊂0⊃
⊂1⊃ ⊂1⊃ ⊂1⊃ ⊂1⊃ ⊂1⊃ ⊂1⊃ ⊂1⊃
⊂2⊃ ⊂2⊃ ⊂2⊃ ⊂2⊃ ⊂2⊃ ⊂2⊃ ⊂2⊃
⊂3⊃ ⊂3⊃ ⊂3⊃ ⊂3⊃ ⊂3⊃ ⊂3⊃ ⊂3⊃
⊂4⊃ ⊂4⊃ ⊂4⊃ ⊂4⊃ ⊂4⊃ ⊂4⊃ ⊂4⊃
⊂5⊃ ⊂5⊃ ⊂5⊃ ⊂5⊃ ⊂5⊃ ⊂5⊃ ⊂5⊃
⊂6⊃ ⊂6⊃ ⊂6⊃ ⊂6⊃ ⊂6⊃ ⊂6⊃ ⊂6⊃
⊂7⊃ ⊂7⊃ ⊂7⊃ ⊂7⊃ ⊂7⊃ ⊂7⊃ ⊂7⊃
⊂8⊃ ⊂8⊃ ⊂8⊃ ⊂8⊃ ⊂8⊃ ⊂8⊃ ⊂8⊃
⊂9⊃ ⊂9⊃ ⊂9⊃ ⊂9⊃ ⊂9⊃ ⊂9⊃ ⊂9⊃

7. SEX
◯ MALE
◯ FEMALE

The Princeton Review

5. YOUR NAME

First 4 letters of last name					FIRST INIT	MID INIT
⊂A⊃	⊂A⊃	⊂A⊃	⊂A⊃		⊂A⊃	⊂A⊃
⊂B⊃	⊂B⊃	⊂B⊃	⊂B⊃		⊂B⊃	⊂B⊃
⊂C⊃	⊂C⊃	⊂C⊃	⊂C⊃		⊂C⊃	⊂C⊃
⊂D⊃	⊂D⊃	⊂D⊃	⊂D⊃		⊂D⊃	⊂D⊃
⊂E⊃	⊂E⊃	⊂E⊃	⊂E⊃		⊂E⊃	⊂E⊃
⊂F⊃	⊂F⊃	⊂F⊃	⊂F⊃		⊂F⊃	⊂F⊃
⊂G⊃	⊂G⊃	⊂G⊃	⊂G⊃		⊂G⊃	⊂G⊃
⊂H⊃	⊂H⊃	⊂H⊃	⊂H⊃		⊂H⊃	⊂H⊃
⊂I⊃	⊂I⊃	⊂I⊃	⊂I⊃		⊂I⊃	⊂I⊃
⊂J⊃	⊂J⊃	⊂J⊃	⊂J⊃		⊂J⊃	⊂J⊃
⊂K⊃	⊂K⊃	⊂K⊃	⊂K⊃		⊂K⊃	⊂K⊃
⊂L⊃	⊂L⊃	⊂L⊃	⊂L⊃		⊂L⊃	⊂L⊃
⊂M⊃	⊂M⊃	⊂M⊃	⊂M⊃		⊂M⊃	⊂M⊃
⊂N⊃	⊂N⊃	⊂N⊃	⊂N⊃		⊂N⊃	⊂N⊃
⊂O⊃	⊂O⊃	⊂O⊃	⊂O⊃		⊂O⊃	⊂O⊃
⊂P⊃	⊂P⊃	⊂P⊃	⊂P⊃		⊂P⊃	⊂P⊃
⊂Q⊃	⊂Q⊃	⊂Q⊃	⊂Q⊃		⊂Q⊃	⊂Q⊃
⊂R⊃	⊂R⊃	⊂R⊃	⊂R⊃		⊂R⊃	⊂R⊃
⊂S⊃	⊂S⊃	⊂S⊃	⊂S⊃		⊂S⊃	⊂S⊃
⊂T⊃	⊂T⊃	⊂T⊃	⊂T⊃		⊂T⊃	⊂T⊃
⊂U⊃	⊂U⊃	⊂U⊃	⊂U⊃		⊂U⊃	⊂U⊃
⊂V⊃	⊂V⊃	⊂V⊃	⊂V⊃		⊂V⊃	⊂V⊃
⊂W⊃	⊂W⊃	⊂W⊃	⊂W⊃		⊂W⊃	⊂W⊃
⊂X⊃	⊂X⊃	⊂X⊃	⊂X⊃		⊂X⊃	⊂X⊃
⊂Y⊃	⊂Y⊃	⊂Y⊃	⊂Y⊃		⊂Y⊃	⊂Y⊃
⊂Z⊃	⊂Z⊃	⊂Z⊃	⊂Z⊃		⊂Z⊃	⊂Z⊃

Start with number 1 for each new section. If a section has fewer questions than answer spaces, leave the extra answer spaces blank.

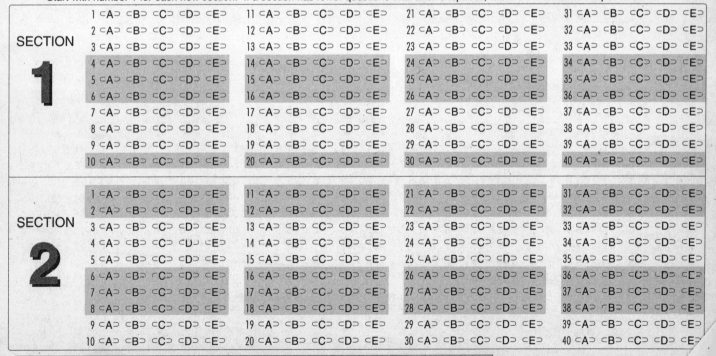

SECTION 1

1 ⊂A⊃ ⊂B⊃ ⊂C⊃ ⊂D⊃ ⊂E⊃	11 ⊂A⊃ ⊂B⊃ ⊂C⊃ ⊂D⊃ ⊂E⊃	21 ⊂A⊃ ⊂B⊃ ⊂C⊃ ⊂D⊃ ⊂E⊃	31 ⊂A⊃ ⊂B⊃ ⊂C⊃ ⊂D⊃ ⊂E⊃
2 ⊂A⊃ ⊂B⊃ ⊂C⊃ ⊂D⊃ ⊂E⊃	12 ⊂A⊃ ⊂B⊃ ⊂C⊃ ⊂D⊃ ⊂E⊃	22 ⊂A⊃ ⊂B⊃ ⊂C⊃ ⊂D⊃ ⊂E⊃	32 ⊂A⊃ ⊂B⊃ ⊂C⊃ ⊂D⊃ ⊂E⊃
3 ⊂A⊃ ⊂B⊃ ⊂C⊃ ⊂D⊃ ⊂E⊃	13 ⊂A⊃ ⊂B⊃ ⊂C⊃ ⊂D⊃ ⊂E⊃	23 ⊂A⊃ ⊂B⊃ ⊂C⊃ ⊂D⊃ ⊂E⊃	33 ⊂A⊃ ⊂B⊃ ⊂C⊃ ⊂D⊃ ⊂E⊃
4 ⊂A⊃ ⊂B⊃ ⊂C⊃ ⊂D⊃ ⊂E⊃	14 ⊂A⊃ ⊂B⊃ ⊂C⊃ ⊂D⊃ ⊂E⊃	24 ⊂A⊃ ⊂B⊃ ⊂C⊃ ⊂D⊃ ⊂E⊃	34 ⊂A⊃ ⊂B⊃ ⊂C⊃ ⊂D⊃ ⊂E⊃
5 ⊂A⊃ ⊂B⊃ ⊂C⊃ ⊂D⊃ ⊂E⊃	15 ⊂A⊃ ⊂B⊃ ⊂C⊃ ⊂D⊃ ⊂E⊃	25 ⊂A⊃ ⊂B⊃ ⊂C⊃ ⊂D⊃ ⊂E⊃	35 ⊂A⊃ ⊂B⊃ ⊂C⊃ ⊂D⊃ ⊂E⊃
6 ⊂A⊃ ⊂B⊃ ⊂C⊃ ⊂D⊃ ⊂E⊃	16 ⊂A⊃ ⊂B⊃ ⊂C⊃ ⊂D⊃ ⊂E⊃	26 ⊂A⊃ ⊂B⊃ ⊂C⊃ ⊂D⊃ ⊂E⊃	36 ⊂A⊃ ⊂B⊃ ⊂C⊃ ⊂D⊃ ⊂E⊃
7 ⊂A⊃ ⊂B⊃ ⊂C⊃ ⊂D⊃ ⊂E⊃	17 ⊂A⊃ ⊂B⊃ ⊂C⊃ ⊂D⊃ ⊂E⊃	27 ⊂A⊃ ⊂B⊃ ⊂C⊃ ⊂D⊃ ⊂E⊃	37 ⊂A⊃ ⊂B⊃ ⊂C⊃ ⊂D⊃ ⊂E⊃
8 ⊂A⊃ ⊂B⊃ ⊂C⊃ ⊂D⊃ ⊂E⊃	18 ⊂A⊃ ⊂B⊃ ⊂C⊃ ⊂D⊃ ⊂E⊃	28 ⊂A⊃ ⊂B⊃ ⊂C⊃ ⊂D⊃ ⊂E⊃	38 ⊂A⊃ ⊂B⊃ ⊂C⊃ ⊂D⊃ ⊂E⊃
9 ⊂A⊃ ⊂B⊃ ⊂C⊃ ⊂D⊃ ⊂E⊃	19 ⊂A⊃ ⊂B⊃ ⊂C⊃ ⊂D⊃ ⊂E⊃	29 ⊂A⊃ ⊂B⊃ ⊂C⊃ ⊂D⊃ ⊂E⊃	39 ⊂A⊃ ⊂B⊃ ⊂C⊃ ⊂D⊃ ⊂E⊃
10 ⊂A⊃ ⊂B⊃ ⊂C⊃ ⊂D⊃ ⊂E⊃	20 ⊂A⊃ ⊂B⊃ ⊂C⊃ ⊂D⊃ ⊂E⊃	30 ⊂A⊃ ⊂B⊃ ⊂C⊃ ⊂D⊃ ⊂E⊃	40 ⊂A⊃ ⊂B⊃ ⊂C⊃ ⊂D⊃ ⊂E⊃

SECTION 2

1 ⊂A⊃ ⊂B⊃ ⊂C⊃ ⊂D⊃ ⊂E⊃	11 ⊂A⊃ ⊂B⊃ ⊂C⊃ ⊂D⊃ ⊂E⊃	21 ⊂A⊃ ⊂B⊃ ⊂C⊃ ⊂D⊃ ⊂E⊃	31 ⊂A⊃ ⊂B⊃ ⊂C⊃ ⊂D⊃ ⊂E⊃
2 ⊂A⊃ ⊂B⊃ ⊂C⊃ ⊂D⊃ ⊂E⊃	12 ⊂A⊃ ⊂B⊃ ⊂C⊃ ⊂D⊃ ⊂E⊃	22 ⊂A⊃ ⊂B⊃ ⊂C⊃ ⊂D⊃ ⊂E⊃	32 ⊂A⊃ ⊂B⊃ ⊂C⊃ ⊂D⊃ ⊂E⊃
3 ⊂A⊃ ⊂B⊃ ⊂C⊃ ⊂D⊃ ⊂E⊃	13 ⊂A⊃ ⊂B⊃ ⊂C⊃ ⊂D⊃ ⊂E⊃	23 ⊂A⊃ ⊂B⊃ ⊂C⊃ ⊂D⊃ ⊂E⊃	33 ⊂A⊃ ⊂B⊃ ⊂C⊃ ⊂D⊃ ⊂E⊃
4 ⊂A⊃ ⊂B⊃ ⊂C⊃ ⊂D⊃ ⊂E⊃	14 ⊂A⊃ ⊂B⊃ ⊂C⊃ ⊂D⊃ ⊂E⊃	24 ⊂A⊃ ⊂B⊃ ⊂C⊃ ⊂D⊃ ⊂E⊃	34 ⊂A⊃ ⊂B⊃ ⊂C⊃ ⊂D⊃ ⊂E⊃
5 ⊂A⊃ ⊂B⊃ ⊂C⊃ ⊂D⊃ ⊂E⊃	15 ⊂A⊃ ⊂B⊃ ⊂C⊃ ⊂D⊃ ⊂E⊃	25 ⊂A⊃ ⊂B⊃ ⊂C⊃ ⊂D⊃ ⊂E⊃	35 ⊂A⊃ ⊂B⊃ ⊂C⊃ ⊂D⊃ ⊂E⊃
6 ⊂A⊃ ⊂B⊃ ⊂C⊃ ⊂D⊃ ⊂E⊃	16 ⊂A⊃ ⊂B⊃ ⊂C⊃ ⊂D⊃ ⊂E⊃	26 ⊂A⊃ ⊂B⊃ ⊂C⊃ ⊂D⊃ ⊂E⊃	36 ⊂A⊃ ⊂B⊃ ⊂C⊃ ⊂D⊃ ⊂E⊃
7 ⊂A⊃ ⊂B⊃ ⊂C⊃ ⊂D⊃ ⊂E⊃	17 ⊂A⊃ ⊂B⊃ ⊂C⊃ ⊂D⊃ ⊂E⊃	27 ⊂A⊃ ⊂B⊃ ⊂C⊃ ⊂D⊃ ⊂E⊃	37 ⊂A⊃ ⊂B⊃ ⊂C⊃ ⊂D⊃ ⊂E⊃
8 ⊂A⊃ ⊂B⊃ ⊂C⊃ ⊂D⊃ ⊂E⊃	18 ⊂A⊃ ⊂B⊃ ⊂C⊃ ⊂D⊃ ⊂E⊃	28 ⊂A⊃ ⊂B⊃ ⊂C⊃ ⊂D⊃ ⊂E⊃	38 ⊂A⊃ ⊂B⊃ ⊂C⊃ ⊂D⊃ ⊂E⊃
9 ⊂A⊃ ⊂B⊃ ⊂C⊃ ⊂D⊃ ⊂E⊃	19 ⊂A⊃ ⊂B⊃ ⊂C⊃ ⊂D⊃ ⊂E⊃	29 ⊂A⊃ ⊂B⊃ ⊂C⊃ ⊂D⊃ ⊂E⊃	39 ⊂A⊃ ⊂B⊃ ⊂C⊃ ⊂D⊃ ⊂E⊃
10 ⊂A⊃ ⊂B⊃ ⊂C⊃ ⊂D⊃ ⊂E⊃	20 ⊂A⊃ ⊂B⊃ ⊂C⊃ ⊂D⊃ ⊂E⊃	30 ⊂A⊃ ⊂B⊃ ⊂C⊃ ⊂D⊃ ⊂E⊃	40 ⊂A⊃ ⊂B⊃ ⊂C⊃ ⊂D⊃ ⊂E⊃

⊂ ⊃

Use a No. 2 pencil only. Be sure each mark is dark and completely fills the intended oval. Completely erase any errors or stray marks.

Start with number 1 for each new section. If a section has fewer questions than answer spaces, leave the extra answer spaces blank.

SECTION

3

1 ⊂A⊃ ⊂B⊃ ⊂C⊃ ⊂D⊃ ⊂E⊃	16 ⊂A⊃ ⊂B⊃ ⊂C⊃ ⊂D⊃ ⊂E⊃	31 ⊂A⊃ ⊂B⊃ ⊂C⊃ ⊂D⊃ ⊂E⊃
2 ⊂A⊃ ⊂B⊃ ⊂C⊃ ⊂D⊃ ⊂E⊃	17 ⊂A⊃ ⊂B⊃ ⊂C⊃ ⊂D⊃ ⊂E⊃	32 ⊂A⊃ ⊂B⊃ ⊂C⊃ ⊂D⊃ ⊂E⊃
3 ⊂A⊃ ⊂B⊃ ⊂C⊃ ⊂D⊃ ⊂E⊃	18 ⊂A⊃ ⊂B⊃ ⊂C⊃ ⊂D⊃ ⊂E⊃	33 ⊂A⊃ ⊂B⊃ ⊂C⊃ ⊂D⊃ ⊂E⊃
4 ⊂A⊃ ⊂B⊃ ⊂C⊃ ⊂D⊃ ⊂E⊃	19 ⊂A⊃ ⊂B⊃ ⊂C⊃ ⊂D⊃ ⊂E⊃	34 ⊂A⊃ ⊂B⊃ ⊂C⊃ ⊂D⊃ ⊂E⊃
5 ⊂A⊃ ⊂B⊃ ⊂C⊃ ⊂D⊃ ⊂E⊃	20 ⊂A⊃ ⊂B⊃ ⊂C⊃ ⊂D⊃ ⊂E⊃	35 ⊂A⊃ ⊂B⊃ ⊂C⊃ ⊂D⊃ ⊂E⊃
6 ⊂A⊃ ⊂B⊃ ⊂C⊃ ⊂D⊃ ⊂E⊃	21 ⊂A⊃ ⊂B⊃ ⊂C⊃ ⊂D⊃ ⊂E⊃	36 ⊂A⊃ ⊂B⊃ ⊂C⊃ ⊂D⊃ ⊂E⊃
7 ⊂A⊃ ⊂B⊃ ⊂C⊃ ⊂D⊃ ⊂E⊃	22 ⊂A⊃ ⊂B⊃ ⊂C⊃ ⊂D⊃ ⊂E⊃	37 ⊂A⊃ ⊂B⊃ ⊂C⊃ ⊂D⊃ ⊂E⊃
8 ⊂A⊃ ⊂B⊃ ⊂C⊃ ⊂D⊃ ⊂E⊃	23 ⊂A⊃ ⊂B⊃ ⊂C⊃ ⊂D⊃ ⊂E⊃	38 ⊂A⊃ ⊂B⊃ ⊂C⊃ ⊂D⊃ ⊂E⊃
9 ⊂A⊃ ⊂B⊃ ⊂C⊃ ⊂D⊃ ⊂E⊃	24 ⊂A⊃ ⊂B⊃ ⊂C⊃ ⊂D⊃ ⊂E⊃	39 ⊂A⊃ ⊂B⊃ ⊂C⊃ ⊂D⊃ ⊂E⊃
10 ⊂A⊃ ⊂B⊃ ⊂C⊃ ⊂D⊃ ⊂E⊃	25 ⊂A⊃ ⊂B⊃ ⊂C⊃ ⊂D⊃ ⊂E⊃	40 ⊂A⊃ ⊂B⊃ ⊂C⊃ ⊂D⊃ ⊂E⊃
11 ⊂A⊃ ⊂B⊃ ⊂C⊃ ⊂D⊃ ⊂E⊃	26 ⊂A⊃ ⊂B⊃ ⊂C⊃ ⊂D⊃ ⊂E⊃	
12 ⊂A⊃ ⊂B⊃ ⊂C⊃ ⊂D⊃ ⊂E⊃	27 ⊂A⊃ ⊂B⊃ ⊂C⊃ ⊂D⊃ ⊂E⊃	
13 ⊂A⊃ ⊂B⊃ ⊂C⊃ ⊂D⊃ ⊂E⊃	28 ⊂A⊃ ⊂B⊃ ⊂C⊃ ⊂D⊃ ⊂E⊃	
14 ⊂A⊃ ⊂B⊃ ⊂C⊃ ⊂D⊃ ⊂E⊃	29 ⊂A⊃ ⊂B⊃ ⊂C⊃ ⊂D⊃ ⊂E⊃	
15 ⊂A⊃ ⊂B⊃ ⊂C⊃ ⊂D⊃ ⊂E⊃	30 ⊂A⊃ ⊂B⊃ ⊂C⊃ ⊂D⊃ ⊂E⊃	

If section 3 of your test booklet has math questions that are not multiple-choice, continue to item 16 below. Otherwise, continue to item 16 above.

ONLY ANSWERS ENTERED IN THE OVALS IN EACH GRID AREA WILL BE SCORED.
YOU WILL NOT RECEIVE CREDIT FOR ANYTHING WRITTEN IN THE BOXES ABOVE THE OVALS.

(Grid-in answer fields numbered 16–25, each with columns for fraction bars, decimal points, and digits 0–9.)

BE SURE TO ERASE ANY ERRORS OR STRAY MARKS COMPLETELY.

PLEASE PRINT YOUR INITIALS

First   Middle   Last

Start with number 1 for each new section. If a section has fewer questions than answer spaces, leave the extra answer spaces blank.

SECTION 4

1 ⊂A⊃ ⊂B⊃ ⊂C⊃ ⊂D⊃ ⊂E⊃
2 ⊂A⊃ ⊂B⊃ ⊂C⊃ ⊂D⊃ ⊂E⊃
3 ⊂A⊃ ⊂B⊃ ⊂C⊃ ⊂D⊃ ⊂E⊃
4 ⊂A⊃ ⊂B⊃ ⊂C⊃ ⊂D⊃ ⊂E⊃
5 ⊂A⊃ ⊂B⊃ ⊂C⊃ ⊂D⊃ ⊂E⊃
6 ⊂A⊃ ⊂B⊃ ⊂C⊃ ⊂D⊃ ⊂E⊃
7 ⊂A⊃ ⊂B⊃ ⊂C⊃ ⊂D⊃ ⊂E⊃
8 ⊂A⊃ ⊂B⊃ ⊂C⊃ ⊂D⊃ ⊂E⊃
9 ⊂A⊃ ⊂B⊃ ⊂C⊃ ⊂D⊃ ⊂E⊃
10 ⊂A⊃ ⊂B⊃ ⊂C⊃ ⊂D⊃ ⊂E⊃
11 ⊂A⊃ ⊂B⊃ ⊂C⊃ ⊂D⊃ ⊂E⊃
12 ⊂A⊃ ⊂B⊃ ⊂C⊃ ⊂D⊃ ⊂E⊃
13 ⊂A⊃ ⊂B⊃ ⊂C⊃ ⊂D⊃ ⊂E⊃
14 ⊂A⊃ ⊂B⊃ ⊂C⊃ ⊂D⊃ ⊂E⊃
15 ⊂A⊃ ⊂B⊃ ⊂C⊃ ⊂D⊃ ⊂E⊃

16 ⊂A⊃ ⊂B⊃ ⊂C⊃ ⊂D⊃ ⊂E⊃
17 ⊂A⊃ ⊂B⊃ ⊂C⊃ ⊂D⊃ ⊂E⊃
18 ⊂A⊃ ⊂B⊃ ⊂C⊃ ⊂D⊃ ⊂E⊃
19 ⊂A⊃ ⊂B⊃ ⊂C⊃ ⊂D⊃ ⊂E⊃
20 ⊂A⊃ ⊂B⊃ ⊂C⊃ ⊂D⊃ ⊂E⊃
21 ⊂A⊃ ⊂B⊃ ⊂C⊃ ⊂D⊃ ⊂E⊃
22 ⊂A⊃ ⊂B⊃ ⊂C⊃ ⊂D⊃ ⊂E⊃
23 ⊂A⊃ ⊂B⊃ ⊂C⊃ ⊂D⊃ ⊂E⊃
24 ⊂A⊃ ⊂B⊃ ⊂C⊃ ⊂D⊃ ⊂E⊃
25 ⊂A⊃ ⊂B⊃ ⊂C⊃ ⊂D⊃ ⊂E⊃
26 ⊂A⊃ ⊂B⊃ ⊂C⊃ ⊂D⊃ ⊂E⊃
27 ⊂A⊃ ⊂B⊃ ⊂C⊃ ⊂D⊃ ⊂E⊃
28 ⊂A⊃ ⊂B⊃ ⊂C⊃ ⊂D⊃ ⊂E⊃
29 ⊂A⊃ ⊂B⊃ ⊂C⊃ ⊂D⊃ ⊂E⊃
30 ⊂A⊃ ⊂B⊃ ⊂C⊃ ⊂D⊃ ⊂E⊃

31 ⊂A⊃ ⊂B⊃ ⊂C⊃ ⊂D⊃ ⊂E⊃
32 ⊂A⊃ ⊂B⊃ ⊂C⊃ ⊂D⊃ ⊂E⊃
33 ⊂A⊃ ⊂B⊃ ⊂C⊃ ⊂D⊃ ⊂E⊃
34 ⊂A⊃ ⊂B⊃ ⊂C⊃ ⊂D⊃ ⊂E⊃
35 ⊂A⊃ ⊂B⊃ ⊂C⊃ ⊂D⊃ ⊂E⊃
36 ⊂A⊃ ⊂B⊃ ⊂C⊃ ⊂D⊃ ⊂E⊃
37 ⊂A⊃ ⊂B⊃ ⊂C⊃ ⊂D⊃ ⊂E⊃
38 ⊂A⊃ ⊂B⊃ ⊂C⊃ ⊂D⊃ ⊂E⊃
39 ⊂A⊃ ⊂B⊃ ⊂C⊃ ⊂D⊃ ⊂E⊃
40 ⊂A⊃ ⊂B⊃ ⊂C⊃ ⊂D⊃ ⊂E⊃

If section 4 of your test booklet has math questions that are not multiple-choice, continue to item 16 below. Otherwise, continue to item 16 above.

ONLY ANSWERS ENTERED IN THE OVALS IN EACH GRID AREA WILL BE SCORED.
YOU WILL NOT RECEIVE CREDIT FOR ANYTHING WRITTEN IN THE BOXES ABOVE THE OVALS.

16 17 18 19 20

21 22 23 24 25

(Grid answer areas with fraction/decimal ovals and digits 0–9 for items 16 through 25)

BE SURE TO ERASE ANY ERRORS OR STRAY MARKS COMPLETELY.

PLEASE PRINT YOUR INITIALS

First   Middle   Last

Start with number 1 for each new section. If a section has fewer questions than answer spaces, leave the extra answer spaces blank.

SECTION 5

#	A B C D E	#	A B C D E	#	A B C D E	#	A B C D E
1	⊂A⊃ ⊂B⊃ ⊂C⊃ ⊂D⊃ ⊂E⊃	11	⊂A⊃ ⊂B⊃ ⊂C⊃ ⊂D⊃ ⊂E⊃	21	⊂A⊃ ⊂B⊃ ⊂C⊃ ⊂D⊃ ⊂E⊃	31	⊂A⊃ ⊂B⊃ ⊂C⊃ ⊂D⊃ ⊂E⊃
2	⊂A⊃ ⊂B⊃ ⊂C⊃ ⊂D⊃ ⊂E⊃	12	⊂A⊃ ⊂B⊃ ⊂C⊃ ⊂D⊃ ⊂E⊃	22	⊂A⊃ ⊂B⊃ ⊂C⊃ ⊂D⊃ ⊂E⊃	32	⊂A⊃ ⊂B⊃ ⊂C⊃ ⊂D⊃ ⊂E⊃
3	⊂A⊃ ⊂B⊃ ⊂C⊃ ⊂D⊃ ⊂E⊃	13	⊂A⊃ ⊂B⊃ ⊂C⊃ ⊂D⊃ ⊂E⊃	23	⊂A⊃ ⊂B⊃ ⊂C⊃ ⊂D⊃ ⊂E⊃	33	⊂A⊃ ⊂B⊃ ⊂C⊃ ⊂D⊃ ⊂E⊃
4	⊂A⊃ ⊂B⊃ ⊂C⊃ ⊂D⊃ ⊂E⊃	14	⊂A⊃ ⊂B⊃ ⊂C⊃ ⊂D⊃ ⊂E⊃	24	⊂A⊃ ⊂B⊃ ⊂C⊃ ⊂D⊃ ⊂E⊃	34	⊂A⊃ ⊂B⊃ ⊂C⊃ ⊂D⊃ ⊂E⊃
5	⊂A⊃ ⊂B⊃ ⊂C⊃ ⊂D⊃ ⊂E⊃	15	⊂A⊃ ⊂B⊃ ⊂C⊃ ⊂D⊃ ⊂E⊃	25	⊂A⊃ ⊂B⊃ ⊂C⊃ ⊂D⊃ ⊂E⊃	35	⊂A⊃ ⊂B⊃ ⊂C⊃ ⊂D⊃ ⊂E⊃
6	⊂A⊃ ⊂B⊃ ⊂C⊃ ⊂D⊃ ⊂E⊃	16	⊂A⊃ ⊂B⊃ ⊂C⊃ ⊂D⊃ ⊂E⊃	26	⊂A⊃ ⊂B⊃ ⊂C⊃ ⊂D⊃ ⊂E⊃	36	⊂A⊃ ⊂B⊃ ⊂C⊃ ⊂D⊃ ⊂E⊃
7	⊂A⊃ ⊂B⊃ ⊂C⊃ ⊂D⊃ ⊂E⊃	17	⊂A⊃ ⊂B⊃ ⊂C⊃ ⊂D⊃ ⊂E⊃	27	⊂A⊃ ⊂B⊃ ⊂C⊃ ⊂D⊃ ⊂E⊃	37	⊂A⊃ ⊂B⊃ ⊂C⊃ ⊂D⊃ ⊂E⊃
8	⊂A⊃ ⊂B⊃ ⊂C⊃ ⊂D⊃ ⊂E⊃	18	⊂A⊃ ⊂B⊃ ⊂C⊃ ⊂D⊃ ⊂E⊃	28	⊂A⊃ ⊂B⊃ ⊂C⊃ ⊂D⊃ ⊂E⊃	38	⊂A⊃ ⊂B⊃ ⊂C⊃ ⊂D⊃ ⊂E⊃
9	⊂A⊃ ⊂B⊃ ⊂C⊃ ⊂D⊃ ⊂E⊃	19	⊂A⊃ ⊂B⊃ ⊂C⊃ ⊂D⊃ ⊂E⊃	29	⊂A⊃ ⊂B⊃ ⊂C⊃ ⊂D⊃ ⊂E⊃	39	⊂A⊃ ⊂B⊃ ⊂C⊃ ⊂D⊃ ⊂E⊃
10	⊂A⊃ ⊂B⊃ ⊂C⊃ ⊂D⊃ ⊂E⊃	20	⊂A⊃ ⊂B⊃ ⊂C⊃ ⊂D⊃ ⊂E⊃	30	⊂A⊃ ⊂B⊃ ⊂C⊃ ⊂D⊃ ⊂E⊃	40	⊂A⊃ ⊂B⊃ ⊂C⊃ ⊂D⊃ ⊂E⊃

SECTION 6

#	A B C D E	#	A B C D E	#	A B C D E	#	A B C D E
1	⊂A⊃ ⊂B⊃ ⊂C⊃ ⊂D⊃ ⊂E⊃	11	⊂A⊃ ⊂B⊃ ⊂C⊃ ⊂D⊃ ⊂E⊃	21	⊂A⊃ ⊂B⊃ ⊂C⊃ ⊂D⊃ ⊂E⊃	31	⊂A⊃ ⊂B⊃ ⊂C⊃ ⊂D⊃ ⊂E⊃
2	⊂A⊃ ⊂B⊃ ⊂C⊃ ⊂D⊃ ⊂E⊃	12	⊂A⊃ ⊂B⊃ ⊂C⊃ ⊂D⊃ ⊂E⊃	22	⊂A⊃ ⊂B⊃ ⊂C⊃ ⊂D⊃ ⊂E⊃	32	⊂A⊃ ⊂B⊃ ⊂C⊃ ⊂D⊃ ⊂E⊃
3	⊂A⊃ ⊂B⊃ ⊂C⊃ ⊂D⊃ ⊂E⊃	13	⊂A⊃ ⊂B⊃ ⊂C⊃ ⊂D⊃ ⊂E⊃	23	⊂A⊃ ⊂B⊃ ⊂C⊃ ⊂D⊃ ⊂E⊃	33	⊂A⊃ ⊂B⊃ ⊂C⊃ ⊂D⊃ ⊂E⊃
4	⊂A⊃ ⊂B⊃ ⊂C⊃ ⊂D⊃ ⊂E⊃	14	⊂A⊃ ⊂B⊃ ⊂C⊃ ⊂D⊃ ⊂E⊃	24	⊂A⊃ ⊂B⊃ ⊂C⊃ ⊂D⊃ ⊂E⊃	34	⊂A⊃ ⊂B⊃ ⊂C⊃ ⊂D⊃ ⊂E⊃
5	⊂A⊃ ⊂B⊃ ⊂C⊃ ⊂D⊃ ⊂E⊃	15	⊂A⊃ ⊂B⊃ ⊂C⊃ ⊂D⊃ ⊂E⊃	25	⊂A⊃ ⊂B⊃ ⊂C⊃ ⊂D⊃ ⊂E⊃	35	⊂A⊃ ⊂B⊃ ⊂C⊃ ⊂D⊃ ⊂E⊃
6	⊂A⊃ ⊂B⊃ ⊂C⊃ ⊂D⊃ ⊂E⊃	16	⊂A⊃ ⊂B⊃ ⊂C⊃ ⊂D⊃ ⊂E⊃	26	⊂A⊃ ⊂B⊃ ⊂C⊃ ⊂D⊃ ⊂E⊃	36	⊂A⊃ ⊂B⊃ ⊂C⊃ ⊂D⊃ ⊂E⊃
7	⊂A⊃ ⊂B⊃ ⊂C⊃ ⊂D⊃ ⊂E⊃	17	⊂A⊃ ⊂B⊃ ⊂C⊃ ⊂D⊃ ⊂E⊃	27	⊂A⊃ ⊂B⊃ ⊂C⊃ ⊂D⊃ ⊂E⊃	37	⊂A⊃ ⊂B⊃ ⊂C⊃ ⊂D⊃ ⊂E⊃
8	⊂A⊃ ⊂B⊃ ⊂C⊃ ⊂D⊃ ⊂E⊃	18	⊂A⊃ ⊂B⊃ ⊂C⊃ ⊂D⊃ ⊂E⊃	28	⊂A⊃ ⊂B⊃ ⊂C⊃ ⊂D⊃ ⊂E⊃	38	⊂A⊃ ⊂B⊃ ⊂C⊃ ⊂D⊃ ⊂E⊃
9	⊂A⊃ ⊂B⊃ ⊂C⊃ ⊂D⊃ ⊂E⊃	19	⊂A⊃ ⊂B⊃ ⊂C⊃ ⊂D⊃ ⊂E⊃	29	⊂A⊃ ⊂B⊃ ⊂C⊃ ⊂D⊃ ⊂E⊃	39	⊂A⊃ ⊂B⊃ ⊂C⊃ ⊂D⊃ ⊂E⊃
10	⊂A⊃ ⊂B⊃ ⊂C⊃ ⊂D⊃ ⊂E⊃	20	⊂A⊃ ⊂B⊃ ⊂C⊃ ⊂D⊃ ⊂E⊃	30	⊂A⊃ ⊂B⊃ ⊂C⊃ ⊂D⊃ ⊂E⊃	40	⊂A⊃ ⊂B⊃ ⊂C⊃ ⊂D⊃ ⊂E⊃

SECTION 7

#	A B C D E	#	A B C D E	#	A B C D E	#	A B C D E
1	⊂A⊃ ⊂B⊃ ⊂C⊃ ⊂D⊃ ⊂E⊃	11	⊂A⊃ ⊂B⊃ ⊂C⊃ ⊂D⊃ ⊂E⊃	21	⊂A⊃ ⊂B⊃ ⊂C⊃ ⊂D⊃ ⊂E⊃	31	⊂A⊃ ⊂B⊃ ⊂C⊃ ⊂D⊃ ⊂E⊃
2	⊂A⊃ ⊂B⊃ ⊂C⊃ ⊂D⊃ ⊂E⊃	12	⊂A⊃ ⊂B⊃ ⊂C⊃ ⊂D⊃ ⊂E⊃	22	⊂A⊃ ⊂B⊃ ⊂C⊃ ⊂D⊃ ⊂E⊃	32	⊂A⊃ ⊂B⊃ ⊂C⊃ ⊂D⊃ ⊂E⊃
3	⊂A⊃ ⊂B⊃ ⊂C⊃ ⊂D⊃ ⊂E⊃	13	⊂A⊃ ⊂B⊃ ⊂C⊃ ⊂D⊃ ⊂E⊃	23	⊂A⊃ ⊂B⊃ ⊂C⊃ ⊂D⊃ ⊂E⊃	33	⊂A⊃ ⊂B⊃ ⊂C⊃ ⊂D⊃ ⊂E⊃
4	⊂A⊃ ⊂B⊃ ⊂C⊃ ⊂D⊃ ⊂E⊃	14	⊂A⊃ ⊂B⊃ ⊂C⊃ ⊂D⊃ ⊂E⊃	24	⊂A⊃ ⊂B⊃ ⊂C⊃ ⊂D⊃ ⊂E⊃	34	⊂A⊃ ⊂B⊃ ⊂C⊃ ⊂D⊃ ⊂E⊃
5	⊂A⊃ ⊂B⊃ ⊂C⊃ ⊂D⊃ ⊂E⊃	15	⊂A⊃ ⊂B⊃ ⊂C⊃ ⊂D⊃ ⊂E⊃	25	⊂A⊃ ⊂B⊃ ⊂C⊃ ⊂D⊃ ⊂E⊃	35	⊂A⊃ ⊂B⊃ ⊂C⊃ ⊂D⊃ ⊂E⊃
6	⊂A⊃ ⊂B⊃ ⊂C⊃ ⊂D⊃ ⊂E⊃	16	⊂A⊃ ⊂B⊃ ⊂C⊃ ⊂D⊃ ⊂E⊃	26	⊂A⊃ ⊂B⊃ ⊂C⊃ ⊂D⊃ ⊂E⊃	36	⊂A⊃ ⊂B⊃ ⊂C⊃ ⊂D⊃ ⊂E⊃
7	⊂A⊃ ⊂B⊃ ⊂C⊃ ⊂D⊃ ⊂E⊃	17	⊂A⊃ ⊂B⊃ ⊂C⊃ ⊂D⊃ ⊂E⊃	27	⊂A⊃ ⊂B⊃ ⊂C⊃ ⊂D⊃ ⊂E⊃	37	⊂A⊃ ⊂B⊃ ⊂C⊃ ⊂D⊃ ⊂E⊃
8	⊂A⊃ ⊂B⊃ ⊂C⊃ ⊂D⊃ ⊂E⊃	18	⊂A⊃ ⊂B⊃ ⊂C⊃ ⊂D⊃ ⊂E⊃	28	⊂A⊃ ⊂B⊃ ⊂C⊃ ⊂D⊃ ⊂E⊃	38	⊂A⊃ ⊂B⊃ ⊂C⊃ ⊂D⊃ ⊂E⊃
9	⊂A⊃ ⊂B⊃ ⊂C⊃ ⊂D⊃ ⊂E⊃	19	⊂A⊃ ⊂B⊃ ⊂C⊃ ⊂D⊃ ⊂E⊃	29	⊂A⊃ ⊂B⊃ ⊂C⊃ ⊂D⊃ ⊂E⊃	39	⊂A⊃ ⊂B⊃ ⊂C⊃ ⊂D⊃ ⊂E⊃
10	⊂A⊃ ⊂B⊃ ⊂C⊃ ⊂D⊃ ⊂E⊃	20	⊂A⊃ ⊂B⊃ ⊂C⊃ ⊂D⊃ ⊂E⊃	30	⊂A⊃ ⊂B⊃ ⊂C⊃ ⊂D⊃ ⊂E⊃	40	⊂A⊃ ⊂B⊃ ⊂C⊃ ⊂D⊃ ⊂E⊃

Completely darken bubbles with a No. 2 pencil. If you make a mistake, be sure to erase mark completely. Erase all stray marks.

1

YOUR NAME: _____
(Print)
          Last   First   M.I.

SIGNATURE: _____   **DATE:** ___ / ___ / ___

HOME ADDRESS: _____
(Print)
          Number and Street

_____
    City   State   Zip Code

PHONE NO.: _____
(Print)

IMPORTANT: Please fill in these boxes exactly as shown on the back cover of your test book.

2. TEST FORM
_____

6. DATE OF BIRTH

Month		Day		Year	
○ JAN					
○ FEB					
○ MAR	⊂0⊃	⊂0⊃	⊂0⊃	⊂0⊃	
○ APR	⊂1⊃	⊂1⊃	⊂1⊃	⊂1⊃	
○ MAY	⊂2⊃	⊂2⊃	⊂2⊃	⊂2⊃	
○ JUN	⊂3⊃	⊂3⊃	⊂3⊃	⊂3⊃	
○ JUL		⊂4⊃	⊂4⊃	⊂4⊃	
○ AUG		⊂5⊃	⊂5⊃	⊂5⊃	
○ SEP		⊂6⊃	⊂6⊃	⊂6⊃	
○ OCT		⊂7⊃	⊂7⊃	⊂7⊃	
○ NOV		⊂8⊃	⊂8⊃	⊂8⊃	
○ DEC		⊂9⊃	⊂9⊃	⊂9⊃	

3. TEST CODE

⊂0⊃	⊂A⊃	⊂0⊃	⊂0⊃	⊂0⊃		
⊂1⊃	⊂B⊃	⊂1⊃	⊂1⊃	⊂1⊃		
⊂2⊃	⊂C⊃	⊂2⊃	⊂2⊃	⊂2⊃		
⊂3⊃	⊂D⊃	⊂3⊃	⊂3⊃	⊂3⊃		
⊂4⊃	⊂E⊃	⊂4⊃	⊂4⊃	⊂4⊃		
⊂5⊃	⊂F⊃	⊂5⊃	⊂5⊃	⊂5⊃		
⊂6⊃	⊂G⊃	⊂6⊃	⊂6⊃	⊂6⊃		
⊂7⊃		⊂7⊃	⊂7⊃	⊂7⊃		
⊂8⊃		⊂8⊃	⊂8⊃	⊂8⊃		
⊂9⊃		⊂9⊃	⊂9⊃	⊂9⊃		

4. REGISTRATION NUMBER

⊂0⊃	⊂0⊃	⊂0⊃	⊂0⊃	⊂0⊃	⊂0⊃	⊂0⊃
⊂1⊃	⊂1⊃	⊂1⊃	⊂1⊃	⊂1⊃	⊂1⊃	⊂1⊃
⊂2⊃	⊂2⊃	⊂2⊃	⊂2⊃	⊂2⊃	⊂2⊃	⊂2⊃
⊂3⊃	⊂3⊃	⊂3⊃	⊂3⊃	⊂3⊃	⊂3⊃	⊂3⊃
⊂4⊃	⊂4⊃	⊂4⊃	⊂4⊃	⊂4⊃	⊂4⊃	⊂4⊃
⊂5⊃	⊂5⊃	⊂5⊃	⊂5⊃	⊂5⊃	⊂5⊃	⊂5⊃
⊂6⊃	⊂6⊃	⊂6⊃	⊂6⊃	⊂6⊃	⊂6⊃	⊂6⊃
⊂7⊃	⊂7⊃	⊂7⊃	⊂7⊃	⊂7⊃	⊂7⊃	⊂7⊃
⊂8⊃	⊂8⊃	⊂8⊃	⊂8⊃	⊂8⊃	⊂8⊃	⊂8⊃
⊂9⊃	⊂9⊃	⊂9⊃	⊂9⊃	⊂9⊃	⊂9⊃	⊂9⊃

7. SEX
○ MALE
○ FEMALE

The Princeton Review

5. YOUR NAME

First 4 letters of last name				FIRST INIT	MID INIT
⊂A⊃	⊂A⊃	⊂A⊃	⊂A⊃	⊂A⊃	⊂A⊃
⊂B⊃	⊂B⊃	⊂B⊃	⊂B⊃	⊂B⊃	⊂B⊃
⊂C⊃	⊂C⊃	⊂C⊃	⊂C⊃	⊂C⊃	⊂C⊃
⊂D⊃	⊂D⊃	⊂D⊃	⊂D⊃	⊂D⊃	⊂D⊃
⊂E⊃	⊂E⊃	⊂E⊃	⊂E⊃	⊂E⊃	⊂E⊃
⊂F⊃	⊂F⊃	⊂F⊃	⊂F⊃	⊂F⊃	⊂F⊃
⊂G⊃	⊂G⊃	⊂G⊃	⊂G⊃	⊂G⊃	⊂G⊃
⊂H⊃	⊂H⊃	⊂H⊃	⊂H⊃	⊂H⊃	⊂H⊃
⊂I⊃	⊂I⊃	⊂I⊃	⊂I⊃	⊂I⊃	⊂I⊃
⊂J⊃	⊂J⊃	⊂J⊃	⊂J⊃	⊂J⊃	⊂J⊃
⊂K⊃	⊂K⊃	⊂K⊃	⊂K⊃	⊂K⊃	⊂K⊃
⊂L⊃	⊂L⊃	⊂L⊃	⊂L⊃	⊂L⊃	⊂L⊃
⊂M⊃	⊂M⊃	⊂M⊃	⊂M⊃	⊂M⊃	⊂M⊃
⊂N⊃	⊂N⊃	⊂N⊃	⊂N⊃	⊂N⊃	⊂N⊃
⊂O⊃	⊂O⊃	⊂O⊃	⊂O⊃	⊂O⊃	⊂O⊃
⊂P⊃	⊂P⊃	⊂P⊃	⊂P⊃	⊂P⊃	⊂P⊃
⊂Q⊃	⊂Q⊃	⊂Q⊃	⊂Q⊃	⊂Q⊃	⊂Q⊃
⊂R⊃	⊂R⊃	⊂R⊃	⊂R⊃	⊂R⊃	⊂R⊃
⊂S⊃	⊂S⊃	⊂S⊃	⊂S⊃	⊂S⊃	⊂S⊃
⊂T⊃	⊂T⊃	⊂T⊃	⊂T⊃	⊂T⊃	⊂T⊃
⊂U⊃	⊂U⊃	⊂U⊃	⊂U⊃	⊂U⊃	⊂U⊃
⊂V⊃	⊂V⊃	⊂V⊃	⊂V⊃	⊂V⊃	⊂V⊃
⊂W⊃	⊂W⊃	⊂W⊃	⊂W⊃	⊂W⊃	⊂W⊃
⊂X⊃	⊂X⊃	⊂X⊃	⊂X⊃	⊂X⊃	⊂X⊃
⊂Y⊃	⊂Y⊃	⊂Y⊃	⊂Y⊃	⊂Y⊃	⊂Y⊃
⊂Z⊃	⊂Z⊃	⊂Z⊃	⊂Z⊃	⊂Z⊃	⊂Z⊃

Start with number 1 for each new section. If a section has fewer questions than answer spaces, leave the extra answer spaces blank.

SECTION 1

1 ⊂A⊃ ⊂B⊃ ⊂C⊃ ⊂D⊃ ⊂E⊃	11 ⊂A⊃ ⊂B⊃ ⊂C⊃ ⊂D⊃ ⊂E⊃	21 ⊂A⊃ ⊂B⊃ ⊂C⊃ ⊂D⊃ ⊂E⊃	31 ⊂A⊃ ⊂B⊃ ⊂C⊃ ⊂D⊃ ⊂E⊃
2 ⊂A⊃ ⊂B⊃ ⊂C⊃ ⊂D⊃ ⊂E⊃	12 ⊂A⊃ ⊂B⊃ ⊂C⊃ ⊂D⊃ ⊂E⊃	22 ⊂A⊃ ⊂B⊃ ⊂C⊃ ⊂D⊃ ⊂E⊃	32 ⊂A⊃ ⊂B⊃ ⊂C⊃ ⊂D⊃ ⊂E⊃
3 ⊂A⊃ ⊂B⊃ ⊂C⊃ ⊂D⊃ ⊂E⊃	13 ⊂A⊃ ⊂B⊃ ⊂C⊃ ⊂D⊃ ⊂E⊃	23 ⊂A⊃ ⊂B⊃ ⊂C⊃ ⊂D⊃ ⊂E⊃	33 ⊂A⊃ ⊂B⊃ ⊂C⊃ ⊂D⊃ ⊂E⊃
4 ⊂A⊃ ⊂B⊃ ⊂C⊃ ⊂D⊃ ⊂E⊃	14 ⊂A⊃ ⊂B⊃ ⊂C⊃ ⊂D⊃ ⊂E⊃	24 ⊂A⊃ ⊂B⊃ ⊂C⊃ ⊂D⊃ ⊂E⊃	34 ⊂A⊃ ⊂B⊃ ⊂C⊃ ⊂D⊃ ⊂E⊃
5 ⊂A⊃ ⊂B⊃ ⊂C⊃ ⊂D⊃ ⊂E⊃	15 ⊂A⊃ ⊂B⊃ ⊂C⊃ ⊂D⊃ ⊂E⊃	25 ⊂A⊃ ⊂B⊃ ⊂C⊃ ⊂D⊃ ⊂E⊃	35 ⊂A⊃ ⊂B⊃ ⊂C⊃ ⊂D⊃ ⊂E⊃
6 ⊂A⊃ ⊂B⊃ ⊂C⊃ ⊂D⊃ ⊂E⊃	16 ⊂A⊃ ⊂B⊃ ⊂C⊃ ⊂D⊃ ⊂E⊃	26 ⊂A⊃ ⊂B⊃ ⊂C⊃ ⊂D⊃ ⊂E⊃	36 ⊂A⊃ ⊂B⊃ ⊂C⊃ ⊂D⊃ ⊂E⊃
7 ⊂A⊃ ⊂B⊃ ⊂C⊃ ⊂D⊃ ⊂E⊃	17 ⊂A⊃ ⊂B⊃ ⊂C⊃ ⊂D⊃ ⊂E⊃	27 ⊂A⊃ ⊂B⊃ ⊂C⊃ ⊂D⊃ ⊂E⊃	37 ⊂A⊃ ⊂B⊃ ⊂C⊃ ⊂D⊃ ⊂E⊃
8 ⊂A⊃ ⊂B⊃ ⊂C⊃ ⊂D⊃ ⊂E⊃	18 ⊂A⊃ ⊂B⊃ ⊂C⊃ ⊂D⊃ ⊂E⊃	28 ⊂A⊃ ⊂B⊃ ⊂C⊃ ⊂D⊃ ⊂E⊃	38 ⊂A⊃ ⊂B⊃ ⊂C⊃ ⊂D⊃ ⊂E⊃
9 ⊂A⊃ ⊂B⊃ ⊂C⊃ ⊂D⊃ ⊂E⊃	19 ⊂A⊃ ⊂B⊃ ⊂C⊃ ⊂D⊃ ⊂E⊃	29 ⊂A⊃ ⊂B⊃ ⊂C⊃ ⊂D⊃ ⊂E⊃	39 ⊂A⊃ ⊂B⊃ ⊂C⊃ ⊂D⊃ ⊂E⊃
10 ⊂A⊃ ⊂B⊃ ⊂C⊃ ⊂D⊃ ⊂E⊃	20 ⊂A⊃ ⊂B⊃ ⊂C⊃ ⊂D⊃ ⊂E⊃	30 ⊂A⊃ ⊂B⊃ ⊂C⊃ ⊂D⊃ ⊂E⊃	40 ⊂A⊃ ⊂B⊃ ⊂C⊃ ⊂D⊃ ⊂E⊃

SECTION 2

1 ⊂A⊃ ⊂B⊃ ⊂C⊃ ⊂D⊃ ⊂E⊃	11 ⊂A⊃ ⊂B⊃ ⊂C⊃ ⊂D⊃ ⊂E⊃	21 ⊂A⊃ ⊂B⊃ ⊂C⊃ ⊂D⊃ ⊂E⊃	31 ⊂A⊃ ⊂B⊃ ⊂C⊃ ⊂D⊃ ⊂E⊃
2 ⊂A⊃ ⊂B⊃ ⊂C⊃ ⊂D⊃ ⊂E⊃	12 ⊂A⊃ ⊂B⊃ ⊂C⊃ ⊂D⊃ ⊂E⊃	22 ⊂A⊃ ⊂B⊃ ⊂C⊃ ⊂D⊃ ⊂E⊃	32 ⊂A⊃ ⊂B⊃ ⊂C⊃ ⊂D⊃ ⊂E⊃
3 ⊂A⊃ ⊂B⊃ ⊂C⊃ ⊂D⊃ ⊂E⊃	13 ⊂A⊃ ⊂B⊃ ⊂C⊃ ⊂D⊃ ⊂E⊃	23 ⊂A⊃ ⊂B⊃ ⊂C⊃ ⊂D⊃ ⊂E⊃	33 ⊂A⊃ ⊂B⊃ ⊂C⊃ ⊂D⊃ ⊂E⊃
4 ⊂A⊃ ⊂B⊃ ⊂C⊃ ⊂D⊃ ⊂E⊃	14 ⊂A⊃ ⊂B⊃ ⊂C⊃ ⊂D⊃ ⊂E⊃	24 ⊂A⊃ ⊂B⊃ ⊂C⊃ ⊂D⊃ ⊂E⊃	34 ⊂A⊃ ⊂B⊃ ⊂C⊃ ⊂D⊃ ⊂E⊃
5 ⊂A⊃ ⊂B⊃ ⊂C⊃ ⊂D⊃ ⊂E⊃	15 ⊂A⊃ ⊂B⊃ ⊂C⊃ ⊂D⊃ ⊂E⊃	25 ⊂A⊃ ⊂B⊃ ⊂C⊃ ⊂D⊃ ⊂E⊃	35 ⊂A⊃ ⊂B⊃ ⊂C⊃ ⊂D⊃ ⊂E⊃
6 ⊂A⊃ ⊂B⊃ ⊂C⊃ ⊂D⊃ ⊂E⊃	16 ⊂A⊃ ⊂B⊃ ⊂C⊃ ⊂D⊃ ⊂E⊃	26 ⊂A⊃ ⊂B⊃ ⊂C⊃ ⊂D⊃ ⊂E⊃	36 ⊂A⊃ ⊂B⊃ ⊂C⊃ ⊂D⊃ ⊂E⊃
7 ⊂A⊃ ⊂B⊃ ⊂C⊃ ⊂D⊃ ⊂E⊃	17 ⊂A⊃ ⊂B⊃ ⊂C⊃ ⊂D⊃ ⊂E⊃	27 ⊂A⊃ ⊂B⊃ ⊂C⊃ ⊂D⊃ ⊂E⊃	37 ⊂A⊃ ⊂B⊃ ⊂C⊃ ⊂D⊃ ⊂E⊃
8 ⊂A⊃ ⊂B⊃ ⊂C⊃ ⊂D⊃ ⊂E⊃	18 ⊂A⊃ ⊂B⊃ ⊂C⊃ ⊂D⊃ ⊂E⊃	28 ⊂A⊃ ⊂B⊃ ⊂C⊃ ⊂D⊃ ⊂E⊃	38 ⊂A⊃ ⊂B⊃ ⊂C⊃ ⊂D⊃ ⊂E⊃
9 ⊂A⊃ ⊂B⊃ ⊂C⊃ ⊂D⊃ ⊂E⊃	19 ⊂A⊃ ⊂B⊃ ⊂C⊃ ⊂D⊃ ⊂E⊃	29 ⊂A⊃ ⊂B⊃ ⊂C⊃ ⊂D⊃ ⊂E⊃	39 ⊂A⊃ ⊂B⊃ ⊂C⊃ ⊂D⊃ ⊂E⊃
10 ⊂A⊃ ⊂B⊃ ⊂C⊃ ⊂D⊃ ⊂E⊃	20 ⊂A⊃ ⊂B⊃ ⊂C⊃ ⊂D⊃ ⊂E⊃	30 ⊂A⊃ ⊂B⊃ ⊂C⊃ ⊂D⊃ ⊂E⊃	40 ⊂A⊃ ⊂B⊃ ⊂C⊃ ⊂D⊃ ⊂E⊃

DO NOT MARK IN THIS AREA

Start with number 1 for each new section. If a section has fewer questions than answer spaces, leave the extra answer spaces blank.

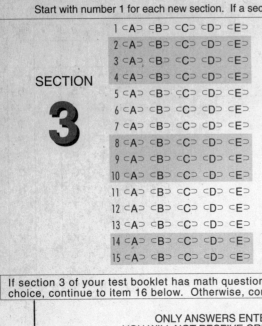

SECTION 3

1 ⊂A⊃ ⊂B⊃ ⊂C⊃ ⊂D⊃ ⊂E⊃
2 ⊂A⊃ ⊂B⊃ ⊂C⊃ ⊂D⊃ ⊂E⊃
3 ⊂A⊃ ⊂B⊃ ⊂C⊃ ⊂D⊃ ⊂E⊃
4 ⊂A⊃ ⊂B⊃ ⊂C⊃ ⊂D⊃ ⊂E⊃
5 ⊂A⊃ ⊂B⊃ ⊂C⊃ ⊂D⊃ ⊂E⊃
6 ⊂A⊃ ⊂B⊃ ⊂C⊃ ⊂D⊃ ⊂E⊃
7 ⊂A⊃ ⊂B⊃ ⊂C⊃ ⊂D⊃ ⊂E⊃
8 ⊂A⊃ ⊂B⊃ ⊂C⊃ ⊂D⊃ ⊂E⊃
9 ⊂A⊃ ⊂B⊃ ⊂C⊃ ⊂D⊃ ⊂E⊃
10 ⊂A⊃ ⊂B⊃ ⊂C⊃ ⊂D⊃ ⊂E⊃
11 ⊂A⊃ ⊂B⊃ ⊂C⊃ ⊂D⊃ ⊂E⊃
12 ⊂A⊃ ⊂B⊃ ⊂C⊃ ⊂D⊃ ⊂E⊃
13 ⊂A⊃ ⊂B⊃ ⊂C⊃ ⊂D⊃ ⊂E⊃
14 ⊂A⊃ ⊂B⊃ ⊂C⊃ ⊂D⊃ ⊂E⊃
15 ⊂A⊃ ⊂B⊃ ⊂C⊃ ⊂D⊃ ⊂E⊃

16 ⊂A⊃ ⊂B⊃ ⊂C⊃ ⊂D⊃ ⊂E⊃
17 ⊂A⊃ ⊂B⊃ ⊂C⊃ ⊂D⊃ ⊂E⊃
18 ⊂A⊃ ⊂B⊃ ⊂C⊃ ⊂D⊃ ⊂E⊃
19 ⊂A⊃ ⊂B⊃ ⊂C⊃ ⊂D⊃ ⊂E⊃
20 ⊂A⊃ ⊂B⊃ ⊂C⊃ ⊂D⊃ ⊂E⊃
21 ⊂A⊃ ⊂B⊃ ⊂C⊃ ⊂D⊃ ⊂E⊃
22 ⊂A⊃ ⊂B⊃ ⊂C⊃ ⊂D⊃ ⊂E⊃
23 ⊂A⊃ ⊂B⊃ ⊂C⊃ ⊂D⊃ ⊂E⊃
24 ⊂A⊃ ⊂B⊃ ⊂C⊃ ⊂D⊃ ⊂E⊃
25 ⊂A⊃ ⊂B⊃ ⊂C⊃ ⊂D⊃ ⊂E⊃
26 ⊂A⊃ ⊂B⊃ ⊂C⊃ ⊂D⊃ ⊂E⊃
27 ⊂A⊃ ⊂B⊃ ⊂C⊃ ⊂D⊃ ⊂E⊃
28 ⊂A⊃ ⊂B⊃ ⊂C⊃ ⊂D⊃ ⊂E⊃
29 ⊂A⊃ ⊂B⊃ ⊂C⊃ ⊂D⊃ ⊂E⊃
30 ⊂A⊃ ⊂B⊃ ⊂C⊃ ⊂D⊃ ⊂E⊃

31 ⊂A⊃ ⊂B⊃ ⊂C⊃ ⊂D⊃ ⊂E⊃
32 ⊂A⊃ ⊂B⊃ ⊂C⊃ ⊂D⊃ ⊂E⊃
33 ⊂A⊃ ⊂B⊃ ⊂C⊃ ⊂D⊃ ⊂E⊃
34 ⊂A⊃ ⊂B⊃ ⊂C⊃ ⊂D⊃ ⊂E⊃
35 ⊂A⊃ ⊂B⊃ ⊂C⊃ ⊂D⊃ ⊂E⊃
36 ⊂A⊃ ⊂B⊃ ⊂C⊃ ⊂D⊃ ⊂E⊃
37 ⊂A⊃ ⊂B⊃ ⊂C⊃ ⊂D⊃ ⊂E⊃
38 ⊂A⊃ ⊂B⊃ ⊂C⊃ ⊂D⊃ ⊂E⊃
39 ⊂A⊃ ⊂B⊃ ⊂C⊃ ⊂D⊃ ⊂E⊃
40 ⊂A⊃ ⊂B⊃ ⊂C⊃ ⊂D⊃ ⊂E⊃

If section 3 of your test booklet has math questions that are not multiple-choice, continue to item 16 below. Otherwise, continue to item 16 above.

ONLY ANSWERS ENTERED IN THE OVALS IN EACH GRID AREA WILL BE SCORED.
YOU WILL NOT RECEIVE CREDIT FOR ANYTHING WRITTEN IN THE BOXES ABOVE THE OVALS.

16 17 18 19 20

21 22 23 24 25

(Grid-in answer boxes with ovals ⊂/⊃ ⊂•⊃ and digits 0–9 for each of items 16 through 25)

BE SURE TO ERASE ANY ERRORS OR STRAY MARKS COMPLETELY.

PLEASE PRINT YOUR INITIALS

First | Middle | Last

Start with number 1 for each new section. If a section has fewer questions than answer spaces, leave the extra answer spaces blank.

SECTION 4

#	A B C D E	#	A B C D E	#	A B C D E	#	A B C D E
1	A B C D E	11	A B C D E	21	A B C D E	31	A B C D E
2	A B C D E	12	A B C D E	22	A B C D E	32	A B C D E
3	A B C D E	13	A B C D E	23	A B C D E	33	A B C D E
4	A B C D E	14	A B C D E	24	A B C D E	34	A B C D E
5	A B C D E	15	A B C D E	25	A B C D E	35	A B C D E
6	A B C D E	16	A B C D E	26	A B C D E	36	A B C D E
7	A B C D E	17	A B C D E	27	A B C D E	37	A B C D E
8	A B C D E	18	A B C D E	28	A B C D E	38	A B C D E
9	A B C D E	19	A B C D E	29	A B C D E	39	A B C D E
10	A B C D E	20	A B C D E	30	A B C D E	40	A B C D E

SECTION 5

#	A B C D E	#	A B C D E	#	A B C D E	#	A B C D E
1	A B C D E	11	A B C D E	21	A B C D E	31	A B C D E
2	A B C D E	12	A B C D E	22	A B C D E	32	A B C D E
3	A B C D E	13	A B C D E	23	A B C D E	33	A B C D E
4	A B C D E	14	A B C D E	24	A B C D E	34	A B C D E
5	A B C D E	15	A B C D E	25	A B C D E	35	A B C D E
6	A B C D E	16	A B C D E	26	A B C D E	36	A B C D E
7	A B C D E	17	A B C D E	27	A B C D E	37	A B C D E
8	A B C D E	18	A B C D E	28	A B C D E	38	A B C D E
9	A B C D E	19	A B C D E	29	A B C D E	39	A B C D E
10	A B C D E	20	A B C D E	30	A B C D E	40	A B C D E

SECTION 6

#	A B C D E	#	A B C D E	#	A B C D E	#	A B C D E
1	A B C D E	11	A B C D E	21	A B C D E	31	A B C D E
2	A B C D E	12	A B C D E	22	A B C D E	32	A B C D E
3	A B C D E	13	A B C D E	23	A B C D E	33	A B C D E
4	A B C D E	14	A B C D E	24	A B C D E	34	A B C D E
5	A B C D E	15	A B C D E	25	A B C D E	35	A B C D E
6	A B C D E	16	A B C D E	26	A B C D E	36	A B C D E
7	A B C D E	17	A B C D E	27	A B C D E	37	A B C D E
8	A B C D E	18	A B C D E	28	A B C D E	38	A B C D E
9	A B C D E	19	A B C D E	29	A B C D E	39	A B C D E
10	A B C D E	20	A B C D E	30	A B C D E	40	A B C D E

SECTION 7

#	A B C D E	#	A B C D E	#	A B C D E	#	A B C D E
1	A B C D E	11	A B C D E	21	A B C D E	31	A B C D E
2	A B C D E	12	A B C D E	22	A B C D E	32	A B C D E
3	A B C D E	13	A B C D E	23	A B C D E	33	A B C D E
4	A B C D E	14	A B C D E	24	A B C D E	34	A B C D E
5	A B C D E	15	A B C D E	25	A B C D E	35	A B C D E
6	A B C D E	16	A B C D E	26	A B C D E	36	A B C D E
7	A B C D E	17	A B C D E	27	A B C D E	37	A B C D E
8	A B C D E	18	A B C D E	28	A B C D E	38	A B C D E
9	A B C D E	19	A B C D E	29	A B C D E	39	A B C D E
10	A B C D E	20	A B C D E	30	A B C D E	40	A B C D E

www.PrincetonReview.com

The Princeton Review
Admissions Services

At The Princeton Review, we care about your ability to get accepted to the best school for you. But, we all know getting accepted involves much more than just doing well on standardized tests. That's why, in addition to our test preparation services, we also offer free admissions services to students looking to enter college or graduate school. You can find these services on our website, *www.PrincetonReview.com*, the best online resource for researching, applying to, and learning how to pay for the right school for you.

No matter what type of program you're applying to—undergraduate, graduate, law, business, or medical—**PrincetonReview.com has the free tools, services, and advice you need to navigate the admissions process.** Read on to learn more about the services we offer.

Research Schools
www.PrincetonReview.com/Research

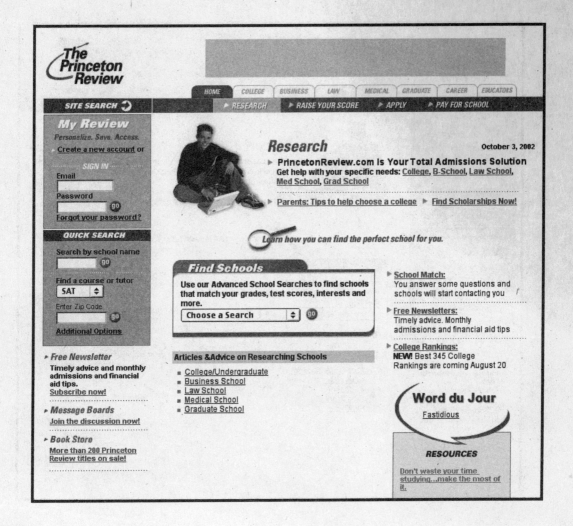

PrincetonReview.com features an interactive tool called **Counselor-O-Matic.** When you use this tool, you enter stats and information about yourself to find a list of your best match schools, reach schools, and safety schools. From there, you can read statistical and editorial information about thousands of colleges and universities. In addition, you can find out what currently enrolled college students say about their schools. Once you complete Counselor-O-Matic, make sure you opt in to School Match so that colleges can come to you.

Our **College Majors Search** is one of the most popular features we offer. Here you can read profiles on hundreds of majors to find information on curriculum, salaries, careers, and the appropriate high school preparation, as well as colleges that offer them. From the Majors Search, you can investigate corresponding careers, read **Career Profiles**, and learn what career is the best match for you by taking our **Career Quiz**.

No matter what type of school or specialized program you are considering, **PrincetonReview.com has free articles and advice, in addition to our tools, to help you make the right choice.**

Apply to School
www.PrincetonReview.com/Apply

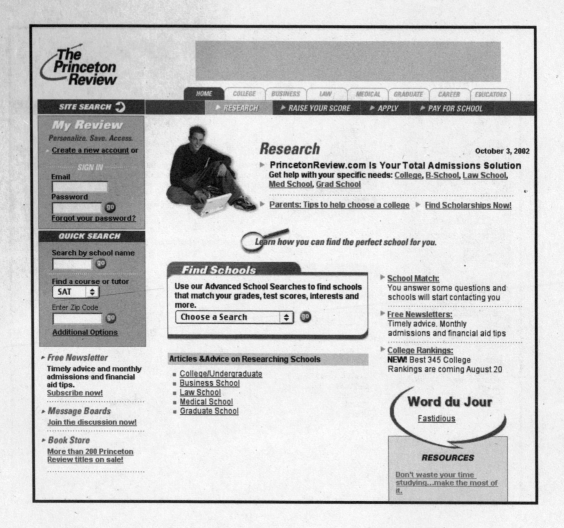

For most students, completing the school application is the most stressful part of the admissions process. PrincetonReview.com's powerful **Online School Application Engine** makes it easy to apply.

Paper applications are mostly a thing of the past. And, our hundreds of partner schools tell us they prefer to receive your applications online.

Using our online application service is simple:

- Enter information once and the common data automatically transfers onto each application.
- Save your applications and access them at any time to edit and perfect them.
- Submit electronically or print and mail them in.
- Pay your application fee online using an e-check, or mail the school a check.

Our powerful application engine is built to accommodate all your needs.

Pay for School
www.PrincetonReview.com/Finance

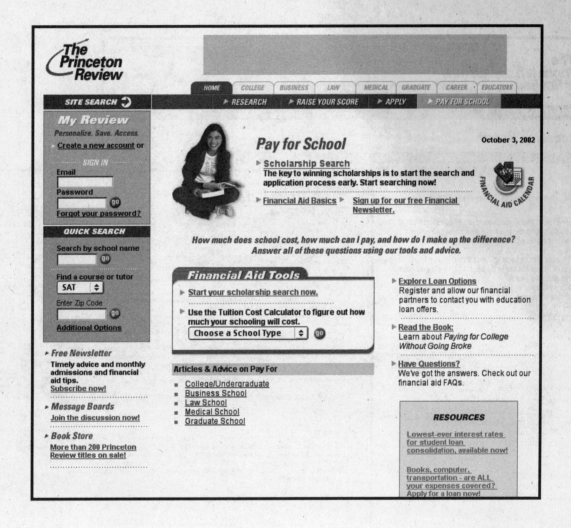

The financial aid process is confusing for everyone. But don't worry. Our free online tools, services, and advice can help you plan for the future and get the money you need to pay for school.

Our **Scholarship Search** engine will help you find free money, although scholarships alone often won't cover the cost of high tuitions. So, we offer other tools and resources to help you navigate the entire process.

Filling out the FAFSA and CSS Profile can be a daunting process; use our **Strategies for both forms** to make sure you answer the questions correctly the first time.

If scholarships and government aid aren't enough to swing the cost of tuition, we'll help you secure student loans. The Princeton Review has partnered with a select group of reputable financial institutions who will help **explore all your loans options**.

If you know how to work the financial aid process, you'll learn you don't have to **eliminate a school based on tuition.**

Be a Part of the PrincetonReview.com Community

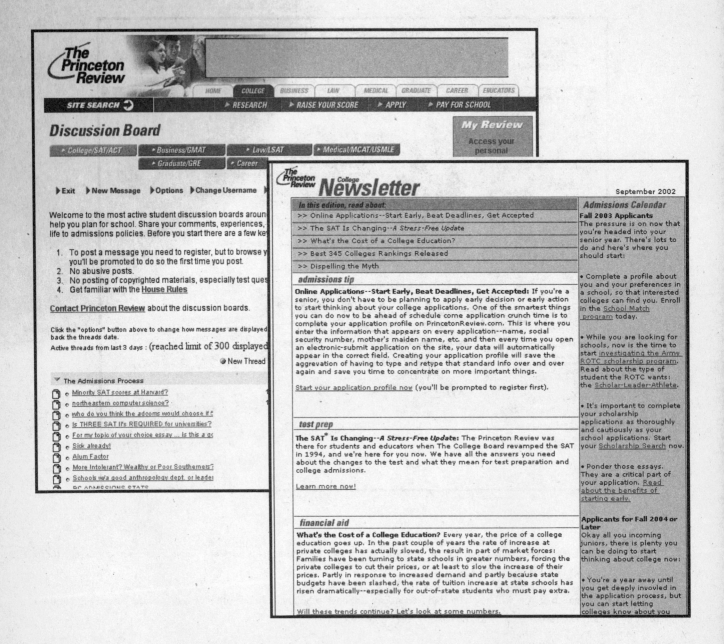

PrincetonReview.com's **Discussion Boards** and **Free Newsletters** are additional services to help you to get information about the admissions process from your peers and from The Princeton Review experts.

Book Store
www.PrincetonReview.com/college/Bookstore.asp

In addition to this book, we publish hundreds of other titles, including guidebooks that highlight life on campus, student opinion, and all the statistical data that you need to know about any school you are considering. Just a few of the titles that we offer are:

- Complete Book of Business Schools
- Complete Book of Law Schools
- Complete Book of Medical Schools
- The Best 345 Colleges
- The K&W Guide to Colleges for Students with Learning Disabilities or Attention Deficit Disorder
- Guide to College Majors
- Paying for College Without Going Broke

For a complete listing of all of our titles, visit our **online book store**:

http://www.princetonreview.com/college/bookstore.asp

NOTES

Find the Right School

BEST 345 COLLEGES
2004 EDITION
0-375-76337-6 • $21.95

COMPLETE BOOK OF COLLEGES
2004 EDITION
0-375-76330-9 • $24.95

COMPLETE BOOK OF
DISTANCE LEARNING SCHOOLS
0-375-76204-3 • $21.00

AMERICA'S ELITE COLLEGES
The Smart Buyer's Guide to the Ivy
League and Other Top Schools
0-375-76206-X • $15.95

Get in

CRACKING THE SAT
2004 EDITION
0-375-76331-7 • $19.00

CRACKING THE SAT
WITH SAMPLE TESTS ON CD-ROM
2004 EDITION
0-375-76330-9 • $30.95

MATH WORKOUT FOR THE SAT
2ND EDITION
0-375-76177-2 • $14.95

VERBAL WORKOUT FOR THE SAT
2ND EDITION
0-375-76176-4 • $14.95

CRACKING THE ACT
2003 EDITION
0-375-76317-1 • $19.00

CRACKING THE ACT WITH
SAMPLE TESTS ON CD-ROM
2003 EDITION
0-375-76318-X • $29.95

CRASH COURSE FOR THE ACT
2ND EDITION
The Last-Minute Guide to Scoring High
0-375-75364-3 • $9.95

CRASH COURSE FOR THE SAT
2ND EDITION
The Last-Minute Guide to Scoring High
0-375-75361-9 • $9.95

Get Help Paying for it

DOLLARS & SENSE FOR COLLEGE STUDENTS
How Not to Run Out of Money by Midterms
0-375-75206-4 • $10.95

PAYING FOR COLLEGE WITHOUT GOING BROKE
2004 EDITION
0-375-76350-3 • $20.00

THE SCHOLARSHIP ADVISOR
5TH EDITION
0-375-76210-8 • $26.00